Wills, Trusts, and Estates Administration

Wills, Trusts, and Estates Administration

Fourth Edition

Suzan D. Herskowitz
Attorney at Law

Boston Columbus Indianapolis New York San Francisco Upper Saddle River
Amsterdam Cape Town Dubai London Madrid Milan Munich Paris Montréal Toronto
Delhi Mexico City São Paulo Sydney Hong Kong Seoul Singapore Taipei Tokyo

Editorial Director: Vern Anthony
Senior Acquisitions Editor: Gary Bauer
Media Project Manager: Karen Bretz
Marketing Manager: Harper Coles
Editorial Project Manager: Linda Cupp
Editorial Assistant: Tanika Henderson
Director of Marketing: David Gesell
Senior Marketing Coordinator: Alicia Wozniak
Production Project Manager: Romaine Denis

Creative Director: Jayne Conte
Cover Designer: Bruce Kenselaar
Image Permission Coordinator: Mike Lackey
Full-Service Project Management: Shylaja Gattupalli
Composition: Jouve India Private Limited
Printer/Binder: Edwards Brothers Malloy
Cover Printer: Lehigh Phoenix
Text Font: MinionPro

Credits and acknowledgments borrowed from other sources and reproduced, with permission, in this textbook appear on the appropriate page within text

© Marzky Ragsac Jr./Fotolia: pages: 1, 9, 30, 61, 94, 142, 187, 220, 280, 321, 336, 372, 390, 400, 415, 463, 529, 532.

Library of Congress Cataloging-in-Publication Data

Herskowitz, Suzan D.,
    Wills, trusts, and estates administration / Suzan D. Herskowitz, attorney at law. — Fourth edition.
      pages cm
    Includes index.
    ISBN-13: 978-0-13-295603-1
    ISBN-10: 0-13-295603-9
  1. Inheritance and succession—United States.   2. Legal assistants—United States—Handbooks, manuals, etc.   I. Title.
    KF753.S58 2012
    346.7305'2—dc23

                                  2012037223

10 9 8 7 6 5 4 3 2

ISBN-13: 978-0-13-295603-1
ISBN-10: 0-13-295603-9

Brief Contents

Contents

Preface

From the Author

At the time I decided to write this book, I had been practicing law for about 10 years and was teaching at Keiser College (now Keiser University) in Fort Lauderdale. I enjoyed teaching. My particular field of expertise for my law practice was estate planning. It was a natural move for me then to write a book as a method I could employ to "teach" estate planning concepts on a broad basis—to my readers and not just to my immediate classroom of students. Overall, I wanted to teach students from the trenches—as a practicing attorney with real clients with real problems and concerns, and not strictly as a scholar or full-time professor.

As my practice has expanded over the intervening 15 years, my expertise has naturally expanded and deepened, and after 25 years in practice, I still enjoy teaching people about estate planning, doing numerous seminars throughout the year, either on my own or through various EAP programs that have asked me to educate different companies' employees. The book, therefore, has expanded to encompass my deepening understanding of the needs of those clients that require estate planning and to address the questions and issues that I am asked on a daily basis.

My view has always been that, unfortunately, estate planning is given the respect of the unwanted "step-child" or "poor relation" in the practice of law and that belief flows from instructor to student in the college setting as well. I'm not suggesting that this treatment is intentional, but stems from a belief in the field of law that estate planning attorney's work is "merely" transactional "grunt" work. Perhaps this mindset comes directly from a lawyer's law school education where litigation and the various topics that usually require litigation are stressed most from day one.

It is my opinion that this belief about the practice of estate planning leads to dry and boring textbooks, which leads to dry and uninspiring classroom instruction. Everyone in the classroom then just grins and bears it, and eventually the student will learn something "interesting" like criminal law or personal injury. No wonder students think estate planning boring!

I wanted to write a book that lets a student see that estate planning can be—and IS—an interesting subject of great importance, and learn and eventually practice it in an engaging and understandable manner. In very few areas of law does a lawyer or paralegal get to actually learn something about their clients beyond the immediate problem. My clients have been some of the most interesting and inspiring people I have ever met, and you can learn so much from the older generations in particular. I want the student reader to know that this is a worthwhile and helpful area of practice and that it is far from boring.

Wills, Trusts, and Estates Administration is a textbook specifically designed for paralegal students and legal professionals. Any book for paralegal or legal assisting students and professionals must be cognizant of the fact that legal assisting training can vary widely. Therefore, a book for paralegals must take all types of readers and their objectives and levels of sophistication into account. This book does not presuppose a prior background in legal studies of any kind. The book is appropriate for the longtime continuing student, and it is ideal for the lifelong learner.

Since the time made available for study of wills, trusts, and estate administration will vary from program to program, this book encompasses the various program modalities, with a focus on two-year and four-year programs. The core materials may easily be covered in a six-week course. There are ample materials for those instructors with the luxury of a longer semester in which to cover the materials, or for the professional needing a comprehensive desk reference. Each chapter is fairly self-contained and, for the most part, can be used independently of the chapters before and after it.

The goal of this book is to cover the information in a clear and concise manner so that a reader will be confident that the knowledge gained and aided by this text will serve the reader throughout his or her career in legal assisting or beyond. Various features motivate the reader and reinforce learning difficult concepts through language that is easy to understand without becoming boring or pedantic. Illustrations, charts and tables, terminology, and appellate court case summaries illustrative of core concepts are found throughout the text. Appendices include wills of some famous people and Form 706 in its entirety. It will be up to the instructor's discretion as to whether or not to assign reading from the appendices or to give detailed instruction on filling out Form 706, although reading the wills of famous people is a lot of fun. Chapter objectives are at the beginning of each chapter and summaries of the materials are at the end of each chapter. Key Terms are also at the end of each chapter so that students are given a snapshot reminder of those terms that they should know at the end of each chapter. Review questions and projects are designed so that instructors can make assignments appropriate for their individual programs and students. Such pedagogical features assist in the retention of learning key concepts. Students may want to tackle the projects, even if they are not assigned, to develop a deeper understanding of the concepts.

Suzan D. Herskowitz

New to the Fourth Edition

Key Pedagogical Changes

A variety of important pedagogical changes have been made in the text for this edition to improve comprehension and concept retention. Major changes in this regard include the following:

- **More Review Questions** have been added to ensure that students master key chapter concepts.
- **New Project Assignments** have been added to develop student's analytical and critical thinking skills.
- **More headings** have been added to the text narrative to make it easier for students to identify and locate key topics within chapters. I have also made greater use of lists and bullet points to help organize information for students.
- **More and varied examples** have been added throughout the text.

Substantive Content Changes

- **New topics** added to this edition include the following:
  - An entire chapter on ethics
  - Additional information on community property distribution especially as it relates to intestacy
  - The risks of writing your own will
  - The Patient Self-Determination Act is explained
  - The problem of elder financial abuse
  - Revocable transfer on death deeds
  - Uniform succession
- **All statistics in the text are up-to-date** and include appropriate source references. These statistics illustrate the aging of America, Americans' beliefs about wills and advance directives, and what drives an American adult to inquire about or require estate planning assistance (or not).
- **Expanded explanations of many topics have been incorporated throughout the textbook.**   In some instances, this was accomplished through a re-write of sections of a chapter and in others by the addition of more and better examples. The decision as to what to add and expand was based on book reviewer recommendations and the author's experience with her own clients and seminar participants, and the types of questions that they have asked over the last 25 years. If clients ask a question enough times, a student will also have the same question and deserves an answer.
- **New Chapter 14, Paralegals and Ethics.**   Reviewers asked for more material on ethics and we decided that an entire chapter should be written. While the chapter is not a comprehensive study of ethics, it is a study of ethics as a paralegal working in an estate planning and elder law environment will likely encounter.

MYLEGALSTUDIESLAB VIRTUAL LAW OFFICE EXPERIENCE FOR WILLS, TRUSTS, AND ESTATES ADMINISTRATION, FOURTH EDITION

The MyLegalStudiesLab Virtual Law Office Experience for *Wills, Trusts, and Estate Administration* is a multi-media course program including an integrated e-book designed to provide students with the tools they need to confirm their mastery of legal concepts and applications and then apply their knowledge and skills in a workplace context. Students watch realistic video scenarios, work with case files and documents, and use the technology tools they will find in the law office to do the work a paralegal will be asked to do in practice. Throughout the course students build a portfolio of work that demonstrates that they have the training and experience employers are looking for.

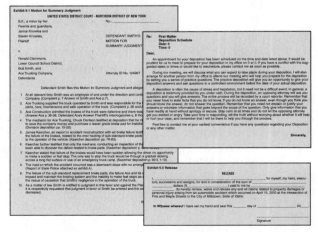

■ **Students engage in a workplace experience as a law office intern**

■ **Students see technology being used in the law office and develop an understanding of how best to deploy technology in practice**

■ **Students build a comprehensive portfolio of workplace products to show potential employers**

■ **Students can test their mastery of concepts and concept application by taking quizzes and receiving feedback and a link to e-book content**

Within the MyLegalStudiesLab students can access a wealth of resources to complete assignments including:

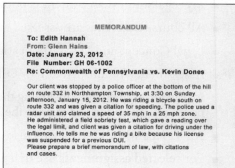

- *Ask the Law Librarian Instructional Videos* to answer student's research and writing questions

- *Ask Technical Support* links to the Technology Resources Website for technology and legal software support

  AbacusLaw Tutorials
  LexisNexis Casemap Tutorials
  SmartDraw Tutorials
  Sanction Tutorials
  Microsoft Office Tutorials

- *Forms File* contains hundreds of examples of commonly used legal documents for the major legal specialties.

- *Case Materials* contain all of the case information and documents needed to complete assignments

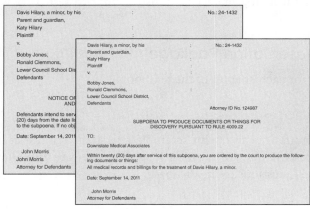

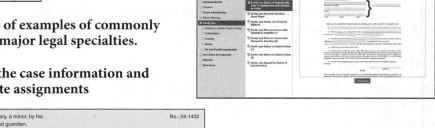

ACCIDENT SCENE

- MyLegalStudiesLab makes it easy for you to confirm that students are achieving measurable outcomes for knowledge of the law, procedural knowledge, and administrative workplace skills.

- MyLegalStudiesLab content is book-specific with an integrated e-book built into the program.

- All course outcomes are assessed and include all AAFPE recommended Learning Objectives.

- Legal Concept and Legal Application quiz questions feed an instructor gradebook.

- Assessments for all Virtual Law Office Experience assignments include grading rubrics.

- Instructor supplements, including the Instructor's Manual, PowerPoint Lecture Screens, and Test Generator have been upgraded and include the Virtual Law Office Assignment teaching notes and rubrics.

- All Videos within the Lab are also available on DVD in a high resolution format for use in the classroom.

- For selected assignments use of legal software is integrated into the Virtual Law Office Experience to be assigned at the instructor's option.

A MyLegalStudiesLab access code with or without the Pearson eText can be packaged with the print textbook at a value price or can be purchased standalone in a bookstore or online. Please consult your local representative for purchasing information or go to www.mylegalstudieslab.com.

Additional Resources for Instructors

To access supplementary materials online, instructors need to request an instructor access code. Go to www.pearsonhighered.com/irc, where you can register for an instructor access code. Within 48 hours of registering, you will receive a confirming e-mail including an instructor access code. Once you have received your code, locate your text in the online catalog and click on the Instructor Resources button on the left side of the catalog product page. Select a supplement, and a log in page will appear. Once you have logged in, you can access instructor material for all Prentice Hall textbooks.

Instructor's Manual

The Instructor's Manual contains suggested course syllabi, chapter outlines, answers to "Questions for Review," and suggestions for additional teaching materials. It also includes a test bank with answers and transparency masters.

PowerPoint Lecture Presentation Package

Lecture screens are available for each chapter of the textbook.

Electronic Test Generator

This program can create custom tests and print scrambled versions of a test at one time, as well as build tests randomly by chapter, level of difficulty, or question type. The software also allows online testing and record-keeping and the ability to add Questions to the database.

CourseConnect Wills, Trusts, & Estates Law Online Course

Looking for robust online course content to reinforce and enhance student learning? We have the solution: CourseConnect! CourseConnect courses contain customizable modules of content mapped to major learning outcomes. Each learning object contains interactive tutorials, discussion questions, MP3 downloadable lectures, assessments, and interactive activities that address different learning styles. CourseConnect courses follow a consistent 21-step instructional design process, yet each course is developed individually by instructional designers and instructors who have taught the course online. Test questions, created by assessment professionals, were developed at all levels of Blooms Taxonomy. When you buy a CourseConnect course, you purchase a complete package that provides you with detailed documentation you can use for your accreditation reviews. CourseConnect courses can be delivered in any commercial platform such as **WebCT, BlackBoard, Angel, Moodle, or eCollege** platforms. For more information contact your representative or call 800-635-1579.

Acknowledgments

The first edition of this book, the very skeletal structure of the book, would not exist but for my former students at Keiser College (now Keiser University), Fort Lauderdale, Florida, who were my "laboratory" during the drafting of that first edition. They listened to lectures, answered sample review questions, participated in many of the projects throughout the text, and offered numerous suggestions and comments, all with good cheer. I have kept in touch with a few over the years, and I thank all of them for their help.

I would again like to thank my dear friend, Jennifer Shea-Roop of Wells Fargo Financial Advisors, for her assistance with certain financial planning questions and my friend and accountant, William A. Lipps, CPA for his assistance regarding income and estate tax questions. It is comforting to know you can have someone on "speed dial" when the need arises.

I have to give credit to my clients over the last 26 years, and to my own family, from whom I have learned so much about family dynamics in the face of aging, financial crises, marriage, birth, illness, and death. Without them, I would not be the estate planning and elder lawyer I have become, and would not have the wealth of information to impart in this fourth edition.

Much thanks to Linda Cupp, Jessica Sykes, and Tanika Henderson, and to Gary Bauer, Senior Acquisitions Editor at Prentice Hall, for his assistance and putting up with me yet again. Thanks to all the wonderful people at Pearson Prentice Hall for bringing this project to fruition.

I would also like to thank the reviewers and instructors who reviewed the text and some of whom wrote directly to me, whose constructive criticism has been most helpful. I hope that I have used their thoughtful comments wisely and that they find the additions and changes to this edition meet their approval:

Laura Alfano, Virginia College Online Division

Steve Dayton, Fullerton College

Terrence P. Dwyer, Western Connecticut State College

Beth R. Pless, Northeast Wisconsin Technical College

Ruth Ann Hall, University of Alabama

Charles R. Splawn, Horry-Georgetown Technical College

Valarie A. Hall, Pima Community College, Downtown Campus

Chapter **one**

PURPOSE AND
NEED FOR A WILL

What is the purpose of a will? Why do we all need one? These questions may not seem interesting or important to most people. Most people don't like to think about wills. And for younger people, death seems a long way off.

For some students who are studying to be paralegals, wills don't seem particularly interesting either. Wills don't hold the same appeal as a custody battle, a car wreck, or a juicy murder trial. Keep in mind that many people will never be involved in custody suits or automobile accidents, if they are lucky. Most people will never be involved in a murder. As Ben Franklin said, however, two things in life are certain—death and taxes. Suddenly, the study of wills becomes much more important.

Why Most People Don't Have Wills

With the exception of those who are not of sound mind or otherwise legally incapacitated, all adults may execute a will. Yet, according to various studies taken in recent years, more than half of all Americans do not have a will. A 2010 study undertaken by Findlaw.com found that 55% of Americans don't have a will, a 3% decrease since its 2008 study. Another survey by EZLaw Blog, however, found that only 36% of survey respondents have a will, although 62% of respondents said it was important to have one! Those who are older and married and those with higher incomes have a will according to the Findlaw.com study, which showed that almost all those polled over age 55 have a will. A similar study undertaken in 2000 by AARP indicated that the older a person was, the more likely he or she was to have executed the documents necessary for end-of-life (44% of those age 50–54, but 85% of those 80 and older). The Findlaw.com study, however, indicated that for those in the age 18–34 category only one in six people had a will.

Wills are not something people look forward to with a sense of happy anticipation. The average person looks forward to enjoying

OBJECTIVES

At the end of this chapter, the student will understand:

- the definition of a will
- why a will is necessary
- common terms used in the study of wills and trust

certain benefits available upon reaching the age of majority (age 18 in most states). He or she can't wait to get a driver's license without restrictions; to vote in state and national elections; to drink legally; and to not require parental permission, to name a few benefits of majority. Yet, while the ability to execute a will is also a privilege of majority, it is not something most healthy adults dream of doing in the near future. Rather, most relegate having a will drafted for them to the area of "someday soon."

Nobody wants to think about his or her death, especially when one is young, healthy, and has an entire lifetime ahead. Procrastination and the fear of one's own mortality are probably the two main reasons why a person does not execute a will.

Another reason is that many people look around at their accumulated property and assume they don't have enough wealth to warrant the time and expense of having a will drafted. One thing a paralegal should keep in mind is that everyone has property, and some people have much more than they realize. Interestingly, a survey conducted by PNC Advisors in Pittsburgh in 2005 found that the wealthier a person is, the less likely it is that he or she has executed a will. The study found that 20% of people with at least $500,000 in investable assets do not have a will, and for those with $10 million or more, a whopping 43% didn't have wills. Yet, according to the 2010 National Statistics Report (most recent), 2,465,936 Americans die every year without executing a will.

Other reasons for not having a will in recent years, as indicated by the EZLaw Blog survey respondents was that they were more focused on paying bills and buying groceries, that estate planning was too time consuming, expensive, complicated, or unnecessary. Thirteen percent believed that their spouse or children would inherit automatically upon their death, which we will later learn may not be the case.

Clearly, having a will and associated documentation, which bundled together are called **estate planning**, is an important field for a paralegal to have knowledge of.

The remainder of this chapter will discuss wills in general (wills will be discussed fully in Chapters 4 and 5), their purpose, and why, despite the average person's seeming aversion to them, they are so very important.

What Is a Will?

A **will** is a written declaration of a person's intent to distribute property after his or her death. As important as letting family and friends know how you want assets to be distributed upon your death, the will, also called a last will and testament, is the method by which **title to property** may be transferred. Wills, executed while the person is alive, are **ambulatory** documents, meaning they are legally binding only upon the person's death. This definition is important to remember since, while a will is a legally binding document, it only becomes effective upon death and therefore is totally and completely *revocable* by the person. That person may also sell or give away any property given to a *beneficiary* in the will and not be concerned that the beneficiary will not receive the property upon his or her death. In practical terms, this means that Ms. *Testator* can, if she desires, *execute* a will in January, change it in March, sell certain property promised to someone in the will in April, buy additional property in June, and effectively change all her beneficiaries in

September—and nothing can be done about it. Until Ms. Testator dies, a will only expresses her intent to leave property to someone. Only upon her death are the expressions made in her will legally binding and potential beneficiaries are powerless to direct or dictate how a person's property will be distributed upon her death. As put more bluntly to his law students, the late Professor E. Reed Quilliam of Texas Tech University School of Law stated that a person doesn't have heirs until he's dead. The corollary is that a person doesn't have a right to your property until you die.

THE PROFESSIONAL PARALEGAL

A paralegal should always consult with his or her supervising attorney before talking directly to a client.

Example: In his will dated March 1, 2011, Jim Simon left his car, a green 2011 Jaguar XKR-S convertible, to his daughter, Beth, and his CrissCraft motorboat to his nephew, Bill Parks. He also left his ski lodge in Aspen to his son, Graham. He gave the rest of his property to various charities.

Jim sold the Jaguar in September 2011 purchasing a new Mercedes SLS AMG Coupe instead. In March 2012, he gave the ski lodge to an old army buddy as a birthday present. Jim then died in April 2012.

Beth will not receive the Jaguar since Jim sold it before his death, and she does not get the Mercedes as the will specified that she was to receive the Jaguar. Graham will not receive the ski lodge since Jim gave that away also. The only beneficiaries that will benefit from Jim's will are his nephew, Bill, and the named charities. In essence, because a will is **ambulatory**, Jim's selling and buying of his cars, and the gift of his ski lodge, revoked those gifts made in the will. Jim was totally within his rights to do with his property as he saw fit during his lifetime, and his will, despite having been executed, was not the controlling factor in his decisions. His named beneficiaries were only his potential beneficiaries until he died and it was determined what property remained in his estate at the time of his death.

The Need for Estate Planning and the Need for a Will

What happens if someone dies without a will? Examine this scenario: Bobbie Black is a successful business person, a divorced single mother with two teenage children, Tina, age 13, and Todd, age 16. One night, driving home from a late meeting, she is killed in a car accident.

An exhaustive search of Bobbie's personal belongings was made—inquiries to friends, family, her ex-husband, and business associates, and a general notice was placed in the local paper asking for information. When all of these methods proved unsuccessful, a court-ordered search of her safe deposit box was performed, but to no avail. The conclusion was that Bobbie died without having executed a will.

Bobbie died **intestate**. This means she died without having executed a legal will. With some exception, the laws of **intestate succession** will determine how and to whom all the property she possessed at the time of her death will be distributed.

Intestate succession is the method that each individual state or jurisdiction uses to determine heirship of a deceased person. The method the state provides may not be what a person intended, but without a will it is the prescribed method used. In no particular order of importance, the following is a list of consequences that may occur if someone dies intestate.

Estate Taxes

When a person dies, the *estate* is subject to taxation in the form of state and federal estate taxes, and in some states, inheritance taxes. If Bobbie had a will, then she could have determined how and from what source any estate taxes (often called "death taxes" by politicians) would be paid.

An **apportionment clause** is a clause in a will allocating the tax burden of the beneficiaries in a will. Since there was no will, state law will determine the method by which the taxes will be paid; without this clause the tax burden is generally borne on the beneficiaries. This person, often the spouse or children, would then bear the largest tax burden of all the beneficiaries. An apportionment clause can spread the burden differently as seen fit.

Distribution of Wealth

Most people consider the ability to determine who will receive their property upon their death to be the paramount reason for executing a will. When someone dies intestate, the state—not the individual—determines how much and to whom all the deceased's property will go. Often, the distribution is not as the deceased intended.

In this case, assume that Bobbie had remarried. Perhaps her husband assumed he would get the lion's share of Bobbie's wealth, or maybe he and Bobbie had already decided that Bobbie's children, Tina and Todd, should receive the biggest share of the pie. Perhaps Bobbie wanted to insure that her sister was well taken care of. Because Bobbie had no will, though, the state statute controlling intestate succession determines which of Bobbie's survivors get her estate and in what proportion.

Appointment of Guardians for Minors

Bobbie left behind two teenage children when she died, Tina and Todd. Without a will that specifically stated whom she wanted to take care of her children and their property, the appointment of the minor children's guardian, or guardians, will be determined by a court.

A **guardian** is a person who is appointed to care for and manage the minor person, the minor's property, or both person and property. The **guardian of the person** is responsible for the care and custody of the minor person. The **guardian of the property** is responsible for a minor's property until the child reaches the age of majority, or is otherwise legally emancipated. While a minor's parents are always the natural guardians of the person, they are not automatically the natural guardians of the property.

In our scenario, we will assume that Bobbie would have wanted the children's father to be their guardian, and in fact, the father would automatically be the guardian of the person of both her children. However, since Bobbie died intestate, a few potential problems might still arise.

While the court will probably appoint the father as the most natural choice as the children's guardian of the person, it may not name him as guardian of their property. This may be an undue hardship if the father has to formally request funds for his children's care and well-being with regularity, and there was no evidence that he was unfit to handle the funds. On the other hand, Bobbie's relatives might decide to contest the ex-husband's custody of the children. Despite being first choice as guardian by any court, it is possible that someone could convince the court that it would not be in the children's best interest for the father to be named as the children's legal guardian.

What would happen if the children's father had predeceased Bobbie? A court will have to select a guardian based on "the best interest of the child." Usually, this will be a blood relative. If Bobbie had a will, she could have named her first choice, her closest friend, Sally, to be her children's guardian. Since Bobbie didn't have a will, it is more likely that the court will appoint Bobbie's mother, despite the fact that Bobbie and her mother did not get along and that Bobbie believed her mother would not raise the children in the manner that Bobbie preferred. In a worst-case scenario, if nobody steps forward to take in Tina and Todd, they could become wards of the state, further complicating matters. This is especially a problem when there are no surviving blood relatives or when the potential guardians cannot take more than one child without hardship. The children may be split up if a family willing to take both children cannot be found (and they are teenagers, making placement difficult from the outset) and the court will have to appoint a special guardian to handle their financial affairs, depleting their funds.

Another potential method of protecting the children is through the use of a pre-need guardianship document, which will be discussed fully in Chapter 6, but is currently valid only in the State of Florida.

Creation of a Testamentary Trust

A trust is a legal agreement in which a person called the **settlor** transfers legal title of property to a **trustee**. The trustee will then manage the property for beneficiaries. A **testamentary trust** is a trust which is drafted as part of the testator's will and only becomes effective upon the testator's death (and, therefore, is as ambulatory as the will it is part of).

Assume Bobbie had amassed a large and lucrative stock portfolio, which upon her death passed to her children (assume they are her only heirs). If she had a will, she then could have established a testamentary trust. This trust would have set many parameters for the care and control of all of her assets, including stocks, as well as the distribution of the dividends and other stock income. For example, she could have determined when the brokerage firm could be replaced, and guidelines for divesting the stocks, as well as how much income the children would receive, how often, and for what purpose. The assets in the trust would not have to be managed by the children's guardian since the trustee would take care of the assets instead. Without a will, however, this type of trust cannot be established. Trusts will be discussed in their entirety in Chapter 7.

Appointment of a Personal Representative

A **personal representative**, or executor, is the person who administers the deceased's estate and carries out the terms of the will. He or she gathers the assets, pays all debts and taxes, and distributes the property as the deceased wished. When someone such as Bobbie dies intestate, the court must appoint a person who will administer the estate. This person no longer called a personal representative and is instead given the name of administrator. This person may not be whom Bobbie would have appointed if she had the choice. The personal representative's duties and obligations will be discussed more fully in Chapter 8.

Funeral Arrangements and Organ Donation

Some people insist that their funeral arrangements be enumerated in the will. Some attorneys agree with this process and will put all the funeral arrangements in the document. Doing so is often comforting to the testator since he or she can state all of his or her wishes in the will, including the costs and arrangements for caskets, funeral services, flowers, cremation or burial plot, and any other service he or she may want. It relieves the testator's mind that he or she is unburdening his loved ones.

In our scenario, Bobbie died without a will. If she made funeral arrangements through some other means including pre-need or pre-planning for the funeral or cremation with the funeral home of her choice, all of her decisions about her funeral arrangements would have been made, relieving her family of a significant burden who will otherwise be required to make the decision at the time of the testator's death, often causing the family to make ill-informed and expensive decisions during their time of grief. The family will make all the arrangements (and often pay for them) without the benefit of knowing what Bobbie may have wanted.

Be aware that even when this clause is drafted into a will, doing so is often an exercise in futility. The will is rarely found, or even looked for, before the testator has been buried. In addition, some families ignore the testator's wishes altogether. Often the family will do only what it thinks is best regardless of what the testator put in a will, or what opinions the testator voiced while alive. They will bury someone who wanted to be cremated, have a religious ceremony for someone who hadn't been to church in 40 years, buy flowers the testator hated, as well as ignore any other desire the testator may have stated. The only portion of most funeral arrangement clauses of use in a will is in regard to how the arrangements shall be paid. Pre-need and prepaid funeral arrangements are generally the best things a person can do for his family concerning the actual arrangements. Unfortunately, however, an attorney and his or her staff have little control over this, other than to have the names of different facilities that could be of assistance to the client if asked.

Wills can also be a vehicle to state a desire to be an organ donor. Like funeral arrangements, a person's organs are no longer useful by the time the will is accessed. Other methods of stating a wish for donation are available. Organ donation and the preferable methods of making this designation will be discussed fully in Chapter 6.

Writing One's Own Will

This subject will be discussed in the chapters on drafting a will, Chapters 4 and 5. There are a few benefits and many pitfalls in writing one's own will.

SUMMARY

While almost 2.5 million Americans die each year, over half of them die without a will despite a will's importance as a means for a person to determine how and to whom all his or her worldly goods will be distributed upon death. Dying intestate (without a legal will) may have unintended consequences, causing many possible problems to arise, including estate taxes, arguments over a minor child's care, property being distributed in a manner not intended or desired, and the need to find someone willing to handle the distribution of the estate assets. These issues can be addressed by the execution of an estate plan, not the least of which includes a will.

KEY TERMS

will
intestate
intestate succession
title to property
estate planning

settlor
trustee
residuary
apportionment clause
guardian

guardian of the person
guardian of the property
testamentary trust
personal representative

REVIEW QUESTIONS

1. According to Findlaw.com how many Americans have not prepared a will as of 2010? What reasons might a person have to forego this planning? What do the other surveys indicate about Americans' propensity to plan their estates?

2. Why does a minor child need a guardian? What types of guardianships are available for a minor child?

3. What are the arguments for and against putting funeral directions in a will?

4. Define *will*. How does a person's execution of a will affect his distribution of his property during his lifetime? Why?

5. What is intestate succession?

6. What is an apportionment clause?

7. Examine this scenario: Bobbie Black died unexpectedly and had executed a will. Bobbie was a single woman with no children. She left $20,000 each to her dear friends Sally and Mona. She also left $20,000 to the local no-kill animal shelter to provide for the care of her dog, Lucky. The remainder of her property was left to her ex-husband, Paul (whom she made a beneficiary specifically after they were divorced). Assume Bobbie had a $4 million taxable estate. Bobbie's will has the following clause:

> I direct that my Executor pay out of my **residuary** estate, without apportionment, all estate, inheritance, succession, and other taxes (together with any penalty thereon), assessed by reason of my death, imposed by the Government of the United States, or any state or territory thereof, or by any foreign government or political subdivision thereof, in respect to all property required to be included in my gross estate for estate or like death tax purposes by any of such governments, whether the property passes under this will or otherwise, including property over which I have a power of appointment, without contribution by any recipient of any such property.

Who will bear the tax burden of Bobbie's estate?

PROJECTS

1. Go to www.findlaw.com and read the excerpts of the study regarding Americans and their estate planning (http://blogs.findlaw.com/law_and_life/2010/12/findlaw-survey-most-americans-dont-have-a-will.html and http://company.findlaw.com/pr/2010/120110.wills.html). Is there anything else you find interesting about this study?

2. Go to www.aarp.org and review the similar study (http://www.aarp.org/research/endoflife/wills/aresearch-import-424.html). Are there any differences from the Findlaw study? What are they and do you think they are significant? Why? What do you think about the EZLaw Blog survey?

MyLegalStudiesLab™   http://www.mylegalstudieslab

MYLEGALSTUDIESLAB VIRTUAL LAW OFFICE EXPERIENCE ASSIGNMENTS

Complete the pre-test, study plan, and post-test for this chapter and answer the Legal Applications questions as assigned.

These will help you confirm your mastery of the concepts and their application to legal scenarios. Then complete the Virtual Law Office assignments as assigned by your instructor. These assignments are designed to develop your workplace skills and result in producing documents for inclusion in your portfolio.

Chapter **two**
PROPERTY

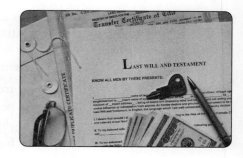

Classification and Definition of Property

All people own property of some kind. You may own a car, a house, clothes, money in checking and savings accounts, a television, or furniture. In addition, you may have 401k retirement plans, bicycles, kayaks, books, and pets. Since the purpose of a will is to distribute property according to the ***testator***'s wishes, a will would be unnecessary without ownership of property. Property, therefore, is the main element behind the entire subject of wills, trusts, and estate administration. This makes the study of the various kinds of property and the ways it can be owned imperative for the paralegal. An understanding of property rights will enable the paralegal to discuss clients' estates with the supervising attorney and with the client, as well as draft the necessary documents properly.

Classification of Property: Real Property and Personal Property
Real Property

Real property, also known as realty or real estate, is any type of property that is immovable, fixed, or permanent. It includes the following:

- The land, including the airspace above the land and the area below the surface of the land. Ownership of the area below the surface will bestow mineral rights on the owner.
- Structures permanently affixed to the land, including houses, offices, barns, or any other building on the land.
- Objects attached to the land or buildings. These are called fixtures.

OBJECTIVES

At the end of this chapter, the student will understand:

- the definitions of real and personal property
- the difference between a joint tenancy, a tenancy in common, a tenancy by the entirety, and community property
- the different estates in property
- what probate and non-probate assets are

Fixtures are objects that were once personal property but have become permanently attached to land or buildings. Once personal property becomes a fixture, it changes its character and becomes real property.

Examples of fixtures are:

- trees
- perennial plants
- shrubs
- built-in appliances (For example, ovens, sinks)
- air conditioner units (not window units)
- hot water heaters

Items that can easily be removed, such as a painting on the wall or a refrigerator, are not fixtures, but keep their original character as personal property.

Personal Property

Personal property is all remaining property that is not realty; that is, not land, permanently affixed structures, or fixtures. Personal property can be further classified as either **tangible personal property** or **intangible personal property**.

Tangible personal property is substantive. It can be touched and is movable. Examples of tangible personal property include the following:

- this book
- dishes and glassware
- cars
- computers
- televisions
- DVDs and DVD players
- cameras
- paintings and photographs
- jewelry
- tools
- houseplants
- window unit air conditioners
- furniture
- your smartphone

Intangible personal property cannot be touched. This concept often confuses clients and often comprises the largest portion of their assets, and it also causes confusion for students, so it is important to understand. Examples of intangible personal property include the following:

- stocks
- patents, copyrights, and trademarks
- royalties, such as oil and gas royalties
- checks
- promissory notes
- 401ks and other individual retirement accounts (IRAs)
- savings accounts, checking accounts, and money market accounts
- cash

While you may have stock certificates or a promissory note, the paper they are written on is worth very little. What that stock certificate is evidence of, however, may be worth a great deal.

Example: John Martinez owns a share in Apple. The stock certificate itself will be worth only the value of the paper and ink, almost nothing, surely not much more than $1. However, that one share is evidence that John owns one share of Apple and its true value is whatever that share's posted value is on the stock exchange on any particular day. Note that in practice, most brokerage firms no longer issue stock certificates and the owners of the shares only receive monthly or quarterly statements showing what they own, how many shares, the current value of those shares, and whether they had a gain or loss. This is called a "street registration" and is truly an intangible asset.

Two types of intangible property that jurisdictions may treat as tangible property are stamp and coin collections. Despite the fact that a collectible coin or stamp may be worth far more than its face value, it is classified as a "collection" rather than merely a series of stamps or coins.

Chose in action is a form of intangible personal property. Specifically, it refers to a personal right you retain when you do not possess the property, but have a right to recover in a lawsuit.

Example: Joan agrees to loan Cindy $1000. They draw up a promissory note in which Cindy agrees to pay the money back at the end of 3 months. When Cindy does not repay Joan in a timely manner, the promissory note is evidence of Joan's right to bring a lawsuit against Cindy for the $1000.

Forms of Property

Once property is properly classified as either real property or personal property, it is important to determine how title to the property was held. Since we are maintaining that a will distributes a testator's property upon his or her death, it is important to know:

1. that the person owned the property, and
2. once we know the person owned the property, how was the title to the property held. Property is either owned by one person alone, or by two or more people at the same time.

Owned in Severalty

Many people see the term "severally," think "several," and therefore, "many" and arrive at the conclusion that property **owned severally** means that two or more people own the property. However, property that is owned *severally* means the opposite. Property owned severally is owned solely by one person, either an individual person or an individual company and no others. This gives that sole owner absolute ownership, the exclusive right to use, sell, lease, give away, or even throw away the property. The person is said to own the property "in severalty."

Example: Jill Hope purchases her home at 100 N. Main Street by herself. Only Jill's name is listed on the **deed**. Jill owns it in severalty. Only Jill has an ownership interest in the home, giving her the sole right to sell it, lease it, mortgage it, or give it away as a gift.

Example: Jill inherits a car from her Aunt Rose. Jill now owns the car in severalty.

Joint Ownership

Joint ownership refers to when two or more persons own property concurrently; that is, at the same time. The most common forms of joint ownership are:

- joint tenancy
- tenancy in common
- tenancy by the entirety
- community property

Joint Tenancy

Joint tenancy is a form of joint ownership of property by two or more persons who are called *joint tenants*. The interest each joint tenant holds at the inception of the initial possession is characterized by the *four unities of title*, which are:

- Time
- Title
- Interest
- Possession

What this means is that all the joint tenants receive an identical interest in the title to the property at the same time and have an equal right to possess the property. All four unities are required for a valid joint tenancy.

Example: Assume Becky Black is a single mother with three adult children: Tina, Todd, and Ted. She decides to retire and go on a round-the-world cruise. Wanting to divest herself of material responsibility, she executes a deed giving her house at 100 N. Main Street to her children equally. The pertinent deed language states "Becky Black, as Grantor, for and in consideration of the love and affection of the Grantor for the Grantees, does hereby grant and convey, without warranty, unto Tina Black, Todd Black, and Ted Black, Grantees, in equal shares as joint tenants."

In this example, a joint tenancy between Tina, Todd, and Ted has been formed:

- Time—one deed
- Title—one deed
- Interest—equal shares, 1/3 each

- Possession—joint tenancy presumes that each owner has an identical right to possess the property (although as a practical matter, families often allow one of the parties to live on and care for the property or they lease it to a tenant)

The unique characteristic of joint tenancy is the concept of **right of survivorship**. Upon the death of one tenant, his or her interest passes automatically to the surviving joint tenants. The sole remaining joint tenant will own the property outright. In many jurisdictions, the term "right of survivorship" must be clearly stated, or it will not be presumed. For this reason, most attorneys will draft a deed to instead state "Becky Black, as Grantor, for and in consideration of the love and affection of the Grantor for the Grantees, does hereby grant and convey, without warranty, unto Tina Black, Todd Black, and Ted Black, Grantees, in equal shares as joint tenants with right of survivorship" so that the Grantor's intent is made clear.

Right of survivorship is unique because upon the death of one of the joint tenants, the other joint tenants immediately own that joint tenant's interest in the property.

Example: Assume similarly in this scenario that Becky Black is a single mother with three adult children, Tina, Todd, and Ted. She decides to retire and go on a round-the-world cruise. Wanting to divest herself of material responsibility, she executes a deed in 2007 giving her house at 100 N. Main Street to her children equally. The pertinent deed language states "Becky Black, as Grantor, for and in consideration of the love and affection of the Grantor for the Grantees, does hereby grant and convey, without warranty, unto Tina Black, Todd Black, and Ted Black, Grantees, in equal shares as joint tenants with right of survivorship." Tina, Todd, and Ted each own a 1/3 share of the house as joint tenants with right of survivorship.

Tina dies in 2008. Immediately upon Tina's death, Todd and Ted each obtain 1/2 of Tina's interest by right of survivorship, so that Todd and Ted now each own a 1/2 interest in the property. See Figure 2.1.

When Ted dies in 2009, Todd obtains Ted's 1/2 interest in the property and by right of survivorship now owns the entire interest in the property in severalty—solely.

Joint tenancy property is often called a ***non-probate asset*** because the property automatically passes to the survivor(s) as a ***matter of law***. Note that once the final survivor owns the property in severalty, that person will have to leave the property by will or it will pass by intestacy. These concepts will be discussed fully in later chapters.

When Tina, Todd, and Ted were given Becky's house, they each obtained an equal right of possession. As stated earlier, this means that each of them has the right to live on the property or lease the property. If they all lived in the house at the same time, their right of possession is undivided, that is, each of them can use the entire house. As also stated earlier, it may not be practical for all three of them and their families to move in (not to mention local zoning laws may prohibit it), so they may let one of them live on the premises or they may lease it to another. In some families, the children who inherited or received the property as a gift in this manner will sell the property and distribute the proceeds equally among themselves.

At any time, any of the tenants may sever his or her interest in the property by selling or giving away, or otherwise partitioning an interest in the property.

Figure 2.1   Distribution of Joint Tenancy

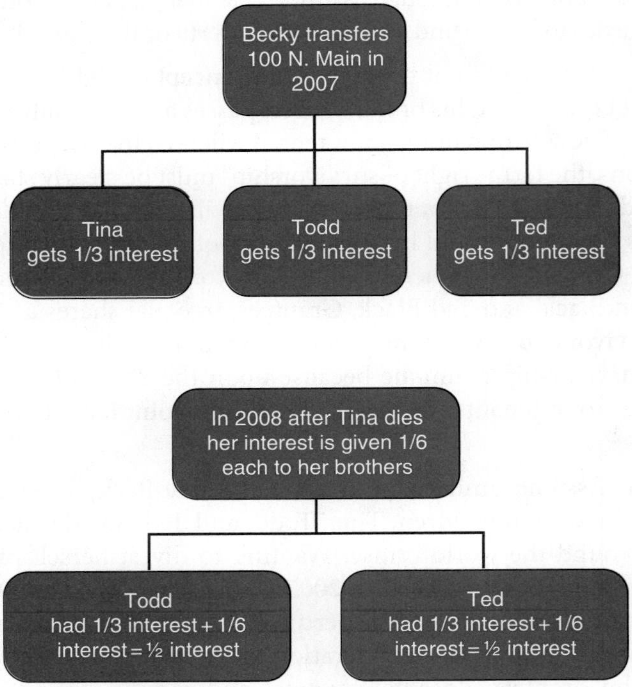

The tenant's act of conveying his or her interest in the property during his or her lifetime destroys one of the four unities and thus ends the joint tenancy. The new tenant does not have a right of survivorship to the other tenants' interests in the property. Instead, the new tenant will be a tenant in common with the other tenants, who will remain joint tenants with right of survivorship with each other. Note that because of local zoning ordinances, severance may require a formal court ordered partition or permission from the local zoning or planning commission. Note this real-life example.

Example: Two brothers Al and Bill, through inheritance, own a 400-acre farm as joint tenants. Al and Bill desire to sever their joint tenancy. Al has a family and he wants his share of the farm to go to his wife and eventually his children upon his death and not to his brother, Bill.

Due to local zoning regulations designed to prevent people from selling to developers, who then create tract housing, and in an effort to maintain the rural setting, the local government required the brothers to obtain an application for subdivision of the property. Part of this process included a promise by the brothers to never redivide the property again. At the end of the process, Al owned 200 acres in severalty and Bill owned 200 acres in severalty.

Joint tenancy is perhaps best known to most people with regard to their bank accounts. It is very common for two or more people to hold checking accounts jointly. Note that state banking regulations promulgate whether or not the words "with right of survivorship" are required to create a true joint tenancy.

The following case illustrates joint tenancy of a checking account, a home, and a business building.

CASE 2.1 **SUMMARY**

DeForge v. Patrick, 76 N.W.2d 733 (Nebraska 1956)

Adelaide Raymond and Nellie Chaplin were sisters who shared a home in Nebraska. Adelaide owned the home and a business building solely. On January 24, 1949, Adelaide conveyed the home and business building to herself and Nellie as joint tenants and not as tenants in common. The deed specifically stated "that in the event of the death of either of said grantees, the entire fee simple title to the real estate described herein shall vest in the surviving grantee."

Similarly, in 1944 the sisters opened a checking account as joint tenants with survivorship rights.

Adelaide died April 15, 1953. She had left debts to be paid but had no other property other than those held jointly with Nellie. Nellie died shortly thereafter on May 15, 1953.

DeForge, the administrator of Adelaide's estate, wanted to know if he could hold the property, requiring Patrick, executor of Nellie's estate, to use the property to pay Adelaide's debts.

The Court responded: "[I]f the purpose to create a joint tenancy is clearly expressed in a deed of conveyance of real estate, the law will permit the intention of the deed to control and a joint tenancy with right of survivorship will be created." The Court had no doubt that Adelaide and Nellie intended to hold both the house and the business building as joint tenants with right of survivorship and that upon the death of one of the sisters, the other would take title to the entire property.

The checking account was opened 8 years before Adelaide's death and the deed was executed 4 years before her death. The Court concluded that it could not be presumed that the debts incurred during Adelaide's last illness were contemplated and that she opened the account or executed the deed with the intent to avoid payment to her creditors. It, therefore, denied DeForge's claim to the property to pay for Adelaide's debts.

Tenants in Common

A tenancy in common occurs when any of the four unities is not present. If the tenants did not receive their respective interests at the same time (on different dates), by the same source (different will, gift, or deed), did not receive the same interest, or each does not have equal right of possession of the property, a **tenancy in common** is formed.

Tenancy in common does not have the benefit of right of survivorship. Each tenant must pass his or her interest by will or it shall be subject to intestacy.

Example: Let's presume in this scenario that Becky Black is a single mother with three adult children, Tina, Todd, and Ted. She decides to retire and go on a round-the-world cruise. Wanting to divest herself of material responsibility, she executes a deed giving her house at 100 N. Main Street to her children. The pertinent deed language states "Becky Black, as Grantor, for and in consideration of the love and affection of the Grantor for the Grantees, does hereby grant and convey, without warranty, a one-half (1/2) interest unto Tina Black, a one-quarter (1/4) interest unto Todd Black, and a one-quarter (1/4) interest unto Ted Black, Grantees."

In this example, a tenancy in common has been formed:

- Time—one deed
- Title—one deed
- Interest—different interests, 1/2 to Tina, 1/4 to Todd, and 1/2 to Ted
- Possession—assumed equal right of possession

Since the unity of interest is not present, a joint tenancy has not been created. When a joint tenancy is not created, a tenancy in common is automatically created.

Example: Becky Black is a single mother with three adult children: Tina, Todd, and Ted. On April 14, 2008, she decides to deed a one-half interest in her house (purchased in 1992) to her children Tina, Todd, and Ted in equal shares (1/6 each), retaining a one-half (1/2) interest. A joint tenancy is not created.

- Time—Becky bought her house in 1992; her children received their interests in 2008.
- Title—Becky by deed in 1992, children by deed in 2008.
- Interest—Becky 1/2, Tina 1/6, Todd 1/6, and Ted 1/6.
- Possession—One assumes that Becky has no intent on giving her children anything beyond an ownership interest in the property and not a right to live there. In fact, assume that Becky continues to pay for all repairs and taxes without any contribution from the children, supporting this.

None of the unities are present in this situation and a tenancy in common has been created.

Example: Let's assume the following instead: Becky Black is a single mother with three adult children: Tina, Todd, and Ted. On April 14, 2007, she deeds one-half (1/2) of the property to Tina, Todd, and Ted in equal shares (1/6 each). On January 15, 2009, Becky dies. Her will leaves the remaining 1/2 of the house (the 1/2 she kept) to Tina, Todd, and Ted equally. At this time, Tina, Todd, and Ted each own a 1/3 interest in the house. Nonetheless, a joint tenancy with right of survivorship has still not been created because the unities were not acquired at the same time.

- Time—1/6 interest to each child in 2007, 1/6 interest to each child in 2009
- Title—by deed in 2007, by will in 2009
- Interest—equal interest, 1/3 each
- Possession—assumed equal right of possession only upon Becky's death when they acquire the remaining interest in the property

Two of the unities are not present and the siblings own the property as tenants in common.

CASE 2.2 **SUMMARY**

Poetz v. Klamberg clearly shows how a court distinguishes between a joint tenancy and a tenancy in common.

Poetz v. Klamberg, 781 S.W.2d 253 (Missouri Court of Appeals, Eastern District, Division Three 1989)

Robert Poetz sued for damages to a car partially owned by him and damaged in a collision between Edward Klamberg and Poetz's daughter, Lisa, the other co-owner of the car.

Klamberg had previously sued Lisa for his injuries and a jury found that Klamberg was 77.5% responsible and Lisa was 22.5% responsible.

The trial court determined that before the accident the car was worth $4700 and afterward only $772 and entered judgment for Poetz for $3928. Klamberg appealed contending that since the car was held by

Poetz and Lisa as tenants in common, he should have been part of the initial lawsuit, therefore barring him from this separate claim. He also contended that if the car was instead held by Poetz and Lisa as joint tenants, Lisa was an essential party to this lawsuit and Lisa was barred because of the prior suit.

The title certificate listed the owners of the car as "Poetz, Robert P. &/or Lisa." State statute said that "every interest in real estate granted or devised to two or more persons, other than executors and trustees and husband and wife, shall be a tenancy in common, unless expressly declared, in such grant or devise, to be a joint tenancy." No similar provision in the statutes existed for personal property, however.

The Court applied case law which said that if the instrument is silent or ambiguous, it will not be construed as creating a joint tenancy. The Court found the use of "&/or" confusing and did not create a joint tenancy, but that the car was owned by Poetz and Lisa as tenants in common, which does not contain the four unities of title.

The Court determined that Poetz was not barred in the present suit, but that his recovery should be limited to his interest in the car and reduced his recovery to $1986.

Tenancy by the Entirety

This form of jointly owned property exists only between husband and wife. It is a special form of joint tenancy that requires the four unities of joint tenancy plus the unity of marriage:

- Time
- Title
- Interest
- Possession
- Marriage

In a **tenancy by the entirety**, both spouses are required to mortgage, sell, or gift the property. In addition, neither spouse may sever the tenancy without written consent of the other.

Not all states recognize tenancy by the entirety. In some states recognizing tenancy by the entirety, any conveyance to spouses automatically creates a tenancy by the entirety regardless of language, while others require explicit language that the property is to be held "by husband and wife as tenants by the entirety" and failure to use the explicit language creates either a joint tenancy with right of survivorship or a tenancy in common.

What makes a tenancy by the entirety desirable, if it is available, is that property held in this manner may be shielded from the reach of creditors. This is especially important if one spouse has debts coming into the marriage or has a business for which he has signed loan guarantees.

It is important to know if your state permits tenancy by the entirety and if it is available for all spousal property, or only real property. For example, in Illinois, only homesteaded real property can be held as tenants by the entirety and not personal property, such as bank accounts.

On the other hand, Virginia Statute §55-20.2 explicitly states "[A]n intent that the part of the one dying should belong to the other shall be manifest from a designation of a husband and wife as "tenants by the entireties" or "tenants by the entirety," but case law states that the simple fact of being husband and wife creates a tenancy by the entirety, as shown in Case Summary 2.4.

Figure 2.2 States That Permit Tenancy by the Entirety by Statute or by Case Law

Alaska	Maryland	Oklahoma
Arkansas	Massachusetts	Oregon
Delaware	Michigan	Pennsylvania
Florida	Missouri	Rhode Island
Hawaii	Mississippi	Tennessee
Illinois	New Jersey	Vermont
Indiana	New York	Virginia
Kentucky	North Carolina	Wyoming

CASE 2.3 **SUMMARY**

Preston v. Burmeister, 52 S.W.3d 386, 389 (Tex.App.-Fort Worth 2001, no pet.)

(Note: Although this case was decided in Texas, the parties stipulated that Florida law be the determining law. This is a divorce and not an estate administration case, but it defines tenancy by the entirety and the unities succinctly.)

Burmeister filed a petition for post-divorce division of property asking for a division of Preston's retirement benefits, which were not addressed in the divorce decree. Preston contributed to his retirement plan with Delta Airlines from 1965 until his retirement in 1996. He was contributing to the plan for almost two years before his marriage to Burmeister and continued to contribute following their 1979 divorce.

The trial court ruled that Burmeister was entitled to an equal share of the retirement benefits already distributed to Preston and to an equal share of all retirement benefits to be distributed to Preston in the future.

Although the appellate court agreed, reversed, and held that the division of the retirement benefits was barred by res judicata, it did discuss the difference between tenancy in common and tenancy by the entirety.

The Court stated that in Florida, "in order to have a tenancy by the entirety in personal property, it must be shown that the husband and wife had unity of possession, unity of interest, unity of title, unity of time, and unity of marriage" and that "once the marriage relationship ends, such property converts to property held by both spouses as tenants in common."

The Court found that Burmeister did not demonstrate to either the trial or appellate courts that the unities necessary to find a tenancy by the entirety existed when Preston began contributing to his retirement account or that they existed during the marriage.

The Court further stated that

given that unity of possession requires joint ownership and control, that unity of time requires the interests to have commenced simultaneously, and that unity of marriage requires the parties to be married at the time the property became titled in their joint names, it is not likely that a Florida court would rule that a tenancy by the entirety in the retirement benefits existed during the marriage.

CASE 2.4 **SUMMARY**

In Re Sampath, 314 B.R. 73 (U.S. Bankr. Court, E.D. Virginia 2004)

In this bankruptcy case, the debtor, Lakshmi Sampath, claimed his interest in a condominium unit, owned by him, his wife, and his daughter, was an exempt asset because it was as tenants by the entirety between him and his wife. When they purchased the property, the deed was titled "as joint tenants with the common-law right of survivorship" and did not mention the marital status of the debtor and his wife. The debtor claimed that he and his wife owned their interest in the property as tenants by the entirety and then with their daughter as joint tenants with right of survivorship. The bankruptcy trustee claimed that because the deed was silent as to the marital relationship between the debtor and his wife, Sampath could not claim the protected status of tenants by the entirety. The significance of the difference, as pointed out by the Court, is that the property would be exempt from the claim of Sampath's individual creditors if it were held as tenants by the entirety. After a lengthy discussion of the common law regarding transfers to husband and wife in Virginia, the Court resolved that "[T]he common-law rule was that a conveyance to a husband and wife—assuming the presence of all the unities—created, by virtue of the legal unity of the husband and wife, a tenancy by the entirety and no other estate." In this case, however, the husband and wife owned the property with their daughter, so the Court continued its analysis. Ultimately, the Court determined that the common-law rule of tenants by the entirety is still valid law in Virginia (although it also discussed other states like Pennsylvania, which by statute, abolished tenants by the entirety).

Community Property

Community property is a form of ownership of property between spouses. In general, community property is all property acquired by a husband or a wife during marriage that is not classified as separate property. *Separate property* is all property acquired prior to marriage or acquired during marriage by gift, will, inheritance, or other means classified as separate by state statute.

Only 10 states permit community property and the law of community property varies in each jurisdiction. Those states are Texas, New Mexico, Arizona, Nevada, California, Idaho, Washington, Louisiana, Wisconsin, and Alaska. The latter two states adopted the Uniform Marital Property Act (UMPA), which uses a community property standard. However, in Alaska, the use of community property by a couple is optional and the default standard is still separate property. In addition, the Commonwealth of Puerto Rico has a form of community property. It is important to note that more than 20% of the U.S. population now lives in a community property state. If you study or work in a community property state at any time, you must become familiar with your state's community property distribution rules (note that portions of the rules may be in the family code and not in the probate code).

In a community property state, each spouse owns 1/2 of the marital estate outright and it is presumed that property acquired during the marriage is community property (although the presumption is rebuttable, it is subject to proof that the property was not a community asset). Upon the death of one spouse, the surviving spouse continues to own his or her half of the estate and the decedent's half is passed by will or intestacy. A spouse may not, under any circumstances, distribute more than his or her 1/2 of the marital estate.

> *Example:* Tex Jones and Jean Jones live in a community property state. When Jean dies in 2007, among their property amassed during their 25-year marriage is their home at 200 Elm Street. Jean did not leave a will. Tex continues to own his 1/2 of the house while Jean's 1/2 passes by intestacy. If Jean had a will and left her half to Tex, he would automatically receive Jean's half; however, under the intestacy laws (discussed in Chapter 3) he may not be the owner of the other half of the house because community property follows different rules for distribution, which will be discussed more fully in Chapter 3.

Clients that move to a separate property jurisdiction from a community property jurisdiction may find, upon the death of a spouse, that the deceased spouse retained his or her community interest in the property. Likewise, clients that move from a separate property jurisdiction to a community property jurisdiction may find that the deceased spouse retained his or her separate property interest.

Advantages and disadvantages of joint tenancy

Advantages:

- automatic transfer of ownership upon death of one joint tenant to other joint tenant(s)
- no probate of that asset—evade certain probate expenses (often called the "poor man's will")
- joint management of the property
- immediate access to the asset by the survivor(s)

Disadvantages:

- disagreement on property management between the tenants
- unintended "inheritance" because the property is not affected by a will
- may destroy estate planning of first to die, since the property automatically belongs to the surviving joint tenant(s) and not necessarily the deceased's beneficiaries
- attachment by joint tenant's creditors (not tenancy by the entirety)
- not affected by contract
- potential tax consequences

Estates

The estate a person holds in property determines the rights and obligations a person has pertaining to that property. Some estates do not convey ownership and knowing that is important when determining if the property is part of a decedent's estate.

Fee Simple

A **fee simple** estate, also called a fee simple absolute or an estate in fee, is the biggest estate a person can hold. It is total ownership of the property and is not subject to restrictions, thereby entitling the owner of this estate to all rights and privileges associated with the property. Subject to the government's right of eminent domain, the estate may not be taken away from the owner or his or her heirs or assigns without consent. While this is total ownership, more than one person may hold a fee interest in the property. In cases such as this, the joint owners are tenants in common. Unless otherwise stated, all conveyances are presumed to create a fee simple estate.

Characteristics of a fee simple estate:

- A fee simple estate is fully transferable during the life of the owner.
  Example: Cassidy Jones owns a mansion in fee simple. Cassidy is free to sell or give away the mansion to any other person during her lifetime. If she sells the mansion to Donald Duck, Donald will own Cassidy's interest, and will own the mansion in fee simple. This is the most recognizable form of ownership and is what most people envisage when they buy their first home from a willing seller.
- A fee simple estate may be transferred by will.

Example: Cassidy Jones owns a mansion in fee simple. She leaves the mansion to her granddaughter, Beth, in her will. When Cassidy dies, Beth will own Cassidy's former interest and owns the mansion in fee simple.

- A fee simple is subject to the claims of creditors. This rule applies both before and after the death of the fee simple owner.

  Example: Cassidy Jones is having some financial troubles. She owes money to Donald Duck. If Cassidy fails to pay Donald, Donald may get a court order requiring Cassidy to sell the mansion and give Donald the money from the proceeds of the sale.

  If Cassidy still owes money to Donald upon her death and the probate estate cannot satisfy the debt with other assets, Donald may be able to require Cassidy's estate to sell the mansion to obtain the money from the proceeds of the sale.

  Perhaps instead, Cassidy had a mortgage on the property (another right of a holder of a fee simple, to mortgage the property); if Cassidy fails to pay her mortgage, the mortgage company may foreclose on the property.

- If the fee simple is not transferred by will, the fee simple will pass through intestacy to the owner's heirs and is subject to the rights of a surviving spouse.

  Example: Bill died without having left a will distributing his property. Upon his death he had two children, Roger and Ernest. He owned his home at 100 Prospect Park in fee simple. Upon his death, the home passes to Roger and Ernest by intestacy, 1/2 share to each of them.

Life Estate

A **life estate** is the right of a person, called the ***life tenant***, to use the property until death.

Example: Regina Smith conveys her house at 100 N. Main Street to her daughter Alex for Alex's life. The pertinent part of the deed states

> Regina smith, Grantor, for and in consideration of the sum of Ten Dollars ($10.00) cash in hand paid by Alex Smith, the Grantee, and for other good and valuable consideration, the receipt and sufficiency of which are hereby acknowledged, hereby grants and conveys, with Special Warranty, unto Alex Smith, Grantee, a life estate in the following described real property.

This is an example of a life estate because Alex has a life estate for the remainder of her life. When she dies, her life estate terminates and her right to the property ceases. She cannot devise this property by will. If she were to sell the property, she could only sell it for her life (a most undesirable purchase, it is rare that a life tenant can sell his or her interest).

A life estate may also be held for the life of another person. If it is held for the life of someone else it is called a ***life estate pur autre vie***. When that person dies, the life estate is terminated and the life tenant must give up the property. The following are examples of life estates.

Example: Bobbie Black conveys her house at 100 N. Main Street to her daughter Tina for the life of Bobbie. The pertinent part of the deed states

> Bobbie Black, Grantor, for and in consideration of the sum of Ten Dollars ($10.00) cash in hand paid by Tina Black, the Grantee, and for other good and valuable consideration, the receipt and sufficiency of which are hereby acknowledged, hereby grants and conveys, with Special Warranty, unto Tina Black, Grantee, a life estate in the following described real property for the life of the Grantor.

> This is an example of a life estate pur autre vie because Tina has a life estate for the life of Bobbie. When Bobbie dies, Tina's life estate terminates and her right to the property ceases.

Another example of a life estate pur autre vie:

> *Example:* Bobbie Black conveys her house at 100 N. Main Street to her daughter Tina for the life of Todd Black, Tina's brother. The pertinent part of the deed states

> Bobbie Black, Grantor, for and in consideration of the sum of Ten Dollars ($10.00) cash in hand paid by Tina Black, the Grantee, and for other good and valuable consideration, the receipt and sufficiency of which are hereby acknowledged, hereby grants and conveys, with Special Warranty, unto Tina Black, Grantee, a life estate in the following described real property for the life of the Todd Black.

> In this example of a life estate pur autre vie, Tina has a life estate for the life of her brother, Todd. When Todd dies, Tina's life estate terminates and her right to the property ceases.

What is interesting about life estate's pur autre vie is that the person retaining the life estate is at the mercy of the other life. If in the situation above, Todd only lives one year, Tina has to find another place to live. These types of life estates are therefore not very popular.

When the grantor conveys the life estate to the life tenant, the grantor may retain a *reversion* in the property. This interest is the right of the grantor to the return of the property upon the termination of the life estate. This is also called a *reversionary interest*.

> *Example:* Bobbie Black conveys her house at 100 N. Main Street to her daughter Tina for the life of Todd Black, Tina's brother. The pertinent part of the deed states

> Bobbie Black, Grantor, for and in consideration of the sum of Ten Dollars ($10.00) cash in hand paid by Tina Black, the Grantee, and for other good and valuable consideration, the receipt and sufficiency of which are hereby acknowledged, hereby grants and conveys, with Special Warranty, unto Tina Black, Grantee, a life estate in the following described real property for the life of the Todd Black.

> When Todd dies, Tina's interest is extinguished. Bobbie has a reversionary interest in the house and the property is returned to her upon Todd's death. This reversionary interest happens automatically because after Todd dies, there is nobody else named as an owner after Tina loses her life estate. The property automatically belongs to Bobbie again, or if she has since died, to her estate.

Instead of having a reversion, a grantor may give someone else the remainder of the property interest. A *remainder* occurs when a grantor gives a life estate to a life tenant and gives the rest to a future owner, someone other than himself or herself. This person is called a **remainderman** (plural, remaindermen).

Example: Bobbie Black conveys her house at 100 N. Main Street to her daughter Tina for the life of Todd Black, Tina's brother. The pertinent part of the deed states

> Bobbie Black, Grantor, for and in consideration of the sum of Ten Dollars ($10.00) cash in hand paid by Tina Black, the Grantee, and for other good and valuable consideration, the receipt and sufficiency of which are hereby acknowledged, hereby grants and conveys, with Special Warranty, unto Tina Black, Grantee, a life estate in the following described real property for the life of the Todd Black, then to Ted Black.

Ted is a remainderman and upon the death of Todd will receive the house in fee simple. Should Ted die before Todd, his remainder will pass to his estate and be distributed by will or by intestacy. The property will not revert to Bobbie and it is important to remember that upon Todd's death, Tina's interest in the property is extinguished.

Another common method, in which estate planners use life estates, is to have the owner of the property transfer the property to himself or herself by deed with the remainder to his or her children. When the owner dies, the property automatically transfers to his or her children and becomes a non-probate asset.

Example: Rachael owns 2500 Peachtree Road in fee simple. She executes a deed conveying the house to herself and her children. The pertinent part of the deed states

> Rachael Grant, Grantor, for and in consideration of the sum of Ten Dollars ($10.00) cash in hand paid by Rachael Grant, Laura Grant, Lance Grant, and Logan Grant, the Grantees, and for other good and valuable consideration, the receipt and sufficiency of which are hereby acknowledged, hereby grants and conveys, without warranty, unto Rachael Grant, Grantee, a life estate in the following described real property, then to Laura Grant, Lance Grant, and Logan Grant as joint tenants with right of survivorship.

In this example, Rachael retains a life estate for her own life, and upon her death, her children have a remainder interest as joint tenants with right of survivorship. This type of deed is often called a "poor man's will" by estate planners because it passes the property to the grantor's children by operation of law instead of by probate, whether by will or intestacy.

Tenancy for Years

In a **tenancy for years**, the time in which the tenant will hold the property is specifically designated. This is a form of *leasehold estate*, however, unlike a lease, in which the landlord retains ownership of the property and the tenant only has the right of use and possession, the person in possession of a tenancy for years has actual ownership of the property for the designated period of time.

Example: Bobbie Black conveys her house at 100 N. Main Street to her daughter Tina only for a period of time. The pertinent part of the deed states

> Bobbie Black, Grantor, for and in consideration of the sum of Ten Dollars ($10.00) cash in hand paid by Tina Black, the Grantee, and for other good

and valuable consideration, the receipt and sufficiency of which are hereby acknowledged, hereby grants and conveys, without warranty, unto Tina Black, Grantee, the following described real property for a period of ten (10) years.

Tina will only hold the house for the 10 years from the date of the conveyance to her. During that period of time, Tina will be able to use and possess the house and even sell the remainder of her 10-year interest (although it is not a desirable purchase). When the 10 years are up, the property will revert to Bobbie.

Probate Versus Non-Probate Assets

Probate assets are all forms of property in a ***decedent's*** estate that require a probate court proceeding to distribute them to the proper beneficiaries or heirs. It does not matter if the property has been conveyed by will ("I give, devise, and bequeath my 1967 Ford Mustang Convertible to my granddaughter, Penelope"), or is being distributed by descent and distribution statutes, that is, intestacy. If it is a probate asset, a court order will be necessary to properly pass title in the property from the decedent's estate to the beneficiaries or heirs.

On the other hand, **non-probate assets** do not require any court proceedings to pass title from the decedent's estate to the beneficiaries or heirs because non-probate assets are neither distributed according to the decedent's will nor by intestacy. In addition, non-probate assets are not subject to the claims of the decedent's creditors, spouse, or children.

In recent years, the goal of many people has been probate avoidance. The need, as well as the understanding, of potential clients to have as few assets as possible be subject to probate proceedings has developed into an entire industry dedicated to assisting clients in the avoidance of probate. Read any special business section of the local newspaper and you are likely to see a myriad of advertisements for free seminars being given by estate planning attorneys and financial planners each promising to teach the layperson the methods necessary to avoid probate. While these seminars are sometimes sponsored by brokerage houses or charitable organizations looking for donations, lending credence to the adage that nothing good in life is free, the methodologies espoused at these seminars are quite valid. Using these methods will often allow a client to, if not totally avoid probate, at least keep the largest portion of his estate out of probate. This has two benefits:

- The property passes to beneficiaries much more quickly; and
- the cost of probate, which can be quite high, is greatly reduced.

Clients must be counseled, however, that it is not always possible to avoid probate totally and while it may be possible to structure a client's assets to avoid probate, it does not necessarily mean that the client will avoid estate taxes. (Estate taxes will be discussed thoroughly in Chapter 11). Any property that does not fall within the specific categories of non-probate assets set forth here is likely to be a probate asset.

Life Insurance

Life insurance is a contract between the insurance company and a person who purchases the insurance benefits. Usually, the person making the purchase contracts for the insurance company to pay a named beneficiary a sum of money upon his death. The sum of money, or proceeds, will be paid directly to the named beneficiary, obviating the need to distribute the property in a probate proceeding.

Example: Doreen Taft buys a life insurance policy with The Life Insurance Company naming her husband, Donald, as her beneficiary. The policy will pay $100,000 to Donald upon Doreen's death. When Doreen dies in 2010, Donald fills out a claim form and sends a copy of the death certificate to The Life Insurance Company. Upon receipt, The Life Insurance Company will send Donald a check for $100,000. No probate proceeding is required for the money to be sent to Donald.

It is important to note, however, that if Doreen had designated her "estate" as the named beneficiary, all the proceeds from the life insurance policy would become probate assets of the estate and would be subject to distribution in probate.

Example: Doreen Taft buys a life insurance policy with The Life Insurance Company naming her husband, Donald, as her beneficiary. The policy will pay $100,000 to Donald upon Doreen's death. When Doreen dies in 2010, Donald was already deceased, having died in 2005. Doreen had not changed the beneficiary designation on the policy and had not named an alternate beneficiary. When Doreen died, the $100,000 life insurance proceeds become part of her probate estate and will pass to her beneficiaries of her will or to her heirs of her intestate estate if she had no will at the time of her death.

Naming an alternate beneficiary prevents non-probate assets from becoming probate assets.

Example: Doreen Taft buys a life insurance policy with The Life Insurance Company naming her husband, Donald, as her beneficiary. The policy will pay $100,000 to Donald upon Doreen's death. When Doreen dies in 2010, Donald was already deceased, having died in 2005. When Doreen purchased the life insurance policy, however, she named Donald as primary beneficiary and their children, Liz and Lawrence, as the alternate beneficiaries. When their mother died, the children only needed to fill out the claim form and send in copies of the death certificates for both Doreen and Donald to The Life Insurance Company. Upon receipt, The Life Insurance Company will send Liz and Lawrence each a check for $33,333.33. No probate proceeding is required for the money to be sent to the children.

Pay-on-Death

Pay-on-death (POD) accounts are savings accounts that a depositor, called the trustee, opens for the benefit of another, called the beneficiary. During the depositor's lifetime, the depositor may withdraw any or all of the money deposited in the account and is considered the rightful owner of the assets on account. Upon the depositor's death, the money automatically passes to the possession of the beneficiary and does not become part of the depositor's probate estate. This type of account is also known as a ***Totten trust***.

Example: Ann Hyde opens a savings account at First Fidelity Savings and Loan for a minor child, Sara. The account shows the depositor as "Ann Hyde for the benefit of Sara Hyde." This is all that is necessary to designate a

POD account or Totten trust. Upon Ann's death, Sara, or her guardian if she is still a minor, only has to produce a death certificate and the ownership of the account will transfer to Sara.

Other Beneficiary-Driven Assets

Trusts

Trusts will be fully discussed in detail in Chapter 8. For now, it is important to know that a trust, as long as it is not a testamentary trust, is not part of a decedent's probate estate because it actually becomes effective during the decedent's lifetime. Any assets that are made part of the trust become non-probate assets.

Life Estates

As was discussed in the previous section on life estates, a life tenant only owns the land in question for his or her life, or for the life of someone else. Any other interest in the property either belongs to the remainderman or will revert to the grantor. This prevents any interest in the property from belonging to the life tenant. Life estates are not, therefore, probate assets. In actuality, however, life estates are not non-probate assets either. Since no interest remains with the life tenant, no interest belongs to the life tenant's estate upon his death. No value attaches to the life tenant's estate at all.

Joint Tenancy with Right of Survivorship

As stated in the section on joint tenancy with right of survivorship earlier in this chapter, the unique characteristic of joint tenancy is the concept of right of survivorship. Upon the death of one tenant, his or her interest passes automatically to the surviving joint tenants. This means that until there is only one remaining joint tenant, no probate proceeding is necessary to pass the deceased's interest to another. The only time a joint tenancy with right of survivorship is a probate asset is when there is only one tenant remaining.

> *Example:* Lucinda White is a single mother with three adult children, Whitney, William, and Wallace. She decides to retire and go on a round-the-world cruise. Wanting to divest herself of material responsibility, she executes a deed giving her house at 100 N. Main Street to her children equally in 2005. The pertinent deed language states "Lucinda White, as Grantor, for and in consideration of the love and affection of the Grantor for Whitney White, William White, and Wallace White, the Grantees, does hereby grant and convey, without warranty, unto Whitney White, William White, and Wallace White, Grantees, in equal shares as joint tenants with right of survivorship."
>
> Each of Lucinda's children owns a 1/3 interest in the house. When Whitney dies in 2006, her interest in the house passes automatically to William and Wallace so that each owns a 1/2 undivided interest in the house. Whitney's interest did not have to be probated for William and Wallace to gain possession and ownership of Whitney's interest. When Wallace dies in 2007, his 1/2 interest in the house automatically passes to William and does not have to be probated for William to gain possession and ownership of Wallace's interest. However, now William is the sole owner of the property.

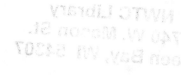

If William were to die in 2012 without having made a will, his ownership of the home would be a probate asset.

As a practical matter, joint tenants should do whatever is necessary in their jurisdiction so as to put other parties on notice that the property passed by right of survivorship to them.

Lady Bird Deed

In a traditional life estate, the life tenant must obtain the signature (permission) of any reversionary interest holder or remainderman to transfer any interest in the property or to mortgage the property, and in fact, cannot sell any more than his or her life interest. *A Lady Bird Deed* is an enhanced life estate deed in which the holder of the life estate also retains the right to transfer the entire property including any reversionary or remainder interest, by sale or gift, without obtaining the consent of the owner of the reversionary holder or remainder interest. If the life estate holder transfers the property, the remainder interest is destroyed. However, if the life estate holder dies before taking any action to transfer the property by sale or gift, it acts as a traditional life estate and passes to the remainderman.

This is considered a better form of life estate in the instances where a parent, attempting to avoid probate, transfers an interest in her property to her children retaining a life estate to herself.

Example: Mabel Smith owns 100 N. Main Street in fee simple. She executes a deed conveying the house to herself and her children. The pertinent part of the deed states

> Mabel Smith, Grantor, for and in consideration of the sum of Ten Dollars ($10.00) cash in hand paid by Richard Smith and Joel Smith, the Grantees, and for other good and valuable consideration, the receipt and sufficiency of which are hereby acknowledged, hereby grants and conveys, without warranty, unto Mabel Smith, Grantee, a life estate in the following described real property, then to Richard Smith and Joel Smith as joint tenants with right of survivorship.

In this example, Mabel's intention was most likely an estate planning tool to convey the property to her children upon her death without the house having to be part of a probate process. However, because it is a traditional life estate, she needs the consent of her children to mortgage the property, or sell it.

However, see this example: Mabel Smith owns 100 N. Main Street in fee simple. She executes a deed conveying the house to herself and her children. The pertinent part of the deed states

> Mabel Smith, Grantor, for and in consideration of the sum of Ten Dollars ($10.00) cash in hand paid by Richard Smith and Joel Smith, the Grantees, and for other good and valuable consideration, the receipt and sufficiency of which are hereby acknowledged, hereby grants and conveys, without warranty, unto Mabel Smith, Grantee, a life estate, *without any liability for waste, with full power and authority in said life tenant to sell, convey, mortgage, lease, or otherwise dispose of the property described herein, in fee simple, with or without consideration, without joinder of the remaindermen, and with full power and authority to retain any and all proceeds generated thereby,* and upon the death of the life tenant, the remainder, if any, to Richard Smith and Joel Smith, as joint tenants with right of survivorship as grantees.

This is an example of an enhanced life estate in which Mabel retains all ownership rights and does not need her children's consent to handle the property however she likes.

Lady Bird deeds are not valid in but a handful of states. They are called Lady Bird deeds because President Johnson allegedly used this type of deed to convey property to his wife, Claudia Taylor "Lady Bird" Johnson.

SUMMARY

Property is the primary reason that wills, trusts, and the administration of estates are needed. Without property ownership, nobody would need a will or a trust because there would be nothing to pass on to family or friends.

Property is classified as either real or personal in nature.

Real property is:

- the land itself, the air above the land, and the area below the surface;
- the buildings affixed to the land; and
- fixtures, which are items of personal property that are permanently attached to the property and are then reclassified as real property. If they can be easily removed, they are not fixtures.

Personal property is all property that is not classified as real property. Personal property can be further classified as either tangible or intangible. Tangible personal property is property that can be touched and moveable, while intangible property is instead evidence of an ownership interest in property. Examples of tangible property are cars, jewelry, furniture, and computers. Examples of intangible personal property are stocks, bonds, and patents.

Title to property can be held in different forms: severally, joint tenancy with right of survivorship, tenancy in common, tenancy by the entirety, and community property. If one person owns property, that property is **owned in severalty**. If more than one person owns property, it is owned jointly. Property owned jointly may be held as joint tenants with right of survivorship, as tenants in common, as tenants by the entirety, or by community, and how the joint property is held is determined by the rules in each jurisdiction.

An estate in property is the form of ownership in property. The estate a person holds in property determines the rights a person has pertaining to that property. Property can be held in fee simple, granting the holder the greatest rights in property; a life estate, which gives the holder all rights for his life; or a tenancy for years, which grants the holder all rights for a period of time only.

For our purposes, property can also be classified as probate or non-probate. Probate property requires a probate proceeding to transfer the title of a decedent's property while non-probate property passes by operation of law and requires simpler proof to transfer the title of the property to the person who should have title.

KEY TERMS

real property	reversion	tenancy in common
fixtures	probate assets	tenancy by the entirety
personal property	pay-on-death	fee simple
tangible personal property	owned in severalty	tenancy for years
intangible personal property	owned severally	remainderman
community property	joint tenancy	non-probate assets
life estate	right of survivorship	

REVIEW **QUESTIONS**

1. What is a right of survivorship?
2. Define *life estate*. What are the characteristics of a life estate that make it a desirable tool for some grantors?
3. What are fixtures?
4. What is the difference between tangible and intangible property? Give examples of both.
5. What are non-probate assets? Give examples.
6. What is a Totten trust? Why are they used?
7. What is the difference between a joint tenancy and a tenancy in common?
8. What unities are required for a tenancy in common? For a tenancy by the entirety?
9. How many states are community property states? Name them.
10. What is a fee simple?

Bonus Question:

James Mitchell owns a home at 100 N. Main Street, Anytown, Anystate with his wife, Wanda. The deed reads "to James Mitchell and Wanda Mitchell, his wife, as joint tenants with right of survivorship and not as tenants by the entirety."

James and Wanda have three adult children, Jim, John, and Dan.

Assume the deed was drafted correctly and that they do not live in a community property state.

a. James dies survived by Wanda. What are the respective rights of Wanda, Jim, John, and Dan in the property, if any?
b. James dies, but Wanda has already predeceased him. What are the children's respective interests in the property?
c. How would scenarios a and b change if the deed specified "James Mitchell and Wanda Mitchell, his wife, as tenants by the entirety"?
d. How would scenarios a and b change if this was a community property state and the deed stated "James Mitchell and Wanda Mitchell, his wife"?

PROJECTS

1. Review a deed to real property. You can use one from your home, your family's, a friend's, or get a random deed from the local land records. One is provided for your use immediately following this chapter as well. Determine how the property is held and how that affects the ownership rights of the parties involved.
2. In the text it was stated that tenancy by the entirety may be protected from the claims of creditors; however, this has been specifically changed in Michigan by United States v. Craft, 535 U.S. 274 (2002). Much has been written about this case and its far-reaching effect on the law of tenancy by the entirety.

   Google the case, read it, and briefly summarize it (you can easily find the case online). How is this result different from the result in In Re: Sampath summarized as Case Summary 2.4.

ONLINE: Find a list of your state statutes and codes and bookmark, or add the list to your "favorites." When in doubt, search engines like Google, Bing, or Yahoo! Search are handy tools for finding state and federal legal information.

MyLegalStudiesLab™   http://www.mylegalstudieslab

MYLEGALSTUDIESLAB VIRTUAL LAW OFFICE EXPERIENCE ASSIGNMENTS

Complete the pre-test, study plan, and post-test for this chapter and answer the Legal Applications questions as assigned. These will help you confirm your mastery of the concepts and their application to legal scenarios. Then, complete the Virtual Law Office assignments as assigned by your instructor. These assignments are designed to develop your workplace skills and result in producing documents for inclusion in your portfolio.

Chapter **three**

TESTATE OR INTESTATE

OBJECTIVES

At the end of this chapter, the student will understand:

- the difference between distribution per stirpes and distribution by representation
- the definition of testate
- the definition of intestacy
- the effect of intestacy upon an estate
- the effect of intestacy upon a decedent's family
- what rights and protections the family has when the decedent dies
- what is ademption

Testacy

Testacy occurs when a person dies and has **_executed_** a valid will. Therefore, when someone who dies is **_testate_**, the person had a valid will at the time of his death.

A will, sometimes called a last will and testament, is valid when the person who makes the will, known as the **_testator_**, creates a document that meets all the statutory requirements. The requirements for a valid will are discussed in Chapter 4.

Assuming the decedent's will is valid ensures that his or her property will be distributed to those he or she wanted to receive the property.

Types of Dispositions

The dispositions in a will are broadly categorized by three types:

- bequests
- legacies
- devises

Bequests are gifts of personal property. **Legacies** are also gifts of personal property and synonymous with bequests. **Devises** are gifts of real property. While these terms are traditional, you may find that most attorneys use the nontraditional vernacular of "give." In fact, many practitioners use the term "give" almost exclusively. Courts will not overturn a disposition in a will when the wrong terminology is used. The Uniform Probate Code (UPC) has done away with the use of different terminology altogether; the UPC utilizes the term "devise" for all dispositions, for example New Mexico's adoption of the UPC, NM Uniform Probate Code, §45-1-201 A (9) defines "devise" as "when used as a noun, means a testamentary disposition of real or personal property and, when used as a verb, means to dispose of real or personal property by will." Regardless, it is important to understand the different kinds of dispositions using traditional terminology. You will then understand and appreciate the subtleties of the different types of dispositions, even if you decide to use the nontraditional vernacular later on in your career.

As stated previously, functionally bequests and legacies are the same—gifts of personal property—while a devise is a gift of real property. Each type of legacy or devise is discussed next. Remember that the UPC does not differentiate between legacies or devises and uses the term "devise" to denote both.

Specific Legacies

Specific legacies, also called specific bequests, are dispositions of specific items of a personal property in a will. As discussed in Chapter 2, personal property includes all tangible and intangible property owned by a decedent that is not classified as real property. Personal property includes such items as cars, jewelry, furniture, computers, and stocks and bonds.

Example: Roberta Roberts writes the following dispositions in her will:

1. I give my classic 2000 Jaguar to my nephew, Alex.
2. I give my shares of stock in IBM to my niece, Amanda.
3. I give my antique desk to my good friend, Stuart Wildenberg, if he survives me.

Each disposition is a gift of a specific item of personal property in the will and is, therefore, a specific legacy.

Demonstrative Legacies

Most practitioners group together demonstrative legacies with specific legacies when drafting wills. Nonetheless, a **demonstrative legacy** is a gift of a specific sum of money that comes from a specific source.

Example: Jacqueline writes the following disposition in her will:

1. I give $5000 to be paid from my money market account at First United Bank in Anytown, Anystate, to my daughter, Tina, if she survives me.
2. I give $10,000 to be paid from the sale of my Microsoft stock to my son, Ted, if he survives me. If he fails to survive me, I give the $10,000 to my grandson, Jacob.

Both of these dispositions are demonstrative legacies. The sums of money each come from a specific source. In the first instance, the money is to be paid from a money market account at a specified bank. Some attorneys draft the disposition so that it states not just the bank and its location, but the account number as well. In the second instance, the testator has directed that the sum is to be given to the beneficiary after a specific item of property is sold to make the gift possible.

General Legacies

General legacies are also dispositions of sums of money. They differ from demonstrative legacies in that they do not specify a source from which the funds must come. General legacies are also called **pecuniary bequests**.

Example: Howie writes the following disposition in his will: I give $10,000 to my son, Arthur, if he survives me. If he fails to survive me, I give $10,000 to my grandson, Martin.

Notice how this gift differs from the disposition in the section on demonstrative legacies. In this disposition, Howie has not directed that the sum be distributed from a particular bank account or that any property be sold. It only requires that the personal representative give Arthur $10,000 from Howie's estate.

Specific Devises

Specific devises are the dispositions of real property made in a will. In states that have adopted the UPC, a specific devise includes dispositions of both real and personal property. In this section, however, we will discuss only gifts of real property. As discussed in Chapter 2, real property includes the land itself as well as fixtures, which are those items of personal property that have become so attached to the land that they have become realty, such as buildings, trees, and crops.

Example: Liz writes the following disposition in her will: I give my vacation home located in Anytown, Anystate, inherited from my father, to my son, Scottie, if he survives me. If he fails to survive me, I give the vacation home to my grandson, Dan.

As long as the disposition is of real property, it is a specific devise.

Residuary Dispositions

After the testator has disposed of individual items of interest to specified members of his or her family and friends, the question about how the rest of his or her property will be distributed must be addressed. The method of disposing of this property is by use of a clause in the will called the **residuary** or ***residue***, which is all the property remaining after the testator has given all of his or her specifically named bequests and devises (as well as paid all lawful debts and taxes, discussed in Chapter 4). The residuary ensures that the remainder of the testator's property is distributed to the person or persons that the testator intends. Failure to draft a residuary clause in a will causes the remainder of the property, usually the bulk of the testator's estate, to pass by intestate succession, discussed later in this chapter. This turn of events may not be what the testator desired and should be avoided, since it defeats the purpose of executing a will in the first place, that is, creating a vehicle which disposes all of a decedent's property as he or she chooses, instead of how the state chooses.

Example: Stephanie writes the following disposition in her will: I give all the rest, residue, and remainder of my personal property, both tangible and intangible, to my husband, Donald, if he survives me. If my husband does not survive me, I give all the rest, residue, and remainder of my personal property, both tangible and intangible, to my children, Jack and Jill, in equal shares.

In this example, the testator states, "I give all the rest, residue, and remainder of my personal property . . . ." This statement denotes the testator's intent to give the remainder of her personal property not already mentioned earlier in the will to her husband. This type of disposition is specifically called a ***residuary legacy*** because it distributes the residue of the testator's personal property only and does not address distribution of real property.

Most typically, however, residuary clauses are worded in such a way as to distribute the entire residue of the testator's property, both personal property and real property.

> *Example:* Claudia writes the following disposition in her will: I hereby give, devise, and bequeath the rest, residue, and remainder of my estate whether real or personal, and wherever located, including all property and interest not otherwise disposed of elsewhere in this document that are acquired by me or my estate after the execution of this document, to my husband, Clarke, if he survives me. If he fails to survive me, I give, devise, and bequeath the rest, residue, and remainder of my estate to my children, Michael and Tommy, in equal shares.

Notice that this residuary clause uses the traditional terminology for dispositions in a will for both real and personal property: devise and bequeath. It also uses the general term "give," such as in "I give, devise, and bequeath." This residuary clause will dispose of any of the testator's property that was not otherwise disposed of in specific legacy or devise clauses and includes all remaining personal property and remaining real property.

Remember that it is also common for attorneys to use the term "give" and leave out the terms "devise" and "bequeath."

Abatement, Ademption, Satisfaction, and Lapse Abatement

Abatement

Abatement means handed down from an ancestor. In estate planning, an **abatement** refers to a reduction in the sums or gifts to a beneficiary to pay the taxes and debts of the estate. As discussed in Chapter 1, most testators specify in their wills how taxes and debts of the estate, as well as funeral and last medical expenses, are to be paid or apportioned. This type of provision, as previously discussed, is called an *apportionment clause*. Situations occur, however, in which either the testator doesn't provide for the payment of debts, expenses, and taxes, or the estate is insufficient to pay all the charges against the estate and satisfy the devises and bequests to each beneficiary as well.

When no provision has been made, or the portion of the estate the testator designated for paying the debts is insufficient to cover them, the personal representative may liquidate, or sell, estate assets to cover the debt. State statute determines the order in which assets are sold. For example, in North Carolina, when there is an absence of the testator's intent as to the order of abatement, abatement occurs, without any preference or priority as between real and personal property, in the following order: (1) property not disposed of by the will; (2) residuary devises; (3) general devises; and (4) specific devises. All assets from each class must be exhausted before any item in the next class may be sold. Note that North Carolina uses the term "devise" for both personal property and real property.

Decedents usually leave general and specific devises to family, friends, and charities and leave the residue to the surviving spouse. As a practical matter, it is important to take into consideration the fact that the residuary estate will be abated before general and specific devises, potentially leaving a surviving spouse with significantly less than anticipated. If the testator had many debts to pay, however, devises to surviving spouses usually abate after all other devises in the same class are exhausted. Despite this safeguard, the surviving spouse will have nothing left, if he or she is the only residuary beneficiary and the entire residuary must be sold to satisfy the decedent spouse's debts. It is difficult to explain this to clients who want to leave the grandchildren and their church demonstrative legacies and how these will get paid before the spouse gets a dime. It is, however, very important to explain this to clients, especially those with small estates who will not see the significance of not depleting their estates to the detriment of a surviving spouse.

Ademption

Ademption, also called extinction, is what happens when property left to a beneficiary is disposed of before the testator's death. If the property is not part of the testator's estate at the time of his or her death, it is said to adeem by extinction.

> *Example:* Richard's will provides, "I devise my vacation cottage on Martha's Vineyard to my daughter, Nikki." If Richard sells the cottage before his death, Nikki will not get the cottage, nor is she entitled to the proceeds of the sale of the cottage. Nikki's gift has been extinguished. It does not matter that Richard may have told Nikki he sold the cottage to provide the cash for Nikki's education. The fact that the money can be traced directly back to the sale of the cottage is immaterial.

The property must be the same as that devised in the will.

> As in the previous example, Richard devised his vacation cottage on Martha's Vineyard to his daughter, Nikki. Richard's will was executed in 2000. In 2005, he sold the cottage and bought another one, also on Martha's Vineyard. Whether Nikki receives the cottage may be dependent upon exactly how the will was worded. If Richard's will stated "I devise my cottage at 123 Tuna Way, Martha's Vineyard to my daughter, Nikki," Tina will not get the new cottage located at 350 Guppy Lane, Martha's Vineyard" as the gift adeemed by extinction.

> If instead, Richard's will stated "I devise my cottage at 123 Tuna Way, Martha's Vineyard, or any other cottage on Martha's Vineyard I may own at my death to my daughter, Nikki," Nikki would indeed inherit the cottage at 350 Guppy Lane, Martha's Vineyard when Richard died.

Ademption does not apply if the property subject to the specific devise was only moved to another location.

> *Example:* Jane's will provides, "I devise the diamond engagement ring that belonged to my grandmother, Ruth, which is in a safe deposit box at First Savings and Loan, to my daughter, Robin." Before her death, Jane moved the contents of the safe deposit box, including the ring, to First United Bank and Trust. Despite the fact that the ring is no longer located where the will has described, the devise does not adeem and Robin still receives the ring.

Examine these scenarios and determine what happens to the property:

Bobbie Black's will has the following disposition: "I devise my home to my son, Todd Black." However, the deed to the property states "Bobbie Black and Donald Black, wife and husband, as tenants by the entirety."

What happens to the house? Does Todd get any portion of the house? Does it matter if his father is alive? Does your answer change, if Donald predeceased Bobbie? Would your answer be different if the deed stated:

- "Bobbie Black and Donald Black as tenants in common"?
- "Bobby Black and Donald Black as joint tenants"?
- "Bobby Black and Donald Black" and was executed in a community property state?
- "Bobbie Black and Donald Smith" and Bobbie and Donald are brother and sister?

There is a line of cases, however, suggesting that courts do not agree with ademption when the property is sold by a guardian or agent under a power of attorney when the testator was incompetent at the time of the sale. There are two lines of authority on this subject. The minority view asks if the property is still part of the testator's estate. If it is not, then the property has adeemed. This is, of course, the customary view of ademption. The majority view that has developed is quite different, however. Review the following two cases and ask yourself the following questions: Were the decisions fair? Do you think the legislature(s) intended the consequences of these decisions? Why or why not?

CASE 3.1 **SUMMARY**

In re Estate of Hegel 76 Ohio St.3d 476, 668 N.E.2d 474 (1996)

On July 24, 1990, Helen Hegel executed her last will and testament, devising her residence and real property to Boettger. In April 1993, Hegel was in an accident and was henceforth unresponsive and could not communicate until her death in January 1994. Two months prior to Hegel's death, Boettger, as Hegel's agent under a power of attorney, sold the residence and contents to a bona-fide purchaser, so that the funds could be used for Hegel's care.

When Hegel's will was admitted to probate, Boettger learned she was the beneficiary of the residence and its contents and submitted a claim of $48,438.86 to the estate as the cash proceeds of the sale of the residence. The executor denied her claim stating that the property had been adeemed due to the sale and the probate court agreed. The appellate court reversed. The Ohio Supreme Court framed the issue before them as "we must determine whether an ademption has occurred where specifically devised property was sold to a third party prior to the testator's death under a durable power of attorney."

The Court relied on Ohio R.C. 2107.501(B), which states, "[i]f specifically devised or bequeathed property is sold by a *guardian*, *** the specific devisee or legatee has the right to a general pecuniary devise or bequest equal to the net proceeds of sale ***." (Emphasis added by Court.) The Court explained that this statute was modeled after former UPC §2-608 and while the UPC itself had been amended to specifically protect property sold by an attorney-in-fact acting under a durable power of attorney (as UPC §2-206), Ohio's statatue had not been so amended.

Thus, the Court stated "The statutory language of R.C. 2107.501(B) is clearly limited to the sale of property by guardians and does not protect specifically devised property sold by attorneys-in-fact. Thus, as applied to this case, when Boettger, as attorney in-fact, sold the testator's residence and its contents prior to the testator's death, Boettger adeemed her specific devise and lost her right to the devised property," reversing the court of appeals and reinstating the probate court decision.

CASE 3.2 **SUMMARY**

In The Matter of the Estate of Pearl Swoyer, Deceased, 439 NW 2d 823 (SD, 1989)

Pearl Swoyer (Pearl) was married to John who died in 1951. They had four children, Teressa, Eldean, Golda, and James. Teressa died prior to 1951 without having married or having children. Pearl's husband, John, died in 1951. James married Marcela and had four children, Jacqueline, Jill, Jerri, and James. Marcela died prior to 1959. Pearl then raised her grandchildren.

Pearl executed her will in 1974 leaving her farm to the grandchildren. Her health started failing in 1980 and in November of that year Eldean obtained guardianship over her. Pearl entered a nursing home in 1981 necessitating a sale of the farm to cover the costs. Eldean petitioned the probate court for permission to sell the farm in 1982 and the sale was approved. Pearl was at that time unable to consent to the sale due to mental incompetency. The farm sale proceeds were $126,000. At the time of Pearl's death in June of 1985, $106,000 of the proceeds remained.

Jacqueline was appointed as executor of Pearl's will and as part of the final accounting, showed the remaining $106,000 being distributed to the four grandchildren as proceeds of the farm sale. Eldean objected, stating that the $106,000 rightfully belonged to the residuary beneficiaries of the will, being himself (1/3), his sister Golda (1/3), and the four grandchildren (sharing 1/3 as James' descendants), because the gift of the farm was adeemed because it had been sold.

At trial, the court determined that the funds belonged to the grandchildren. The appellate court affirmed the trial court's decision. The Court said that the question revolved around the testator's intent to adeem or revoke the devise but noted that the statute for ademption of property did not address an incompetent testator and a guardianship sale of the property. Obviously, Pearl was incapable of forming the intent to adeem or voluntarily revoke the devise.

The Court discussed the two lines of authority; the one that says if the property is not part of the estate, the gift adeems; and the view that says that there is no ademption when the property is sold by a guardian because the testator cannot form the intent to adeem or avoid the effect of an ademption by executing a new will. The Court stated that the ademption only extends to those proceeds that were used to provide care and maintenance for Pearl. The remaining property was not adeemed and such proceeds remaining from the sale belonged to the grandchildren.

Satisfaction

Satisfaction is simply what occurs when the testator gives the gift to the beneficiary before the testator dies. The presumption is that the gift was given in lieu of the testamentary gift.

> *Example:* Olivia's will provides, "I devise the diamond engagement ring that belonged to my grandmother, Ruth, to my daughter, Madison." Before her death, Olivia gave the ring to Madison on the occasion of her 30th birthday. When Olivia dies, the estate will not give another diamond ring to Madison, nor will she receive the value of the ring because she already has the gift.

Anti-Lapse

At common law, a beneficiary of a will had to survive the testator to receive the gift. When the beneficiary did not survive the testator, the gift lapsed and passed either as part of the residue of the estate (to the residuary beneficiaries), or by intestacy, if there was no other provision made for the devise.

Anti-lapse statutes prevent the gift from lapsing by substituting the beneficiary's issue for the beneficiary.

> *Example:* Bobbie executed a will leaving $100,000 to her brother, Paul. The residue of Bobbie's estate was left to her sister, Mary. Paul predeceased

Bobbie. Assume Bobbie was single and had no children. Under the common law, the gift of $100,000 passed into the residuary and, therefore, to Mary. However, an anti-lapse statute would prevent the gift from passing into the residuary, if Paul had issue (heirs, children, grandchildren) of his own. Assume that Paul had two children, June and Joan. The effect of the anti-lapse statute is that June and Joan would each receive $50,000 from Bobbie's estate and Mary would not receive the $100,000.

It should be noted that anti-lapse statutes tend to favor lineal ascendants and descendants, as well as collateral kin whose nearest common ancestor is a grandparent (discussed later in this chapter). For this reason, anti-lapse statutes usually don't apply when a spouse, foster child, or stepchild is involved.

Anti-lapse statutes do not apply when the testator has indicated to the contrary in the will. As in the example above, Bobbie leaves her brother, Paul, $100,000 in her will. Bobbie's will provides, "I give, devise, and bequeath $100,000 to my brother, Paul, if he survives me," indicating that the gift to Paul was conditioned upon Paul surviving Bobbie. If Paul predeceases Bobbie, the gift does lapse into the residuary and therefore Mary receives the $100,000, not Paul's children.

As a drafting technique, it is common for wills to state "if he survives me," followed by another named beneficiary, or to specifically state that if the beneficiary does not survive, the gift becomes part of the residue. The purpose of this type of clause is to ensure that the gift to the original beneficiary does, in fact, lapse and not be disposed of pursuant to an anti-lapse statute.

CASE 3.3 **SUMMARY**

This case addresses the issue of the New York anti-lapse statute but also addresses the issue of "per capita" which is discussed in the next section of this chapter.

Matter of Edwards, 13 Misc 3d 210 (2006)

Josephine Edwards (Josephine) died in June 2005 leaving a last will and testament that provided as follows:

"article second: I hereby give, devise and bequeath all the rest, residue and remainder of my estate, real, personal or mixed, wheresoever situated, whereof I may be seized or possessed or to which I may be in any manner entitled or in which I may be interested at the time of my death as follows: "A. a twenty-five (25%) percent share to my brother, robert edwards, per capita, absolutely and forever; "B. a twenty-five (25%) percent share to my brother, john edwards, per capita, absolutely and forever; "C. a twenty-five (25%) percent share to my niece, ann kaufman, per capita, absolutely and forever; "D. a twenty-five (25%) percent share to my nieces and nephews, robert m. edwards, suzanne ingrasia, patricia purrman, fred koestlich, pamela heidtmann and john v. edwards, share and

share alike, per capita, absolutely and forever." (all non-capitalization [sic])

Both Robert Edwards and Ann Kaufman predeceased Josephine.

First, the Court set about deciding "the operation of the antilapse statute (EPTL 3-3.3) in connection with the words "per capita" in the bequest to Robert Edwards." The Court opined that if the words "per capita" were meant to be an "otherwise provision," the anti-lapse statute would not apply and Robert M. Edwards would not take his father's devise. If, however, the words had no effect, Robert M. Edwards would take his father's share of the residuary.

The Court stated "[A] distribution "per capita" is an equal division among beneficiaries (EPTL 1-2.11). When used in connection with the words "issue" or "descendents," the term per capita may describe a substitutional gift." However, if the term "per capita" is used by itself, it does not describe a substitutional gift, and in this case, the Court concluded that the phrase was added inadvertently and should be disregarded.

The second issue before the Court concerned the division of the bequest to Ann Kaufman who died without issue. The Court asked "whether Ann's share is to be divided (1) among John Edwards and the beneficiaries named in paragraph D (including Robert M. Edwards), or (2) among John Edwards, the beneficiaries named in paragraph D (including Robert M. Edwards) and Robert M. Edwards as a "substitute taker" under paragraph A."

According to the Court, pursuant to New York EPTL 3-3.3, when a bequest is made to the issue or siblings of a testator but the beneficiary has predeceased the testator, the gift will not lapse and instead is distributed to that beneficiary's surviving issue. This abrogates the common-law rule stating that devise to a predeceased child lapses and the predeceased child's children then inherit. Presumably, this was to substitute what likely was the testator's goal as well as to prevent a devise from being distributed to other beneficiaries that might not have a relationship of any note with the testator. The purpose of EPTL 3-3.4 is to prevent an ineffective residuary bequest or devise from falling into intestacy and that the devise then is distributed to the "remaining residuary beneficiaries." The Court held that Robert M. Edwards would receive a share of the lapsed bequest to Ann Kaufman in his own right and as a substitute taker of his father's share.

Methods of Distribution—Per Stirpes Versus Per Capita

A decedent's property may be distributed by either of two methods:

- **per stirpes** (by the roots), or
- **per capita** (by the head).

These methods of distribution are used when a testator leaves property to a group of people and some of that group die before the testator. For example:

Bobbie Black is unmarried and has three adult children, Tina, Todd, and Ted. Tina dies in 2005. Bobbie dies in 2009 not having changed her will which states, "All of my property in equal shares to my descendants per capita who survive me." She has left her property to a group, her descendants, in this instance Tina, Todd, and Ted. If all three of them were alive, they would each receive 1/3 of Bobbie's estate. In this example, Tina has predeceased Bobbie and her will states to my descendants *per capita*. So what exactly does that mean? Examine this scenario:

Bobbie Black is unmarried and has three adult children, Tina, Todd, and Ted. Tina has three children when she dies in 2005. Bobbie dies in 2009 not having changed her will which states, "All of my property in equal shares to my descendants per capita who survive me." This is an example of ***per capita distribution***, in which the surviving beneficiaries each receive an equal share. Because Bobbie's will refers to "descendants," and ***descendants*** are those people that come from an ancestor or source; issue. ***Issue*** are a person's **lineal descendants** or offspring. Todd and Ted are Bobbie's children, and therefore come from a lineal ancestor (Bobbie). Tina was Bobbie's child but is deceased. Tina's three living children are therefore Bobbie's lineal descendants. Because Bobbie's will made no distinction between children or grandchildren, Todd and Ted share in Bobbie's estate equally with Tina's three children, each receiving 1/5 of Bobbie's estate. Tina's children may be seen to have been overcompensated for their mother's death. See Figure 3.1.

Examine this scenario instead: Bobbie's will states "All of my property in equal shares to my children who survive me." In this example, Bobbie has specified that the group that takes is her children but she specifies that they must survive her. In this instance of per capita distribution, Todd and Ted each receive 1/2 of Bobbie's

Figure 3.1 Per capita distribution

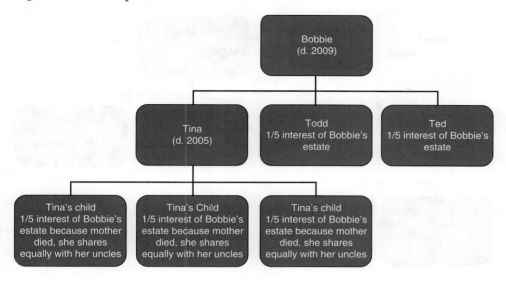

Figure 3.2 Per capita distribution with a "must survive me" provision

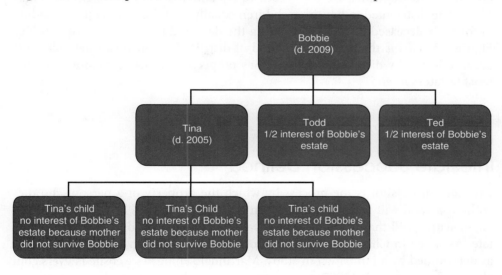

estate. Tina's children are left out because Tina did not survive Bobbie, therefore being undercompensated for their mother's death. See Figure 3.2.

In ***per stirpes distributions***, also called distributions by representation, the beneficiaries receive their shares based upon the level of lineal descendant they are from their ancestor, the decedent. Should any of the decedent's children predecease the decedent, that child's issue will take the child's share of the estate. Examine this scenario:

Bobbie's will states "All of my property in equal shares per stirpes to my descendants who survive me." Bobbie had three children, Tina, Todd, and Ted and each of these living descendants should receive 1/3 of Bobbie's estate. Since Tina

Figure 3.3   Per stirpes distribution

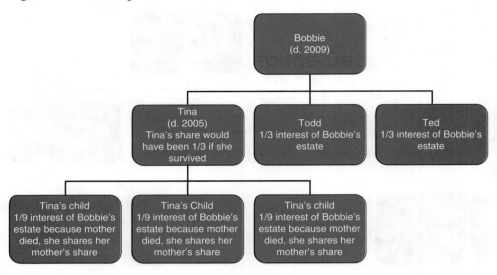

is deceased however and Bobbie's will specifies that the property is to be distributed to her descendants, Todd will receive 1/3 and Ted will receive 1/3 but Tina's 1/3 will be distributed to her three children equally, or 1/9 each, in effect standing in for their deceased parent and splitting the deceased parent's share equally. See Figure 3.3. This is the preferred method of distributing for most estate planners because it usually distributes the testator's property in a manner closest to what most testators intend.

Intestacy

Intestate Succession Defined

Intestate succession is the process by which the property of a person who dies without a valid will is distributed. When a decedent dies either without a will at all, or with a will that is found to be invalid, he or she is said to have died intestate. As stated in Chapter 1, more than one-half of American adults die *intestate* as determined by a Findlaw.com study. Martindale Hubbell's website lawyers.com also conducted a study (2007) on Americans and wills and drew the same conclusion. In addition, the study showed that only one in three African-American adults (32%), and one in four Hispanics (26%) have wills.

Intestate Succession Laws

The decedent's failure to have a will triggers the intestacy laws of the state in which the testator was domiciled at the time of death. See Figure 3.4 for a list of the intestacy laws by state. Domicile refers to where the testator resided. Proof of domicile include:

- where the testator had a driver's license
- where he filed his federal and state taxes

- where Social Security payments were sent
- where he had his primary residence
- where he had registered to vote

The state's intestacy laws determine who among the decedent's heirs receive the decedent's property and in what proportion each takes the property. These laws of succession are designed to ensure that a decedent's next of kin, that is, family, receives the property. In practice, however, the property may be distributed to family members to whom the decedent did not want his or her property to go or to family members the decedent did not know. For example, it is well known that when multimillionaire Howard Hughes' estate was finally distributed, the lion's share of it went to his distant cousins. In most cases, this is not the intent of the decedent, but when no will is found or the will is found to be invalid, the law must distribute the property to the next available kin. A will may be considered

Figure 3.4　Intestacy Laws by State

Alabama	Title 43 Chapter 8 Section 40
Alaska	Title 13 Chapters 11 and 12
Arizona	Title 14 Division 6, Part 2
Arkansas	Title 28
California	Division 2, Part 6, Chapter 1
Colorado	Title 15 Article 11, Part 1
Connecticut	Title 45a
District of Columbia	Division III Title 19
Florida	Title XLII Chapter 732, Part 1
Georgia	Title 53 Chapter 2
Hawaii	Title 30A Chapter 560, Article II, Part 1
Idaho	Title 15 Chapter 2 Part 1
Illinois	Chapter 755
Indiana	Title 29 Chapter 2
Iowa	Title XV Chapter 633 Division IV, Parts 1 and 2
Kansas	Chapter 59 Article 5
Kentucky	Title XXXIV, Chapter 391
Louisiana	LA CC 871 et seq.
Maine	Title 18A Part I
Maryland	Maryland Code, Estates and Trusts, Title 3
Massachusetts	Part II, Title II, Chapter 190
Michigan	Chapter 700
Minnesota	Chapter 524
Missouri	Title XXXI, Chapter 474

(continued)

Figure 3.4 (continued)

Montana	Title 72 Chapter 2, Part 1
Nebraska	Chapter 30
Nevada	Title 12, Chapters 133 and 134
New Hampshire	Title LVI, Chapter 561
New Jersey	Title 3B
New Mexico	Chapter 45, Article 2
New York	Chapter 17-B, Article 4
North Carolina	Chapter 29
North Dakota	Title 30.1, Chapter 30.1–04
Ohio	Title XXI, Chapter 2105
Oklahoma	Title 84
Oregon	Chapter 112
Pennsylvania	Title 20, Chapter 21
Rhode Island	Title 33, Chapter 33.1
South Dakota	Title 29A, Chapter 2
South Carolina	Title 62, Chapter 2
Tennessee	Title 31, Chapter 2
Texas	Texas Probate Code, Chapter II, Section 38
Utah	Title 75, Chapter 2
Vermont	Title 14, Part 2, Chapter 41
Virginia	Title 64.1, Chapter 1
Washington	Title 11, Chapter 11.04
West Virginia	Chapter 42, Article 1
Wisconsin	Chapter 852
Wyoming	Title 2, Chapter 4

invalid for any number of reasons, including the testator's lack of capacity to execute a will, the lack of proper witnesses, or perhaps fraud or duress upon the testator inducing him or her to execute the will. These will be discussed later in this text.

THE PROFESSIONAL PARALEGAL

Paralegals often have the tedious but important job of locating the decedent's heirs at law. In some states, such as New York, the Probate Court (called "Surrogate Court" in New York) requires detailed family trees to be drawn for the court's benefit. This task also typically is undertaken by the paralegal. See Figure 3.5 for the New York Family Tree Form and Figures 3.6 and 3.7 for brief examples of a family tree.

Figure 3.5

FAMILY TREE

Cross Out Class That is Not Applicable	Children or Brothers/Sisters	Grandchildren or Nieces/Nephews	Great Grandchildren or Grandnieces/Grandnephews

_____ Decedent

_____ Name of Spouse

_____ Deceased _____ Date

_____ Divorced _____ Date

_____ Never Married

STATE OF NEW YORK
COUNTY OF _____

_____ being duly sworn, states that the charts contained on this paper are correct.

Sworn to me on _____

_____
NOTARY PUBLIC

NOTE: Complete reverse side of family tree form also

(continued)

Figure 3.5 (continued)

Form FT-1

Grandparents	Aunts and Uncles	First Cousins \#	**First Cousins Once Removed \#

Paternal Grandfather

Paternal Grandmother

Father of Decedent

Maternal Grandfather

Maternal Grandmother

Mother of Decedent

STATE OF NEW YORK
COUNTY OF _____

_____ being duly sworn, states that the charts contained on this paper are correct.

Sworn to before me on _____

_____
NOTARY PUBLIC

**List First Cousins Once Removed by # that corresponds
with deceased first cousin.

Figure 3.6

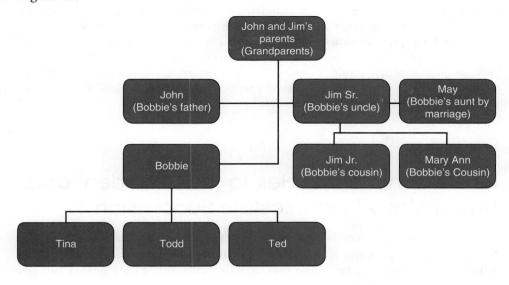

Figure 3.7

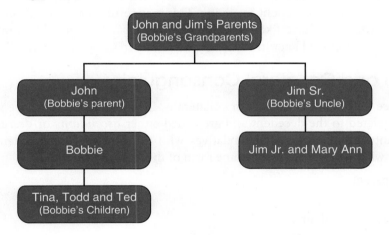

CASE 3.4 **SUMMARY**

Note the unintended consequence of dying intestate in this recent case.

Estate of Shellenbarger, 169 Cal. App. 4th 894; 86 Cal. Rptr. 3d 862 (review denied March 25, 2009)

In this case, Laura A. Barnes, administrator of the Estate of Lesley Loren Shellenbarger, and mother of the deceased, appealed an order denying her petition to exclude Lesley Shellenbarger's natural father's entitlement to distribution of his estate.

Lesley was born in June of 1963 and died intestate in April 2005, having no surviving spouse, registered domestic partner, child, or issue from a predeceased child. Lesley was survived by his mother, Laura Barnes, and his natural father, Clifford Shellenbarger, who were married briefly more than 40 years prior.

After Lesley died, Laura petitioned to probate Lesley's estate and was appointed administrator. Laura also filed a petition for instructions to determine entitlement to the estate, alleging that Clifford abandoned Lesley and hence should not take as an intestate heir.

The trial court asked "[C]an a bad guy luck into an inheritance, and is there an equitable way to avoid it?" It answered the second question with a "no."

The appellate court said that "it does not matter that Clifford never even saw his son." It stated that while Clifford's parental neglect may have been grounds for terminating parental rights when Lesley was a minor, Laura never had his rights terminated. It concluded that the California Supreme Court stated repeatedly that "[i]ntestate succession is wholly statutory. Any inequality which results from the operation of [law] has been engendered by the Legislature itself." The Court stated at the outset that they thought the result of their decision was unfair because Clifford never "saw his son for the 42 years he lived" and that "the father should reap a financial windfall after the death of his son." Nonetheless, the appellate court held that a probate court "may not, on principles of equity, disinherit a natural parent who abandons a child who later dies intestate."

Relationship of the Heir to the Decedent and How It May Affect Intestate Succession

In general, intestate succession laws, or laws of succession, are based upon the idea that a decedent's property should pass by **consanguinity**, or blood relationships. With the exception of a surviving spouse, who is obviously only related by marriage, but who nonetheless is given a special status to the decedent, all people to whom a decedent's property will be distributed when he dies intestate, must be blood relatives of the decedent surviving. This may result in a distribution that the decedent would not have liked or intended. Some of these possible unintended scenarios are discussed later in the text, particularly in Chapter 7.

Lineal and Collateral Consanguinity

People are related either lineally or collaterally. Lineal relations are those who are directly related to the decedent and are called either **ascendants** or **descendants**. Ascendants are ancestors, those relatives who came before the decedent. Each ancestor will be designated with some form of the word "parent":

- parent
- grandparent
- great-grandparent

Descendants are those relatives who follow the decedent, commonly called **issue** or offspring. They are designated with some form of the word "child":

- children
- grandchildren
- great-grandchildren

Collateral relations are those that, while related by blood to the decedent, are not directly ascending or descending, so are relatives that are not ancestors or descendants such as

- siblings
- aunts and uncles
- cousins

Note that your father's brother's wife (your uncle's wife), while usually called your "aunt," is only related by marriage, not by blood, and is therefore not collaterally related. Her children, your cousins, however, *are* collaterally related to you.

Example: Rob's father, John, has a brother, Jim. Jim is married to May. Jim and May have two children, Jim Jr. and Maryann. Based on these facts, Rob's lineal relation is his father (his ancestor, a "parent"). Rob's collateral relations are his uncle Jim (John's brother), and his cousins, Jim Jr. and Maryann (Jim's children). May, as Jim's wife, is not a blood relative and is therefore not a collateral relationship at all. See Figure 3.6.

Determining Degree of Kinship

Determining how closely related someone is to the decedent usually requires some type of family tree. Drawing a family tree gives a two-dimensional picture of the decedent's family, making determinations about kinship easier.

The degree of kinship of lineal relatives is calculated by counting each step above the decedent and each step below the decedent.

Now see it drawn in this fashion as shown in Figure 3.7.

Bobbie's lineal relatives are her ancestors (father and grandparents) and her descendents (children), because they are immediately above and below her on the tree. Jim Sr., Jim Jr., and Maryann are collateral relatives because they are not directly in a line above or below her on the tree. Drawing the family tree in this manner makes it readily apparent who all the lineal relatives of Bobbie are. Bobbie's ancestors are all those people directly in line above her and her descendants are those people directly in line below her. Her parents are one degree away, her children are one degree away, and her grandchildren would be two degrees away.

If Maryann has two children, what is their degree of kinship with Bobbie? Where would they be placed on the family tree?

Calculating the degree of kinship of collateral relatives requires finding the nearest common ancestor and then counting downward. Bobbie's parents are her ancestors. Assume she has no siblings. Her nearest common ancestor is her father John. Since John's brother, Jim Sr., and Jim Sr.'s children are in the column alongside the column for lineal relatives, Jim Sr., Jim Jr., and Maryann, along with her two children, are Bobbie's collateral relatives. In this instance, determining the degree of kinship between Bobbie and Maryann's children requires counting from John, Bobbie's common ancestor with her. John is the first degree and his brother, Jim Sr., is the first degree; Maryann is the second degree and Maryann's children are therefore a third-degree relative with Bobbie.

Relationship by Affinity

People related by **affinity** are related not by blood but instead by marriage, such as in-laws or "step" relations like stepchildren and stepparents. In general, those related to the decedent by affinity are not entitled to a portion of the decedent's estate under the laws of succession. Currently two prominent exceptions to affinity rules exist—a spouse and adopted children—who are entitled to a portion of the decedent's estate although not related by marriage. The rules regarding affinity have been changing, as will be discussed in Chapter 7 on the changing face of families and its effect on estate planning.

Example: Using the previous example of Bobbie's family, Jim Sr.'s wife, May, is related to Bobbie and her father, John, by affinity since she is a blood relation of neither and is related only by marriage.

Other Relationships by Kinship

Surviving Spouse

One such exception is that the decedent's surviving spouse always takes first under the laws of succession.

Using the example of Bobbie's family again, Jim Sr.'s wife, May, is related to Jim Sr. by affinity. Despite this, she would inherit at least a portion of Jim Sr.'s property as his surviving spouse.

The amount that the surviving spouse inherits from the decedent varies from state to state. Often, the amount the surviving spouse inherits is based upon who else has survived the decedent. For example, in Virginia, if the surviving spouse is the mother or father of all of the decedent's children, she or he will receive the entirety of the decedent's property. If, however, the surviving spouse is not the parent of all of the decedent's children, she or he may receive only 1/3 of the decedent's property. This often leads to interesting distributions and often is not what the decedent intended.

Divorce usually terminates a former spouse's ability to inherit from the decedent since the divorce ends the marriage. When a couple is only separated when the decedent dies, the spouse is still considered a surviving spouse and will inherit his or her intestate share of the decedent's estate. If a couple divorces and remarries, the ability to inherit from the decedent spouse is not adversely affected.

Adopted Children

Another prominent exception pertains to adopted children. Most modern statutes consider adopted children as blood relatives of the adopting parents. The adoptive child will receive property as if he or she was the natural-born child of his or her adoptive parents. Conversely, the relationship between the adopted child and his or her natural parents is severed, precluding inheritance from the natural parents. The severance also precludes inheritance of the adopted child's estate by the natural parents.

Nonmarital Children

In the past, an ***illegitimate*** or nonmarital child was considered a bastard and was therefore unable to inherit from either of his or her natural parents. After a time, it became accepted that the child should not be punished because his or her parents did not marry. The illegitimate child, as the child is still called in various statutes (even as it may be considered politically incorrect), was then permitted to inherit only from his or her natural mother and her family. In recent years, however, the illegitimate child has been able to inherit from his or her father and his father's family, if paternity is established, or if the parents marry after the child is born. While the natural mother and her family can inherit from the child, neither the father nor his family can inherit from the child unless the father has openly accepted the child as his.

Half Blood

Half-blood children are those that have either the same mother or the same father, but do not have both the same mother and father. In most states, half-blood children inherit as if they were "whole-blood" children of the parent.

Pretermitted Children

People often write wills before they have children. Sometimes they write wills after they have one or two children, but then have one or two more. If a person dies before writing a new will providing for those afterborn children, the afterborn children are called "pretermitted," which means omitted or disregarded. **Pretermitted children** then are children who were left out of their parent's estate planning, often simply by omission and the forgetfulness of the parent. A pretermitted child, whether natural born or adopted, receives an intestate share of his or her deceased parent's estate. This is not generally what a parent intends because it often gives the child a share of the estate that is greater than his or her other children and in some circumstances dips into the amount that the surviving spouse receives. It should be noted that, if the children are adults when the parent dies, the child does not necessarily take an intestate share as these statutes are meant to protect the decedent's minor children.

In general, there are two situations in which the children do not receive an intestate share:

- It is apparent from the will that the child was intentionally omitted. This occurs when a child, perhaps already born to the parent at the time the will was executed, was omitted from the will. If the child can prove that the omission was unintentional, he or she will receive an intestate share of his or her deceased parent's estate. For example, John's will states, "I have three children, Roger, Pete, and Keith. It is my intent to not leave a portion of my estate to my son, Keith."

- The parent has one or more children at the time the will was executed but left all or most of the estate to the other parent of the pretermitted child. For example: Amanda White is married to Adam. Amanda and Adam have two children at the time Amanda executes a will leaving all of her estate to Adam. Two years after Amanda executes the will, Amanda and Adam have a third child. Amanda is busy and neglects to update her will. Amanda dies three years after the third child was born. The third child, although a pretermitted child, may not receive an intestate share of Amanda's estate because all of the estate was left to Adam, the child's father.

The law of pretermitted child has recently also taken a few interesting turns. In the Massachusetts case of *Woodward v. Commissioner of Social Security*, 760 N.E.2d 257, 260 (Mass. 2002), the Massachusetts Supreme Judicial Court asked whether twins that were conceived from frozen sperm and born 2 years after the father's death have specific inheritance rights under state law making them eligible for certain federal survivor benefits. The determination was based upon whether the twins were the deceased father's natural children for the disposition of his personal property under the Massachusetts law of intestate succession.

The Court determined that under limited circumstances, posthumously conceived children do have inheritance rights under state intestacy law. To claim inheritance rights, the Court concluded that:

1. The child's surviving parent or legal representative must establish a genetic relationship between the child and the decedent.
2. The parent or representative must demonstrate that the decedent "affirmatively consented" to posthumous conception and the support of any resulting child.

3. Notice be given to all interested parties in any action brought to establish such inheritance rights.

However, other courts have not found that these children are pretermitted at all. We will discuss this topic further in Chapter 7 on the changing face of families and its effect on estate planning.

Pretermitted Spouse

If a person executes a will, marries, and then dies without executing a new will providing for the new spouse, the surviving spouse is called "pretermitted." The **pretermitted spouse** is entitled to an intestate share of his or her deceased spouse's estate.

In general, there are three situations in which the pretermitted spouse will not receive an intestate share of the deceased spouse's estate:

- The pretermitted spouse had signed either an antenuptial or a postnuptial agreement in which he or she waived all rights to the deceased spouse's estate, or when the agreement made provision for the pretermitted spouse's support.
- The pretermitted spouse was provided for in the deceased spouse's will that was executed before the marriage. For example, if Amanda White had executed a will before her marriage to Adam in which she left Adam $100,000, Adam may not be able to take an intestate share because he was otherwise provided for in Amanda's will.
- The deceased spouse intentionally leaves the pretermitted spouse out of the will. This is usually accomplished by use of an explicit statement, such as "to the extent allowed by law, I intend to disinherit Adam." In this situation, Adam may still be able to take a share of the estate by elective share, which is discussed later in this chapter.

Community Property and Intestacy

Community property rules make for interesting distributions because the division of decedent's property is dependent upon whether the asset was a separate asset or a community asset.

Separate property is property that is owned before marriage or is acquired during marriage by gift or inheritance (and perhaps property acquired in another state or as proceeds of a lawsuit for bodily injury). Such property must be kept separate and not be comingled with the spouse's assets.

Community property is all property that is not classified as separate property and in most instances, the presumption is that all property acquired during a marriage is community property unless it can be proved otherwise.

So unlike in a noncommunity property state wherein all the decedent's property is treated the same, in a community property state, first the nature of the property has to be accounted for (probate or non-probate) and then whether it is community or separate before you can determine who inherits the property under the intestacy laws. In fact, the distribution may be entirely different depending upon whether it's community or separate property.

For example, in Texas, when there is a surviving spouse, she keeps her half of the community asset, which was hers to begin with, but her deceased husband's

Figure 3.8   Texas Probate Code Sec. 45. COMMUNITY ESTATE.

a. On the intestate death of one of the spouses to a marriage, the community property estate of the deceased spouse passes to the surviving spouse if:

1. no child or other descendant of the deceased spouse survives the deceased spouse; or
2. all surviving children and descendants of the deceased spouse are also children or descendants of the surviving spouse.

b. On the intestate death of one of the spouses to a marriage, if a child or other descendant of the deceased spouse survives the deceased spouse and the child or descendant is not a child or descendant of the surviving spouse, one-half of the community estate is retained by the surviving spouse and the other one-half passes to the children or descendants of the deceased spouse. The descendants shall inherit only such portion of said property to which they would be entitled under Section 43 of this code. In every case, the community estate passes charged with the debts against it.

Figure 3.9   Washington RCW 11.04.015—Descent and Distribution of Real and Personal Estate.

The net estate of a person dying intestate, or that portion thereof with respect to which the person shall have died intestate, shall descend subject to the provisions of RCW 11.04.250 and 11.02.070, and shall be distributed as follows:

(1) Share of surviving spouse or state registered domestic partner. The surviving spouse or state registered domestic partner shall receive the following share:

(a) All of the decedent's share of the net community estate; and
(b) One-half of the net separate estate if the intestate is survived by issue; or
(c) Three-quarters of the net separate estate if there is no surviving issue, but the intestate is survived by one or more of his or her parents, or by one or more of the issue of one or more of his or her parents; or
(d) All of the net separate estate, if there is no surviving issue nor parent nor issue of parent.

(2) Shares of others than surviving spouse or state registered domestic partner. The share of the net estate not distributable to the surviving spouse or state registered domestic partner, or the entire net estate if there is no surviving spouse or state registered domestic partner, shall descend and be distributed as follows:

(a) To the issue of the intestate; if they are all in the same degree of kinship to the intestate, they shall take equally, or if of unequal degree, then those of more remote degree shall take by representation.
(b) If the intestate not be survived by issue, then to the parent or parents who survive the intestate.

(continued)

Figure 3.9   (continued)

> (c) If the intestate not be survived by issue or by either parent, then to those issue of the parent or parents who survive the intestate; if they are all in the same degree of kinship to the intestate, they shall take equally, or, if of unequal degree, then those of more remote degree shall take by representation.
>
> (d) If the intestate not be survived by issue or by either parent, or by any issue of the parent or parents who survive the intestate, then to the grandparent or grandparents who survive the intestate; if both maternal and paternal grandparents survive the intestate, the maternal grandparent or grandparents shall take one-half and the paternal grandparent or grandparents shall take one-half.
>
> (e) If the intestate not be survived by issue or by either parent, or by any issue of the parent or parents or by any grandparent or grandparents, then to those issue of any grandparent or grandparents who survive the intestate; taken as a group, the issue of the maternal grandparent or grandparents shall share equally with the issue of the paternal grandparent or grandparents, also taken as a group; within each such group, all members share equally if they are all in the same degree of kinship to the intestate, or, if some be of unequal degree, then those of more remote degree shall take by representation.

half only goes to her if all the children of the marriage belong to both of them or if he had no children at the time of his death.

How does this work? Review this scenario: Yvette and David were married for 20 years at the time of David's death. Neither of them had any children. In this scenario, Yvette would take all of David's interest in the community property.

However, review this scenario; the results are different: Yvette and David were married for 20 years at the time of David's death. Both of them had children from prior marriages. All of their children are grown. They did not own their house as joint with right of survivorship but as community property. Because he had no will leaving the property to Yvette, upon David's death, Yvette retained her ownership interest in the community property (1/2) and David's children own the other 1/2 interest in the marital home. If Yvette does not get along with her stepchildren, they could force her to buy them out of their interest. Is this what David intended? Probably not.

Note that this is not the case in Washington State where the net community estate of the decedent passes to the surviving spouse or domestic partner. Therefore, it is extremely important to understand your state's intestacy laws if you live in one of the 10 community property states.

Summary of Intestate Succession

It is important to remember that the laws of each jurisdiction are different, so it is important for you, as a paralegal, to become familiar with the intestate succession laws of the state in which you plan to work.

Bobbie and Donald Black are married with three children, Tina, Todd, and Ted. In this scenario, Donald dies leaving an estate of $500,000 and has no debts or tax liabilities. He also dies without a will. What is the outcome in each of the following situations?

1. Donald dies with Bobbie surviving but no children or grandchildren.
2. Donald dies with Bobbie surviving and all three of their children survive as well.
3. Donald dies with Bobbie surviving and all three of their children survive as well. Donald has a daughter, Beth, from a prior marriage. In your jurisdiction, would it matter if it was not Donald but Bobbie who had a child from a prior marriage?
4. Donald dies in 2011. Bobbie died in 2008. All three of their children survive Donald.
5. Donald dies with Bobbie surviving. Todd predeceases Donald and had two children upon his death.
6. Donald dies in 2011. Bobbie predeceased him. They had no children or issue.

Escheat

When a person dies without a surviving spouse, children, parents, siblings, or any other ascertainable kin, that person's estate **escheats** to the state. This means that the property passes to the state. Real property always escheats to the state in which the property is located. Most states provide that personal property escheats to the state in which the deceased was domiciled. Counseling clients usually entails discussing this possibility and that, even if the client has no real family, it is often best to write a will leaving the estate to friends or charity and avoid "giving" the property to the state. It should be noted, however, that it is very rare for an estate to escheat.

Issues Affecting Distribution

Homestead Exemption

The **homestead exemption** generally allows the family or the head of the household to characterize the family residence as the homestead. In some states, only married persons can claim the homestead, while in others, the head of household must be the husband. Many states today allow single persons as well as the wife to claim the homestead.

In states that allow this exemption, the homestead is free from all claims and creditor's execution. The purpose of this exemption is to ensure that the family does not lose the roof over their heads. The homestead itself is not just the physical building but the surrounding property as well. While the property allowance varies from state to state, it is generally accepted that the amount of acreage allowed for rural land is greater than that for urban land. For example, in Florida the homestead is up to 160 contiguous acres for rural land and up to one acre for urban land, limited to the family's actual residence. Rural land is often determined by the property's use. So, a Florida family living on five acres may still only claim up to one acre unless the property is farmland. A family that lives on five acres and puts a cow to pasture on that land may then claim the entire five acres. In Texas, another state with a homestead exemption, the residential homestead consists of a lot or lots of 10 acres or less that is located within a city or town, while a rural homestead may be up to 200 acres. There is no limit on the value of the land and its improvements entitled to homestead protection. Homestead is based solely on the size or acreage of the land involved and it must be the person's primary residence.

Family Allowance

States may allow a cash allowance for the benefit of the surviving spouse and minor children. This may be in lieu of, or in addition to, the homestead exemption and is shielded from the claims of creditors. Since this is an amount for the maintenance of the deceased's family while the estate is probated, it is a priority payment which is made in addition to any property the family may obtain by will, inheritance, or elective share, discussed below.

Exempt Property

States may allow a portion of a decedent's property to be exempt and free from creditor's claims up to a specified dollar amount.

The property is usually limited to household furniture, furnishings and appliances, autos and personal effects and only applies when there is a surviving spouse or minor children.

Surviving Spouse's Elective Share

Elective share is a choice a surviving spouse has to make when his or her spouse dies. The choice is either to take a statutorily mandated share of his or her deceased spouse's estate, or to take what the spouse was left in the will, if there was a will or if anything was left to the surviving spouse. The purpose of the elective share is to protect a surviving spouse from being disinherited by the decedent spouse. The elective share creates a situation in which a spouse may not be disinherited by his or her deceased spouse.

The choice the surviving spouse makes is called a ***Right of Election***. The surviving spouse must elect either to take what was left for him or her under the decedent spouse's will, if anything at all, or to renounce the will provisions pertaining to spousal distributions altogether. The election must be made within a statutory period of time and if the survivor fails to make the election, he or she must take the amount provided for in the will. If the election to take a share of the estate is made, the surviving spouse then takes an amount of the decedent spouse's estate as set by statute. The elective share is usually a percentage of the decedent's estate, often the amount the spouse would have received if the decedent died intestate and is applied after deductions for the estate's debts, as well as mortgages and liens against the estate and estate property. The property is valued at its fair market value as of the date of the decedent spouse's death.

The elective share will not apply if the surviving spouse waived his or her rights to the decedent spouse's estate in either an antenuptial or a postnuptial agreement. In addition, if the surviving spouse has been found to have abandoned the deceased spouse, grounds for denying the surviving spouse's right to the election may be claimed.

The elective share is in addition to homestead, exempt property, and family allowances.

CASE 3.5 **SUMMARY**

This case illustrates both the concept of elective share of a surviving spouse and that of a pretermitted spouse. Note that the Michigan Court extensively quotes *Mongold v Mayle*, a West Virginia Court of Appeals case (although calling it the West Virginia Supreme Court in the opinion) which also illustrates the two concepts.

In re Estate of IDA SPRENKLE-HILL, Deceased

474 Mich. 878, 704 N.W.2d 697 (Mich. Ct. App. 2005), appeal to Mich. Sup. Ct. den

The decedent, Ida Sprenkle-Hill, executed a will and trust in 1999, providing that on her death, her entire estate would pour into a trust, which in turn would disburse specific amounts totaling $9000 to two individuals and the remainder to her two sons. Sprenkle-Hill died in 2001 having married George Hill 6 months earlier. Sprenkle-Hill never changed her will, however.

Hill filed a spouse's election and the probate court determined that the spousal election was not available to him because he was entitled to a portion of the estate under the state's pretermitted statute.

MCL 700.2202, which is titled "election of surviving spouse," states:

> (2) The surviving spouse of a decedent who was domiciled in this state and who dies testate may file with the court an election in writing that the spouse elects 1 of the following:
>
> a. That the spouse will abide by the terms of the will.
> b. That the spouse will take 1/2 of the sum or share that would have passed to the spouse had the testator died intestate, reduced by 1/2 of the value of all property derived by the spouse from the decedent by any means other than testate or intestate succession upon the decedent's death.

MCL 700.2301, which is titled "entitlement of spouse; premarital will," states:

> (1) [I]f a testator's surviving spouse marries the testator after the testator executes his or her will, the

surviving spouse is entitled to receive, as an intestate share, not less than the value of the share of the estate the surviving spouse would have received if the testator had died intestate as to that portion of the testator's estate, if any, that is not any of the following:

> a. Property devised to a child of the testator who was born before the testator married the surviving spouse and who is not the surviving spouse's child.
> b. Property devised to a descendant of a child described in subdivision (a).
> c. Property that passes under section 2603 or 2604[3] to a child described in subdivision (a), or to a descendant of such a child.

As the Court explained, "In other words, under §2202, a surviving spouse may elect either to abide by the will or to receive a share of the decedent's estate, which is referred to as the spouse's "elective share." Under §2301, a "pretermitted spouse"—that is, a surviving spouse who married the decedent after the will was executed—is entitled to receive an intestate share of a specified portion of the estate."

As Hill did not claim a share of the estate as a pretermitted spouse under §2301, but instead decided to claim an elective share under §2202, the Court asked whether Hill was entitled to take his elective share as a surviving spouse, or whether, as a pretermitted spouse, he was limited to the remedy afforded under §2301. The Court concluded that as a surviving spouse, Hill, who married Sprenkle-Hill after her will was executed, was not barred from claiming an elective share.

The Court quoted a West Virginia case, *Mongold v Mayle*, 452 SE2d 444, 447 (W Va, 1994) in which a surviving spouse appealed the trial court's ruling that she was not entitled to claim her elective share because the statutory provision governing pretermitted spouses, which the court referred to as the "premarital will provision," was exclusively controlling. The West Virginia appellate court observed that the purpose of an elective-share statute "is to prevent disinheritance of the spouse," and that this form of spousal protection has existed since the Code of Hammurabi. The West Virginia appellate court found that modern elective-share statutes reflect "the contemporary view of marriage as an economic partnership," and are based on the rationales that all surviving spouses have contributed in some way toward the deceased's ability to acquire property, and that the surviving spouse will need to be supported. The West Virginia appellate court concluded that the purpose behind West Virginia's elective-share provision was "to prevent spousal disinheritance in order to ensure that the surviving spouse's contribution to the acquisition of property during the marriage is recognized and in order to ensure that the surviving spouse has continuing financial support after the death of his or her spouse."

The West Virginia appellate court then observed that this purpose was "obviously different than the purpose of the premarital will provision," which considers "the possibility that the decedent spouse may have forgotten about the pre-existing will when marrying the surviving spouse, and if the decedent spouse had remembered the will, he would have included the surviving spouse in the will." The West Virginia appellate court then concluded that "[c]ommon sense dictates" that the premarital will provision "does not preclude a surviving spouse from taking an elective share" because "[t]o hold otherwise, would allow a spouse to disinherit his or her spouse, thereby defeating the purpose behind the elective-share theory of the Revised Uniform Probate Code." The Michigan Court of Appeals found the reasoning persuasive and adopted it.

It concluded that a surviving spouse who satisfied the conditions of §2301 may take an elective share under §2202, if that provision yielded a larger amount. The amount to which the surviving spouse was entitled under §2301 would be considered part of the elective share. Conversely, if the share available to a surviving spouse under §2301 was greater than the elective share under §2202, the surviving spouse may receive the full amount to which he or she is entitled under §2301 by electing to abide by the terms of the will pursuant to §2202.

Dower and Courtesy

Dower and courtesy refer to a surviving spouse's right of inheritance of real property regardless of the devise of such property in the deceased spouse's will.

Dower refers to the common law right of a surviving wife in her husband's real property. The interest the wife was entitled to under dower at common law was a life estate in one-third of the property.

Courtesy refers to the common law right of a surviving husband in his wife's real property. The interest the husband was entitled to under courtesy at common law was a life estate in the entire property, if there was a living child of the marriage.

The purpose of dower and courtesy was to provide the surviving spouse a place to live despite a deceased spouse's attempt to disinherit the survivor. Notice that under the common law, the wife's interest was considerably less. While most states have abolished dower and courtesy in favor of elective share or community property, those that maintain them have generally statutorily changed the rights of both spouses to give them an equal life estate in the decedent spouse's real property, usually the whole thereof.

Other Issues That Affect Distribution of the Estate

Homicide by Beneficiary or Heir

The effect of the decedent's homicide by either a beneficiary to a will or heir of the decedent's estate is governed by "felonious slayer" statutes. The general rule, as stated in the UPC, is that a beneficiary who intentionally kills or hires someone to kill the decedent, is unable to inherit from the decedent, whether by will or intestate succession. The decedent's estate will pass through to the next "innocent" beneficiary or heir as if the killer had predeceased the decedent.

The UPC also provides for the distribution of a decedent's non-probate assets, such as joint tenancies, tenancies by the entirety, and life insurance proceeds, which are distributed if the remaining tenant or insurance beneficiary is the killer, since they do not require disposition by the probate court. Many states, however, consider the death of the decedent by the remaining joint tenant to constitute a severance of the decedent's interest in the tenancy. This ensures that the joint tenant-killer does not retain his or her right of survivorship. It would apply to all joint tenancies with right of survivorship and tenancies by the entirety in both real and personal property. This includes tenancies in joint bank, savings, and credit union accounts. Should the killer be a life insurance beneficiary, many state laws treat the killer-beneficiary as if he or she predeceased the decedent, allowing the life insurance proceeds to pass to the alternate beneficiary, or if there is no alternate, by intestacy to the next "innocent" heir.

Simultaneous Death of Decedent and Beneficiary

When the decedent predeceases the beneficiary, the decedent's property is devised as mandated either by the provisions in the decedent's will or by the laws of succession. If both the decedent and the beneficiary die simultaneously, however, disposition of the decedent's assets becomes a vexing problem.

True **simultaneous death** requires both parties to die at the same time. For example, a husband and wife have a fatal car crash. Police and rescue units are on the scene within minutes of the accident. The officer in charge notes that both the husband and the wife were already dead. It will be presumed they died simultaneously and each will be presumed to have predeceased the other.

The problems with simultaneous death occur when the decedent and beneficiary die within a short time of each other but not truly simultaneously. Unless it can be proved that a decedent and beneficiary died at the same time, the parties will be treated as if they had survived each other. The decedent's estate passes to the beneficiary as if the beneficiary was still alive.

> *Example:* Ronald Berger and Kelly Berger, husband and wife, have a car crash. Kelly dies at 1:20 P.M., while still at the scene of the accident. Ronald dies at 1:25 P.M., also at the scene, however, the paramedics don't know that Ronald survived Kelly. They appear to have died simultaneously and the consequences can be disastrous. In this instance, Kelly's estate passes to Ronald and Ronald's estate passes to Kelly.
>
> How is this problematic? If, for example, Ronald and Kelly each had assets totaling $4 million when they died in 2011, each would have died with an $8 million estate! This would be a real treat for the tax man as they would collect estate taxes based upon assets from both estates, reducing the amount of property that would actually pass to their kin and/or will beneficiaries.

To prevent this from happening, the UPC, as well as some state statutes, provides that, if the beneficiary does not survive the decedent by 120 hours, the beneficiary will be deemed to have predeceased the decedent. This is still a small window of time, but makes provision for those instances in which a common disaster, such as a car accident, causes a decedent and a beneficiary to die within a few hours or days of each other. In this instance then, Kelly's property would not pass to Ronald.

Another method of curing this problem is to write a will provision which addresses this issue. A testator may write a provision that states a specified time in which the beneficiary must survive the testator. For example, Ronald's will may provide, "Should my wife, Kelly, predecease me or die within 30 days after my death, then and in that event, I give, devise and bequeath all rest, residue, and remainder to my children, Rhonda and Stacy." If Ronald's will made this provision, his estate would bypass Kelly and pass directly to the three children. The testator can designate any time frame, although 30 days to 6 months is most common.

SUMMARY

A person dies testate when he or she has executed a valid will. The dispositions the person makes via the will are called bequests, legacies, and devises, depending upon the type and character of the property involved. Bequests and legacies are synonymous and refer to the distribution of personal property in a will while devises refer to the distribution of real property in a will.

Abatement occurs when the decedent's will does not provide for how the debts and other expenses of the estate are to be satisfied or when the assets are insufficient. State statute prescribes the order in which an estate's assets will be appropriated if either of these situations occurs. A testator can cure this by having an apportionment clause in the will. Ademption occurs when property the testator devises in his or her will is no longer part of his or her estate when he or she dies. When this occurs, the gift is said to have adeemed by extinction. At common law, when a beneficiary did not survive the testator, the gift to the beneficiary lapsed and passed either as part of the residue of the estate or by intestacy (if there was no residue clause in the will). Anti-lapse statutes prevent the gift from lapsing by allowing the beneficiary's descendants to take the gift.

Intestate succession is the method by which a person's estate is distributed when the person dies without a valid will. The laws of succession are determined by state statute. They are enacted as a measure of protection for the decedent's family, but may not reflect the true wishes of the decedent. For this very reason, it is important that the client engage in proper estate planning while alive and that he or she is made aware of the consequences of not having a plan in the event of the client's death. Property is distributed either per stirpes or per capita. Per stirpes is Latin for "by the roots"; per capita is Latin for "by the head." When a testator intends to leave property to a group, that is, "my children," or "my grandchildren," or "my descendants," the method by which his or her property is distributed upon his or her death determines how much of the property each beneficiary receives when one person of the group has predeceased the testator.

A person has ancestors or descendants, who are direct blood relatives and are considered lineal descendants. A person also has **collateral descendants** who are blood relatives but are not directly related, such as aunts, uncles, and cousins. A person who is related only by marriage is considered a relationship by affinity. Whether a person is a surviving spouse, an adopted child, a pretermitted child, or spouse, or related by the whole or half blood, may have an impact on inheritance. A person rarely dies without any relatives either lineally or collaterally, so a person's estate rarely escheats, or is given to the state for lack of an heir.

When a decedent spouse dies, states often give the surviving spouse and minor children additional protections to ensure that they have sufficient means of support. These protections include homestead, family allowance, exempt property, and elective share. An elective share is the ability of the surviving spouse to take a statutory amount of the decedent spouse's estate so as to prevent the spouse from being left a small amount of the estate or being disinherited.

The intentional homicide of a decedent by a beneficiary, or by someone the beneficiary directs, prevents the beneficiary from inheriting any of the decedent's estate. The decedent's estate passes to the next "innocent" beneficiary or heir as if the killer had predeceased the decedent.

If the beneficiary dies simultaneously with the testator, the beneficiary will be deemed to have predeceased the testator. However, the Uniform Probate Code, as well as many state statutes, provides that unless the beneficiary survives the testator by 120 hours, he or she will be deemed to have predeceased the testator. A testator may provide in his or her will for a specified period of time in which the beneficiary must survive the testator or be deemed to have predeceased him or her.

KEY **TERMS**

legacies	bequests	general legacy
demonstrative legacy	pecuniary bequest	ademption
residuary	abatement	per stirpes
satisfaction	per capita	collateral descendants
intestate succession	lineal descendants	pretermitted child
affinity	pretermitted spouse	elective share
escheat	homestead exemption	anti-lapse
simultaneous death	devises	

REVIEW **QUESTIONS**

1. What are the disadvantages of having an estate disposed of by descent and distribution?

2. Can a person disinherit his or her spouse?

3. From whom do adopted children inherit today?

4. Explain the difference between testate and intestate.

5. Define *escheat*.

6. What are the differences between lineal and collateral relatives? What are relationships by affinity?

7. What is the purpose of the homestead?

8. What are pretermitted children and what effect do they have on an estate?

9. What is an elective share and what is its purpose?

10. What is an anti-lapse statute and what is its purpose?

11. What is the difference between a demonstrative bequest and a general bequest?

12. What are children by half-blood? How are they distinguished from whole-blood children? Do you think this is fair?

PROJECTS

1. You are a paralegal working for a probate attorney. Judy's will provides $100,000 to her brother, Paul. The residue of Judy's estate was left to her sister, Mary. Paul predeceased Judy. Assume Judy was single and had no children. Your supervising attorney has asked you to research your state's intestate succession laws to determine who of Judy's family will receive the estate. Does it make a difference if Paul had children of his own?

2. Prepare your own family tree.

3. Janet dies at the advanced age of 100, leaving only her three grandchildren, Bobbie, Jim Jr., and Maryann, as her nearest kin. Janet's son, John, was the father of Bobbie, while Janet's son, Jim Sr., was Jim Jr. and Maryann's father. Janet's estate was worth $240,000 at the time of death. What is the per capita distribution to each of Janet's grandchildren? What is the per stirpes distribution to each of them?

4. Thomas left a validly executed will that stated in part:

I devise $10,000 to my son Alec.

I devise $5000 to my stepson Bill.

I devise $5000 to my friend Jerry.

I devise the residue of my estate one-half to the United Way and one-half to my son Steven.

Unfortunately, Alec, Bill, Jerry, and Steven all predecease Thomas.

Alec leaves one daughter Cheryl, surviving him.

Bill leaves two daughters, Ann and Mitzi, surviving him.

Jerry leaves three daughters, Harriet, Marilyn, and Jennifer surviving him.

Steven leaves one daughter, Robin surviving him.

At Thomas's death, Cheryl, Ann, Mitzi, Harriet, Marilyn, Jennifer, and Robin are alive.

All other persons are deceased.

Assume an anti-lapse statute is in effect in your jurisdiction.

Under state law, who receives the $10,000 devise to Alec, the $5000 devise to Bill, the $5000 devise

to Jerry, and Steven's share of the residue of the estate? Explain your answers.

Do you think this is what Thomas intended? Why or why not?

MyLegalStudiesLab™   http://www.mylegalstudieslab

MYLEGALSTUDIESLAB VIRTUAL LAW OFFICE EXPERIENCE ASSIGNMENTS

Complete the pre-test, study plan, and post-test for this chapter and answer the Legal Applications questions as assigned. These will help you confirm your mastery of the concepts and their application to legal scenarios. Then complete the Virtual Law Office assignments as assigned by your instructor. These assignments are designed to develop your workplace skills and result in producing documents for inclusion in your portfolio.

Chapter **four**
THE WILL

A Short History of Wills

The law of wills has a long history, beginning in the 1200s, and is rooted in the English feudal system. Under this system, real property was required to be passed from the father to his eldest son, then from the son to his eldest son, and so on, called primogeniture. Primogeniture excluded female children altogether. It also excluded the wife (think Mrs. Dashwood and her daughters in Jane Austen's *Sense and Sensibility*).

Property in primitive societies tended to belong either to the group as a whole or to the king. In medieval England, the king gave property to his lords who had limited ownership of real property under the feudal system. The common people did not own land at all.

The only property that could be freely distributed was personal property. This was done by using a document called a testament. Jurisdiction of testaments was held by the church (at that time, the Roman Catholic Church); the testaments were taken orally by the priest at the time of last confession.

After a time, people devised ways to get around the restrictions on the disposition of real property. The government, not liking these methods of circumvention because they often enabled landowners to forego the payment of taxes upon distribution, passed in 1536 the Statute of Uses, which put new restrictions on distribution. A mere 4 years later (1540), however, England under Henry VIII was forced to enact the Statute of Wills, which allowed most landowners to distribute real property by written will. The Statute of Wills also permitted a father to distribute property by will to any of his male children, disinheriting the eldest son if he wished, bypassing the law of primogeniture. Among the rules set forth for a valid will in the Statute of Wills was that the will must be in writing and must have two witnesses.

Distribution continued in this fashion until feudalism ended in 1660, when all land could be disposed of by written will instead of by primogeniture. In addition, with the installation of England's king as head of the Church of England, the church's dominance over

OBJECTIVES

At the end of this chapter, the student will understand:

- the history of wills
- the statutory requirements for a valid will
- how to change or revoke a will
- what joint and mutual wills are
- the concept of will contests

disposition of personal property also ended. Eventually, only one document was required to dispose of both real and personal property, hence the term "last will and testament." Today the term "will" suffices to describe distribution of both real and personal property.

Validity
Statutory Requirements

Many factors go into determining whether or not a will is valid. Since the ability to execute a will is still considered a privilege granted by the government, all the factors are statutory in nature, that is, set out by statute, code, or law. In the United States, the individual states are the sole grantors of this privilege. Federal statutes do not govern the factors or formalities that must be observed for a will to be valid. As a paralegal, you must learn your own state's requirements for executing a will. While there are a few variations, the laws from state to state follow basic common law concepts.

The statutory requirements are a means of preventing fraud and of insuring to the best of anyone's capability that the will was drafted properly and that the testator's wishes are carried out.

Note: Throughout this book, as a matter of convenience, we may use the term "probate court" to denote the entity in charge of carrying out a decedent's wishes if a will was drafted, or the statutory requirements in the case of intestacy. Nonetheless, the term "probate court" may not be accurate in your jurisdiction. For example, in New York State, the entity that handles probate matters is the Surrogate Court. In West Virginia and Virginia, no judicial process is involved at all unless the beneficiaries or heirs are contesting the distribution of the decedent's estate. In West Virginia, the entity handling probate matters is the Office of the Fiduciary Commissioner; and in Virginia, all matters are filed with the Circuit Court Clerk, but are referred to a Commissioner of Accounts, usually a local lawyer appointed to the position. It is up to the student to determine what entity has oversight of probate matters in his or her jurisdiction.

THE PROFESSIONAL PARALEGAL

A paralegal must become familiar with his or her state's requirements for executing a valid will. Don't wait to be told. Look it up and memorize the requirements.

Intent and Capacity

The document being offered as the testator's will in any probate proceeding must be proven to be the testator's last valid will. Remember that the only person who can unequivocally let all interested parties know what was really meant by certain statements in the document, or if the document itself was really intended to be a will, is the testator himself or herself, but that person is deceased and certainly isn't telling! Therefore, the deceased's testamentary **intent** must be clear from the face of the document. The will must be able to stand on its own without any outside evidence (called parole evidence), meaning that the procedure to determine the intent is taken from the "four corners of the document."

Intent   It is important, therefore, that the will reveals the testator's intent. The form, language, and words used are all indications of intent. This means that the attorney drafting the will with the help of her paralegal must demonstrate the testator's intent using clear language of the testator's wishes. For example, in a document that says "last will and testament" across the top of the page, the words "last will and testament" are indicative of the intent to create a will. If the document does not say "last will and testament" or "last will," but instead says "Grandma's Best Brownies," a court may question whether the deceased meant for the document to indeed be a will. Perhaps, the court will reason the document was just a page of jottings on which the deceased was deciding which of his or her personal effects and other property would be given and to whom.

Testamentary Capacity   For a testator to create a valid will, he or she must also have **testamentary capacity**. Testamentary capacity is the legal ability of a person to create a will. Testamentary capacity has two factors:

- age
- sound mind

Age   The age of legal majority has nothing to do with the age at which one may legally drink, join the military, get married, or leave compulsory education. It is, however, tied to the age at which you can vote.

A testator must be of majority age to make a valid will. For most purposes, the age of majority in the United States is 18, except for two states with the age of 19 (Nebraska and Alabama) and one state with the age of 21 (Mississippi). A person turns 18 on his or her actual birth date of his or her 18th year. Some states allow people who are under the age of 18 to execute wills for various reasons, such as marriage, emancipation, and being in the armed service. Paralegals should become familiar with any variations their states may have.

CASE 4.1 **SUMMARY**

This paternity case illustrates what constitutes the age of majority.

C.M.R. v. L.S.A.
Tennessee Court of Appeals, Knoxville, Case No. E2001-0292-COA-R3-JV (2002)

In this paternity action, the trial court dismissed the case stating that it was filed outside the statute of limitations, which is the period of time in which a cause of action must be brought or be barred from suit.

The statute of limitations is statutory in nature and is dependent upon what type of action it is (i.e., no statute of limitations on murder but a statute of limitations on breach of contract). The court dismissed this action because it concluded that the statute of limitations for paternity actions began on the child's 18th birthday.

C.M.R. filed a paternity action on June 5, 2001. C.M.R. was born out of wedlock on June 18, 1979. L.S.A., the alleged father moved to dismiss the case based on T.C.A. §36-2-306(a) which stated, "An action to establish the parentage of a child may be instituted before or after the birth of the child and until three (3) years beyond the child's age of majority." C.M.R. argued that a person is "age 18 until you turn age 19 on your next birthday."

The Court stated, however, that they had "no doubt that the legislature intended the phrase "until three (3) years beyond the child's age of majority" to mean three years beyond the date on which the child attained the age of majority."

The Court concluded that as the trial court found that the action was filed more than 3 years after June 19, 1997, the trial court properly dismissed the suit.

Sound Mind

Testamentary capacity also requires the testator to be of **sound mind** at the time the will was executed. If a person was mentally incapacitated at the time of death, it does not matter as long as he or she was of sound mind at the time the will was signed.

The concept of sound mind has four components:

- **Objects of One's Bounty**—The testator must know the "natural objects of his bounty." These are members of his or her immediate family, as well as other people for whom the testator has a familial relationship or for whom he or she has affection. This does not mean the testator must leave anything to all of them, or any of them, however. The requirement is only that he or she be aware of who these people are. It is common for a clause to be put in a will, stating who the testator's family members are to illustrate this point. Example: In Lucinda Clark's will, there is a clause regarding family that states:
  REGINALD CLARK is my spouse.
  I have three children, HUEY CLARK, BILLY CLARK, and WILLARD CLARK. References to my children are to them and any child that may be borne to or adopted by me.
  References to my descendants are to my children and their descendants.
  Example of another family clause: Lucinda Clark's will states in part:
  SECTION 1—DECLARATION CONCERNING FAMILY
  I hereby declare that I am married to REGINALD CLARK. I have three children, to-wit: HUEY CLARK, BILLY CLARK, and WILLARD CLARK. Any references to my "husband" shall refer to Reginald Clark. Any references to my "child" or "children" shall refer to Huey Clark, Billy Clark, and Willard Clark. I have no other children born to or adopted by me.
- **His or Her Bounty**—The testator must know the nature and extent of his or her bounty. A testator's "bounty" is the property that he or she owns.

Figure 4.1   **Georgia Code Section 53-4-11.** Testamentary Capacity

> a. Testamentary capacity exists when the testator has a decided and rational desire as to the disposition of property.
> b. An incapacity to contract may coexist with the capacity to make a will.
> c. An insane individual generally may not make a will except during a lucid interval. A monomaniac may make a will if the will is in no way connected with the monomania. In all such cases, it must appear that the will expresses the wishes of the testator unbiased by the insanity or monomania with which the testator is affected.
> d. Neither advancing age nor weakness of intellect nor eccentricity of habit or thought is inconsistent with the capacity to make a will.

- **That He or She Is Making a Will**—The testator must know that he or she is making a will and that this document is a plan for disposing of his or her property upon his or her death. He or she must understand the effect executing this document will have on his or her property. This is usually done by showing "Will" or "Last Will and Testament" at the top of the first page and a first clause, called an opening clause, exordium clause, or publication clause.

> *Example:* I, **LUCINDA CLARK,** a resident of the City of Anytown, Anystate, being of sound and disposing mind, memory, and understanding, and mindful of the uncertainties of this life, and not acting under duress, menace, fraud, or undue influence, do hereby make, publish, and declare this my Last Will and Testament and revoking any and all former wills and codicils that I previously have made.

> Notice how this opening clause states the testator's name, current domicile, and that she is of sound mind and not acting under undue influence. Sound mind is a component of testamentary capacity and is discussed immediately below. The concept of undue influence is also a component of intent and testamentary capacity and is also discussed below. This does not insure that Lucinda Clark is of sound mind, but just the fact that it is stated is considered evidence that she knew this was her will and that she intended to make a will.

- **Mental Competence**—The testator must be free from what courts have called "insane delusions" that would influence his or her decisions regarding the formulation of his or her estate plan. The concept of delusions is interesting because courts have decided that someone who is generally considered mentally incompetent may, in a *lucid interval*, properly execute a valid will. As long as the testator had a rational moment while executing the will, the "lucid interval," the document is valid. Courts have also held that a will is valid despite the testator's low IQ, lack of personal hygiene, or other eccentricities.

A number of cases illustrate this point.

CASE 4.2 **SUMMARY**

Matter of Estate of Roosa
1988 WY 59, 753 P.2d 1028 (1988)

This case illustrates that a person's eccentricities may not automatically categorize a person as being of "unsound" mind.

In this case, Roosa was by any standards a strange individual. The Court, however, quoted at length from 1 Bowe-Parker, Page on Wills, §12.21 at 606–608 (1960), on the standard of testamentary capacity which it had determined, had been adopted in Wyoming.

' * * * Testator must have sufficient strength and clearness of mind and memory, to know, in general, without prompting, the nature and extent of the property of which he is about to dispose, and nature of the act which he is about to perform, and the names and identity of the persons who are to be the objects of his bounty, and his relation towards them. He must have sufficient mind and memory to understand all of these facts, and to comprehend these elements in their relation to each other, and a charge, in negative form, that capacity is lacking if testator is not able to know all of these facts, is erroneous, since he lacks capacity if he is unable to understand any one of them. He must be able to appreciate the relation of these factors to one another, and to recollect the decision which he has formed.

The appellants filed affidavits from Barbara Barker and Gabriel Barker, employees of Barker Brothers, Inc. from whom Roosa rented a trailer. Barbara and Gabriel knew Roosa from 1963 through 1983. The Court stated that their affidavits contained conclusion and opinions, such as: "Roosa lived in a dream world; he did not operate in reality; he did not have a clear understanding of his business affairs; and he lacked capacity to sign a will." Barbara and Gabriel supported their conclusions based on specific instances of what they considered eccentric or even delusional behavior on the part of Roosa. The incidents relied upon included such things as: Roosa calling himself, "Craig R." and "Major Craig R."; his statement of belief that he was a partner with Barker Brothers, Inc. in a number of large projects; his attempt to contribute large sums of money to those projects in 1978; his statement that he was working for the Attorney General of the United States; and his periodic billing to Barker Brothers, Inc. for "work" he believed he was doing for that firm. Roosa did "putter around" on Barker Brothers, Inc. property to "occupy Mr. Roosa's time and keep him happy," but he was not on the payroll.

The appellants filed the affidavit of Mary Lou Sare's which also discussed Roosa's eccentric behavior. She said that Roosa had mentioned a connection with a car factory in Colorado. He also made "vague" requests that she transfer his money to a Montana bank. He poured a package of sugar on her desk, and complained that it was not processed properly and discussing the fact that it should be reported to someone. On one occasion, she said, Roosa suggested that she might have to assist him to prevent aliens from coming across the border, in connection with his perceived duties as a guard for Barker Brothers, Inc.

The Court stated that one could certainly infer that Roosa was an eccentric. However, "[A] conclusion of eccentricity, though, does not foreclose the possession of testamentary capacity." The Court stated the general rule as "* * * Eccentricity has no effect on testamentary capacity; * * *."

The Court continued, quoting 1 Bowe-Parker Page on Wills, supra, §12.37 at 644–645:

> The fact that the testator was filthy, forgetful, and eccentric, * * * believed in witchcraft, and had dogs eat at the same table with him, * * * or that testator thought that others were plotting against him and was afraid to go out in the dark, * * * does not establish lack of capacity.

Ultimately, this court concluded that Roosa was eccentric but understood his property, that he had made a will and who he wanted the property to go to and therefore had the requisite mental capacity (sound mind) to make a valid will.

CASE 4.3 **SUMMARY**

Sellers v. Qualls, 206 Md. 58, 66 (1954)

This is another case regarding a testator's eccentricities and claims of unsound mind.

In this case, the Court stated that there is no extraordinary mental capacity for making a will required by the law. "Mere eccentricity" is not enough to void a will and the eccentricities in this matter did not rise to a level of incapacity. The eccentricities were described as follows:

> …the effects of diseases (diabetes) from which she suffered; her rather frequent falls both indoors and outside, her rummaging through a garbage dump, which she permitted to be established on her place (and on which she sometimes fell), and eating moldy bread and other food which she retrieved from it; once eating

food which she had vomited; eating food given her by hucksters for her chickens; eating large quantities of cheese, liverwurst, braunschweiger or bacon, regardless of dietary restrictions; licking her plate; making unfounded accusations of theft against a tenant, against her sister, Mrs. Sellers, and against others; hitting Mrs. Sellers with a saucer at some unspecified date in 1950; making unfounded allegations of attempts to poison her; hiding money in odd places; laughing, crying, or talking to herself and seeming nervous or upset; and on one occasion wanting to put roomers out of her house and then letting them return almost immediately.

The Court concluded that her eating habits were "an odd and extreme form of miserliness; but miserliness is not necessarily the hallmark of insanity, and is more likely to indicate the reverse."

Undue Influence

Sound mind and intent of the testator also raise issues of **undue influence**. Often, a friend or family member will try to induce the testator to write a will favoring a particular beneficiary, usually the friend or family member herself or a relative of that friend or family member. This often occurs with older people who are reliant upon the friend or family member for assistance with everyday events, such as shopping, paying bills, driving them to doctor's appointments, and general advice. While it is understandable that the older person would want to give them a gift as a reward for their assistance, it may be considered undue influence, especially if the gift was unduly large or caused some or all of the person's family to be left out in favor of the "helper."

CASE 4.4 **SUMMARY**

Orwick v. Moldawer, 822 A.2d 506 (Md. App., 2003)

In this case, the son of the decedent alleged that his half-sister had exerted influence on their father, causing him to largely be disinherited from his father's will.

Dana Orwick, the decedent, lived with his daughter, Jackie, who was his daughter from his second marriage. Kurt Orwick was a son from a prior marriage. Dana was admitted to a hospital with terminal cancer on May 15, 2000. On May 24, 2000, 3 days before his death, Dana executed a will that only noted Kurt once, as trustee for Dana's grandson (Kurt's son) to whom Dana left his library and record collection. Otherwise, the remainder of the estate, totaling $653,000, was left to Jackie and her brother, Michael, Dana's other child from his second marriage.

Kurt alleged that Dana was not competent to make a will and that Jackie and Michael exerted undue influence on him. The trial court concluded that Kurt had not made a case against Jackie (Kurt had dropped his case against Michael) and dismissed the suit.

The appellate court stated that "undue influence which will avoid a will must be unlawful on account of the manner and motive of its exertion, and must be exerted to such a degree as to amount to force or coercion, so that free agency of the testator is destroyed." The Court determined that a jury could have found that the will did give substantial benefit to Jackie and that Jackie caused or assisted the execution of the will, that she had opportunity to exert influence and that the will contained an unnatural disposition of Dana's estate. It noted that if Dana had died intestate, the three children would have each received about $217,666. The Court determined that a jury could have found that Jackie assisted Dana in the execution of the will; that she told her father where to sign and sought the location of the attorney because she contacted the drafting attorney; and that she requested the hospital to provide witnesses to sign the will. The Court said that, by themselves, these facts do "even hint of under influence" but that, together with other factors, could support a jury's

finding of undue influence. The Court also determined that a jury could find that Jackie had the opportunity to exert influence as she lived in the house with her father since 1999. Finally, the Court determined that the jury could find that Jackie exerted undue influence because of the "unnatural disposition of Dana's assets by completely cutting Kurt out of the will."

However, the Court stated that it must determine if there was a confidential relationship between Jackie and Dana and that Dana was highly susceptible to undue influence. The Court stated that "testamentary gifts are natural and expected, and people who receive gifts under a will, usually a parent, child, spouse, sibling, close friend, or trusted employee, often stand in a fiduciary or confidential relationship with the testator," making the burden of proving undue influence difficult. The Court stated that "the mere existence of a familial relationship is not indicative of a confidential relationship," quoting 3 Bowe-Parker: Page on Wills, §29.84 (1961). It continued that the "issue is whether a level of trust and confidence exists between two people to the point that the testator trusts another to conduct the testator's business and that trusted person abuses that trust in some way to gain a benefit in the testator's will."

The Court concluded that there was "simply no evidence to support even the inference that Jackie maintained a confidential relationship with her father of the kind sufficient" for Kurt to sustain his burden of proof. The Court noted that no testimony that Jackie took over Dana's day-to-day finances was proffered. It also noted that Dana's attorney indicated in the notes, he provided, that Dana had every intention of excluding Kurt from the will and went to the attorney's office alone to take care of the will's provisions. The attorney's notes also indicated that correspondence between Dana and his attorney went back to at least January of 2000. The Court concluded that Dana was "very much in control of his finances and estate, and sought the financial advice of an attorney, not that of his daughter." The Court upheld the trial court's dismissal of the suit.

As shown in the prior case, the person contesting the will on the grounds that the testator was coerced into executing the will because of a lack of mental capacity (contest is discussed at the end of this chapter) has the burden of proving that the testator lacked the requisite mental capacity to execute a valid will. In general, the witnesses to the will, the testator's physician, other health-care providers, family members, and friends may be asked to testify as to the testator's mental soundness. The paralegal who is asked to witness a will, a common task, should assess the testator's capacity before witnessing. If there are any doubts about the testator's capacity, the paralegal should call those doubts to the supervising attorney's attention privately.

According to the Alzheimer's Association, as many as 5.4 million Americans are living with Alzheimer's today. Undue influence and the soundness of mind of the testator, already likely the number one cause of action in probate contests, will surely rise as the number of Americans of advanced age continues to grow. See Alzheimer's from the Frontlines: Challenges a National Alzheimer's Plan Must Address, Alzheimer's Association, 2011; www.alz.org/documents_custom/napareport.pdf

Is the Will Written or Oral

Holographic Wills

In most instances, a will must be in writing. "In writing" means that it must be handwritten, printed, or typed. A will that is completely handwritten is called a **holographic will**. Holographic wills do not require the signatures of witnesses, although they must otherwise follow all statutory requirements for executing a valid will, meaning one with intent and testamentary capacity. It is presumed that, if the will is completely in the hand of the testator, he or she intended to make a will. Holographic wills are not permitted in all states. Alaska, Arizona, Arkansas, California, Colorado, Idaho, Kentucky, Louisiana, Maine, Michigan, Mississippi, Montana, Nebraska, Nevada, New Jersey, North Carolina, North Dakota, Oklahoma, Pennsylvania, South Dakota, Tennessee, Texas, Utah, Virginia, West Virginia, and Wyoming permit holographic wills. Connecticut, Hawaii, South Carolina, Washington, and Wisconsin, while not accepting one written in its state boundaries, permit holographic wills that were validly created in another state. Maryland and New York only permit holographic wills made by members of the armed forces while serving out of state (Maryland) or in armed conflict (New York). In both states, the wills are voided one year after discharge.

Nuncupative Wills

A few states allow **nuncupative**, or oral, wills in limited circumstances. Usually made during the last moments of a terminal illness or military service in time of war, they must be declared in the presence of witnesses. In fact, they are often called "Soldiers and Sailors Wills" because they are most often permitted for active duty military personnel. Nuncupative wills may only dispose of personal property.

Signature of the Testator

A will must be signed by the testator. When the testator is physically unable to sign his name, he may affix his mark to the document. The usual mark is an "X," but any mark including a single initial or what looks like scribble suffices as long as

CASE 4.5 **SUMMARY**

Estate of Norman F. Shelly, Deceased,
27 Fiduc. Rep. 2d 170 (O.C. Franklin
2007), aff'd 950 A.2d 1021 (Pa. Super.
2008), alloc. denied, 962 A.2d 1198
(Pa. Super. 2008)

Norman Shelly died on July 27, 1999. On August 25, 1999, Thomas Steigner submitted a cardboard panel of a cigarette carton for probate and the Register of Wills issued letters of administration c.t.a. (c.t.a. means with will annexed) to Michael J. Cook. Cook was not related to Shelly. The cardboard panel was written totally in Shelly's hand but contained no witness **attestations** nor was it notarized.

Together with the cardboard panel, Steigner filed an Oath of Non-Subscribing Witnesses who said they knew Shelly and recognized his signature.

None of the beneficiaries listed on the panel were Shelly's heirs. Shelly's four heirs appealed the admittance of the purported will to probate and the trial court found in their favor.

The Court stated that the only term that could be construed on the panel which would dispose of any property is "DEVIDE" which the trial court presumed meant "divide." The cardboard panel specifically stated:

MONEY, DEVIDE

MICHAEL COOKS SONS

However, as the Court pointed out, Shelly also placed an arrow leading from the previous section of his writing which read "FARM MACH + MACHINES AND TOOLS MICHAEL COOK SR LIVING MY AGE" into the section regarding "MONEY, DEVIDE." The Court concluded that the writing did not indicate what money was to be divided, into what shares, or if it was to be divisible to Michael Cook Sr. and his sons, or only to Michael Cook's sons. The Court determined that "the cigarette carton does not include the one essential element for the creation of a will, a disposition of property" and therefore cannot be considered a will.

The cardboard panel also stated the following:
FIRST AND LAST ONLY WILL
D?"
NORMAN F. SHELLY

The Court concluded that Shelly using the term "draft" indicated that he did not intend a testamentary writing to be created on the cardboard panel but instead intended for the writing to be only a draft in contemplation of creating a will at a later time, taking the common meaning of the word draft from Black's Law Dictionary.

The Court affirmed the trial court which found in favor of the four heirs.

Figure 4.2   New York Statute Regarding Nuncupative and Holographic Wills

§ 3-2.2 Nuncupative and holographic wills

(a) For the purposes of this section, and as used elsewhere in this chapter:
   (1) A will is nuncupative when it is unwritten, and the making thereof by the testator and its provisions are clearly established by at least two witnesses.
   (2) A will is holographic when it is written entirely in the handwriting of the testator, and is not executed and attested in accordance with the formalities prescribed by 3-2.1.
(b) A nuncupative or holographic will is valid only if made by:
   (1) A member of the armed forces of the United States while in actual military or naval service during a war, declared or undeclared, or other armed conflict in which members of the armed forces are engaged.

(continued)

Figure 4.2 (continued)

(2) A person who serves with or accompanies an armed force engaged in actual military or naval service during such war or other armed conflict.

(3) A mariner while at sea.

(c) A will authorized by this section becomes invalid:

(1) If made by a member of the armed forces, upon the expiration of one year following his discharge from the armed forces.

(2) If made by a person who serves with or accompanies an armed force engaged in actual military or naval service, upon the expiration of one year from the time he has ceased serving with or accompanying such armed force.

(3) If made by a mariner while at sea, upon the expiration of three years from the time such will was made.

(d) If any person described in paragraph (c) lacks testamentary capacity at the expiration of the time limited therein for the validity of his will, such will shall continue to be valid until the expiration of one year from the time such person regains testamentary capacity.

(e) Nuncupative and holographic wills, as herein authorized, are subject to the provisions of this chapter to the extent that such provisions can be applied to such wills consistently with their character, or to the extent that any such provision expressly provides that it is applicable to such wills.

CASE 4.6 **SUMMARY**

In the matter of the Estate of Stephen Ellis Alexander, Deceased, 188 S.W.3d 327 (Tex.App.-Waco [10th Dist.] 2006), Rehearing Overruled March 21, 2006

This case involved the question of whether the decedent, Stephen Ellis Alexander, made a nuncupative will before his death or died intestate.

In April 2001, Stephen, Cheryl, and Deborah Alexander each received a substantial inheritance, when their paternal grandmother died according to the terms of a testamentary trust established by their grandfather in his will. Stephen consulted with an attorney on several occasions regarding the need to prepare a will but none was ever executed.

Stephen suffered from several chronic conditions and was hospitalized in Temple, Texas, from June 18 to July 8, 2002. He allegedly made the nuncupative will on July 4 while hospitalized.

According to the affidavits of several "friends," (Court's use of quotes), Stephen was taken to the hospital in Waco, Texas, for "a few days" sometime after his release from the hospital in Temple and he was then sent home.

Stephen was taken by ambulance to another Waco hospital on July 24, 2002 due to extreme intoxication. He died 2 days later.

Cheryl Alexander filed an application to determine heirship and for an independent administration of Stephen's estate. The application was submitted with affidavits of heirship executed by herself, her sister Deborah, Ben Lambeth, and another person, each affirming that Cheryl and Deborah were Stephen's sole heirs and that he had died intestate. Independent administration of Stephen's estate was granted by the probate court, giving letters of administration to Cheryl, and declaring Cheryl and Deborah to be Stephen's sole heirs. Cheryl filed an inventory, appraisement, and list of claims for Stephen's estate which the probate court approved.

Ben Lambeth later filed an application to probate Stephen's alleged nuncupative will a few months later. Cheryl and Deborah denied the existence of a valid, nuncupative will. The probate court granted a summary judgment for Cheryl and Deborah and rendered a take-nothing judgment in their favor.

The Court, determining whether Stephen made a valid nuncupative will, quoted the relevant section of the Texas Probate Code.

No nuncupative will shall be established unless it be made in the time of the last sickness of the deceased, at his home or where he has resided for ten days or more next preceding the date of such will, except when the deceased is taken sick away from home and dies before he returns to such home; nor when the value exceeds Thirty Dollars, unless it be proved by three credible witnesses that the testator called on a person to take notice or bear testimony that such is his will, or words of like import.

Tex. Prob. Code Ann. §65 (Vernon 2003).

The Court stated that first, they must determine whether Stephen was "in the time of the last sickness" when he made the alleged nuncupative will and that the rule in Texas has long been that the testator must be "in extremis" or "overtaken by sudden and violent sickness, and has not time or opportunity to make a written will."

The Court determined that "Stephen suffered from several chronic conditions which ultimately contributed significantly to his death. He allegedly made the nuncupative will while hospitalized in Temple for complications associated with these conditions. He died eighteen days after his release from the Temple hospital, with one brief intervening hospitalization of 'a few days.'" However, it then stated that

the fact that the chronic conditions which afflicted Stephen when he was admitted to the VA hospital in Temple (and apparently many months before) were the very same chronic conditions which substantially contributed to his death thirty-eight days later is no evidence that Stephen was "in extremis" during his hospitalization in Temple.

The Court quoted the case of *McClain v. Adams*, 135 Tex. 627, 146 S.W.2d 373 (1941), which in turn quoted *Prince v. Hazleton*, 20 Johns. 502, 514 (N.Y. 1822), which specifically addressed the issue of chronic illness.

If nuncupative wills can be permitted at all, in the cases of chronic disorders, which make silent and slow, but sure and fatal approaches, it is only in the very last stage and extremity of them. In no other period can such a disorder be deemed, within any reasonable construction of the Statute of Frauds, a man's last sickness. Such diseases continue for months, and sometimes for years. In one of Captain Cook's voyages he states that he lost his first lieutenant, Mr. Hicks, near the conclusion of the voyage of three years, and almost within sight of the English coast. But he adds that as his disease was the consumption, and as it existed when he left England, it might be truly said that he was dying during the whole voyage. What would the law call that man's last sickness? Not the whole voyage surely, and probably it would be narrowed down to the last day, and to the last hour of his existence. We must give a reasonable interpretation to the Statute, in reference to the mischief, and to the remedy. We cannot safely apply a man's last sickness to the whole continuance of a protracted disease, without giving to the Statute an absurd construction.

The Court was in favor of Cheryl and Deborah, stating that the evidence conclusively established that Stephen was not "in extremis" during his hospitalization in Temple and had not made a nuncupative will.

the witnesses attest that the mark was indeed the testator's "signature." If the testator is completely unable to sign or mark the document, the will may be signed by another person who does so at the testator's direction and in his presence. In some states, the signature must be affixed at the end of the will. In most states, however, the signature does not need to be at the end. It is very important to follow this requirement since a signature in the wrong place may invalidate the document. For example, in New York, a will may be signed only at the end of the document because the act of signing marks the "end of the will." A signature anywhere else, therefore, marks the will's end, potentially many pages before the testator intended. It is common for attorneys to direct testators to sign or initial the bottom of each page so as to avoid the possibility of the will being changed in any manner, including the addition or removal of pages, especially when a long document is involved. As a practical matter, a testator should not do this in New York since it may invalidate the will. It is most common for all wills to be signed at the end of the document regardless of jurisdiction.

THE PROFESSIONAL PARALEGAL

Older clients are often worried that their signatures are no longer nice, straight, even, or have any number of other "imperfections." It is important for the paralegal to be sympathetic to the older clients' emotions regarding their own frailties of age, and together with the supervising attorney, assure clients that nobody is giving them a penmanship grade and however they mark the page is adequate as long as the witnesses watch them do it.

Witnesses

Witnesses are required to prove that the document being executed as a will is genuine. Almost all states require that a will be signed by two competent witnesses. (Note: Vermont requires three witnesses.) Most times the witnesses do not need to read the will or be informed about the will's content. They only need to be told that they are witnessing the execution of the testator's will.

In most states, the witnesses must sign in the testator's presence. The laws of the states vary concerning whether or not they must also sign in each other's presence. Many states do not require that the witnesses sign in each other's presence as long as each was present when the testator signed. In a smaller percentage of states, the witnesses must sign not only in the presence of the testator, but also in the presence of each other. Attorneys, however, generally require all parties to remain in the room and witness each other's signatures as this assures everyone that the will was properly executed.

Witnessing consists of two parts: ***attesting*** and **subscribing**. A witness *attests* when he or she sees the signature or makes a mental note that the signature exists. A witness *subscribes* when he or she signs below or following the testator's signature.

A witness must be competent. Factors that help ascertain a witness's competency include the following:

- whether the witness is capable of testifying to the facts of the will's execution;
- whether the witness can testify concerning the testator's mental capacity; and
- whether the witness is "interested." An interested witness is a witness that somehow may benefit from the will. A beneficiary that witnesses the will is an interested witness. As a practical matter, a beneficiary to a will should not be allowed to witness the will; since, in some states any gift in the will to that beneficiary is void, and in other states it may invalidate the will entirely. An interested witness signing the will opens the will up for challenge by others who may claim fraud or undue influence.

Many states do not have an age requirement for a witness to a will, although as a practical matter, most lawyers require witnesses to be at least 18 years of age.

Notary Public—Self-Proof Clauses and Affidavits

A notary public is not required to sign a will to ensure its validity. Most attorneys however affix a **self-proof affidavit** or clause to the will and that requires a notary's signature and seal. A self-proving or self-proof affidavit is a document in which the testator and the witnesses swear and affirm before a notary public to the will's execution and substitutes for the live testimony of the witnesses when the will is probated. Traditionally, probate rules require at least one witness to testify concerning the will's execution. The witness testifies that:

- he or she was the witness who signed the will as a witness at the testator's direction;
- he or she observed the testator, who appeared to be of sound mind; and
- the testator signed the will in their presence and, if necessary, that the witnesses signed in the presence of the testator and each other.

The testator swears that he or she:

- is over the age of majority,
- is of sound mind,
- is not under any duress or influence, and
- has asked the witnesses to witness the signing of his or her will.

A will that has an affidavit attached attests and verifies all of that information. It is therefore self-proving, preventing a very serious problem, that being the unavailability of the witnesses either due to their death or the inability to find them at the time the will is probated. Wills are often probated many years after their execution. It is often impossible to locate the witnesses when it is time to probate the will, and many times, the witnesses are either incapacitated or deceased themselves. The legal fees to prove the will without a witness can be substantial.

> For example: Samantha Smart's father, John, executes a will in 1952 and never updates the will. John's will was signed and witnessed by two competent witnesses in accordance with state law and is entirely valid. No self-proof affidavit is executed. John dies in 2005. Samantha's mother Brenda has come to your supervising attorney for the probate of John's estate and informs you and the attorney that she worked as a legal secretary for years and that her former employer drafted the will. When the lawyer inquires about how to contact the witnesses, she informs that both witnesses are deceased, as is the drafting lawyer. The only way to probate the will is to go through a complicated legal proceeding of proving the will without witnesses.
>
> Had John's will been supplemented with the self-proof affidavit, no live witnesses would be required. The affidavit would have substituted for live witness testimony and the will would have been admitted to probate without delay.

It should be noted that since the self-proof affidavit is a separate document and is not required to validate a will, a testator may choose to execute one well after the will has been executed. All that is required is the signature of the testator, the original witnesses, and a notary. The witnesses must then be able to swear to the notary that at the time of the execution the testator met all testamentary requirements of being able to execute a valid will. It is prudent, however, to execute the affidavit at the same time the will is executed to avoid complications, including the death and unavailability of the testator or the witnesses. It is best to secure their signatures immediately upon will execution and most attorneys have all parties sign the affidavit as a matter of course.

THE PROFESSIONAL PARALEGAL

The paralegal would do well to become a notary public on his or her own volition. Becoming a notary in most states is not difficult and is a vital service to perform in most law offices, especially in an office with a heavy estate planning concentration. It will increase your value to your employers.

Changing or Revoking a Will
Changing a Will

As a person's needs change—financially, in familial responsibility, and in health, as well as in mobility, because we are such a mobile society today—that person's estate planning requirements also change.

It is prudent for someone to write a will at age 35 and keep it in a safe deposit box until death without giving it a second glance. As already discussed, Americans are living longer, making it much more likely that their financial and other goals, as well as desires and health needs, will change dramatically over the course of those years.

As a rule, wills, and other estate planning documents, should be reviewed by the testator every 3–5 years, not just by the testator's relatives 30 years after execution and after the testator has died. In every situation in which finances or relationships have changed, the testator should consider reviewing the will, even if it is sooner than the 3–5 year window, such as in cases where there has been a marriage, a divorce, inheritance, children who have been born or who have died, grandchildren born or when the testator has retired, and when the testator moves to a new state.

Codicils   One method of changing the terms of a will is to execute a **codicil**. A codicil is an addition or supplement to a will that modifies certain sections of it.

A codicil must be executed with the same formalities as the will it modifies, meaning that the codicil has been executed with:

- testator's intent
- testamentary capacity of the testator
- testator's signature
- required number of witnesses
- all parties witnessing each other sign if required by statute
- self-proving affidavit (preferred)

When the will is properly referenced by the codicil, the codicil has the effect of republishing the will. Referencing the will in the codicil is called *incorporation by reference*.

Republication has the interesting effect of restoring the will referenced in the codicil. This means that even a defective will, such as a will with only one witness, or one that was revoked, is reestablished when the codicil is properly executed.

Paralegals and law students alike often wonder why someone would go to the trouble of drafting a codicil since it requires the same formalities as a will. As a practical matter, with the common use of computers today, it is just as easy to draft a new will. In fact, it may be safer since a codicil can be lost or "misplaced" by a beneficiary that doesn't agree with the changes made in the codicil. Also, the original will and the codicil have to be read together, and sometimes, the changes made in the codicil are so significant that it makes more sense to do an entirely new will revoking the old one. Until the advent of computers in law offices, however, codicils were an excellent alternative to redrafting an entire will when the only means of drafting was a typewriter, and before typewriters, when the only method of drafting was to scribe the document by hand. A codicil was a short and relatively simple method of changing a document that may have been 10 or more pages long. The shorter the document, the less likely typographical errors would be made. Codicils saved time. An example of a modern codicil is shown in the will of actor Paul Newman which may be found in Appendix B.

Cross-Out Marks and Other Writings

Sometimes a testator will cross out will provisions and write in new ones. The testator will sometimes do this to save legal expenses but often does it simply because he does not realize that his actions may have grave consequence.

While it is possible that the deletions and additions may be accepted as valid by a probate court, it is more likely they will not be accepted, considered instead to be a spoliation of the document. To still be considered valid, the markings must be shown to be the testator's intent, a difficult task, since the markings have to be made with the same testamentary formalities as the will, which is impossible to prove. All cross-outs and markings must therefore be made while the testator, witnesses, and notary are still at the table and the testator and witnesses initial each change. Otherwise, courts will have difficulty determining if the markings were actually the testator's or those of someone who attempted to make changes after the fact.

In most instances, the effect of cross-out marks and additions is the revocation of those provisions. In extreme circumstances, the entire document is invalidated. Hopefully, your supervising attorney lets clients know to never mark on the original documents. Unfortunately, as a paralegal, there is little you can do about this error made often enough by clients. All cross-outs and markings must therefore be initialed.

Revoking a Will

Since wills are **ambulatory**, methods for revoking as well as changing wills are necessary. The methods for revoking, or canceling, a will are set by state statute, requiring the paralegal to ascertain what his or her state's laws are regarding revocation.

Methods of revocation:

- by physical act
- by operation of law
- by subsequent writing

Revocation by Physical Act

Methods of **revocation by physical act** are:

- burning
- tearing
- canceling, usually by writing, "canceled" across the front of each page

- obliterating, such as shredding
- otherwise destroying

Examples of revocation by physical act include the following:

- Bobbie writes "canceled" across each page of her will.
- John puts his will in the fireplace and burns it.
- Todd tears his will into little, confetti-like pieces while Tina puts hers through a shredder.
- Ted asks his friend, Adam, to destroy the will for him. When a testator asks someone else to destroy the will on his behalf, the testator must follow state statute very carefully to be sure of proper compliance. Some states require two witnesses to the destruction. For obvious reasons, this is not the preferred method of destruction.

Dependent Relative Revocation   What happens when the testator has made a new will and destroyed the old one believing it to have been revoked, but then it is discovered that the new will is void? The old, canceled will is considered valid under the doctrine of **dependent relative revocation (DRR)**. The origins of dependent relative revocation are in the 1716 English case of *Onions v. Tyrer*. In that case, the testator executed a first will, and four years later made another expressly revoking the first. The testator then had his wife tear up the first will. The court found that the second will was not properly executed and held that the first will was still valid despite being torn up. The idea behind dependent relative revocation is the presumption that the testator would not have canceled the original will but for the belief that the new one was valid. This doctrine is used to avoid the problem of intestacy.

> *Example:* Bobbie executes a will in 1995. In 2005 she executes a new will and destroys the 1995 will. Unfortunately, the 2005 will is invalid and void. It is presumed that Bobbie's 1995 will is still valid and that she would not have destroyed the 1995 will had she known the 2005 will was void. The presumption can be overcome by testimony that she did not want the provisions in the 1995 will to determine her bequests and devises.

However, in *First Union National Bank of Florida v. Estate of Mizell*, 807 So. 2d 78 (Fla. Dist. Ct. App. 2001), the testator properly executed a will in 1978. In 1993, due to deteriorating health, he executed a new will expressly revoking the 1978 will but did not tear up or destroy it. The trial court held that the will was "procured through undue influence," and that the testator was incompetent to make a will. It also found that the 1978 will was revoked by the express revocation clause in the 1993 will. The appellate court reversed, finding that the 1978 will could not have been revoked because the 1993 will revoking it was invalid. The court never discussed dependent relative revocation and in Schiavo, *Dependent Relative Revocation Has Gone Astray: It Should Return to Its Roots*, 13 Widener Law Review 73 (2006), the author maintains that the case law on this subject indicates that the decision was made in that manner because the 1978 will had not been destroyed.

Revocation by Operation of Law   A will can be **revoked by operation of law**. This means that the testator does not have to know about or agree to the revocation.

State statute may automatically revoke the will. Two methods in which a will may be either partially or wholly revoked by operation of law are:

- by the subsequent marriage, or
- subsequent divorce of the testator.

By Subsequent Marriage   The marriage of the testator after executing a will may result in the following:

- revocation of the entire will unless it specifically states that it was being executed in contemplation of marriage;
- revocation of the will only if a child is born of the marriage;
- revocation of the will if a child is born and no provision was made in the will for the child;
- revocation if there are provisions that would have benefited a former spouse; and
- have no effect at all.

  It is important to know what effect a subsequent marriage may have in the state in which the will shall be probated. Depending upon state statute, it will be determined if the testator's will should be changed or not. In most instances, a marriage gives rise however to the implementation of a pretermitted spouse statute and in the case of a child born of the marriage, a pretermitted child statute, both of which are discussed elsewhere in this book.

Divorce, Dissolution, or Annulment of Marriage   In most states, a divorce or dissolution of marriage or an annulment of the marriage revokes the bequest to former spouse but does not revoke the entire will. Only in Connecticut and Georgia will a divorce revoke the entire will. In Iowa, Louisiana, Mississippi, New Hampshire, and Vermont, a divorce has no effect on the will whatsoever and the former spouse receives all gifts enumerated in the will.

In most states, annulments only revoke gifts made to the "former spouse" and do not affect the entire will.

REMINDER: Whenever a testator has an important change in her life, she should review her will, even if it is not within the 3–5 year window of review.

Revocation by Subsequent Writing   The best way to revoke a will is to write a new will. Most wills expressly revoke the prior will by declaring that any prior wills and codicils are revoked. Failure to put such a clause in the new will most often has the effect of making the new will a codicil of the old one unless, of course, the testator takes the steps necessary to destroy the original will.

Joint and Mutual Wills

Joint Wills

A **joint will** is one document in which two or more people dispose of property and restrict the revocation of the document without the express written consent of both parties. The document is probated after each co-testator dies.

Joint wills are not usually recommended, since changing or revoking the will requires consent of both parties, which is a difficult task. You could have one spouse outlive the other for a prolonged period of time, the parties could divorce or separate and refuse to consent to changes, one of the parties may have sole custody of the document, one of them may become incapacitated necessitating a significant change in their estate planning and one of them may destroy the document without the consent of the other causing the other to become intestate.

Mutual Wills

Mutual wills are separate documents that contain the identical provisions and often include an agreement that neither testator will change his or her will after the death of the other. Mutual wills are also called *reciprocal wills*. Although the provisions in mutual wills providing that neither testator changes or revokes the will after the other's death have been upheld by courts as a contract between the parties, the provisions place a great burden on the survivor.

For example: Janet and Michael marry in 2000. The following year they execute mutual wills with provisions agreeing that neither will change nor revoke his or her will after the death of the other spouse. Michael dies in a car crash in 2011. Janet is only 36 years old. She will be prevented from changing her will for the remainder of her life, which barring unforeseen tragedy is statistically another 40+ years. Should Janet decide to remarry and have children, how will she provide for them after her death? Mutual wills without these provisions are quite common and acceptable. A clause in a will demonstrating that the parties do not intend to create a contractually binding mutual will may be written as follows:

> My husband has executed on this date a will with provisions substantially similar to this will. These wills are not mutual wills, and there is no contractual understanding or agreement between my husband and me to execute these wills.

Will Contests

A **will contest** is a lawsuit that challenges the validity of a will after the death of the testator. Someone who has standing must bring suit. To have standing, a person must claim an interest or right in the decedent's estate. This person is almost always someone who would be a beneficiary under a prior will or can claim an interest under the intestacy laws. This person must be able to prove by clear and convincing evidence that the will was not valid based on the following objections:

- The will wasn't executed properly.
- The testator lacked testamentary capacity.
- The will was revoked.
- The will was forged.
- Notice was not given to the heirs.
- The testator was forced by duress, fraud, or undue influence to sign the will.
- The will contained material mistakes.

Most will contests cases are based upon allegations of a lack of testamentary capacity and undue influence. As you will notice, many of the cases illustrated throughout this book for other reasons are at first predicated on whether or not the testator was of sound mind or was unduly influenced. The easiest explanation of this is simply based upon the fact that the majority of estate planning clients are older and are more likely to be considered enfeebled or otherwise in mental decline by family (whether or not it is actually true). In addition, it is not uncommon for older Americans to be taking a number of prescribed medications some of which could have side effects that affect a person's mental capacity. It is perhaps the easiest of avenues to contest a will, although will contests are far from easy.

The burden of proof for a will contest is on the proponent of the contest. In other words, it isn't for the proponent of the will to prove that the testator had capacity. It is for the person contesting the will to prove that the testator lacked capacity. Note the following two will contests, both of which discuss testamentary capacity and undue influence and one of which also questions the proper execution of the will.

CASE 4.7 **SUMMARY**

ANDREWS v RENTZ , 266 Ga. 782, 470 SE2d 669 (1996)

Bignon died testate in 1993 at the age of 83. His estate consisted of approximately $150,000 on deposit and two residences valued in excess of $100,000. His first will, executed in 1988, left most of his estate to his granddaughter and $200 to his daughter Patricia Andrews. He executed a new will in 1991 leaving his granddaughter nothing, Patricia $200, and Mary Rentz, a friend who took care of him since his wife's death, the bulk of his estate. He also appointed Rentz as his executor. Rentz filed the will for probate and Patricia contested on grounds of undue influence and lack of testamentary capacity. The probate court ruled in favor of probate and Andrews appealed.

Testimony at trial showed that Rentz was a close personal friend of the decedent's, and was paid $500 a month to help him with his financial and personal needs. Rentz admitted to a close personal relationship with Bignon but stated that she did not discuss his estate with him. Other evidence indicated that Bignon was depressed about his wife's death but that his mental state was normal and that he was not disoriented.

Patricia presented a doctor's testimony that Bignon had a "moderate degree of brain atrophy in 1979 which caused forgetfulness, but the physician further testified that such atrophy was not unusual in a person of Bignons' age, and that Bignon was otherwise oriented and able to comprehend and understand." The appellate court determined that this evidence fell "short of showing a lack of testamentary capacity, and certainly fails to show such at the time that Bignon executed the will in 1991."

The appellate court then turned to the issue of undue influence. It stated, "[A] presumption of undue influence arises when it is shown that the will was made at the request of a person who receives a substantial benefit, who is not a natural object of the maker's estate, and who held a Confidential relationship with the testator." The court found that while Rentz had a confidential relationship with Bignon and was present when he executed his 1991 will, she never discussed the disposition of his estate with him, did not participate in testamentary planning or requested or coerced him to make her his beneficiary, nor did Bignon feel coerced to do so. The court also found that the evidence at trial did not indicate that "Bignon did not make the disposition freely and voluntarily or that his free agency to dispose of his estate as he wished was destroyed." Concurring in part and dissenting in part, Justice Carley wrote for himself and Justice Sears and found that "there was sufficient evidence from which a jury could find that Ms. Rentz exercised such undue influence over the testator as would invalidate his will." Justice Carley also found that while "the testator had sufficient mental capacity to execute a will, a mere diminution in, rather than a total absence of, his mental capacity is nevertheless relevant when considering the sufficiency of the circumstantial evidence of Ms. Rentz's exercise of undue influence over him. This is true because "the amount of influence necessary to dominate a mind impaired by age or disease may be decidedly less than that required to control a strong mind." He stated that Bignon had moderate brain atrophy and that he was susceptible to the influence of others. The judge noted that Bignon relied on Rentz to make decisions and write his checks and placed her name on his accounts. Bignon insisted that Rentz remain present when family members visited. The judge stated that Rentz participated in the "substantive discussions regarding the testamentary disposition of the testator's estate. In those discussions, Ms. Rentz often purported to act more as the testator's independent surrogate than as a mere conduit for the expression of the testator's own testamentary intent."

Justice Carley concluded that "there was a confidential relationship and, considering the evidence as to the age and mental condition of the testator and the control and domination of the testator by Ms. Rentz over a long period of time, a verdict in favor of Ms. Andrews was, in my opinion, authorized and a verdict in favor of Ms. Rentz was not demanded."

CASE 4.8 **SUMMARY**

In the Matter of Estate of Walker, 80 A.D.3d 865, 914 N.Y.S.2d 379 (2011)

Delanor A. Perry-Davis, Formerly Known as Delanor A. Perry, As Executor of Susie M. Walker, Deceased, Appellant; Tommy B. Walker, Respondent.

The decedent died in June 2009 and was survived by the respondent and her great-grandson, Anthony D. Walker. In an August 2007 will, she gave her entire estate to her grandson, who is the child of the petitioner and the respondent. When her grandson died suddenly, she executed a new will, dated October 26, 2007, naming her great-grandson as the sole beneficiary of her estate and specifically disinherited the respondent. Petitioner, as executor of decedent's estate, offered the will for probate and respondent filed objections, alleging that the will was not properly executed, that the decedent lacked testamentary capacity, and the will was the product of undue influence and fraud.

The appellate court found that the will execution was supervised by the drafting attorney, witnessed and notarized as evidenced by a self-proving affidavit. This created a presumption of due execution and the respondent, having failed to challenge it, and therefore warranted a dismissal of his objection to the proper execution of the will by the trial court.

Regarding the decedent's testamentary capacity, it stated that "the appropriate inquiry is whether the decedent was lucid and rational at the time the will was made" and that "the burden of proving capacity rests with the proponent of the will, who must demonstrate that decedent understood the consequences of executing the will, knew the nature and extent of the property being disposed of and knew the persons who were the natural objects of her bounty, and her relationship to them."

The appellate court found that the executor presented an affidavit of the attesting witnesses affirmatively "stating that decedent was of sound mind and memory and was competent to make a will" creating "a presumption of testamentary capacity and prima facie evidence of the facts attested to." In addition, the drafting attorney testified that the decedent was alert and rational at the time of execution, as well as the fact that the decedent was clear that she did not want to leave anything to her son, the respondent, instead leaving everything to her grandson. The trial record indicated that the decedent "regularly expressed her dissatisfaction with respondent and disappointment in the manner in which he treated her and, for that reason, did not want him to inherit anything." An affidavit of a home aide who cared for the decedent stated that while the decedent was "physically infirm, was at all times mentally acute, engaged in various daily activities and managed her own financial affairs, including paying the bills and expenses for the property she owned in Brooklyn."

The appellate court stated that "[C]ontrary to respondent's contention, a decedent need only have a general, rather than a precise, knowledge of the assets in his or her estate." It also found that since "decedent handled her own financial affairs during the year preceding her death supports an inference that she apprehended the size of her estate."

The court stated that "[T]o prove undue influence, a respondent must demonstrate that the decedent was actually constrained to act against [his (or her)] own free will and desire by identifying the motive, opportunity and acts allegedly constituting the influence, as well as when and where such acts occurred." It stated that "[M]ere speculation and conclusory allegations, without specificity as to precisely where and when the influence was actually exerted, are insufficient to raise an issue of fact."

The court found that the "crux of respondent's contention" was that the petitioner, his ex-wife, resided with the decedent, accompanied her to the attorney's office, and was present when it was signed. However, the court found that there was no direct evidence that she in any way influenced the distribution of decedent's estate.

The court then admitted the will to probate.

In Terrorem Clauses

In terrorem **clauses**, also known as no contest clauses, are clauses in a will that provide for the forfeiture of all benefits under the will to any beneficiary objecting to probate or challenging the will. See Blanco and Whitacre, *The Carrot and Stick Approach: In Terrorem Clauses in Texas Jurisprudence*, 43 Tech. L. Rev. 1127 (2011), in which the authors state "[E]veryone is familiar with the oft-cited "carrot-and-stick" idiom, which may conjure up the image of a donkey or other beast of burden being enticed along by the potential reward of a carrot dangling in front of the animal's face. The other half of the expression—the stick—serves as a threatened punishment, which will be used if the carrot is not sufficient inducement to persuade the animal to move. The phrase "carrot-and-stick" is, in fact, defined as "characterized by the use of both reward and punishment to induce cooperation." Inducing behavior is exactly what testators and trust settlors hope to accomplish by including in terrorem clauses in their wills and trusts. The purpose of such clauses is to effectuate the intent of the testator or settlor to avoid will or trust contests by offering potential contestants a "carrot" in the form of a gift or bequest under the terms of the instrument, but threatening a "stick" in the form of forfeiture of such gift or bequest if they contest the instrument."

Clients find them extremely popular and ask for them to be added even after being told they are not enforceable because just the appearance of them in a will, they believe, discourages the beneficiaries and those left out from contesting.

Some states have held these clauses to be void as a matter of policy and they are largely unfavorable to courts or legislatures. For example, Texas recently ameliorated the strict "all or nothing" of the no contest clause by amending its statutes to provide that an in terrorem clause is unenforceable if a beneficiary contests a will (or trust) in good faith and upon just cause. As this "just cause" language is still new, it is not clear as to how the courts in Texas will interpret it but the purpose is clear; the clauses can have a chilling effect on will contests that may be for very good reason. These clauses are also referred to as penalty or forfeiture clauses. For an interesting case which pits New York law, which enforces in terrorem clauses, against Florida law, which holds them void as against public policy, see *Shumash v. Stark*, reproduced at the end of this chapter.

SUMMARY

Wills are the primary method of distributing a person's estate after his or her death. While wills are a common method of distribution, they must be executed following very strict formalities as set by state statute. Violation of these formalities may invalidate either part of, or the entire will.

Wills may either be written or oral. If written entirely in the testator's handwriting, the will is called holographic. If oral, it is called nuncupative. Both holographic and nuncupative wills may be used only in certain limited circumstances and are not valid in some jurisdictions. In addition, couples may write their wills jointly, that is, one will for more than one

person, or mutually, that is, two or more wills with identical provisions. In both these instances, the wills are considered binding contractual agreements between the two and may not be changed or revoked without the express written consent of the other.

Of utmost importance to the validity of a will is the testator's intent and capacity. Intent refers directly to the testator's express instructions regarding how and to whom his or her property will be bequeathed or devised. The memorialization of those instructions is the document known as the will. The testator's intent must be clear from the four corners of the document.

Testamentary capacity refers to the legal ability of a person to create a will and may be comprised of two factors. If the testator is not of majority age, he or she may not execute a will. In all but three states, the age of majority is 18. The other factor refers to the testator's sound mind, which is his or her ability to know that the document being executed is a will, what he or she owns at the time of the document's execution, who his family and close friends are, and that he or she is giving property to certain chosen beneficiaries. The testator must also attest that he or she is executing the will of his or her own free will and is not under any duress or being influenced in any manner.

Wills are ambulatory, meaning as long as the testator is of sound mind they can be changed or revoked at any time before the testator's death. Wills can be changed either by codicil or by an entirely new will. They can be revoked by canceling them, destroying them in some fashion, by operation of law, and by writing an entirely new will.

Will contests are lawsuits in which a person with an interest in the outcome of the probate of a will challenges the will's validity. Certain factors, such as improper execution and undue influence, may be argued to persuade a court that the will as executed by the testator is invalid and that the dispositions made in the document should not be followed.

KEY **TERMS**

intent
objects of one's bounty
self-proof (or self-proving) affidavit
revocation by physical act
revocation by operation of law
will contest

attestation
testamentary capacity
holographic will
codicil
ambulatory
mutual wills
undue influence

dependent relative revocation
subscription
sound mind
nuncupative will
joint will
in terrorem clause

REVIEW **QUESTIONS**

1. What is a will?
2. Define *ambulatory*.
3. What are the four components of soundness of mind? Describe each.
4. What is the age of majority in your state?
5. Describe how a person may revoke a will by physical act.
6. What is a codicil?
7. How does a testator's subsequent marriage generally affect a will? A subsequent divorce?
8. What is a holographic will?
9. What is a nuncupative will?
10. What factors may be raised to contest a will?
11. What is testamentary capacity and how does it affect a will's validity?
12. What is the difference between attesting and subscribing to a will?
13. What is a self-proof affidavit and what effect does it have?
14. How may a will be signed?
15. What is dependent relative revocation? Does this doctrine make sense to you in its application? Why or why not?
16. Does your state permit in terrorem clauses? Do you think they are fair and if so, under what circumstances? Why?

PROJECTS

1. Does your state allow holographic wills? Look up the statute and note the requirements.
2. Does your state allow nuncupative wills? What does your state statute provide?
3. What happens in your state if a will is not self-proved? Describe the process.
4. Read In the Matter of the Estate of Spicer H. Breeden, 992 P.2d 1167 (Colo. 2000),

reprinted at the end of this chapter and discuss the following: effect of the purported holographic writing, testamentary capacity, and competency of witnesses. For background on Spicer Breeden and his family, see http://www.nytimes.com/1997/03/18/us/a-web-of-money-drugs-and-death.html?pagewanted=2 and for more information about this Estate, see the 2003 case at caselaw.findlaw.com/co-court-of-appeals/1346335.html

5. Read Shumash v. Stark, reprinted at the end of this chapter, and discuss how the New York court came to its decision despite the fact that the decedent died in Florida.

NOTES

(**Note:** The probate court opinion is numbered 96PRS62 and can be found easily with a Google search, as can a number of articles on Spicer Breeden and his family. This appellate case has been used as precedent a number of times since 2000, and a Google search will also yield some of those cases for those students that care to explore these issues more fully.)

1. Vic E. Breeden, the decedent's father, was a named party in the contested probate proceeding and in the appeal to the court of appeals. However, on April 19, 1999, Petitioners filed a motion for amendment to caption and suggestion of death, stating that on April 16, 1998, Vic E. Breeden died, leaving Holly Breeden Connell and Vic E. Breeden, III, as his heirs. Accordingly, on May 3, 1999, the court granted the motion to amend the caption to reflect Holly B. Connell and Vic E. Breeden, III, as Petitioners.

2. *Cunningham v. Stender*, 127 Colo. 293, 255 P.2d 977 (1953).

3. *See* §13-90-102(1), 5 C.R.S. (1999).

4. Petitioners also alleged at the probate hearing lack of testamentary intent and that the will did not conform to section 15-11-502, 5 C.R.S. (1999), but these issues are not before us.

5. In particular, McSpadden testified that at a March 14, 1996, lunch meeting, the decedent told him that he intended to leave his estate to McSpadden and Respondent.

6. We granted certiorari on the following issues:
   1. Whether the court of appeals improperly applied the "Insane Delusions Test" for testamentary capacity by merging the mutually exclusive jury instructions test for "unsound mind."
   2. Whether the court of appeals improperly applied the Dead Man's Statute to affirm the probate court's denial of Objectors' Motion to Dismiss Holly Breeden Connell and Vic E. Breeden as parties, thus precluding testimony regarding their conversations with the deceased, Spicer Breeden.

7. Fistula is "an abnormal passage leading from an abscess or hollow organ to the body surface … and permitting the passage of fluids or secretions." *Webster's Ninth New Collegiate Dictionary* 467 (1988).

8. Although some of these cases predate *Cunningham* or occurred in other states, the tests applied are substantially the same.

9. Monomania is defined as "insanity upon a particular subject only, and with a single delusion of the mind," while paranoia is defined as "chronic delusional insanity" that is marked by "a false premise, pursued by a logical process of reasoning to an insane conclusion." 1 William J. Bowe & Douglas H. Parker, *Page on Wills* §12.31 (W.H. Anderson Co. ed., 4th ed. 1960 & Supp. 1999).

10. Footnote 2 to CJI-Civ. 4th 34:9 directs one to use "whichever parenthesized and bracketed portions of the instruction are appropriate in light of the evidence in the case."

11. Although the probate court did not specifically use the phrase "materially affect or influence" in its decision, we find from our review of the court order that the probate court applied this standard.

12. As noted above, Breeden Sr. passed away during the pendency of the appeal proceedings. As such, this issue as applied to him is moot. *See Van Schaack Holdings v. Fulenwider*, 798 P.2d 424, 426–427 (Colo. 1990) (holding an issue moot where judgment would have no practical legal effect upon the existing controversy). However, for ease of comprehension, we have chosen to refer to both Breeden Sr. and Connell in analyzing the probate court's denial of Petitioners' motion to dismiss these two parties.

13. There are a few exceptions to the general prohibition against parties testifying, such as when the party offering the testimony is a nominal party who has no real interest in the outcome of the proceedings. *See generally Risbry v. Swan*, 124 Colo. 567, 577–578, 239 P.2d 600, 606 (1951) (stating that although administrator of estate is a

necessary party to the action, he is not a party to the issue and has no personal interest in the result of the controversy); *David v. Powder Mountain Ranch*, 656 P.2d 716, 718–719 (Colo. App. 1982) (holding that in a quiet title action, where all parties who have an interest in a property must be named, fact that all those named as defendants might be necessary parties does not make them parties to the issue and thus preclude their testimony under the Dead Man's Statute).

14. We do not reach the issue of whether Breeden Sr. or Connell are interested persons pursuant to the Dead Man's Statute.

15. The probate judge stated:

On the motion to dismiss that was filed this morning by Mr. Bosworth on behalf of Vic E. Breeden, Sr., … and on behalf of Holly B. Connell, Mr. Bosworth, I think that the case that Mr. Sterling distributed to us this morning, *In re Estate of Gardner*, [31 Colo. App. 361, 505 P.2d 50 (1972)] is helpful on this point and it's consistent with the Court's analysis of your motion, which is that parties ought not to be allowed on the day of trial or from the witness box to disavow their interest in the estate in order to get out from under the application of the Dead Man's Statute.

There's an additional reason … that even if Mr. Breeden, Sr. and Holly B. Connell were permitted to be dismissed at this point … they still retain their status as … heirs … who … would have taken if there had been no will …

I also note … the pleading which brought the issue which we're facing this morning before the Court which was filed … on behalf of Vic E. Breeden [and] Holly B. Connell … [who you indicate] are beneficiaries under a will, and for those reasons you asked their objection to the probate, which I'm being asked to grant this morning, be heard by the Court and that brought the matter before the Court. Accordingly, I'm going to deny the motion to dismiss these individuals from the case.

Tr. of Hr'g at 25–26.

16. In addition, Petitioners did not identify Breeden Sr. or Connell as testifying witnesses until August 29, 1996, when they filed a trial witness list two working days prior to the hearing.

MyLegalStudiesLab™   http://www.mylegalstudieslab

MYLEGALSTUDIESLAB VIRTUAL LAW OFFICE EXPERIENCE ASSIGNMENTS Complete the pre-test, study plan, and post-test for this chapter and answer the Legal Applications questions as assigned. These will help you confirm your mastery of the concepts and their application to legal scenarios. Then, complete the Virtual Law Office assignments as assigned by your instructor. These assignments are designed to develop your workplace skills and result in producing documents for inclusion in your portfolio.

In the Matter of the Estate of Spicer H. Breeden, Deceased, 992 P.2d 1167 (Colo. 2000)

Petitioners challenge the decision of the court of appeals affirming the probate court's determination that the decedent, Spicer H. Breeden, possessed testamentary capacity at the time he executed his holographic will and the probate court's ruling denying Petitioners' motion to dismiss Vic E. Breeden and Holly Breeden Connell as parties to the action. The supreme court affirms the court of appeals and holds that the probate court correctly applied the two exclusive tests for testamentary capacity to find that the testator, Spicer H. Breeden, was of sound mind at the time he executed his holographic will. In addition, the supreme court holds that the probate court did not abuse its discretion when it denied Petitioners' motion to dismiss Vic E. Breeden and Holly Breeden Connell as parties.

The decedent, Spicer H. Breeden, hand wrote a will that left his estate to Respondent, Sydney Stone. When Respondent offered the document for probate, Petitioners filed objections, alleging that the decedent lacked testamentary capacity at the time he executed the will because he was suffering from insane delusions. The probate court held that the decedent was of sound mind at the time he executed the holographic will. Petitioners appealed to the court of appeals, who affirmed the decision of the probate court. The supreme court granted certiorari to review the decision by the court of appeals.

Petitioners allege that in any will contest involving a testator's soundness of mind, only one of the two tests for sound mind should be applied. The supreme court finds that either or both of the two tests for sound mind may apply to a given case; a testator both must satisfy the *Cunningham* elements test and must not suffer from an "insane delusion" that materially affected the disposition in the will.

In addition, Petitioners contend that the probate court erred when it denied their motion to dismiss Vic E. Breeden and Holly Breeden Connell as parties, thus precluding their testimony under the Dead Man's Statute, §13-90-102(1), 5 C.R.S. (1999). The supreme court finds that the probate court did not abuse its discretion in denying the motion to dismiss two of the three named parties on the first day of the hearing, in light of the unfair surprise to Respondent and the prejudice that may have resulted.

SUPREME COURT, STATE OF COLORADO   January 18, 2000
No. 98SC570

In The Matter of the Estate of
Spicer H. Breeden, Deceased:

HOLLY BREEDEN CONNELL,
and VIC E. BREEDEN, III, Petitioners,

v.

SYDNEY STONE, Respondent.

Certiorari to the Colorado Court of Appeals
EN BANC   Judgment Affirmed

Semler & Associates, P.C.
R. Parker Semler
Denver, Colorado

Attorneys for Petitioners
Gelt, Fleishman & Sterling, P.C.
Dana E. Steele
Harry W. Sterling
Denver, Colorado

Attorneys for Respondent
Justice Rice delivered the Opinion of the Court.
Justice Bender does not participate.

This court granted certiorari to address two issues raised by Petitioners Holly Breeden Connell and Vic E. Breeden, III (Petitioners). [1] First, Petitioners argue that the probate court incorrectly applied both the "insane delusion" and the *Cunningham* [2] elements tests for testamentary capacity and improperly merged the insane delusion test with the *Cunningham* elements test. Second, Petitioners challenge whether the probate court erred when it denied their motion to dismiss Vic E. Breeden (Breeden Sr.) and Holly Breeden Connell (Connell) as parties based on an improper application of the Dead Man's Statute. [3] We now hold that the probate court correctly applied the two exclusive tests for testamentary capacity to find that the testator, Spicer Breeden, was of sound mind at the time he executed the holographic will. In addition, we hold that the probate court did not abuse its discretion when it denied Petitioners' motion to dismiss Breeden Sr. and Connell as parties, thus precluding their testimony under the Dead Man's Statute.

I. Facts and Procedural History

This case involves a contested probate of a handwritten (holographic) will executed by Spicer Breeden, the decedent. Mr. Breeden died in his home on March 19, 1996, from a self-inflicted gunshot wound 2 days after he was involved in a highly publicized hit-and-run accident that killed the driver of the other vehicle.

Upon entering the decedent's home following his suicide, the Denver police discovered on his desk a handwritten document that read: "I want everything I have to go to Sydney Stone— 'houses,' 'jewelwry,' [sic] stocks[,] bonds, cloths [sic]. P. S. I was *Not* Driving the Vehical— [sic]." At the bottom of the handwritten document, the decedent printed, "SPICER H. BREEDEN" and signed beneath his printed name.

Sydney Stone (Respondent) offered the handwritten document for probate as the holographic will of the decedent. The decedent had previously executed a formal will in 1991 and a holographic codicil leaving his estate to persons other than Respondent. Several individuals filed objections to the holographic will, including Petitioners, who alleged lack of testamentary capacity. [4]

On September 3–6, 1996, a hearing was held on the petition for formal probate. Both parties presented evidence in the form of testimony of factual and expert witnesses, handwriting samples, and other documents. On September 26, 1996, the probate court formally admitted the decedent's holographic will to probate. The court made several findings based on the evidence presented. First, the court found that the decedent used cocaine and alcohol for several years prior to his death, based on the testimony of his friends Jennifer Chelwick and Michael Crow. Relying on the autopsy report and testimony from the decedent's sister, the court found that the decedent used alcohol and cocaine on the evening of March 17 and between March 17 and 19, and that substantial alcohol was consumed proximate to the time of death. Based on the testimony of a number of the decedent's friends, the court found that the decedent's moods were alternately euphoric, fearful, and depressed, and that he was excessively worried about threats against himself and his dog from government agents, friends, and others.

In addition, the probate court considered the testimony of a number of expert witnesses, including two forensic toxicologists, two forensic psychiatrists, a forensic document examiner, and two handwriting experts. After considering conflicting evidence from the various expert witnesses, the court concluded that the decedent possessed the motor skills necessary to write his will and that his handwriting on the holographic will was unremarkable when compared to other writing exemplars. The court also considered the testimony of the decedent's friends Ken McSpadden and Rick Eagan, who testified that in the two weeks prior to his death, the decedent had indicated to each of them in separate conversations that he did not intend to leave his estate to his family. [5]

After considering the evidence, the probate court found that Petitioners did not prove by a preponderance of the evidence that, because of the decedent's chronic use of alcohol and drugs or their use between March 17 and 19, he was not of sound mind when he executed the holographic will. In addition, the probate court held that the stress and anxiety that compelled the decedent to commit suicide did not deprive him of testamentary capacity. The court also found that the decedent's insane delusions regarding his friends, government agencies, and others, did not affect or influence the disposition of his property. In reaching the conclusion that the decedent was of sound mind at the time he executed the will, the probate court relied on the will itself, which evidenced a sufficient understanding of the general nature of his property and the disposition under the will, the testimony of two doctors regarding the decedent's motor skills at the time he wrote the will, evidence that the decedent had omitted his father and sister from his will in the past, and testimony from two friends that indicated the decedent had been considering revising his will in the future.

Petitioners appealed to the court of appeals, asserting that the probate court erred by applying and merging both tests for sound mind contained in Colorado Jury Instruction 34:9 and by refusing to dismiss Connell and Breeden Sr. as parties to the case, thus precluding their testimony under the Dead Man's Statute. The court of appeals affirmed the decision of the probate court, holding that the probate court order, when read in its entirety, indicated that the probate court correctly applied the appropriate tests for sound mind and correctly applied the Dead Man's Statute to find that Holly Breeden Connell and Vic E. Breeden should not be dismissed as parties. *See In re Breeden*, No. 96CA2012 (Colo. App. July 2, 1998) (not selected for official publication).

We granted certiorari to address whether the probate court correctly applied the insane delusion and *Cunningham* elements tests and whether the probate court correctly denied Petitioners' motion to dismiss Connell and Breeden Sr. as parties. [6]

II. Testamentary Capacity

Underlying Colorado's law of wills is the fundamental concept of freedom of testation; namely that a testator "may dispose of his property as he pleases, and that [he] may indulge his prejudice against his relations and in favor of strangers, and that, if he does so, it is no objection to his will." *Lehman v. Lindenmeyer*, 48 Colo. 305, 313, 109 P. 956, 959 (1909). This principle, however, is subject to the requirement that the maker of the will possesses testamentary capacity at the time he executes the will. A person has testamentary capacity if he is an "individual eighteen or more years of age who is of sound mind." §15-11-501, 5 C.R.S. (1999).

Until 1973, the proponents of a will assumed the burden of proving that the testator had testamentary capacity at the time he executed a will. However, in 1973, the legislature shifted this burden to the contestants of a will. *See* Ch. 451, sec. 1, §153-13-407, 1973 Colo. Sess. Laws 1538, 1576 (codified as amended at §15-12-407, 5 C.R.S. (1999)). Under section 15-12-407, once a proponent of a will has offered prima facie proof that the will was duly executed, any contestant then assumes the burden of proving a lack of testamentary capacity, including a lack of sound mind, by a preponderance of the evidence. *See id.; see also In re Estate of Olschansky*, 735 P.2d 927, 929 (Colo. App. 1987); *In re Estate of Grobman*, 635 P.2d 231, 233 (Colo. App. 1981). The issue of what constitutes sound mind has developed along two separate lines of inquiry, summarized below.

A. The *Cunningham* Test

We initially defined sound mind as having sufficient understanding regarding

> the extent and value of [one's] property, the number and names of the persons who are the natural objects of [one's] bounty, their deserts with reference to their conduct and treatment toward [oneself], their capacity and necessity, and that [one] shall have sufficient active memory to retain all of these facts in [one's] mind long enough to have [one's] will prepared and executed.
>
> *Lehman, 48 Colo. at 312, 109 P. at 958.*

After *Lehman*, this court further refined the test for sound mind in 1953 in the landmark case *Cunningham v. Stender*, when we held that mental capacity to make a will requires that: (1) the testator understands the nature of her act; (2) she knows the extent of her property; (3) she understands the proposed testamentary disposition; (4) she knows the natural objects of her bounty; and (5) the will represents her wishes. 127 Colo. 293, 301, 255 P.2d 977, 981-82 (1953).

B. The Insane Delusion Test

This court has also held that a person who was suffering from an insane delusion at the time he executed the will may lack testamentary capacity. We first defined an insane delusion in 1924 as "a persistent belief in that which has no existence in fact, and which is adhered to against all evidence." *In re Cole's Estate,* 75 Colo. 264, 269, 226 P. 143, 145 (1924). We held that a party asserting that a testator was suffering from an insane delusion must meet the burden of showing that the testator suffered from such delusion. *See id.*

We also have addressed the issue of the causal relationship necessary between an individual's insane delusion and his capacity to contract. *See Hanks v. McNeil Coal Corp.,* 114 Colo. 578, 585, 168 P.2d 256, 260 (1946). In *Hanks,* we noted that contractual capacity and testamentary capacity are the same. *Id.* In that case, a prosperous farmer suffered mental and physical deterioration after being diagnosed with diabetes. He became irritable and critical of his son's work, and in 1934 he developed a "secret formula" for a medicine to cure fistula [7] in horses that was comprised of ground china, brick dust, burnt shoe leather and amber-colored glass. This mixture was to be poured into the ear of the horse opposite the shoulder suffering from the fistula infection. In 1937, the farmer began to devote most of his time and money to peddling his medicine. In 1940, he was adjudicated insane and his son was appointed conservator of his estate. His son subsequently brought suit against a coal manufacturer to put aside a contract, alleging that his father was insane at the time he entered the contract. The lower court held that, although the farmer was suffering from insane delusions related to his fistula cure, there was no evidence of delusions in connection with his other businesses at that time. We affirmed, holding that

> [o]ne may have insane delusions regarding some matters and be insane on some subjects, yet [be] capable of transacting business concerning matters wherein such subjects are not concerned, and such insanity does not make one incompetent to contract unless the subject matter of the contract is so connected with an insane delusion as to render the afflicted party incapable of understanding the nature and effect of the agreement or of acting rationally in the transaction.

Id. at 585, 168 P.2d at 260.

The *Hanks* case sets out a standard for the requisite causal connection between insane delusions and contractual capacity that is equally applicable to testamentary capacity. A number of other courts have applied a similar standard in the context of testamentary capacity by phrasing the inquiry as whether the delusion *materially* affects the contested disposition in the will. *See Akers v. Hodel,* 871 F.2d 924, 934 (10th Cir. 1989) (holding that test under Oklahoma law is whether an insane delusion materially affected the will); *Velez v. Metropolitan Life Ins.,* 723 F.2d 7, 9 (10th Cir. 1983) (applying the "materially affect" test of testamentary capacity to the Oklahoma law of contracts); *Benjamin v. Woodring,* 303 A.2d 779, 784 (Md. 1973) (stating that to set a will aside based on an insane delusion, will must be the consequence or product of the delusion); *In re Estate of Aune,* 478 N.W.2d 561, 564 (N.D. 1991) (requiring that the will is the consequence or product of an insane delusion in order to set it aside); *In re Estate of Kesler,* 702 P.2d 86, 88 (Utah 1985) (holding that there was substantial evidence to support that the testator suffered from insane delusions that materially affected the contested will and trust); *In re Estate of Watlack,* 945 P.2d 1154, 1158 (Wash. App. 1997) (finding that facts supported the conclusion that the will was the product of insane delusions); *In re Estate of Evans,* 265 N.W.2d 529, 534-35 (Wis. 1978) (stating that "a testamentary document will not be disallowed unless … the insane delusion materially affected the disposition embodied in the will").

Based on Colorado precedent and the persuasive authority from other jurisdictions discussed above, we hold that before a will can be invalidated because of a lack of testamentary capacity due to an insane delusion, the insane delusion must materially affect the disposition in the will.

C. *Cunningham* and Insane Delusion Tests Are Not Mutually Exclusive

As the preceding case law indicates, the *Cunningham* and the insane delusion tests for sound mind have developed independently of each other.

The *Cunningham* test is most commonly applied in cases in which the objectors argue that the testator lacked general testamentary capacity due to a number of possible causes such as mental illness, physical infirmity, senile dementia, and general insanity. *See, e.g., White v. White,* 149 Colo. 166, 170, 368 P.2d 417, 419 (1962) (holding that physical illness was insufficient to render a testator incapacitated to make a will where there was no evidence that she did not understand the nature of the transaction); *Deeds v. Proudfit,* 133 Colo. 85, 89, 293 P.2d 643, 645 (1956) ("proponent established to the satisfaction of the jury that deceased knew and understood the business she was transacting at the time of the execution of the will and understood the nature and extent of her property and the natural objects of her bounty"); *In re Shapter's Estate,* 35 Colo. 578, 580–581, 585 P. 688, 690 (1905) (holding that despite "enfeebled" condition, direct and circumstantial evidence indicated that the testator understood the nature of his actions); *Calloway v. Miller,* 266 P.2d 365, 368 (N.M. 1954) (effects of advanced age do not establish lack of testamentary capacity where the testator had knowledge of meaning of making a will, of character and extent of the estate, and of the natural objects of his bounty). [8]

The insane delusion test ordinarily involves situations in which the testator, although in possession of his general faculties, suffers from delusions that often take the form of monomania or paranoia. [9] *See, e.g., Davis v. Davis,* 64 Colo. 62, 170 P. 208 (1917) (father who believes his son is not his son, suffers from an insane delusion); *see also In re Haywood's Estate,* 240 P.2d 1028, 1032–1033 (Cal. App. 1952) (fact that a testator dislikes the natural objects of his bounty, is not an insane delusion); *McReynolds v. Smith,* 86 N.E. 1009, 1012 (Ind. 1909) (belief that property worth several million dollars is only worth ten thousand dollars is an insane delusion); *Power v. Overholt,* 101 A. 733 (Pa. 1917) (a testator's belief, not based on any evidence, that his niece stole from him is an insane delusion); *In re Hanson's Estate,* 52 P.2d 1103, 1111–1112 (Utah 1935) (holding that a testator did not suffer from insane delusions, though she was afraid of men, was afraid to go out at night, was self-conscious about a deformed back, was untidy and disheveled, was sensitive, believed that others were plotting against her, and disliked talking to more than one person at a time).

As such, the *Cunningham* and insane delusion tests, although discrete, are not mutually exclusive. In order to have testamentary capacity, a testator must have a sound mind. In Colorado, a sound mind includes the presence of the *Cunningham* factors *and* the absence of insane delusions that materially affect the will. As noted above, insane delusions are often material to the making of the will, and thus will defeat testamentary capacity. *See Akers v. Hodel,* 871 F.2d at 934; *Benjamin v. Woodring,* 303 A.2d at 784; *In re Estate of Aune,* 478 N.W.2d at 564; *In re Estate of Kesler,* 702 P.2d at 88; *In re Estate of Watlack,* 945 P.2d at 1157–1159; *In re Estate of Evans,* 265 N.W.2d at 534–535. However, just as in the *Hanks* case, not all insane delusions materially affect the making of a will. Nonetheless, a testator suffering from an immaterial insane delusion must still meet the *Cunningham* sound mind test.

Accordingly, we hold that an objector may challenge a testator's soundness of mind based on both, or either of the *Cunningham* and insane delusion tests.

D. The Jury Instruction

Instruction 34:9 of the Colorado Jury Instructions is consistent with this holding. The Instruction informs the jury that:

> A will which was executed at a time when the person making the will lacked testamentary capacity is not valid and is not entitled to be admitted to probate. (*name of alleged testator*) [10] lacked testamentary capacity if it is proved that (he) (she) …(was not of sound mind) at the time the will was … executed.

(A person is not of sound mind if, when executing a will, [that person is afflicted with an insane delusion that affects or influences the dispositions of property made in the will] [or] [that person does not understand all of the following:

1. That he or she is making a will;
2. The nature and extent of the property he or she owns;
3. How that property will be distributed under the will;
4. That the will distributes the property as he or she wishes; and
5. Those persons who are the natural ones to receive his or her property.])

CJI-Civ. 4th 34:9 (italics, brackets, and parentheses in original).

The definition of an insane delusion is contained in Colorado Jury Instruction 34:10, which defines it as "a persistent belief, resulting from illness or disorder, in the existence or non-existence of something which is contrary to all evidence." CJI-Civ. 4th 34:10.

The structure and wording of Jury Instruction 34:9 preserves the discrete nature of these two tests for sound mind. The Instruction employs the use of the word "or" in brackets and sets off each test from the other by enclosing them each in brackets to clearly present the tests as independent. *See* CJI-Civ. 4th 34:9. In addition, note two of the "Notes on Use" following Instruction 34:9 states that one should "use whichever parenthesized and bracketed *portions* of the instruction are appropriate in light of the evidence in the case." *Id.* at n.2 (emphasis added). This language indicates that either or both tests may be applicable to a particular will and more than one portion may apply to any given case. A plain reading of the Instruction, and particularly the use of the word "or," leads to the conclusion that, while exclusive, an objector to a will may challenge a testator's capacity based on both or either of these two tests.

E. Probate Court Decision

Petitioners argue that the trial court erred with respect to its analysis of the *Cunningham* and the Insane Delusion tests. They contend that because this case involves insane delusions, the insane delusion test should have been exclusively applied. By extension, they argue that the *Cunningham* test should not have been applied at all. Based upon this logic, Petitioners argue that the trial court erred by: (1) applying both the *Cunningham* and the insane delusion tests in a case which involves only insane delusions; and (2) merging the *Cunningham* and the insane delusion tests.

Upon reviewing the decision of the probate court, we hold that the court correctly applied these two exclusive tests for testamentary capacity to find that the decedent was of sound mind at the time he executed his holographic will. The court found that the decedent had used alcohol and cocaine for several years prior to his death, had used alcohol and cocaine between March 17 and 19, suffered from mood swings, and worried excessively about threats against his and his dog's life. Despite these adverse findings, the court found that the decedent was of sound mind.

First, the court applied the *Cunningham* test and found that the decedent: (1) could index the major categories of the property comprising his estate; (2) knew his home and rental addresses; and (3) identified the devisee by name and provided her current address. The court noted that the will was "legible, logical in content, and reasonably set[] out [the decedent's] intent." In addition, the probate court considered the testimony of handwriting experts that indicated that at the time the decedent wrote the will, he was in command of his motor skills and his handwriting was unremarkable when compared to other exemplars. Based upon these factors, the trial court found that the decedent met the *Cunningham* test for sound mind.

Then, the probate court applied the insane delusion test to hold that although the decedent was suffering from insane delusions at the time he executed his will, "[his] insane delusions did not affect or influence the disposition of property made in the will." *Cf. In re Haywood's Estate*, 240 P.2d at 1033 (finding that a testator's hallucination of a headless wolf was not related to the making of the will). In so finding, the probate court considered the decedent's delusions regarding listening devices in his home and car and assassination plots against himself and his dog. In addition, the court weighed the testimony of numerous expert witnesses regarding the decedent's handwriting, his mental state near the time he executed the will, and the impact of his drug and alcohol use on his mental faculties. Further, the court considered testimony from several persons who stated that the decedent was not close to Petitioners, had infrequent contact with them, indicated to friends that he believed his father was irresponsible with money, disliked his sister's husband, and that his relationship with his brother was distant. *Cf. id.* (holding no insane delusion where testator disliked his son and thought he was a drunkard). In fact, the decedent had not made provisions for either Breeden Sr. or Connell in his earlier 1991 will. *Cf. In re Estate of Hayes,* 55 Colo. 340, 351, 135 P. 449, 453 (1913) ("upon question of mental capacity … it is of special importance to note that [two years earlier, the testator] executed a will which was quite similar in the disposition"). As such, the probate court concluded that the insane delusions from which the decedent suffered did not materially affect or influence the disposition made in the holographic will. [11]

The Petitioners also contend that the trial court erred by "merging" the *Cunningham* and insane delusion tests, and point for support to the probate court's statement that the

> [o]bjectors did not prove by a preponderance of the evidence that [the decedent's insane delusions] caused [him] to misapprehend the nature of his property, the identities of or his relationship with objectors, or the manner in which he wished to dispose of his property at the time the will was written.

Our decision that the probate court correctly applied both tests for sound mind, by implication, holds that the court did not incorrectly merge the two tests. Although, at times, the probate court merged language from the *Cunningham* and insane delusion tests, the decision as a whole indicates that the court thoroughly analyzed all of the evidence presented and applied each of the tests to find that the decedent was of sound mind.

In sum, the probate court order reflects that the court thoroughly considered all of the evidence presented by the parties and concluded that (1) the testator met the *Cunningham* test for sound mind and (2) the insane delusions from which the decedent was suffering did not materially affect or influence his testamentary disposition.

III. Probate Court's Denial of Petitioners' MOTION TO DISMISS BREEDEN SR. AND CONNELL

Petitioners contend that the probate court erred when it denied their motion to dismiss Breeden Sr. [12] and Connell as parties so that they could testify to conversations with the decedent arguably barred by the Dead Man's Statute. Petitioners argue that the probate court erred because neither Breeden Sr., nor Connell had a disqualifying direct interest to justify an invocation of the Dead Man's Statute. We now hold that the probate court did not err when it denied Petitioners' motion to dismiss two of the three named parties because the Dead Man's Statute bars their testimony as parties to the suit, and therefore, dismissing them as parties on the first day of the hearing would have resulted in unfair surprise and potential prejudice to Respondent.

A. The Dead Man's Statute

Under section 13-90-101, 5 C.R.S. (1999), all persons with an interest in a cause of action are presumed competent to testify. *See Patterson v. Pitoniak,* 173 Colo. 454, 457, 480 P.2d 579, 580 (1971). However, this general rule of competency is limited by a number of exceptions, including section 13-90-103, 5 C.R.S. (1999), known as the "Dead Man's Statute." The Dead Man's Statute is a less limiting codification of the common law rule that excluded as incompetent the testimony of all parties and all persons who stood to gain or lose by the outcome of a case. *See Wise v. Hillman,* 625 P.2d 364, 366 (Colo. 1981). The policy underlying the Dead Man's Statute is to guard against perjury by living interested witnesses when deceased persons cannot refute the testimony, thus protecting estates against unjust claims. *See Coon v. Berger*, 41 Colo. App. 358, 360, 588 P.2d 386, 388 (1978), *aff'd*, 199 Colo. 133, 606 P.2d 68 (1980); *Wise*, 625 P.2d at 366 (stating that the "purpose [of the Dead Man's Statute] is to promote equal justice between the parties"). *See generally* Herbert E. Tucker, *Colorado Dead Man's Statute: Time for Repeal or Reform?*, Colo. Law., Jan. 2000, at 45.

The Dead Man's Statute states:

> No party to any civil action, suit, or proceeding *or* person directly interested in the event thereof shall be allowed to testify therein of such person's own motion or in such person's own behalf ... when any adverse party sues or defends as the ... heir, legatee, or devisee of any deceased person....

§ 13-90-102(1), 5 C.R.S. (1999) (emphasis added).

We have interpreted this statute to hold that a potential witness is disqualified if, at the time of the proceedings, he is a party to the suit, [13] or he will gain or lose by the direct legal operation of the judgment, and his testimony is being offered against an heir, legatee, devisee, or other person listed in the statute. *See In re Eder's Estate*, 94 Colo. 173, 180, 29 P.2d 631, 634 (1934) ("the statute contemplates *either* a party *or* one who has a direct interest") (emphasis added); *see also Wise*, 625 P.2d at 366 (stating that "parties and other interested persons are ... barred from testifying"). A contest of a probate falls within the statute because the purpose of the suit is to divest legatees and devisees of all rights in the estate of the testator. *See In re Shapter's Estate*, 35 Colo. at 578, 85 P. at 688.

In the present case, Petitioners Breeden Sr. and Connell were parties to the suit;[14] accordingly, their testimony was barred by application of the Dead Man's Statute.

B. The Probate Court Did Not Err When It Denied Petitioners' Motion to Dismiss Breeden Sr. and Connell

A petition for formal probate of the decedent's will was filed on April 5, 1996. On June 3, 1996, Petitioners filed an objection to petition for formal probate. On September 3, 1996, the first day of the probate hearing, Petitioners filed a motion to dismiss Breeden Sr. and Connell as parties to the suit. The trial court denied the motion. In denying the motion, the probate court stated three reasons for its decision: (1) the motion was filed on the first day of the hearing; (2) the parties would be barred from testifying under the Dead Man's Statute regardless; and (3) having identified themselves as beneficiaries and having objected to the probate of the decedent's will, the parties should not be permitted to disclaim their interest. [15]

The probate court's denial of the motion to dismiss filed by Petitioners Breeden Sr. and Connell is subject to an abuse of discretion review. *Cf. Draper v. School Dist. No. 1*, 175 Colo. 216, 218, 486 P.2d 1048, 1049 (1971) (denial of motion for joinder of a party not necessary to the litigation will be overturned only if it amounts to an abuse of discretion). *See generally Tillery v. District Court*, 692 P.2d 1079, 1085 (Colo. 1984) (holding that although the standard of review is abuse of discretion, a plaintiff's motion to dismiss the action without prejudice should be granted, unless it will result in legal prejudice to the defendant).

We hold that the probate court did not abuse its discretion when it denied Petitioners' motion to dismiss. Despite having sufficient time to prepare for the probate hearing, Petitioners chose to wait until the day of the hearing to file a motion to dismiss two of the three named parties to the suit. [16] This motion was a surprise to both the court and opposing counsel. As such, the trial court correctly noted that, if the motion were to be granted, the result would be unfair surprise and potential prejudice. *See generally Todd v. Bear Valley Village Apts.*, 980 P.2d 973, 979 (Colo. 1999).

Accordingly, we hold that the probate court did not abuse its discretion when it denied Respondents' motion to dismiss Breeden Sr. and Connell as parties. Because Breeden Sr. and Connell were parties, the probate court correctly excluded their testimony regarding conversations with the decedent pursuant to the Dead Man's Statute.

IV. Conclusion

We hold that the probate court correctly applied the two exclusive tests for testamentary capacity to find that the testator, Spicer Breeden, was of sound mind at the time he executed the holographic will. Additionally, we hold that the probate court did not abuse its discretion when it denied Petitioners' motion to dismiss Breeden Sr. and Connell as parties, thus precluding their testimony as parties under the Dead Man's Statute. Accordingly, we affirm the decision of the court of appeals upholding the probate court's ruling that the decedent was of sound mind and upholding the probate court's denial of Petitioners' motion to dismiss Breeden Sr. and Connell. http://www.nyestatelitigationblog.com/uploads/file/ShamashDecision.pdf.

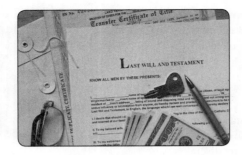

Chapter **five**

WILL PREPARATION AND DRAFTING

OBJECTIVES

At the end of this chapter, the student will understand:

- his or her role in collecting information from the client
- his or her role in drafting a will for the client
- the clauses that are part of a will
- the importance of having the will drafted and then executed correctly

Client Conference

Before an attorney can draft a will, a conference must be held with the client. At the conference, the attorney will obtain all information necessary to determine what provisions will be required to effectuate an estate plan for the client that will properly dispose of the client's property upon death with the minimum of time and expense. Information that the attorney may ask the client includes what property is held by the client, who his or her family and friends are, to whom he or she intends to leave his or her property, and who his or her outstanding creditors are. The paralegal may be asked to sit in on the conference to take notes. This interview is to collect preliminary information from the client. Many attorneys use a written data information sheet, which is either sent to the client in advance of the initial interview or given to the client to fill out while waiting to be seen by the attorney.

It is imperative that the paralegal hone the skills necessary to talk to clients, if he or she has any client contact. It is important for the client to obtain a level of comfort with both the attorney and the paralegal, because there are occasions that will necessitate the discussion of sensitive subjects for the client. If the paralegal has contact with the client from the outset, it will be very important for the paralegal to assure the client that the law office personnel, from the secretaries to the attorney, are there to serve the client and make the client comfortable. This is often done solely by a respectful demeanor. Remember that estate planning is a difficult subject for many clients. Older clients may be unsure, difficult, confrontational, timid, sensitive, or frail. If the client has made an appointment, he or she already knows how important planning for his or her death is, but it still may be difficult to discuss. The client needs to know that the law firm will be thoroughly professional and that any information imparted to any staff member will be held in the strictest confidence.

Figure 5.1   Client Data Sheet

FILE NO. _____

CLIENT DATA SHEET

DATE _____ REFERRED BY _____

YOUR NAME _____ BIRTH DATE _____

YOUR SPOUSE'S NAME _____ BIRTH DATE _____

HOME ADDRESS _____

CITY _____ STATE _____ ZIP _____

HOME TELEPHONE (_____)_____

WORK PLACE: YOURS _____

ADDRESS _____

WORK TELEPHONE (_____)_____

WORK PLACE: SPOUSE'S _____

ADDRESS _____

WORK TELEPHONE (_____)_____

SOCIAL SECURITY #: YOURS _____ SPOUSE'S _____

MARITAL STATUS: [ ] MARRIED [ ] SINGLE [ ] WIDOW(ER)
          [ ] DIVORCED [ ] LEGALLY SEPARATED

UNITED STATES CITIZEN: YOU: [ ] YES [ ] NO; SPOUSE [ ] YES [ ] NO

FOR OFFICE USE ONLY

DATE FILE OPENED _____ DATE FILE CLOSED _____

ORIGINATING ATTORNEY _____

PRIMARY ATTORNEY _____

DATE TO BE COMPLETED BY _____

COPY TO CLIENT FOR REVIEW [ ] YES [ ] NO

(continued)

Figure 5.1   (continued)

FEE ARRANGEMENT–FIXED FEE FROM $ _____ TO $ _____

HOURLY RATE OF $ _____ OTHER _____

ADVANCE FEE PAID (IN TRUST ACCOUNT) $ _____

NEXT APPOINTMENT DATE _____

_____

_____

_____

_____

COMMENTS

_____

_____

_____

_____

ESTATE PLANNING DATA SHEET

PART I

CLIENT(S) _____ **FILE #** _____

PLEASE BRING TO THE FIRST CONFERENCE AS MANY OF THE FOLLOWING DOCUMENTS AS ARE APPLICABLE TO YOU (check those which apply):

[ ] Existing Wills or Trust Agreements

[ ] Life Insurance Policies

[ ] Divorce Decrees and Property Settlement Agreements

[ ] Deeds and Lease Agreements for Real Estate

[ ] Employee Benefit and Retirement Plans

[ ] Corporation Documents and Shareholder Agreements

(continued)

Figure 5.1 (continued)

[ ] Partnership Agreements

[ ] Deeds of Trust and Notes for Money Owed to You

[ ] Last Year's Income Tax Returns

[ ] Gift Tax Returns

[ ] Any Other Information That Might Be Important

I. CHILDREN

A. NAME _____ BIRTH DATE _____

   CHILD'S SPOUSE _____ MINOR CHILDREN? [ ] YES [ ] NO

   CITY AND STATE _____

B. NAME _____ BIRTH DATE _____

   CHILD'S SPOUSE _____ MINOR CHILDREN? [ ] YES [ ] NO

   CITY AND STATE _____

C. NAME _____ BIRTH DATE _____

   CHILD'S SPOUSE _____ MINOR CHILDREN? [ ] YES [ ] NO

   CITY AND STATE _____

D. NAME _____ BIRTH DATE _____

   CHILD'S SPOUSE _____ MINOR CHILDREN? [ ] YES [ ] NO

   CITY AND STATE _____

If any children listed are from a prior marriage or are adopted, please indicate.

II. BACKGROUND INFORMATION (VERY IMPORTANT, PLEASE COMPLETE)

YOURS

   A. PREVIOUS MARRIAGES

      FORMER SPOUSE _____

      DATE & PLACE OF MARRIAGE _____

(continued)

Figure 5.1 (continued)

HOW TERMINATED _____

DATE TERMINATED _____

B. DIVORCE OBLIGATIONS (PAY/RECEIVE)

CHILD SUPPORT _____

ALIMONY _____

LIFE INSURANCE _____

OTHER TERMS _____

YOUR SPOUSE'S

C. PREVIOUS MARRIAGES

FORMER SPOUSE _____

DATE & PLACE OF MARRIAGE _____

HOW TERMINATED _____

DATE TERMINATED _____

D. DIVORCE OBLIGATIONS (PAY/RECEIVE)

CHILD SUPPORT _____

ALIMONY _____

LIFE INSURANCE _____

OTHER TERMS _____

E. ARE THERE SPECIAL NEEDS FOR ANY CHILD? [ ] YES [ ] NO

IF YES, PLEASE EXPLAIN _____

F. DO YOU OR YOUR SPOUSE SUPPORT OR EXPECT TO
SUPPORT ANYONE ELSE SUCH AS A PARENT OR
OTHER PERSON? [ ] YES [ ] NO

IF YES, PLEASE EXPLAIN _____

(continued)

Figure 5.1   (continued)

G. MILITARY SERVICE (BRANCH, RANK, SERIAL #, DATES):

YOURS _____

YOUR SPOUSE'S _____

H. DESCRIBE ANY SIGNIFICANT HEALTH PROBLEMS:

YOURS

YOUR SPOUSE'S _____

I. NAME & ADDRESS OF PHYSICIAN _____

J. HAVE YOU EVER LIVED IN A COMMUNITY PROPERTY STATE?

(AZ, CA, TX, ID, LA, NM, NV, WA, & WI)   [ ] YES [ ] NO

K. NAMES OF OTHER COUNTRIES IN WHICH YOU HAVE LIVED, IF

ANY _____

L. HAVE YOU OR YOUR SPOUSE EVER HAD A NAME
CHANGE (OTHER THAN BY REASON OF MARRIAGE)?   [ ] YES [ ] NO

M. DID YOU MAKE GIFTS BEFORE 1982 IN EXCESS
OF $3000 IN VALUE TO ANY PERSON IN ANY YEAR?   [ ] YES [ ] NO

AFTER 1981 IN EXCESS OF $10,000 IN VALUE TO ANY
PERSON IN ANY YEAR?   [ ] YES [ ] NO

AFTER 2001 IN EXCESS OF $11,000 IN VALUE TO ANY
PERSON IN ANY YEAR?   [ ] YES [ ] NO

N. DID YOUR SPOUSE MAKE GIFTS BEFORE 1982
IN EXCESS OF $3000 IN VALUE TO ANY PERSON
IN ANY YEAR?   [ ] YES [ ] NO

AFTER 1981 IN EXCESS OF $10,000 IN VALUE TO
ANY PERSON IN ANY YEAR?   [ ] YES [ ] NO

AFTER 2001 IN EXCESS OF $11,000 IN VALUE TO ANY
PERSON IN ANY YEAR?   [ ] YES [ ] NO

O. DO YOU OR YOUR SPOUSE WISH TO FORGIVE ANY
LOANS AT DEATH?   [ ] YES [ ] NO

(continued)

Figure 5.1   (continued)

P. ARE THERE ANY SPECIFIC INSTRUCTIONS FOR
   YOUR OR YOUR SPOUSE'S BURIAL?   [ ] YES [ ] NO

Q. DO YOU OR YOUR SPOUSE HAVE A PRE- OR
   POSTNUPTIAL AGREEMENT?   [ ] YES [ ] NO
   (If so, bring a copy with you.)

R. DO YOU WANT YOUR RESIDENCE TO PASS:

   _____ Upon death to your spouse

   _____ Other _____

III. KEY PEOPLE IN YOUR ESTATE PLAN

   A. **EXECUTORS** OF WILLS (List persons, banks, or trust companies that
   you would like to consider as potential executors of your estate.)

FIRST [ ] Spouse [ ] Other _____

ADDRESS _____

ALTERNATE _____

ADDRESS _____

SECOND ALTERNATE _____

ADDRESS _____

   B. **TRUSTEES** OF TESTAMENTARY OR REVOCABLE LIVING TRUSTS
   (List persons, banks, or trust companies that you would like to consider as
   potential trustees.)

ORIGINAL [ ] Spouse [ ] Other _____

FIRST SUCCESSOR _____

SECOND SUCCESSOR _____

THIRD SUCCESSOR _____

   C. **GUARDIANS** FOR MINOR CHILDREN

FIRST _____

SECOND _____

THIRD _____

(*continued*)

Figure 5.1   (continued)

IV. DISPOSITION OF YOUR ESTATE (where your assets are to go after death) (Use this as a guide for further discussion.)

[ ] YES [ ] NO   Would you like to prepare a separate written list of specific items of property as a guide for your Executor/Trustee in the distribution of your personal estate, such as jewelry, furniture, furnishings, vehicles, art, antiques, china, silver, and the like?

A. If you plan to make specific bequests, complete the following:

Beneficiary _____

Address _____

Asset/Cash Sum _____

Alternate _____

Beneficiary _____

Address _____

Asset/Cash Sum _____

Alternate _____

Beneficiary _____

Address _____

Asset/Cash Sum _____

Alternate _____

Beneficiary _____

Address _____

Asset/Cash Sum _____

Alternate _____

B. If your spouse survives you

_____ All to spouse

(continued)

Figure 5.1 (continued)

_____ All to spouse except the following specific items

_____

_____

C. If your spouse predeceases you

1. To children

_____ Outright, equal shares, no trust

_____ Outright, no trust

_____ % to _____

_____ % to _____

_____ % to _____

_____ Trust

        _____ equal shares

        _____ unequal shares

_____ % to _____

_____ % to _____

_____ % to _____

_____ Separate trusts for each beneficiary; distribution at age _____.

_____ One trust for all beneficiaries; distribution when each reaches age _____.

_____ One trust for all beneficiaries; distribution when youngest reaches age _____.

_____ Tier distribution

        _____ % at _____ years

        _____ % at _____ years

        Balance at _____ years

(_continued_)

Figure 5.1 (continued)

_____ Distributions other than for support, education, welfare, and/or medical _____

_____ Special trust instructions _____

2. Other beneficiaries _____

_____

_____

3. Charitable beneficiaries _____

_____

V. ADVISORS

	NAME	ADDRESS	PHONE
A. ACCOUNTANT			
B. OTHER ATTORNEY			
C. STOCKBROKER			
D. FINANCIAL PLANNER			
E. LIFE INSURANCE AGENT			
F. OTHER ADVISORS			

VI. OTHER INFORMATION YOU WOULD LIKE TO PROVIDE

_____

_____

_____

_____

(_continued_)

Figure 5.1   (continued)

ESTATE PLANNING DATA SHEET

PART II

I. INVENTORY OF ASSETS (please complete with full information):

To indicate ownership, please use the following:

C owned entirely by you
S owned entirely by your spouse
J owned jointly with your spouse with right of survivorship
O other partial ownership (provide details)

Include the full value of the property except in the case of property designated O. For property designated O, include only the value of your interest or your spouse's interest.

A. REAL ESTATE (including condominium apartment)

DESCRIP-TION	DATE PUR-CHASED	COST PLUS IMPROVE-MENTS	CURRENT VALUE	MORTGAGE PAYABLE	CURRENT NET VALUE	OWNED BY

B. OWNERSHIP INTEREST IN BUSINESS (Put additional businesses on back of page.)

1. Name of business or company _____

2. Business address _____

3. Type of business entity (e.g., S-Corporation, LLP) _____

4. Your ownership interest (percentage, # of shares, units, etc.) _____

Spouse's ownership interest (percentage, # of shares, units, etc.) _____

5. Value of your ownership interest _____

Value of spouse's ownership interest _____

Value of entire business _____

(continued)

Figure 5.1   (continued)

6. Names and ownership interests of other owners

_____

_____

_____

7. Do you have a plan for transferring your interest at death or retirement? _____ If so, provide details. _____

8. Do you have a buy–sell agreement? _____ If so, include a copy.

9. Do you have key-person and/or disability insurance for you or your spouse? _____ If so, include details. _____

For the "owned by" column of the following sections, please continue to use these ownership codes:

  C owned entirely by you
  S owned entirely by your spouse
  J owned jointly with your spouse with right of survivorship
  O other partial ownership (provide details)

Include the full value of the property except in the case of property designated O. For property designated O, include only the value of your interest or your spouse's interest.

C. STOCKS AND BONDS (You may attach copies of brokerage or investment accounts.)

1. Listed securities (stocks and bonds)

DESCRIPTION	NO. OF SHARES OR FACE VALUE	DATE ACQUIRED	MARKET ORIGINAL COST	VALUE VALUE	OWNED BY

(continued)

Figure 5.1   (continued)

2. U.S. Government Bonds (e.g., Series "E" or "EE" bonds)

FACE VALUE	PAYABLE ON DEATH TO	ISSUE DATE	CURRENT VALUE	OWNED BY

D. CASH AND NOTES

1. Cash

NAME & ADDRESS OF BANK	ACCOUNT NUMBER	CHECKING OR SAVINGS	TRUST ACCOUNT BENEFICIARY	CURRENT BALANCE	OWNED BY

2. Mortgages and promissory notes owed to you

NAME OF MORTGAGEE OR CREDITOR	UNPAID FACE VALUE	REPAYMENT BALANCE	INTEREST TERMS	RATE	OWNED BY

E. LIFE INSURANCE   (Please show values in this section without reduction for loans, but be sure to include life insurance policy loans in part II.)

Policies owned by and insuring you:

COMPANY AND POLICY NUMBER	POLICY TYPE (GROUP, TERM, WHOLE LIFE, ETC.)	ANNUAL PREMIUM	CASH SURRENDER VALUE	FACE VALUE OR DEATH BENEFIT	DESIGNATED BENEFICIARY

(*continued*)

Figure 5.1   (continued)

Policies owned by you and insuring others:

COMPANY AND POLICY NUMBER	POLICY TYPE (GROUP, TERM, WHOLE LIFE, ETC.)	ANNUAL PREMIUM	CASH SURRENDER VALUE	FACE VALUE OR DEATH BENEFIT	DESIGNATED BENEFICIARY

Policies owned by spouse and insuring spouse:

COMPANY AND POLICY NUMBER	POLICY TYPE (GROUP, TERM, WHOLE LIFE, ETC.)	ANNUAL PREMIUM	CASH SURRENDER VALUE	FACE VALUE OR DEATH BENEFIT	DESIGNATED BENEFICIARY

Policies owned by spouse and insuring others:

COMPANY AND POLICY NUMBER	POLICY TYPE (GROUP, TERM, WHOLE LIFE, ETC.)	ANNUAL PREMIUM	CASH SURRENDER VALUE	FACE VALUE OR DEATH BENEFIT	DESIGNATED BENEFICIARY

Policies owned by others and insuring you or your spouse:

COMPANY AND POLICY NUMBER	POLICY TYPE (GROUP, TERM, WHOLE LIFE, ETC.)	ANNUAL PREMIUM	CASH SURRENDER VALUE	FACE VALUE OR DEATH BENEFIT	DESIGNATED BENEFICIARY

(continued)

Figure 5.1   (continued)

F. TRUSTS CONTAINING GENERAL POWERS OF APPOINTMENT HELD BY YOU

INSTRUMENT CONFERRING POWER	DATE POWER CREATED	VALUE OF PROPERTY SUBJECT TO POWER

(Provide copy of instrument creating power.)

G. TRUSTS CONTAINING GENERAL POWERS OF APPOINTMENT HELD BY YOUR SPOUSE

INSTRUMENT CONFERRING POWER	DATE POWER CREATED	VALUE OF PROPERTY SUBJECT TO POWER

(Provide copy of instrument creating power.)

H. YOUR ANNUITIES AND RETIREMENT BENEFITS (include Keogh plans and IRAs)

For "type of plan" indicate nonqualified, deferred compensation, pension, profit-sharing, IRA, or the like.

TYPE OF PLAN	ANNUITY OR LUMP SUM PAYOUT	DESIGNATED BENEFICIARY	AMOUNT OF YOUR CONTRIBUTION	APPROXIMATE VALUE

(Provide copies of contracts, plans, etc.)

I. YOUR SPOUSE'S ANNUITIES AND RETIREMENT BENEFITS (include Keogh plans and IRAs)

(*continued*)

Figure 5.1   (continued)

For "type of plan" indicate nonqualified, deferred compensation, pension, profit-sharing, IRA, or the like.

TYPE OF PLAN	ANNUITY OR LUMP SUM PAYOUT	DESIGNATED BENEFICIARY	AMOUNT OF YOUR CONTRIBUTION	APPROXIMATE VALUE

(Provide copies of contracts, plans, etc.)

J. MISCELLANEOUS PROPERTY INTERESTS

NATURE OF THE PROPERTY	APPROXIMATE VALUE	OWNED BY

II. DEBTS, LOANS, AND LIENS   Current Value

Debts owed

  By you   _____

  By your spouse   _____

  By you and your spouse jointly   _____

Bank loans

  To you   _____

  To your spouse   _____

  To you and your spouse jointly   _____

Insurance policy loans

  On policies owned by you   _____

  On policies owned by your spouse   _____

Installment contracts

  Payable by you   _____

  Payable by your spouse   _____

  Payable by you and your spouse jointly _____

Contingent liabilities (guaranty, indemnity agreements)

(*continued*)

Figure 5.1   (continued)

	Amount
Yours	_____
Your spouse's	_____
III. APPROXIMATE ANNUAL INCOME	Amount
Salary	
Yours	_____
Your spouse's	_____
Fees	
Paid to you	_____
Paid to your spouse	_____
Commissions	
Paid to you	_____
Paid to your spouse	_____
Interest income	
Yours	_____
Your spouse's	_____
Dividend income	
Yours	_____
Your spouse's	_____
Pensions received	
Yours	_____
Your spouse's	_____
Annuities	
Paid to you	_____
Paid to your spouse	_____
Royalties received	
By you	_____
By your spouse	_____
Trust income	
Received by you	_____
Received by your spouse	_____
Payments received on mortgages, installment sales, etc.	
By you	_____
By your spouse	_____
TOTAL	_____

(*continued*)

Figure 5.1   (continued)

IV. FUTURE INHERITANCES

Do you or your spouse expect to inherit property from parents or others?

From Whom?   Estimated Amount

_____

_____

_____

SUMMARY

(Recapitulation—For Lawyer Use)

ASSETS	CURRENT INCLUDABLE VALUE			
	C	S	J	O
1. Real estate (current value)				
2. Value of business interests				
3. Listed securities				
4. U.S. Government Bonds				
5. Cash				
6. Mortgages and promissory notes owed to client(s)				
7. Life insurance includable in estate				
8. General powers of appointment				
9. Annuities, retirement benefits				
10. Miscellaneous property interests				
11. Gift tax paid on gifts within last 3 years				
	C	S	J	O
TOTAL ASSETS:				

LIABILITIES
1. Mortgages payable
2. Bank loans
3. Insurance policy loans
4. Debts, etc.

(continued)

Figure 5.1   (continued)

	C	S	J	O
TOTAL LIABILITIES:				
	C	S	J	O
NET CURRENT ESTATE				

THE PROFESSIONAL PARALEGAL

Paralegals are often asked to review client data sheets to determine if any necessary information is missing or must be supplemented. After this task is completed, the paralegal will brief the attorney about the client. If a data sheet is used by the supervising attorney, the paralegal will have the opportunity to fill in missing and incomplete information. If a data sheet is not used, the paralegal will collect all preliminary information directly from the client if he or she is sitting in on the initial client interview, or will collect the information afterward from the supervising attorney.

It is very important that the paralegal take down as much information as possible. It is also important to pay attention during the meeting. Sometimes when a client seemingly drones on and on, it is easy to get lulled into a bit of a daze. Avoid that as you never really know when something will be said that will prove to be enlightening. And remember no smartphone gazing!

Personal and Family Information

The first thing the paralegal must be certain to have available, if asked to do an initial draft of a will, is the client's full name, any names by which he or she might otherwise be known currently or formerly, his or her domicile, age, and marital status. All of this information aids in determining how to approach the drafting process.

Other important information gathered during the client conference is that regarding family and friends. It is important for the attorney to determine the extent of the client's family relationships, and not just to whom the client intends to leave his or her property. Many clients balk at giving such extensive information when they only want to leave property to one child or grandchild, a sister, or even a distant cousin. The client must nonetheless be persuaded that this information may assist the attorney in drafting a will that is less susceptible to contest. Very few clients anticipate a fight over their property when they die, but the attorney must. Nothing brings out the worst in good people than the chance of obtaining "free" money from a deceased relative. If the attorney is made aware of any potential family squabbles in advance, the will's provisions can be drafted to minimize any problems that might arise during the probate of the client's estate.

Consider this example from a real situation: Older clients make an appointment to have wills drawn up. They have been married over 40 years and have two adult daughters. Their desire is to leave everything to each other and then equally to the daughters. More than half-hour into the client interview, it comes to light that the daughters are the wife's children and not the husband's. Despite being married over 40 years, the wife had been married before and came to this marriage with two young children and an absentee father. The current husband was the only father the girls really knew; they considered him their father and he considered them his daughters. However, he had never legally adopted them. If his will had said, "if my wife does not survive me, I give my estate to my daughters," the daughters would not receive the property. Morally, the daughters should have received the property, but not legally. The will was ultimately drafted to provide that the daughters and the grandchildren would be considered his daughters for purposes of the document so that upon his death, they would in fact, receive the property as he intended. For example:

> Any references to my "child" or "children" shall refer to Tina Black and Terry Black without distinction to whether they are natural born, or born of my wife. I have no other children born to, or adopted by me. Any references to my "grandchildren" shall refer to my wife's grandchildren without distinction to whether they are my natural grandchildren or my wife's.

Information about family members should include their names, domicile, ages, relationship to the client, and marital status. It should also be noted if the family members have children, their ages, and their marital status. Knowing a child's or grandchild's age assists in determining whether or not that beneficiary should receive property outright or be held in some sort of trust for his or her benefit and distributed later on. Adopted and nonmarital children and grandchildren must be included, although some families fail to tell attorneys about nonmarital children and it goes unacknowledged to the detriment of the estate plan. Some attorneys will ask the paralegal to draw a family tree to illustrate the client's family. As discussed in Chapter 3, family trees are helpful when the client has an extensive family since it makes each family member and their relationships to each other easily identifiable.

Client Assets and Liabilities

The client must also disclose a list of all assets he or she may possess, as well as any liabilities. Assets include all property, both real and personal, that the client owns solely or jointly with others. Personal property that should be disclosed includes stocks and bonds, furniture, jewelry, money, cars, patents and copyrights, insurance policies of any type, Social Security or veteran's benefits, pensions or annuities, and interests in any business. It is important to note if any of the client's real property is homesteaded, as this may affect the testator's ability to distribute the property. Clients often balk at this as well, usually brushing it off as "oh, I don't have much." Its importance cannot be emphasized enough, however, as the client may have enough to trigger a tax issue. This has not been of much concern over the last few years (due to the high exemption rate) but as we approach 2013 (at the time of this writing), we do not know how Congress will amend the laws and some people may in fact find themselves either above an exemption limit or bumping very close to it. You and your supervising attorney cannot assist the client with proper estate planning with only part of the puzzle that is your client completed.

Any powers of appointment the client may possess are also included in this list. A **power of appointment** is created when a donor confers the authority upon another, the donee, to select and nominate who will receive the donor's property or income either by will or in a trust. In some circumstances, the donee is given the authority to select himself or herself as a beneficiary of the power; in other circumstances, the potential list consists of the donor's family or other restricted class of people. When the list is restricted by the donor, it is called a ***limited power of appointment***. When the power is unlimited in scope, it is called a ***general power of appointment***. When the donee is able to select himself or herself, the property over which he or she has been given the power of appointment may be included in his or her estate. In addition, if the client is a beneficiary or trustee of a revocable living trust that he or she created for the benefit of himself or herself or others, the property will be included in his or her estate as well.

Example: Laurie Smithfield's will gives a power of appointment to her husband, Reginald.

I give to my husband, Reginald, a limited power of appointment, exercisable only by his Last Will and Testament and only by specific reference to such power, to appoint the entire principal and undistributed income of my trust to a class of persons consisting of our children and the descendants of our children and subject to any conditions, trusts and restrictions as may be determined by Reginald.

Any liabilities that the client may have must also be disclosed, including the following:

- credit card debt
- outstanding mortgages
- business debts
- medical, legal, or other professional expenses
- payments due on promissory notes or contracts

This allows the attorney to determine if there are issues that need to be addressed when the client wants to give property away; for example, when Ben wants to give his house to his son, George, does the house come free of the mortgage, or does George get the house subject to the mortgage. In addition, knowing the amount of debt in a client's estate enables the attorney to determine the amount of exemption the client may be subject to for estate taxes.

Once this information is collected, the attorney, with assistance from the paralegal, can scrutinize each asset and liability to determine what type of will is necessary to effectuate the best possible estate plan for the client.

THE PROFESSIONAL PARALEGAL

It cannot be stressed enough that any information given by a client is confidential. Be very careful when discussing your job with roommates, friends, family, or spouses. Your supervising attorney is directly responsible for your ethical violations and can be disciplined by the Bar. A client may sue for malpractice if the client believes he or she is harmed to any degree. You will likely also be fired from your job.

Other Important Information

When clients sit down with their lawyer and you, as the assigned paralegal, they come armed with a bevy of beliefs about their estates, some of which are incorrect. It is important that they should be disavowed of those beliefs before they leave the law office. One incorrect belief is that they "only need a simple will" because they "don't have very much." Incorrect beliefs often stem from the plethora of articles in magazines and the business sections of newspapers across the country, as well as television infomercials and shows, which advise that you save on probate costs if you have life insurance and other non-probate assets as the major portion of the estate. While it is true that you save probate expenses, it does not mean, however, that the face value of the life insurance or trust escapes the decedent's taxable estate. Except in rare circumstances, the face value of life insurance is included in the taxable estate. In fact, it may be the face value of the insurance proceeds that pushes the client's taxable estate beyond the amount covered by the exclusion amount. (As discussed in Chapter 12.)

> *Example:* Barry and Georgia Milton lived a very average middle-class existence during 40 years of marriage. Barry worked in the town lumber mill until retirement, and Georgia was a stay-at-home mom. They had a modest but nice home and two cars, went on a few vacations, and put their two children through college. Each had life insurance that named the other as the primary beneficiary. The two policies on Barry's life had a combined face value of $350,000, while the one policy on Georgia's life had a face value of $200,000. When Georgia died, Barry collected the insurance proceeds on her life. When Barry went to a lawyer's office to inquire about a will that would leave the lion's share of his estate to his grandchildren, ages 17, 15, 10, and 4, he immediately told the paralegal that he only needed "a simple will. That's all. I don't have much." When the paralegal tallied up all of Barry's assets, however, it was determined that Donald might need more sophisticated estate planning. How? The modest home had appreciated in value, and was now worth $650,000. The $200,000 Barry collected from the life insurance policy on Georgia's life was sitting in a bank certificate of deposit account drawing interest. Barry had a 401k as well, the value of which totaled $275,000. If the value of Barry's life insurance is added to the value of home, the proceeds and interest from his wife's life insurance, as well as any other assets Barry may have, his estate is worth far more than he assumed. Even if Barry's estate escapes estate taxes, it is questionable whether such a large estate should be left outright to young children, the likely consequence of drafting only a "simple will."

For this reason, information regarding life insurance, as well as any other non-probate asset, must be disclosed by the client when the initial client interview is held.

As shown in Barry's example, it is not unusual for a client to come to the initial client interview and exclaim, "I only need a simple will," when in reality the client needs more detailed estate planning due to a large and perhaps taxable estate. In other situations, the client may say, he or she wants a "simple will," and explain later that he or she wants a trust for the benefit of his or her children or grandchildren. When told that this type of will is not a simple one, the client might say that he or she believed it would be a simple matter, with a shrug of the shoulders, or exclaim, "but you just have it on the computer, right?" Obtaining additional information will reveal if the client's significant non-probate assets require tax planning, or if the client will require either a living or testamentary trust for the benefit of himself or herself or his family.

If the client offers information suggesting that he or she is having a "new" will made, a copy of the old will should be obtained from the client, if possible. If the client asks, why it is needed, the client should be told that the will should be reviewed and that after its review by the attorney, the client will be informed about what changes should be made, if any are necessary. In addition, the previous will may give the attorney information about the client's estate that was not discussed during the interview.

Example: Ray's prior will provides for a small fishing boat with an inboard/outboard motor to be left to his son, Todd, but Ray makes no mention of it during the client interview. The attorney can now inquire about the boat. He or she may find out that Ray sold the boat two years prior, or perhaps that Ray forgot about the boat and still wants Todd to receive it. Perhaps, Ray decides that he wants the boat to go to his 17-year-old grandson instead. Having the old will often offers a new "window" of review of the client's estate.

THE PROFESSIONAL PARALEGAL

Remember that only a lawyer can give legal advice. If the client has questions, you must tell the client that the attorney will be happy to answer any questions the client has, and offer to set an appointment for the client to meet with the attorney or relay the message to the attorney with a phone number to call the client back. At all costs, refrain from giving the client any information, including saying things like "I'm not the attorney, so I can't be sure but..." and giving an "opinion."

Drafting

Once the client has left the office, the work really begins. If a paralegal works in a law office that specializes in estate planning, his or her job duties will certainly include drafting clients' wills.

Drafting a client's will necessitates following the lawyer's and the client's instructions carefully. The client's wishes should be followed to the full extent of the law. Following are the various clauses that are always or often added to a will.

Opening Clause

The opening clause in a will is called the **exordium clause**. It is also known as the publication clause. The purpose of this clause is to identify the testator, to state his or her domicile, to specifically state that the document is his or her last will and testament (showing the testator's intent to make a will), and to revoke any prior wills and codicils, if any.

Example: I, ROSE REDTHORN, a resident of Anytown, Anycounty, Anystate, being of sound and disposing mind, memory and understanding, and mindful of the uncertainties of this life, and not acting under duress, menace, fraud, or undue influence, do hereby make, publish and declare this my Last Will and Testament, and revoking any and all former wills and codicils that I previously have made.

This clause is simple but its importance cannot be understated—it recites that the testator is of sound mind and is signing this last will of her own free will. Of course, this can be contested, but it is evidence that she understood what she was doing—making a will.

Instruction to Pay Debts

Called an **apportionment clause,** this provision lets the personal representative and the probate court know how debts and other charges to the estate are to be paid. For more discussion on this clause, see Chapter 3 under the topic of abatement.

Example: I direct that my Executor pay, as a cost of the administration of my estate, all of my funeral expenses and interment (burial or cremation), including the cost of a suitable monument or marker over my grave. I direct that my Executor pay all my just debts, expenses incurred during my last illness, and the costs of administration of my estate as soon as practicable after my death, and shall be paid by my executor out of the assets of my residuary estate. My executor may, in his sole discretion, pay from my domiciliary estate all or any portion of the costs of **ancillary administration** and similar proceedings in other jurisdictions.

I direct that my Executor pay out of my residuary estate, without apportionment, all estate, inheritance, succession, and other taxes (together with any penalty thereon), assessed by reason of my death imposed by the Government of the United States, or any state or territory thereof, or by any foreign government or political subdivision hereof, in respect to all property required to be included in my gross estate for estate or like death tax purposes by any of such governments, whether the property passes under this will or otherwise, including property over which I have a power of appointment, without contribution by any recipient of any such property.

Note the use of the term ancillary administration in the example above. Ancillary administration refers to a secondary probate in a jurisdiction other than in the testator's domicile. Ancillary administrations are performed when the testator (or intestate) has real property in a jurisdiction other than his legal residence. Ancillary administration will be discussed fully in Chapter 11.

Dispositive Provisions

Usually, the clauses following the apportionment clause are those in which the testator gives his or her property to the beneficiaries. It is in this section that specific, demonstrative, general, and residuary dispositions are made. Read this example showing distribution to a trust: I give the residue of my estate, whether real or personal and wherever located, including all property and interests not otherwise disposed of elsewhere in this document that are acquired by me or my estate after the execution of this document, to my children, Chastity White Rosemont, Chelsea

White, and Charles White, and any other children born to or adopted by me, if they survive me, in equal shares. Should my child fail to survive me, I give such residue to the remaining of my children who survive me, in equal shares. Said shares are to be distributed subject to the following terms:

Until such time that my children attain the age of twenty-five (25) years, the property shall be held IN TRUST by JOHN BLACK, as Trustee ("Trustee"), during which time, my Trustee may expend all of the income and as much of the principal which, in his sole and absolute discretion, he deems necessary for my children's health, education, maintenance, and support. Upon each of my children's attainment of the age of twenty-five years, she or he shall receive her or his share of the remainder of the property, including all principal and interest, if any, outright and free of trust.

See this example of specific bequests: All items of tangible personal property shall be distributed to my husband, if he survives me. If my husband does not survive me, I give and bequeath certain items of tangible personal property as follows:

1. All of the antique toys to Jacob Rosemont.
2. All of the green glassware originally belonging to Granny and Pappy White, to Chelsea White.
3. Antique small nativity scene originally belonging to my mother, Brenda Black, to Charles White.
4. Antique trunk to Charles White.
5. Antique children's school desk to Jacob Rosemont.
6. All the china, crystal, and Lenox vases to Chastity White Rosemont.

See this example of **demonstrative bequests**:

1. I give the sum of One Thousand Dollars ($1000.00) to DAILY HARVEST FOOD BASKET OF ANYTOWN, ANYSTATE.
2. I give the sum of Five Hundred Dollars ($500.00) to JACK PEPPER.

See this example of residuary clause; the disposition to the trust above was also a residuary clause:

A. I give the residue of my estate, whether real or personal and wherever located, including all property and interests not otherwise disposed of elsewhere in this document that is acquired by me or my estate after the execution of this document, to my husband, JERRY DAWSON, if he survives me.
B. If my husband does not survive me, I give such residue to my children, JENNY DAWSON, ALICE DAWSON NEWBURG, AND BRIANNA DAWSON, and any other child that may be born to or adopted by me at the time of my death, in equal shares, if they survive me.
C. If any of my children does not survive me, I give her share of the residue to her children, my grandchildren, per stirpes, if they survive me.
D. If neither my children nor my grandchildren survive me, I give the residue of my estate, whether real or personal and wherever located, including all property and interests not otherwise disposed of elsewhere in this document that is acquired by me or my estate after the execution of this document to my descendants who survive me.

E. Whenever property is to be distributed to the descendants of a person (the "ancestor"), such property shall be divided into equal shares, one share for each then living descendant in the first generation below the ancestor in which at least one descendant is living, and one share for each deceased descendant in such generation who has a descendant then living. Each share created for a living descendant shall be distributed to such descendant. Each share created for a deceased descendant shall be divided and distributed according to the directions in the two preceding sentences until no property remains undistributed.

F. A person who has a relationship by or through legal adoption shall take under this will as if the person had the relationship by or through birth, except that a person adopted after reaching age twenty-one and descendants of such a person shall not so take.

Note how the residuary clause leaves the testator's property first to the husband if he survives. Then it leaves the property to the children if they survive and if a child doesn't survive, to her children per stirpes. This is done so that if both of the testator's children predecease her, the grandchildren take their mother's share equally. If the residuary clause had given it to them per capita, the grandchildren would have taken an equal share of the entire residuary.

Also, note that the clause directs that all descendants, even those by adoption will take a share of the testator's property. Some clients specifically ask for that clause to be changed so that only biological descendants take a share of their estate. It is rarely done but as stepparents adopt their spouses' children, it is being seen more and more, mostly by the grandparents who do not have a relationship with those children or who insist that family property and heirlooms stay "within the family."

Appointment of the Personal Representative

The clause immediately after the residuary clause is usually the clause in which the personal representative is appointed, as well as any successors should the original be unable or unwilling to attend to her duties. This clause usually states if the **personal representative** must post a **bond,** which is a surety, insurance, to assure that the personal representative performs her duties and if she doesn't, compensates the estate for any losses due to negligence or outright theft. Simple mistakes are not reimbursed by a bond. While we are using the term personal representative to denote the person with the authority to administer the testator's estate, the term used may also be executor or independent executor, depending upon state statute.

Personal Representative's Duties and Obligations

After the personal representative is appointed, the duties and obligations he or she will have must be included in the will. The clause may be a short recitation of the state statute providing for the duties and obligations of the personal representative, or it may be a long section denoting all of the acts a personal representative may perform as part of his or her duties. It is important to make sure the personal representative maintains as many powers as possible. Clients often question the need for the personal representative to have all these powers so it is important that the client be reassured that without those powers expressly being given, the personal representative may have to seek court approval for any acts done in furtherance of duties, failure to state the personal representative's power of sale over real property being the most common reason to need court approval.

Appointment of Guardian for Minor Children

If the testator has minor children, a clause appointing a guardian for them must be included in the will. This author tells people all the time that if a client has children, this may be the most important clause in the will and that when a client says, "I don't need a will because I don't have anything," the best answer is "you have children don't you? They are your most important asset."

The guardian is the person that is legally responsible for the children upon the death of both parents. Clients often believe that they don't have to name a guardian because the family will take care of Jimmy Jr. or that the child's godparent will do it. It is vitally important, however, that the client make clear who the guardian will be because otherwise the child's care and custody will be subject to court resolution of the issue. That throws the child's upbringing into confusion as family members argue over who would be the best caretaker for Jimmy Jr. If there are no adults readily willing and able to take care of Jimmy Jr., he could become part of the foster care system.

The testator can appoint one guardian that will handle both the persons and the property of his or her children, or appoint separate guardians; one to take care of the children themselves and another to manage their assets. The guardian of the person is the person who has custody of the child while the guardian of the property handles the child's assets. If the clause just says "guardian," that person takes charge of both the child and his or her assets. Most times, the position is split into person and property only when the assets the child inherits are large, and it is believed by the parent that someone who is perfect to take care and custody of the child may not be the proper person to manage the money. In those instances, it is most likely that a trust is set up for the management of the child's assets.

> *Example:* If the natural parent of my minor child does not survive me, or is unable to act as my child's guardian, I name TODD BLACK, currently of Albuquerque, New Mexico, to have custody and be the guardian of the person of my minor child. I request that any guardian designated herein or pursuant to the provisions hereof be allowed to qualify as such without being required to give security on any fiduciary bond.

In Terrorem Clause

As stated in Chapter 4, **in terrorem clauses** are also known as "no contest" clauses or penalty clauses, and provide for the forfeiture of all benefits under the will to any beneficiary objecting to probate or challenging the will. Some states have held these clauses to be void as a matter of policy.

> *Example:* Except as otherwise specified in this Will, I have intentionally and with full knowledge omitted to provide for my heirs at the time of my death. If any beneficiary under this Will or heir at law of mine or person claiming through any of them shall contest or otherwise challenge the validity of this Will or attack any of its provisions or the trust described in Section 6 herein, directly or indirectly, any share or interest in my estate given to such person under this Will is hereby revoked, and such share or interest shall be distributed in the same manner provided herein as if such person had predeceased me.

Simultaneous Death

As discussed in Chapter 3, if a testator and his or her beneficiary die simultaneously, how to dispose of the testator's assets may become a question for the personal representative.

True simultaneous death requires both parties to die at the same time. The real problems with simultaneous death occur when the testator and beneficiary die within a short time of each other, but not truly simultaneously. Unless proved that they died at the exact same time, the parties will be treated as if they had survived each other.

The Uniform Probate Code, as well as some state statutes, provide that if the beneficiary does not survive the testator by 120 hours, the beneficiary will be deemed to have predeceased the testator. This is still a small window of time, but makes provision for those instances in which a common disaster, such as a car accident, causes a testator and a beneficiary to die within a few hours or days of each other. Another method to address the issue is to write a will provision.

Example: I shall be deemed for purposes of this will to have survived my husband if we die simultaneously, or if there is no sufficient evidence (in the opinion of my Executor) that my husband and I have died otherwise than simultaneously.

Last Clauses in the Will

Testimonium Clause   The **testimonium clause** is the one that is immediately above the testator's signature. For this reason, it is also called the signature clause. Its primary purpose is to establish the end of the will by presenting the testator's signature and affixing the date of execution.

Example: IN TESTIMONY WHEREOF, I have set my hand and seal to this my last will and testament consisting of six (6) typewritten pages, and on all pages of which I have placed my initials for security and identification this _____ day of _____, 2005.

_____ (SEAL)

GEORGE ROGERS

Attestation Clause   The **attestation clause** follows the testator's signature and comes immediately before the witnesses' signatures. The purpose of this clause is to assert that the witnesses saw the testator execute (sign) the document in their presence and that each witness signed in each other's presence, if required. They also attest that, to the best of their knowledge, the testator was over the age of majority, was of sound mind, and executed the will of his or her own accord.

Example: The undersigned certify that the Testator has initialed each page of this document and signed, sealed, acknowledged and declared the document to be the Will of the Testator, in the presence of us, who, in the presence of the Testator, and at the request of the Testator, and in the presence of each other, all present together at the same time, have subscribed our names as witnesses. We declare that at the time of the signing and acknowledgment of this document, the Testator, according to our best knowledge and belief was over the age of eighteen (18) years, of sound mind and disposing memory, and under no constraint.

Self-Proof Affidavit

As explained in Chapter 4, the self-proof affidavit is not required by law, but precludes the problems involved with finding witnesses to testify after the death of the testator since it substitutes for their live courtroom testimony. A notary public signs and seals this document after watching the testator and all witnesses sign the will and the *affidavit.*

Review Figures 5.2 and 5.3 carefully. Each illustrates a will in full, and points out the different possible will clauses. Figure 5.2 is an example of a simple will, while Figure 5.3 is a sample of a will with a testamentary trust, meaning a trust set up to take effect only when the testator dies. Review each will going over each individual clause and review what each clause is meant to accomplish. Make note of the language used for each clause. Other sample forms in Chapters 6 and 8 will help the paralegal draft a complete estate plan specifically designed for the client's needs. Remember to insure that the provisions in each document conform to the law in your jurisdiction.

Figure 5.2   Will of an Unmarried Woman

Assume for this example that Bobbie's father and mother from prior examples are deceased and that Bobbie is not married and has no children. She has only one sister, Cynthia Smith.

Last Will and Testament of Bobbie Black

I, BOBBIE BLACK, a resident of the County of Anycounty, State of Anystate, being of sound and disposing mind, memory and understanding, and mindful of the uncertainties of this life, and not acting under duress, menace, fraud, or undue influence, do hereby make, publish, and declare this my Last Will and Testament and revoking any and all former wills and codicils that I previously have made.

Section 1—Family

I hereby declare that I am not married and there are no children born to or adopted by me. I have one sister, CYNTHIA SMITH. Any reference to my "sister" shall refer to her.

Section 2—Costs of Administration

I direct that my Executor pay all my just debts, expenses incurred during my last illness and the costs of administration of my estate be paid as soon as practicable after my death and shall be paid by my Executor out of the assets of my residuary estate. My Executor may, in his sole discretion, pay from my domiciliary estate all or any portion of the costs of ancillary administration and similar proceedings in other jurisdictions.

I direct that my Executor pay out of my residuary estate, without apportionment, all estate, inheritance, succession and other taxes (together with any penalty thereon), assessed by reason of my death imposed by the Government of the United States, or any state or territory thereof, or by any foreign government or political subdivision hereof, in respect to all property required to be

Exordium Clause—what does this show? It shows that the testator intended to make a will and wasn't just jotting down notes. Formality in a will is important. The more formal, the more likely it will survive a will contest.

Declaration concerning family. Shows that she knew the objects of her bounty.

Clause regarding payment of debts—note that this says all "lawful and just debts." The purpose of this wording is to give the personal representative the ability to decline payment of any debt that is frivolous or unlawful, such as a gambling debt.

(continued)

Figure 5.2   (continued)

included in my gross estate for estate or like death tax purposes by any of such governments, whether the property passes under this will or otherwise, including property over which I have a power of appointment, without contribution by any recipient of any such property.

Section 3—Disclaimer

Any beneficiary or the legal representative of any deceased beneficiary shall have the right, within the time prescribed by law, to disclaim any benefit or power under my will. When property is to be distributed to the descendants of a person and one such descendant disclaims his interest in all or a portion of such property, the disclaimed interest, determined as if the disclaimant were living at the time of distribution, shall be distributed to the then living descendants of the disclaimant; provided, however, that if the disclaimant has no descendants then living, the interest shall be distributed as if the disclaimant had predeceased the event that results in the distribution of the property.

Section 4—List of Tangible Personal Property

During my lifetime, I intend to create and maintain from time to time a list of specific bequests of personal items and other tangible personal property. I incorporate the same herewith and I direct my Executor to make distribution in accordance with my wishes expressed therein. I intend this writing to be binding upon my Executor pursuant to Section _____ of the Code of Anystate, as amended from time to time before my death. Tangible personal property includes stamp or coin collections, but does not include other money or stock certificates or other evidences of intangible rights or interests. Tangible personal property does not include any property that is held primarily for investment purposes or used in connection with any business in which I may be engaged, or in which I may have any interest at the time of my death.

If no such list is found by my Executor within thirty (30) days of the issuance of letters of administration, then it shall be conclusively presumed that no such list exists, and my Executor shall not substitute cash or any other assets for any such property.

Section 5—Distribution of Residue

A. I give the residue of my estate, whether real or personal and wherever located, including all property and interests not otherwise disposed of elsewhere in this document that is acquired by me or my estate after the execution of this document, to my sister, CYNTHIA SMITH, if she survives me.

B. If my sister shall not survive me, I give the residue of my estate, whether real or personal and wherever located, including all property and interests not otherwise disposed of elsewhere in this document that is acquired by me or my estate after the execution of this document, as follows:

1. I give the sum of One Thousand Dollars ($1000.00) to my friend, JAMES JONES.

2. I give the sum of Five Hundred Dollars ($500.00) to my friend, ERICA ELLISON.

Apportionment Clause. In this situation, the testator has directed that all taxes be paid from the residuary without apportionment, meaning that the taxes are taken off the top. This means that the person or persons getting the majority of her assets will pay all the taxes. This clause, although most commonly used, may put an unfair burden on a surviving spouse (the usual residuary beneficiary when there is a surviving spouse) if there is a large tax bill.

Disclaimer Clause. In this situation a beneficiary may, before accepting their gift, disclaim or renounce his or her legal claim to the property in favor of other beneficiaries. For example, in this will, the testator leaves money to certain individuals but if they disclaim the funds, the funds will belong to the remaining beneficiaries because the disclaimer will, for that one bequest, treat the beneficiary as if he or she predeceased the testator.

Declaration of personal belongings. Not all states allow this type of clause. In states that do, the testator may leave personal property to beneficiaries by means of a separate piece of paper, which may be written at any time before the testator's death and without a will's formalities.

(continued)

Figure 5.2 (continued)

3. I give the sum of One Thousand Dollars ($1000.00) to my friends, BARBARA HARRISON and STEVEN HARRISON, in equal shares, or to the survivor of them.

4. I give Thirty-Five Percent (35%) of the remainder of my estate to the Church of Anytown currently located at 210 Elm Street, Anytown, Anystate to be used to feed the homeless through its breadline.

5. I give Forty-Five Percent (45%) of the remainder of my estate to Anytown College, Anytown, Anystate.

6. I give Twenty Percent (20%) of the remainder of my estate to the animal shelter, Anytown, Anystate.

Section 6—Appointment of Executor and Powers

A. I nominate and appoint my sister, CYNTHIA SMITH, to be my Executor. If my Executor should, for any reason, fail to qualify, or having qualified, cease to act in such capacity, I nominate and appoint JAMES JONES, to be my Executor, as successor, upon like terms. If administration of my estate should be necessary in any jurisdiction where my Executor is unable to qualify, or if my Executor deems it necessary for any other reason, I give to my Executor the power to designate any individual or corporation with trust powers to serve with my Executor or in my Executor's stead. I request that no security or bond be required of any Executor, except for any corporate Executor named, or appointed in the preceding sentence, which shall be required to post security or a bond. References in my will to my "Executor" are to the one or ones acting at the time, except where otherwise specifically provided.

B. Any corporate Executor shall receive for its services the compensation for which it is willing to undertake similar services for others at the time such services are rendered, as evidenced by its published fee schedule in effect from time to time, unless it is willing to agree upon a fee that is less than its customary fee.

C. I direct that the provisions hereinafter contained with respect to the powers, authorities, discretion, and immunities of my Executor shall be liberally and broadly construed; and I further direct that such powers, authorities, and discretion may be exercised without the joinder, acquiescence, or approval of any beneficiary of my estate, and no person taking any property from my Executor by sale, conveyance, assignment, lease, exchange, or mortgage shall be required to see to the application or distribution of the purchase money or other proceeds, or to inquire as to the authority of my Executor in the premises; and I further direct that in the exercise of such powers, authorities, and discretion, my Executor shall not be liable for any losses to my estate so long as my Executor acts in good faith and upon reasonable premises.

D. In addition to the powers granted by law, I grant my Executor the powers set forth in Section _____ of the Code of Anystate, as in force from time to time, and I incorporate that Code Section in my will by this reference. My Executor may select assets for allocation to a particular share as my Executor shall deem to be in the best interests of the beneficiaries of my estate created under this will, and assets allocated to one share need not

Residuary Clause—all remaining property of the testator after all debts and taxes have been paid as well as all other bequests have been made.

Appointment of Personal Representative, here called Executor

Providing for a corporate executor to be paid for its services

Authority of personal representative

(continued)

Figure 5.2 (continued)

be of the same character as assets allocated to another share; and, without limiting the generality of the foregoing, my Executor may allocate assets having different income tax bases in such manner, amounts, and proportions as my Executor shall deem appropriate. The powers and discretion granted to my Executor are exercisable only in a fiduciary capacity and may not be used to enlarge or shift any beneficial interest except as an incidental consequence of the discharge of the duties of my Executor. My Executor may distribute tangible personal property passing to a minor to any adult person with whom the minor resides, and that person's receipt shall be a sufficient voucher in the accounts of my Executor.

Additional powers granted

Section 7—Miscellaneous Provisions

A. Except as otherwise provided in this will, if any share of my estate shall vest in absolute ownership in any minor, or to a person who is incapacitated by reason of legal incapacity, or physical or mental illness or infirmity, my Executor in his absolute, unreviewable, and uncontrolled judgment and discretion, shall be authorized, in each such case, to hold, administer, invest, and reinvest such share for the benefit of such person or minor during his or her minority or incapacity, and to apply so much of the net income and of the then principal of said share as my Executor in his absolute discretion, may deem necessary to the proper care, maintenance, education, and comfort of such person, or to make such payments to the legal guardian of such person, or to the person with whom such person resides, or directly to such person, or otherwise as my Executor from time to time deems expedient, and to accumulate for the benefit of such minor or incapacitated person any income not applied or paid as aforesaid.

Providing authority for personal representative to hold property in trust under certain circumstances.

1. The term minor shall mean any person who has not reached his or her eighteenth (18) birthday.

What constitutes a minor. Testator may set this higher than the age of minority.

2. The term incapacitated shall mean any person who is under legal disability or by reason of illness, or mental or physical disability is, in the written opinion of two impartial doctors currently practicing medicine, unable to properly manage his or her affairs.

Defining incapacity for purposes of this will

B. For simplicity, I may have expressed pronouns and other terms in one number and gender, but where appropriate to the context these terms shall be deemed to include the other number and genders. Any headings herein are for convenience and shall not affect interpretation.

Clause regarding use of gender and pronouns

IN TESTIMONY WHEREOF, I have set my hand and seal to this my last will and testament consisting of six (6) typewritten pages, and on all pages of which I have placed my initials for security and identification this _____ day of _____, 2012.

_____(SEAL)

BOBBIE BLACK

Testimonium Clause

The undersigned certify that the Testator has initialed each page of this document and signed, sealed, acknowledged, and declared the document to be the Will of the Testator, in the presence of us, who, in the presence of the

(continued)

Figure 5.2 (continued)

Testator and at the request of the Testator, and in the presence of each other, all present together at the same time, have subscribed our names as witnesses. We declare that at the time of the signing and acknowledgment of this document, the Testator, according to our best knowledge and belief was over the age of eighteen (18) years, of sound mind and disposing memory, and under no constraint.

Signed on _____, 2012.

_____

_____

STATE OF ANYSTATE

COUNTY OF ANYCOUNTY, to wit:

Before me, the undersigned authority, on this date personally appeared **BOBBIE BLACK,** _____ and _____, known to me to be the Testator and witnesses, respectively, whose names are signed to the foregoing instrument and, all of these persons being by me first duly sworn, BOBBIE BLACK, the Testator, declared to me and to the witnesses in my presence that said instrument is her last will and testament and that she had willingly signed and executed it in the presence of said witnesses as her free and voluntary act for the purposes therein expressed, that said witnesses stated before me that the foregoing will was executed and acknowledged by the Testator as her last will and testament in the presence of said witnesses who in her presence and at her request and in the presence of each other did subscribe their names thereto as attesting witnesses on the day of the date of said will and that the Testator, at the time of the execution of said will, was over the age of eighteen years and of sound and disposing mind and memory.

_____
BOBBIE BLACK

_____
Witness

_____
Witness

Sworn and acknowledged before me by Bobbie Black, the testator, _____, witness, and _____, witness, this _____ day of _____, 2012.

_____
Notary Public

My commission expires: _____.

Attestation Clause

This is written into documents (not just wills) so that anyone reading the document knows that the space left at the end of this page is deliberate and that nothing is missing but that there is at least one more page to this document.

Self-proving affidavit. Must conform to state statute

Figure 5.3   Will of a Married Woman

Last Will and Testament of Bobbie Black

I, **VIRGINIA MASON JAMES,** a resident of the County of Anycounty, State of Anystate, being of sound and disposing mind, memory and understanding, and mindful of the uncertainties of this life, and not acting under duress, menace, fraud, or undue influence, do hereby make, publish and declare this my Last Will and Testament and revoking any and all former wills and codicils that I previously have made.

Section 1—Declaration Concerning Family

I hereby declare that I am married to Ian J. James. I have three natural born children to-wit: May Wright, Amber Wright Bishop, and Robert Wright, and two stepchildren, to-wit: Susan James Christopher and Jennifer James Loftis. Any references to my "husband" shall refer to Ian J. James. Any references to my "child" or "children" shall refer to May Wright, Amber Wright Bishop, Robert Wright, Susan James Christopher, and Jennifer James Loftis without distinction to whether they are natural born or born of my husband. I have no other children born to or adopted by me.

Section 2—Funeral and Payment of Taxes, Debts, and Expenses

I have made pre-paid arrangements for direct cremation with Anytown Funeral Home, 300 Elm Street, Anytown, Anystate; Contract # 123456B.

I direct that my Executor pay all my just debts, expenses incurred during my last illness and the costs of administration of my estate be paid as soon as practicable after my death and shall be paid by my Executor out of the assets of my residuary estate. My Executor may, in his sole discretion, pay from my domiciliary estate all or any portion of the costs of ancillary administration and similar proceedings in other jurisdictions.

I direct that my Executor pay out of my residuary estate, without apportionment, all estate, inheritance, succession, and other taxes (together with any penalty thereon), assessed by reason of my death imposed by the Government of the United States, or any state or territory thereof, or by any foreign government or political subdivision hereof, in respect to all property required to be included in my gross estate for estate or like death tax purposes by any of such governments, whether the property passes under this will or otherwise, including property over which I have a power of appointment, without contribution by any recipient of any such property.

Section 3—Right of Disclaimer

Any beneficiary or the legal representative of any deceased beneficiary shall have the right, within the time prescribed by law, to disclaim any benefit or power under my will. When property is to be distributed to the descendants of a person and one such descendant disclaims his interest in all or a portion of such property, the disclaimed interest, determined as if the disclaimant were living at the time of distribution, shall be distributed to the then living descendants of the disclaimant; provided, however, that if the disclaimant has no descendants then living, the interest shall be distributed as if the disclaimant had predeceased the event that results in the distribution of the property.

Exordium Clause—what does this show? It shows that the testator intended to make a will and wasn't just jotting down notes. Formality in a will is important. The more formal, the more likely it will survive a will contest.

Declaration concerning family showing that testator knows the objects of her bounty.

Funeral arrangements—while it may not be the best place for these arrangements, clients like seeing it in their will.

Clause regarding payment of debts—note that this says all "lawful and just debts." The purpose of this wording is to give the personal representative the ability to decline payment of any debt that is frivolous or unlawful, such as a gambling debt.

Apportionment Clause

Disclaimer Clause

(continued)

Figure 5.3   (continued)

This will pre-supposes a community property state. Notice that Bobbie is declaring that she is disposing of her separate property and her share of the community. In addition, she is stating that if she holds a power of appointment in her trust, she is not exercising it.

Disposition of personal property. Notice that it directs that any personal property is not taxed unless it becomes part of the residue of the estate.

Residuary Clause: First to husband

If husband predeceases, then equally to children—Note that this will considers all of her children and her husband's children to be her children for purposes of distribution

If not to children, then to grandchildren, including her stepchildren's children

If no grandchildren, then to descendants

Definition of descendants

Section 4—Disposition of All Property and Power of Appointment

It is my intention by this Will to dispose of my separate property, if any, and also my share of the community property of my husband, IAN J. JAMES, and myself. I do not intend hereby to exercise any power of appointment that I may have.

Section 5—Disposition of Personal Property

Except as provided in any written instructions to my Executor regarding the disposition of personal effects, I give any interest I may have in all personal property, including all of my separate property, if any, and my share of the community personal property of my husband and myself, including but not limited to, automobiles, clothing, jewelry, china, silver, books, pictures and other works of art, household furniture and furnishings and all other items of domestic, household or personal use to my husband, if he survives me. If my husband fails to so survive me, such gift shall lapse and become part of the residuary.

The bequests made by this paragraph shall be free and clear of estate and inheritance taxes, which I direct my Executor to charge against the residue of my estate.

Section 6—Disposition of Residue of Estate

A. I give the residue of my estate, whether real or personal and wherever located, including all property and interests not otherwise disposed of elsewhere in this document that is acquired by me or my estate after the execution of this document, to my husband, IAN J. JAMES, if he survives me.

B. If my husband does not survive me, I give such residue to my children, MAY WRIGHT, AMBER WRIGHT BISHOP, ROBERT WRIGHT, SUSAN JAMES CHRISTOPHER, AND JENNIFER JAMES LOFTIS, and any other child that may be born to or adopted by me at the time of my death, in equal shares, if they survive me.

C. If any of my children does not survive me, I give his or her share of the residue to his or her children, my grandchildren, without regard as to whether they are my biological grandchildren or the biological grandchildren of my husband.

D. If neither of my children nor grandchildren survive me, I give the residue of my estate, whether real or personal and wherever located, including all property and interests not otherwise disposed of elsewhere in this document that is acquired by me or my estate after the execution of this document to my descendants who survive me.

E. Whenever property is to be distributed to the descendants of a person (the "ancestor"), such property shall be divided into equal shares, one share for each then living descendant in the first generation below the ancestor in which at least one descendant is living, and one share for each deceased descendant in such generation who has a descendant then living. Each share created for a living descendant shall be distributed to such descendant. Each share created for a deceased descendant shall be divided and distributed according to the directions in the two preceding sentences until no property remains undistributed.

F. A person who has a relationship by or through legal adoption shall take under this will as if the person had the relationship by or through birth,

(continued)

Figure 5.3 (continued)

except that a person adopted after reaching age twenty-one and descendants of such a person shall not so take.

What constitutes adoption

Section 7—Appointment and Powers of Executor

I nominate and appoint my husband, Ian J. James, to be my Executor. If he should, for any reason, fail to qualify, or having qualified, cease to act in such capacity, I nominate and appoint May Wright, as my husband's successor, upon like terms. If May Wright should, for any reason, fail to qualify, or having qualified, cease to act in such capacity, I nominate and appoint Susan James Christopher, as alternate successor, upon like terms. If administration of my estate should be necessary in any jurisdiction where my Executor is unable to qualify, or if my Executor deems it necessary for any other reason, I give to my Executor the power to designate any individual or corporation with trust powers to serve with my Executor or in my Executor's stead. I request that no security or bond be required of any Executor, except for any corporate Executor named or appointed in the preceding sentence, which shall be required to post security or a bond. References in my will to my "Executor" are to the one or ones acting at the time, except where otherwise specifically provided.

Nomination of Personal Representative, called Executor in this document

Any corporate Executor shall receive for its services the compensation for which it is willing to undertake similar services for others at the time such services are rendered, as evidenced by its published fee schedule in effect from time to time, unless it is willing to agree upon a fee that is less than its customary fee.

I direct that the provisions hereinafter contained with respect to the powers, authorities, discretion, and immunities of my Executor shall be liberally and broadly construed; and I further direct that such powers, authorities, and discretion may be exercised without the joinder, acquiescence, or approval of any beneficiary of my estate, and no person taking any property from my Executor by sale, conveyance, assignment, lease, exchange, or mortgage shall be required to see to the application or distribution of the purchase money or other proceeds, or to inquire as to the authority of my Executor in the premises; and I further direct that in the exercise of such powers, authorities, and discretion, my Executor shall not be liable for any losses to my estate so long as my Executor acts in good faith and upon reasonable premises.

In addition to the powers granted by law, I grant my Executor the powers set forth in Sections _____ of the Anystate Probate Code, as in force from time to time, and I incorporate those Code Sections in my will by this reference. My Executor may select assets for allocation to a particular share as my Executor shall deem to be in the best interests of the beneficiaries of my estate created under this will, and assets allocated to one share need not be of the same character as assets allocated to another share; and, without limiting the generality of the foregoing, my Executor may allocate assets having different income tax bases in such manner, amounts, and proportions as my Executor shall deem appropriate. The powers and discretion granted to my Executor are exercisable only in a fiduciary capacity and may not be used to enlarge or shift any beneficial interest except as an incidental consequence of the discharge of the duties of my Executor. My Executor may distribute tangible

(*continued*)

Figure 5.3 (continued)

personal property passing to a minor to any adult person with whom the minor resides, and that person's receipt shall be a sufficient voucher in the accounts of my Executor.

Section 8—Gifts to Minors and Incompetents

Except as otherwise provided in this will, if any share of my estate shall vest in absolute ownership in any minor, or to a person who is incapacitated by reason of legal incapacity, or physical or mental illness or infirmity, my Executor in his absolute, unreviewable, and uncontrolled judgment and discretion, shall be authorized, in each such case, to hold, administer, invest, and reinvest such share for the benefit of such person or minor during his or her minority or incapacity, and to apply so much of the net income and of the then principal of said share as my Executor in his absolute discretion, may deem necessary to the proper care, maintenance, education, and comfort of such person, or to make such payments to the legal guardian of such person, or to the person with whom such person resides, or directly to such person, or otherwise as my Executor from time to time deems expedient, and to accumulate for the benefit of such minor or incapacitated person any income not applied or paid as aforesaid. In the alternative, my Executor in his absolute, unreviewable, and uncontrolled judgment and discretion is authorized to turn such property over to the Trustee of that certain Trust Agreement described in Section 6 hereinabove to be maintained as part of said Trust Agreement and the duties of the Executor under this Section 8 shall cease.

The term minor shall mean any person who has not reached his or her eighteenth (18) birthday.

The term incapacitated shall mean any person who is under legal disability or by reason of illness, or mental or physical disability is, in the written opinion of two impartial doctors currently practicing medicine, unable to properly manage his or her affairs.

Section 9—Gender and Headings

For simplicity, I may have expressed pronouns and other terms in one number and gender, but where appropriate to the context these terms shall be deemed to include the other number and genders. Any headings herein are for convenience and shall not affect interpretation.

Clause regarding use of gender

Section 10—Partial Invalidity

Should any part, clause, provision, or condition of this Will be held void, invalid, or inoperative, then I direct that such invalidity shall not affect any other provision hereof, which shall be effective as though such invalid revisions had not been made.

Section 11—Simultaneous Death

I shall be deemed for purposes of this will to have survived my husband if we die simultaneously or if there is no sufficient evidence (in the opinion of my Executor) that my husband and I have died otherwise than simultaneously.

Simultaneous death clause in which testator states that she is to have survived her husband. His will's clause shall say that it is presumed that he will have predeceased her.

(continued)

Figure 5.3   (continued)

Section 12—Omitted Heirs and Will Contests

Except as otherwise specified in this Will, I have intentionally and with full knowledge omitted to provide for my heirs at the time of my death. If any beneficiary under this Will or heir at law of mine or person claiming through any of them shall contest or otherwise challenge the validity of this Will or attack any of its provisions or the trust described in Section 6 herein, directly or indirectly, any share or interest in my estate given to such person under this Will is hereby revoked, and such share or interest shall be distributed in the same manner provided herein as if such person had predeceased me.

Omitted heirs and in Terrorem Clause

    IN TESTIMONY WHEREOF, I have set my hand and seal to this my last will and testament consisting of eight (8) typewritten pages, and on all pages of which I have placed my initials for security and identification this _____ day of _____, 2012.

Testimonium Clause

_____(SEAL)
VIRGINIA MASON JAMES

    The testator declared to us, the undersigned, that this instrument, consisting of eight (8) typewritten pages, including the page signed by us as witnesses, was the testator's Will.

    The testator then signed this Will in our presence, all of us being present at the same time.

    The testator appears to us to be over eighteen (18) years of age and of sound mind, and we have no knowledge of any facts indicating that this instrument or any part of it was procured by duress, menace, fraud, or undue influence.

    We understand that this instrument is the testator's Will, and we now subscribe our names as witnesses.

    We declare under penalty of perjury under the laws of the State of Anystate that the foregoing is true and correct.

Attestation Clause

_____
Witness signature

_____
Witness name printed

_____
Witness signature

_____
Witness name printed

THE STATE OF ANYSTATE

COUNTY OF ANYCOUNTY

    Before me, the undersigned authority, on this day personally appeared VIRGINIA MASON JAMES, _____, and _____, known to me to be the testator and the witnesses, respectively, whose names are subscribed to the annexed or foregoing instrument in their respective capacities, and, all of said persons being by me duly sworn, the said BOBBIE BLACK, testator, declared

(continued)

Figure 5.3   (continued)

to me and to the said witnesses in my presence that said instrument is her last will and testament, and that she had willingly made and executed it as her free act and deed; and the said witnesses, each on his oath stated to me, in the presence and hearing of the said testator, that the said testator had declared to them that said instrument is her last will and testament, and that she executed same as such and wanted each of them to sign it as a witness; and upon their oaths each witness stated further that they did sign the same as witnesses in the presence of the said testator and at her request; that she was at that time eighteen years of age or over (or being under such age, was or had been lawfully married, or was then a member of the armed forces of the United States or of an auxiliary thereof or of the Maritime Service) and was of sound mind; and that each of said witnesses was then at least fourteen years of age.

_____
VIRGINIA MASON JAMES,
Testator

_____
Witness

_____
Witness

Subscribed and sworn to before me by the said VIRGINIA MASON JAMES, testator, and by the said _____ and _____, witnesses, this _____ day of _____, 2012.

_____(SEAL)

Notary Public in and
for _____

My Commission Expires: _____

Self-proving affidavit. Must conform to state statute

What Are the Risks of Writing Your Own Will?

We all know that there are a number of books and software available these days that coach you on how to write your own will. But is that a good idea? Why would you do it and what are the risks of doing so?

The first thing to note is that people tend to believe that all wills are "simple." To some degree, lawyers ourselves have fostered that belief because we usually call basic wills "simple wills." You, however, are reading this book and already know that drafting a will is not that simple. A "simple will" is merely the most uncomplicated will we can draft for a client. There is, however, nothing simple about it. It is, despite its basic nature, a complex legal document and it is easier than most people think to cause more harm than good when you draft any legal document, wills included, without understanding what you are doing.

So why else do people draft their own wills? Probably, the biggest factor beyond the belief that it's easy to do is cost. A basic will drafted by your lawyer will cost between $125 and $350 on average. That's per person. So for a couple that is struggling to make ends meet or has to pay for braces or college, or the senior couple that is worried if their retirement assets will last, this could be the sole factor in deciding to buy a form at the local big box office supply store and fill it out.

What are the risks? You can already guess some of them. Before reading further, take a moment to jot down what you think are risks in drafting your own will.

- Most laypeople do not understand what is required to properly execute a will. Unless the will is holographic (remember that means written *totally* in the testator's own hand), a will must be witnessed by *two* competent witnesses. It is not uncommon for laypeople to believe that if they get any document notarized, they are making the document legal. This is not so with wills. A will does not require a notary. It does require two witnesses. What happens when the will is not properly witnessed? In most cases, the will fails. In some states, this is obviated by statute. For example, in Virginia, a statute enacted in 2007 provides that if a will was not properly executed, it may be proved in court to be the decedent's will. Notice, however, that this requires a court action and as we already know, this can be costly, especially if other family members would rather that the purported will was not valid.
- Is the property the layperson is giving in the will a probate asset? It's all well, fine, and good to leave "the bank account at First Union Bank of Anytown" to the local animal shelter. It's admirable. However, what's the outcome of this scenario?

Figure 5.4   Virginia Statutes §64.1-49.1. Writings Intended as Wills, Etc.

Although a document, or a writing added upon a document, was not executed in compliance with §64.1-49, the document or writing shall be treated as if it had been executed in compliance with §64.1-49 if the proponent of the document or writing establishes by clear and convincing evidence that the decedent intended the document or writing to constitute (i) the decedent's will, (ii) a partial or complete revocation of the will, (iii) an addition to or an alteration of the will, or (iv) a partial or complete revival of his formerly revoked will or of a formerly revoked portion of the will.

The remedy granted by this section (i) may not be used to excuse compliance with any requirement for a testator's signature, except in circumstances where two persons mistakenly sign each other's will, or a person signs the self-proving certificate to a will instead of signing the will itself and (ii) is available only in proceedings brought in a circuit court under the appropriate provisions of this title, filed within one year from the decedent's date of death and in which all interested persons are made parties.

- Billy Budd leaves "my bank account at First Union Bank of Anytown to the Anytown Humane Society for care of the dogs and cats at the shelter." Billy owns the account as "joint tenants with right of survivorship" with his daughter Audrey. Does the Humane Society receive the property upon Billy's death? No, because the bank account is a non-probate asset and upon Billy's death, the proceeds of the account automatically belong to Audrey. It is very common for laypeople to draft wills that purport to give property that is either a non-probate asset or is not even theirs to give. For example, "I want the Colt 45 I gave my son Billy Budd Jr. to be given to his son Trey Budd when Trey turns 13." Two problems arise with this attempt at a testamentary gift. First, "I want" can be construed as **precatory language** and therefore may be considered only a suggestion and not a requirement. Second, and most importantly, the gun doesn't belong to Billy, it belongs to his son. He can't bequest the gun to his grandson because it's not his to give away.

- Laypeople fail to address second marriages and the consequences of leaving everything to "my spouse." Take this scenario: Calista Carter had two children when she married John Carter. John also had two children previously. They had no children together. They bought wills on the Internet and filled them out, her will leaving everything to John if he survived her and then everything to her children if he didn't. John's will was substantially the same. Calista dies and John inherits all of Calista's property. When John dies two years later, John's children get all of the property including that property that John inherited from Calista. Calista's children receive nothing. Is this what they intended when they drafted their own wills? Chances are not.

- Laypeople do not properly provide for disabled children. We will discuss special needs trusts in a later chapter; however, at this point, it is important to note that an inheritance by a disabled child of any age will likely disqualify him or her from receiving government assistance. Government assistance is an all or nothing system so while the inheritance may be small, even $1 over the allowable amount will likely cause all benefits to be discontinued. This is most certainly not what was intended.

- Laypeople do not think about the actual value of their assets. It is not uncommon for folks even with a few million dollars in assets to believe that a "simple will" is adequate. While the probate estate is not enough to trigger an estate tax by itself, the non-probate assets added to the probate estate often bring a person's total assets above the estate tax exemption amount. They fail to provide for the need for estate tax planning so their estates pay as much as half of those assets that are over the exemption to the Internal Revenue Service (IRS) instead of those assets going to their children and grandchildren. For example, John died in 2000 with $1,500,000, his wife having predeceased him. His estate would have had to pay the IRS a quarter million dollars.

- Laypeople do not consider the fact that their young children may in fact inherit a large sum of money that will be distributed to them at age 18 because the "simple will" does not provide any mechanism to keep the money in trust for them until they are older and more capable of handling the funds.

- Laypeople with businesses fail to determine the fate of their business upon their death. This often requires far more than a basic will and should be discussed with business partners, accountants, and lawyers to assure that the business is continued or wound up and that the business owner's family is provided for. For example: Ryan Seascape owns a successful beach umbrella company with his partner Jim Bookman. Ryan and his wife, Lea, buy do-it-yourself wills from the big box office supply store and leave everything to each other. Ryan dies in a boating accident the following year. The business he had with Jim is worth $10 million. Lea, as executor of Ryan's will, demands that Jim pay over Ryan's share of the net proceeds and capital of the business to Ryan's estate. Of course, this is almost impossible for any business to do. Assets are often tied up in production and supplies, receivables, and goodwill of the business. To give Lea the assets would likely destroy the company. Ryan (and Jim) should have taken better precautions and prepared for business succession through proper planning.

- Laypeople believe that online programs are positively compliant and take their state's rules and regulations into account. One such program makes you a fine will (and possibly trust) legal in the State of California and references community property throughout the document (and what have you already learned about community property states?) and another makes you a will compliant with the laws of the State of New York. Is this in the layperson's best interest if that person lives in Nebraska?

- In addition, all of these websites have significant disclaimer clauses. One such site has the following information: "Therefore, if you need legal advice for your specific problem, or if your specific problem is too complex to be addressed by our tools, you should consult a licensed attorney in your area." How does the layperson even know their problem is too complex? That's what a lawyer is for. Most clients do not understand the complexity of their issues until they discuss it within the confines of the client interview process.

- People should think very carefully before doing their own legal documents. The law is fraught with people that draft their own wills, contracts, and leases to save money and wind up costing themselves or their families many thousands of dollars in legal fees to correct the errors made because someone wanted to save a few dollars. It is a common lawyer "joke" that we love when people do their own legal work because it funds our childrens' college tuitions and our vacations. However, the reality is that seeing the poor work laypeople do when they draft their own documents is very sad and sometimes heartbreaking.

Execution of the Will

All wills, with the exception of holographic and nuncupative wills, require that the testator's signature be witnessed. The process of having the testator and witnesses sign the will in each others' presence is called "execution."

THE PROFESSIONAL PARALEGAL

The paralegal's duties regarding a will's execution is dependent upon his or her supervising attorney's requirements. In some offices, it is a paralegal's responsibility to act as one of the witnesses to the will or as the notary. In others, the paralegal's duties may be more detailed. A paralegal may be required to greet and settle the client in a conference room or firm library, have the client read over the will, then either witness or notarize the will, and otherwise be present during all phases of the will's execution.

The following checklist will be helpful should the paralegal be given the greater responsibility and have the opportunity to insure that all proper formalities of execution are carried out:

- Is the testator of legal age, usually 18 years old?
- Does the testator appear to be of sound mind at the time of execution?
- Is someone available to sign on behalf of and at the testator's direction should the testator be physically unable to sign? If the testator cannot sign, the person signing must be directed by the testator to do so. After signing for the testator, the person that did so should write that he or she wrote at the testator's direction and then sign his or her own name. If this occurs, the paralegal should have prepared the will so that this clause is evident.
- In general, the testator should let the people in the room at the time of execution know that he or she is signing the will as this shows the testator's intent to execute a will. It is not necessary for the testator to read the will to the witnesses since they are only witnessing his or her signature and do not have to know the contents of the will for the will to be valid. This may be done in the form of a question by the attorney asking the testator, if he or she is signing a will instead so that the testator replies in the affirmative.
- Depending upon state law, the testator should initial the bottom of each page of the will before signing. Initials are used to insure that a family member or friend does not substitute new pages to the will after it has been executed. This should *never* be done in New York State, however, since initials are considered a form of signature. In New York, any form of signature indicates the end of the will. If the first page is initialed, the will may be considered invalid since "the end" of the document will be page one, hardly a complete will.
- Are the proper number of witnesses available? Most states require two witnesses that are of sound mind and meet the age requirement for witnesses in that state. Witnesses that may be beneficiaries of the will or who are related to the testator are called *interested witnesses*. It is best not to have a relative of the testator sign as a witness since the relative may be a beneficiary or potential beneficiary to the will. Such a signature may invalidate the bequest to that beneficiary, or in some circumstances, invalidate the

Figure 5.5   Washington Statute RCW 11.12.160. Interested Witness—Effect on Will

(1) An interested witness to a will is one who would receive a gift under the will.

(2) A will or any of its provisions is not invalid because it is signed by an interested witness. Unless there are at least two other subscribing witnesses to the will who are not interested witnesses, the fact that the will makes a gift to a subscribing witness creates a rebuttable presumption that the witness procured the gift by duress, menace, fraud, or undue influence.

(3) If the presumption established under subsection (2) of this section applies and the interested witness fails to rebut it, the interested witness shall take so much of the gift as does not exceed the share of the estate that would be distributed to the witness if the will were not established.

(4) The presumption established under subsection (2) of this section has no effect other than that stated in subsection (3) of this section.

Figure 5.6   Missouri Revised Statutes Section 474.330—Who May Witness Will—Effect of Interest in Will

474.330. 1. Any person competent to be a witness generally in this state may act as attesting witness to a will.

2. No will is invalidated because attested by an interested witness; but any interested witness shall, unless the will is also attested by two disinterested witnesses, forfeit so much of the provisions therein made for him as in the aggregate exceeds in value, as of the date of the testator's death, what he would have received had the testator died intestate.

3. No attesting witness is interested by reason of being a creditor of the estate or because he is named executor in the will or unless the will gives to him some personal and beneficial interest.

entire will. Note that in Washington State, shown as Figure 5.5 below, the signature of an interested witness does not invalidate the will or its provision giving the gift to the beneficiary but creates a rebuttable presumption that the gift was procured by fraud or duress. That means potential court hearing, which means time and money that an estate may not have to spend. See that in Missouri, however, the provisions pertaining to that interested witness are indeed invalidated unless two uninterested witnesses also signed.

- The witnesses and notary must be physically present in the room to watch the testator sign the will. It is important that signatories are not running in and out of the room or answering a phone or checking smartphones for text messages (or worse, Facebook). Remember that, in some states, the witnesses must also sign in each other's presence, making it imperative that both witnesses are present at the same time to watch each other sign. As a matter of practice, it is not unusual for a receptionist who is still trying to cover the reception desk to be a witness, often causing the witness to not really be present when the testator or the other witness is signing. The paralegal should prevent this if at all possible and make sure that everyone is present in the room and paying attention. A court could invalidate a will because the witness had his or her back turned to the testator when either the testator was signing, or when the witness was signing if a family member chooses to contest the will. Not being physically present is a definite ground for invalidation, should anyone decide to contest the will.

- Remember that while a self-proof affidavit or clause is not necessary to validate a will, it is best to have one to prevent having to look for the witnesses when the testator dies some years later. The only time a witness has to attend court for a probate matter is during a will contest. The paralegal should insure that someone other than a witness is available to notarize the will. This person must also be present during the execution and watch both the testator and witnesses sign the document. As per most state laws, the notary should not be related to the testator. In some states, the notary should not be related to the witnesses or the beneficiaries either.

Where to Keep the Will After Execution

Lawyers' opinions concerning where clients' wills should be kept vary greatly. It is best to leave the original will in one of five possible places:

- If the lawyer has a vault, he or she may keep his or her clients' wills in it. Many lawyers decline to keep clients' wills on the premises, not wanting the responsibility of housing the wills for fear of loss due to theft or fire. A lawyer who does store clients' wills should have a fireproof safe. In addition, if a lawyer keeps the will, the client's family will have to contact the lawyer to retrieve it, and the family may feel obligated to use that lawyer for the probate of the estate even if that is not what they would prefer. Some lawyers do not want the appearance of soliciting business, so won't keep the wills on premises. Other lawyers keep clients' wills for precisely this reason. They hope the families will hire them for business upon the deaths of the testators. Still other lawyers will retain clients' wills as a service to clients that do not want the responsibility, or do not have a safe place, such as a safe deposit box, to keep the documents themselves. It is important for the paralegal to be informed about his or her supervising lawyer's preference concerning this matter, so the client may be properly advised.

- An alternative to having the lawyer retain the document is to give it to the personal representative for safekeeping. Some clients give the will to the personal representative since that is the person who will most need the document upon the client's death. It is important, however, to insure that the personal representative has a safe place for the will. If the personal representative is a bank, for example, the will may be kept with the bank's other important documents, usually in the bank vault. If a safe place cannot be provided, however, the personal representative should not retain the document. One aspect of giving the will to the personal representative is often overlooked—that the client may decide to amend or revoke the will at a later date, sometimes changing the personal representative's designation. The client may be embarrassed about asking the personal representative for the will. If it appears that a client will be embarrassed or afraid to ask the personal representative for the will, the document should not be left in the personal representative's possession. Still another aspect of leaving the will with someone other than the client or a corporate personal representative (such as a bank's trust department) is that the personal representative, especially if a relative, may be tempted to alter or even destroy the document if it does not appear to favor whom the personal representative believes it should. If the client has any belief or fear that the designated personal representative will be unhappy with the client's gifts, that personal representative should not retain control of the document. In addition, the lawyer may want to counsel the client to choose a more trustworthy personal representative.

- The will may be deposited in the client's safe deposit box. This may not be the best possible avenue to take, however, since the will may not as accessible as it would otherwise be. When a testator dies, the bank is usually required to seal the safe deposit box as soon as it receives notification of the death. This may delay probate proceedings since an order for permission to open the box must be obtained. This may be a simple task in some jurisdictions but a more cumbersome and time-consuming task in others. Once the order is received, bank officials will often accompany the family member to the vault, and inventory the items found in the box when it was opened. The person that asked to have the box opened may only take the will from the box. After the will is taken, the box will be resealed until the personal representative has the authority to access the box again. In spite of the difficulties that may occur if the will is kept in a safe deposit box, this is often the only secure method of filing that a testator has and should not be discouraged, although the ramifications must be thoroughly explained.

- In some states, the will can be filed with the clerk of the court. A receipt for the will is given, and whoever presents the receipt to the clerk may retrieve it as long as the testator is alive. Once the testator dies, the probate court keeps the original will and gives copies to the personal representative. Some people do not like this method of housing a will since it essentially puts a will on public file while it is still ambulatory. For those testators that do not have a safe place to deposit the will, however, it is a viable option.

- The client can always take the will and all copies home. This method is only recommended when the client can assure that the will can be placed in a fireproof box or safe. Most clients, however, do not house their documents properly, so it is important to have the client counseled on the importance of keeping the will in a safe, fireproof, and watertight place. (Believe it or not, the refrigerator is considered a good place if the items are kept water- and airtight.)

SUMMARY

A paralegal's duties concerning the initial client interview vary from office to office. In some offices, the attorney meets with the clients alone, while in others, the paralegal is invited to sit in and take notes. If the paralegal is invited to the client interview, it is very important for the paralegal to make note of all names, addresses, dates, information concerning family and friends that is offered, and information about all assets and liabilities. The paralegal's observations will be invaluable to the attorney concerning the client's demeanor as well. How the client's estate plan, memorializing the client's desires and needs, is drafted is dependent upon what information is received from the client. A paralegal's ability to glean all important information is essential to drafting a good estate plan for the client. It is a necessary skill for a paralegal to talk to clients so that the client will obtain a level of comfort with the law office staff. A paralegal must always comport himself or herself with professionalism and project that

professionalism to the client. Law office staff should always treat clients with the utmost respect although some clients may be difficult, especially those who are older. The client must always feel that their matters will be held in the strictest of confidence.

A paralegal's duties in an office that relies on estate planning may very well be to draft the initial documents for the supervising attorney's review. A paralegal must always insure that the documents comport with state statute.

After the will and other supporting documents are drafted, the document must be executed. To execute legal documents means to have them signed with all requisite formalities, so as to insure validity. After the documents are executed, they must be stored in a safe place. Supervising attorneys have different views concerning what constitutes a safe place. Some possible safe places are bank safe deposit boxes or in vaults at a bank, at the client's home, or in the supervising attorney's office. Another possible depository is with the court clerk.

KEY TERMS

exordium clause
testimonium clause

attestation clause
power of appointment

demonstrative bequests
in terrorem clause

REVIEW QUESTIONS

1. What is an exordium clause? What is its purpose?
2. What is an attestation clause?
3. What is a demonstrative bequest?
4. Where should a client keep a will for safekeeping and why?
5. Why should a will include a self-proving affidavit? What is the risk of not having one?

6. What are some of the tasks a paralegal may be asked to handle concerning the drafting and execution of a will?
7. What is an in terrorem clause?
8. What is a testimonium clause?
9. Must a notary assist in the signing of a will?
10. What is an apportionment clause?

PROJECT

1. Go to your local law library and find a form book on will drafting specific to your state. Draft the appropriate simple will for yourself. Please note that this document should not ever be executed

without having it properly reviewed by a professional. *You should not do a will for a friend or family member as you would be practicing law without a license, a criminal offense.*

2. Refer to the wills in Appendix B and answer the following questions about the various wills. Make note of any very well-drafted clauses and of any you thought were poorly drafted and why:
   - Which clause is the exordium clause?
   - Which one provides for guardianship?
   - Does the will provide for a trust?
   - Is there a demonstrative bequest?
   - Is there an apportionment clause?
   - Is there an in terrorem clause?
   - Does the will clearly state the objects of the testator's bounty?
   - Does the will have a self-proving affidavit?

MyLegalStudiesLab™   http://www.mylegalstudieslab

MYLEGALSTUDIESLAB VIRTUAL LAW OFFICE EXPERIENCE ASSIGNMENTS

Complete the pre-test, study plan, and post-test for this chapter and answer the Legal Applications questions as assigned.

These will help you confirm your mastery of the concepts and their application to legal scenarios. Then, complete the Virtual Law Office assignments as assigned by your instructor. These assignments are designed to develop your workplace skills and result in producing documents for inclusion in your portfolio.

Chapter six

ADVANCE DIRECTIVES

OBJECTIVES

At the end of this chapter, the student will understand:

- the history of the right to die
- what advance directives are
- the purpose of a living will
- the purpose of a do-not-resuscitate order (**DNRO**)
- the purpose of health-care surrogates and proxies
- the purpose of durable powers of attorney
  - What the Physician Orders for Life-Sustaining Treatment Paradigm Program is
  - What death with dignity statutes are
- what anatomical gifts are and how they are made

Illness and death and dying. These topics may be more difficult to discuss with a client than talking about wills or trusts because this area impacts directly upon the client's core beliefs. The client must confront his or her beliefs regarding debilitating illnesses, vegetative states, and the very act of dying.

A client may come into the law office and blithely say "I need a living will," but not understand the ramifications of executing one. Frankly, most clients don't really even understand what a "living will" is, which is no fault of their own; the terminology for advance directives, as they are properly classified, is a jumble. The client may have heard about them from family, friends, or coworkers. The newspapers, especially the business sections, are filled with seminars on estate planning and why it is necessary to have wills, trusts, powers of attorney, and living wills. During a recent hospital visit, a client was undoubtedly asked if one had been prepared for him or her (as is required by federal law). The client may have even gone to a free seminar in which the opportunity to fill out a living will was provided. The terminology isn't even the same from jurisdiction to jurisdiction. No wonder everyone is confused!

History of the Right to Die

Once upon a time, the question of whether a person had the right to die was a foregone conclusion. If a person became gravely ill, and there was little a physician could do, that person was made comfortable and was left to die in peace, often at home with friends and family in attendance. This was most often the norm and not the exception. When medical science improved to the point of being able to prolong the process of dying through machinery, medications, and complicated surgeries, the right to die and management of the dying became a greater issue.

(**Note:** The cases described here, *Cruzan, Anderson,* and *Schiavo,* are reproduced in Appendix A "Important Cases Concerning the Right to Die.")

This delicate issue first came to national attention with the plight of Karen Ann Quinlan. In the summer of 1974, Quinlan had told her boyfriend and two other friends that she was going to die young. In April of 1975, she was admitted in a New Jersey hospital, in a coma of unknown origins (although she had ingested alcohol and tranquilizers that evening). Her parents requested that Karen be removed from the ventilator that assisted her breathing, and the hospital refused because it believed its obligation was to keep her alive regardless. In September of 1975, her parents instituted legal proceedings to have her removed from the ventilator. In March of 1976, the Supreme Court in New Jersey concluded that Karen had a right to privacy, which included her right to be removed from the machine.

THE PROFESSIONAL PARALEGAL

While the legal processes are within the purview of the supervising attorney, the paralegal is in the perfect position to assess the client's understanding of these matters and to brief the attorney in advance about any questions and concerns the client may have. Perhaps the result of the initial contact between client and paralegal will persuade the lawyer to counsel the client differently. The lawyer may ask the client to talk to his or her family, doctors, clergy, and other potentially interested parties *before* executing any advance directive. THE PARALEGAL MUST ALWAYS REMEMBER, HOWEVER, NOT TO ENGAGE IN GIVING ADVICE TO THE CLIENT!

The next case that brought this issue to the forefront of public debate, forcing more state legislatures to shine a brighter light on the issue, was *Cruzan v. Director, Missouri Health Dept.*, 497 U.S. 261 (1990).

Facts relating to Nancy Cruzan:

- Car accident in January of 1983.
- U.S. Supreme Court decision in 1990.
- A new case was filed in the Circuit Court of Jasper County on August 30, 1990 and Jasper County Circuit Court Judge Charles E. Teel, Jr., ordered removal of the tubes on December 10, 1990.
- Nancy died December 26, 1990, shortly after her tubes were removed.

In this case, Nancy Cruzan was in a *permanent vegetative state* for five years after a serious car accident. A persistent vegetative state is defined as the patient showing no evidence of awareness of self or environment, and an inability to interact with others; no evidence of sustained, reproducible, purposeful, or voluntary behavioral responses to visual, auditory, tactile, or noxious stimuli; and no evidence of language comprehension or expression (Persistent Vegetative State & Minimally Conscious State: Audrius V. Plioplys MD, FRCPC, FAAP, CMD, AMDA's 29th Annual Symposium, Dallas, Texas, March 17, 2006). Cruzan was nourished by a feeding and hydration (gastro) tube. Cruzan's coworkers claimed that on different occasions before the accident, Cruzan told them that she did not want to be maintained on life support if she ever became a "vegetable." Cruzan's parents brought a lawsuit in an effort to have their daughter's life support removed. Ultimately, Cruzan was maintained on life support because her statements to her coworkers were not specific as to Cruzan's wishes concerning the withdrawal of artificial hydration and nutrition and Cruzan's parents could not prove by clear and convincing evidence that Nancy Cruzan would have not wanted to be kept on life support.

Concern about a person's "right to die" has raised some interesting questions for courts to answer. In the not so distant past, courts often only had to determine if a medical care practitioner was responsible for the "wrongful death" of a patient. Wrongful death is a claim of negligence made against the physician, also known as medical malpractice. A negligence claim requires proof of a duty of care to the patient, a breach of that duty, causation, and damages. The medical care practitioner would be liable only for harms giving rise to damages proximately caused by the negligent act. It was presumed that if a physician didn't do everything possible to save a patient, she could be found negligent of her duties as a medical provider.

Courts now, however, also wrestle with the issue of "wrongful living," which occurs when the patient, through what is proper and competent medical care, is kept alive. It is difficult to define the harm in such a case, as the Supreme Court of Ohio stated in October 1996 in *Anderson v. St. Francis–St. George Hospital, Inc.*, 671 N.E. 2d 225.

The Ohio court explained it this way:

> Because a person has a right to die, a medical professional who has been trained to preserve life, and who has taken an oath to do so, is relieved of that duty and is required by a legal duty to accede to a patient's express refusal of medical treatment. Whether intentional or negligent, interference with a person's legal right to die would constitute a breach of that duty to honour the wishes of the patient.

The latest court battle regarding the right to die concerns Terry Schiavo. This case was on the front page of every newspaper and on every newscast nationwide for a number of months. Clients who may not remember a neighbor's name all seem to know the name of "that woman in Florida, Schiavo." Terry Schiavo was brain damaged following a heart attack in 1990, when oxygen was cut off to her brain causing a persistent vegetative state. Her husband and guardian, Michael Schiavo, petitioned the Pinellas County, Florida County Court to allow him to have her feeding tube removed. Schiavo's parents vehemently disagreed and fought to have the life sustaining treatments maintained. The Court, in 2003, after a long battle with Schiavo's parents, permitted the removal. Florida Governor Jeb Bush intervened and the Florida Legislature passed a law commonly known as "Terri's Law," which permitted Bush to order the feeding tubes reinserted. Terri's Law stated that the only way a feeding tube or other life-prolonging measures could be withheld was through a living will or similar written document, or if there was proof by clear and convincing evidence of express consent to withholding such measures while competent to consent, as in the Supreme Court decision in Cruzan. The law would not have allowed parents, spouses, adult children, or other family members to have the tubes of a minor or incompetent person removed. On September 23, 2004, the Florida Supreme Court struck down Terri's Law as unconstitutional. The unanimous Court stated, "It is without question an invasion of the authority of the judicial branch for the Legislature to pass a law that allows the executive branch to interfere with the final judicial determination in a case."

While more Americans are aware of this important issue, the question remains, however, if Americans are doing anything about it. This question comes up often during the client consultation and clients are as confused about what to do as ever.

A poll conducted by the Pew Research Center for the People and the Press published on February 1, 2011 found that 7% of Internet users look online for information about end-of-life decisions but that "women, non-Hispanic whites, younger adults, and those with higher levels of education and income are more likely than other demographic groups to gather health information online." A prior study from the Pew Research Center for the People and the Press conducted from November 9 to November27, 2005, and written about again by Pew in August 2009, found that only 3 in 10 people or 29% now have a living will, although that is much higher than it was in 1990 (12%). Among married couples, 69% have talked with their spouse about end-of-life care compared to 51% in 1990. The Pew Research Center found that those who had to make end-of-life decisions, or dealt with illnesses in the prior five years, were more likely to have made decisions about their own end-of-life care afterward.

While not preparing documents, people are, however, talking about end-of-life care. According to a Pew Research Center's Social & Demographic Trends project, "among those ages 65 and older with at least one living child, 63% have talked to their children about how to handle their medical care if they can no longer make their own decisions; 35% have not discussed this with their children. Older adults are more likely to have discussed their will and what to do with family belongings than they are to have discussed end-of-life medical decisions (76% have discussed their will with their children)." Elderly parents bring up the subject 70% of the time while their children bring it up only 10% of the time.

The 2005 Pew Research Center poll also found that by more than eight-to-one (84%–10%), the American public approved of laws letting terminally ill patients make the decision about whether to be kept alive through medical treatment compared to 79% in 1990, which the Pew Research Center found to be a "small but significant increase." The poll also found that 70% said that patients should "sometimes be allowed to die" and that only 22% thought that doctors should always try to save a patient. Additionally, the poll found that, while Americans were evenly divided over physician-assisted suicide, they overwhelmingly support laws allowing patients to make decisions about whether they should be kept alive with artificial means. Newer studies question the government's role in these decisions however, and so the arena of end-of-life care is likely to remain in flux as long as the health-care debate continues.

How does the patient, then, express his or her wishes? Nancy Cruzan told coworkers and still wound up on life support. What is the best way to ensure that a patient's determination concerning his or her medical treatment is followed? The only surefire way to ensure that a client's expressions are actualized is to have the client execute various **advance directives**. The importance of these documents may best be depicted by various statistics regarding America's population and the need for care among an aging population:

- The U.S. Census Bureau reported that on April 1, 2010, the number of Americans age 65 and older was 40.3 million. The 2010 census indicated that 71,991 Americans were age 100 or older. Compare that with the approximately 3500 the U.S. had in 1960. (Source: The Older Population: 2010, 2010 Census Briefs, United States Census Bureau, November 2011.)

- The states with the greatest projected age of 85+ from 2007 to 2030 are Alaska (+297%), Nevada (+176%), Arizona (+135%), Wyoming (+126%), and

New Mexico (+123%), according to the AARP Public Policy Institute. The Institute also found that the same age group was projected to be more than double during that time period in Virginia, Vermont, Colorado, and Texas. (The Institute's source documents were various U.S. Census Bureau reports.)

Advance directives are witnessed written documents or oral statements containing instructions concerning a person's health. It should be noted that in almost all instances, these documents should be written to avoid complications. Most jurisdictions require the statements to be in writing in any case, and it is difficult to get a hospital or nursing facility risk manager to accept anything but a written document.

In this chapter, we will discuss the following major advance directives: living wills, do-not-resuscitate orders (DNRO), health care surrogates and proxies, durable powers of attorney, POLST (the Physician Orders for Life-Sustaining Treatment Paradigm Program), death with dignity statutes, and anatomical gifts (organ donation).

Living Wills

A **living will** is a declaration that directs the kind of medical care a person wants in the event that person suffers from a terminal condition, or is in a persistent vegetative state. Most clients refer to this document as their ability to ensure that they can have life-prolonging procedures either withheld or withdrawn. Most commonly they refer to it as the "pull the plug" document. However, a person may also execute a living will expressing that he or she wants life-prolonging procedures, effectively preventing family members from getting permission to withdraw life support, even though there may not be a written declaration stating that life support should be withdrawn.

A *life-prolonging procedure* is usually defined as any treatment, procedure, or intervention that uses mechanical or artificial means to restore, sustain, or replace a bodily function without which the individual's life would cease (such as breathing). The definition also applies to a patient with a terminal condition if the procedure would only serve to prolong the process of dying. It does not include the administration of medication or procedures that serve to provide comfort or care, or alleviate the individual's pain.

A *terminal condition* is one caused by injury, disease, or illness from which there is no reasonable probability of recovery, and in which without treatment the individual will die, or be in a *persistent vegetative state* (PVS). A PVS is characterized by the absence of voluntary action or cognitive behavior and the inability to communicate or interact with the environment in a purposeful manner. This type of advance directive is called a "living" will because it takes effect during the life of the individuals who executed them, but is sadly misnamed. The term "living will" itself causes much confusion among clients who believe the document is, in fact, a will, as in a last will and testament. This type of advance directive has been enacted in approximately 80% of the states.

Requirements for a Living Will's Validity

Each jurisdiction has its own specific requirements and it is difficult for one textbook to go into details for each jurisdiction's provisions, but the following list illustrates the general requirements for a living will. A paralegal will have to follow and use the applicable state statute and form. If a jurisdiction has a promulgated form, it must be used; if the form is recommended, the supervising attorney may use a different format and the paralegal should use his or her supervising attorney's preferred form.

- name, address, and telephone number of the declarant (the individual executing the living will)
- statement that the declarant is willfully and voluntarily making his or her desire known that he or she does not want life to be artificially prolonged in the event that there is no medical probability of recovery from an incurable injury, disease, or illness that is terminal and that use of artificial, extraordinary, extreme, or radical medical or surgical means or procedures will only serve to prolong the moment of death and that the declarant's physician has determined that death is imminent
- statement that the declarant wants life-prolonging procedures to be withheld or withdrawn and that he or she be permitted to die naturally and with dignity
- statement that the directive will be honored by the declarant's family and physicians in the absence of the declarant's ability to give directions
- statement holding harmless any person, hospital, or medical facility carrying out the directive
- signature of witnesses and declarant, and the date signed
- statement concerning HIPAA regulations. *HIPAA* refers to the Health Insurance Portability and Accountability Act of 1996 in which a patient's health and records privacy is regulated. HIPAA regulations dictate what institutions and which people have the right to a patient's "protected health information" and therefore, most attorneys now make reference to an agent's authority to obtain such information pursuant to the HIPAA regulations

Living wills may also include the following requirements:

- the date and notification of the diagnosis given by the physician
- name, address, and telephone number of treating physician, if there is one; and of the medical facility, if there is one
- statement that if the declarant is pregnant, the directive will have no force or effect during such pregnancy
- notary public's acknowledgment

In the following examples, note the similarities and the differences in the recommended statutory language of each jurisdiction.

Do Not Resuscitate Orders

Another advance directive is the do not resuscitate order or **DNRO**. Although state laws vary widely on this matter, there are similarities from state to state. Most DNR statutes are very specific regarding the language to be used. Following state statute, administrative guidelines and orders will be very important.

In general, the DNRO may only be executed by a patient with a terminal condition and in most cases is prepared by the patient's physician, not her attorney. This contrasts with a living will since the latter document may be prepared by an attorney on behalf of a perfectly healthy individual in anticipation of that person contracting a terminal illness or injury sometime in the future. A DNRO may not.

The DNRO declares that the patient does not want resuscitation efforts to be initiated if the patient suffers cardiac arrest or respiratory failure and for whom resuscitation is not warranted. The terminal condition of the patient, as determined by the requisite number of physicians (usually two), will be stated on the face of the document. The patient or his or her surrogate, if allowed by state law, must sign the document.

The DNRO is usually drafted on colored paper (often yellow) and will say "DO NOT RESUSCITATE" in large letters. It is most often mandated that the document be a form printed by a state agency. The effective date will be prominent.

Many patients with DNROs also wear medical identification (EMS) bracelets that alert emergency medical personnel (paramedics) that the DNRO exists. In some states, the bracelet itself will be treated like a DNRO, while in others, it is only evidence that one exists.

If a DNRO meets state requirements, it must be honored. See Figure 6.1 for an example of a DNRO statute.

Figure 6.1   Ohio Administrative Code §3701-62-04 Do-not-resuscitate identification

---

3701-62-04 Do-not-resuscitate identification.

A. The following items are approved as DNR identification:
1. A do-not-resuscitate order documented on the form depicted in appendix A to this rule. This form may be reproduced as needed;
2. Documentation on the form depicted in appendix A to this rule that the person named on the form has executed a declaration that authorizes the withholding or withdrawal of CPR and that has not been revoked pursuant to section 2133.04 of the Revised Code and that the declaration has become operative in accordance with section 2133.03 of the Revised Code;
3. A transparent hospital-type bracelet with an insert as depicted in appendix B to this rule;
4. A necklace bearing both the logo depicted in appendix C to this rule and the person's name. If the person is a "DNR Comfort Care—Arrest" patient as specified in rule 3701-62-05 of the Administrative Code, the necklace shall include the word "arrest" under the logo;
5. A bracelet bearing both the logo depicted in appendix C to this rule and the person's name. If the person is a "DNR Comfort Care—Arrest" patient as specified in rule 3701-62-05 of the Administrative Code, the bracelet shall include the word "arrest" under the logo;
6. A wallet card as depicted in appendix D to this rule. This card may be reproduced as needed; and
7. A printed form of a declaration sold or otherwise distributed in accordance with section 2133.07 of the Revised Code, if the declarant specifies on the form that the declarant wishes to use it as DNR identification.

(continued)

Figure 6.1 (continued)

B. A person is eligible to obtain DNR identification if either of the following circumstances exist:
   1. The person has executed a declaration that authorizes the withholding or withdrawal of CPR and that has not been revoked pursuant to section 2133.04 of the Revised Code, and the declaration has become operative in accordance with section 2133.03 of the Revised Code; or
   2. The person's attending physician, or CNP or CNS as provided in rule 3701-62-02 of the Administrative Code, has issued a current do-not-resuscitate order, in accordance with the do-not-resuscitate protocol specified in rule 3701-62-05 of the Administrative Code, for that person, and has documented the grounds for the order in that person's medical record. The do-not-resuscitate order itself may be used as DNR identification if it is documented on the form depicted in appendix A to this rule.
C. A person may obtain DNR identification in the following manner:
   1. In the case of the form specified in paragraphs (A)(1) and (A)(2) of this rule, by obtaining a copy of the form from a physician, CNP, CNS, or health care facility and completing the form in conjunction with the person's attending physician, or CNP or CNS as provided in rule 3701-62-02 of the Administrative Code.
   2. In the case of the wallet card specified in paragraph (A)(6) of this rule, by doing both of the following:
      a. Obtaining both the form specified in paragraph (A)(1) of this rule and the wallet card from a physician, CNP, CNS, or health care facility; and
      b. Completing both the form and card in conjunction with the person's attending physician, or CNP or CNS as provided in rule 3701-62-02 of the Administrative Code.
   3. In the case of the hospital-type bracelet specified in paragraph (A)(3) of this rule, by doing both of the following:
      a. Obtaining a DNR order from the person's attending physician, or CNP or CNS as provided in rule 3701-62-02 of the Administrative Code; and
      b. Acquiring a bracelet containing a completed insert from a physician, CNP, CNS, health care facility, or pharmacy. The physician, CNP, CNS, facility, or pharmacy shall not issue a bracelet to the person unless the person presents a DNR order.
   4. In the case of the necklace specified in paragraph (A)(4) of this rule and the bracelet specified in paragraph (A)(5) of this rule, by doing both of the following:
      a. Obtaining a DNR order from the person's attending physician, or CNP or CNS as provided in rule 3701-62-02 of the Administrative Code; and
      b. Acquiring a necklace or bracelet from a person or government entity that manufactures or distributes it. The order for the necklace or bracelet shall be accompanied by a copy of the DNR order.
   5. In the case of a declaration form specified in paragraph (A)(7) of this rule, by obtaining and completing the form in the manner required by sections 2133.01 to 2133.15 of the Revised Code and specifying on the form that the declarant wishes to use it as DNR identification. If the declarant wishes to be a "DNR Comfort Care—Arrest" patient, as specified in rule 3701-62-05 of the Administrative Code, the declarant shall include a statement in the declaration that in the event of a cardiac arrest or a respiratory arrest, the declarant is not to receive CPR. Effective: 06/11/2009

   For more on Ohio's DNR rules and other identification information, see http://www.odh.ohio.gov/rules/final/f3701-62.aspx.

Figure 6.2   Massachusetts General Laws. Chapter 201D. Health Care Proxies. Section 2. Appointment of health care agents; execution of proxy; alternate agents.

Section 2.

Every competent adult shall have the right to appoint a health care agent by executing a health care proxy. Said health care proxy shall be in writing signed by such adult or at the direction of such adult in the presence of two other adults who shall subscribe their names as witnesses to such signature. The witnesses shall affirm in writing that the principal appeared to be at least eighteen years of age, of sound mind, and under no constraint or undue influence. No person who has been named as health care agent in a health care proxy shall act as a witness to the execution of such proxy. For the purposes of this section, every adult shall be presumed to be competent and every health care proxy shall be presumed to be properly executed unless a court determines otherwise.

A competent adult may designate an alternate health care agent as part of a valid health care proxy. Said alternate may serve when the designated health care agent is not available, willing, or competent to serve and the designated health care agent is not expected to become available, willing, or competent to make a timely decision given the patient's medical circumstances; or, the health care agent is disqualified from acting on the principal's behalf pursuant to other requirements of this chapter.

Figure 6.3   "Living Will" and Advance Medical Directive for Virginia (effective July 1, 2009)

Virginia Advance Medical Directive

I, **BOBBIE BLACK**, willfully and voluntarily make known my wishes in the event that I am incapable of making an informed decision, as follows:

I understand that my advance directive may include the selection of an agent in addition to setting forth my choices regarding health care. The term **"health care"** means the furnishing of services to any individual for the purpose of preventing, alleviating, curing, or healing human illness, injury, or physical disability, including but not limited to medications; surgery; blood transfusions; chemotherapy; radiation therapy; admission to a hospital, nursing home, assisted living facility, or other health care facility; psychiatric or other mental health treatment; and life-prolonging procedures and palliative care.

The phrase **"incapable of making an informed decision"** means unable to understand the nature, extent, and probable consequences of a proposed health care decision; unable to make a rational evaluation of the risks and benefits of a proposed health care decision as compared with the risks and benefits of alternatives to that decision; or unable to communicate such understanding in any way.

The determination that I am incapable of making an informed decision shall be made by my attending physician and a second physician or licensed clinical psychologist after a personal examination of me and shall be certified in writing. The second physician or licensed clinical psychologist shall not be otherwise currently involved in my treatment, unless such independent second physician or licensed clinical psychologist is not reasonably available. Such certification shall be required before health care is provided, continued, withheld, or withdrawn; before any named agent shall be granted authority to make health care decisions on my behalf; and before, or as soon as reasonably

(continued)

Figure 6.3 (continued)

practicable after, health care is provided, continued, withheld, or withdrawn, and every 180 days thereafter while the need for health care continues.

    If at any time I am determined to be incapable of making an informed decision, I shall be notified, to the extent I am capable of receiving such notice, that such a determination has been made before health care is provided, continued, withheld, or withdrawn. Such notice also shall be provided, as soon as practical, to my named agent or person authorized by §54.1-2986 of the *Code of Virginia* to make health care decisions on my behalf. If I am later determined to be capable of making an informed decision by a physician, in writing, upon personal examination, then any further health care decisions will require my informed consent.

    This advance directive shall not terminate in the event of my disability.

Section I: Appointment of Agent

I hereby appoint the following as my primary agent to make health care decisions on my behalf as authorized in this document:

    Name of Primary Agent: DONALD BLACK
    Telephone: (000) 555-1212
    Address:

    If the above-named primary agent is not reasonably available or is unable or unwilling to act as my agent, then I appoint the following as successor agent, to serve in that capacity:

    Name of Successor Agent: TINA BLACK
    Telephone: (000) 555-1111
    Address:

    I hereby grant to my agent named above full power and authority to make health care decisions on my behalf as described below whenever I have been determined to be incapable of making an informed decision. My agent's authority is effective as long as I am incapable of making an informed decision.

    In exercising the power to make health care decisions on my behalf, my agent shall follow my desires and preferences as stated in this document or as otherwise known to my agent. My agent shall be guided by my medical diagnosis and prognosis and any information provided by my physicians as to the intrusiveness, pain, risks, and side effects associated with treatment or non-treatment. My agent shall not make any decision regarding my health care which he or she knows, or upon reasonable inquiry ought to know, is contrary to my religious beliefs or my basic values, whether expressed orally or in writing. If my agent cannot determine what health care choice I would have made on my own behalf, then my agent shall make a choice for me based upon what he or she believes to be in my best interests.

    My agent shall not be liable for the costs of health care that he or she authorizes, based solely on that authorization.

Section II: Powers of My Agent

(CROSS THROUGH ANY LANGUAGE YOU DO NOT WANT AND ADD ANY LANGUAGE YOU DO WANT.)

    The powers of my agent shall include the following:

A. To consent to or refuse or withdraw consent to any type of health care, treatment, surgical procedure, diagnostic procedure, medication, and the use of mechanical or other procedures that affect any bodily function, including, but not limited to, artificial respiration, artificially administered nutrition and hydration, and cardiopulmonary resuscitation. This authorization

(continued)

Figure 6.3   (continued)

specifically includes the power to consent to the administration of dosages of pain-relieving medication in excess of recommended dosages in an amount sufficient to relieve pain, even if such medication carries the risk of addiction or of inadvertently hastening my death;

B. To request, receive, and review any information, verbal or written, regarding my physical or mental health, including but not limited to, medical and hospital records, and to consent to the disclosure of this information;

C. To employ and discharge my health care providers;

D. To authorize my admission to or discharge (including transfer to another facility) from any hospital, hospice, nursing home, assisted living facility, or other medical care facility. If I have authorized admission to a health care facility for treatment of mental illness, that authority is stated elsewhere in this advance directive;

E. To authorize my admission to a health care facility for the treatment of mental illness for no more than 10 calendar days provided I do not protest the admission and a physician on the staff of or designated by the proposed admitting facility examines me and states in writing that I have a mental illness and I am incapable of making an informed decision about my admission, and that I need treatment in the facility; and to authorize my discharge (including transfer to another facility) from the facility;

F. To authorize my admission to a health care facility for the treatment of mental illness for no more than 10 calendar days, even over my protest, if a physician on the staff of or designated by the proposed admitting facility examines me and states in writing that I have a mental illness and I am incapable of making an informed decision about my admission, and that I need treatment in the facility; and to authorize my discharge (including transfer to another facility) from the facility.

(If you give your agent the powers described in this Subsection F, your physician must complete the following attestation.)

Physician attestation: I am the physician or licensed clinical psychologist of the declarant of this advance directive. I hereby attest that the declarant is capable of making an informed decision and that the declarant understands the consequences of this provision of this advance directive.

Physician Signature:
Date:
Physician Name Printed:

G. To authorize the specific types of health care identified in this advance directive, specify cross-reference to other sections of directive even over my protest.

(If you give your agent the powers described in this Subsection G, your physician must complete the following attestation.)

Physician attestation: I am the physician or licensed clinical psychologist of the declarant of this advance directive. I hereby attest that the declarant is capable of making an informed decision and that the declarant understands the consequences of this provision of this advance directive.

Physician Signature:
Date:
Physician Name Printed:

(continued)

Figure 6.3 (continued)

H. To continue to serve as my agent even in the event that I protest the agent's authority after I have been determined to be incapable of making an informed decision;

I. To authorize my participation in any health care study approved by an institutional review board or research review committee according to applicable federal or state law that offers the prospect of direct therapeutic benefit to me;

J. To authorize my participation in any health care study approved by an institutional review board or research review committee pursuant to applicable federal or state law that aims to increase scientific understanding of any condition that I may have or otherwise to promote human well-being, even though it offers no prospect of direct benefit to me;

K. To make decisions regarding visitation during any time that I am admitted to any health care facility, consistent with the following directions: . . . . ; and

L. To take any lawful actions that may be necessary to carry out these decisions, including the granting of releases of liability to medical providers.

Further, my agent shall not be liable for the costs of health care pursuant to his authorization, based solely on that authorization.

Section III: Health Care Instructions

(CROSS THROUGH PARAGRAPHS A AND/OR B IF YOU DO NOT WANT TO GIVE ADDITIONAL SPECIFIC INSTRUCTIONS ABOUT YOUR HEALTH CARE.)

A. I specifically direct that I receive the following health care if it is medically appropriate under the circumstances as determined by my attending physician: . . . .

B. I specifically direct that the following health care not be provided to me under the following circumstances (you may specify that certain health care not be provided under any circumstances): . . . .

Section IV: End of Life Instructions

(CROSS THROUGH THIS OPTION IF YOU DO NOT WANT TO GIVE INSTRUCTIONS ABOUT YOUR HEALTH CARE IF YOU HAVE A TERMINAL CONDITION.)

If at any time my attending physician should determine that I have a terminal condition where the application of life-prolonging procedures—including artificial respiration, cardiopulmonary resuscitation, artificially administered nutrition, and artificially administered hydration—would serve only to artificially prolong the dying process, I direct that such procedures be withheld or withdrawn, and that I be permitted to die naturally with only the administration of medication or the performance of any medical procedure deemed necessary to provide me with comfort care or to alleviate pain.

OPTION: OTHER DIRECTIONS ABOUT LIFE-PROLONGING PROCEDURES. (If you wish to provide your own directions, or if you wish to add to the directions you have given above, you may do so here. If you wish to give specific instructions regarding certain life-prolonging procedures, such as artificial respiration, cardiopulmonary resuscitation, artificially administered nutrition, and artificially administered hydration, this is where you should write them.) I direct that:

_____

_____

_____

_____ ;

(continued)

Figure 6.3   (continued)

OPTION: My other instructions regarding my care if I have a terminal condition are as follows:

_____

_____

_____

_____ ;

In the absence of my ability to give directions regarding the use of such life-prolonging procedures, it is my intention that this advance directive shall be honored by my family and physician as the final expression of my legal right to refuse health care and acceptance of the consequences of such refusal.

Section V: Appointment of an Agent to Make an Anatomical Gift or Organ, Tissue, or Eye Donation

(CROSS THROUGH IF YOU DO NOT WANT TO APPOINT AN AGENT TO MAKE AN ANATOMICAL GIFT OR ANY ORGAN, TISSUE, OR EYE DONATION FOR YOU.)

Upon my death, I direct that an anatomical gift of all of my body or certain organ, tissue, or eye donations may be made pursuant to Article 2 (§32.1-289.2 et seq.) of Chapter 8 of Title 32.1 and in accordance with my directions, if any. I hereby appoint my primary agent and if he is not available, my successor agent, to make any such anatomical gift or organ, tissue, or eye donation following my death. I further direct that: . . . . (declarant's directions concerning anatomical gift or organ, tissue, or eye donation).

This advance directive shall not terminate in the event of my disability.

AFFIRMATION AND RIGHT TO REVOKE: By signing below, I indicate that I am emotionally and mentally capable of making this advance directive and that I understand the purpose and effect of this document. I understand I may revoke all or any part of this document at any time (i) with a signed, dated writing; (ii) by physical cancellation or destruction of this advance directive by myself or by directing someone else to destroy it in my presence; or (iii) by my oral expression of intent to revoke.

_____

BOBBIE BLACK

The declarant signed the foregoing advance directive in my presence.

_____   _____
Witness   Witness

Figure 6.4   "Living Will" for West Virginia

STATE OF WEST VIRGINIA LIVING WILL

The Kind of Medical Treatment I Want and Don't Want If I Have a Terminal Condition or Am In a Persistent Vegetative State

Living will made this 15th day of February, 2009.

I, **BOBBIE BLACK,** being of sound mind, willfully and voluntarily declare that I want my wishes to be respected if I am very sick and not able to communicate my wishes for myself. In the absence of my ability to give directions regarding the use of life-prolonging medical intervention, it is my desire that my dying shall not be prolonged under the following circumstances:

If I am very sick and not able to communicate my wishes for myself and I am certified by one physician, who has personally examined me, to have a terminal condition or to be in a persistent vegetative state (I am unconscious and am neither aware of my environment nor able to interact with others), I direct that life-prolonging medical intervention that would serve solely to prolong the dying process or maintain me in a persistent vegetative state be withheld or withdrawn. I want to be allowed to die naturally and only be given medications or other medical procedures necessary to keep me comfortable. I want to receive as much medication as is necessary to alleviate my pain.

I give the following SPECIAL DIRECTIVES OR LIMITATIONS: (Comments about tube feedings, breathing machines, cardiopulmonary resuscitation, dialysis, and mental health treatment may be placed here. My failure to provide special directives or limitations does not mean that I want or refuse certain treatments.)

NO SPECIAL INSTRUCTIONS

It is my intention that this living will be honored as the final expression of my legal right to refuse medical or surgical treatment and accept the consequences resulting from such refusal.

I understand the full import of this living will.

_____

BOBBIE BLACK

_____

Address

I did not sign the principal's signature above for or at the direction of the principal. I am at least eighteen years of age and am not related to the principal by blood or marriage, entitled to any portion of the estate of the principal to the best of my knowledge under any will of principal or codicil thereto, or directly financially responsible for principal's medical care. I am not the principal's attending physician or the principal's medical power of attorney representative or successor medical power of attorney representative under a medical power of attorney.

_____   _____

WITNESS   DATE

_____   _____

WITNESS   DATE

Figure 6.5 Texas Directive to Physicians

Instructions for completing this document:

This is an important legal document known as an Advance Directive. It is designed to help you communicate your wishes about medical treatment at some time in the future when you are unable to make your wishes known because of illness or injury. These wishes are usually based on personal values. In particular, you may want to consider what burdens or hardships of treatment you would be willing to accept for a particular amount of benefit obtained if you were seriously ill.

You are encouraged to discuss your values and wishes with your family or chosen spokesperson, as well as your physician. Your physician, other health care provider, or medical institution may provide you with various resources to assist you in completing your advance directive. Brief definitions are listed below and may aid you in your discussions and advance planning. ***Initial the treatment choices that best reflect your personal preferences.*** Provide a copy of your directive to your physician, usual hospital, and family or spokesperson. Consider a periodic review of this document. By periodic review, you can best assure that the directive reflects your preferences.

In addition to this advance directive, Texas law provides for two other types of directives that can be important during a serious illness. These are the Medical Power of Attorney and the Out-of-Hospital Do-Not-Resuscitate Order. You may wish to discuss these with your physician, family, hospital representative, or other advisers. You may also wish to complete a directive related to the donation of organs and tissues.

Directive

I, **DONALD BLACK**, recognize that the best health care is based upon a partnership of trust and communication with my physician. My physician and I will make health care decisions together as long as I am of sound mind and able to make my wishes known. If there comes a time that I am unable to make medical decisions about myself because of illness or injury, I direct that the following treatment preferences be honored:

If, in the judgment of two (2) physicians, one of which is my personal family care physician, I am suffering with a terminal condition from which I am expected to die within six months, even with available life-sustaining treatment provided in accordance with prevailing standards of medical care:

_____ I request that all treatments other than those needed to keep me comfortable be discontinued or withheld and my physician allow me to die as gently as possible;

OR

_____ I request that I be kept alive in this terminal condition using available life-sustaining treatment. (THIS SELECTION DOES NOT APPLY TO HOSPICE CARE.)

If, in the judgment of two (2) physicians, one of which is my personal family care physician, I am suffering with an irreversible condition so that I cannot care for myself or make decisions for myself and am expected to die without life-sustaining treatment provided in accordance with prevailing standards of care:

_____ I request that all treatments other than those needed to keep me comfortable be discontinued or withheld and my physician allow me to die as gently as possible;

OR

_____ I request that I be kept alive in this irreversible condition using available life-sustaining treatment. (THIS SELECTION DOES NOT APPLY TO HOSPICE CARE.)

(continued)

Figure 6.5 (continued)

Additional requests: (After discussion with your physician, you may wish to consider listing particular treatments in this space that you do or do not want in specific circumstances, such as artificial nutrition and fluids, intravenous antibiotics, etc. Be sure to state whether you do or do not want the particular treatment.)

I direct that I be permitted to die naturally with only the administration of medication including barbiturates and narcotics, or the performance of any medical procedure deemed necessary to provide with comfort care or to alleviate pain.

After signing this directive, if my representative or I elect hospice care, I understand and agree that only those treatments needed to keep me comfortable would be provided and I would not be given available life-sustaining treatments. If I do not have a Medical Power of Attorney, and I am unable to make my wishes known, I designate the following person(s) to make treatment decisions with my physician compatible with my personal values:

PURSUANT TO MY MEDICAL POWER OF ATTORNEY

If I do **not** have a Medical Power of Attorney, and I am unable to make my wishes known, I designate the following person(s) to make treatment decisions with my physician compatible with my personal values:

1. _____

2. _____

(If a Medical Power of Attorney has been executed, then an agent already has been named and you should not list additional names in this document.)

If the above persons are not available, or if I have not designated a spokesperson, I understand that a spokesperson will be chosen for me following standards specified in the laws of Texas. If, in the judgment of my physician, my death is imminent within minutes to hours, even with the use of all available medical treatment provided within the prevailing standard of care, I acknowledge that all treatments may be withheld or removed except those needed to maintain my comfort. I understand that under Texas law this directive has no effect if I have been diagnosed as pregnant. This directive will remain in effect until I revoke it. No other person may do so.

Signed:

_____

DONALD BLACK

February 15, 2009

Date
In Anycounty, State of Texas
Residence: 123 Main Street
          Anytown, Texas

Two competent adult witnesses must sign below, acknowledging the signature of the Declarant. The witness designated as Witness 1 may not be a person designated to make a treatment decision for the patient and may not be related to the patient by blood or marriage. This witness may not be entitled to any part of the estate and may not have a claim against the estate of the patient. This witness may not be the attending physician or an employee of the attending physician. If this witness is

(*continued*)

Figure 6.5 (continued)

an employee of a health care facility in which the patient is being cared for, this witness may not be involved in providing direct patient care to the patient. This witness may not be an officer, director, partner, or business office employee of a health care facility in which the patient is being cared for or of any parent organization of the health care facility.

_____   _____
Witness 1 Signature   Witness 2 Signature

_____   _____
Witness 1 Printed Name   Witness 2 Printed Name

Definitions:

"Artificial nutrition and hydration" means the provision of nutrients or fluids by a tube inserted in a vein, under the skin in the subcutaneous tissues, or in the stomach (gastrointestinal tract).

"Irreversible condition" means a condition, injury, or illness:

1. that may be treated, but is never cured or eliminated;
2. that leaves a person unable to care for or make decisions for the person's own self; and
3. that, without life-sustaining treatment provided in accordance with the prevailing standard of medical care, is fatal.

Explanation: Many serious illnesses such as cancer, failure of major organs (kidney, heart, liver, or lung), and serious brain disease such as Alzheimer's dementia may be considered irreversible early on. There is no cure, but the patient may be kept alive for prolonged periods of time if the patient receives life-sustaining treatments. Late in the course of the same illness, the disease may be considered terminal when, even with treatment, the patient is expected to die. You may wish to consider which burdens of treatment you would be willing to accept in an effort to achieve a particular outcome. This is a very personal decision that you may wish to discuss with your physician, family, or other important persons in your life.

"Life-sustaining treatment" means treatment that, based on reasonable medical judgment, sustains the life of a patient and without which the patient will die. The term includes both life-sustaining medications and artificial life support such as mechanical breathing machines, kidney dialysis treatment, and artificial hydration and nutrition. The term does not include the administration of pain management medication, the performance of a medical procedure necessary to provide comfort care, or any other medical care provided to alleviate a patient's pain.

"Terminal condition" means an incurable condition caused by injury, disease, or illness that, according to reasonable medical judgment, will produce death within 6 months, even with available life-sustaining treatment provided in accordance with the prevailing standard of medical care.

Explanation: Many serious illnesses may be considered irreversible early in the course of the illness, but they may not be considered terminal until the disease is fairly advanced. In thinking about terminal illness and its treatment, you again may wish to consider the relative benefits and burdens of treatment and discuss your wishes with your physician, family, or other important persons in your life.

Health-Care Surrogates and Proxies

A **health-care surrogate** is a person who is named by the declarant to make all medical decisions in the event the declarant is unable to give consent. Some states like Massachusetts that do not allow living wills, allow health-care surrogates instead. Others, like Florida, allow for both.

A **health-care surrogate** is a person designated to make health-care decisions on your behalf if you are incapable of making decisions for yourself. In general, the health-care surrogate may make any legally permissible decision on your behalf without your consent and does not require your authority. In states, like Florida and Massachusetts as well as California, you may name a health-care surrogate. If you do not name a health-care surrogate, state statute determines who will act as surrogate on your behalf.

Any competent adult may be named as the surrogate, but it should not be a person with a possible conflict of interest. Conflicts of interest might include the treating medical care provider or the operator or employee of the health-care facility at which the declarant is being treated or lives, such as the administrator of a nursing home. When you designate a health care surrogate, the designation must be made in writing in the presence of two adult witnesses. In some states, if the declarant names someone other than his or her spouse or adult children, the surrogate must give the spouse and the children notice when the surrogacy becomes effective. It often becomes the responsibility of the paralegal to ensure that the notice is sent in a manner that requires signature upon receipt for the surrogate's protection.

The surrogate may only act if the declarant becomes incompetent, or is otherwise unable to act of his or her own accord (for example, he or she is anesthetized during a surgical procedure). Usually the incapacity of a patient to make health-care decisions is made by the patient's attending physician with at least one other physician concurring. In general, a court ruling is not required, unless the purpose for the surrogacy is to have the patient committed to a mental facility. In those instances, a judge or magistrate may be required to make the declaration of incapacity despite a written declaration to nominate a surrogate. This is a matter of state statute and will vary by jurisdiction.

The surrogate will be able to do the following:

- review medical records
- consult with health-care providers
- give medical consent
- apply for medical benefits, such as Medicare and Medicaid
- make other health-care decisions

Some states differentiate between a health-care surrogate and a health-care proxy but others don't. A **health-care proxy** is usually defined as a person who is authorized by state law to make health-care decisions for an individual who has not expressly designated a surrogate, although in some states, like Massachusetts, the use of the term "proxy" is used instead of surrogate. As a paralegal, you will have to learn what terminology your state uses for each document and what each document purports to accomplish. The proxy is usually designated by the health-care provider, following preferences set by state law. These preferences usually include the patient's legal guardian, spouse, adult children, adult siblings, other adult relatives, or close friends.

Medical Powers of Attorney

Medical powers of attorney are another form of advance directive in which the person authorizes another to act on his or her behalf concerning medical care. The person making the authorization is called the **principal**, while the person who is being authorized is called the ***attorney in fact*** or **agent**. (The Uniform Powers of Attorney Act only uses the term "agent" so any state that has adopted the UPOAA will use that term exclusively. We are using the term agent in this book as well.)

The authorization may include any number of powers such as the ability to consent to or refuse or withdraw consent to any type of medical care or treatment including surgery and diagnostic procedures, medication, artificial respiration, artificially administered nutrition and hydration, and cardiopulmonary resuscitation; to request, receive, and review medical and hospital records; to employ and discharge health care providers; and to authorize the principal's admission or discharge to or from any hospital, hospice, nursing home, adult home, or other medical care facility for services. Unlike a standard power of attorney, the authorization to act survives the incapacity of the principal. In fact, *under medical powers of attorney, the agent may only make decisions concerning the principal's medical care if the principal is unable to do so.* The **medical power of attorney** has no effect unless the principal is incapacitated.

It is this ability to take effect upon the incapacity of the principal that makes it a powerful document. It enables the agent to advocate for the principal's medical care and comfort without obtaining a guardianship, which is often time-consuming and costly. It is also an emotional strain on families, who deal with mom or dad being unable to handle his or her own affairs, but cannot cope with having to have them declared legally incompetent. This form of power of attorney, like all powers of attorney, ceases to be effective upon the death of the principal. The principal must be mentally competent at the time the power is executed.

In general, neither surrogates and agents under a medical power of attorney nor proxies may give consent for abortions, sterility procedures, shock therapy, psychosurgery, experimental treatments that are not FDA approved, or admission to a mental facility, unless the patient gave permission in writing, or the surrogate or proxy receives court approval.

Issues Surrounding Advance Directives

Estate planning practitioners (the author included) urge clients to have advance directives prepared. We understand that without them, a family may be compelled to spend time and money to obtain guardianships on behalf of a loved one that can no longer fend for him or her. We appreciate that it is far less expensive and time-consuming to have an advance directive prepared while you are competent, than to worry how a family will cope with the ravages of illness and an inability to have the documents handy. We understand that a proxy, surrogate, or agent should be consulted in advance to make sure that she is comfortable with that role and that the client should discuss his or her wishes fully at that time. No family should have to deal with getting a medical directive prepared while in the midst of a medical crisis. It is always better to do so when things are calm and decisions can be made from a rational instead of panicked state of mind.

That said, a study by Dr. Joan Ten and Dr. Joanne Lynn at the George Washington University Center to Improve Care for the Dying and their colleagues found that advance directives make little or no difference in medical care, a bitter pill for those of us in the field.

The study performed at GWU and seven other medical centers and reported in *The Journal of the American Geriatrics Society* involved 4804 terminally ill patients. Only 688 of those patients, however, had written directives describing the medical care he or she wanted or financial directives (described below in the section on Durable Powers of Attorney). The study found that, of the 688 directives, only 22 contained instructions which guided medical care explicitly. Their own doctors only knew about their advance directives 25% of the time, begging the questions why not and why weren't the directives noted in the patient's chart? When you add these statistics to the statistics at the beginning of this chapter indicating that only 3 in 10 people even have a directive, it is apparent that a patient's physicians and their families have no idea what the patient really wants. Indeed a bitter pill.

Figure 6.6 Medical Power of Attorney (West Virginia form)

Note how some states, such as West Virginia, below, have promulgated forms that they prefer you use even for Medical Powers of Attorney. Other states do not have preferred forms.

STATE OF WEST VIRGINIA
MEDICAL POWER OF ATTORNEY

> **The Person I Want to Make Health Care Decisions For Me When I Can't Make Them Myself**

Dated: _____, 2007

I, **BOBBIE BLACK,** currently of Anycounty County, West Virginia, hereby appoint **DONALD BLACK** as my representative to act on my behalf to give, withhold, or withdraw informed consent to health care decisions in the event that I am not able to do so myself.

If my representative is unable, unwilling, or disqualified to serve, then I appoint **TINA BLACK** as my alternate successor representative.

This appointment shall extend to, but not be limited to, health care decisions relating to medical treatment, surgical treatment, nursing care, medication, hospitalization, care and treatment in a nursing home or other facility, and home health care. The representative(s) appointed by this document is specifically authorized to be granted access to my medical records and other health information and to act on my behalf to consent to, refuse or withdraw any and all medical treatment or diagnostic procedures, or autopsy if my representative(s) determines that I, if able to do so, would consent to, refuse, or withdraw such treatment or procedures. Such authority shall include, but not be limited to, decisions regarding the withholding or withdrawal of life-prolonging interventions.

_____ Initials

I appoint this representative(s) because I believe this person understands my wishes and values and will act to carry into effect the health care decisions that I would make if I were able to do so, and because I also believe that this person will act in my best interest when my wishes are unknown. It is my intent that my family, my physician, and all legal authorities be bound by the decisions that are made by the representative(s) appointed by this document and it is my intent that these decisions should not be the subject of review by any health care provider or administrative or judicial agency.

It is my intent that this document be legally binding and effective and that this document be taken as a formal statement of my desire concerning the method by which any health care decisions should be made on my behalf during any period when I am unable to make such decisions.

(continued)

Figure 6.6 (continued)

In exercising the authority under this medical power of attorney, my representative(s) shall act consistently with my special directives or limitations as stated below. I am giving the following SPECIAL DIRECTIVES OR LIMITATIONS ON THIS POWER: (Comments about tube feedings, breathing machines, cardiopulmonary resuscitation, dialysis, funeral arrangements, autopsy, and organ donation may be placed here. My failure to provide special directives or limitations does not mean that I want or refuse certain treatments.)

For example: NO ANATOMICAL GIFTS SHALL BE MADE.

THIS MEDICAL POWER OF ATTORNEY SHALL BECOME EFFECTIVE ONLY UPON MY INCAPACITY TO GIVE, WITHHOLD, OR WITHDRAW INFORMED CONSENT TO MY OWN MEDICAL CARE.

I understand the full import of this medical power of attorney.

_____

BOBBIE BLACK

I did not sign the principal's signature above. I am at least eighteen years of age and am not related to the principal by blood or marriage. I am not entitled to any portion of the estate of the principal or to the best of my knowledge under any will of the principal or codicil thereto, or legally responsible for the costs of the principal's medical or other care. I am not the principal's attending physician, nor am I the representative or successor representative of the principal.

_____   _____
WITNESS   DATE

_____   _____
WITNESS   DATE

_____ Initials

STATE OF WEST VIRGINIA

COUNTY OF ANYCOUNTY, TO-WIT:

I, _____, a Notary Public of said County, do certify that BOBBIE BLACK, as principal, and _____ and _____, as witnesses, whose names are signed to the writing above bearing, have this day acknowledged the same before me.

Given under my hand this ____ day of _____, 2007.

_____
Notary Public

My commission expires:_____

_____ Initials

Figure 6.7 Medical Power of Attorney (Texas Form)

INFORMATION CONCERNING THE MEDICAL POWER OF ATTORNEY

THIS IS AN IMPORTANT LEGAL DOCUMENT. BEFORE SIGNING THIS DOCUMENT, YOU SHOULD KNOW THESE IMPORTANT FACTS:

Except to the extent you state otherwise, this document gives the person you name as your agent the authority to make any and all health care decisions for you in accordance with your wishes, including your religious and moral beliefs, when you are no longer capable of making them yourself. Because "health care" means any treatment, service, or procedure to maintain, diagnose, or treat your physical or mental condition, your agent has the power to make a broad range of health care decisions for you. Your agent may consent, refuse to consent, or withdraw consent to medical treatment and may make decisions about withdrawing or withholding life-sustaining treatment. Your agent may not consent to voluntary inpatient mental health services, convulsive treatment, psychosurgery, or abortion. A physician must comply with your agent's instructions or allow you to be transferred to another physician.

Your agent's authority begins when your doctor certifies that you lack the competence to make health care decisions.

Your agent is obligated to follow your instructions when making decisions on your behalf. Unless you state otherwise, your agent has the same authority to make decisions about your health care as you would have had.

It is important that you discuss this document with your physician or other health care provider before you sign it to make sure that you understand the nature and range of decisions that may be made on your behalf. If you do not have a physician, you should talk with someone else who is knowledgeable about these issues and can answer your questions. You do not need a lawyer's assistance to complete this document, but if there is anything in this document that you do not understand, you should ask a lawyer to explain it to you.

The person you appoint as agent should be someone you know and trust. The person must be eighteen years of age or older or a person under eighteen years of age who has had the disabilities of minority removed. If you appoint your health or residential care provider (e.g., your physician or an employee of a home health agency, hospital, nursing home, or residential care home, other than a relative), that person has to choose between acting as your agent or as your health or residential care provider; the law does not permit a person to do both at the same time.

You should inform the person you appoint that you want the person to be your health care agent. You should discuss this document with your agent and your physician and give each a signed copy. You should indicate on the document itself the people and institutions who have signed copies. Your agent is not liable for health care decisions made in good faith on your behalf.

Even after you have signed this document, you have the right to make health care decisions for yourself as long as you are able to do so and treatment cannot be given to you or stopped over your objection. You have the right to revoke the authority granted to your agent by informing your agent or your health or residential care provider orally or in writing or by your execution of a subsequent medical power of attorney. Unless you state otherwise, your appointment of a spouse dissolves on divorce. This document may not be changed or modified. If you want to make changes in the document, you must make an entirely new one. You may wish to designate an alternate agent in the event that your agent is unwilling, unable, or ineligible to act as your agent. Any alternate agent you designate has the same authority to make health care decisions for you.

(continued)

Figure 6.7 (continued)

THIS POWER OF ATTORNEY IS NOT VALID UNLESS IT IS SIGNED IN THE PRESENCE OF TWO COMPETENT ADULT WITNESSES. THE FOLLOWING PERSONS MAY NOT ACT AS ONE OF THE WITNESSES:

1. the person you have designated as your agent;
2. a person related to you by blood or marriage;
3. a person entitled to any part of your estate after your death under a will or codicil executed by you or by operation of law;
4. your attending physician;
5. an employee of your attending physician;
6. an employee of a health care facility in which you are a patient if the employee is providing direct patient care to you or is an officer, director, partner, or business office employee of the health care facility or of any parent organization of the health care facility; or
7. a person who, at the time this power of attorney is executed, has a claim against any part of your estate after your death.

MEDICAL POWER OF ATTORNEY DESIGNATION OF HEALTH CARE AGENT

I, DONALD BLACK appoint:

Name:	BOBBIE BLACK
Address:	100 N. Main Street
	Anytown, TEXAS
Phone:	(100) 555-1212

as my agent to make any and all health care decisions for me, except to the extent I state otherwise in this document. This medical power of attorney takes effect if I become unable to make my own health care decisions and this fact is certified in writing by my physician.

LIMITATIONS ON THE DECISION-MAKING AUTHORITY OF MY AGENT ARE AS FOLLOWS: **NONE**

DESIGNATION OF ALTERNATE AGENT

(You are not required to designate an alternate agent, but you may do so. An alternate agent may make the same health care decisions as the designated agent if the designated agent is unable or unwilling to act as your agent. If the agent designated is your spouse, the designation is automatically revoked by law if your marriage is dissolved.)

If the person designated as my agent is unable or unwilling to make health care decisions for me, I designate the following persons to serve as my agent to make health care decisions for me as authorized by this document, who serve in the following order:

A. First Alternate Agent
    Name: TINA BLACK
    Address: 400 S. White Street
                Anytown, Texas
        Phone: _____

B. Second Alternate Agent
    Name: TODD BLACK
    Address: 250 Running Brook Court

(continued)

Figure 6.7   (continued)

Phone: Anytown, Texas
_____

The original of this document is kept at: First Anytown Bank

120 S. Main Street, Anytown, Texas

The following individuals or institutions have signed copies:
Notice how the document specifically states who already is on notice that the document exists.

Name:	Donald Black
Address:	100 N. Main Street, Anytown, Texas
Name:	Tina Black
Address:	400 S. White Street, Anytown, Texas
Name:	Todd Black
Address:	250 Running Brook Court, Anytown, Texas
Name:	Anytown Senior Health Care Medical Center
Address:	300 Campus Way, Anytown, Texas

Duration

I understand that this power of attorney exists indefinitely from the date I execute this document unless I establish a shorter time or revoke the power of attorney. If I am unable to make health care decisions for myself when this power of attorney expires, the authority I have granted my agent continues to exist until the time I become able to make health care decisions for myself.

Prior Designations Revoked

I revoke any prior medical power of attorney.

Acknowledgment of Disclosure Statement

I have been provided with a disclosure statement explaining the effect of this document. I have read and understand that information contained in the disclosure statement.

I sign my name to this medical power of attorney on the 15th day of June, 2006, at Anytown, Anytown County, Texas.

DONALD BLACK

Statement and Signature of First Witness

I am not the person appointed as agent by this document. I am not related to the principal by blood or marriage. I would not be entitled to any portion of the principal's estate on the principal's death. I am not the attending physician of the principal or an employee of the attending physician. I have no claim against any portion of the principal's estate on the principal's death. Furthermore, if I am an employee of a health care facility in which the principal is a patient, I am not involved in providing direct patient care to the principal and am not an officer, director, partner, or business office employee of the health care facility or of any parent organization of the health care facility.

Signature:_____

Print Name:_____ Date:_____

Address:_____

(continued)

Figure 6.7 (continued)

Signature of Second Witness Signature:_____ Print Name:_____ Date:_____ Address:_____

Another study found that the use and impact of living wills on patient care has not been adequately studied. This study conducted at the Hamot Medical Center in Erie, Pennsylvania, and published in February 2009 issue of *The Journal of Emergency Medicine* found that there is a lack of education and understanding about when a living will is used in a pre-hospital setting. The study sought to determine how a living will impacts patient care, for those who call 911 in an emergency, by determining how the living will is interpreted by Emergency Medical Service (EMS) personnel. It importantly also sought to establish how that interpretation impacted lifesaving care. The results of the study suggested that the majority of pre-hospital care providers, including EMS personnel, interpreted a living will to be a DNRO, incorrectly so. (TRIADII: Do Living Wills Have an Impact on Pre-Hospital Lifesaving Care? *Journal of Emergency Medicine,* 2009.)

A third study was published in March 2004 in the Hastings Center Report by Angela Fagerlin, Ph.D., a research scientist at the University of Michigan Medical School and Veterans Administration Healthcare System, and Carl Schneider, Professor at the University of Michigan Law School and the University of Michigan Medical School. This study said that living wills don't and can't work for their intended purpose stating that the documents fail to meet five key criteria for success, and therefore offer false promise of control over end-of-life treatment. They fail five criteria in that:

1. most people don't have living wills;
2. those who do rarely know what care they want in the future;
3. it is difficult to express their wishes accurately and understandably;
4. the document itself is often unavailable when decisions are being made; and
5. even when available, surrogate decision makers cannot reliably apply its instructions to the current health situation.

Professor Schneider stated "living wills don't fail for lack of effort, education, intelligence, or good will. They fail because of basic traits of human psychology." Doctor Fagerlin surmises that since many Americans are functionally illiterate it adds to the problem.

Additional studies have been performed on discrete portions of American society. In one study in rural eastern North Carolina (Department of Medicine, East Carolina University School of Medicine), 75 ambulatory elderly persons were interviewed at community dining sites about their beliefs concerning living wills and medical care for terminal illness. The study, while small, covered all of the important questions that as legal practitioners we should be thinking about when consulting with clients. Fifty-two percent of them said they were familiar with living wills and 64% were able to correctly state what the North Carolina living will says. Eighty-six percent expressed a desire to receive basic medical care for comfort only in the face of terminal illness; however, none of those 65 persons had in fact signed the living will document provided by the state, and only 3% (2 of them) had even discussed a living will with their physicians. Ninety-three percent wanted family or spouses to make decisions about their terminal care if they couldn't decide for themselves; they only discussed these decisions with their health care proxies 45% of the time, however. Eighty-one percent wanted to discuss end-of-life care with their physicians, but only 11% actually did so, and in most instances (five of the eight) the discussions were instigated by the patients. The researchers concluded that "living will legislation is congruent with the desire of many elderly persons to limit medical care in terminal illness. However, this elderly population did not make use of living wills as a means of indicating their wishes." They recommended that communication between physicians and their patients, and patients and their proxies, be improved. They also believed that alternatives to living wills should be explored.

Still another study undertaken in 2005 by Carmen Santiago, a doctoral student at the University of North Texas Science Center, found that Mexican-Americans knew little about advance directives. Santiago reviewed research on advance directives in the U.S. and Mexican-Americans in the Dallas-Fort Worth area to determine the level of knowledge as well as attitudes, and how culture, religion, and family influenced decisions regarding advance directives.

Santiago found that the patients who were hospitalized or receiving home health care, or family and caregivers of elderly persons who were either hospitalized or receiving home health care, showed a lack of knowledge about advance directives and that both groups were also confused about them. Some of the participants thought that living wills distributed property. She found that the elderly persons were more likely to allow their adult children to make decisions for them. (Source: University of North Texas Health Science Center at Fort Worth, http://www.hsc.unt.edu/news/newsrelease.cfm?ID=310)

Despite the fact that since 1990, the Federal *Patient Self-Determination Act* has required hospitals to ask patients whether they have a living will, and if not, whether they want information to help them make one, these studies as well as others, indicate that advance directives cause uncertainty for patients and their families and their doctors, who often do not apply living wills properly and as the patient actually would have wished. A new model of advance directive has been developed and there is hope that it will improve patient care for end-of-life treatment (POLST, discussed in the following section), as well as certain death with dignity statutes, which are also discussed later in this chapter.

Patient Self-Determination Act

At the time of a patient's admission to a health-care facility, the Federal Patient Self-Determination Act requires those health-care facilities to give the patient a written summary of her health-care decision-making rights. Although this Act was enacted at the federal level, it is administered, like many laws, at the state level and each state has enacted its own summary of rights. Facilities included in the Act include hospitals, nursing homes, home health agencies, and assisted living facilities. Doctors and doctors' offices, however, are not bound by the Act.

In addition, at the time of admission, the patient shall also be given a copy of the facility's policies with respect to recognizing advance directives. This is important because not all facilities will accept all directives. For example, it is entirely possible that a hospital will not honor a living will that directs for the removal of life-prolonging procedures. At that point, it is up to the patient and the patient's family to use that facility's services or seek the services of another.

The facility will also ask the patient if she has an advance directive and document that the directive is part of the patient's medical records. The patient has the responsibility to bring the directive with her at the time of admission. The facility may not, however, require a patient to have a directive. To require a patient to have or not have a directive is prohibited by the Act.

It should be noted that despite the studies indicating that advance directives are not a panacea, they are, in this author's opinion, certainly better than nothing at all. Nothing at all leads to the cases found in Appendix A "Important Cases Concerning the Right to Die," and studies show that Americans don't want that, even if they aren't sure how to avoid the problems of having nothing at all.

Durable Powers of Attorney

A standard general *power of attorney* is a document that gives another person the authorization to act on one's behalf. The person authorizing the other to act is called the **principal** while the person who is being authorized is called the *attorney in fact* or **agent**. The Uniform Power of Attorney Act only uses the term "agent" and the term "attorney-in-fact" is falling from favor. (It often confuses lay people as they think of "lawyer" when they hear or read the term "attorney.") The authorization may include any number of powers such as the ability to mortgage, sell, or lease property; sell, buy, or trade stocks and bonds; institute lawsuits; and run a business. This authorization does not survive the incapacity of the principal. A general power of attorney does not survive the incapacity of the principal because under the general laws of agency "qui facit per alium, facit per se," which means "he who acts through another is deemed in law to do it himself." If the principal could not act, neither could the agent, who merely stepped into the principal's shoes. If the principal was no longer capable of handling his or her own affairs, the agent couldn't handle the principal's affairs either. All powers of attorney cease to be effective upon the death of the principal.

The first durable power of attorney statute was enacted in Virginia and allowed an agent to continue to act even after the principal became disabled, incompetent, or incapacitated. A **durable power of attorney** then is a document which is a creature of statute and provides for the document to have additional language which allows the powers and authority of the agent to survive the principal's incapacity, or permits the powers to become effective upon the principal's incapacity. For obvious reasons, the principal must be mentally competent at the time the power is executed. These new durable powers of attorney opened new avenues for estate planners because a person could name an agent in advance of incapacity and potentially avoid the future need for a guardian or conservator.

Durable powers of attorney are often titled "General and Durable Powers of Attorney" or "Durable Powers of Attorney" and most often refer to an agent handling the principal's personal and financial decisions, but not usually his or her medical decisions. Those are most often handled separately in a document called either a "Medical Directive" or a "Medical or Health Care Power of Attorney" or "Power of Attorney for Health Care Decisions" (discussed above in this chapter). It is important to note, however, that if the client's power of attorney, such as the one in the example below, did not have the language stated or similar language showing the intent to survive the client's incapacity, it would be a general power of attorney.

Example: Marilyn Mondo's durable power of attorney states the common language used to express a durable power of attorney:
"This power shall not terminate on disability of the principal, and such disability shall not affect the authority herein granted."

CASE 6.1 **SUMMARY**

In Re: Marjorie H. Weidner a/k/a Marjorie H. Ross, deceased, 938 A.2d 354 (2007) (Supreme Court of Pennsylvania, Middle District)

In April, 1993, Marjorie H. Ross, executed a "Durable General Power/Letter Of Attorney" appointing her daughters, Susan L. Rhodes and Carol A. Doersom, to act together or separately as her attorney-in-fact. The power of attorney provided Rhodes and Doersom with the authority to act as Ross's

true and lawful attorney, for me and in my name and on my behalf to execute notes, checks, drafts and bills of exchange and to pledge my general credit, without any limitation whatsoever; to endorse notes, checks, drafts and bills of exchange which may require my endorsement and to collect the proceeds thereof; to collect all coupons, dividends, rents or other income whatsoever due me; to draw checks or any other instruments in my name for all or any part of any deposit that I may have in any banking or savings institution whatsoever; to take charge and custody of all my assets, real, personal and mixed, whatsoever, and wheresoever situate; to pay over to me from time to time, and whenever by me demanded, my net income; to endorse, sign and transfer stock certificates, or any other document or paper that may require my signature; to sell, lease, or convert any or all my assets, real, personal and mixed whatsoever, and to reinvest the proceeds thereof from time to time; to receive full or partial payment of debts owing to me including those secured by judgement [sic], mortgage or security agreement and to enter full or partial satisfaction on the record of such debt,

judgement [sic], mortgage or security agreement and to release from the lien thereof, any property bound by such debt, judgement [sic], mortgage or security agreement; to prepare, sign and execute all tax returns or other statements that may be required of me by law; and this Power of Attorney shall not be affected by disability of the principal, whether physical or mental, and the authority conferred herein shall be exercisable notwithstanding his/her disability, and later uncertainty as to whether the Principal is dead or alive in accordance with Act No. 295 effective December 10, 1974 (20 Pa.C.S. 5601). This Power of Attorney includes the authority to deal fully and in all respects, including purchasing and selling, with any and all now owned or after acquired real estate and/or personal property; and I also hereby grant unto my said Attorney, the power and authority to do any act which is set forth in Chapter 56 of Title 20 of the Pennsylvania Consolidated Statutes Annotated, (20 Pa.C.S.A. 5601 through 5607), known as "Powers of Attorney", as amended from time to time. I incorporate herein by reference thereto, all of the provisions set forth in said Act; and the authority herein conferred shall also extend to my Attorney-in-Fact being authorized to enter any safe deposit box in my name at any lending institution, and to sign, seal, execute, acknowledge and deliver all instruments, agreements and contracts necessary or proper for the carrying out of the powers herein granted, with the same powers and to all intents and purposes with the same validity as I could if personally present; hereby ratifying and confirming whatsoever my said attorney shall or may do by virtue hereof. And I declare it to be my intent and purpose that none of the specific powers conferred hereby on my said attorney shall in any manner limit or diminish the effect of the general language contained herein or the general powers conferred hereby.

In April 1994, Ross married Walter J. Weidner. Weidner and Ross executed a prenuptial agreement acknowledging each had children from a previous marriage and desired to maintain their separate property for the benefit of their children. The agreement provided the parties could name each other as beneficiaries on their life insurance policies, but could not do so on annuities.

In July 1994, Ross purchased a life insurance policy from the Metropolitan Life Insurance Company (MetLife), naming Weidner as the beneficiary, using funds from the conversion of an annuity policy she owned before her marriage to Weidner.

In June 1999, at the request of Rhodes (Ross's attorney-in-fact under her power of attorney), the beneficiary on the policy was changed to Rhodes, Doersom, Donald Ross, Elizabeth Tickner, and Jane Kabai. In November 1999, MetLife wrote Rhodes regarding the change. Rhodes responded in March 2000, stating that Ross suffered from advanced Alzheimer's Disease and that she was Ross's attorney-in-fact and wanted the beneficiary changed immediately, claiming that this request was consistent with her earlier request (and that of her mother, as expressed in the prenuptial agreement).

Ross died September 16, 2003. When Weidner contacted MetLife, MetLife told Weidner that his claim would not be honored because the policy's beneficiary had been changed in 1999 at Rhodes's request.

Weidner filed a petition for declaratory judgment seeking the determination that the power of attorney was insufficient to empower Rhodes to change the policy's beneficiary, and that Rhodes breached her fiduciary obligations because the change provided no benefit to the principal. The trial court found that the language of the power of attorney was sufficient to authorize Rhodes to change the policy's beneficiary designation. The trial court further determined that Rhodes's change of the beneficiary to benefit herself was proper since she was Ross's child.

Weidner appealed asking the Superior Court if the power of attorney authorized Rhodes to change the policy's beneficiary designation. The Superior Court reversed the trial court stating that the power of attorney's incorporation of Chapter 56 of Title 20 by reference was "insufficient to grant powers as it does not apprise the principal of the type of powers listed in the power of attorney statute." Since the Superior Court determined that the power of attorney didn't have specific language authorizing Rhodes to engage in any insurance matters, the power of attorney did not authorize her to change the designation of a beneficiary.

The Supreme Court reversed the Superior Court and remanded for consideration of all the issues that were raised at the Superior Court. It relied on In re Estate of Reifsneider, 610 A.2d 958 (Pa. 1992) which asked "whether a principal wishing to grant one of the powers referred to in section 5602(a) must explicitly identify the power using specific language either identical or similar to the statutory language."

In Reifsneider the Supreme Court determined that the powers of attorney statute did not

> limit the subjects that may properly be addressed by powers of attorney, nor does it confine the way such powers may be defined." And "[s]imply put, general language can 'show a similar intent on the part of the principal' to empower the attorney-in-fact to do one or more of the listed things if the general language, according to its common usage, would be understood as encompassing such power or powers.

The Supreme Court found that the powers of attorney statute did not

> confine the way powers given in a power of attorney may be defined. Section 5602 provides a principal may empower his attorney-in fact to do any of an enumerated list of tasks, by including specific language or by including language showing a similar intent. 20 Pa.C.S. §5602(a). Here, [Ross] chose to incorporate by reference the powers enumerated in the statute, and by doing so evinced her intent to confer broad authority to her attorneys-in-fact. She specifically stated no specific powers were intended to limit the general powers conferred.

The Court found that Ross's power of attorney expressly incorporated the Powers of Attorney statute and expressly granted Rhodes the power and authority to do any act therein.

The Court found that the document's general language showed Ross's intent to empower Rhodes to do any or all of the things permitted by the statute, which included engaging in insurance transactions.

The Supreme Court held that the power of attorney was sufficient to allow Rhodes the ability to change the beneficiary designation on the MetLife policy.

Checklist for What May Be and Should Be Added to a Power of Attorney

1. Name and address of principal
2. Name and address of agent
3. The scope and extent of the power to be given the agent
4. The property subject to the power
5. The agent's authority to delegate his or her duties
6. The extent to which the agent must report to a third person or the principal
7. The power of the third person to veto the agent's actions
8. When the power takes effect: the date and time
9. How long the power will remain in effect
10. The principal's authority to revoke the power given
11. Compensation for the agent
12. The date the power of attorney will be executed
13. An acknowledgment: the place for the signature of the principal and witnesses
14. Recordation, if necessary
15. The agent's written acceptance

Uniform Power of Attorney Act and Safeguarding the Principal from Financial Abuse

According to Linda S. Whitton, Reporter Professor of Law, Valparaiso University School of Law, as she wrote in National Durable Power of Attorney Survey Results and Analysis, National Conference of Commissioners on Uniform State Laws (2002) as well as The New Uniform Power of Attorney Act: Balancing Protection of the Principal, the Agent, and Third Persons, 41st Annual Heckerling Institute on Estate Planning (2007), "[T]here exists an inherent tension between two objectives: 1) preservation of the effectiveness of durable powers as a low-cost, flexible, and private form of surrogate decision making; and 2) protection of incapacitated principals from financial abuse. Professor Whitton also stated that complicating reform efforts was the very real problem of trustworthy agents who are reluctant to serve as agent because of "contentious family dynamics and the fear of liability."

The National Commission on Uniform Laws (discussed further in Chapter 13) has explicitly stated that the UPOAA provides "mandatory provisions that provide safeguards for the protection of the principal, the agent, and persons who are asked to rely on the agent's authority; [M]odernizes the various areas of authority that can be granted to an agent and requires express language authorization by the principal where certain authority could dissipate the principal's property or alter the principal's estate plan; [P]rovides step-by-step prompts are given for designation of agent, successor agents, and the grant of authority through an optional statutory form; and [O]ffers clearer guidelines for the Agent, who is often a trusted family members [sic]." In addition, the UPOAA encourages acceptance of a power of attorney by third parties.

The UPOAA was finally promulgated in 2009. The effort to have the UPOAA adopted in all states so that there is uniformity among the states has paid off. Every state except Louisiana has adopted the law. It is unclear, however, if the localities take elder financial abuse as seriously as they should. Some state and district attorneys' offices will prosecute and others still consider this a "family matter" best left to the civil courts.

Figure 6.8   Powers of Attorney Statutes

State	Citation
Alabama	Ala. Code §§26-1-2 to 26-1-2.1
Alaska	Alaska Stat. §§13.26.332 to 13.26.358
Arizona	Ariz. Rev. Stat. Ann. §§14-5501 to 14-5507
Arkansas	Ark. Code Ann. §§28-68-101 to 28-68-419
California	Cal. Prob. Code §§4000-4034, 4050-4054, 4100-4102, 4120-4130, 4150-4155, 4200-4207, 4230-4238, 4260-4266, 4300-4310, 4400 4409, 4450-4465
Colorado	Colo. Rev. Stat. Ann. §§15-1-1301 to 15-1-1320, 15-14-501 to 15-14-509
Connecticut	Conn. Gen. Stat. Ann. §§1-42 to 1-56, 1-56a to 1-56b; Conn. Gen. Stat. Ann. 45a-562
Delaware	Del. Code Ann. tit. 12, §§4901-4905
District of Columbia	D.C. Code §§21-2081 to 21—2085, 21-2101 to 21-2118
Florida	Fla. Stat. Ann. §709.08
Georgia	Ga. Code Ann. §§10-6-1 to 10-6-39
Hawaii	Haw. Rev. Stat. Ann. §§551D-1 to 551D-7
Idaho	Idaho Code §§15-5-501 to 15-5-507
Illinois	755 Ill. Comp. Stat. Ann. 45/1-1, 45/2-1 to 45/2-11, 45/3-1 to 45/3-4
Indiana	Ind. Code Ann. §§30-5-1-1 to 30-5-10-4
Iowa	Iowa Code Ann. §§633B.1 to 663B.2
Kansas	Kan. Stat. Ann. §§58-650 to 58-665
Kentucky	Ky. Rev. Stat. Ann. §386.093
Louisiana	La. Civ. Code Ann. art. 2985-3032
Maine	Me. Rev. Stat. Ann. tit. 18-A, §§5-501 to 5-510
Maryland	Md. Code Ann., Est. & Trusts §§13-601 to 13-602
Massachusetts	Mass. Ann. Laws ch. 201B §§1-7
Michigan	Mich. Comp. Laws Ann. §§700.5501 to 700.5520
Minnesota	Minn. Stat. Ann. §§523.01 to 523.24
Mississippi	Miss. Code Ann. §§87-3-101 to 87-3-113
Missouri	Mo. Ann. Stat. §§404.700 to 404.737
Montana	Mont. Code Ann. §§72-5-501, 72-5-502, 72-31-201 to 72-31-238
Nebraska	Neb. Rev. Stat. §§30-2664 to 30-2672, Neb. Rev. Stat. §§49-1501 to 49-1561
Nevada	Nev. Rev. Stat. Ann. §§111.450 to 111.470
New Hampshire	N.H. Rev. Stat. Ann. §§506:5 to 506:7
New Jersey	N.J. Stat. Ann. §§46:2B-8.1 to 46:2B-l9
New Mexico	N.M. Stat. Ann. §§46B-1-101 to 46B-1-403
New York	N.Y. Gen. Oblig. Law §§5-1501 to 5-1506
North Carolina	N.C. Gen. Stat. Ann. §§32A-1 to 32A-3, 32A-8 to 32A-14.12, 32A-40 to 32A-43

(continued)

Figure 6.8   (continued)

North Dakota	N.D. Cent. Code §§30.1-30-01 to 30.1-30-06
Ohio	Ohio Rev. Code Ann. §§1337.01 to 1337.10
Oklahoma	Okla. Stat. Ann, tit. 58, §§1071 to 1077, 1081; Okla. Stat. Ann. tit. 15, §§ 1001 to l020
Oregon	Or. Rev. Stat. §§127.005 to 127.045
Pennsylvania	20 Pa. Cons. Stat. Ann. §§5601-5611
Rhode Island	R.I. Gen Laws §§34-22-6 to 34-22-7
South Carolina	S.C. Code Ann. §§62-5-501 to 62-5-505
South Dakota	S.D. Codified Laws §§59-7-1 to 59-7-9
Tennessee	Tenn. Code Ann. §§34-6-101 to 34-6-111
Texas	Tex. Prob. Code Ann. §§481 to 506)
Utah	Utah Code Ann. §§75-5-501 to 75-5-504
Vermont	Vt. Stat. Ann. tit. 14 §§3501-3516
Virgin Islands	V.I. Code Ann. tit. 15, §§1261 to 1267
Virginia	Va. Code Ann. §§11-9.1 to -11-9.7
Washington	Wash. Rev. Code Ann. §§11.94.010 to 11.9.150
West Virginia	W. Va. Code Ann. §§39-4-1 to 39-4-7
Wisconsin	Wis. Stat. Ann. §§243.07, 243.10
Wyoming	Wyo. Stat. Ann. §§3-5-101 to 3-5-103

Anatomical Gifts

An **anatomical gift** is the donation of all or part of a human body upon death. Organs are used for both research and transplantation. Most organ transplants are successful. The lives of transplant recipients are often saved, or their quality of life is greatly improved. Many recipients' transplants function for more than twenty years. The one-year success rates range from 70% for liver and lung transplants to over 90% for kidney transplants, and these percentages are continually improving.

The sad statistics, however, according to the Healthcare Systems Bureau (HSB), Division of Transplantation, an agency of the U.S. Department of Health Resources and Services Administration (HRSA), are that as of June 2009, 102,042 people were waiting for transplants. More than 2200 were under the age of 18, and 47% were minorities. Approximately one-quarter of those waiting for transplants will die because an organ will not be available. In fact, at least eight people die each day for lack of an available donor. (Source: www.organdonor.gov.)

Clients are frequently confused about the concept of organ donation. The paralegal can assure a client that neither the donor nor the donor's family are charged for the donation and that the donation will not delay funeral arrangements. In all instances, it is a good idea for the potential donor to discuss donation with his or her friends, family, and clergy.

A donor must be at least 18 years of age to voluntarily donate his or her organs. There are currently three methods by which a person may become an organ donor.

Figure 6.9 Sample Durable and General Power of Attorney, Following Virginia Law After Adoption of the UPOAA

DURABLE GENERAL POWER OF ATTORNEY

OF

JACK C. BLACK

Prepared by/Return to John Jones,
Jones, Jones and Brown, P.C.,
121 Main Street, Noplace,
Virginia 11112, (555) 555-1333;
jjones@jonespc.com

(continued)

Figure 6.9 (continued)

DURABLE GENERAL POWER OF ATTORNEY
OF
JACK BLACK

I, **JACK C. BLACK**, a/k/a **JACKSON C. BLACK**, of Noplace, Virginia, "principal," do hereby appoint JOAN C. BLACK of 999 South Street, Noplace, Virginia 11111, to serve as my "agent" under this general durable power of attorney. In addition, in order to provide for succession, in the event that my agent dies, resigns, or is incapacitated, I appoint the following persons to serve as consecutive successors to my agent named above and who shall serve in the order specified below (in which case all references herein to my "agent" shall refer to my "successor agent"): **JOHNNY C. BLACK** of 111 West Street, Someplace, Virginia 22222, first successor agent. **JANE R. BLACK** of 333 West Place, Anyplace, Virginia 22222, second successor agent.

If any successor agent dies, resigns, or is incapacitated, then the next successor agent named above shall serve as my agent. Any party dealing with any person named as successor agent hereunder may rely upon as conclusively correct an affidavit or certificate under penalties of perjury of such agent that those persons named as prior agents have died, resigned, or are incapacitated.

I intend to create a General, Durable Power of Attorney with this instrument.

GRANT OF GENERAL AUTHORITY

I grant my agent and any successor agent general authority to act for me with respect to the following subjects as defined in the Uniform Power of Attorney Act (Virginia Code §26-72 et seq.):

1. Real Property (Va. Code §26-98), including, but not limited to, my residence located at 999 South Street, Noplace, Virginia 11111
2. Tangible Personal Property (Va. Code §26-99).
3. Stocks and Bonds (Va. Code §26-100).
4. Commodities and Options (Va. Code §26-101).
5. Banks and Other Financial Institutions (Va. Code §26-102).
6. Operation of Entity or Business (Va. Code §26-103).
7. Insurance and Annuities (Va. Code §26-104).
8. Estates, Trusts, and Other Beneficial Interests (Va. Code §26-105).
9. Claims and Litigation (Va. Code §26-106).
10. Personal and Family Maintenance (Va. Code §26-107).
11. Benefits from Governmental Programs or Civil or Military Service (Va. Code §26-108).
12. Retirement Plans (Va. Code §26-109).
13. Taxes (Va. Code §26-110).

GRANT OF SPECIFIC AUTHORITY

Granting any of the following will give your agent the authority to take actions that could significantly reduce your property or change how your property is distributed at your death.

I grant my agent and any successor agent general authority to exercise the following specific powers defined in the Virginia Uniform Power of Attorney Act (Va. Code §26-95):

(Initial each for validity)

1. _____ Create, amend, revoke, or terminate an inter vivos trust (Va. Code §26-95(A)(1)).
2. _____ Create or change rights of survivorship (Va. Code §26-95(A)(3)).
3. _____ Create or change a beneficiary designation (Va. Code §26-95(A)(4)).

(continued)

Figure 6.9 (continued)

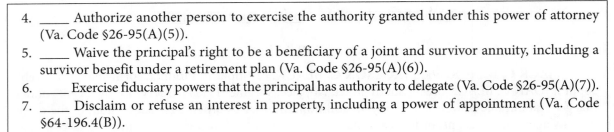

4. _____ Authorize another person to exercise the authority granted under this power of attorney (Va. Code §26-95(A)(5)).
5. _____ Waive the principal's right to be a beneficiary of a joint and survivor annuity, including a survivor benefit under a retirement plan (Va. Code §26-95(A)(6)).
6. _____ Exercise fiduciary powers that the principal has authority to delegate (Va. Code §26-95(A)(7)).
7. _____ Disclaim or refuse an interest in property, including a power of appointment (Va. Code §64-196.4(B)).

GRANT OF SPECIFIC AUTHORITY TO MAKE GIFTS

Make a gift of my property subject to the limitations of the Va. Code §26-111 and the special instructions set forth below: (Va. Code §26-95(A)(2)).

1. **Limitation on Recipients of Gifts.** In exercising the authority granted herein to make gifts, my agent shall only make gifts of my property to or for the benefit of my spouse or my spouse and descendants or my descendants or to any charitable organization, the gifts to which qualify for the Federal income and gift tax charitable deduction, and to which I shall have previously made gifts, and pay my charitable pledges and dues in a manner that my agent shall determine reflects my general donative history.
2. **Gifts to Agent.** I specifically authorize gifts under this power of attorney to my spouse and my descendants when my spouse is serving as my agent.

LIMITATION ON AGENT'S AUTHORITY

1. **Personal Benefit.** My agent that is not my ancestor, spouse, or descendant MAY NOT use my property to benefit the agent or a person to whom the agent owes an obligation of support unless I have included that authority in the Special Instructions. (Va. Code §26-95(B)).
2. **Life Insurance on Agent's Life.** My Agent shall have no authority whatsoever concerning any interest in or incidents of ownership in any policy of insurance I may own on my agent's life.
3. **Avoid Disrupting Estate Plan.** I direct my agent to make reasonable efforts to review my estate plan and, to the extent possible, avoid disrupting the provisions of my estate plan known to my agent. I authorize any person having knowledge of my estate plan, or possession of my estate plan, or possession of my estate planning documents to make disclosure of my estate plan to my agent. If my agent sells any of my assets, I direct that my agent, to the extent possible, avoid selling any asset that I have specifically given away as part of my estate plan.
4. **Reside At Home.** I want to reside at home for as long as it is reasonable for me to do so under the circumstances. To the extent necessary for me to reside at my home, I direct my agent to pay for in-home care. I realize that the cost of in-home care may exceed the cost of nursing home or assisted living facility.

REVOCATION OF EXISTING GENERAL DURABLE POWER OF ATTORNEY

I hereby revoke all general durable powers of attorney previously created by me and terminate all agency relationships created thereunder except for powers created by me on forms provided by financial institutions granting the right to write checks on deposit funds to, and withdraw funds from accounts to which I am signatory or granting access to a safe deposit box.

SPECIAL INSTRUCTIONS

1. **Expenses.** My Agent shall be entitled to reimbursement for expenses reasonably incurred on my behalf (Va. Code §26-83).

(continued)

Figure 6.9 (continued)

2. **Compensation.** My agent is entitled to reasonable compensation for services rendered as my agent. In determining what constitutes "reasonable compensation," the following factors may be considered: (i) the time spent by my agent in managing my affairs, (ii) my net worth, (iii) the nature of my assets, and (iv) the fees charged by professional fiduciaries. My agent is authorized to pay himself or herself such compensation from my funds. Additionally, my agent shall be entitled to be repaid for all reasonable expenses incurred on my behalf under this instrument.

3. **Duties.** My agent shall have the following fiduciary duties: (i) to act loyally for my benefit; (ii) to act so as not to create a conflict of interest that impairs the agent's ability to act impartially in the principal's best interest; (iii) to act with the care, competence, and diligence ordinarily exercised by agents in similar circumstances; (iv) to keep a record of all receipts, disbursements, and transactions made on behalf of the principal; (v) to cooperate with a person that has authority to make health care decisions for the principal to carry out the principal's reasonable expectations to the extent actually known by the agent and otherwise act in the principal's best interest; and (vi) to attempt to preserve the principal's estate plan, to the extent actually known by the agent, if preserving the plan is consistent with the principal's best interest based on all relevant factors, including (A) the value and nature of the principal's property; (B) the principal's foreseeable obligations and need for maintenance; (C) minimization of taxes, including income, estate, inheritance, generation-skipping transfer, and gift taxes; and (D) eligibility for a benefit, a program, or assistance under a statute or regulation (Va. Code §26-85(B)).

4. **Commingling Funds and Assets.** My agent, if my spouse, may commingle my funds and assets with those of my spouse. However, my agent shall maintain separate accounting records concerning my funds and assets.

5. **Exoneration.** I relieve my agent from liability to me or my estate for (i) breach of a fiduciary duty or (ii) the failure to exercise any of the authority granted by this power of attorney (Va. Code §26-86).

6. **Prudent Investor Act.** My agent shall comply with the provisions of the Virginia Uniform Prudent Investor Rule, unless my agent is my spouse, in which case, my agent shall not be required to comply with the provisions of the Virginia Uniform Prudent Investor rule. (Va. Code §45.3 et. seq.)

7. **Employment of Principal's Attorney.** I authorize my agent to employ the attorney who drafted this power of attorney or who assisted me with my estate planning or business affairs. I waive any conflicts of interest that may arise from such employment. I authorize the attorney to make full disclosure to my agent of estate plan and business, financial and personal affairs, and authorize the attorney to accept the employment.

8. **Disclosure.** My agent shall not be required to disclose information nor permit inspection of any of my records (Virginia Code §26-85(1)).

EFFECTIVE DATE

This power of attorney is effective immediately. (Va. Code §26-80(A)).

NOMINATION OF CONSERVATOR OR GUARDIAN

It is my intention by executing this Durable Power of Attorney to provide for the administration of my affairs without the necessity of court action or the appointment of a representative payee. Accordingly, I request in the strongest possible terms that any court or government agency that may receive or act upon a petition for the appointment of a conservator, guardian, or representative payee should deny such petition so long as my agent is acting under this power of attorney. If any court or government agency should deem it necessary to appoint a fiduciary (including a guardian,

(continued)

Figure 6.9 (continued)

conservator, or representative payee) in spite of this request, then I nominate and appoint my agent to serve, and request that my agent be given priority for appointment. In the event that my agent is unavailable or unable to serve as agent, or as conservator or guardian, then I request that my desires, as expressed in this document, be given full force and effect as a written expression of my wishes and intent. (Va. Code §26-79).

RELIANCE ON THIS POWER OF ATTORNEY

Any person, including my agent, may rely upon the validity of this power of attorney or a copy of it unless that person knows it has terminated or is invalid. (Va. Code §26-77(D))

DURABLE

I intend for this power of attorney to be durable. This power of attorney and my agent's authority shall not terminate upon my incapacity. (Va. Code §26-75)

GOVERNING LAW

The meaning and effect of this power of attorney shall be determined by the law of the Commonwealth of Virginia. (Va. Code §26-78).

SIGNATURE AND ACKNOWLEDGMENT

I, **JACK C. BLACK**, sign my name to this Power of Attorney this 30th day of June, 2012, and being first duly sworn, do declare to the undersigned authority that I sign and execute this instrument as my power of attorney, that I sign it willingly or willingly direct another to sign for me, that I execute it as my free and voluntary act for the purposes expressed in the power of attorney, and that I am eighteen years of age or older, of sound mind, and under no constraint or undue influence.

_____(SEAL)

JACK C. BLACK

_____   _____

Witness   Address

_____   _____

Witness   Address

COMMONWEALTH OF VIRGINIA

CITY OF NOPLACE, to-wit:

This power of attorney was acknowledged before me this 30th of June, 2012 by **JACK C. BLACK**, principal, and _____and _____, witnesses.

_____

NOTARY PUBLIC

My Commission Expires: _____

My registration number:_____

See www.unos.org/default.asp for up-to-date information on transplant and donation statistics.

By Will

As stated in Chapter 1, a will can be a vehicle for making an anatomical gift. The problem with putting a gift clause in the will is that transplants must be made within a very short time after death. The will is often not found, or even looked for, until after the potential donor has been buried or cremated. This defeats the purpose of making an anatomical gift.

By Signed Document

Another method that is common and much preferable is the use of an organ tissue donor card. These cards must be signed by the donor in the presence of two witnesses, who must sign the document in the presence of the donor and of each other. The donor should keep this card on his or her person at all times. Many states will affix a sticker directly onto the donor's driver's license. This will instantly alert EMS personnel, or anyone else looking at the donor's license of that person's donor status.

A donor card may specify that all organs and tissues or only certain, specific organs are being donated. The donation may specify a donee if preferred. Some donors may also want to specify certain religious restrictions. A donor with these concerns should speak with his or her clergy of choice to see if there is a special organ donation card that applies. See www.organdonor.gov for a model donor card.

By Others

If no preference for donation has been made, or in the case of minors (who may not themselves make an anatomical gift), other people may make the gift on the decedent's behalf. In order of priority, these people are the surviving spouse, adult child, parent, sibling, or guardian.

The HRSA makes how to donate easy, recommending the following:

- Register with the state donor registry. Most states have donor registries.
- Designate your decision on your driver's license. Do this when you obtain or renew your license.
- Sign a donor card now. Carry the donor card until the designation is made on the driver's license or a donor registry is joined.
- Talk to family now about the donation decision so they are prepared.

POLST: Physician Orders for Life-Sustaining Treatment Paradigm Program

According to a report in October 2007 by Charles P. Sabatino, J.D. for the American Bar Association, Commission on Law and Aging, a "small but growing number of states have recognized that patient wishes, no matter how communicated, must be methodically factored into or translated into the medical decision making engine." The first state to recognize this was Oregon, which in the early 1990s started a program called the Physicians Orders for Life-Sustaining Treatment, or **POLST**. According to the website for the Physician Orders for Life-Sustaining Treatment Paradigm (www.polst.org), the "program is designed to ensure that seriously ill person's wishes regarding life-sustaining treatments are known, communicated, and honored across all health care settings." The program hopes that through its efforts they will (from its website):

- facilitate the development, implementation, and evaluation of POLST Paradigm Programs in the U.S.,
- educate the public and health care professionals regarding the POLST Paradigm,
- support, perform, and fund research related to end-of-life care, and
- improve the quality of end-of-life care.

According to Mr. Sabatino, "POLST is not an advance directive in the conventional sense but is an advance care planning tool that reflects the patient's here-and-now goals for medical decisions that could confront the patient in the immediate future."

States with implemented POLST programs are:

- Washington
- Oregon
- California
- Colorado
- Hawaii
- Idaho
- Montana
- Pennsylvania
- West Virginia (Physician Orders for Scope of Treatment or POST)
- Tennessee
- North Carolina
- New York
- Utah
- Wisconsin

For states that are developing programs, of which there are many, and those that don't have any programs, see http://www.ohsu.edu/polst/programs/state-contacts.htm.

Does POLST work? Studies show that it does. A telephone survey undertaken by Hickman, Nelson, Moss, Hammes, Terwilliger, Jackson, and Tolle, M.D. found that POLST is widely used in Oregon hospices (100%) and West Virginia hospices (85%), but only regionally in Wisconsin (6%). Of the survey respondents, 97% believed the POLST form was useful in preventing unwanted resuscitations by emergency medicine personnel, and 96% found the form useful in initiating conversations about treatment preferences. A review of charts in those three states showed that preferences for treatment limitations were respected in 98% of cases, and no one received unwanted CPR, intubation, intensive care, or feeding tubes. The researchers found that "POLST is well regarded by hospice staff and allows for greater individualization of care plans than traditional approaches focused on code status."

Death with Dignity Acts

In 1994, Oregon voters adopted a measure which would become law in 1997 (Or. Rev. Stat. §§127.800-.995 (2005)). According to the State of Oregon website, The Oregon **Death with Dignity Act** (DWDA) "allows terminally-ill Oregonians to end their lives through the voluntary self-administration of lethal medications, expressly prescribed by a physician for that purpose." In addition, the Oregon Department of Human Services is required "to collect information about the patients and physicians who participate in the Act, and publish an annual statistical report." Such a decision to end one's life under the statute requires an informed decision whereby the physician explains the nature of the person's illness, the prognosis, the risk involved, and the alternate treatment modalities. Under the DWDA, a person must have less than six months life expectancy, and the diagnosis must be confirmed by a second physician. Oregon's data as of February 29, 2012, states that since the Act was passed in 1997, 935 patients have had DWDA prescriptions written and 596 patients have died from ingesting medications prescribed under the DWDA. The data also indicates that "[O]f the 71 DWDA deaths during 2011, most (69.0%) were aged 65 years or older; the median age was 70 years. As in previous years, most were white (95.6%), well-educated (48.5% had at least a baccalaureate degree), and had cancer (82.4%). Most (94.1%) patients died at home; and most (96.7%) were enrolled in hospice care either at the time the DWDA prescription was written or at the time of death. Most (96.7%) had some form of healthcare insurance, although the number of patients who had private insurance (50.8%) was lower in 2011 than in previous years (68.0%), and the number of patients who had only Medicare or Medicaid insurance was higher than in previous years (45.9% compared to 30.4%)." Voters in the State of Washington adopted Initiative Measure 1000, the Washington Death with Dignity Act, by a margin of 59–41% on November 4, 2008. The provisions of the Washington Act have the same safeguards and procedures as Oregon's DWDA. The State of Washington's Department of Health website provided that there were 103 participants in 2011. Of those, 94 individuals died: 70 of these people died after ingesting the medication, 19 of these people died without having ingested the medication, and of the remaining 5 people who died, ingestion status was unknown; for the remaining 9 people, no documentation was received as to whether or not death had occurred.

Of the 94 participants who died, they ranged in age between 41 and 101, 94% were white-non-Hispanic, 46% were married, 75% had at least some college education, 78% had cancer, 12% had a neurodegenerative disease, such as Amyotrophic Lateral Sclerosis, and another 10% had other illnesses such as heart and respiratory disease. Of the 70 participants that ingested the medication, 93% were at home, 83% were receiving hospice care, 87% of all participants had private, Medicare, Medicaid, or a combination of health insurance coverage.

On December 5, 2008, in *Baxter v. Montana,* the Montana Supreme Court held that Montana law prevents the prosecution of a physician who authorizes a lethal dose of medication as long as the terminally ill patient is competent, and requests the prescription. Its analysis was based upon patient consent of the doctor's actions. In that situation, the court reasoned, there could be no criminal prosecution so long as the consent did not violate public policy. In this situation, the court determined that no public policy issues were violated.

Figure 6.10 Estate and Probate Statutes

Alabama	Title 43 Chapter 2 Administration of Estates
	Title 43 Chapter 8 Probate Code
Alaska	Title 13 Decedents' Estates, Guardianships, Transfers, and Trusts
	Title 13 Chapter 16 Probate of Wills and Administration
Arizona	Title 14 Trusts, Estates, and Protective Proceedings
Arkansas	Title 28 Wills, Estates, and Fiduciary Relationships
California	California Probate Code
Colorado	Title 15 Probate, Trusts, and Fiduciaries
Connecticut	Title 45 Probate Courts and Procedure
District of	Division III Title 18 Wills
Columbia	Division III Title 19 Descent Distribution and Trusts
	Division III Title 20 Probate and Administration of Decedents' Estates
Florida	Title XLII Estates and Trusts
Georgia	Title 53 Wills, Trusts, and Administration of Estates
Hawaii	Title 30A Uniform Probate Code
Idaho	Title 15 Uniform Probate Code
Illinois	Chapter 755 Estates
	Chapter 760 Trusts and Fiduciaries
Indiana	Title 29 Probate
	Title 30 Trusts and Fiduciaries
Iowa	Title XV Chapter 633 Probate Code
	Title XV Chapter 634 Private Foundations and Charitable Trusts
	Title XV Chapter 635 Administration of Small Estates
	Title XV Chapter 636 Sureties-Fiduciaries-Trusts-Investments
Kansas	Chapter 59 Probate Code
Kentucky	Chapter 140 Inheritance and Estate Taxes
	Chapter 386 Administration of Trusts—Investments
	Chapter 391 Descent and Distribution
	Chapter 394 Wills
	Chapter 395 Personal Representatives
	Chapter 396 Claims Against Decedents' Estates
Louisiana	Book III, Title I of Successions
	Uniform Probate Law
Maine	Title 18 Decedents' Estates and Fiduciary Relations
	Title 18A Probate Code
Maryland	Titles 1 to 16 Estates and Trusts
Massachusetts	MGL Part II, Title II Descent and Distribution, Wills, Estates
Michigan	Chapters 701–713 Probate Code
Minnesota	Chapters 524–532 Estates of Decedents; Guardianships
Missouri	Title XXXI, Chapters 456–475 Trusts and Estates of Decedents

(continued)

Figure 6.10 (continued)

Montana	<u>Title 72</u> Estates, Trusts and Fiduciary Relationships
Nebraska	<u>Chapter 30</u> Decedents' Estates; Protection of Persons and Property
Nevada	<u>Title 12</u> Wills and Estates of Deceased Persons
	<u>Title 13</u> Guardianships; Conservatorships; Trusts
New Hampshire	<u>Title 56</u> Probate Courts and Decedents' Estates
New Jersey	<u>Titles 3A and 3B</u> Administration of Estates—Decedents and Others
New Mexico	<u>Chapter 45</u> Uniform Probate Code
	<u>Chapter 46</u> Fiduciaries and Trusts
New York	<u>Chapter 17-B</u> Estates, Powers, and Trusts
North Carolina	<u>Chapter 41</u> Estates
	<u>Chapter 47</u> Probate and Registration
North Dakota	<u>Title 30.1</u> Uniform Probate Code
Ohio	<u>Title XXI</u> Courts—Probate—Juvenile
Oklahoma	<u>Title 58</u> Probate Procedure
	<u>Title 84</u> Wills and Succession
Oregon	<u>Chapter 111</u> Probate Law
	<u>Chapter 112</u> Intestate Succession and Wills
	<u>Chapter 113</u> Initiation of Estate Proceedings
	<u>Chapter 114</u> Administration of Estates
	<u>Chapter 115</u> Claims, Actions, and Suits Against Estates
Pennsylvania	<u>Title 20</u> Decedents, Estates and Fiduciaries
Rhode Island	<u>Title 33</u> Probate Practice and Procedure
South Dakota	<u>Title 29A</u> Uniform Probate Code
	<u>Title 55</u> Fiduciaries and Trusts
South Carolina	<u>Title 21</u> Estates, Trusts, Guardians and Fiduciaries
	<u>Title 62</u> Probate Code
Tennessee	<u>Title 30</u> Administration of Estates
	<u>Title 31</u> Descent and Distribution
	<u>Title 32</u> Wills
	<u>Title 35</u> Fiduciaries and Trust Estates
Texas	<u>Texas Probate Code</u>
	<u>Texas Probate Code Chapter V</u> Estates of Decedents
	<u>Texas Probate Code Chapter IV</u> Execution and Revocation of Wills
	<u>Texas Probate Code Chapter XIII</u> Guardianship
Utah	<u>Title 22</u> Fiduciaries and Trusts
	<u>Title 75</u> Uniform Probate Code
Vermont	<u>Title 14</u> Decedents' Estates and Fiduciary Relations
Virginia	<u>Title 64.1</u> Wills and Decedents' Estates
Washington	<u>Title 11</u> Probate and Trust Law
West Virginia	<u>Chapter 41</u> Wills

(*continued*)

Figure 6.10   (continued)

	Chapter 42 Descent and Distribution
	Chapter 44 Administration of Estates and Trusts
Wisconsin	Chapter 701 Trusts
	Chapter 853 Wills
	Chapters 851–882 Probate
Wyoming	Title 2 Wills, Decedents' Estates and Probate Code
	Title 2 Chapter 2 Probate Court
	Title 2 Chapter 6 Wills
	Title 2 Chapter 7 Administration of Estates

This case is reproduced in Appendix A "Important Cases Concerning the Right to Die." In 2011, three bills were introduced to the Montana legislature regarding death with dignity. One was based upon the Oregon and Washington laws, and would codify the Montana Supreme Court's ruling. The other two tried to overturn the court's ruling. None of the bills passed.

SUMMARY

Advance directives are documents that set forth a person's directions to a family member or friend concerning the kind of medical care and treatment, as well as the method of living and dying, if the person becomes incapacitated and unable to make such decisions. This subject is very delicate, and the paralegal will be at the forefront when discussing advance directives with the client. The paralegal should become familiar with all forms of advance directives—living wills, DNRO, health-care surrogates and proxies, medical powers of attorney, durable powers of attorney, and anatomical gifts, as well as POLST and **Death with Dignity Act**, if you are in Washington, Oregon, or Montana—and be prepared to speak with the supervising attorney about the client's wishes, questions, and concerns.

Living wills are declarations that direct the kind of medical care a person wants in the event that person suffers from a terminal condition, or is in a persistent vegetative state. Often this directive is made to a physician and does not require a family member or friend to step in. Living wills contain a statement that the person is willfully and voluntarily making his or her desire known that he or she does not want life to be artificially prolonged in the event that there is no medical probability of recovery from an incurable injury, disease, or illness that is terminal

and that use of artificial, extraordinary, extreme, or radical medical or surgical means or procedures will only serve to prolong his or her dying.

A DNRO declares that the patient does not want resuscitation efforts to be initiated if the patient suffers cardiac arrest or respiratory failure, and for whom resuscitation is not warranted. The terminal condition of the patient, as determined by the requisite number of physicians (usually two), will be stated on the face of the document. The patient or his or her surrogate, if allowed by state law, must sign the document.

In some states, a person names a health-care surrogate who is a person named by an individual to make all medical decisions in the event the individual is unable to give consent. The designation of the surrogate must be in writing. A health-care proxy is a person authorized by state law to make health-care decisions for an individual who has not expressly designated a surrogate. The proxy is usually designated by the health-care provider, following preferences set by state law. Under medical powers of attorney, the agent may only make decisions concerning the principal's medical care if the principal is unable to do so. The medical power of attorney has no effect unless the principal is incapacitated.

A durable power of attorney is a document in which the principal gives an agent the authorization to act on one's behalf, usually for financial and business concerns. The authorization may include the ability to mortgage, sell, or lease property; sell, buy, or trade stocks and bonds; institute lawsuits; and run a business. The powers and authority of the agent survive the principal's incapacity or permits the powers to become effective upon the principal's incapacity so that the agent may act for the principal if in fact, the principal becomes incapacitated.

Anatomical gifts are the donation of all or part of a human body upon death. Organs are used for both research and transplantation. Most people do not make anatomical gifts, and more than 100,000 people are waiting for transplants in the U.S. alone.

POLST (Physicians Orders for Life-Sustaining Treatment), while not really an advance directive, is a program designed to "ensure that seriously ill person's wishes regarding life-sustaining treatments are known, communicated, and honored across all health-care settings."

Death with Dignity act permits terminally ill individuals to end their lives through the voluntary self-administration of lethal medications, expressly prescribed by a physician for that purpose. Only three states currently have Death with Dignity laws, two by statute: Oregon and Washington, and one by legal precedent (court decision): Montana. Those states that have statutes have stringent standards regarding the administration of the act and penalties for noncompliance.

KEY **TERMS**

living will	POLST	health-care proxy
advance directive	principal	anatomical gifts
medical power of attorney	agent	DNRO
durable power of attorney	health-care surrogate	Death with Dignity Act

REVIEW **QUESTIONS**

1. What is the purpose of a living will?
2. How may a gift of organs be made?
3. What is a health-care surrogate?
4. Explain the difference between a power of attorney and a durable power of attorney.
5. How does a do not resuscitate order differ from a living will?
6. How has medical technology influenced the subject of the right to die?
7. What is a Death with Dignity Act and how does it work?
8. What is the POLST program? Review the POLST paradigm website. What is its purpose?
9. What is the function of an agent under a durable power of attorney?
10. What is a do not resuscitate order and when are they used?
11. In your opinion, should the paralegal have the task of assisting the client with advance directive documents if his or her religious, ethical, or moral beliefs are contradictory to those of the client? Why?

PROJECTS

1. Determine if your state has a preferred or mandated living will form. Do you think your state's form is adequate, based upon your knowledge of these documents? Print it out and prepare to discuss it in class.
2. Assist a local nursing facility in preparing advance directives for their clients (as allowed by state and federal law only).
3. Determine if your jurisdiction has established an "Outside the Hospital Do-Not-Resuscitate Act" to permit the execution of do-not-resuscitate orders for use by emergency medical providers for patients receiving treatment outside a hospital.

MyLegalStudiesLab™ http://www.mylegalstudieslab

MYLEGALSTUDIESLAB VIRTUAL LAW OFFICE EXPERIENCE ASSIGNMENTS

Complete the pre-test, study plan, and post-test for this chapter and answer the Legal Applications questions as assigned. These will help you confirm your mastery of the concepts and their application to legal scenarios. Then complete the Virtual Law Office assignments as assigned by your instructor. These assignments are designed to develop your workplace skills and result in producing documents for inclusion in your portfolio.

Chapter **seven**

PLANNING FOR NON-TRADITIONAL FAMILIES

Introduction

Where does one begin when discussing such topics as same-sex marriage, grandparents raising grandchildren, and artificial insemination using frozen eggs or sperm after divorce or death? It would be safe to say, very carefully. These topics are fraught with peril—political landmines, and religious, moral, and ethical issues are often raised and debated.

The goal here in this chapter is not to enter the fray of the argument, but to dispassionately talk about the ramifications of the law as it is or is being proposed by the various authorities concerning an individual's estate planning. Questions that are raised include the following:

- Is the will effective regarding the same-sex spouse?
- Is a grandchild being raised by a grandparent an heir?
- Who gets to be the health-care proxy or surrogate when a partner is in a medical crisis?
- Is a child born after artificial insemination the heir of her deceased sperm or egg donor parent?
- Will a stepchild inherit from a stepparent if the stepparent was the person who raised the child?

The law continues to be in great flux in these areas and so, unfortunately, we will not necessarily have the answers. We can, however, raise the questions that a paralegal will need to examine if a client with any of these issues walks in the door—because they will.

Same-Sex Marriage and Civil Unions

History and Issues Regarding Same-Sex Marriages

Same-sex marriage, also known as gay marriage, is the legally recognized marriage between two people of the same sex, which is in opposition to the time-honored tradition of two persons of the opposite sex being married. The debate over same-sex marriage is not strictly an American issue either. Europe also has been dealing with the issue. As of July 2012, eight European countries, Belgium, Denmark, Iceland, the Netherlands, Norway, Portugal, Spain, and Sweden, have legalized gay marriage; so has Canada and South Africa. Israel recognizes same-sex marriages performed abroad, although you cannot be married in Israel unless you are a heterosexual couple. The Caribbean islands of Aruba and the Netherland Antilles also recognize same-sex marriage, but do not perform them on the islands. Fourteen European countries have a form of civil union or unregistered cohabitation.

The debate over same-sex unions in the United States has been rocky. In 1993, the Massachusetts Supreme Judicial Court held that Massachusetts must allow gay and lesbian couples to marry. The debate has raged ever since.

The **Defense of Marriage Act** (DOMA) was signed by President Bill Clinton on September 21, 1996. The bill was passed by Congress by a vote of 85–14 in the Senate and a vote of 342–67 in the House of Representatives. As passed by Congress, DOMA specifically defines marriage in the federal government system as a legal union exclusively between one man and one woman. In addition, the Act permits each state to deny recognition of same-sex marriages from other states where same-sex marriage is legal despite the **Full Faith and Credit Clause** of the United States Constitution. The Full Faith and Credit Clause is Section 1 of Article IV of the Constitution and states "Full faith and credit shall be given in each state to the public acts, records, and judicial proceedings of every other state. And the Congress may by general laws prescribe the manner in which such acts, records, and proceedings shall be proved, and the effect thereof." The clause is used to ensure that judicial decisions in one state are recognized and honored in other states. It has also been used to recognize the validity of a marriage performed in another state. Traditionally, each state honored a marriage legally performed in another state, and for that matter, in another country.

Passage of the Act was in response to two court cases, *Baehr v. Lewin* and *Romer v. Evans*. In *Baehr*, the Hawaii Supreme Court held that the denial of the right of marriage to same-sex couples was gender discrimination. In *Romer*, the United States Supreme Court struck down Colorado's Constitutional Amendment 2 prohibiting government action or policies that would have protected gay men and lesbians from discrimination. In *Romer*, however, the Court also stated that any government action that showed what amounted to deliberate prejudice toward a group could not be justified. Since *Baehr* and *Romer*, the law's constitutionality has been appealed to the United States Supreme Court several times, but the Court has declined to review the appeals.

On June 11, 2009, a new lawsuit filed in United States District Court for the Central District of California in which Arthur Smelt and Christopher Hammer questioned whether their marriage must be recognized nationwide by states that have not approved gay marriage. In August 2009, the case was dismissed, the federal judge holding that the two men could not show personal harm suffered because of the law. The Obama Administration has shown varying support for a repeal of DOMA; the administration's website, www.whitehouse.gov, stated in May 2009, "[Obama] supports full civil unions and federal rights for LGBT [lesbian, gay, bisexual and transgendered] couples and opposes a constitutional ban on same-sex marriage." On June 17, 2009, the website stated,

> I am also proud to announce my support for an important piece of legislation introduced in both Houses of Congress last month—the Domestic Partners Benefits and Obligations Act of 2009. This legislation will extend to the

same-sex partners of Federal employees the same benefits already enjoyed by the opposite-sex spouses of Federal employees.

It has yet to pass through the Congress, usually dying in committee.

That same day, President Obama issued an executive memorandum requesting that the Secretary of State and the Director of the Office of Personnel Management, in consultation with the Department of Justice, "extend the benefits they have respectively identified to qualified same-sex domestic partners of Federal employees where doing so can be achieved and is consistent with Federal law." You may review the memorandum at:

http://www.whitehouse.gov/assets/documents/2009fedbenefits_mem_rel.pdf.

Many state legislatures have called for an amendment to the United States Constitution specifically stating that marriage is between one man and one woman. On September 30, 2004, however, the House of Representatives failed to pass a proposed amendment with a vote of 227 for and 186 against. According to The Human Rights Campaign, as of July 1, 2012, the following states have enacted constitutional amendments restricting marriage to one man and one woman: Alabama, Alaska, Arizona, Arkansas, California, Colorado, Florida, Georgia, Kansas, Idaho, Kentucky, Louisiana, Michigan, Mississippi, Missouri, Montana, Nebraska, Nevada, North Carolina, North Dakota, Ohio, Oklahoma, Oregon, South Carolina, South Dakota, Tennessee, Texas, Utah, Virginia, and Wisconsin. States with statutory laws restricting marriage to one man and one woman are Delaware, Hawaii, Illinois, Indiana, Maine, Maryland, Minnesota, Pennsylvania, Washington, West Virginia, and Wyoming.

As of July 2012, Massachusetts, Connecticut, Vermont, New Hampshire, and Iowa recognize same-sex marriages. In 2009, the District of Columbia decided that while you cannot have a same-sex marriage performed in the District, a same-sex marriage performed in another state is valid in the District for all purposes. New York courts have ruled similarly that same-sex marriages conducted in states where same-sex marriages are legal are recognized, but that same-sex marriage licenses cannot be issued. The irony is that in the District and New York, courts can rule on same-sex divorces. In May 2009, the California Supreme Court upheld Proposition 8, a voter-approved ban on same-sex

CASE 7.1 **SUMMARY**

Varnum et al v. Brien, 763 N.W.2d 862 (Iowa 2009) Iowa Supreme Court

http://www.judicial.state.ia.us/Supreme_Court/Recent_Opinions/20090403/07-1499.pdf. The Court in Varnum unanimously found that the Iowa marriage statute was unconstitutional and that marriage licenses should be issued to gay and lesbian couples and heterosexual couples alike.

It is true the marriage statute does not expressly prohibit gay and lesbian persons from marrying; it does, however, require that if they marry, it must be to someone of the opposite sex. Viewed in the complete context of marriage, including intimacy, civil marriage with a person of the opposite sex is as unappealing to a gay or lesbian person as civil marriage with a person of the same sex is to a heterosexual. Thus, the right of a gay or lesbian person under the marriage statute to enter into a civil marriage only with a person of the opposite sex is no right at all. Under such a law, gay or lesbian individuals cannot simultaneously fulfill their deeply felt need for a committed personal relationship, as influenced by their sexual orientation, and gain the civil status and attendant benefits granted by the statute. Instead, a gay or lesbian person can only gain the same rights under the statute as a heterosexual person by negating the very trait that defines gay and lesbian people as a class—their sexual orientation. *In re Marriage Cases*, 183 P.3d at 441. The benefit denied by the marriage statute—the status of civil marriage for same-sex couples—is so "closely correlated with being homosexual" as to make it apparent the law is targeted at gay and lesbian people as a class.

marriage, but permitted the approximately 18,000 same-sex marriages that had already been performed to remain valid. At various times over the last few years, same-sex marriages have been both allowed and banned in California due to various voter initiatives, legislative decisions, and court decisions. New Mexico and Rhode Island are the only states that have no law either banning or allowing same-sex marriage.

As you can see, the laws regarding this issue are totally confusing and continue to be at issue and a political hot potato, being discussed much on the election circuit.

An August 2007 survey by the Pew Forum on Religion & Public Life and the Pew Research Center for the People & the Press found that 55% of Americans opposed gay marriage while 36% favored it. It also found that those with a higher frequency of church attendance opposed gay marriage by a margin of 73% opposed to 21% in favor. Opposition among white evangelicals was higher still at 81%. Opposition among black Protestants was 64%, Latino Catholics was 52%, white, non-Hispanic Catholics was 49%, and white mainline Protestants was 47%. Sixty percent of those without a religious affiliation expressed support for gay marriage.

Similar polls taken in 2008 and 2009 suggest that Americans are changing their minds, however. A *Washington Post/ABC* poll taken in March 2009 found that 49% of Americans supported gay marriage and 53% want their state to recognize gay marriages from other states.

A *New York Times/CBS News* poll released in early 2009 also found that 42% of Americans supported gay marriage. A recent Quinnipiac poll found that 55% of Americans were against gay marriage but that 57% support civil unions.

Civil Unions and Domestic Partnerships

So, how does a **civil union**, defined as the legal recognition of the marriage-like partnership of two individuals, differ from marriage? As Steven Goldstein, director of Equality, New Jersey, said in 2006 upon New Jersey's passing of its civil union law, "[N]obody knows what civil unions are in the real world. That's the problem." While everyone knows what a marriage is from state to state and jurisdiction to jurisdiction, civil unions and their related domestic partnerships are creatures of statute and, as such, their definitions change depending upon the reading of the law in a particular jurisdiction. For example, when Vermont passed its civil union law in 2000, it stated, "Parties to a civil union shall have all the same benefits, protections and responsibilities under Vermont law, whether they derive from statute, policy, administrative or court rule, common law, or any other source of civil law, as are granted to spouses in a marriage." In some jurisdictions and countries, civil unions are open to heterosexual couples who do not want to get married, but want the same benefits granted to married couples. In Europe, where civil unions are often between heterosexual couples as well as between same-sex couples, some heterosexual couples see civil union as the step between living together and marriage.

What Are the Issues and Problems of Not Permitting Same-Sex Marriages or Civil Unions or of Only Permitting Civil Unions?

In the United States, findings concerning civil unions have not been uniformly positive. For example, the New Jersey Civil Union Review Commission in 2008, two years after New Jersey's civil union law passed, found that the civil union law did not give same-sex couples the same protections as their heterosexual counterparts. It stated, "This commission finds that the separate categorization established by the Civil Union Act invites and encourages unequal treatment of same-sex couples and their children." In its report, the commission found that individuals were prevented from visiting their partners in hospitals and making medical decisions on their behalf.

Colorado's new civil union law passed in 2009, however, permits all unwed couples the power to make end-of-life decisions for his or her partner, and ensures that a dependent partner receives wrongful death and insurance benefits and other estate-planning rights.

Unlike marriage, civil unions are not portable from state to state. DOMA makes it entirely possible that a civil union or same-sex marriage in one state will not be recognized in another. Certainly, without President Obama's memorandum regarding equal benefits for same-sex couples, federal benefits would be denied for any couple that is not legally married. If you wonder how many benefits a non-married couple does not have benefit of, consider that in 2004, the United States Government Accountability Office determined that there were 1138 federal statutory provisions classified in the United States Code "in which benefits, rights, and privileges are contingent on marital status or in which marital status is a factor."

For some, the concept of denying same-sex couples the ability to marry smacks of the interracial laws in this country in prior decades. For example in 1959, Richard and Mildred Loving were put in jail for the crime of being an interracial couple. At the time, Virginia held that their marriage was not only invalid, it was also a felony. After marrying in Washington, D.C., where interracial marriage was permitted, the Lovings were arrested in the early morning of July 11, 1959, when they were removed by police from their bed in their Virginia home. Under Virginia's Racial Integrity Act of 1662, they were charged with and pleaded guilty to the felony charge. The case was eventually determined in their favor by the United States Supreme Court in *Loving v. Virginia*, 388 U.S. 1 (1967). In that case, the United States Supreme Court held that Virginia's anti-miscegenation law was unconstitutional. While no same-sex couples have been arrested as the Lovings were, the facts are eerily similar in that the Lovings' marriage was valid in one jurisdiction and invalid just a few miles away.

You might recall that at the beginning of this book, we stated that if you are of sound mind and legal age, you can leave your property, no matter how much or how little you own, whether real or personal in nature, to whomever you want, and in whatever amounts you choose.

How is this concept affected by the laws being passed by the various legislatures? Should these rights be altered based on sexual orientation, or perhaps based upon a conscientious choice by a heterosexual couple not to marry, but to live together in a long-term committed relationship?

For example, the Virginia Legislature passed the Affirmation of Marriage Act in April of 2004, an amendment to Virginia's Defense of Marriage law. This law is considered the most stringent of the DOMA laws and, in fact, Virginia is considered the most anti-gay, pro-marriage state in the United States. The amendment went into effect from July 1, 2004. It states,

> Be it enacted by the General Assembly of Virginia:
> 1. That the Code of Virginia is amended by adding a section numbered 20-45.3 as follows:
> §20-45.3. Civil unions between persons of same sex.

> A civil union, partnership contract or other arrangement between persons of the same sex purporting to bestow the privileges or obligations of marriage is prohibited. Any such civil union, partnership contract or other arrangement entered into by persons of the same sex in another state or jurisdiction shall be void in all respects in Virginia and any contractual rights created thereby shall be void and unenforceable.

At first blush, and according to the legislative intent and proponents of the law, the law only purports to prevent the patina of "marriage" on same-sex couples, especially those who obtained legal marriages or the right of civil union in other states, as other states have also prevented same-sex marriages from being valid in their states. However, constitutional scholars and activists have argued that if a judge chose to interpret the Virginia law broadly, he or she could, in fact, overturn, or nullify, a gay person's will, trust, power of attorney, medical directive, or deed among other legal documents. In Defense of Marriage, laws might also affect heterosexual committed couples depending upon their wording. If you read Virginia's statute for example, the law specifically bans any civil union, even those between heterosexual couples. If interpreted broadly such a law, which abridges a same-sex couple's rights to contract, might be extended to encompass domestic heterosexual partners. For example, in the private sector, many companies, including Microsoft, Boeing, and Disney, have extended certain employee family benefits to domestic partners. Boeing specifically excluded domestic heterosexual partners from the benefit plan citing that a heterosexual couple could legally marry and that if they wanted the benefits, they would in fact, have to marry. A law such as Virginia's DOMA would consider such decision by Boeing to be within its rights and could negate Microsoft's and Disney's decision to give benefits to domestic partners.

Yet, the United States Census Bureau indicates that 43% of all Americans, or 99.6 million people, are single. That number includes 6.5 million unmarried-partner households, of which 581,300 were same-sex households. Interestingly, the number of Americans aged 65 and older who choose to cohabit instead of marry has also increased. It is clear from the data that the face of the family is changing in the United States and that perhaps the law should change to meet the face of the American family.

Opponents of the Virginia law and scholars base their argument upon the language "… partnership contract or other arrangement entered into by persons of the same sex … and any contractual rights created thereby shall be void and unenforceable." Their argument is that same-sex couples might have their constitutional right to contract abridged. In June 2004, Jonathan Rauch, a commentator in *The Washington Post*, surmised that a gay man from California on business in Virginia, if injured in a car accident, might have his medical directive naming his partner as power of attorney denied legitimacy. He likened Virginia's law to the Jim Crow laws before Civil Rights. In another article Rauch wrote for *The Atlantic* in 2004, he illustrated the problem with a humorous example:

"Wait a minute," a gay person might protest. "How is this supposed to work? I get married in Maryland (say), but every time I cross the border into Virginia during my morning commute, I'm single? Am I married or not?" As Rauch points out, unlike marriage which is portable from state to state, a same-sex marriage or civil union is not. [Note: "Same sex marriage will be legal in Maryland starting January 2103 but at the time was not available in Maryland: Rauch only used it as an example because people routinely commute between Maryland and Virginia on a daily basis.]

Unlike Virginia, the Texas Defense of Marriage Act, which was passed in May 2003, denies the right to marriage for same-sex couples, but does not prevent same-sex couples from living together, or deny them the right to leave property to each other, or enter into powers of attorney and other contracts.

To understand what civil union would provide all unmarried but committed domestic partners, one only needs to look to Vermont, which has permitted civil union since 2000. In Vermont, the following is a list of some of the rights and obligations that are granted to unmarried but committed partners:

- Intestacy rights, similar to those granted to spouses, and protection for the surviving partner (such as family allowance and elective share).
- The right to make the decision regarding disposal (burial or cremation) of the partner's remains upon the partner's death.
- Preference as a partner's guardian or conservator upon the partner's incapacity.
- Ability to make health-care decisions for a partner who is unable to do so.
- The right to visit the partner in the hospital. In many situations, life partners have been barred from their partners' hospital room by family members and hospital staff.
- Ability to sue for wrongful death.
- Ability to sue for loss of consortium.
- Family medical leave.
- Parental leave to raise children.
- Greater access to family health insurance benefits.
- Alimony payments if the couple splits up.

It should be noted that these rights do not extend beyond the borders of Vermont, or to the federal government.

The American Law Institute (ALI) has tried to set forth working guidelines for what constitutes a "domestic partner." The ALI defines a domestic partnership as follows:

- Two persons of the same or opposite sex;
- Who are not married to each other;
- Who share a primary residence; and
- Who live together as a couple.

In addition, the ALI stated that if such a family should dissolve, a court should consider such other factors as the couple's physical intimacy, whether they participated in a commitment or "marriage" ceremony; registered as domestic partners with their employers; named each other as health-care agent for medical decisions; made joint gifts to charity; celebrated holidays, birthdays, and "anniversaries" together; agreed to be buried together, or determined who would take possession of the deceased partner's ashes; and what their reputation in the community as a couple was. Monogamy was stressed as the cornerstone of a domestic partnership. It stands to reason that these factors would easily factor in whether or not a couple was a domestic partnership for probate purposes as well.

Other factors that would be considered include whether they relocated together as a couple, co-parented, co-mingled finances, and if one of the partners sacrificed a career for the benefit of the family unit. The couple's attempt to grant or devise property to each other, using wills and will substitutes, and statements made to other parties would also be of utmost importance.

Consider, however, a state's attempt to make heretofore traditional marriage the only legitimate expression of a family unit. It appears that laws similar to Virginia's statute, if taken to its extreme, could very well be extended to preclude the ability of domestic couples to grant or devise property to each other, if a family can so easily contest such documents.

Currently in Virginia, as stated before, a court could invalidate a deed between "John Smith and Bob Jones" if they were a same-sex couple and the family contested. It appears on the face of the law that a court could also uphold a lawsuit by a sibling contesting a deed his sister executed with her domestic partner in which the heterosexual couple took title as joint tenants with right of survivorship.

> *Example:* Todd Black files a lawsuit upon his sister Tina Black's death, claiming that the deed recorded by his sister, Tina, and her domestic partner, Steven White, was not valid. The document stated that Tina and Steven took title to the property as "Tina Black and Steven White as joint tenants with right of survivorship." Under a broad interpretation of the Virginia statute, Todd would be able to have a court render the deed invalid. The outcome of such a court decision would be that one-half of the title to the home that Tina and Steven lived in would be subject to either Tina's will or intestacy.

Under the schema of domestic partnership laws, if a family member can demonstrate that the surviving partner committed infidelities against the deceased, he or she can claim that the couple was not a domestic partnership. No such requirement of monogamy is required for couples who are in a "traditional" marriage.

It stands to reason that if state legislatures are willing to nullify legal documents executed for the express purpose of protecting loved ones in civil unions, gay and lesbian relationships, and committed but not traditionally married partnerships, legislatures would not be willing to add these partnership schemes to their intestacy laws. Yet, E. Gary Spitko, Associate Professor of Law at Santa Clara University, stated in 81 Oregon L.R. 255, 269 that "[T]here is widespread acceptance among succession law scholars that it is and should be an important goal of any intestacy scheme to further the donative intent of the intestate property owner." If the goal of intestacy statutes is to carry out the most logical donative intent of a deceased person, the question that begs answering is whether the statutes should be changed to provide for these family structures.

Unfortunately, many couples believe that the law will protect them and that they are considered their partner's heir and would inherit from the partner. This misguided belief, that the committed partner has legal standing, can have grave consequences. Estate and financial planners encourage domestic partners to execute all manner of estate planning documents, so that the partners will provide for each other and their children because the law generally does not. When partners have estate plans drafted, the inheritance schemes may become the subject of will contests by the deceased's excluded family members, still considered by the law to be the "natural bounty" of the deceased. Whether the children of these relationships will be allowed to inherit from the father may very well be based on the state's laws concerning children born out of wedlock; that is, did the parent acknowledge the child, legally adopt the child, or give the child his or her name, or is the name of the parent on the birth certificate. Professor Spitko, quoting Milton C. Regan, Jr., states that "current research suggests that cohabitation has become less of an 'engagement' that serves as a prelude to marriage and more of an intimate arrangement that may serve as an alternative to it." Similarly, the law only considers a child of a same-sex marriage as the child of the mother who gave birth to the child, or the mother or father that adopted the child. Since most state laws prohibit gay couples from adopting together, this means that the child may only inherit from one parent. This would seem to indicate that the intestacy laws should be changed to protect these family members, but whether they will be in the foreseeable future remains to be seen.

Domestic Partner Registries

A **domestic partnership** is a legal or personal relationship between two individuals who live together and share a common domestic life, but are not legally married or bound by a civil union. Registries are available in many municipalities and states. Registries are noted to provide a standard for employers to allow workers to share benefits with their partners. According to the Maine Department of Health Data and Program Management, Bureau of Health of the Department of Health and Human Services, in Maine, which enacted a statewide domestic partnership registry, "registered domestic partners are accorded a legal status similar to that of a married person with respect to matters of probate, guardianships, conservatorships, inheritance, protection from abuse, and related matters. Typically, **domestic partner registry** laws do not afford domestic partners as many rights as are afforded to married couples, but the registries are seen as a step in the right direction. Domestic registry options are available in several localities with other localities debating whether or not such registries should be allowed or banned.

Grandparents Raising Grandchildren

According to U.S. census data for 2010, 4.9 million children (7%) under age 18 live in grandparent-headed households. This is not the same family situation as a grandparent living with a family unit consisting of at least one parent, children, and a grandparent figure. This is a situation where the grandparent is raising the grandchild because of some sort of parental failure due to the death of a parent, a parent who is incarcerated or drug-addicted, or is otherwise unavailable to parent his or her own children.

This issue has become so prevalent in the United States that the government has an entire website dedicated to grandparents raising grandchildren which lists resources for grandparents to use to assist them in this difficult task: http://www.usa.gov/Topics/Grandparents.shtml#vgn-data-and-publications-vgn

U.S. census data suggest that two million grandparents are responsible for their grandchildren's basic needs, such as food, shelter, and clothing. Almost half a million of grandparents have income below the poverty level. In addition, 1.4 million grandparents responsible for the basic care of their grandchildren are still in the work force. Three-quarters of a million grandparents caring for grandchildren have a disability.

As previously stated, parental failure takes many forms. It may occur because the parents are deceased. Often, however, the grandparent raises grandchildren because of an absent parent due to incarceration or drug and alcohol problems of the parent, as well as other mental or physical ailments of the parent. Grandparents become caregivers for grandchildren when family violence takes place in the parental home, when the parents get divorced and can no longer support the children, when the parents become unemployed or homeless, or when the parents are abusive or neglectful of the children. In addition, grandparents often bear the burden of raising grandchildren after the teen pregnancy of the parent.

Legal Issues

Important legal issues are raised when a grandparent is raising a grandchild. This book cannot address issues of child support. What we most want to know in the realm of estate planning are as follows:

- Can a grandparent make medical decisions for the grandchildren?
- Can a grandparent enroll a grandchild in school and receive reports from the school concerning the grandchild's education?
- Will a grandchild inherit from his or her grandparent?

Medical Decisions

A parent can create a power of attorney, which gives the grandparents the authority to make medical decisions for the grandchildren. Of course, as we have already learned, a person must be capable of executing a power of attorney. If the parent is already neglectful of the children, drug addicted, or simply absent, the authorization is just not given. A power of attorney will not remove the parents' rights and the parent can revoke the power of attorney at any time. Many states and the District of Columbia have enacted medical consent legislation permitting parents to authorize a grandparent (or other adult) to obtain medical treatment for children in their absence. While all jurisdictions have permitted medical treatment for minors without parental consent in emergency situations, a grandparent would not otherwise be able to consent for routine medical or dental care without such authorization.

Figure 7.1   Parent Authorizing Medical Consent to a Non-Parent (Pennsylvania)

Medical Consent Authorization

Act 52 of 1999 Medical Consent Act

I, _____, am the Parent/ Legal Guardian (if Legal Guardian, attach copy of court order) of the child(ren) listed below and there are no court orders now in effect that would prohibit me from conferring the power to consent upon another person.

I, _____, do hereby confer upon
    (Name of Parent or Legal Guardian or Custodian)

_____
    (Name of Person Bringing Child(ren) for Care)

residing at _____

the power to consent to necessary medical or mental health treatment for the following child(ren):
1) Name: _____ Born on: _____

Residing at: _____

(continued)

Figure 7.1   (continued)

2) Name: _____ Born on: _____

Residing at: _____

3) Name: _____ Born on: _____

Residing at: _____

and on the child(ren)'s behalf do hereby state that the power to consent that I confer shall not be affected by my subsequent disability or incapacity.

The power that I confer is specifically limited to health care and mental health care decision making, and it may be exercised only by the person named above.

The person named above may consent to the following examinations and treatment for my child(ren) (check all that apply):

_____ Medical _____ Surgical _____ Mental Health

_____ Immunizations _____ Development _____ Dental

_____ Other (specify)

and may have access to any and all records, including, but not limited to, insurance records regarding any such services.

I confer the power to consent freely and knowingly in order to provide for the child(ren) and not as a result of pressure, threats or payments by any person or agency. This document (which consists of two pages) shall remain in effect until it is revoked by my written notification to my child(ren)'s medical, mental health care, and insurance providers, and the person named above.

In witness hereof, I have signed my name to this medical consent authorization, on this _____ day of _____, 20_____ in _____, Pennsylvania.

_____

(Printed Name) of Parent or Legal Guardian

_____

(Signature) of Parent or Legal Guardian

_____

(Witness Signature)

_____

(Witness No. 1 Printed Name and Address)

_____

(Witness Signature)

_____

(Witness No. 2 Printed Name and Address)

_____

(Signature of Adult Person who is Being Given Power to Consent)

(Forms/Medical of Adult Person who is Being Given Power to Consent)

Inheritance by the Grandchild from a Grandparent Who is Raising the Child

Perhaps the most troublesome issue surrounding grandparents raising grandchildren, however, is in inheritance.

As pointed out by Professor Kristine S. Knaplund of Pepperdine University in 42 *Arizona Law Review* 1 (2006), entitled "Grandparents Raising Grandchildren and the Implications for Inheritance," if a grandparent dies without executing a will, intestacy laws will distribute everything to the parent and not the grandchild, who was for the most part abandoned by the parent to begin with.

Professor Knaplund and other legal scholars have suggested several methodologies to solve this problem:

- Equitable adoption: The doctrine of **equitable adoption** follows common law principles that a child may become "equitably" adopted by judicial declaration and is followed by a majority of states. As stated by Professor Irene D. Johnson of the Pace University School of Law,

  > The doctrine of equitable adoption, as devised by courts of equity, recognizes the child as an heir of the 'parent' or 'parents' in very limited circumstances. Other than satisfaction of the requirements for an equitable adoption in those states that recognize the doctrine, the only way to become an heir for intestate succession purposes is to be born into or adopted into a family.

  [To read Professor Johnson's article, go to http://digitalcommons.pace.edu/lawfaculty/555] Equitable adoption is limited because in most instances, the grandchild may only be adopted if the grandparent formally attempted to adopt the grandchild, or there was a clear agreement that the grandparent would adopt. Professor Johnson stated that she "believes that the law should be changed to recognize the reality of domestic arrangements in this country, to the benefit of children who usually do not have any say in the matter when they are removed from their families of birth, and who often are from disadvantaged economic circumstances."

  The problem with equitable adoption is that the parent most often believes that as soon as he or she gets back on his or her feet, the child will be returned, setting up a situation in which the parties trust that the care giving by the grandparent is only a temporary measure. As we have already stated, statistically this belief does not pan out, however, since almost half of the grandchildren live with the grandparents for at least five years. Clearly, in this most common of situations, the grandparent never attempted to adopt the children, nor was there an agreement between the grandparents and parent to allow the grandchildren to be adopted by the grandparents.

- A Will: Possibly the best solution to inheritance by the grandchildren, who have come to rely on their grandparents and are usually still minors at the time of the grandparent's death, is to execute a will which leaves the property to the grandchild in trust (testamentary trust). Leaving the property in trust usually eliminates the necessity for a conservator to be appointed to manage the property during the grandchild's minority. Of course, care must be taken to ensure that large amounts of property should not be given to a grandchild outright so that a potentially unsuitable guardian is not put in charge of the property, and that control of the property does not pass to the grandchild immediately upon reaching his or her majority.

- An Inter Vivos Trust: An equally good solution to a testamentary trust is a living trust, which also leaves the grandchild property in trust, and prevents the property from being mismanaged or given to the grandchild upon his or her majority.

- Transfer under the Uniform Transfer to Minors Act: Professor Knaplund suggests that leaving a gift utilizing the **Uniform Transfer to Minors Act** (UTMA), which is available in some form in all states, except South Carolina and Vermont, might be a good solution when there is only a small amount of personal property and no real property, and only one minor child. Under a UTMA transfer, the property is left to the minor in the care of a custodian. Professor Knaplund sees a few drawbacks to UTMA transfers including the fact that the property automatically must transfer to the custody of the grandchild upon his or her majority; however, such a transfer may be better than nothing at all.

- Change the Definition of "Child" in the Intestacy Statutes: Professor Johnson suggests a change favoring the grandchildren in such a situation, as being raised by a grandparent, as "intestate succession statutes to include such children in the definition of 'child.'" The statute would then include biological and legally adopted children in the definition of "child," but would add to "child" a person who had been raised in a family as a "family member." She states, "There is no reason to make distinctions based on circumstances outside of the child's control and about which, at the point when such a matter would be raised—upon the death of one of the family heads without a will in place—no issue should be made."

- Beneficiary Designation: Specifically naming a grandchild as the beneficiary under retirement benefits, pension benefits, insurance benefits, and other POD accounts will ensure that the grandchild receives the property. As with leaving property to a grandchild in a will, care must be taken to ensure that large amounts of property should not be given to a grandchild outright so that a potentially unsuitable guardian is not put in charge of the property and that control of the property does not pass to the grandchild immediately upon reaching his or her majority.

Stepparents and Stepfamilies

Once upon a time in a faraway land there was a tiny kingdom, peaceful, prosperous, and rich in romance and tradition. Here in a stately chateau there lived a widowed gentleman and his little daughter, Cinderella. Although he was a kind and devoted father who gave his beloved child every luxury and comfort, still he felt she needed a mother's care. And so he married again, choosing for his second wife a woman of good family with two daughters just Cinderella's age, by name, Anastasia and Drisella. It was upon the untimely death of this good man, however, that the stepmother's true nature was revealed. Cold, cruel, and bitterly jealous of Cinderella's charm and beauty, she was grimly determined to forward the interests of her own two awkward daughters. Thus as time went by, the chateau fell into disrepair for the

> family fortunes were squandered on the vain and selfish step-sisters while Cinderella was abused, humiliated, and finally forced to become a servant in her own house.
>
> — "*Cinderella*" *from Grimm's Fairy Tales.*

Similar to some of the issues of grandparents raising grandchildren are the issues of stepparents raising stepchildren.

Professor Mary Ann Mason, Dean of the Graduate Division at the University of California at Berkeley, 36 *Fam. L.Q.* 227 (2002), wrote that "the stepfamily affects large percentage of American families, and yet has been virtually ignored as a family issue. It is estimated that about one-fourth of the children born will live with a stepparent before they reach majority." Professor Mason rightly noted that, like grandchildren, stepchildren have no right of inheritance when a stepparent dies. This can cause great hardship for children who have relied on a stepparent for basic support, such as food, housing, and other financial assistance. Similarly, to those issues raised above in the section on grandparents raising grandchildren, possible solutions to the problem of stepchildren not inheriting from a stepparent include the following:

- equitable adoption
- executing a will or inter vivos trust
- transferring property under the UTMA
- changing the definition of "child" in intestate succession statutes

Like those dealing with grandchild inheritance, some courts have provided that if the stepchild could show that the stepparent was *in loco parentis* or otherwise the de facto parent or the subject of an equitable adoption, some form of inheritance may succeed. The stepparent is considered a de facto parent because he or she had the intent to support the child and take on parental obligations. As previously stated, equitable adoption takes into account that the natural parent might still be living and would not allow the stepparent to adopt the child. Proof that the child would have been adopted but for the natural parent's objection is often required. Whether a stepparent is a de facto parent for the stepchild is predicated on the involvement in the child's life. The child must live with the stepparent and be financially dependent upon the stepparent, but the stepparent must be more than a source of financial support for the child. The stepparent must be involved in the child's life, that is, the child's activities, and in the discipline of him or her. In *Estate of Joseph*, 53 Cal. App. 4th 684, 61 Cal. Rptr. 2d 803 (1997), the California Supreme Court held that the relationship had to begin during the child's minority and continue through their joint lifetimes. The California Law Commission that same year, relying on *Estate of Joseph* and other cases holding similarly, published a recommendation that would "codify case law holding that the legal barrier to adoption need only exist at the time the adoption was contemplated or attempted, and rejects cases holding that the legal barrier must exist throughout their joint lifetimes." As of 2012, the provisions of §6454 of the California Probate Code have not been modified to contain those recommendations, however.

It is therefore as uncertain whether a stepchild will be able to inherit from a stepparent who does not provide for the child in his or her estate planning documentation, similar to intestacy by grandchildren who were raised by a now deceased grandparent. Under current law, in most circumstances, stepchildren do not inherit under intestate succession laws and there has been little movement to change the law despite the changing demographics to suggest that change is necessary. In fact, as recently as October 2006, in a report to the Drafting Committee to Amend the Intestacy Provisions of the Uniform Probate Code, Laura M. Twomey, the ABA Advisor to the committee, wrote,

> The committee did not feel comfortable having step children inherit before any of the step parents' relatives, but considered the possibility of letting step children inherit if the property would otherwise escheat to the state. One concept discussed was to permit step children to inherit if the step child shared a common household with the step parent during minority. We discussed the fact that in some cases, the relationship between the step parent and step child are not harmonious and people would rather have the property pass to the state than to their step children. We also discussed that while the provision might not fulfill the decedent's intent in some cases, there were perhaps more cases where it would. We noted that there is currently no definition of step child.

Perhaps, executing a will or trust for a minor or even an adult stepchild is the surest way to provide for that child upon the stepparent's death. However, even when a stepparent makes a will, the stepparent doesn't always make sure they are leaving property to their stepchildren.

Example: Michael and Nicole Lopez make an appointment with a lawyer. They tell the lawyer they have been married 52 years and have two adult daughters and that each daughter has children of her own. They are clearly proud of their daughters and dote on their grandchildren. The Lopezes require "simple" estate planning and decide that in their wills they want to leave everything to each other and then everything to their daughters should either Michael or Nicole predecease the other. Toward the end of the appointment, Michael casually mentions that Nicole had been married before and that the girls were only babies when he and Nicole got married. Of course, this raised a red flag to the attorney, who questioned Michael and Nicole further. Upon further discussion, the attorney learned that indeed Michael was not the natural parent of either daughter and that he had not formally adopted them. Nonetheless, he considered them his daughters for all intents and purposes and always referred to them as his "daughters" and they referred to him as "Dad." The attorney drafted Michael's will to state among other provisions, as follows:

> I hereby declare that I am married to NICOLE LOPEZ. I have two stepchildren, to-wit: TINA SMITH WHITE and JANICE SMITH GRAY. Any references to my 'wife' shall refer to NICOLE LOPEZ. Any references to my 'child' or 'children' shall refer to TINA SMITH WHITE and JANICE SMITH GRAY without distinction to whether they are natural born or born of my wife. I have no other children born to or adopted by me. Any references to my 'grandchildren' shall refer to my wife's grandchildren without distinction to whether they are my natural grandchildren or my wife's.

The purpose of this clause was to put all parties and the probate court and clerk on notice that Tina and Janice were to take as his "children" under his will although they were not his natural or adopted children.

Further provisions in the will stated,

"If my wife does not survive me, I give such residue to my children as defined in Section 2 above, in equal shares, if they survive me. If either of my children does not survive me, I give her share of the residue to her children, my grandchildren."

Post-Mortem Conception and a Parent's Last Will

What if a man or woman has his or her eggs or sperm frozen for future use and later, perhaps years later, the deceased individual's spouse or girlfriend (or boyfriend through a surrogate mother) gives birth to a child using that egg or sperm?

Professor Kristine S. Knaplund of Pepperdine University in 46 *Arizona Law Review* 91 (October 2008), entitled "Postmortem Conception and a Father's Last Will," asked a similar question concerning a man in the military freezing sperm for the future and dying in combat. Professor Knaplund asked, "But what if the man dies, and his widow or girlfriend gives birth to a baby years later? What effect will this child have on the man's will?" She states that as early as 1962, Professor W. Barton Leach of the Harvard Law School predicted that the then new phenomenon of sperm banks, which were created to protect children of astronauts from mutations caused by space radiation, would pose a threat to the Rule Against Perpetuities, in which a bequest must vest within 21 years of a life in being. He feared that because the sperm could be preserved indefinitely, the astronaut's widow could have his children long after a life in being plus twenty-one years invalidating will bequests. Professor Knaplund wrote that "[F]ifteen years after Professor Leach's prediction, an Australian newspaper reported that a widow had given birth to a child using her deceased husband's cryopreserved sperm." As stated by Amanda Horner, Comment, 33 S. Ill. U. L.J. 157 (2008), "I Consented To Do What?: Posthumous Children And The Consent To Parent After-Death," "… recent technology makes it increasingly easier for a parent to have a posthumous child."

A handful of cases have determined whether or not children, conceived after their fathers' deaths, were entitled to inherit in intestacy and thus eligible to receive Social Security benefits. In *Woodward v. Comm. of Soc. Sec.*, 760 N.E.2d 257 (Mass. 2002), the Supreme Judicial Court of The State of Massachusetts held that

> In certain limited circumstances, a child resulting from posthumous reproduction may enjoy the inheritance rights of "issue" under the Massachusetts intestacy statute. These limited circumstances exist where, as a threshold matter, the surviving parent or the child's other legal representative demonstrates a genetic relationship between the child and the decedent. The survivor or representative must then establish both that the decedent affirmatively consented to posthumous conception and to the support of any resulting child. Even where such circumstances exist, time limitations may preclude commencing a claim for succession rights on behalf of a posthumously conceived child.

As in *Woodward*, the couple in *Gillett-Netting v. Barnhart*, 231 F. Supp. 2d 961 (2002), faced the husband's cancer by postponing chemotherapy and freezing and depositing sperm for later use. Both husbands died from their cancer. Rhonda Gillett-Netting had two children using her deceased husband's sperm, Juliet and Piers. She then filed for Social Security benefits based on her husband's earnings. The trial court in the case held that "Juliet and Piers do not qualify for child's insurance benefits because they are not Netting's 'children' under the Act and they were not dependent on Netting at the time of his death." The appellate court stated that

> Under Arizona law, Netting would be treated as the natural parent of Juliet and Piers and would have a legal obligation to support them if he were alive, although they were conceived using in-vitro fertilization, because he is their biological father and was married to the mother of the children. *See* Ariz. Rev. Stat. §25-501 (providing that children have a right to support from their natural parents; the biological father of a child born using artificial insemination is considered a natural parent if the father is married to the mother). Although Arizona law does not deal specifically with posthumously-conceived children, *every* child in Arizona, which necessarily includes Juliet and Piers, is the legitimate child of her or his natural parents.

The appellate court remanded the case so that benefits could be determined.

However, in 1994, in the case of *Hart v. Shalala*, No. 94-3944, Judith Hart, a child conceived three months after her father's death from cancer, was denied Social Security survivor's benefits. In a surprise twist, however, when Mrs. Hart appealed to the federal court in Louisiana, the Social Security Administration decided to award benefits rather than have the court render a decision on posthumous children. How the court would have decided the case remains a mystery.

In *Estate of Kolacy*, 753 A.2d 1257 (N.J. Super. Ct. Ch. Div. 2000), the New Jersey court held that posthumously conceived children were the heirs of the decedent father, even if there was no estate to distribute, because it could have an effect on the children in the future if a relative left a will providing for the deceased father's "issue" or "heirs."

In *Stephen v. Commissioner of Social Security*, 386 F. Supp. 2d 1257 (M.D.Fla. 2005), the Florida court refused to extend benefits to posthumously conceived children, but in that case the decedent parent never gave consent for the removal of the father's sperm. However, the Court gave a glimpse into how it would have held, even if the father had given consent when it stated that "In vitro fertilization and other methods of assisted reproduction are new technologies that have created new legal issues not addressed by already existing law." It also stated,

> Were we to define the term "conceive," we would be making a determination that would implicate many public policy concerns, including, but certainly not limited to, the finality of estates. That is not our role. The determination of public policy lies almost exclusively with the legislature, and we will not interfere with that determination in the absence of palpable errors.

The latest case in this field was determined in March 2012 by the U.S. Supreme Court. In *Astrue v. Capato*, 566 U. S. ____, 2021 AS IN 132 S.Ct. 2021, the Court determined that "the undisputed biological children of a deceased wage earner and his widow" qualified for Social Security survivor benefits.

The Supreme Court first questioned whether the twins were Robert's children under the law. It found that "[U]nder Florida law, a marriage ends upon the death of a spouse," and that the twins, conceived after the death of their father, did not qualify as "marital" children because their parents were not married under Florida law when they were born.

The Supreme Court case is likely to pave the way for other cases. In the meantime, such children's rights of inheritance may be in jeopardy.

SUMMARY

The topics such as same-sex marriage, grandparents raising grandchildren, and artificial insemination using frozen eggs or sperm after divorce or death must be discussed carefully because of the political, religious, moral, and ethical issues they raise.

Unfortunately, for the most part, at this time, more questions are raised than answered, such as:

- Is a will effective regarding a same-sex spouse or domestic partner?
- Is a grandchild, being raised by a grandparent, an heir?
- Who gets to be the health-care proxy or surrogate when a same-sex or non-married partner is in a medical crisis?
- Is a child, born after artificial insemination, the heir of her deceased's sperm or egg donor parent?
- Will a stepchild inherit from a stepparent if the stepparent was the person who raised the child?

As we have seen, same-sex marriage is legal in some states and confers all the benefits of that state's laws that are given to heterosexual married couples. The validity of a same-sex marriage is not portable from state to state, however, as most states refuse to acknowledge them. The federal Defense of Marriage Act (DOMA) signed in 1996 specifically defines marriage in the federal government system as a legal union exclusively between one man and one woman and permits states to refuse, despite the United States Constitution's Full Faith and Credit Clause, which holds that the laws and judgments of a sister state shall be given acceptance. It is the Full Faith and Credit Clause which has been traditionally used to recognize the validity of a marriage performed in another state or in another country.

A civil union is a statutory creature providing that unmarried couples have all the same benefits, protections, and responsibilities under law, whether they derive from statute, policy, administrative or court rule, common law, or any other source of civil law, as are granted to spouses in a marriage. Not all states have civil unions and in those that do, some are for same-sex couples only, while others are for heterosexual couples as well. Domestic partnerships are similar to civil unions and are defined as a legal or personal relationship between two individuals who live together and share a common domestic life, but are not legally married or bound by a civil union. Registries are available for domestic partners in many municipalities and states.

As per U.S. census data for 2010, 4.9 million children live in a household with a grandparent that is the head of household. A parent may create a power of attorney giving the grandparent authority to make medical decisions for the grandchildren. In jurisdictions with medical consent legislation, a parent may authorize a grandparent to obtain medical treatment for the grandchildren in the parent's absence. A parent must be capable of executing a power of attorney in favor of the grandparent and consent to the medical directive for the grandchildren. Often the consent is not granted.

Grandchildren have difficulty inheriting from their grandparents when the grandparents do not have a will devising anything to them. If a grandparent dies without executing a will, intestacy laws distribute everything to the parent and not the grandchild. Methods to prevent disinheritance by a grandparent, who has been raising the grandchild, include the following: equitable adoption in which a court determines that the child was the heir of the "parent" or "parents" in very limited circumstances; execution of a will or trust; a transfer under the Uniform Transfer to Minors Act; or use of a beneficiary designation form or pay-on-death account. Scholars have suggested that the intestate succession laws be changed to add grandchildren to the definition of "child"; however, no state has chosen to do so.

Similar issues surround a stepchild that has been raised by a stepparent.

To date, only a handful of cases have determined whether or not children conceived after their fathers' deaths were entitled to inherit in intestacy and thus eligible to receive Social Security benefits. Most have determined that the child was eligible to inherit as the father's legal child. One court, however, stated that "The determination of public policy lies almost exclusively with the legislature, and we will not interfere with that determination in the absence of palpable errors." It denied benefits based on the fact that the father had not consented to the withdrawal and use of his sperm before he died. The latest case decided in early March 2012 by the United States Supreme Court said that under Florida law, the children were not the deceased biological parent's children because the parents were not married at the time of their birth.

KEY **TERMS**

same-sex marriage

civil unions

domestic partnerships

post-mortem conception

Uniform Transfer to Minors Act

Defense of Marriage Act

equitable adoption

Full Faith and Credit Clause

domestic partner registry

REVIEW **QUESTIONS**

1. What is the Defense of Marriage Act?

2. Are civil unions and same-sex marriages portable? Why or why not?

3. Does a stepchild inherit from a stepparent if the stepparent was the person who raised the child? Why or why not?

4. Does a grandchild inherit from his or her grandparent if the grandparent raised the grandchild? Why or why not?

5. What is **post-mortem conception**?

6. Do children conceived post-mortem inherit from their parents? Explain.

7. What is the Full Faith and Credit Clause?

8. What is the doctrine of equitable adoption?

9. What are the requirements for an equitable adoption?

10. What are the steps a grandparent or stepparent can take to ensure that a grandchild or stepchild inherits?

11. What is a domestic partnership and what is a domestic partner registry?

PROJECTS

1. Determine if your state or locality has a domestic registry. What are its requirements? Is there a form to fill out available online? If so, print it out.

2. Read and review the working paper of Browne C. Lewis, Assistant Professor of Law, Cleveland-Marshall College of Law, entitled "Dead Men Reproducing: Responding to the Existence of Afterdeath Children" dated August 25, 2008. You can retrieve it for no charge at http://ssrn.com/

abstract=1256442. Do you agree or disagree with his arguments? Explain.

3. After reading the *Astrue v. Capato* case found at "download PDF" at http://supreme.justia.com/cases/federal/us/566/11-159/, determine if you agree or disagree and how it compares with the Lewis article in Project 2. Explain.

4. Read Case 7.2 below and answer the questions posed by the court under its heading "Issues." Do you agree or disagree and why?

MyLegalStudiesLab™   http://www.mylegalstudieslab

MYLEGALSTUDIESLAB VIRTUAL LAW OFFICE EXPERIENCE ASSIGNMENTS

Complete the pre-test, study plan, and post-test for this chapter and answer the Legal Applications questions as assigned. These will help you confirm your mastery of the concepts and their application to legal scenarios. Then, complete the Virtual Law Office assignments as assigned by your instructor. These assignments are designed to develop your workplace skills and result in producing documents for inclusion in your portfolio.

CASE 7.2

In The Matter of the Estate of Seader 2003
Wy 119, 76 P.3d 1236 (2003)

Before HILL, C.J., and GOLDEN, LEHMAN, KITE, and VOIGT, JJ.
VOIGT, Justice, delivered the opinion of the Court; *GOLDEN*, Justice, filed a dissenting opinion with which *HILL*, Chief Justice, joined.

VOIGT, Justice.

[1] The district court refused to apply the doctrines of equitable adoption, adoption by estoppel, and virtual adoption to avoid the operation of the anti-lapse statute. The district court also concluded that the testator's will did not evidence an intention that the share of a predeceased devisee pass to that devisee's children. The devisee's children appealed. We affirm.

Issues

1. Whether the doctrines of equitable adoption, adoption by estoppel, and virtual adoption are available under Wyoming law to allow the descendents of a predeceased stepchild to be considered lineal descendents of their step-grandfather under the anti-lapse statute?

2. Whether the district court erred in concluding that the testator's will did not evidence an intention that the share of a predeceased devisee pass to that devisee's children?

Facts

[2] Julie L. Schroeder (Julie) was born on August 13, 1943 to Mary Allen Cirksana (Mary) and Louis Sylvester Burke.[1] When Julie was two years old, Mary married Neil Adam Seader (Neil). At the time of the marriage, Neil agreed to adopt Julie. Over the years, Neil voiced his intention to adopt Julie, and he treated her as if she were his natural daughter. At one time, Mary and Neil discussed adoption with an attorney, but decided not to follow through because of the expense. Neil never did adopt Julie. Nevertheless, she used the surname "Seader" as a youth.[2]

[3] Neil and Mary had two sons, Neil J. Seader (Neil J.) and Charles Lee Seader (Charles). Mary died in 1966, leaving her entire estate to Neil. Julie had two children, Kim Sanderson (Kim) and Kirk Olive (Kirk). In his Last Will and Testament, dated August 30, 1996, after a few specific bequests, Neil left the residue of his estate to Neil J., Charles, and Julie. Julie died on May 7, 2000. Neil died on July 10, 2000.

[4] Neil's will was admitted to probate on July 21, 2000. On May 2, 2001, the personal representative of the estate filed a Preliminary Report, Accounting and Petition for Distribution, in which he noted that Julie had predeceased Neil and he proposed distributing her one-third residuary interest to Kim and Kirk. Subsequently, Neil J. filed an Objection to Preliminary Report, Accounting and Petition for Distribution, in which he contended that the testamentary devise to Julie had failed pursuant to Wyo. Stat. Ann. §§2-6-106 and 2-6-107 (LexisNexis 2003).[3] Charles soon thereafter filed a similar objection. That was followed by a Petition for Declaration of Status as Beneficiaries of Estate filed by Kim and Kirk. Finally, Neil J. and Charles filed a Motion for Summary Judgment.

[5] On February 22, 2002, the district court issued its Order Granting Summary Judgment. The district court concluded that the residuary devise to Julie failed because she predeceased Neil and she was not Neil's "grandparent" or a "lineal descendent" of Neil's grandparent, as required by the anti-lapse statute.[4] The district court also held that Neil's will was clear and unambiguous and that it contained no indication that it was Neil's intention to have Kim and Kirk inherit their mother's share of the estate. Several months later, the Order Approving Accounting, and Decree of Distribution incorporated the provisions of the summary judgment order. This appeal followed.

Standard of Review

[6] We recently reiterated our standard for review of summary judgments granted under W.R.C.P. 56:

> When a motion for summary judgment is before this court, assuming there is a complete record, we have exactly the same duty and materials as did the district court and must follow the same standards. *Hoblyn v. Johnson*, 2002 WY 152, ¶11, 55 P.3d 1219, ¶11 (Wyo.2002). The propriety of granting summary judgment depends upon the

correctness of a court's dual findings that there is no genuine issue as to any material fact and the prevailing party is entitled to judgment as a matter of law. *Id.* This court looks at the record from the viewpoint most favorable to the party opposing the motion, giving to him all the favorable inferences which may be drawn from the facts contained in affidavits, depositions, and other materials appearing in the record. *Id.*

The party moving for summary judgment bears the initial burden of establishing a prima facie case for a summary judgment. If the movant carries this burden, the party opposing the summary judgment must come forward with specific facts to demonstrate that a genuine issue of material fact does exist. *Eklund v. PRI Environmental, Inc.*, 2001 WY 55, ¶10, 25 P.3d 511, ¶10 (Wyo.2001). A material fact has been defined as a fact upon which the outcome of the litigation depends in whole or in part. *Hoblyn*, 2002 WY 152, ¶11, 55 P.3d 1219, ¶11.

Bertagnolli v. Louderback, 2003 WY 50, ¶¶ 10-11, 67 P.3d 627, 630-31 (Wyo. 2003).

Discussion

The Adoption Issues

[7] Julie died two months before Neil died. Had she survived him, she would have taken one-third of his residuary estate under his will. Had she been his biological daughter or his legally adopted daughter, her share of his estate would have gone to Kim and Kirk pursuant to Wyo. Stat. Ann. §2-6-106. Likewise, had she been his biological daughter or his legally adopted daughter, and had he died intestate, her share of his estate would have gone to Kim and Kirk.[5] She was not, however, legally adopted. As a result, in an effort to take in her stead under Neil's will, Kim and Kirk now seek equitable recognition of adoptive status for their mother.[6]

[8] We previously have held that "adoption at common law was unknown and, therefore, the adoption of minor children as well as the rights and liabilities emanating there from are governed by statutory provisions concerning descent, distribution, and adoption." *In re Randall's Estate*, 506 P.2d 432, 432-33 (Wyo. 1973).[7] We also previously have held that substantial conformity with all statutory requirements is necessary to effectuate a legal adoption. *Matter of Adoption of AMD*, 766 P.2d 550, 552 (Wyo. 1988). The present question is whether, under the circumstances of this case, equity should interpose itself where no legal adoption took place.

[9] It will be helpful to preface our discussion of this issue with a consideration of the basic concepts that are involved, beginning with the meaning of "adoption." Where, as in Wyoming, that term is not statutorily defined, the courts have supplied a definition:

> In this regard, "adoption" has been defined by some courts as the establishment or creation of a legal relationship of parent and child between persons who were not so related by nature or law, whereupon the person adopted becomes the legal heir of his or her adopter, and the rights and duties of domestic relation with the adoptee's natural parents are terminated. It has been said that adoption is the legal equivalent of biological parenthood, so that a decree of adoption renders the adoptee, for all intents and purposes, the child of the adoptive parent.
>
> *2 Am.Jur.2d, Adoption §1 at 869 (1994) (footnotes omitted).*[8]

[10] In their Petition for Declaration of Status as Beneficiaries of Estate, Kim and Kirk set forth equitable adoption, adoption by estoppel, and virtual adoption as separate causes of action. Where these doctrines have been recognized, however, they have largely been treated as interchangeable, and all are based on the same theory: "[O]ne who had agreed to adopt a child during his life, but for some reason did not, for inheritance purposes alone, will be considered to have [...] adopted [the child]." 2 Am.Jur.2d, *Adoption, supra*, §43 at 918-19. Equitable adoption has been described as follows:

> While a child to be adopted pursuant to an agreement between his natural parent and the adoptive parent cannot specifically enforce its adoption by the deceased adoptive

parent, nevertheless, because of the agreement, he can obtain specific enforcement of the benefits that would accrue from such adoption—this remedy is sometimes referred to as an equitable adoption.

The terms "equitable adoption," "virtual adoption," and "adoption by estoppel," have been used interchangeably by the courts. Generally speaking, the theory of recovery in an equitable adoption case is founded upon either equitable principles or upon the theory of estoppel. In the former it is a judicial remedy for an unperformed contract of legal adoption or, in the alternative, the ordering of specific performance of an implied contract to adopt. The estoppel theory operates to preclude a party from asserting the invalidity of a status of an "adopted" child for inheritance purposes. It has been said that a so-called "equitable adoption" is no more than a legal fiction permitting specific performance of a contract to adopt. Furthermore, the descriptive phrase "adoption by estoppel" has been described as a shorthand method of saying that because of the promises, acts and conduct of an intestate deceased, those claiming under and through him are estopped to assert that a child was not legally adopted or did not occupy the status of an adopted child.

An adoption by estoppel is an equitable remedy to protect the interests of a person who was supposed to have been adopted as a child but whose adoptive parents failed to undertake the legal steps necessary to formally accomplish the adoption; the doctrine is applied in an intestate estate to give effect to the intent of the decedent to adopt and provide for the child.

The doctrine is predicated on principles of contract law and equitable enforcement of the agreement to adopt for the purpose of securing the benefits of adoption that would otherwise flow from the adoptive parent under the laws of intestacy had the agreement to adopt been carried out; as such it is essentially a matter of equitable relief. Being only an equitable remedy to enforce a contract right, it is not intended or applied to create the legal relationship of parent and child, with all the legal consequences of such relationship, nor is it meant to create a legal adoption. The need for the doctrine arises when the adoptive parents die intestate; the doctrine is invoked in order to allow the supposed-to-have-been adopted child to take an intestate share. It is not applicable where the decedent dies testate.

2 Am.Jur.2d, Adoption, supra, §53 at 929-30 (footnotes omitted). See also Rebecca C. Bell, Comment, Virtual Adoption: The Difficulty of Creating an Exception to the Statutory Scheme, XXIX Stetson L. Rev. 415, 419-30 (1999) (comparing estoppel and contract as bases for the theory) and Harvey A. Schneider, Comment, Equitable Adoption: A Necessary Doctrine?, 35 S. Cal. L. Rev 491, 492-96 (1962) (problems with contract theory).

[11] Equitable adoption must be distinguished from adoption by contract, deed, or notarial act, a process recognized by statute in some jurisdictions. Where such methods of adoption are legislatively sanctioned, they result in a legal adoption status that is no different from the status that arises from a decree of adoption in a judicial proceeding. 2 Am.Jur.2d, *Adoption, supra*, §43 at 918. Equitable adoption, on the other hand, "is never viewed as the equivalent of a formal adoption, in terms of establishing a parent-child relationship, and is merely a status invented by courts of equity as a means of allowing a child in an appropriate case to enjoy part of the advantage of adoptive status." 18 Proof of Facts 2d, *Equitable Adoption* §1 at 543 (1979).

[12] The elements of equitable adoption are (1) an implied or express agreement to adopt the child; (2) reliance on that agreement; (3) performance by the natural parents in giving up custody; (4) performance by the child in living in the home of, and in acting as the child of, the adoptive parents; (5) partial performance by the foster parents in taking the child into their home and treating the child as their child; and (6) the intestacy of the foster parents. *Lankford v. Wright*, 347 N.C. 115, 489 S.E.2d 604, 606-07 (1997); 2 Am.Jur.2d, *Adoption, supra*, §54 at 932-33. In granting summary judgment to Neil J. and Charles, the district court made no findings of fact in regard to any of these elements. Instead, summary judgment was granted on the ground that Wyoming has not recognized equitable adoption. In this situation, we will assume that the facts favor Kirk and Kim, as the opponents of summary judgment, although we are troubled by the lack of verified facts in the record.

[13] The majority of states recognize equitable adoption in one form or another, although the doctrine has been explicitly rejected in others.[9] Almost exclusively, the application of the doctrine has been limited to intestate estates. *See, for example, Calista Corp. v. Mann,* 564 P.2d 53, 61 (Alaska 1977); *Estate of Wilson,* 111 Cal.App.3d 242, 168 Cal. Rptr. 533, 534 (1980); *Barlow v. Barlow,* 170 Colo. 465, 463 P.2d 305, 306 (1969); *Miller v. Paczier,* 591 So.2d 321, 322 (Fla.App. 1991); *Roberts v. Caughell,* 65 So.2d 547, 547 (Fla. 1953); *Franzen v. Hallmer,* 404 Ill. 596, 89 N.E.2d 818, 821 (1950); and *Lankford,* 489 S.E.2d at 607. It generally has not been applied to testate estates. *In re Estate of Wall,* 502 So.2d 531, 532 (Fla.App. 1987). *See also* Rebecca C. Bell, *supra,* XXIX Stetson L. Rev. at 435-39 (does not apply to testate estates, but only to intestate estates where the decedent's intent is unknown).[10] In addition, the doctrine is generally limited to the equitably adopted person's attempt to inherit from an intestate adoptive parent, and is not used to enforce the right of the adoptee to inherit from collateral kindred, nor to enforce the right of collateral kindred to inherit from the adoptee. *Heien v. Crabtree,* 369 S.W.2d 28, 30 (Tex. 1963); Stanley P. Atwood, Comment, *Virtual Adoption and Rights of Inheritance,* XXI Wash. & Lee L. Rev. 312, 317 (1964).

[14] Wyoming has not incontrovertibly recognized equitable adoption, even in intestate estates. Three cases, however, deserve mention because they touch on similar or related issues. In *Nugent v. Powell,* 4 Wyo. 173, 33 P. 23, 24 (1893), the mother of a child, who had been abandoned by the father, consented to the child's adoption by a childless couple. Statutory adoption was pursued to completion, with the exception of the probate court's failure to enter the adoption order of record. *Id.* at 25. Upon the intestate death of the adoptive father subsequent to the death of the adoptive mother, the siblings of the deceased adoptive father sought distribution of his estate to themselves, claiming that the child's adoption was ineffective. This Court reversed the district court's decree favoring the deceased's siblings on the ground that there had been substantial compliance with the adoption statutes. *Id.* at 25.

[15] *Nugent* has been cited for the following proposition:

> The equitable adoption doctrine first appeared in the late nineteenth and early twentieth centuries in Missouri and Wyoming when these two pioneer states held that an agreement to adopt that did not fulfill the statutory provision of adoption could be enforced under the principles of equity.

> *Beth Ann Yount, Note, Lankford v. Wright: Recognizing Equitable Adoption in North Carolina, 76 N.C. L. Rev. 2446, 2455 (1998) (footnotes omitted). Our reading of Nugent leads us to the considerably more limited conclusion that the case merely stands for the proposition that substantial, rather than absolute, compliance with the adoption statutes is sufficient to create a legal adoption. The emphasis in Nugent is upon legal adoption under a statutory scheme, not equitable adoption based upon an agreement.*

[16] Commentators have noted that courts have not always done well at distinguishing between contracts to adopt and contracts to make a will or leave an inheritance:

> The courts often speak in terms of specific performance of the contract to adopt. In according this remedy courts have sometimes failed to distinguish between a contract to leave a child's share of the adopting parent's estate to the adopted child—which of course limits the right of the adopting parent to dispose of his estate by will—and a contract to adopt, *i.e.,* to comply with the statutory adoption procedure. The latter type of contract leaves the adopting parent free to disinherit the adopted child just as he could disinherit a natural child.

> *Edward D. Bailey, Adoption "By Estoppel," 36 Tex. L. Rev. 30, 32-33 (1957); see also J.C.J., Jr., Note, Equitable Adoption: They Took Him Into Their Home and Called Him Fred, 58 Va. L. Rev. 727, 729-30 (1972) ("Of course, a single case may involve both a contract to make a will and a contract to adopt, and courts sometimes fail to distinguish between them; but the essence of equitable adoption is the provision of a judicial remedy for an unperformed adoption agreement.") (footnote omitted).*

[17] *Pangarova v. Nichols*, 419 P.2d 688 (Wyo. 1966), is just such a case, largely because the parties, long before the matter got to court, blurred the distinctions between adoption and inheritance. In *Pangarova*, a man and his wife wrote numerous letters to their adult niece in Bulgaria, offering to adopt her and to make her their heir if she would come to Casper, Wyoming, to live with them. *Id.* at 690. The niece eventually did come to Casper and moved into the home of her uncle and his new wife, his first wife having died. *Id.* And the uncle did, indeed, make a will naming his niece as the sole beneficiary of his estate. *Id.* at 690-93. Unfortunately, the niece and the new wife did not get along, the niece moved out, and the uncle drafted a new will leaving everything to his new wife. Upon the uncle's death, the niece filed an action seeking damages for breach of the contract to adopt her and to make her an heir. *Id.* at 693-94.

[18] The district court directed a verdict against the niece. In reversing and remanding for a new trial, this Court emphasized that the alleged contract did not deal solely with adoption, but promised that the uncle would make the niece his heir. We concluded that "[s]uch contracts are not uncommon in the case of minor children and are 'generally construed to impose upon the adoptive parent an obligation to make the child an heir, which equity will specifically enforce.'" *Id.* at 695 (*quoting* R.P. Davis, Annotation, *Specific Performance of, or Status of Child Under, Contract to Adopt Not Fully Performed*, 171 A.L.R. 1315, 1318 (1947)). This quoted language, taken from an annotation concerning enforcement of a contract to adopt, appears to be at least an indirect acceptance of the concept of equitable adoption. However, the quoted language is followed immediately in the opinion by this sentence: "Our difficulty here is that an adult is involved." *Pangarova*, 419 P.2d at 695. Thereafter, we pursued neither that general issue—adoption of an adult—nor the specific issue of equitable adoption of an adult. Instead, we cited several cases where the contract being enforced in equity was not simply a contract to adopt, but also contained a promise to make the adoptee an heir. *Id.* at 695-96.[11]

[19] On appeal after retrial, a jury verdict in favor of the niece was affirmed. *Nichols v. Pangarova*, 443 P.2d 756 (Wyo. 1968). While reference is made in the second opinion to "a contract that decedent would adopt her and make her his heir," the concept of equitable adoption is not directly discussed. *Nichols*, 443 P.2d at 758. Instead, the discussion focuses on "a contract to devise or bequeath property," "an oral contract to make a will," and "an agreement to will property." *Id.* at 759, 761 and 762. In the final analysis, *Pangarova* is fundamentally not an equitable adoption case.

[20] One other Wyoming case must be mentioned. We have already cited *Matter of Adoption of AMD*, 766 P.2d at 552, for the proposition that substantial compliance with the adoption statutes is required for a legal adoption to occur. The case also holds as follows:

> Adoption in Wyoming is a statutory proceeding and cannot be accomplished by private contract. It is held that: "If the relation of adoptive parent and child cannot be created by a private contract, it is equally certain that it cannot arise by estoppel."
>
> *Id.* at 554 (quoting 2 Am.Jur.2d, Adoption, §8 (1962)). Upon first reading, this language might appear to be an outright renunciation of the concept of equitable adoption (adoption by estoppel), but the facts and procedural status of the case indicate otherwise. The appellant had filed a petition to adopt his fiancée's two children. After the couple married, a decree was entered purporting to be a final decree of adoption. The couple soon separated, however, and the appellant filed a petition to have the adoptions vacated. He contended that the adoptions had been granted without compliance with statutory mandates.[12] Matter of Adoption of AMD, 766 P.2d at 551-52.

[21] The district court held that the appellant was estopped from contesting the validity of the adoptions because he had invoked the jurisdiction of the court, because he had failed to show material misrepresentations, and because it was in the best interests of the children that the adoption be confirmed. *Id.* at 552. This is the context in which this Court, in agreeing with the appellant, held that the legal status of adoption may only be created by statutory compliance, and that estoppel cannot be applied to avoid statutory mandates. *Id.*

at 553-54. Clearly, that holding had nothing to do with the traditional concept of utilizing equitable adoption to protect a promised inheritance in an intestate estate.

[22] *Matter of Adoption of AMD*, like *Nugent* and *Pangarova*, left considerable doubt as to the status of equitable adoption in Wyoming. Because the instant case also fails to resemble the typical situation in which the doctrine is applied, it will have the same effect. If Neil had died intestate, Wyo. Stat. Ann. §2-4-101(c)(i) (LexisNexis 2003) would apply and his estate would have gone "[t]o his children surviving, and the descendents of his children who are dead...." The "simple" question then would be whether to apply equitable adoption, so that Julie would be considered Neil's child for purposes of intestate succession. But that is not the question that is being asked in this case. Neil *did* leave a will, and he *did* make Julie a beneficiary. Consequently, this case is quite unlike the usual equitable adoption case because its focus is not upon enforcing specific performance of a contract. Instead, its focus is upon statutory construction.

[23] Neither party presented this case below as a question of statutory construction, so the district court made no findings and reached no conclusions in that regard. However, "[i]f the evidence in the record supports the summary judgment granted by the district court on any legal basis . . . we will affirm." *Grose v. Sauvageau*, 942 P.2d 398, 402 (Wyo. 1997). Because the inter-related issues of adoption and the distribution of decedents' estates are purely statutory, we must apply our standard rules of statutory construction to the questions before us.[13] We recently reiterated those rules at length:

> This court interprets statutes by giving effect to the legislature's intent.... We begin by making an inquiry relating to the ordinary and obvious meaning of the words employed according to their arrangement and connection.... We give effect to every word, clause, and sentence and construe together all components of a statute *in pari materia*.... Statutory interpretation is a question of law.... We review questions of law de novo without affording deference to the district court's decision.
>
> *Worcester v. State*, 2001 WY 82, ¶13, 30 P.3d 47, 52 (Wyo.2001). *If a statute is clear and unambiguous, we simply give effect to its plain meaning.... Only when we find a statute to be ambiguous, do we resort to the general principles of statutory construction.... An ambiguous statute is one whose meaning is uncertain because it is susceptible to more than one interpretation ...*
>
> It is a basic rule of statutory construction that courts may try to determine legislative intent by considering the type of statute being interpreted and what the legislature intended by the language used, viewed in light of the objects and purposes to be accomplished.... Furthermore, when we are confronted with two possible but conflicting conclusions, we will choose the one most logically designed to cure the mischief or inequity that the legislature was attempting to accomplish.
>
> *In re Collicott*, 2001 WY 35, ¶9, 20 P.3d 1077, 1080 (Wyo.2001). *We presume that statutes are enacted by the legislature with full knowledge of existing law, so we construe statutes in harmony with existing law, particularly other statutes relating to the same subject or having the same purpose....*
>
> Statutes must be construed so that no portion is rendered meaningless.... Interpretation should not produce an absurd result.... We are guided by the full text of the statute, paying attention to its internal structure and the functional relation between the parts and the whole.... Each word of a statute is to be afforded meaning, with none rendered superfluous.... Further, the meaning afforded to a word should be that word's standard popular meaning unless another meaning is clearly intended.... If the meaning of a word is unclear, it should be afforded the meaning that best accomplishes the statute's purpose.... We presume that the legislature acts intentionally when it uses particular language in one statute, but not in another.... If two sections of legislation appear to conflict, they should be given a reading that gives them both effect.

Rodriguez v. Casey, 2002 WY 111, ¶¶ 9-10, 50 P.3d 323, 326-27 (Wyo. 2002). In addition, it is a well-known principle of law that courts are not free to legislate. The first rule of statutory construction is that legislative intent, not a court's perception of fairness, controls. *State Dept. of Revenue and Taxation v. Pacificorp*, 872 P.2d 1163, 1166 (Wyo. 1994); *Olheiser v. State ex rel.*

Wyoming Workers' Compensation Div., 866 P.2d 768, 770 (Wyo. 1994). It is not the court's prerogative to usurp the power of the legislature by deciding what should have been said. *Barber v. State Highway Commission*, 80 Wyo. 340, 342 P.2d 723, 725 (1959). The courts must follow, and cannot extend, statutory definitions. *State v. Weeden*, 17 Wyo. 418, 100 P. 114, 115 (1909). For over a century, Wyoming courts have recognized that it is their duty only to interpret and declare what the law is, not to be responsible for its defects. *Hamilton v. Territory of Wyoming*, 1 Wyo. 131, 135 (1873). And of specific importance to the instant case is the precept that exceptions not made by the legislature in a statute cannot be read into it. *State ex rel. Peterson v. Ellsworth*, 59 Wyo. 288, 139 P.2d 744, 748 (1943). Courts should be particularly chary of applying equity to negate statutory intent. Equity "arose in response to the restrictive and inflexible rules of the common law, and not as a means of avoiding legislation that courts deemed unwise or inadequate." *Lankford*, 489 S.E.2d at 608 (Mitchell, C.J., dissenting).

> A court of equity has no more right than has a court of law to act on its own notion of what is right in a particular case; it must be guided by the established rules and precedents. Where rights are defined and established by existing legal principles, they may not be changed or unsettled in equity. A court of equity is thus bound by any explicit statute or directly applicable rule of law, regardless of its views of the equities.
>
> *Id. (quoting 27A Am.Jur.2d, Equity §109 (1994)).*

[24] Kim and Kirk oversimplify the task presented to this Court. They argue, correctly, that the question is whether their mother should be considered Neil's adopted daughter for purposes of the anti-lapse statute. But they incorrectly characterize that statute as allowing the "children" of a predeceased "family member" to take the share of an estate that was bequeathed to the deceased family member under a will, but denying such treatment to "non-family members." If that were the question, we would only have to determine whether Julie was a "family member." But the statutory construct is much more complex than that.

[25] Neil left the residuary portion of his estate to Julie, Neil J., and Charles. Julie died before Neil did. As applied to the facts of this case, Wyo. Stat. Ann. §2-6-107(b) provides that, if Julie's residuary devise lapsed, then the entire residue is to be divided equally between Neil J. and Charles. Whether or not the devise to Julie lapsed depends on Wyo. Stat. Ann. §2-6-106, which provides, in effect, that if Julie is a lineal descendent of Neil's grandparent, the residuary devise to her did not lapse, and her share will go to Kim and Kirk. The question is whether the legislature intended that result.

[26] The phrase "lineal descendent" is not defined in the statute. The word "lineal" connotes "a direct blood relative," and "lineal descent" indicates "[d]escent in a direct or straight line, as from father or grandfather to son or grandson." *Black's Law Dictionary* 456, 941 (7th ed. 1999). "Lineal descent" is contrasted with "collateral descent," which refers to "descent in a collateral or oblique line, from brother to brother or cousin to cousin." *Id.* at 456. "With collateral descent, the donor and donee are related through a common ancestor." *Id.*

[27] The problem in the instant case, of course, is not that Julie was Neil's collateral relative. The problem is that Julie was not the lineal descendent of Neil's grandparent either biologically or by legal adoption. Legislative intent is certainly clear that, had Julie been adopted, she would be considered Neil's child, and would then be a lineal descendent under the statutes. Wyo. Stat. Ann. §1-22-114(b) (LexisNexis 2003). But, on its face, the anti-lapse statute just as clearly makes no provision for step-children or other persons who have not been legally adopted. And in that regard, the words of the statute are not ambiguous. A lineal descendent is a lineal descendent. We cannot create an ambiguity within the statute by asking whether we should apply an equitable doctrine to broaden the class of persons identified by the statute.[14]

[28] The primary function of equitable adoption is to enforce a child's right to inherit from someone who promised, but failed to adopt that child, and then died intestate.

Because the putative adoptive parent died without a will, there was neither a testamentary inheritance, nor a testamentary disinheritance, either of which was an available option for the decedent (unless there was also a specific promise to make a will, or leave an inheritance). Equitable adoption is used to fill that intent "gap" by allowing the child to inherit as if she had been adopted. Where a will has been made, however, there is no gap to be filled. We know the decedent's intent from the terms of the will. In the instant case, we do not need equitable adoption to enforce Neil's intent to leave a portion of his estate to Julie—Neil did that himself in his will.[15]

[29] This case serves as a good example of why the doctrine of equitable adoption should not be applied to testate estates—the result may negate both legislative and testamentary intent.[16] The specific facts of this case also raise another consideration: when the child seeking recognition of adoptive status is a step-child brought into the home by the marriage of her mother to the putative adoptive father, the inference does not necessarily follow that there was a promise to adopt. A court may infer such a promise in cases where biological parents relinquish their child to others. The same inference may not be appropriate, however, when a mother brings her child into the home of her new husband. In that situation, there may be an equal inference that the father-child or stepfather-stepchild relationship merely arose out of the domestic status of the parties. J.C.J., Jr., Note, *supra*, 58 Va. L. Rev. at 737-38; George A. Locke, Annotation, *Modern Status of Law as to Equitable Adoption or Adoption by Estoppel*, 97 A.L.R.3d 347, §26 at 65-67 (June 2003 Supp.). *See also*, Rebecca C. Bell, *supra*, XXIX Stetson L. Rev. at 430 and George C. Sims, Comment, *Adoption by Estoppel: History and Effect*, XV Baylor L. Rev. 162, 168-69 (1963).

> As for the stepparent-stepchild relationship in this case, that relationship calls for particular circumspection before recognizing an equitable adoption. Courts have seldom applied the doctrine of equitable adoption or its equivalents to treat a stepparent as an adoptive parent.... One reason is the appreciation that it is in the public interest for stepparents to be generous and loving with their stepchildren. Such conduct could be discouraged if a consequence of such kindness toward a stepchild would be the imposition on the stepparent of the legal incidents of parenthood, such as a duty to provide child support after divorce or a reallocation of the stepparent's estate after death.

> *Otero v. City of Albuquerque, 965 P.2d 354, 362 (N.M.App. 1998).*

[30] Finally, although it is part of the probate code chapter dealing with intestate succession, Wyo. Stat. Ann. §2-4-104 (LexisNexis 2003) should also be considered when determining the intent of the legislature as to the inheritance rights of children who have not been legally adopted: "Persons of the half-blood inherit the same share they would inherit if they were of the whole blood, but stepchildren and foster children and their descendents do not inherit."

Testamentary Intent

[31] In their second issue, Kim and Kirk contend that the district court erred in concluding that Neil's will did not evidence an intention that their mother's share of his estate should go to them. They argue that, even if the anti-lapse statute does not preserve the devise to her, this Court should give effect to Neil's intention, as provided by Wyo. Stat. Ann. §2-6-105 (LexisNexis 2003):

> The intention of a testator as expressed in his will controls the legal effect of his dispositions. The rules of construction expressed in the succeeding sections of this article apply unless a contrary intention is indicated by the will.

We note that Wyo. Stat. Ann. §2-1-102(a)(ii) (LexisNexis 2003) also emphasizes the importance of testamentary intent:

> a.   This code shall be liberally construed and applied, to promote the following purposes and policies to:

> . . .

(ii) Discover and make effective the intent of a decedent in distribution of his property[.]

[32] Before we address the parties' arguments as to testamentary intent, we will briefly review our standards for the construction of wills. Consistent with the above statutory directives, "the intention of the testator must govern." *Hammer v. Atchison*, 536 P.2d 151, 155 (Wyo. 1975). Furthermore, the intent of the testator must be ascertained solely from the meaning of the words used in the will. *Churchfield v. First Nat. Bank of Sheridan*, 418 P.2d 1001, 1003 (Wyo. 1966); *In re Boyd's Estate*, 366 P.2d 336, 337 (Wyo. 1961). Where the will is clear and unambiguous, the court may not read into a will something the testator did not place there. *Dainton v. Watson*, 658 P.2d 79, 81 (Wyo. 1983); *Kortz v. American Nat. Bank of Cheyenne*, 571 P.2d 985, 987 (Wyo. 1977). The courts will not supply words for the testator. *In re Lendecke's Estate*, 329 P.2d 819, 822 (Wyo. 1958). Wyo. Stat. Ann. §2-6-112 (LexisNexis 2003), which requires wills to be in writing, precludes ascribing to a testator any intention not expressed in the instrument itself. *Churchfield*, 418 P.2d at 1003; *In re Boyd's Estate*, 366 P.2d at 337.

[33] In granting summary judgment to Neil J. and Charles on this issue, the district court made the following findings:

> The Last Will and Testament of Neil Adam Seader is clear and unambiguous. Based on the clear and unambiguous language of the Last Will and Testament there is no indication that it was the decedent's intention to have Ms. Schroeder's children inherit the share. Ms. Schroeder would have inherited had she survived the decedent. To the contrary, such a provision is nowhere to be found within the Last Will and Testament.

[34] The argument of Kim and Kirk that Neil intended for them to take their mother's share of his estate is contained in one paragraph of their appellate brief:

> Under the will, Neil Adam Seader left the residue of his estate to three individuals. The will does not identify the relationship of any of these individuals to the testator and the testator made no distinction between them in the residuary clause. This evidences an intention that these three individuals be treated identically under the residuary clause. In the specific bequest clause, the testator left his coins to the same three individuals equally, "share and share alike." Again, evidence of an intention that these three be treated equally. Finally, in the specific bequest clause, Julie Schroeder is given a Thomas Organ but the decedent's two biological sons are given nothing additional. If this adds anything to the testator's intentions about Julie Schroeder, it is that she should be given preference over the biological sons—certainly not treated worse.

[35] The specific provisions of the will upon which this argument is based read as follows:

> SECOND: (SPECIFIC BEQUESTS) I make the following specific bequests: (1) my Thomas Organ to Julie Schroeder; (2) the sum of $500.00 to Ronald Bathrick. Also, (3) my coins in the safe deposit box to be divided equally among Charles Lee Seader, Neil J. Seader and Julie L. Schroeder, share and share alike.
>
> THIRD: All the rest, residue and remainder of my property, of every nature and description, real, personal or mixed, wheresoever the same may be situate, and whether acquired before or after the execution of this Last Will and Testament, and including is [sic] such rest, residue and remainder, any property over which at the time of my death I shall have the power of testamentary disposition, is directed to be sold and I give, bequeath and devise the proceeds to [be] divided to:
>
> *Neil J. Seader   Charles Lee Seader   Julie L. Schroeder*
> *[Address]   [Address]   [Address]*

[36] We agree with the district court that these provisions are clear and unambiguous and that they simply do not contain any hint of an intention on Neil's behalf that the bequest and devise to Julie should be exempt from the anti-lapse statute. The will does not even refer to Julie as "my child" or to Julie, Neil J., and Charles as "my children." There is nothing within the language of the will from which we can infer that Julie was intended to be

considered a "lineal descendent." It must be remembered that we cannot create an ambiguity within the will by application of the knowledge that Neil did not adopt Julie or by the assertions of others that he had allegedly previously intended to adopt her.

[37] Even if we were to accept the contention that, at the time of his marriage to Julie's mother, Neil agreed to adopt Julie, that adds nothing to our assessment of Neil's testamentary intent. An adopted child, like a natural child, could have been left out of the will altogether. We would have to speculate to conclude that, because Neil included Julie in his will, he meant for the gifts to her to pass to her children if she predeceased him. Such speculation is simply not justified; the terms of the will and the statutory provisions are equally unambiguous.

Conclusion

[38] We decline to apply the doctrine of equitable adoption to affect the distribution of a testate estate. Equity should not be available to countermand clear legislative mandates. Adoption and probate are both statutory procedures, with formalities designed to ensure certainty. Where neither the applicable statutes nor the last will and testament are ambiguous, neither legislative intent nor testamentary intent depends upon resort to equity. Furthermore, there is no language within the unambiguous Last Will and Testament of Neil Adam Seader from which we can discern an intent that the provisions of Wyo. Stat. Ann. §§2-6-106 and 2-6-107 not apply to the testamentary gift to Julie L. Schroeder.

[39] The district court's Order Granting Summary Judgment and Order Approving Accounting, and Decree of Distribution are affirmed.

GOLDEN, J., dissenting, with whom HILL, C.J., joins.

[40] Because I believe there is room for equity under the unique facts of this case, I dissent. With regards to the first issue, the application of the principles of equity to these facts, I disagree with the reasoning of the majority opinion. The Wyoming Probate Code specifically provides that principles of equity should be applied to supplement Code provisions to the extent the equitable principles do not directly contradict express probate provisions. Wyo. Stat. Ann. §2-1-102(b) (LexisNexis 2003). The majority opinion finds such an express contradiction where I believe none exists. The majority opinion relies heavily on a dissent in a North Carolina intestate succession case to support its reasoning, *Lankford v. Wright*, 489 S.E.2d 604, 607 (N.C. 1997). In *Lankford*, the North Carolina Supreme Court recognized and applied the doctrine of equitable adoption under a more standard set of facts, ultimately allowing a woman to inherit from the intestate estate of a woman who had held her out as her child. *Id*. at 606-07.

[41] The dissent in the North Carolina case was based upon a statute that is substantially different from Wyoming's statutes. The North Carolina statute, included in the provisions governing intestate succession, provided that a person **adopted in accordance with the adoption statutes** is entitled by succession to any property by, through and from his adoptive parents.[17] The dissent argued that the statute evinced a legislative policy decision that **only** those children legally adopted could inherit. *Id*. at 608. Continuing this line of reasoning, the dissent interpreted the statute as a legislative mandate precluding the application of equitable adoption by courts for purposes of intestate succession.

[42] The majority in *Lankford* refused to accept the reasoning of the dissent, stating:

> [W]e again note that an overwhelming majority of states that have addressed the question have recognized and applied the doctrine [of equitable adoption]. More importantly, it is the unique role of the courts to fashion equitable remedies to protect and promote the principles of equity such as those at issue in this case. We are convinced that acting in an equitable manner in this case does not interfere with the legislative scheme for adoption, contrary to the assertions of the dissent. Recognition of the

doctrine of equitable adoption does not create a legal adoption, and therefore does not impair the statutory procedures for adoption.

Lankford, 489 S.E.2d at 607. I believe that the majority in *Lankford* has the better argument, especially concerning the role of equity and the courts. Equity is always available, and indeed is intended, to fill gaps in compliment with the law, whether common law or statutory law.

> Equity follows the law except in those matters which entitle the party to equitable relief, although the strict rule of law be to the contrary. It is at this point that their paths diverge. As the archer bends his bow that he may send the arrow straight to the mark, so equity bends the letter of the law to accomplish the object of its enactment.

Holloway v. Jones, 246 S.W. 587, 591 (Mo. 1922). A reading of the Wyoming Probate Code as a whole reveals that the legislature intends and expects Wyoming courts to apply equity when necessary to "discover and make effective the intent of a decedent in distribution of his property." §2-1-102(a)(ii).

[43] Thus, equity may be applied when necessary unless prohibited by an express probate provision. The majority opinion finds such an express prohibition in the anti-lapse statute. To save a bequest from lapsing, the anti-lapse statute requires the deceased devisee be a lineal descendant. The majority opinion claims that the term "lineal descendant" is unambiguous and this Court cannot apply equity to "broaden the class of persons identified by the statute." "Lineal descendant" means no more, or less, than in a direct line, *e.g.* a child or grandchild. The definition of "child" remains to be supplied. In *In re Cadwell's Estate*, this Court quoted with approval a definition of "lineal descendant" that included "an adopted child." 26 Wyo. 412, 419-20, 186 P. 499, 501 (Wyo. 1920). "Child" is defined by Wyo. Stat. Ann. §2-1-301(v) (LexisNexis 2003) as including "an adopted child." No definition expressly states, or even implies, that the definition of "adopted child" is limited to a legally adopted child, to the exclusion of an equitably adopted child. As such, I see no direct conflict in reading "equitably adopted child" into the definition of lineal descendant.

[44] Which brings me back to the initial enquiry – should equity be applied to these facts? I would approach the question in a slightly different manner. Certainly, this case does not present the standard set of facts for the application of equitable adoption. Because Neil died testate, equitable adoption in the traditional sense does not apply. The Wyoming Probate Code clearly directs that "[t]he intention of a testator as expressed in his will controls the legal effect of his dispositions." Wyo. Stat. Ann. §2-6-105 (LexisNexis 2003). Thus, the critical inquiry is Neil's intentions as expressed in his will.

[45] In determining the intent of a testator, it is important to note that the Wyoming Probate Code is set up as an "opt out" code. In other words, the provisions of the probate code apply, unless the testator evinces a contrary intention in the will. Thus, the anti-lapse statute automatically applies, unless the testator indicates otherwise in his will. In this case, Neil's will provides no indication that he did not want the anti-lapse statute to apply. Thus, Neil's intent is for the anti-lapse statute to apply. There is no question that if one or both of the biological sons had predeceased their father, their heirs would have taken "in place" of the deceased devisee.

[46] It is critical to note that the anti-lapse statute is not a statute of devise, but rather only limits the conditions upon which an inheritance will lapse. The inheritance does not lapse if it is made to a lineal descendent. If made to a lineal descendant, the "issue of the deceased devisee take in place of the deceased devisee." Wyo. Stat. Ann. §2-6-106 (LexisNexis 2003). Thus, Kim and Kirk are not attempting to inherit in their own name or in their own right; they will only take in the place of Julie. It is still Julie's inheritance that is at stake.

[47] Neil's will clearly indicated that he did want Julie to receive an inheritance from him. The question is: did he want her to receive the inheritance as his daughter or as a non-relative? The majority opinion decides the issue against Julie based upon the lack of any

express language in the will referring to Julie as his daughter. I believe this oversimplifies the process. Neil never clarified anyone's status in his will. I believe this lack of clarification renders the terms of the will ambiguous.

[48] "[T]he construction of the will is to be resolved by determining the intent of deceased as such appears from a full and complete consideration of the entire will when read in the light of the surrounding circumstances." *Douglas v. Newell*, 719 P.2d 971, 973 (Wyo. 1986). The circumstances in this case indicate that Neil consistently treated and referred to Julie as his daughter. Julie was his wife's daughter. When Julie's mother died, she left her entire estate to Neil, leaving nothing to Julie. Then Neil executed his will, treating all three children equally in at least two provisions of the will, including the residuary clause. I believe the family context creates a strong implication that Neil considered Julie his daughter, thus creating an ambiguity in his will requiring extrinsic evidence to resolve his true intent.

[49] The complication in this case is that, even if Neil intended Julie to take as his daughter, Julie was never legally adopted by Neil. Julie is legally not a lineal descendant of Neil. I do not believe, however, that the inquiry is automatically at an end with the determination of Julie's legal status. This case is presented to this Court as a plea to recognize Julie as adopted in equity. If Julie is recognized as adopted in equity, for purposes of inheritance only, Julie would be a lineal descendant, her share would not lapse, and her children would take her share as her representatives. This, I believe, is where there is room for the application of equity to affect Neil's testamentary intent.

[50] This case was decided on summary judgment. I would reverse and remand this case for further proceedings to determine Neil's testamentary intent. Starting with his will, we know Neil wanted Julie to inherit from him, but we do not know from the will what status Neil accorded Julie. I believe the first issue to determine is if there is clear and convincing evidence to support equitable adoption. If there is not, the inquiry is at an end because Neil could not have considered Julie an adopted daughter. Julie's share would thus lapse.

[51] If there is clear and convincing evidence supporting equitable adoption, then the question returns to Neil's testamentary intent. Did Neil intend for Julie to take only if she survived him, or did Neil take for granted that Julie was his daughter and her inheritance would not lapse? If it can be proven that Neil did want Julie to take as his daughter, then I believe it would be appropriate to apply the principle of equitable adoption, thus preventing Julie's share from lapsing. This would then allow for Neil's testamentary intent to be fulfilled. Applying principles of law and equity is exactly what this court is expected to do to "discover and make effective the intent of a decedent in distribution of his property." §2-1-102(a)(ii).

[52] However, I note that many jurisdictions accept that "adoption by estoppel" precludes not just the foster parents but also their heirs from challenging the status of a child as equitably adopted. *See e.g. Shaw v. Scott*, 252 N.W. 237 (Iowa 1934) (collecting cases); *Fiske v. Lawton*, 144 N.W. 455 (Minn. 1913). In both *Shaw* and *Fiske*, the foster child predeceased the foster parents and the foster parents then died intestate. The respective courts, after finding clear and convincing evidence of an agreement to adopt, estopped the heirs of the foster parents from challenging the status of the foster child as equitably adopted, thus clearing the way for the foster child's children to inherit their parent's share.

NOTES

1. "Julie" is sometimes spelled "Julia" in the court file.
2. None of the relevant motions, petitions, and legal memoranda in the record are verified or accompanied by sworn affidavits, perhaps because there does not appear to be any controversy as to the basic facts. The facts stated herein are taken from the various pleadings and are set forth in the light most favorable to the appellants.

3. Wyo. Stat. Ann. §2-6-106 states:

> If a devisee who is a grandparent or a lineal descendent of a grandparent of the testator is dead at the time of execution of the will, fails to survive the testator, or is treated as if he predeceased the testator, the issue of the deceased devisee take in place of the deceased devisee and if they are all of the same degree of kinship to the devisee they take equally, but if of unequal degree then those of more remote degree take per stirpes. One who would have been a devisee under a class gift if he had survived the testator is treated as a devisee for purposes of this section whether his death occurred before or after the execution of the will.

Wyo. Stat. Ann. §2-6-107(b) states:

> Except as provided in W.S. 2-6-106, if the residue is devised to two (2) or more persons and the share of one (1) of the residuary devisees fails for any reason, his share passes to the residuary devisee, or to other residuary devisees in proportion to their interests in the residue.

4. "In general, a devise or legacy left to a beneficiary in his individual capacity, and not jointly with others, will lapse upon his death prior to that of the testator, unless the testator has expressed a contrary intention, or unless a controlling statute otherwise dictates." *Matter of Stroble's Estate*, 6 Kan.App.2d 955, 636 P.2d 236, 239 (1981). *See also* 80 Am.Jur.2d, *Wills*, §§1423-1430 (2002).

5. Wyo. Stat. Ann. §1-22-114(b) (LexisNexis 2003) states: "Adopted persons may assume the surname of the adoptive parent. They are entitled to the same rights of person and property as children and heirs at law of the persons who adopted them." Wyo. Stat. Ann. §2-4-101(c) (LexisNexis 2003) states, in pertinent part:

> Except in cases above enumerated, the estate of any intestate shall descend and be distributed as follows:
>
> (i) To his children surviving, and the descendents of his children who are dead, the descendents collectively taking the share which their parents would have taken if living[.]

6. Equitable adoption does not create an adoption; rather, it merely recognizes its existence for limited purposes. *Holt v. Burlington Northern R. Co.*, 685 S.W.2d 851, 858 (Mo.App. 1984).

7. Wyoming's adoption statutes are found at Wyo. Stat. Ann. §§1-22-101 through 1-22-203 (LexisNexis 2003).

8. While adoption is not defined in Wyo. Stat. Ann. §1-22-101, which is the definitions section of Wyoming's adoption statutes, Wyo. Stat. Ann. §1-22-114, which sets forth the effects of adoption, contains language similar to that cited above:

   a. Upon the entry of a final decree of adoption the former parent, guardian or putative father of the child shall have no right to the control or custody of the child. The adopting persons shall have all of the rights and obligations respecting the child as if they were natural parents.

   b. Adopted persons may assume the surname of the adoptive parent. They are entitled to the same rights of person and property as children and heirs at law of the persons who adopted them.

9. *See* 2 Am.Jur.2d, *Adoption, supra*, §53 at 931-32 n.10-n.13; George A. Locke, Annotation, *Modern Status of Law as to Equitable Adoption or Adoption by Estoppel*, 97 A.L.R.3d 347, §3, 359-66 (1980); Rebecca C. Bell, *supra*, XXIX Stetson L. Rev. at 417 n.12; Beth Ann Yount, Note, *Lankford v. Wright: Recognizing Equitable Adoption in North Carolina*, 76 N.C. L. Rev. 2446, 2446 n.5 (1998); and J.C.J., Jr., Note, *Equitable Adoption: They Took Him Into Their Home and Called Him Fred*, 58 Va. L. Rev. 727, 727-28 n.7 and n.10 (1972).

10. *But see Thomas v. Malone*, 142 Mo.App. 193, 126 S.W. 522, 523-24 (1910), where an equitably adopted child was allowed to pursue a claim against a will as a pretermitted heir. Further, some courts have begun to apply the doctrine to other claims, such as life insurance benefits, inheritance tax considerations, wrongful death actions, worker's compensation benefits, child support, and will contests. George A. Locke, *supra*, 97 A.L.R.3d at 353.

11. *Hicks v. Simmons*, 271 F.2d 875, 877 (10th Cir. 1959) (oral promise to adopt and to leave adopting parents' property to adoptee); *In re Gary's Estate*, 69 Ariz. 228, 211 P.2d 815, 818 (1949) (oral promise to feed, clothe, educate, and make heir); *Foster v. Cheek*, 212 Ga. 821, 96 S.E.2d 545, 546-50 (1957) (oral promise to adopt and to make heir to inherit as natural child); *Fredrick v. Christensen*, 73 S.D. 130, 39 N.W.2d 529, 531-32 (1949) (legal adoption coupled with promise to make heir); *In re McLean's Estate*, 219 Wis. 222, 262 N.W. 707, 708 (1935) (no adoption promised, but oral promise to provide in will).

12. The children had not lived in his home for six months, as required by Wyo. Stat. Ann. §1-22-111 (a) (iii) (W.S. 1977).

13. The adoption statutes and the probate code must be read together to determine legislative intent. *In re Cadwell's Estate*, 26 Wyo. 412, 186 P. 499, 500 (1920).

14. That was the point of Chief Justice Mitchell's dissent in *Lankford*, 489 S.E.2d at 608.

15. Alternatively, what Kim and Kirk are asking this Court to do is to presume that Neil made his will in ignorance of the adoption statute and in ignorance of the anti-lapse statute, and that he actually intended a result opposite from the statutory results. There is no evidence to support that theory.

16. We are not herein determining whether equitable adoption may be applied in an intestate setting.

Wyo. Stat. Ann. §2-1-102(b) (LexisNexis 2003) allows for the appropriate exercise of equity in a probate case: "Unless displaced by the particular provisions of this code, the principles of law and equity supplement the code provisions." *See Calista Corp.*, 564 P.2d at 61 n.18.

17. N.C. Gen. Stat. §29-17 (2001). Succession by, through and from adopted children

   a. A child, adopted in accordance with Chapter 48 of the General Statutes or in accordance with the applicable law of any other jurisdiction, and the heirs of such child are entitled by succession to any property by, through and from his adoptive parents and their heirs the same as if he were the natural legitimate child of the adoptive parents.

Chapter **eight**

TRUSTS: ELEMENTS AND PURPOSE

OBJECTIVES

At the end of this chapter, the student will understand:

- trust terminology
- the trust elements
- how to create a trust
- the different types of trusts
- how to terminate a trust

Overview of Trusts

What is a trust? A trust is an estate planning vehicle in which a person, called the trustor, transfers property to a trustee. The trustee then holds the property in the trust ("in trust") for the benefit of certain third parties, called beneficiaries. A trust is essentially a contract between the trustor and the trustee in which the trustee agrees to manage the trust property and distribute the assets pursuant to the agreement's terms.

- There are two kinds of trusts: Those that are created in a will, called **testamentary trusts;** and
- Those that are created as stand-alone documents of which there are two basic types:
  - revocable trusts (also called inter vivos or living trusts), meaning they can be altered or amended
  - irrevocable trusts, meaning that once put into effect, they may not be altered or amended

Trust Elements

Every trust must contain certain elements to be valid. A trust that is missing any of these elements (with the exception of the one for a trustee) will cause the trust to fail.

Five elements are required for a valid trust of any type:

1. a trustor
2. a trustee
3. trust property
4. beneficiary(ies)
5. trust purpose

As already stated, if any one of these trust elements are missing, the trust will fail, causing the property to be distributed in one of two ways. If the trust was a testamentary trust, the property will be distributed through a residuary clause. If the will either did not have a residuary clause, or if the residuary beneficiary predeceases the testator or refuses to accept the bequest, the trust property will be distributed by intestate succession. If a revocable or irrevocable trust was involved, the property will either revert to the trustor, or in some circumstances, to the beneficiaries outright.

Trustor

The **trustor,** also called the settlor or grantor, is the person who establishes the trust as a method for holding, investing, and eventually distributing the property to certain beneficiaries. A trustor may create a trust for different reasons including:

- Management of the trust property by someone other than him or herself.
- Tax savings.
- Prevent a beneficiary from getting property outright, in effect doling it out to the beneficiary. This may be because the beneficiary is a minor. It also is used to prevent a beneficiary's creditors, spouse or former spouse from obtaining the funds.

Who Can Be a Trustor   A trustor can be any individual with the legal capacity to execute the trust (sound mind to create a contract). A trustor may also be a legal entity, including corporations, limited liability companies or partnerships, or foundations, or other charitable entities, as long as that company's chartering documents permit creation of the trust. In fact, many trusts are created by corporations that wish to endow some of their wealth for the benefit of society. Examples of such trusts are those set up for the benefit of the arts and medical research.

Sound Mind of Trustor   The concept of sound mind is the same as is used when dealing with wills if the trust is testamentary, meaning part of a will. The trustor must have the requisite mental capacity to execute the will, otherwise the entire will, including the testamentary trust provisions, will be invalid.

Revocable trusts (also called "living trusts") are contracts however, so the trustor must have contractual capacity. A prerequisite of contractual capacity is that the person making the contract is of sound mind. If the trustor lacks sound mind, he or she will be considered incapable of executing the living trust. If a potential trustor is old and enfeebled, incapable of making an independent decision about his or her affairs, or generally unaware of the full extent of his or her property, or the beneficiaries to whom the property would be given, the trustor may be considered incapable of making a trust. As in wills, however, mere age, illness, foul disposition or temper, eccentricity, stinginess, or excessive spending do not automatically mean that the trustor lacks mental capacity. These traits are only evidence of the possibility that the trustor is not of sound mind, and would subject the trust to a contest by interested parties, such as heirs who were not named as beneficiaries of the trust, or were not given as much as they believed they were entitled to.

The Trustee

The **trustee** is either an individual or a legal entity to whom the trustor gives legal title to the trust property. Any legal entity, including corporations such as bank trust departments, may be a trustee. Anyone who can legally hold or own property can be a trustee. The trustee must also have the ability to enter into contracts (have contractual capacity). In general, if a person is under no legal disability, he or she can be a trustee. Examples of legal disability include mental illness or being under guardianship. A minor can, however, be a trustee despite the fact that being a minor is a form of legal disability. You may recall that a basic rule of contracts is that a minor may enter into contracts, but all his or her contractual acts must be ratified once he or she reaches the age of majority. Therefore, *all* acts the minor performed as an underaged trustee must be ratified or affirmed when the minor reaches his or her majority. As a practical matter, it is always best to name a trustee who is of legal age at the time the trust is executed so that any potential problems are avoided, such as (1) that the trustee either will not ratify or is under another disability at the time and cannot ratify, and (2) that many people and companies will not contract with a minor at the outset because they are fearful of the possibility that the acts will not be ratified later.

The trustee is, as previously stated, given **legal title** to the property, which means the trustee is the legal owner of the property.

Fundamental Fiduciary Duties   A trustee, however, takes the ownership interest as a **fiduciary**, meaning that the trustee has an affirmative duty to act in the best interest of the trustor and primarily the beneficiaries of the trust, and not for his or her or its personal interests. As such, the trustee is subject to duties and obligations that restrict his or her use of the property, which are either explicitly stated in the trust document or by statute. Examples of fiduciaries that are bound to act in the best interest of their clients, beneficiaries, or charges are stockbrokers, real estate brokers, and lawyers (and their paralegals). The trustee of a trust is held to the same standards as other fiduciaries.

The Trustee shall administer the trust in good faith and according to its terms and the law. Except as otherwise provided, the following fundamental provisions apply to all aspects of the Trustee's investment, management, and administration of its estate. The following provisions may be found in a trust:

A. General Standard of Care.   A Trustee shall exercise the standard of care, skill, and caution generally exercised by compensated trustees with respect to comparable estates in the same geographic area. A Trustee who has special skills or expertise, or is selected as a Trustee in reliance upon the Trustee's representation that the Trustee has special skills or expertise, has a duty to use those special skills or expertise.

B. Loyalty and Impartiality; Primary and Secondary Beneficiaries. The Trustee shall act solely in the interest of the beneficiaries of its estate, not in the interest of the Trustee personally. If a Fiduciary's estate has two or more beneficiaries, the Trustee shall act impartially, taking into account any differing interests of the beneficiaries. However, the Trustee (i) may favor present income beneficiaries over future beneficiaries and (ii) shall favor "primary" beneficiaries over other beneficiaries, and "secondary" beneficiaries over beneficiaries who are neither primary nor secondary.

C. Conflict Resolution.   The Trustee shall make a reasonable effort to resolve any conflicts (including conflicts as to favorable or adverse tax consequences) between or among the Trustee and those persons who are beneficially interested in its estate, by mutual agreement. If after reasonable efforts the Trustee, in the Trustee's discretion, determined that a mutual agreement is not likely to be reached, the Trustee shall resolve the conflicts in the Trustee's discretion.

D. Duty to Verify Facts.   The Trustee shall make a reasonable effort to verify relevant facts. However, the Trustee may rely on (and need not independently verify): (i) the advice of any professional (including an agent, attorney, advisor, accountant, fiduciary, or other professional or representative) who was hired (or to whom duties were delegated) in accordance with this instrument and with reasonable care; and (ii) any written instrument or other evidence that the Trustee reasonably believes to be accurate. (But a corporate Trustee shall always be liable for the acts, omissions and defaults of its affiliates, officers, and regular employees.)

E. Duty to Keep Beneficiaries Informed.   The Trustee shall keep all current beneficiaries of a trust, who have attained the age of 25 years, reasonably informed concerning the administration of the trust and material facts necessary for the beneficiaries to protect their interests.

F. Reliance on Predecessor Fiduciary.   A Trustee may rely on the records and other representations of a Predecessor Fiduciary (meaning a predecessor Trustee under this instrument or a personal representative or trustee of any estate or trust from which distributions may be made to the Trustee), and need not request an accounting from or contest any accounting provided by a Predecessor Fiduciary. However, the preceding shall not apply to any Trustee to the extent that the Trustee (i) has received a request from a beneficiary having a vested material interest in its estate, to secure an accounting or to conduct an investigation, or (ii) has actual knowledge of facts that would lead a reasonable person to believe that, as a consequence of any act or omission of a Predecessor Fiduciary, a material loss has occurred, or will occur.

G. Special Rule for Uncompensated Individual Trustees.   Notwithstanding any contrary provision, whenever an uncompensated individual is serving as Trustee (meaning an individual serving with no right to compensation, or who, at all relevant times, has waived his or her right to compensation), he or she: (i) may continue any style of investing that is consistent with the style of investing we undertook during our lifetimes; and (ii) shall exercise that standard of care, which is commensurate with his or her particular skills and expertise, or, to the extent lower, the general standard of care required of Trustees without special skills or expertise.

A trustee's duties and obligations are generally very broad within the categories listed above. A fiduciary must uphold standards in order to perform properly. Such standards include:

- high degree of good faith, loyalty, and care in the management of his or her duties
- use of ordinary and reasonable skill and prudence in his or her functions
- preservation and protection of the trust assets
- refrain from self-dealing, meaning he or she may not personally benefit from his or her management of trust assets

  Example: The trust property of the "Richard Wiggins Revocable Trust" includes a tract of land that has not appreciated in value for some time, and the trustee, George Dunkin, wants to sell it and invest the proceeds in other property that would increase the value of the trust. The fair market value of the land is $400 per acre and George could easily sell the land for that amount. George is prohibited from selling the property to himself, unless he is willing to spend at least $400 per acre. If he sold it to himself for anything less, he would be self-dealing because he would be receiving a personal benefit from the trust to the detriment of the beneficiaries. In addition, if George has an offer for more than $400 per acre, George must at least match the offer, or again, he would be self-dealing.

- not delegate the performance of trust duties to anyone else. A trustee may hire professionals, such as accountants, stockbrokers, and lawyers to assist him or her in his or her duties, but he or she may not hire someone else to manage the trust in his or her stead. The trustee must manage the trust personally. For example: George Dunkin is the trustee of the "Richard Wiggins Revocable Trust." He is doing a fine job of managing the trust, but he has received notice that a portion of the trust assets, land on the east side of town, is being appropriated by the county, which will use the land as part of a road-widening project. George may hire a lawyer to assist in protecting the trust's assets. George may not ask his friend, James Harkness, to manage the trust while he goes to Europe for the summer, however. George once a trustee is always a trustee unless he dies, becomes disabled, or resigns, or is removed.
- maintain accurate records and accounts. These records must be periodically given to the beneficiary(ies). The beneficiary is also given a reasonable right of inspection. Any refusal to open the books to the beneficiaries is grounds for removal.
- take possession of the trust property and make it profitable. Should the trustee refuse to take possession, and therefore, deny ownership of the property, he or she will not be a trustee and an alternate trustee must be found.
- pay all legally enforceable trust debts
- collect all debts owed to the trust

Trust Property

Trust property is also called the:

- res
- corpus
- principal
- fund
- assets
- estate

Trust property is any property that can be freely transferred from one party to another. This includes real and personal property. Only property with restrictions on transferability may not be trust property.

Example: A government pension or annuity is generally nontransferable as they often have restrictions limiting to whom the principal and/or the proceeds may be given (usually they may be given only to a spouse, child, or other dependent), as well as how and when they may be distributed.

Property transferred to a trust must generally be income producing. If it is not income producing, a trustee will usually sell the property in favor of other income producing property. The purpose of making the property income producing is to provide *income* to the beneficiaries without having to invade the *principal* of the trust, thereby preserving the assets for the future. A trust's principal is all of the original assets and those assets added to the trust during the time the trust is in effect. A trust's income is all of the interest, dividends, and gain that the trust's principal has during the time the trust is in effect. A trust's goal is to expend only income for the beneficiaries and preserve the principal for the future (so that it can accumulate more income, and be distributed to beneficiaries when the trust terminates). However, certain grantor trusts, usually those in which the grantor is also the trustee and the primary beneficiary, will permit the trustee to maintain trust property that is non-income producing, such as the grantor's primary residence or another home, such as a vacation property, as well as the grantor's regular checking account or savings, which likely make little if any interest, or household furnishings and other items in regular household usage. It is understood that these assets are not in the trust for the purpose of creating income.

As stated, the trustee holds only the legal title to the property in the trust and holds the property for the benefit of the beneficiaries. The beneficiaries hold the **equitable title** to the trust property, meaning they have the right of enjoyment of the property. In practical terms, this means that while the trustee has the sole right to buy, sell, mortgage, or lease the property, or for that matter, do anything else with the property as is permitted under the trust agreement, and comports with his or her fiduciary duties, the trustee's right to the property is subservient to the beneficiaries' right to the property. The trustee's duty to the equitable title holders prevents the trustee from abusing any legal ownership rights he has in the property. If the trustee abuses his or her position in any way, he or she will have breached his or her fiduciary duties to the beneficiaries. A breach of duty is grounds for removal as trustee, and therefore, is a powerful restriction on his or her actual ownership of the property.

The Beneficiary

The **beneficiary** is the party that holds the equitable title to the trust property and derives the benefit and enjoyment of the property. This means that the beneficiaries of a trust are entitled to receive the trust's income and profits as prescribed in the trust agreement, and in some but not all cases, the principal of the trust as well.

The beneficiary, also called the *cestui que trust,* must be identified clearly by name, "Huey Duck, Dewey Duck, and Louie Duck," or by class, "to all of my grandchildren" or "to all of the graduates of the class of 2012." Beneficiaries need not have either mental or contractual capacity to hold the equitable title to the property. In fact, trusts are often created to protect persons who have neither the mental nor contractual capacity to hold property on their own. It is not uncommon for parents to create a trust for the benefit of their minor, or mentally or physically disabled, children in the event that the parents become unable to provide for their children in the future.

If there is more than one beneficiary to the trust, they will hold the equitable title as tenants in common, a form of property ownership which is discussed fully in Chapter 2. The trust agreement determines the extent to which the principal and income of the trust are distributed to each beneficiary and how often.

Trust Purpose

A trust may be created for any lawful purpose, but may never be created if it will violate any criminal or civil laws. The **trust purpose** must be clearly stated in the trust agreement, for the agreement to be valid.

Example: Lisa Low's trust states in part:

As Trustor, I have established this trust in order to provide a means for the management of certain of my property, for the management of such further property interests as may be deposited with the trustee by me, and for my maintenance, comfort, and support during my lifetime, and for the benefit of my children after my death, all in the manner hereafter provided.

Examples of a valid trust purpose include providing for the health, maintenance, support, and welfare of the trustor, his or her family, or friends. Trustors often provide for the education of their children or grandchildren through a trust. Trusts are natural vehicles for such a purpose because the money can be properly invested until such time that the children require it for college or trade school, at which time the trustee will distribute as much as is necessary.

Example: Lisa Low's trust, leaving property to her daughters with her brother-in-law as trustee, states in part:

I give the residue of my estate, whether real or personal and wherever located, including all property and interests not otherwise disposed of elsewhere in this document that is acquired by me or my estate after the execution of this document, to my children LINDA LOW AND LINDSAY LOW, if they survive me, in equal shares. Said shares are to be distributed subject to the following terms:

Until such time that my children attain the age of twenty-one (21) years, the property is to be held IN TRUST by JOHN LOW as Trustee ("Trustee"), during which time my Trustee may expend all of the income and as much of the principal which, in his sole and absolute discretion, he deems necessary for my children's health, education, maintenance and support.

Often, only the income will be necessary to effectuate the purpose of the trust, leaving the principal available for distribution when the children are old enough to handle large sums of money responsibly.

CASE 8.1 **SUMMARY**

This case explains the duties of a trustee and the concept of self-dealing.

Ledbetter v. First State Bank & Trust Co., 85 F.3d 1537 (11th Cir. 1996).

Ledbetter was the trustor and beneficiary of a revocable trust. First State Bank was the trustee. Ledbetter sued the bank alleging, among other things, that the bank had conflicts of interest in its dealings and violated its duties by not acting in Ledbetter's best interest.

The bank was wholly owned by First State Corporation (FSC), and owned, as trustee for Ledbetter, a small percentage (1/2–1%) of FSC stock. However, the bank held nearly 40% of the stock when it considered the shares owned on behalf of Ledbetter's relatives. The bank's and FSC's principal officers and directors were substantially the same. Through two of its senior officers, the bank and FSC rejected an offer for merger with another bank (First Alabama), which Ledbetter contended would have led to benefits to himself and other trust beneficiaries. The possibilities of this sale and merger were never communicated to the bank or its trust committee, which never had the opportunity to be consulted about the merger, or to consider it. In addition, FSC made a public offering of its treasury stock which diminished the voting power of the bank as trustee, and the bank made no effort to stop the FSC offering, which Ledbetter contended was an act of disloyalty by the bank.

The Court stated that the foremost duty of a fiduciary to its beneficiary is undivided loyalty, and that if a trustee "places itself in a position where its interests might conflict with the interests of the beneficiary, the law presumes that the trustee acted disloyally."

"Trustees must be entirely at the service of the trust and above suspicion." This requires a "trustee to maintain a position where his every act is above suspicion, and the trust estate, and it alone, can receive not only his (the trustee's, author added) best services, but his unbiased and uninfluenced judgment." The Court found that the bank had conflicts of interest that ran "broadly" and "pervasively." It was a wholly owned subsidiary of FSC. As trustee it owned nearly 40% of FSC's stock. Management of the bank and FSC was "overlapping and interlocking." "[T]he bank and the holding company are tightly bound together by a web of overlapping duties, responsibilities, and relationships, by crossassignment of principal officers and directors of the bank and of the principal officers."

The Court also found that some of the bank's officers and directors were unfamiliar with their obligations under the law. Evidence showed that some officers had never seen the trust department's policies and procedures manual.

One expert witness in the case testified that the bank's trust committee should have obtained independent legal counsel and advice on behalf of the beneficiaries of the trusts that held FSC stock. The bank claimed it was a waste of shareholders' money. Ledbetter asserted that the bank breached its duty by "not encouraging, prompting or joining with others to require FSC … to negotiate with First Alabama." The Court recounted the bank's draft of the trust agreement which Ledbetter specifically rejected. In part, the draft stated that

> Trustor has the utmost confidence in the First State Bank and Trust Company and its affiliates, and he expressly relieves Trustee from any and all restrictions or claims of self-dealing or undivided loyalty that may arise hereunder. ******In carrying out the foregoing, TRUSTOR expressly relieves TRUSTEE from any liability in connection there with and expressly waives any requirements or restrictions relative to self-dealing or undivided loyalty.

The Court noted that a trustee may not hold its own, or an affiliate's stock, unless given authority to do so. Even when a trustee has discretion, the Court will not permit abuse of the discretion, meaning that the trustee must act in good faith and with proper motives, and within "the bounds of a reasonable judgment."

The cause was reversed and remanded to the lower court for further findings.

Trust Classifications

Trusts may be classified by whether they are written or oral, revocable or irrevocable.

Express or Implied

Trusts are either

- express; or
- implied.

Express Trusts

Express trusts are those that are deliberately created by a trustor. They may be either written or oral, and must clearly state the purpose for which the trust is being formed. An express trust will fail for lack of a trust purpose.

> *Example:* Lisa Low wants to set up a trust for the education of her children, Linda and Lindsey. She has a lawyer draft a trust with explicit provisions pertaining to their ability to use the trust's income and principal for their education. This trust is an express written trust.

> Until such time that my children attain the age of twenty-one (21) years, the property is to be held IN TRUST by JOHN LOW as Trustee ("Trustee"),

during which time my Trustee may expend all of the income and as much of the principal which, in his sole and absolute discretion he deems necessary for my children's education, including study at institutions of higher learning and vocational institutions.

Example: Instead of having a lawyer draft a trust agreement, Linda tells her brother-in-law, John, that she's set up a bank account in her own name but that she intends for the income from the account to be for Linda and Lindsey's education. She also tells John that when the children finish schooling, the account's principal should be divided between Linda and Lindsey. This is an express oral trust.

Of course, express written trusts have a distinct advantage over oral trusts simply because any written document can be verified, and it is much more difficult to verify provisions of an oral trust. Proving oral trusts often requires courtroom testimony of witnesses, some of whom may have spotty memories, or may lie (although you hope not). In the second example, the only people privy to the information about the trust provisions were Lisa and John. If Lisa dies before Linda and Lindsey complete schooling, it is possible that the bank account may be distributed as part of Lisa's estate, unless John can convince a court that Lisa intended the money to be expended only for her children's education. It undoubtedly saves a great deal of time and money, not to mention aggravation, to have any trust put in writing.

Implied Trusts

Implied trusts, sometimes called involuntary trusts, are those that are created by operation of law, meaning they are created through the application of established legal principles. Their creation is rooted in the idea that someone would be unjustly enriched unless the law imposed a trust on the situation. Two types of trusts are generally created in these situations:

- resulting trusts
- constructive trusts

Resulting trusts often arise when an express trust fails. As you will recall, when a trust is created, the trustee holds the legal title to the property. If the trust fails, the trustee still holds the legal title to the property, but the beneficiary does not hold equitable title to the property (because the trust failed and that's what gave the beneficiary equitable title). This leads to a situation whereby a person (the trustee), who was not meant to have the benefit and enjoyment of the property, does in fact now own the property outright without restriction. Since this was not the intent of the trustor, a court will impose an implied resulting trust on the property, so that the former trustee only holds the property for the benefit of the person to whom the benefit was intended, the former beneficiary.

Example: Lisa sets up a trust with her brother-in-law, John, as trustee, for the benefit of her children, Linda and Lindsey. As trustee, John has ownership of a bank account with a balance of $100,000. For some reason, the trust that Lisa sets up is found to be invalid. John is now the legal owner of the bank account and John claims the funds for himself; however, Linda and Lindsey petition a court to impose an implied resulting trust on the bank account because Lisa never intended for John to own the $100,000 for himself. The resulting trust is imposed because the legal title to the money is being held by John, and should be for the benefit of Linda and Lindsey. If John had been allowed to keep the bank account funds for himself, it would have been manifestly unfair and not what Lisa intended. The imposition of the resulting trust means that John has legal title, while Linda and Lindsey have equitable title. At all times, the proceeds of the bank account belong to Linda and Lindsey. Most likely, the funds will be given directly to Linda and Lindsey, if they are of age and if not, to a new trustee to maintain the funds on their behalf.

A **constructive trust** arises when a person has title to property, or takes possession of property under circumstances for which there may never have been a formal trust agreement.

Example: Scott and Susie are a fairly well-to-do elderly couple that live in an exclusive area of Anytown, Anystate. They have three children, Kurt, Keith and Kristina. In spite of their advancing age, both Scott and Susie are in good health and can expect to live for quite a few more years. Their two adult sons, Kurt and Keith, kill Scott and Susie, so they can inherit their parents' wealth sooner rather than later. In some states, the sons will be unable to inherit Scott and Susie's property at all. In other states, however, they will inherit despite their heinous crime. In those states that do not block the inheritance, the states will impose an implied trust. This is called an implied constructive trust, which is imposed by operation of law as a means of preventing unjust enrichment on the part of someone who obtained title to the property through fraud or some other kind of wrongdoing. In this instance, legal title to Scott and Susie's property will be held by Kurt and Keith, while the equitable title will be held by the person that should hold title, Kristina.

CASE 8.2 **SUMMARY**

At issue in this case is the authority of a court to impose a constructive trust on the proceeds of a life insurance policy that was to have been maintained by a decedent for the benefit of his child and former wife.

Tupper v. Roan v. Tupper, Court Of Appeals Of The State Of Oregon, 349 Or. 211, 243 P.3d 50 (2010)

Heather Tupper married Jerry Tupper in 1999. They had a child in 2002, and began divorce proceedings in 2003. A stipulated dissolution judgment was entered in January 2004, which granted Heather custody of the child and required Jerry to pay child support. The judgment also provided that "[S]o long as either party has a legal obligation to support any child of the parties, each party shall maintain an insurance policy insuring his or her life in an amount of not less than

$100,000, naming the other parent as trustee on behalf of any supported child." The judgment also included a provision stating

> [A] constructive trust shall be imposed over the proceeds of any insurance owned by either party at the time of either party's death if either party fails to maintain insurance in said amount, or if said insurance is in force but another beneficiary is designated to receive said funds. The trustee shall make distribution as described herein.

However, at the time of the judgment, Jerry owned no life insurance policy of any kind.

Shortly after the entry of the judgment, Jerry began living with Danette Roan. In February 2006, Jerry and Danette each purchased a life insurance policy with a death benefit of $600,000, and named each other as sole beneficiary. Jerry died 3 months later, and Danette received $600,000 in life insurance proceeds as sole beneficiary of Jerry's life insurance policy.

At his death, Jerry was still obligated to pay child support to Heather, but owned no life insurance policy other than the one naming Danette as beneficiary.

Heather sued Danette alleging that Danette knew about Jerry's breach of the life insurance obligation when he purchased the life insurance policy naming Danette as sole beneficiary. Heather asserted a claim for unjust enrichment against Danette, requesting a constructive trust on $100,000 of the proceeds Danette had received. (In the alternative, she asserted a claim for money received, requesting $100,000 in damages instead.)

Danette denied knowing about Jerry's life insurance obligation before his death. (She also asserted a claim for unjust enrichment against the personal representative of Jerry's probate estate on the ground that the estate should be liable for Jerry's contractual obligations.)

At trial, a constructive trust in favor of Heather on $100,000 of Danette's proceeds was entered.

On appeal, the Court had to determine if Heather should prevail on her unjust enrichment claim. The Court stated that

> [C]onstructive trusts are remedies employed by courts "to avoid unjust enrichment when no other adequate remedy is available." Justification of the imposition of a constructive trust is "the existence of a confidential or fiduciary relationship, a violation of a duty imposed by that relationship, and unjust enrichment."

The court stated that for Heather to prevail on her unjust enrichment claim, she had to prove that Jerry, in designating Danette as beneficiary of his life insurance policy, gave Danette property that belonged to Heather, and that Danette knew or should have known of his wrongful conduct. The Court concluded that there was a genuine issue of material fact as to whether Danette knew about any wrongful conduct of Jerry's. However, the Court determined that Heather failed to offer admissible evidence that Jerry gave Danette property that belonged to Heather.

The Court quoted from *McDonald v. McDonald*, 57 Or App 6, 643 P2d 1280, *rev den*, 293 Or 373 (1982), in which the decedent was also obligated under the terms of a dissolution judgment to provide life insurance for his children. The decedent in that case had a policy that complied with the obligation, but he allowed the policy to lapse. The decedent remarried and acquired new policies, each designating his new wife as beneficiary, and none designating his children. When the decedent died, the children requested the imposition of a constructive trust on the proceeds of those life insurance policies. In that case, the Court concluded that imposition of a constructive trust was not appropriate because there was no evidence that the decedent had transferred any property that had belonged to the children.

> [A] constructive trust may be imposed only when the putative trustee holds property which rightfully belongs to another and is thereby unjustly enriched. There is no trust property or unjust enrichment here. *Although father may have been obligated to carry a life insurance policy for the benefit of plaintiffs, that he happened to carry life insurance policies for the benefit of defendant does not mean that anything she held was, or ever had been plaintiffs' property.*

The Court in this case stated

> [A]s was the decedent in *McDonald*, in this case, Jerry was obligated under a dissolution judgment to maintain insurance for another person, Heather. Like the decedent in *McDonald*, in this case, Jerry did not do so. As did the decedent in *McDonald*, in this case, Jerry acquired a *new* policy and designated someone else as the beneficiary, Danette. And, as in *McDonald*, in this case, although that may have constituted a breach of the dissolution judgment, it did not involve the transfer of any property to Danette that originally belonged to Heather.

The Court found that Heather failed to offer any evidence that, when Jerry designated Danette as the beneficiary on his life insurance policy, he gave her property that belonged to Heather and that the trial court erred and should not have imposed a constructive trust.

CASE 8.3 **SUMMARY**

This case illustrates why you should always get it in writing!

Fenderson v. Austin, 685 A.2d 600, 454 Pa. Super. 412 (1996).

Members of the family involved in this case included: Lydia (mother), Bryan (son), Lewis (son), Elizabeth (daughter), Rosemarie (Bryan's wife), Lettie (Lewis's wife) and Charles Craft (Elizabeth's husband).

Lydia, Bryan, Elizabeth and Charles lived with Bryan in his home. In 1961, they purchased 15 Pelham Road and Lewis, who lived in Washington, D.C., paid the deposit of $2300. Charles paid $6890.32 cash and Bryan paid $4388.37, which was the settlement from the sale of his home. The remainder of the $24,279.11

purchase price was taken as a $13,000.00 mortgage acquired by Lewis.

Lewis, Elizabeth, and Lydia took title to the property as joint tenants with right of survivorship. Bryan was not on the deed because at the time of the conveyance he had a lawsuit against him (which was later dismissed with prejudice, meaning that the case was dismissed and the party suing him could not bring another lawsuit on that matter). Nonetheless Bryan, Rosemarie, Lydia, Elizabeth and Charles lived on the property until 1969.

Charles died in 1964. Elizabeth moved out in 1969. Lydia died in 1972. Bryan and Rosemarie continued to live on a portion of the property and rented the remainder. Brian reimbursed Lewis and Elizabeth for 50% of the expenses and mortgage payments on the property and paid $2254 directly to the mortgage company.

Lewis died in 1983, after which time Elizabeth and Bryan were the only parties to the original transaction still living; Elizabeth, Bryan and Rosemarie continued to live on the property until Elizabeth's death in early 1991 at which time the property was distributed according to Elizabeth's will which gave a life estate in the property to Bryan.

Brian died in March of 1991, and his wife, Rosemarie, filed suit seeking an ownership interest in the property based upon:

- an express oral agreement to add Bryan to the deed, or
- a resulting trust, or
- a constructive trust

The trial court refused to find that Bryan had an interest in the property. It gave Rosemarie a life estate in the property finding that Elizabeth promised to make a will in which Rosemarie would have a life estate. The appellate court reversed the trial court finding that the trial court could not grant Rosemarie a life estate because neither Rosemarie nor Lettie raised the theory of a promise to make a will benefiting Rosemarie.

The appellate court also found that the trial court erred by not imposing a resulting trust in favor of Bryan's estate. "Based on the chancellor's findings of fact, supported by clear, precise, direct and unequivocal evidence, a resulting trust exits. Furthermore, the resulting trust is not invalid."

The appellate court stated that a resulting trust arises when a "person makes a Disposition of property under circumstances which raise an inference that he does not intend that the person taking or holding the property should have a beneficial interest in the property." In this case, the court found that this was a purchase-money resulting trust. A purchase-money resulting trust requires:

- a transfer from one person with the purchase price paid by another
- the payor does not have the intention that no resulting trust would arise
- the transferee is not the natural object of the payor's bounty.

The appellate court stated that this type of trust may occur even when several people contribute to the payment of the purchase price and title is not in all their names. In this situation, "a resulting trust arises in favor of the person who paid the purchase price in the proportion that the amount paid bears to the total purchase price."

The cash portion of the acquisition of the property was provided in part by Bryan's settlement check, which was 1/6 the amount of the purchase price at the time title passed to Lewis, Elizabeth and Lydia. The appellate court found that it was apparent Bryan intended to acquire a beneficial interest in the property based on his payment toward the purchase price and that a resulting trust was created at the time of settlement. Additionally, the court found that since the deed to the property provided for a joint tenancy with right of survivorship, the parties taking title to the deed also intended for Bryan's interest to be as a joint tenant with right of survivorship, that the resulting trust does not destroy the four unities of title required for a joint tenancy with right of survivorship, those being time, possession, title and interest.

Therefore, as the last remaining survivor of the property, Bryan had the sole ownership and control of the property prior to his death and that once he passed away, the property should have been disposed of pursuant to his estate, not Elizabeth's.

Is the Trust Testamentary or Inter Vivos?

Trusts may be either testamentary or inter vivos.

Testamentary Trusts

As previously stated in Chapter 1, a testamentary trust is a trust which is drafted as part of the testator's will and only becomes effective upon the testator's death. The entire trust document is part of the testator's will. Since the testamentary trust is part of the will, it is ambulatory like the will and is of no effect until the death of the testator. In addition, the trust will not take effect until the will is entered into probate and validated. The personal representative will only be authorized to distribute the estate property properly belonging to the trust only after the will has been entered into probate, and the personal representative has been given the authority to act. Until such time, the named trustee will be unable to manage the trust or distribute income or principal as stated in the trust.

Remember the example from Chapter 1:

Assume Bobbie Black has just died. Prior to her death she had amassed a large and lucrative stock portfolio, which upon her death passed to her children (assume they are her only heirs and are minors). If she had a will, she could have established a testamentary trust. This trust would have set many parameters for the care and control of all of her assets, including stocks, as well as the distribution of the dividends and other stock income. She could have determined when the brokerage firm could be replaced, guidelines for divesting the stocks, and how much income the children would receive, how often, and for what purpose. The assets in the trust would not have to be managed by the children's guardian since the trustee would take care of the assets instead.

Examine this example which also protects minors:

> *Example:* Bobbie Black is married to Donald and has three children, Tina (age 15), Todd (age 13), and Ted (age 10). Her will reads in part,
>
>> I leave all the rest, residue and remainder of my estate to my husband, Donald, if he survives me. If my husband fails to survive me, I leave all the rest, residue and remainder of my estate to my children Tina, Todd, and Ted in equal shares. Such shares shall be held IN TRUST however under the following terms:
>>
>> Until such time that my children attain the age of twenty-five (25) years, the property shall be held IN TRUST by ROGER WATERS as Trustee ("Trustee"), during which time, my Trustee may expend all of the income and as much of the principal which, in his sole and absolute discretion, he deems necessary for my children's health, education, maintenance and support. Upon my children's attainment of the age of twenty-five years he or she shall receive his or her share of the remainder of the property, including all principal and interest, if any, outright and free of trust.

This is a testamentary trust because the trust's terms are embedded in Bobbie's will, and the terms do not become effective until the will becomes effective upon her death. Therefore, the trust must be drafted according to all prerequisites for a will, including testamentary intent and capacity.

Inter Vivos Trusts

Inter vivos trusts are also called *living trusts*. They are drafted to take effect during the trustor's lifetime and usually take effect upon their execution. As such, they are not bound by the rules surrounding probate proceedings, giving them a distinct advantage over testamentary trusts. Unless recorded in the land (deed) records, or other records for some purpose, they are private documents and, unlike testamentary trusts which are filed in the probate records where anyone may read their provisions, remain private and therefore, unseen by prying eyes of the public and the community. They become effective immediately upon execution, allowing the trustee to manage the trust property without delay, and the testator's death will not affect its management, except if a new trustee must take over the trust duties. The document creating an inter vivos trust may also be called a declaration of trust.

Revocable or Irrevocable

Inter vivos trusts may be:

- revocable
- irrevocable

Revocable inter vivos trusts are a popular choice for estate planning because they are highly flexible. If the trust is **revocable**, the trustor has the right to change, amend, or terminate the trust at any time during his or her lifetime as long as he or she is not under any legal disability and remains of sound mind. The trustor may also be a trustee, allowing him or her to maintain a good deal of control over the trust property and the trust beneficiaries (often called a grantor trust). This right to control the trust during life must be explicit. A clause such as the following is essential for creating a revocable inter vivos trust:

> *Example:* I, Sophia Sanchez, reserve the right to revoke or terminate this trust in whole or in part during my lifetime. In addition, I reserve the right to amend or modify this agreement during my lifetime. Such amendment or revocation shall be made by written instrument delivered to the Trustee.

During her lifetime, Sophia can revoke the trust as well as amend its terms to suit her needs as time goes on. Upon her death, however, the revocable trust's terms will become **irrevocable**, meaning that the terms may no longer be changed.

Trustors tend to maintain a great deal of control over the assets during their lifetimes, usually all of the control. Because of this, trusts of this type do not therefore afford the trustor any real tax savings during life since the Internal Revenue Service considers the trust and the trustor to be the same entity as long as the trustor maintains control. Despite this disadvantage, revocable trusts are a popular choice for estate planning.

Trustors often place most or all of their assets in these revocable living trusts, allowing them to maintain control over their property during life, but affording them the ability to give management and control to another if they become too old to care for their property themselves, or just don't want to.

> *Example:* Geraldine Branch is a single mother with three adult children, Mark, Martin, and Michelle. She creates a revocable trust in which she is the trustee and the sole primary beneficiary. The trust provides her with all the income and principal that she needs to maintain her lifestyle. She names her son, Mark, as her alternate trustee to take effect upon her death or disability or resignation. Geraldine decides to retire, and go on a round-the-world cruise. She resigns as trustee and Mark immediately takes over the management of the trust. Geraldine and he decide that she will email, text, or call him whenever she needs additional funds which he will deposit into an agreed upon account for her use. Geraldine can go on the cruise knowing that the management of the trust assets will continue according to the trust's terms without any disruption.

Compare this example:

Geraldine Branch is a single mother with three adult children, Mark, Martin and Michelle. Geraldine is diagnosed to have the beginning of Alzheimer's. While she is still competent and able to do so, she has her attorney draft a revocable trust for her to execute in which she is the trustee and the sole primary beneficiary. The trust provides her with all the income and principal that she needs to maintain her lifestyle. She names her son, Mark, as her alternate trustee to take effect upon her death or disability or resignation. When Geraldine either believes she is no longer capable of handling her own affairs or her doctors confirm that she can no longer do so, Mark will take over as trustee immediately and manage the trust assets for Geraldine's benefit. All of her needs are managed by the new trustee, Mark.

Revocable trusts also allow trustors to avoid probate's time constraints and costs.

Example: Geraldine Branch is a single mother with three adult children, Mark, Martin, and Michelle. She creates a revocable trust in which she is the trustee and the sole primary beneficiary. The trust provides her with all the income and principal that she needs to maintain her lifestyle. She names her son, Mark, as her alternate trustee to take effect upon her death or disability or resignation. When Geraldine dies, Mark takes over the trust as trustee. At that time, he will distribute the trust assets pursuant to its terms. The trust may terminate or it may continue for the benefit of other beneficiaries, paying income and principal according to its terms.

In those states where probate is a long, drawn out and often expensive proposition, a revocable trust is a great time saver as well as a tremendous cost savings to the family. Revocable trusts can also save estate taxes in certain circumstances (which will be discussed in Chapter 9).

It is always important when drafting trusts, however, to determine if the trustor will lose certain benefits, such as homestead tax savings on a residence (rarely). It is also important to determine if the cost of preparing the trust and transferring the property to the trust will be too expensive for the client. Often, elderly clients on limited incomes will want inter vivos trusts because their families will avoid probate and its attendant costs. While this is commendable, a client with limited income may find the cost of the preparation outweighs the benefit. Only your attorney can assist the client in making that decision, however.

Irrevocable trusts, which as stated, may not be altered, modified, revoked, or terminated, will be discussed fully in Chapter 9.

Pourover Wills

A **pourover will**, called a pourover trust by some legal experts, is created when a provision in the will states that the testator leaves the residuary of his or her estate to the trustee of a living trust. The effect of this provision is to take a portion or all of the testator's property away from the jurisdiction of the probate court. The only chore that the personal representative of the will has to perform is to distribute the property to the trustee. After distribution, the property will be held, managed, and disposed of pursuant to the provisions of the trust, which takes all of the management and control of the decedent's estate out of the probate arena.

Example: David Washington's residuary clause in his will states in part:

I give the residue of my estate, including all property over which I have a general power of appointment, to the DAVID WASHINGTON REVOCABLE TRUST executed immediately preceding this Will, as amended from time to time hereafter, to be administered and distributed in accordance with the terms of said Trust in effect at my death.

Termination of a Trust

Situations exist in which trusts either must be terminated or in which the termination is desired. Trusts may be terminated in five situations:

1. The trust's purpose has been fulfilled.

    Example: Martina Lopez executes a trust in which the purpose is to pay income to herself and her husband, George for their lifetimes. When both of them are deceased, the remaining trust principal and any unpaid income is to be distributed to their children, Anabella and Christophe. Once the trust property is distributed to the children, the trust's purpose will have been fulfilled and the trust will terminate. When the purpose is impossible to attain, the trust terminates and the trust principal is held either by the trustee in an implied trust for the beneficiaries, or is distributed to the beneficiaries outright.

    "Upon the death of the Surviving Spouse, this trust shall terminate and the remaining property of this trust (including any property payable to the Trustee by Will, by beneficiary designation, or otherwise) (the "Surviving Spouse's Trust Property") shall be disposed of as provided in this Article. Gifts of personal effects and other specific gifts shall only be made to the extent that the items are included among the Surviving Spouse's Trust Property."

2. The trust's terms require termination after a period of time.

    Example: Frances Wright executes a trust to provide quarterly income to her children for 20 years. At the end of the 20-year period, the trust will terminate.

3. The trust allows for revocation by the trustor.

    Example: Gerald Jones executes a trust that specifically provides that the trust is revocable by the trustor at any time. After five years, Gerald decides to revoke the trust. His formal revocation of the trust will terminate it.

4. The legal title and equitable title of the trust are held solely by the same person.

    Example: Marta Deluca creates a trust to pay quarterly income for herself and her daughter, Chris. Marta names herself as Trustee and Chris as successor trustee. Ten years after the creation of the trust, Marta dies, leaving Chris as the sole beneficiary of the trust. Since Chris now holds the legal title (as trustee) and the equitable title (as sole beneficiary), the interests merge and the trust terminates. Note that for grantor trusts whereby Marta would be the trustor, the trustee, and the beneficiary, the trust will not terminate despite the fact that on its face, it appears that the legal and equitable titles are merged from the beginning.

5. The beneficiaries agree that the trust's purpose does not require the continuation of the trust.

Example: Billie executes a trust to pay quarterly income to her three children. If the children all agree that the trust does not have to continue, the trust will terminate. A trust may also terminate if the trust terms explicitly provide that the trustee determines that it is no longer economical to administer a trust.

Her trust states in part:

If, in the Trustee's discretion, the property of this trust becomes so depleted as to be uneconomical to be administered as a trust, the Trustee may terminate the trust and distribute the property of the trust as follows: (i) if the trust is named for or identified by reference to a single then living beneficiary, to the named beneficiary; otherwise, (ii) if the Surviving Spouse is then living and a beneficiary of the trust, to the Surviving Spouse; otherwise, (iii) to the then living beneficiaries of the trust in proportion to their then respective presumptive interest in the trust.

Drafting a Trust

A paralegal can draft a trust by following the guidelines set forth in this chapter. The paralegal would, however, be wise in discussing it fully with his or her supervising attorney before drafting one word of it, especially until he or she becomes more proficient in trust drafting. Trusts are very complicated documents and should be drafted with great care.

THE PROFESSIONAL PARALEGAL

A paralegal can use any number of excellent practice manuals to assist in drafting documents that will suit the client's wishes. Most, if not all, of the manuals now have online and downloadable forms to assist with the process and reduce the time needed for drafting. Remember, however, that even though clauses and forms are printed in a book, it doesn't make them right. If you think a clause does not fit your client's situation, discuss it with your supervising attorney or do not use it.

Name of the Trust

A trust does not have to be named; however, giving the trust a name ensures that the trust is distinguishable from other legal documents in the client's possession, and the document will appear polished. In addition, clients like to see their legal documents named. Trusts may be named simply: "Trust Agreement," or they may be named "The Bobbie Black Revocable Trust," "The Bobbie and Donald Black Trust," "The Black Family Trust," or "Declaration of Trust of Bobbie and Donald Black." They can also be named after the client's property, such as "Crossroads Trust." All such names are appropriate.

Trust Purpose

A trust will fail for want of a purpose. The trust purpose must be clearly specified and cannot be for any purpose that is illegal or may be construed as such.

> *Example:* As Trustors, we have established this trust in order to provide a means for the management of certain of our property, for the management of such further property interests as may be deposited with the trustee by us, and for our maintenance, comfort, and support during our lifetimes, and for the benefit of our children after our deaths, all in the manner hereafter provided.

Appointment of a Trustee

While a trust will not fail if a specific person or corporation is named as trustee, a trust will fail if the trust does not make provision for the position of trustee.

Trustee's Powers

All trustees are given general powers of trust management by state law. The trust may be drafted, however, to either limit or expand those powers. Powers can be expressed in a clause that gives the trustee very broad discretion, such as

> The Trustee may, in his or her sole discretion, pay to or apply for the benefit of each child for whom a trust is then held, as much of the net income of that child's share of my estate as the Trustee shall determine to be in the best interest of and tending to promote the welfare of such child, after taking into consideration, to the extent the Trustee deems advisable, any other income or resources of such child.

Powers can also be expressed in a series of clauses, making the trustee's duties and obligations more specific. These clauses often take many pages, making up a significant portion of the trust agreement. A sampling of such clauses may be studied in Figure 8.1.

Trust Beneficiaries

It is important to name beneficiaries in the trust. Beneficiaries should be named by individual legal name, such as "to my son, Ted Black," or by class, such as "to my nieces and nephews," or "to my children who survive me."

Trust Property

A trust will fail if it is not properly funded. It is important that all property to be placed in trust be described as specifically as possible, including the legal description of real property and certificate numbers of stocks. Many trusts are opened with less than ten dollars ($10.00) and are effectively "dry trusts." They are however funded, no matter how small the amount. The trustor then has the ability to add property to the trust as he or she sees fit.

Figure 8.1   The Donald Black and Bobbie Black Revocable Trust

Declaration that they are the trustors even though they don't explicitly say that they are

Statement that the trust is revocable; also notice the title.

Declaration that they are the trustees.

Trust is not dry.

Another statement of the name of the trust and that it is revocable.

Appointment of successor.

How trust assets will be distributed if they are incapacitated.

The residence does not have to be productive property.

We are DONALD BLACK and BOBBIE BLACK of Anytown, Anystate. We revocably transfer to ourselves as Co-Trustees, and declare ourselves the Co-Trustees of the sum of One Dollar. This property and all investments, reinvestments and additions shall be administered as provided in this instrument. This instrument, as from time to time amended, may be designated the "THE DONALD BLACK AND BOBBIE BLACK REVOCABLE TRUST."

We have three children, TINA BLACK, TODD BLACK, and TED BLACK. Every reference in this instrument to a "child" or "children" of ours is of them and all other children who may be borne to or adopted by us in the future.

Article 1—Trustee Appointment

If either one of us fails or ceases to serve as Co-Trustee of any trust created under this instrument, the other shall serve as sole Trustee of that trust. If both of us fail or cease to serve as Trustee of any trust, we appoint TODD BLACK. If all of the above (and any successors) fail or cease to serve as Trustee of any trust and the resulting vacancy is not filled under the provisions of Section 10.1, the Trustee Appointer (designated in Section 10.1) shall appoint a Trustee of that trust in accordance with the provisions of Section 10.3.

Article 2—Disposition During our Lives

So long as either or both of us is living, all property transferred to the Trustee shall be administered as THE DONALD BLACK AND BOBBIE BLACK REVOCABLE TRUST as provided in this Article, Article 3, and Article 4. Except as otherwise provided, the words "this trust" as used in this Article, Article 3, and Article 4 means THE DONALD BLACK AND BOBBIE BLACK REVOCABLE TRUST.

2.1   Direct Distributions

During our joint lifetimes, each one of us who is not Incapacitated (defined in Section 14.5) may direct the Trustee to distribute all or part of his or her respective separate property and all of our marital property by delivering to the Trustee a written instrument which designates to whom the distribution is to be made.

2.2   Distributions during Period of Incapacity

In addition, whenever the Trustee considers that either (or both) of us is Incapacitated, the Trustee shall distribute so much or all of the income and principal of this trust (even though exhausting this trust) as the Trustee considers advisable for the health, maintenance and support of that one (or both) of us and that of any minor child dependent on us for support.

2.3   Principal Residence

We reserve the right to reside upon any real property placed in this trust as our permanent residence during our lifetimes, it being the intent of this provision for us to retain all requisite beneficial interests and possessory rights in and to such real property as tenants by the entirety pursuant to Anystate Code §55-20.2.

(continued)

Figure 8.1 (continued)

Article 3—Death of First Spouse

3.1 Partial Termination and Division of Trust

Upon the death of the first of us to die (the "Deceased Spouse"), the property of this trust (including any property payable to the Trustee by Will, by beneficiary designation, or otherwise) shall be divided into two shares.

A. **Surviving Spouse's Trust Property.** As to that part of the trust property which is the separate property of the "Surviving Spouse" or which represents the Surviving Spouse's interest in our marital property, this trust shall not terminate. Instead, that property shall be retained by the Trustee in this trust and shall continue to be administered as provided in Article 2 for the Surviving Spouse's life.

B. **Deceased Spouse's Trust Property.** As to the remaining property of this trust (the "Deceased Spouse's Trust Property"), this trust shall terminate and the Trustee shall distribute the Deceased Spouse's Trust Property as provided in the remaining provisions of this Article. Gifts of personal effects and other specific gifts shall only be made to the extent that the items are included among the Deceased Spouse's Trust Property.

3.2 Retained General Power of Appointment

The Deceased Spouse shall have a Testamentary General Power of Appointment (defined in Section 14.4) over all of the Deceased Spouse's Trust Property. To the extent that the Deceased Spouse does not fully exercise this Power of Appointment, the following distributions shall be made.

> The spouses have a power of appointment to use in their will over their own property.

3.3 Personal Effects

All of our jewelry, pictures, photographs, works of art, books, household furniture and furnishings, clothing, automobiles, boats, recreational vehicles and equipment, club memberships, burial plots, and articles of household or personal use or ornament of all kinds, shall be distributed to the Surviving Spouse, subject to the provisions of Section 11.11.

3.4 The Surviving Spouse's Retirement Accounts

All of the Deceased Spouse's interest in the Surviving Spouse's employee or self-employed benefit plans and individual retirement accounts shall be distributed to the Surviving Spouse.

3.5 Principal Residence

The right to reside upon any real property placed in this trust as the Surviving Spouse's permanent residence shall be retained, it being the intent of this provision for the Surviving Spouse to retain all requisite beneficial interests and possessory rights in and to such real property.

3.6 Marital Deduction Amount

A Marital Deduction Amount (defined in Article 13) shall be distributed to the Trustee of the Marital Trust, to be administered as provided in Article 5.

(continued)

Figure 8.1 (continued)

3.7 Disclaimer of Marital Deduction Amount

If the Surviving Spouse disclaims all or any portion of his or her interest in the Marital Deduction Amount, the disclaimed portion (including all interests of persons other than the Surviving Spouse) shall be distributed to the Trustee of the Bypass Trust, to be administered as provided in Article 6.

3.8 Deceased Spouse's Remaining Trust Property

After providing for payment of Debts, Expenses and Death Taxes, if any, as directed by Article 12, the "Deceased Spouse's Remaining Trust Property" shall be distributed to the Trustee of the Bypass Trust to be administered as provided in Article 6. For purposes of the preceding, the "Deceased Spouse's Remaining Trust Property" means the then remaining Deceased Spouses' Trust Property, net of (i) all specific transfers in this Article that do not lapse, and (ii) all Debts and Expenses.

Article 4—Death of Second Spouse

4.1 Termination of Trust

Upon the death of the Surviving Spouse, this trust shall terminate and the remaining property of this trust (including any property payable to the Trustee by Will, by beneficiary designation, or otherwise) (the "Surviving Spouse's Trust Property") shall be disposed of as provided in this Article. Gifts of personal effects and other specific gifts shall only be made to the extent that the items are included among the Surviving Spouse's Trust Property.

4.2 Retained General Power of Appointment

The Surviving Spouse shall have a Testamentary General Power of Appointment (defined in Section 14.4) over all of the Surviving Spouse's Trust Property. To the extent that the Surviving Spouse does not fully exercise this Power of Appointment, the following distributions shall be made.

4.3 Personal Effects

All of the Surviving Spouse's jewelry, pictures, photographs, works of art, books, household furniture and furnishings, clothing, automobiles, boats, recreational vehicles, and equipment, club memberships, burial plots, and articles of household or personal use or ornament of all kinds (collectively, the Surviving Spouse's "personal effects"), shall be distributed as follows, subject to the provisions of Section 11.11.

A. **Memorandum on Personal Effects.** The Surviving Spouse may leave a memorandum making one or more personal effects gifts. If the memorandum is wholly in his or her own handwriting or typewritten and signed by him or her, and dated on or after the date of this instrument: (i) it shall be deemed to be an amendment to this trust instrument; (ii) all gifts specified in the memorandum shall be made prior to making any of the following gifts; and (iii) if the memorandum conflicts with any of the following gifts, the memorandum shall control.

B. **Gift of Remaining Personal Effects.** To the extent not disposed of by the above, all of the Surviving Spouse's remaining personal effects shall be

Termination of the trust upon the death of the survivor of them.

(continued)

Figure 8.1 (continued)

distributed to our children who survive the Surviving Spouse, in equal shares. However, if any child fails to survive the Surviving Spouse but leaves one or more descendants who survive the Surviving Spouse, the share that child would have received (if he or she had survived) shall be distributed per stirpes to his or her descendants who survive the Surviving Spouse.

C. **Division of Personal Effects.** Any personal effects given to two or more individuals shall be divided among them as they may agree among themselves. If they cannot agree on a division within a reasonable time following the Surviving Spouse's death, the Trustee shall make the division for them.

4.4   Surviving Spouse's Remaining Trust Property

After providing for payment of Debts, Expenses and Death Taxes as directed by Article 12, the "Surviving Spouse's Remaining Trust Property" shall be distributed to our children who survive the Surviving Spouse. However, if any child who fails to survive the Surviving Spouse leaves one or more descendants who survive the Surviving Spouse, the share that child would have received (if he or she had survived) shall be distributed per stirpes to his or her descendants who survive the Surviving Spouse, subject to the provisions of Article 7 (providing for lifetime Grandchild's Trusts for our grandchildren) and Article 8 (providing for lifetime Descendant's Trusts for our great grandchildren and more remote descendants). For purposes of the preceding, the "surviving Spouse's Remaining Trust Property" means the then remaining Surviving Spouse's Trust Property, net of (i) all specific transfers in this Article that do not lapse, and (ii) all Debts and Expenses.

> Remaindermen are the children to whom the property is distributed upon the death of the surviving spouse.
>
> If Tina, Todd, or Ted predecease Bobbie and Donald, his or her share of the trust will go to his or her children.

4.5   Contingent Disposition

Any part of the Surviving Spouse's Remaining Trust Property not effectively disposed of by the above provisions shall be distributed one-half to DONALD BLACK's then living Heirs (defined in Section 14.6.C) and one-half to BOBBIE BLACK's then living Heirs, subject to the provisions of Article 9 (providing for Contingent Trusts for beneficiaries who are under age or Incapacitated.

> If none of the children or grandchildren or great-grandchildren (lineal descendants) of Bobbie and Donald survive, the property is then distributed to other lineal descendants and collateral heirs.

Article 5—Marital Trust

5.1   Distributions during the Life of the Surviving Spouse

Beginning at the Deceased Spouse's death and during the life of the Surviving Spouse, the Trustee shall distribute to the Surviving Spouse the income of the Marital Trust, at least quarterly, plus so much or all of the trust principal (even though exhausting the trust) as the Trustee determines to be appropriate to provide for his or her continued health, maintenance and support.

5.2   Termination and Final Distribution upon the Death of the Surviving Spouse

Upon the death of the Surviving Spouse, the Marital Trust shall terminate. The Trustee shall distribute any income accumulated, but remaining undistributed at the Surviving Spouse's death, to the Surviving Spouse's estate, and shall provide for payment of taxes attributable to the trust as provided in Section 12.5. The remaining trust property, if any, shall be distributed as provided in Section 4.4 or Section 4.5, whichever applies, as if it were the Surviving Spouse's Remaining Trust Property.

(continued)

Figure 8.1   (continued)

Article 6—Bypass Trust

6.1   Distributions during the Trust Term

During the term of the Bypass Trust, it shall be administered as follows:

A. **General Discretionary Distributions to the Surviving Spouse, Our Children and Our Descendants.** The Trustee shall distribute to the Surviving Spouse, as primary beneficiary, and may distribute to our children and other descendants, as secondary beneficiaries, so much or all of the trust income and principal as the Trustee determines to be appropriate to provide for their continued health, maintenance, support, and education (including college or vocational, graduate or professional school education).

6.2   Termination and Final Distribution

On the death of the Surviving Spouse, the Bypass Trust shall terminate and the remaining trust property, if any, shall be distributed as provided in Section 4.4 or 4.5, whichever applies, as if it were the Surviving Spouse's Remaining Trust Property, and as if the Surviving Spouse had died on the termination date of the trust.

Article 7—Grandchild's Trusts

How property is distributed if it goes to grandchildren.

7.1   Creation of Trusts.

All property that passes subject to the provisions of this Article that otherwise would be distributable to a grandchild of ours, shall instead be distributed to the Trustee as a separate Grandchild's Trust named for the grandchild, to be administered as provided in the Article. When used in this Article, the words "the trust", "the grandchild's trust", "his or her trust" means the Grandchild's Trust named for a particular grandchild and the words "the grandchild" mean that grandchild.

7.2   Distributions during Grandchild's Life

During the life of the grandchild, the grandchild's trust shall be administered as follows.

A. **General Discretionary Distributions to Grandchild and Descendants.** The Trustee shall distribute to the grandchild, as primary beneficiary, and may distribute to his or her descendants (if any), as secondary beneficiaries, so much or all of the income and principal of the grandchild's trust (even though exhausting the trust) as the Trustee determines to be appropriate to provide for their continued health, maintenance, support, and education (including college or vocational, graduate or professional school education).

B. **Distributions to Guardians.** To the extent the Trustee believes the above distributions will not be unduly jeopardized, the Trustee may distribute to the court appointed guardian of the person of the grandchild so much of the trust income and principal as the Trustee determined to be appropriate to provide for a reasonable proportion of any additional housing costs or other expenses of the guardian incurred as a result of caring for the grandchild.

(continued)

Figure 8.1   (continued)

C. **Special Additional Distributions to Grandchild and Descendants.** At any time after the grandchild or any descendant of the grandchild has reached the age of twenty-five years, and to the extent the Trustee believes the above distributions will not be unduly jeopardized, the Trustee may distribute to the grandchild or descendant so much of the income and principal of the grandchild's trust as the Trustee determines to be appropriate:

1. **Business or Profession.** To enable the grandchild or descendant to enter into or continue a business or profession in which the Trustee believes there are reasonable prospects for success; or

2. **Home Purchase**. To provide a down payment of a home for the grandchild or descendant, and his or her family, the value of which would be reasonably related to the type of home the grandchild or descendant might be expected to own, occupy and support.

Any payments made under this Subsection to a grandchild's descendant shall be charged without interest as an advancement against the unappointed share of the grandchild's trust, if any, otherwise distributable to the descendant (or his or her ascendant or descendants) on the termination of the grandchild's trust.

7.3   Termination and Final Distribution upon Grandchild's Death

Upon the grandchild's death, the grandchild's trust shall terminate and the remaining trust property, if any, shall be disposed of as follows.

A. **Testamentary Powers Of Appointment.** The grandchild shall have a Testamentary General Power of Appointment over the GST Taxable portion of his or her trust. As to the remaining property of the trust, if any, the grandchild shall have a Testamentary Limited Power of Appointment, exercisable in favor of any one or more of the following: our descendants, the spouses of our descendants, the surviving spouses of any deceased descendants of ours, and any public, charitable and religious organizations. (The terms Testamentary General Power of Appointment and Testamentary Limited Power of Appointment are defined in Section 14.4, and the term GST Taxable portion is defined in Section 14.6.G.)

B. **Distribution to Descendants.** If the grandchild does not fully exercise his or her Powers of Appointment, the remaining unappointed property of the trust, if any, shall be distributed per stirpes to the following individuals who survive the grandchild: (i) the grandchild's descendants, if any, otherwise, (ii) the descendants of the grandchild's parent who is a child of ours, if any, otherwise, (iii) our descendants. The preceding distributions are subject to the provisions of the Article 7, Article 8 (providing for lifetime Child's Trusts for our children), and Article 9 (providing for lifetime Descendant's Trusts for our great grandchildren and more remote descendants).

C. **Contingent Disposition.** Any property of the grandchild's trust not effectively disposed of by the preceding provisions shall be distributed as provided in Section 4.5 as if it were the Surviving Spouses' Remaining Trust Property, and as if the Surviving Spouse had died on the termination date of the grandchild's trust.

(continued)

Figure 8.1 (continued)

Article 8—Descendant's Trusts

8.1 Creation of Trusts

All property that passes subject to the provisions of this Article that otherwise would be distributable to a descendant of ours (other than a child or grandchild of ours) shall instead be distributed to the Trustee as a separate Descendant's Trust named for the descendant, to be administered as provided in this Article. When used in this Article, the words "the trust", "the Beneficiary's trust", or "his or her trust" mean the Descendant's Trust named for a particular descendant and the words "the Beneficiary" mean that descendant.

8.2 Distributions during Beneficiary's Life

During the life of the Beneficiary, the Beneficiary's trust shall be administered as follows.

A. **General Discretionary Distributions to Beneficiary and Descendants and Spouse.** The Trustee shall distribute to the Beneficiary, as primary beneficiary, and may distribute to his or her descendants and spouse (if any), as secondary beneficiaries, so much or all of the income and principal of the Beneficiary's trust (even though exhausting the trust) as the Trustee determines to be appropriate to provide for their continued health, maintenance, support, and education (including college or vocational, graduate or professional school education).

B. **Distributions to Guardians.** [As to any beneficiary who is a child of ours.] To the extent the Trustee believes the above distributions will not be unduly jeopardized, the Trustee may distribute to the court appointed guardian of the person of the Beneficiary so much of the trust income and principal as the Trustee determines to be appropriate to provide for a reasonable proportion of any additional housing costs or other expenses of the guardian incurred as a result of caring for the Beneficiary.

C. **Special Additional Distributions to Beneficiary and Descendants.** At any time after the Beneficiary of any descendant of the Beneficiary has reached the age of twenty-five years, and to the extent the Trustee believes that above distributions will not be unduly jeopardized, the Trustee may distribute to the Beneficiary or descendant so much of the income and principal of the Beneficiary's trust as the Trustee determined to be appropriate:

   1. **Business or Profession**. To enable the Beneficiary of descendant to enter into or continue a business or profession on which the Trustee believes there are reasonable prospects for success: or

   2. **Home Purchase.** To provide a down payment on a home for the Beneficiary or descendant, and his or her family, the value of which would be reasonably related to the type of home the Beneficiary of descendant might be expected to own, occupy and support.

8.3 Termination and Final Distribution upon Beneficiary's Death

Upon the Beneficiary's death, the Beneficiary's trust shall terminate and the remaining trust property, if any, shall be disposed of as follows.

(continued)

Figure 8.1 (continued)

A. **Testamentary Powers Of Appointment.** The Beneficiary shall have a Testamentary General Power of Appointment over the GST Taxable portion of his or her trust. As to the remaining property of the trust, if any, the Beneficiary shall have a Testamentary Limited Power of Appointment, exercisable on favor of any one of more of the following: our descendants, the spouses of our descendants, the surviving spouses of any deceased descendants or ours, and any public, charitable and religious organizations. (The term Testamentary General Power of Appointment and Testamentary Limited Power of Appointment are defined in Section 14.4 and the term GST Taxable portion is defined in Section 14.6.G).

B. **Distribution to Descendants.** If the Beneficiary does not fully exercise his or her Powers of Appointment, the remaining unappointed property of the trust, if any, shall be distributed per stirpes to the following individuals who survive the Beneficiary: (i) the Beneficiary's descendants, if any, otherwise, (ii) the descendants of the nearest ancestor of the Beneficiary who is a descendant of ours and who has surviving descendants, if any, otherwise, (iii) our descendants. The preceding distributions are subject to the provisions of this Article and Article 7 (providing for lifetime Grandchild's Trusts for our grandchildren).

C. **Contingent Disposition.** Any property of the Beneficiary's trust not effectively disposed of by the preceding provisions shall be distributed as provided in Section 4.5 as if it were the Surviving Spouse's Remaining Trust Property and as if the Surviving Spouse had died on the termination date of the Beneficiary's trust.

Article 9—Contingent Trusts

9.1 Creation of Trusts

All property that passes subject to the provisions of this Article that otherwise would be distributable by the Trustee to any beneficiary (other than the Surviving Spouse, or a child, grandchild or other descendant of ours) who has not reached the age of twenty-five years or who, in the discretion of the Trustee, is Incapacitated (defined in Section 14.5) may instead be distributed to the Trustee as a separate Contingent Trust named for the beneficiary, to be administered as provided in this Article. When used in this Article, the words "the trust," "the beneficiary's trust," or "his or her trust" means the Contingent Trust named for a particular beneficiary and the words "the beneficiary" mean that beneficiary.

9.2 Distributions during the Beneficiary's Life

During the life of the beneficiary, the beneficiary's trust shall be administered as follows.

A. **General Discretionary Distributions.** The Trustee shall distribute to the beneficiary so much or all of the income and principal of the beneficiary's trust (even though exhausting the trust) as the Trustee determines to be appropriate to provide for the beneficiary's continued health, maintenance, support, and education (including college or vocational, graduate or professional school education).

(continued)

Figure 8.1   (continued)

B. **Mandatory Terminating Distribution to Beneficiary at Age Twenty-Five.** Whenever the beneficiary (i) reaches the age of twenty-five years and, (ii) in the Trustee's discretion, is not Incapacitated, the Trustee shall distribute to the beneficiary the remaining property of his or her trust.

9.3   Termination and Final Distribution upon the Beneficiary's Death

If the beneficiary dies before the complete distribution of his or her trust, the trust shall terminate and the remaining trust property, if any, shall be disposed of as follows.

A. **Distribution to Descendants.** The remaining property of the beneficiary's trust shall be distributed per stirpes to the following individuals who survive the beneficiary: (i) the beneficiary's descendants, if any, otherwise, (ii) the descendants of the beneficiary's parent who is more closely related to us, if any, otherwise, (iii) our descendants, if any. All of the preceding distributions are subject to the provisions of this Article, Article 7 (providing for lifetime Grandchild's Trusts for our grandchildren), and Article 8 (providing for lifetime Descendants' Trusts for our great grandchildren and more remote descendants).

B. **Contingent Disposition.** Any property of the beneficiary's trust not effectively disposed of by the preceding provisions shall be distributed as provided in Section 4.5 as if it were the Surviving Spouse's Remaining Trust Property, and as if the Surviving Spouse had died on the termination date of the beneficiary's trust.

Article 10—Trustee Provisions

The provisions of this Article govern the fiduciary relationship of the Trustee. When used in this instrument, where the context permits, the term Trustee means the trustee or co-trustees from time to time serving and the "estate" of the Trustee means the particular trust estate being administered by the Trustee.

What happens if a trustee cannot or will not act.

10.1   Trustee Succession

A. **Surviving Spouse's Appointment of Co-Trustee.** Whenever the Surviving Spouse is serving as sole Trustee of any trust created under this instrument, he or she may appoint a Co-Trustee to serve with him or her. If a Co-Trustee is still serving with the Surviving Spouse, then the appointed Co-Trustee shall also cease serving as Trustee (unless otherwise eligible to continue to serve as a Trustee in accordance with the provisions of this instrument). Each Co-Trustee appointment must comply with the general provisions of Section 10.3.

B. **Trustee Appointer.** We name the following persons, in the following order, to serve as the Trustee Appointer: (i) DONALD BLACK and BOBBIE BLACK, (ii) either DONALD BLACK or BOBBIE BLACK, (iii) otherwise TODD BLACK, (iv) otherwise as to any Grandchild's Trust or Descendant's Trust, the named beneficiary, if legally competent, otherwise the parent or guardian of the named beneficiary, if any, (v) otherwise all of our then living adult descendants, if any (acting by majority vote).

(continued)

Figure 8.1   (continued)

C. **Resignation.** A Trustee may resign as Trustee of any one or more trusts created under this instrument at any time, with or without cause, by delivering a resignation notice in recordable form (i) to each of us who is then living, or, if neither of us is then living, to each adult beneficiary of the trust who is then permitted to receive distributions from the trust; (ii) to each serving Co-Trustee, if any; and (iii) to the next successor Trustee named in this instrument, if any, otherwise, to the Trustee Appointer (but only if the Trustee Appointer's action is required to fill the resulting vacancy). The Trustee's resignation shall be effective only upon the acceptance and qualification of the successor.

10.2   Corporate Trustee Removal without Cause

The first named Trustee Appointer who is then living and not Incapacitated may remove any bank or other corporation serving as Trustee of any trust at any time with or without cause and appoint a Qualified Corporation as successor Trustee of such trust. Every such Trustee removal must comply with the general provisions of Section 10.3.

10.3   Trustee Appointment and Removal Procedures

A. **Generally.** Every appointment (or removal) of a Trustee must be evidenced by a written instrument in recordable form, signed by the person (or the requisite number of persons) required to approve the appointment (or removal), and delivered to the appointee (or Trustee being removed). The instrument must identify the appointee (or Trustee being removed), state the effective time and date of appointment (or removal), and every appointment must contain an acceptance by the appointee. Except as otherwise provided, every Trustee appointed under this instrument must be either a Qualified Corporation or one of more Qualified Individuals (defined below).

B. **Qualified Individual.** The term Qualified Individual means any legally competent individual who has attained the age of 25 years and who is willing to serve under this instrument.

C. **Qualified Corporation.** The term Qualified Corporation means any corporation having trust powers that is qualified and willing to serve under this instrument, and that has, as of the relevant time, either (i) a minimum capital and surplus of at least five million dollars ($5,000,000 U.S.), or (ii) at least one hundred million dollars ($100,000,000 U. S.) in trust assets under administration.

Corporations often have requirements that show that they are solvent.

10.4   Trustee Compensation

A. **Expense Reimbursement and Reasonable Compensation.** Each Trustee shall be reimbursed from its estate for the reasonable costs and expenses incurred in condition with the administration of its estate and also shall be entitled to receive fair and reasonable compensation from its estate (payable at convenient intervals selected by the Trustee) considering: (i) the duties, responsibilities, risks, and potential liabilities undertaken; (ii) the nature of its estate; (iii) the time and effort involved; and (iv) the customary and prevailing charges for services of a similar character at the time and at the place the services are performed.

What compensation a trustee may have. In some trusts family members receive no compensation.

(continued)

Figure 8.1 (continued)

B. **Professional Serving As Trustee.** A professional individual serving as Trustee may receive compensation for Trustee services based on his or her customary hourly rates (or other customary charges for professional services). If the professional has hired himself or herself (or any professional organization with which he or she is affiliated) in a professional capacity with respect to his or her estate, Trustee compensation shall be in addition to compensation for professional services; however, each service shall be compensated for only once (as either a Trustee service or professional service but not both).

C. **Corporate Co-Trustee.** Where appropriate and customary, a bank or other corporate Co-Trustee may receive compensation in amounts not exceeding the customary and prevailing charge for services of a similar character at the time and at the place the services are performed as if it were serving as sole Trustee.

D. **Waiver of Right to Compensation.** Any Trustee may at any time waive a right to receive compensation for services rendered or to be rendered as Trustee.

10.5 Trustee Liability

Regarding losses to the trust estate.

A. **Generally.** A Trustee who has made a reasonable, good faith effort to exercise the standard of care and other fundamental duties applicable to the Trustee in Section 11.3 and the other provisions of this instrument shall not be liable: (i) for any loss that may occur as a result of any actions taken or not taken by the Trustee; (ii) for the acts, omissions or defaults of any other individual or entity serving as Trustee or as ancillary trustee; nor (iii) to any person dealing with the Trustee in the administration of its estate, unless the Trustee expressly contracts and binds itself personally. For purposes of the preceding, a Trustee's conduct shall be judged in light of the facts and circumstances existing at the time and not by hindsight.

B. **Reimbursement.** An individual or entity serving as Trustee shall be entitled to reimbursement from its estate for any liability or expense, whether in contract, tort or otherwise, reasonably incurred by the Trustee in the administration of its estate.

10.6 Transactions in Which the Trustee Has an Interest

Notwithstanding any contrary provisions of the Anystate Code or other applicable law: (i) any individual or entity serving as Trustee under this instrument may engage his or her estate in transactions with himself or herself personally (or otherwise), so long as the Trustee established that the consideration exchanged in the transaction is fair and reasonable to his or her estate; and (ii) any Trustee may engage its estate in transactions with itself personally (or otherwise) pursuant to the terms of any valid and enforceable executory contract signed by either or both of us. [For example, the Trustee may (i) buy or sell property of its estate from or to such person, or from or to a relative, employee, business associate or affiliate of such person serving as Trustee; (ii) sell or exchange and transact other business activities involving properties of its estate with any other estate under the control of any such person serving as Trustee; and (iii) sell to or purchase from its estate the stock, bonds, obligations or other securities of the

(continued)

Figure 8.1 (continued)

person serving as Trustee or its affiliate.] Whenever the office of Trustee is filled by more than one person, any transaction in which a Trustee has a personal interest must be approved by all Trustees.

10.7 Independent Administration without Bond

So far as can be legally provided, all of the powers and discretions granted to the Trustee shall be exercised without the supervision of any court. No bond or other security shall be required of any primary or successor Trustee in any jurisdiction, whether acting independently or under court supervision.

No bond required of a trustee.

10.8 Ancillary Trustee

If at any time and for any reason the Trustee is unwilling or unable to act as Trustee as to any property subject to administration in any jurisdiction (other than the jurisdiction in which the Trustee is serving), then, to the extent permitted by applicable law, the Trustee may appoint (and remove) any one or more Qualified Individuals or a Qualified Corporation (both terms defined in Section 10.3) to act as ancillary trustee on such terms as the Trustee may deem appropriate. Except as specifically limited or provided in the appointing instrument: (i) the ancillary trustee shall account to the Trustee for all property, which it may receive in connection with the administration of such property and shall have all of the rights, titles, powers, duties, discretions, and immunities of the Trustee; (ii) the ancillary trustee may resign at any time by giving thirty days advance written notice to the Trustee; and (iii) the ancillary trustee may be removed at any time by the Trustee upon such notice (or no notice) as the Trustee may deem appropriate.

10.9 Beneficiary Serving As Trustee

If an individual is both a Trustee and beneficiary of a trust created under this instrument, he or she may make distributions to himself or herself pursuant to the terms of the trust, except that he or she shall neither possess or exercise any powers with respect to, nor authorize or participate in any decision as to: (i) any discretionary distribution or loan to or for the benefit of himself or herself, except to the extent that the distributions or loans are limited to amounts necessary for his or her health, maintenance, support, and education; (ii) any discretionary distribution to any other beneficiary, if the distribution would discharge any of the Trustee's legal obligations; (iii) the termination of the trust because of its small size, if the termination would result in a distribution to himself or herself or if the distribution would discharge any of his or her legal obligations; (iv) the treatment of any estimated income tax payment as a payment by him or her, except to the extent that the payment is limited to an amount necessary for his or her health, maintenance, support and education; nor (v) any action to be taken regarding an insurance policy held in the trust insuring his or her life, unless expressly authorized by other provisions of this instrument. These decisions shall be made solely by the other then serving Trustee or Trustees of the trust ("Independent Trustee"). If necessary, the currently acting Trustee may appoint the individual or entity (if any) next designated under this instrument to act as Trustee as an Independent Co-Trustee of the trust; otherwise, upon written

(continued)

Figure 8.1 (continued)

request of the currently acting Trustee, an Independent Co-Trustee of the trust shall be appointed by the Trustee Appointer. However, if an Independent Co-Trustee is appointed under these circumstances, the sole power and responsibility of the Independent Co-Trustee shall be to make decisions reserved to the Independent Co-Trustee. The provisions of this Section do not apply to either of us when serving as Trustee of the Donald and Bobbie Black Revocable Trust.

10.10   Co-Trustee Provisions

Except as otherwise provided, Co-Trustees shall act (i) by unanimous consent if two are serving, and (ii) by majority vote if three or more are serving. Any individual Co-Trustee may revocably delegate to any other Co-Trustee any or all of his or her rights, powers, and discretions as a Co-Trustee. Any delegation shall be by written instrument specifying the extent and duration of the delegation. Whenever we are both serving as Co-Trustees, either of us may sign checks or provide directions to banks, brokerage firms, and other financial institutions without the joinder of the other. Whenever a corporate Co-Trustee is serving, it shall have custody of all investments and records of its estate to the exclusion of all individual Co-Trustees (but it may revocably waive this right in whole or in part from time to time), and it shall have the primary responsibility for preparing and distributing accountings.

10.11   Reorganization or Insolvency of Corporate Trustee

If a corporation nominated to serve or serving as the Trustee ever changes its name, or merges or is consolidated with or into any other bank or trust company, the corporation shall be deemed to be a continuing entity and shall continue to be eligible for appointment, or shall continue to act as the Trustee. If a corporation serving or designated to serve as the Trustee becomes insolvent and its assets are sold, transferred to, or otherwise acquired by another entity by any form of governmental or regulatory process, the successor entity shall not succeed to appointment as Trustee, and if it does so succeed by operation of laws, we direct the Trustee to resign from its office as Trustee unless the Trustee Appointer agrees that it may continue to serve.

Article 11—Administrative Provisions

11.1   Trust Revocation

How and when the trust may be revoked.

While we are both living, either of us who is legally competent may from time to time amend or revoke this instrument and the trusts evidenced by it, in whole or in part, by written instrument delivered to the Trustee, except that, if amended, the duties, powers and responsibilities of the Trustee shall not be changed without the Trustee's written consent. Whenever neither of us is legally competent, neither of us nor our court appointed guardians shall have any power of authority to amend or revoke this instrument or any trust evidenced by it. After the death of the Deceased Spouse, all trusts created under this instrument other than the Bock Revocable Trust shall become irrevocable. After the Surviving Spouse's death, this instrument and all the trusts evidenced by it shall be irrevocable.

(continued)

Figure 8.1 (continued)

11.2 Duties at Inception of Estate

Within a reasonable time after accepting a fiduciary appointment or receiving assets as a part of its estate, the Trustee shall (i) review the records, assets, beneficiaries, purposes, terms, distribution requirements, and all other relevant circumstances of its estate, and (ii) make and implement a distribution plan and an investment plan that are consistent with the purposes of its estate generally and that bring the estate portfolio into compliance with Sections 11.4 and 11.5.

11.3 Fundamental Fiduciary Duties

Fiduciary duties.

The Trustee shall administer the trust in good faith and according to its terms and the law. Except as otherwise provided, the following fundamental provisions apply to all aspects of the Trustee's investment, management and administration of its estate:

A. **General Standard of Care.** A Trustee shall exercise the standard of care, skill, and caution generally exercised by compensated trustees with respect to comparable estates in the same geographic area. A Trustee who has special skills or expertise, or is selected as a Trustee in reliance upon the Trustee's representation that the Trustee has special skills or expertise, has a duty to use those special skills or expertise.

B. **Loyalty and Impartiality; Primary and Secondary Beneficiaries.** The Trustee shall act solely in the interest of the beneficiaries of its estate, not in the interest of the Trustee, personally. If a Fiduciary's estate has two or more beneficiaries, the Trustee shall act impartially, taking into account any differing interests of the beneficiaries. However, the Trustee (i) may favor present income beneficiaries over future beneficiaries, and (ii) shall favor "primary" beneficiaries over other beneficiaries and "secondary" beneficiaries over beneficiaries who are neither primary nor secondary.

C. **Conflict Resolution.** The Trustee shall make a reasonable effort to resolve any conflicts (including conflicts as to favorable or adverse tax consequences), between or among the Trustee and those persons who are beneficially interested in its estate, by mutual agreement. If after reasonable efforts the Trustee, in the Trustee's discretion, determined that a mutual agreement is not likely to be reached, the Trustee shall resolve the conflicts in the Trustee's discretion.

D. **Duty to Verify Facts.** The Trustee shall make a reasonable effort to verify relevant facts. However, the Trustee may rely on (and need not independently verify): (i) the advice of any professional (including an agent, attorney, advisor, accountant, fiduciary, or other professional or representative) who was hired (or to whom duties were delegated) in accordance with this instrument and with reasonable care; and (ii) any written instrument or other evidence that the Trustee reasonably believes to be accurate. (But a corporate Trustee shall always be liable for the acts, omissions and defaults of its affiliates, officers and regular employees).

E. **Duty To Keep Beneficiaries Informed.** The Trustee shall keep all current beneficiaries of a trust who have attained the age of twenty-five years reasonably informed concerning the administration of the trust and material facts necessary for the beneficiaries to protect their interests.

(continued)

Figure 8.1 (continued)

> F. **Reliance on Predecessor Fiduciary.** A Trustee may rely on the records and other representations of a Predecessor Fiduciary (meaning a predecessor Trustee under this instrument or a personal representative or Trustee of any estate or trust from which distributions may be made to the Trustee), and need not request an accounting from or contest any accounting provided by a Predecessor Fiduciary. However, the preceding shall not apply to any Trustee to the extent that the Trustee (i) has received a request from a beneficiary having a vested material interest in its estate to secure an accounting or to conduct an investigation, or (ii) has actual knowledge of facts that would lead a reasonable person to believe that, as consequence of any act or omission of a Predecessor Fiduciary, a material loss has occurred or will occur.
>
> G. **Special Rule for Uncompensated Individual Trustees.** Notwithstanding any contrary provision, whenever an uncompensated individual is serving as Trustee (meaning an individual serving with no right to compensation or who, at all relevant times, has waived his or her right to compensation), he or she: (i) may continue any style of investing that is consistent with the style of investing we undertook during our lifetimes; and (ii) shall exercise that standard of care which is commensurate with his or her particular skills and expertise, or, to the extent lower, the general standard of care required of Trustees without special skills or expertise.
>
> **11.4 Prudent Investor Rule**
>
> Except as otherwise provided, the prudent investor rule, as set forth in the following provisions, governs all aspects of the Trustee's investments.
>
> A. **Generally.** The Trustee shall invest and manage the assets of its estate as a prudent investor would by considering the purposes, terms, distribution requirements, and other relevant circumstances of its estate [including the following, to the extent relevant: (i) general economic conditions; (ii) the possible effect of inflation or deflation; (iii) the expected tax consequences of investment decisions or strategies; (iv) the role that each investment or course of action plays within the overall estate portfolio; (v) the expected total return from income and the appreciation of capital; (vi) other resources of the beneficiaries; (vii) needs for liquidity, regularity of income, and preservation or appreciation of capital; (viii) an assets special relationship of special value, if any, to their purposes of its estate or to one or more of the beneficiaries; and (ix) any other relevant circumstances].
>
> B. **Portfolio Theory.** The Trustee shall make investment and management decisions respecting individual assets not in isolation but in the context of its estate portfolio as a whole and as a part of an overall investment strategy having risk and return objectives reasonably suited to its estate.
>
> C. **Diversification.** Generally, the Trustee shall diversify the investments of its estate unless the Trustee reasonably determined that, because of special circumstance, the purposes of its estate are better served without diversifying.

Prudent investing is the process that the trustee must follow. If the process the trustee follows when making investment decisions is prudent (based on what is known), the decisions are considered prudent even if the outcome loses money for the trust.

Refers to the Modern Portfolio Theory.

(continued)

Figure 8.1 (continued)

D. **Originally Contributed Properties.** Notwithstanding the preceding (but subject to Section 13.6), the Trustee may continue to hold and maintain all assets, without liability for any depreciation or loss that may result.

E. **Unproductive or Wasting Assets.** Except as otherwise provided in Section 13.6, the Trustee may receive, acquire, and maintain unproductive or underproductive assets, if the Trustee believes it is reasonable to do so. Upon the sale or disposition of any unproductive or underproductive asset, the Trustee may (but need not) allocate an appropriate portion of the principal element of such sale proceeds to income for fiduciary accounting purposes.

11.5   Permitted Investments; Management Authority

Except as otherwise provided, and to the extent consistent with the provisions of Sections 11.3 and 11.4 and the circumstances of its estate, the Trustee may invest its estate in any kind of property or type of investment, and may exercise the broadest managerial discretion that is consistent with the management and administration of its estate. This includes, but is not limited to, the following powers.

A. **Securities and Business Interests.** The Trustee may acquire securities, whether traded on a public securities exchange or offered through a private placement, and may trade on margin, borrow upon, and purchase or sell securities in such accounts as the Fiduciary may deem appropriate or useful. The Trustee may form, reorganize or dissolve corporations, give proxies to vote securities, enter into or oppose (alone or with others) voting trusts, buy-sell, stock restriction or stock redemption agreements, mergers, consolidations, foreclosures, liquidations, reorganizations, or other changes in the financial structure of any corporation, and generally exercise all rights of a stockholder. The Trustee may continue, initially form, expand, and carry on business activities, whether in proprietary, general, or limited partnership, joint venture, corporate, or other form with any persons and entities as the Trustee deems proper. Business activities conducted by the Trustee should be sufficiently related to the administration and investment of its estate so that its estate never becomes taxable as an association for federal tax purposes.

B. **Real Estate.** The Trustee may purchase, sell, exchange, partition, subdivide, develop, manage, and improve real property. A Trustee may grant or acquire easements, may impose deed restrictions, may adjust boundaries, may raze existing improvements, and may dedicate land or rights in land for public use.

C. **Mineral Properties.** The Trustee may acquire, maintain, manage, or sell mineral interests, and make oil, gas and mineral leases covering any lands or mineral interests forming a part of its estate, including leases for periods extending beyond the duration of its estate. A Fiduciary may pool or unitize any or all of the lands, mineral leaseholds, or mineral interest of its estate with others for the purpose of developing and producing oil, gas or other minerals, and make leases or assignments containing the right to pool or unitize. A Fiduciary may enter into contracts and agreements in relation to the installation or operation of absorption, repressuring and other processing

(continued)

Figure 8.1 (continued)

plants, drill or contract for the drilling of wells for oil, gas, or other minerals, enter into, renew, and extend operating agreements and exploration contracts, engage in secondary and tertiary recovery operations, make "bottom hole" or "dry hole" contributions, and deal otherwise with respect to mineral properties as an individual owner might deal with his own properties. A Fiduciary may enter into contracts, conveyances, and other agreements or transfers deemed necessary or desirable to carry out these powers, including division orders, oil, gas or other hydrocarbon sales contracts, processing agreements, and other contracts in relation to the processing, handling, treating, transporting and marketing of oil, gas or other mineral production. The term "mineral" means minerals of whatever kind and wherever located, whether surface or subsurface deposits, including (without limitation) coal, lignite, and other hydrocarbons, iron, ore, and uranium.

D. **Life Insurance.** The Trustee may acquire, maintain in force, and exercise all rights of a policyholder under policies of life insurance, insuring the life of a beneficiary of its estate, or an individual in whom such beneficiary has an insurable interest.

E. **Joint Investments; Accounts with the Trustee.** The Trustee may invest its estate in undivided interests in any otherwise appropriate investment and may hold separate estates under this or any other instrument in one or more common accounts in undivided interests. A corporate Trustee may deposit the cash portion of its estate with itself and may invest its estate in its common trust funds or those of an affiliate. In determining where to invest cash resources, a Trustee may consider all factors, including facility of access and security of funds invested, as well as the stated rate of return.

F. **Manage, Sell, And Lease.** The Trustee may manage, sell, lease (for any term, even beyond the anticipated term of its estate), grant or exercise options to purchase, convey, exchange, partition, improve, repair, insure, and otherwise deal with all property of its estate without the consent or ratification of any court, remainderman, or third party, upon the terms, for the consideration and with the covenants and warranties of title (general or special) as the Fiduciary deems appropriate.

G. **Nominee Title.** The Trustee may hold title to any property in the name of one or more nominees without disclosing the fiduciary relationship, and may allow its nominees to take possession of assets of its estate with direct custodial supervision by the Trustee.

H. **Loans and Guarantees.** The Trustee may lend money to any individual or entity, may endorse, guarantee, become the surety of, provide security for, or otherwise become obligated for or with respect to the debts or other obligations of any individual or entity. All these transactions (except those for the benefit of any current beneficiaries of the particular estate involved) shall be on commercially reasonable terms, including adequate interest and security.

I. **Borrow.** The Trustee may assume, renew, and extend any indebtedness previously created, and borrow for any purpose (including the purchase of investments or the payment to taxes) from any source (including a Trustee

(continued)

Figure 8.1 (continued)

individually) at the then usual and customary rate of interest, and mortgage or pledge any property of its estate to any lender.

J. **Pay Expenses.** The Trustee may pay all taxes and all reasonable expenses, including reasonable compensation to the agents and counsel (including investment counsel) of the Trustee.

K. **Claims.** The Trustee may institute and defend suits and release, compromise, or abandon claims.

11.6   Agents and Attorneys

The Trustee may employ and compensate agents, attorneys, advisors, accountants, and other professionals (including the Trustee individually and any professional organization with which the Trustee is affiliated) and may rely on their advice and delegate to them any authorities (including discretionary authorities).

11.7   Principal and Income

Subject to Section 13.6, the Trustee shall allocate receipts and disbursements between principal and income in a reasonable manner and may establish a reasonable reserve for depreciation or depletion and fund this reserve by appropriate charges against the income of its estate. For purposes of determining an appropriate reserve for depreciable or depletable assets, a Trustee may (but need not) adopt the depreciation or depletion allowance available for federal income tax purposes. For purposes of determining income from a partnership or proprietorship, a Trustee may (but need not) utilize the partnership or proprietorship's income as reported for federal income tax purposes.

> How principal and income are allocated.

11.8   Records, Books of Account, and Reports

The Trustee shall maintain proper books of account which shall be, at all reasonable times, open for inspection or audit by us and all current permissible beneficiaries of its estate who are not Incapacitated. Within a reasonable time after receiving written request from a beneficiary entitled to inspect books of account, the Trustee shall make a written financial report of its estate to the beneficiary. The natural or court appointed guardian of an Incapacitated beneficiary otherwise entitled to request a report may request (and receive) a report on the beneficiary's behalf. No Trustee shall ever be required to deliver reports of its estate more frequently than quarterly. Whenever the Surviving Spouse is serving as Trustee, he or she may provide copies of bank, brokerage, and other financial statements and that shall constitute a sufficient report of all assets and transactions disclosed on the statements.

11.9   Discretionary Distribution Considerations

Except as otherwise provided, in making discretionary distributions under this instrument, the Trustee making the distribution decision may consider all circumstances and factors the Trustee deems pertinent, including: (i) the beneficiaries' accustomed standard of living and station in life; (ii) all other income and resources reasonably available to the beneficiaries and the advisability of supplementing their income or resources; (iii) the beneficiaries' respective character and habits, their diligence, progress, and aptitudes in acquiring an education, and their ability to handle money usefully and prudently and to assume the

(continued)

Figure 8.1 (continued)

responsibilities of adult life and self-support in light of their particular abilities and disabilities; and (iv) the tax consequences of the Trustee's decision to make (or not to make) the distributions, and out of which trust, any distributions should be made. Except as otherwise provided, as to any trust with more than one beneficiary, the Trustee may make discretionary distributions in equal or unequal proportions and to the exclusion of any beneficiary. The Trustee shall not allow a beneficiary, who reasonably should be expected to assist in securing his or her own economic support, to become so financially dependent upon distributions from any trust that he or she loses an incentive to become productive in a manner that is reasonably commensurate with any other individual having the ability and being in the circumstance of the beneficiary. Whenever this instrument provides that the Trustee "may" make a distribution, the Trustee may, but need not, make the distribution.

11.10   Form of Payment to Beneficiaries

Distributions to a beneficiary may be made: (i) directly to the beneficiary; (ii) to the guardian or other similar representative (including the Trustee) of an Incapacitated beneficiary; (iii) to a Custodian (including the Trustee) for a minor beneficiary under the Uniform Gifts to Minors Act or Uniform Transfers to Minors Act of any State; or (iv) by expending the same directly for the benefit of the beneficiary or by reimbursing a person who has advanced funds for the benefit of the beneficiary. The Trustee shall not be responsible for a distribution after it has been made to any person in accordance with this Section.

11.11   Personal Effects; Personal Residence

A. **Division and Distribution of Personal Effects.** As to any personal effects item distributable to a minor or other Incapacitated person, the Trustee may: (i) hold the item for future distribution to the distributee; (ii) sell the item and distribute the proceeds to the distributee or any trust named for him or her, or (iii) distribute the item (or sales proceeds) in any manner authorized by Section 11.10. In exercising this discretion, the Trustee shall consider the age of the distributee, the practical utility of the item to him or her, and any sentimental or family significance of the item. In dividing personal effects among multiple distributees, each distributee who is a minor or Incapacitated person shall be represented by his or her parent or guardian, if any, otherwise by the Trustee.

B. **Personal Effects Expenses.** All reasonable expenses of packing, insuring and shipping any personal effects to a distributee, or storing personal effects for later distribution, shall be paid by the Trustee as an administration expense.

C. **Insurance Proceeds and Liens.** Except as otherwise provided, all gifts of personal effects or residential or other real property (i) include the proceeds of any insurance policies on the property, and (ii) are subject to all liens other than liens for real property taxes or assessments.

D. **Homestead Occupancy Right.** We shall each have the right to use and occupy as a principal residence (rent free and without charge except for

How distributions are made is important because a trustee may make a distribution on behalf of a beneficiary instead of to a beneficiary. Example: Payment of tuition directly to a university instead of to the student beneficiary.

(continued)

Figure 8.1 (continued)

taxes and other costs and expenses as may be specified elsewhere in this instrument) any residential property held in any trust of which either of us is a current beneficiary. This right lasts for life or until the trust terminates or is revoked (as to the property).

11.12 Character of Beneficial Interests

All interests provided under this instrument (whether principal or income, and whether distributed or held in trust): (i) shall belong solely to the particular estate (not any beneficiary) prior to actual distribution, and (ii) upon distribution, shall be received as a gift from us and shall not be the marital property of the beneficiary and his or her spouse.

11.13 Distributions Not Treated as Advancements

Except as otherwise provided, no discretionary distribution to a beneficiary of any trust created under this instrument shall be treated as an advancement.

11.14 Spendthrift Trust

To the maximum extent allowed by law, each trust created under this instrument shall be a "spendthrift trust," as defined by the Anystate Code §55-545.02. Prior to actual receipt by any beneficiary, no income or principal distributable from a trust created under this instrument shall be subject to anticipation or assignment by a beneficiary or to attachment by any creditor of, person seeking support from, person furnishing necessary services to, or assignee of any beneficiary.

11.15 Early Trust Termination

Subject to Section 11.9, if in the Trustee's discretion the property of any trust becomes so depleted as to be uneconomical to be administered as a trust, the Trustee may terminate the trust and distribute the property of the trust as follows: (i) if the trust is named for or identified by reference to a single then living beneficiary, to the named beneficiary; otherwise, (ii) if the Surviving Spouse is then living and a beneficiary of the trust, to the Surviving Spouse; otherwise, (iii) to the then living beneficiaries of the trust in proportion to their then respective presumptive interest in the trust.

11.16 Maximum Duration of Trusts

Despite any other provision of this instrument, to the extent that any trust created under this instrument had not previously vested in a beneficiary, the trust shall terminate upon the expiration of the period of the applicable Rule Against Perpetuities (determined using as measuring lives of both of us, all of the descendants of our parents, and all persons who are mentioned by name or as a class as beneficiaries of any trust created by or pursuant to this instrument who are living on the date the trust or any predecessor trust becomes irrevocable), and the Trustee shall distribute any property then held in the trust (i) to the beneficiary for whom the trust is named, if any; otherwise (ii) per stirpes to the then living descendants of the named beneficiary, if any; otherwise (iii) the trust estate shall be distributed as provided in Section 4.5 as if it were the Surviving Spouse's Remaining Trust Property and as if the Surviving Spouse had died on the termination date of the trust.

(continued)

Figure 8.1   (continued)

11.17   Combination of Trusts

The Trustee may terminate (or decline to fund) any trust created by this instrument and transfer the trust assets to any other trust (created by this instrument or otherwise) having substantially the same beneficiaries, terms and conditions, regardless of whether the Trustee under this instrument also is serving as the trustee of the other trust and without liability for delegation of its duties nor for defeating or impairing the interest of remote, unknown, or contingent beneficiaries. Similarly, the Trustee of any trust created by this instrument may receive and administer as part of its trust, the assets of any other substantially similar trust. In exercising either discretion, the Trustee shall consider the trusts' inclusion ratios for generation-skipping transfer tax purposes, but may combine trusts with different inclusion ratios if the Trustee shall deem the combination to be advisable.

11.18   Creation of Multiple Trusts

The Trustee may divide any trust created under this instrument into two or more separate identical trusts (in any proportion) if the Trustee deems it advisable. The Trustee shall divide any trust created under this instrument into two or more separate identical trusts (in the appropriate proportion) in order: (i) to segregate assets having different presumed or actual transferors for GST purposes into separate trusts, (ii) to segregate assets except from the generation-skipping transfer tax from other assets, and (iii) to ensure that every trust has a GST inclusion ratio of either one or zero. The Trustee may exercise discretionary powers held with respect to the new trusts independently. Where the original trust specifies a dollar amount to be distributed at a specified time, the aggregate dollar amount shall not change but the Trustee may distribute the amount from any new trust or partly from one or more in any ratio. If the Trustee allocates assets between the new trusts based on values as of a date prior to the allocation date, the assets allocated to each trust shall have an aggregate fair market value that is fairly representative of the appreciation and depreciation in value of all available assets from the valuation date to the date or dates of allocation (or the Trustee may use an alternate allocation approach so long as the method of asset allocation does not jeopardize an otherwise allowable estate tax deduction or generation-skipping transfer tax exemption).

11.19   Division and Distribution of Trust Estate

The Trustee may divide, allocate, or distribute property of its estate in undivided interests, non pro rata, and either wholly or partly in kind. Except as otherwise provided, all required distributions shall be made on the basis of the fair market value of the assets to be distributed at the time of distribution. If non pro rata distributions are to be made, the Trustee should attempt to allocate the tax basis of the assets distributed in an equitable manner among the beneficiaries of its estate, but the Trustee may at all times rely upon the written agreement of the beneficiaries as to the apportionment of assets. To the extent non pro rata distributions are made and the tax basis of the assets so distributed is not uniformly apportioned among beneficiaries, the Trustee may, but need not, make equitable adjustments among the beneficiaries as a result of any non-uniformity in basis.

(continued)

Figure 8.1 (continued)

11.20 Successive Distributions Not Required

To the extent that the Trustee is authorized to distribute property to any trust (created under this instrument or otherwise) and under the terms of that trust (or by virtue of the exercise of a discretionary power or for any other reason), the property would be immediately distributable to or among any one or more persons or other trusts; the Trustee may distribute the property directly to those persons or trusts in lieu of the directed distribution.

11.21 Additional Contributions

Subject to Section 11.18, the Trustee may receive (or refuse to receive for tax or other reasons) contributions of additional property to its estate from any source and in any manner.

11.22 Collection of Nonprobate Assets

The Trustee may receive (or refuse to receive for tax or other reasons) the proceeds of life insurance policies, employee benefit plans, and other contractual rights that are payable to the Trustee (collectively, "Nonprobate Assets"). The Trustee may take whatever action, if any, the Trustee considers best to collect Nonprobate Assets [without regard to whether the Nonprobate Assets are of a character generally authorized for trust investments or are subject to conditions (including reasonable written rights of withdrawal and directions to allocate such property to or among one or more trusts created under this trust instrument) that are acceptable to the Trustee. The Trustee (i) need not incur expense or initiate legal proceedings unless indemnified; (ii) may give a full discharge to an obligor of such obligor's liability under any such policy or plan; (iii) may elect optional modes of settlement available to it, after giving consideration to the tax effect upon all of the beneficiaries of my estate and any trust created by me by this trust instrument or otherwise; and (iv) may make any election that the Trustee believes is reasonable or proper under the circumstances. A Trustee may, but need not, make economic adjustments among the beneficiaries of its estate as a consequence of the tax ramifications resulting from any such election made or not made by the Trustee]. Subject to the other provisions in this instrument, any Nonprobate Assets shall be allocated: in accordance with the directions contained in the beneficiary designation or other instrument of transfer, if any; otherwise, in satisfaction of any specific pecuniary gift for which the available properties are insufficient, if any; otherwise, Nonprobate Assets received with respect to the death of the Deceased Spouse shall be disposed of as a part of the Deceased Spouse's Remaining Trust Property and Nonprobate assets received with respect to the death of the Surviving Spouse shall be disposed of as a part of the Surviving Spouse's Remaining Trust Property.

11.23 Plan Benefits Trusts

To the extent that the Trustee is designated as the beneficiary of any qualified benefit plan or individual retirement account or other Nonprobate Asset subject to the Minimum Required Distribution Rules (the "MRD Rules") (collectively "Plan Benefits"), the following provisions apply: (i) a Plan Benefits Trust corresponding to each trust provided for in this instrument is created; (ii) all Plan Benefits shall be allocated (A) in accordance with the directions, if any, contained in the beneficiary designation or other instrument of transfer;

Refers to what happens if the trust becomes the owner of certain benefit plans or retirement accounts with minimum distribution rules.

(continued)

Figure 8.1 (continued)

otherwise, (B) subject to Section 14.1 (allocating all income in respect of a decedent in the Deceased Spouse's estate to the Marital Deduction Amount), Plan Benefits received with respect to the death of the Deceased Spouse shall be allocated to or among the trusts or individuals receiving the Deceased Spouse's Remaining Trust Property and Plan Benefits received with respect to the death of the Surviving spouse shall be allocated to or among the trusts of individuals receiving the Surviving Spouse's Remaining Trust Property, substituting Plan Benefits Trusts for their corresponding trusts; (iii) each Plan Benefits Trust shall be irrevocable; (iv) each Plan Benefits Trust shall be identical to its corresponding trust except that all of the following persons, if any, who would otherwise be beneficially interested in the trust (other than those whose interests are contingent solely upon the death of a prior beneficiary living as the DB Determination Date, defined below), are completely excluded as beneficiaries and permissible appointees of the trust: (A) individuals having a shorter life expectancy than the measuring beneficiary and (B) entities not having a life expectancy; and (v) the Trustee shall deliver a copy of this instrument or alternate descriptive information to the plan administrator in the form and content and with the time limits required by applicable statute and treasury regulations. For purposes of the section, the "measuring beneficiary" of a Plan Benefits Trustee means the oldest individual who is both living and ascertainable specified in this instrument (by name or by class) as a current permissible beneficiary of the trust as of the date for determination of the "Designated Beneficiary" under applicable statute and treasury regulations (the "DB Determination Date"). We intend that, except for persons whose interests are contingent solely upon the death of a prior beneficiary living at the DB Determination Date, only individuals eligible as designated beneficiaries (as defined in Internal Revenue Code ("IRC") Section 401 (a) (9) and applicable treasury regulations) for purposes of the MRD Rules shall ever be permissible distributees or appointees of Plan Benefits Trusts. This instrument shall be administered and interpreted in a manner consistent with this intent. Any provision of this instrument which conflicts with this intent shall be deemed ambiguous and shall be construed, amplified, reconciled, or ignored as needed to achieve this intent.

11.24   Creation of S Trusts

If: (i) any trust created under this instrument (an "Original Trust") holds or is to receive any stock in a corporation eligible to be an S corporation ("S Stock"); (ii) the Original Trust has a Current Beneficiary; (iii) the Current Beneficiary is a U.S. citizen or resident; and (iv) the current Beneficiary elects or intends to elect to qualify the trust as a Qualified Subchapter S Trust ("QSST") under IRC §1361(d), then, the Trustee is authorized to allocate the S Stock to a separate "S Trust" to be administered as provided in this Section. In addition to any distributions provided for in the Original Trust, whenever an S Trust holds any S Stock, the Trustee shall distribute all the income of the S Trust to the Current Beneficiary in quarterly or more frequent installments. During the life of the current Beneficiary: (i) the Current Beneficiary shall be the sole beneficiary of the S Trust; (ii) no distributions shall be made to anyone other than the Current Beneficiary; and (iii) if the S

(*continued*)

Figure 8.1 (continued)

Trust terminates during the Current Beneficiary's life, the remaining property of the S Trust, if any, shall be distributed to the Current Beneficiary. If the Current Beneficiary dies before the complete distribution of the S Trust: (i) the trust shall terminate upon his or her death; (ii) the Trustee shall distribute any undistributed income of the trust to his or her estate; and (iii) the remaining property of the trust shall be disposed of pursuant to the terms of the Original Trust. In the case of any Child's Trust, Grandchild's Trust, Descendant's Trust or Contingent Trust, the term "Current Beneficiary" means the child, grandchild, other descendants or other beneficiary for whom the trust is named. In the case of the Marital Trust or the Bypass Trust, the term "Current Beneficiary" means the Surviving Spouse. The Trustee may amend an S Trust in any manner necessary for the sole purpose of ensuring that the S Trust qualifies and continues to qualify as a QSST. Each amendment must be in writing and must be filed among the trust records. We intend that every S Trust qualify as a QSST within the meaning of IRC §1361(d)(3). This instrument shall be interpreted in a manner consistent with this intent and any inconsistent provisions shall be construed, amplified, reconciled, or ignored as needed to achieve this intent.

11.25   Governing Law

A. **Generally.** To the extent consistent with the other provisions of this instrument, (i) the Trustee shall have the powers, duties, and liabilities of trustees set forth in the Anystate Code, as amended and in effect from time to time, and (ii) the construction, validity of every trust created under this instrument shall be governed by Anystate Law.

Allows the trustee to change the situs of the trust

B. **Change of Governing Law.** The Trustee of any trust may designate any other jurisdiction's law as the governing law with respect to the administration of that trust, on the following conditions: (i) The change of governing law must be in the best interests of the trust's beneficiaries and must not jeopardize any otherwise allowable estate tax deduction or generation-skipping transfer tax exemption, (ii) The Trustee (or at least one Co-Trustee) of the trust must be domiciled (in the case of an individual Trustee) or have its principal place of business (in the case of a bank or other corporate trustee) in the designated jurisdiction, (iii) The designated jurisdiction may be any nation, state, district, territory, political subdivision, or similar jurisdiction, (iv) The designation must be by signed, acknowledged declaration which states that effective date of the designation and is filed among the trust records, (v) There is no limit on the number of successive designations of governing law for any trust, and (vi) Notwithstanding any designation, Anystate law shall continue to apply to the extent that the powers of the Trustee are broader under Anystate law than under the designated jurisdiction's law.

Article 12—Debts, Expenses and Taxes

12.1   Payment of Debts, Expenses and Death Taxes

Except as otherwise provided, and to the extent that the personal representative of the Deceased Spouse's (or the Surviving Spouse's) probate estate shall certify in writing to the Trustee that the Readily Marketable Assets (as defined in his or

(continued)

Figure 8.1 (continued)

her Will) included in the principal of the residue of his or her probate estate are insufficient, the Trustee shall provide for payment out of the Deceased Spouse's Remaining Trust Property (or the Surviving Spouse's Remaining Trust Property, as appropriate) of all Debts, Expenses and Death Taxes (as defined in his or her Will).

How debts are paid.

12.2 Source of Payment

A. **Generally.** Except as otherwise provided: (i) Debts and Expenses shall be charged without apportionment against the Deceased Spouse's Remaining Trust Property (or the Surviving Spouse's Remaining Trust Property, as appropriate); (ii) Death Taxes shall be charged without apportionment against that portion of the Deceased Spouse's Remaining Trust Property (or the Surviving Spouse's Remaining Trust Property, as appropriate) that does not qualify for the marital or charitable deduction, until exhausted, then against the balance of the Deceased Spouse's Remaining Trust Property (or the Surviving Spouse's Remaining Trust Property, as appropriate); and (iii) Interest concerning any tax (including Death Taxes) shall be charged in the same manner as the tax.

B. **Disclaimer by the Surviving Spouse.** In the event of a qualified disclaimer by the Surviving Spouse of any interest in any property, any resulting increase in Death Taxes shall be charged against the disclaimed interest.

C. **Non-Elected Marital Trust.** In the event of the non-election under IRC Section 205(b) (7) of the IRC to qualify all (or any portion) of the Marital Trust for the marital deduction, any resulting increase in Death Taxes shall be charged against that trust (or portion).

D. **Direct Skips.** Generation-skipping transfer taxes on direct skips shall be charged against the property involved in the direct skip.

E. **Principal and Income Apportionment.** Debts, Expenses, and Death Taxes shall be apportioned between principal and income in accordance with Title 5, Chapter 20.1, Sections 55.277.1 et seq. of the Anystate Code; however, no Debts, Expenses, or Death Taxes shall be charged against the income of any marital or charitable share (both terms defined above) to the extent it would result in a material limitation on the share's right to income.

12.3 Charges against Exempt Assets

Notwithstanding any contrary provision, and to the maximum extent allowed by law, no Debts, Expenses or Death Taxes shall be charged against or satisfied out of any interest in any Exempt Assets, including: (i) insurance and annuities; (ii) any stock, bonus, pension, profit sharing, or similar plan (including any individual retirement account or retirement plan for self employed individuals); and (iii) any other property or interest in property that is not chargeable with the claims of the creditors of this trust or our estates (collectively, "Exempt Assets"). However, the following may be charged against a particular Exempt Asset: (i) Debts secured by a lien or other security interest in that Exempt Asset; (ii) Administrative expenses properly and fairly allocable to the administration of that Exempt Asset, and (iii) Death Taxes imposed with respect to that Exempt Asset.

(continued)

Figure 8.1 (continued)

12.4 Tax Elections

The Trustee shall make elections under tax laws solely in fiduciary capacity and in the manner as appears advisable to the Trustee to minimize taxes and expenses payable out of our estates, the trust property of trusts created by either of us, and by the beneficiaries of each. For example: (i) the Trustee, in its discretion, may elect or not elect to treat all or any portion of federal estimated taxes paid by any trust to be treated as a payment made by any one or more beneficiaries of that trust who are entitled to receive current distributions of income or principal from that trust (the election need not be made in a pro rata manner among all trust beneficiaries); and (ii) equitable adjustments may (but need not) be made to compensate for the effect of tax elections on the interests of beneficiaries or the amount of recovery of Death Taxes as directed above.

12.5 Taxes in the Surviving Spouse's Estate

Upon termination of any trust created under this instrument that results in any Increased Death Taxes in the Surviving Spouse's estate, unless the Surviving Spouse provides to the contrary by specific reference to marital deduction property in his or her Will, the Trustee shall pay from the trust, either directly or to the Surviving Spouse's estate, the amount of the Increased Death Taxes imposed with respect to the trust.

A. **Increased Death Taxes.** In this Section, Increased Death Taxes means that amount of the total estate, inheritance, succession, capital gains at death, and other death taxes (including interest and penalties), imposed under the laws of any jurisdiction with respect to the Surviving Spouse's estate that the personal representative of the Surviving Spouse's estate shall rightfully request in accordance with his or her will or applicable law giving due regard to the "taxable value" of all property determined in accordance with the Anystate Code.

B. **Multiple Trusts.** If there is more than one such trust that results in any Increased Death Taxes in the Surviving Spouse's estate, all Increased Death Taxes shall be paid pro-rata out of all such trusts based on relative taxable values (as determined above).

12.6 GST Taxes on Trust Distributions

If the Trustee considers any distributions or termination of an interest or power in a trust created under this instrument to be a taxable distribution (a "Distribution"), a taxable termination (a "Termination"), or a direct skip (a "Direct Skip") for generation-skipping transfer tax purposes, the Trustee may exercise the following authorities with respect to any such Distribution, Termination, or Direct Skip. In the case of a Distribution, the Trustee may increase the amount otherwise distributable by an amount estimated to be sufficient to permit the beneficiary receiving such Distribution to pay the estimated generation-skipping transfer tax as imposed in part with respect to other property held in trust under this instrument, taking into consideration deductions, exemptions, credits, and other factors that the Trustee deems appropriate. The Trustee may, but need not, make equitable adjustments among beneficiaries of a trust as a consequence of additional distributions or generation-skipping transfer tax payments made with respect to Distributions, Terminations, or Direct Skips.

(continued)

Figure 8.1 (continued)

Article 13—Marital Deduction Amount

13.1 Marital Deduction Amount

The Marital Deduction Amount is the sum of (i) all income in respect of a decedent and rights to income in respect of a decedent included in Eligible Marital Deduction Property, if any, which, if allowed as a federal estate tax marital deduction, would result in the lowest possible total of federal estate tax and state death taxes (but only those state death taxes which are estate taxes computed by reference to the credit allowable under IRC Section 2011, or successor provisions) payable from all sources by reason of the Deceased Spouse's death.

13.2 Pre Distribution Income

The distribution of the Marital Deduction Amount shall entitle the recipient to the net income of this trust, without material limitation, that is attributable to the Marital Deduction Amount from the date of the Deceased Spouse's death to the dates of distribution.

13.3 Eligible Marital Deduction Property

The term Eligible Marital Deduction Property means property (including any Nonprobate Assets payable to the Trustee) or the proceeds of property, the value of which is included in the Deceased Spouse's gross estate for federal estate tax purposes, that is available for distribution in satisfaction of the Marital Deduction Amount, and as to which (if distributed in satisfaction of the Marital Deduction Amount) it is possible (by election or otherwise) to obtain a federal estate tax marital deduction. The gift of the Marital Deduction Amount shall abate to the extent that it cannot be fully satisfied with Eligible Marital Deduction Property. To the extent that there is an excess of Eligible Marital Deduction Property, assets for which a foreign tax credit is available under Section 2014 of the IRC shall not be distributed in satisfaction of the Marital Deduction Amount gift.

13.4 Computational Guidelines

The Marital Deduction Amount shall be determined: (i) as if a federal estate tax marital deduction is allowed for property distributed to the Marital Trust; (ii) without regard to any qualified disclaimer that the Surviving Spouse may file with respect to the gift of the Marital Deduction Amount or any other interest passing from the Deceased Spouse to the Surviving Spouse under this instrument or otherwise; and (iii) in all other respects, after accounting for all other deductions and credits allowed to the Deceased Spouse's estate and after giving effect to the exercise or proposed exercise of tax elections.

13.5 Valuation of Distributed Property

Each item of property distributed in kind in satisfaction of the Marital Deduction Amount shall be valued for purposes of satisfying the gift at its value as finally determined for federal estate tax purposes in the Deceased Spouse's gross estate, or, if such item is an investment or reinvestment of property included in the Deceased Spouse's gross estate for federal estate tax purposes or the proceeds of any sale or other disposition of property so included or of any such investment

---

(continued)

Figure 8.1   (continued)

or reinvestment, the item shall be valued at its federal income tax basis at the actual date or dates of distribution. Notwithstanding any contrary provision, the total of all property distributed in satisfaction of the Marital Deduction Amount shall have an aggregate fair market value at the date or dates of distribution which is fairly representative of the appreciation and depreciation in value from the Deceased Spouse's death to the date or dates of such distribution of all such property then available for distribution. In estimating the date of distribution values of assets distributed in kind, the Trustee may use its best judgment; the Trustee need not obtain an independent distribution date appraisal.

13.6   Statement of Intent

We intend that the distribution of the Marital Deduction Amount to the Marital Trust qualify in full for the federal estate tax marital deduction and any similar stated death tax marital deduction. The Surviving Spouse may require the Trustee to make property held in the Marital Trust productive of income within a reasonable time. For each calendar year in which an interest is held by the Marital Trust in any Plan Benefits (defined in Section 11.23): (i) the Trustee shall allocate distributions from each Plan Benefits interest (A) to trust income, to the extent of the income earned that year by the interest, and (B) to trust principal, to the extent of any excess distributions; and (ii) to the extent that distributions from a Plan Benefits interest are less than the income earned by the interest, the Surviving Spouse may require the Trustee to remedy the shortfall by demanding additional distribution, allocating principal receipts from other assets to trust income, or taking other appropriate measures, at the Trustee's option. This instrument shall be administered and interpreted in a manner consistent with this intent. Any provision of this instrument which conflicts with this intent shall be deemed ambiguous and shall be construed, amplified, reconciled, or ignored as needed to achieve this intent. However, this Section shall not require that the election provided for in IRC Section 2056(b) (7) be made in whole or in part with respect to the Marital Trust.

Article 14—General Provisions

14.1   No Contest

If any individual beneficiary (other than the Surviving Spouse) under any of the provisions of either of our Wills or this instrument shall at any time commence or join, directly or indirectly, in the prosecution of proceedings in any court to oppose the admission of either of our Wills to probate or to have either of our Wills or this instrument set aside or be declared invalid (in whole or in part), regardless of whether the proceedings are instituted in good faith or with probable cause, that beneficiary shall forfeit any and all right, title, or interest in or to this trust (in addition to a similar forfeiture of interest under our Wills), legal or equitable, and the property disposed of under this instrument shall be distributed in the same manner as would have occurred had the beneficiary predeceased both of us. Moreover, if any individual beneficiary (other than the Surviving Spouse) shall at any time commence or join, directly or indirectly, in the prosecution of proceedings in any court to challenge the actions by either or both of us in administering the trusts created by this instrument, or the exercise of any discretion by either or both of us in our capacity as trustee, that beneficiary shall

In Terrorem Clause

(continued)

Figure 8.1 (continued)

Disclaimers; similar to those in wills.

forfeit any and all right, title, or interest in or to this trust (in addition to a similar forfeiture of interest under our Wills), legal or equitable, and the property disposed of under this instrument shall be distributed in the same manner as would have occurred had the beneficiary predeceased both of us.

14.2 Disclaimers

Except as otherwise provided, if a beneficiary under this instrument is surviving but is deemed to be deceased by virtue of a qualified disclaimer (as defined under IRC Section 2518), then the beneficiary shall only be deemed to be deceased with respect to the specific interest in property specified in the qualified disclaimer and the qualified disclaimer shall not affect any other rights or interests granted under this instrument, including but not limited to rights or interest in trusts to which the disclaimed interest passes as a result of the qualified disclaimer. If the qualified disclaimer is of a life estate or the Disclaimant's entire interest in property (or an undivided portion of such property) in trust, the termination provisions of such estate or trust with respect to the disclaimed interest shall be applied as if the Disclaimant failed to survive.

14.3 Disclaimer Trusts

This Section applies whenever an individual (the "Disclaimant") files a qualified disclaimer with respect to any property that passes to (or remains in) a trust under this instrument (the "Recipient Trust") by virtue of such qualified disclaimer, but only if the Disclaimant: (i) is a Trustee (or named successor Trustee) of the Recipient Trust; (ii) has the power to remove a Trustee of the Recipient Trust; (iii) holds any Power of Appointment (defined in Section 14.4) over the Recipient Trust; (iv) has any beneficial interest in the Recipient Trust; or (v) has any power to direct the beneficial enjoyment of the Recipient Trust. Notwithstanding any contrary provision of this instrument, unless the Disclaimant disclaims all of his or her rights, powers, and interests with respect to the Recipient Trust as described above, the property which would otherwise pass to (or remain in) the Recipient Trust shall instead be distributed to a separate Disclaimer Trust on terms identical to the terms of the Recipient Trust except as follows.

A. **Power Of Appointment**. The Disclaimant shall possess no Power of Appointment over the Disclaimer Trust.
B. **Ascertainable Limitation on Discretionary Powers**. Neither the Disclaimant nor any Trustee whom the Disclaimant may remove from office without cause, shall possess or exercise any powers with respect to, or be authorized to participate in any decision as to, any discretionary distribution or any loan to or for the benefit of any beneficiary of the Disclaimer Trust, except to the extent that such distributions or loans are limited to amounts necessary for the beneficiary's health, maintenance, support, and education.
C. **Discretionary Termination**. The Disclaimant shall have no authority to terminate the Disclaimer Trust because of its small size.
D. **Estimated Tax Payments**. The Disclaimant shall have no authority to treat any estimated income tax payment by the Disclaimer Trust as an estimated income tax payment by a beneficiary.

(continued)

Figure 8.1 (continued)

> E. **Beneficial Interest**. If the Disclaimant is not the Surviving Spouse, the Disclaimant shall have no beneficial interest in the Disclaimer Trust.
>
> F. **Independent Trust Administration**. As to persons who remain as beneficiaries of both the Disclaimer Trust and the Recipient Trust, the Trustee may exercise discretionary powers held with respect to the Disclaimer Trust and the Recipient Trust (including discretionary distributional powers) on an independent basis, and where the Recipient Trust specifies a dollar amount to be distributed at a specified time, the aggregate dollar amount so specified shall not change but the Trustee may distribute such amount from either the Recipient Trust or the Disclaimer Trust or partly from each in any ratio.
>
> **14.4   Testamentary Powers of Appointment Created in This Instrument**
>
> Except as otherwise provided, the following provisions shall apply to every Testamentary Limited Power of Appointment ("Limited Power") and Testamentary General Power of Appointment ("General Power") (collectively, "Power of Appointment") created in this instrument which may be exercisable at any particular time by any person (the "Donee").
>
> *Exercise of powers of appointment*
>
> A. **Exercise Powers of Appointment**. Every exercise of a Power of Appointment must specifically refer to the Section in this instrument creating the Power of Appointment. A Power of Appointment may be exercised solely by language in the duly probated Will of the Donee. The Trustee may assume the Donee had no Will if, six months after the Donee's death, the Trustee has no actual knowledge of the existence of a Will.
>
> B. **Permissible Appointees of Limited Powers**. The Donee may exercise a Limited Power only in favor of any one or more then living or subsequently born individuals and other entities who are members of the group or class specified, in such proportions among them (even to the complete exclusion of any one or more of them) and subject to such trusts and such other conditions as the Donee may choose. Notwithstanding any contrary provision, the Donee of a Limited Power shall never have the power to exercise the Limited Power on favor of himself or herself, his or her creditors, his or her estate, or the creditors of his or her estate, nor may he or she appoint trust property in discharge of his or her legal obligations.
>
> C. **Permissible Appointees of General Powers**. The Donee may exercise a General Power in favor of his or her estate or the creditors of his or her estate, as well as any one or more then living or subsequently born individuals or other entities in such proportions and subject to such trusts and such other conditions as the Donee may choose.
>
> **14.5   Determination of Incapacity**
>
> Except as otherwise provided, an adult individual generally shall be considered to have full legal capacity absent a presently existing adjudication of incapacity or insanity by a court or other judicial tribunal having jurisdiction to make such a determination.
>
> *Standard for determining incapacity of a trustee or beneficiary*
>
> A. **Fiduciaries**. For purposes of qualification to serve as a Trustee or in any other fiduciary capacity under this instrument, an adult individual shall

(continued)

Figure 8.1 (continued)

be considered legally incapacitated to act when two physicians who have examined such person within the prior two years have certified that in their judgment such person does not have the physical or mental capacity to effectively manage his or her financial affairs.

B. **Beneficiaries**. An adult individual beneficiary under this instrument shall be considered Incapacitated upon a good faith determination made by the fiduciary charged with making such evaluation that such individual lacks the physical or mental capacity, personal or emotional stability, or maturity of judgment needed to effectively manage his or her personal or financial affairs (whether because of injury, mental or medical condition, substance abuse or dependency, or any other reason). Individuals under the age of majority shall be considered legally incapacitated.

14.6 Definitions

In connection with the construction and interpretation of this instrument the following definitions apply, unless otherwise expressly provided.

A. **Children and Descendants**. Except as otherwise provided, a "child" of another individual means a child determined in accordance with Section 20-49.1 of the Anystate Code. An adopted person shall be a child of the adopting parent(s) but only if legally adopted before attaining age eighteen. A posthumous child who survives birth shall be treated as living at the age of death of his or her parent. An individual's "descendants" means the individual's children, the children of those children, and so on, determined in accordance with the preceding.

B. **Spouse**. A "spouse" of a beneficiary does not include any individual who, at the relevant time, is divorced or legally separated from the beneficiary, or engaged in pending divorce proceedings with the beneficiary.

C. **Heirs**. A person's Heirs or then living Heirs means those individuals who would be that person's heirs at law as to separate personal property if that person were to die single, intestate, and domiciled in Anystate at the referenced time.

D. **Per Stirpes**. Whenever a distribution (or allocation) of property is to be made "per stirpes" to (or to trusts for) the descendants of any person, the property shall be divided into as many shares as there are then living children of the person and deceased children of the person who left descendants who are then living. One share shall be distributed to (or to the trust for) each living child and the share for each deceased child shall be divided among his or her then living descendants in the same manner.

E. **Pronouns**. Pronouns, nouns, and terms as used in this instrument shall include the masculine, feminine, neuter, singular, and plural forms wherever appropriate to the context.

F. **Survive**. If we have both died and either of us survived the other by any period to time, he or she shall be treated as having survived the other for all purposes; however, if the order of our deaths cannot be determined, Bobbie Black shall be presumed to have survived Donald Black for all purposes. In all other cases a requirement that an individual "survive" a specified person or event or be "surviving" or "living" means survival be at least ninety days;

(continued)

Figure 8.1 (continued)

however, the Trustee may make advance distributions within that period of any gift to any beneficiary to the extent necessary to provide for his or her health, maintenance, and support.

G. **GST Taxable Portion**. The "GST Taxable" portion of any terminating trust is, collectively, each portion or fraction of the trust, if any, with a positive inclusion ratio that would pass to a skip person with respect to the presumed or actual transferor of the trust in a transfer subject to the generation-skipping transfer tax (all as determined under Chapter 13 of the IRC) if no Powers of Appointment over any part of the trust existed.

H. **Section 2514(e) Amount**. The "Section 2514(e) Amount" means (i) the greater of Five Thousand Dollars ($5,000) or five percent (5%) of the aggregate value of the assets out of which, or the proceeds of which, the exercise of the Withdrawal Right could have been satisfied, or (ii) such other amount, the lapse of a power of appointment over which will not be treated as a release of the power, as may from time to time be allowed under IRC Section 2514(e).

I. **Code**. References to the IRC or any Section of the IRC mean the Internal Revenue Code of 1986, or the Section, as amended and in effect from time to time, or the appropriate successor provision.

14.7 Notice

Any notice required to be given or delivered under this instrument shall be deemed given or delivered when an acknowledged written notice is actually delivered to the person or organization entitled to notice or mailed certified mail, return receipt requested, to the address then appearing on the Trustees record for the person or organization.

14.8 Actions By and Notice to Incapacitated Persons

Any action permitted to be taken by a minor or other incapacitated person shall be taken by the person's parents or guardian. Any notice or report required to be delivered to a minor or other incapacitated person shall be delivered to such person's parents or guardian. If both parents of a minor are living, any such action shall be taken by, and any such notice shall be given to, the parent to whom we are more closely related.

14.9 Trust Not Contractual

This instrument is not being executed by us as a result of any agreement, express or implied, between us, or between us collectively and any other party.

14.10 Headings

The headings employed in this instrument are for reference purposes only and shall not in any way affect the meaning or interpretation of the provisions of this instrument.

We have signed this instrument this _____ day of _____, 2011.

_____   _____ (SEAL)

Witness   DONALD BLACK,
                                                                   Grantor and Trustee

(continued)

Figure 8.1 (continued)

_____   _____ (SEAL)
Witness   BOBBIE BLACK,
                                  Grantor and Trustee

COMMONWEALTH OF ANYSTATE,
CITY OF ANYTOWN, to-wit:

The foregoing document was acknowledged before me on _____,
2011 by DONALD BLACK as Grantor and Trustee.

_____
Notary Public

My commission expires:_____
Notary ID no.: _____

COMMONWEALTH OF ANYSTATE,
CITY OF ANYTOWN, to-wit:

The foregoing document was acknowledged before me on _____,
2011 by BOBBIE BLACK as Grantor and Trustee.

_____
Notary Public

My commission expires:_____
Notary ID no.: _____

Should follow state law

THE PROFESSIONAL PARALEGAL

Clients who fail to fund their trusts abound. The paralegal is often given the task of assisting the client in funding the trust. This may mean helping the client fill out bank transfer documents, stock transfer documents although most brokerage firms have this task down to a science and it has become very easy to do, and assisting with changing beneficiaries on life insurance forms. This is extraordinarily important because clients often fail to put their property in the trust and erroneously think that just executing the trust does the job. It is important for the law firm to explain to the clients that execution of the trust alone does not fund the trust, and to assist the client in transferring assets to the trust properly. Not ensuring that assets are transferred to the trust, means that the trust is dry, and the purpose for executing the trust will essentially have failed.

Method of Distribution

How the trust property is to be distributed by the trustee is very important. While the powers clause tells the trustee and the beneficiaries what the trustee may and may not do with the property, a distribution clause, or series of distribution clauses, will leave no doubt in anyone's mind as to the testator's intentions regarding who is to benefit from the trust estate.

Example: The trust for Miriam and Robbie Balchek states in part:

ARTICLE 4—DEATH OF SECOND SPOUSE

4.1. Termination of Trust. Upon the death of the Surviving Spouse, this trust shall terminate and the remaining property of this trust (including any property payable to the Trustee by Will, by beneficiary designation, or otherwise) (the "Surviving Spouse's Trust Property") shall be disposed of as provided in this Article. Gifts of personal effects and other specific gifts shall only be made to the extent that the items are included among the Surviving Spouse's Trust Property.

4.2. Retained General Power of Appointment. The Surviving Spouse shall have a Testamentary General Power of Appointment (defined in Section 14.4) over all of the Surviving Spouse's Trust Property. To the extent that the Surviving Spouse does not fully exercise this Power of Appointment, the following distributions shall be made.

4.3. Personal Effects. All of the Surviving Spouse's antiques, pictures, photographs, works of art, books, household furniture and furnishings, clothing, automobiles, boats, recreational vehicles, and equipment, club memberships, burial plots, and articles of household or personal use or ornament of all kinds (collectively, the Surviving Spouse's "personal effects"), shall be distributed as follows, subject to the provisions of Section 11.11).

A. Memorandum on Personal Effects. We may leave a memorandum making one or more personal effects gifts as an exhibit to this Trust. If the memorandum is wholly the handwriting of either or both of us, or typewritten and signed by either or both of us, or is video-taped by a licensed professional videographer, and dated on or after the date of this instrument: (i) it shall be deemed to be an amendment to this trust instrument; (ii) all gifts specified in the memorandum shall be made prior to making any of the following gifts; and (iii) if the memorandum conflicts with any of the following gifts, the memorandum shall control.

B. Gift of Remaining Personal Effects. To the extent not disposed of by the above, all of the Surviving Spouse's remaining personal effects shall be distributed to our children who survive the Surviving Spouse, in equal shares. However, if any child fails to survive the Surviving Spouse, but leaves one or more descendants who survive the Surviving Spouse, the share that child would have received (if he or she had survived) shall be distributed per stirpes to his or her descendants who survive the Surviving Spouse.

C. Division of Personal Effects. Any personal effects given to two or more individuals shall be divided among them as they may agree among themselves. If they cannot agree on a division within a reasonable time following the Surviving Spouse's death, the Trustee shall make the division for them.

4.4. Surviving Spouse's Remaining Trust Property. After providing for payment of Debts, Expenses, and Death Taxes as directed by Article 12, the "Surviving Spouse's Remaining Trust Property" shall be distributed to our children who survive the Surviving Spouse, in equal shares.

For purposes of the preceding, the "surviving Spouse's Remaining Trust Property" means the then remaining Surviving Spouse's Trust Property, net of (i) all specific transfers in this Article that do not lapse, and (ii) all Debts and Expenses.

4.5. Contingent Disposition. Any part of the Surviving Spouse's Remaining Trust Property not effectively disposed of by the above provisions shall be distributed one-half to BOBBIE BLACK's then living heirs (defined in Section 14.6.C) and one-half to DONALD BLACK's then living Heirs, subject to the provisions of Article 9 (providing for Contingent Trusts for beneficiaries who are under age or incapacitated).

Note that in the trust clause above, the trust anticipates that upon the death of both Miriam and Robbie, the trust will terminate. At that time the trustee will distribute the property, taking into effect any power of appointment that the surviving spouse had (the surviving spouse being either Miriam or Robbie upon the other's death), debts and taxes, as well as any memorandum distributing personal effects, similar to the one that testators can use as we saw in Chapters 4 and 5. At that point, the trust estate is to be distributed to their children and if the children do not survive them, it is distributed one-half to Miriam's heirs and one-half to Robbie's, based upon intestate succession. In most cases, this will be the other remaining children or their grandchildren.

Termination of the Trust

All trusts should indicate when they will be terminated. As shown in the example above, or as in the example here:

Example: Scott Peters is married to Barbara Peters. They have no children, but Scott wants to provide for his siblings Jim Peters and Susan Mangrove during their lifetime and then give the remainder to a charity. His trust states in part:

Upon the death of the survivor of Grantor and Grantor's spouse, the Family Trust, or so much there of as remains and is not disposed of by virtue of Grantor's spouse's limited power of appointment, as the case may be, shall be divided into two shares, one for JIM JENSEN and one for SUSAN MANGROVE.

a. The Trustee shall pay to Grantor's siblings, JIM JENSEN and one for SUSAN MANGROVE, or expend for their benefit, in convenient installments, all the net income arising from their respective shares of the Family Trust. In addition to such income payments, so long as Grantor's siblings shall live, the Trustee is authorized, from time to time, to pay or expend so much of the **corpus** of their respective shares of the Family Trust as the Trustee, in Trustee's sole discretion, deems necessary for their health, support and maintenance, if living at the time of the particular payment.

b. Upon the death of either or both JIM JENSEN and SUSAN MANGROVE, the remainder of his or her share shall be distributed by the Trustee to Hospice Care of Anytown, First Religious Center of Anytown, and Anytown Animal Shelter, in equal shares. If a charity is not in existence at the time of my death, then pursuant to the *Doctrine of Cy Pres,* a Court with jurisdiction over this matter, the Trustee shall insure that the bequest be given to a similar charity.

Signature

All trusts must be signed by the testator. It should also be witnessed by at least two competent witnesses and notarized if state law requires notarization.

Study Figure 8.1 carefully. It illustrates an inter vivos trust and points out the different possible trust clauses. We will re-visit this form in Chapter 9 when we discuss trusts with marital deduction clauses.

The Professional Paralegal Sample forms in Chapters 5, 6, and 9 will help the paralegal draft a complete estate plan specifically designed for the client's needs. Remember to ensure that the provisions in each document conform to state law.

SUMMARY

A trust is a legal agreement in which a person called the trustor (also grantor or settlor) transfers legal title of property to a trustee. The trustee will then manage the property for the benefit of the beneficiaries. The trustor is the trust's creator and the trustee is a fiduciary who will manage the trust assets for the benefit of beneficiaries. A fiduciary has an affirmative duty to act in the best interest of the trustor and the beneficiaries of the trust, and not for his or her or its personal interests. The trustee is subject to duties and obligations that restrict his or her use of the property, which are either explicitly stated in the trust document or enumerated by statute. Standards of a fiduciary include:

- high degree of good faith, loyalty, and care in the management of his or her duties
- use of ordinary and reasonable skill and prudence in his or her functions
- preservation and protection of the trust assets
- refrain from self-dealing, meaning he or she may not personally benefit from his or her management of trust assets

The beneficiaries of a trust receive trust income and sometimes trust principal from the trustee periodically as the trust terms provide.

There are two kinds of trusts. A testamentary trust is incorporated into a will. Since it is part of the will, it is ambulatory and subject to probate upon the death of the trustor. An inter vivos trust is also called a living trust because it takes effect during the testator's lifetime. An inter vivos trust may be revocable, meaning it can be amended and modified during the trustor's lifetime, or irrevocable, meaning its terms are not subject to amendment or modification at any time.

Trusts may be express or implied. An express trust is either written or oral and clearly states the purpose for which it is being formed. Implied trusts, or involuntary trusts, are created by operation of law. Implied trusts are either resulting or constructive. Resulting trusts are imposed when it is apparent that the holder of the property was not the true owner and the property was, in fact, being held for the benefit of another. Constructive trusts are imposed as a means of preventing unjust enrichment on the part of a titleholder who obtained the property through fraud or other wrongdoing.

Pourover wills are will provisions in which the testator leaves the entire residuary of the estate to the trustee of the living trust as its beneficiary. For this reason, they are also called pourover trusts by some legal experts.

A trust may be terminated in five situations:

- The trust's purpose has been fulfilled.
- The trust's terms require termination after a period of time.
- The trust allows for the trustor's revocation.
- The legal title and equitable title merge.
- The beneficiaries agree that the trust's purpose does not require the trust's continuation.

KEY TERMS

trustor	trust purpose	fiduciary
trustee	inter vivos trust	implied trust
corpus	legal title	constructive trust
beneficiary	revocable	pourover will

equitable title   express trust   testamentary trust
irrevocable   resulting trust

REVIEW **QUESTIONS**

1. List five names used to describe the property that is held in a trust.

2. How is a testamentary trust created? When does it come into existence?

3. What is a pourover will?

4. How may a trust be terminated?

5. What is the distinction between a resulting trust and a constructive trust?

6. List five of the trustee's duties.

7. For what purposes may a trust be created?

8. What is the difference between legal title and equitable title?

9. What are the elements of a valid trust?

10. What is a cestui que trust?

11. Will a trust fail for lack of a trustee? May a trustee be a corporation or other legal entity that is not a person?

PROJECT

Read Moneyhon and Parrish-Moneyhon v. Moneyhon, reproduced as Case 8.4 and briefly state the facts of the case. What did the court decide? Do you think the decision was fair and just? Why or why not?

MyLegalStudiesLab™   http://www.mylegalstudieslab
MYLEGALSTUDIESLAB VIRTUAL LAW OFFICE EXPERIENCE ASSIGNMENTS
Complete the pre-test, study plan, and post-test for this chapter and answer the Legal Applications questions as assigned.

These will help you confirm your mastery of the concepts and their application to legal scenarios. Then complete the Virtual Law Office assignments as assigned by your instructor. These assignments are designed to develop your workplace skills and result in producing documents for inclusion in your portfolio.

CASE 8.4 **SUMMARY**

Reversed and Rendered and Opinion filed February 12, 2009.
In The
Fourteenth Court of Appeals

NO. 14-06-00873-CV

BRIAN D. MONEYHON AND CHERYL PARRISH-MONEYHON, Appellants

V.

PATRICIA MONEYHON, Appellee

On Appeal from the 412th District Court

Brazoria County, Texas

Trial Court Cause No. 37527

OPINION

A husband and wife appeal a judgment from the trial court ordering the couple to convey title to a home, which the couple shared with the husband's mother, to the husband's mother. In five issues, the couple complains that (1) the judgment imposing a constructive trust on the home based on an alleged breach of fiduciary duty is improper because the judgment does not comport with the pleadings; (2) the trial court's judgment cannot be affirmed on any other basis; (3) the mother is precluded from seeking judicial assistance to re-acquire title to the home that allegedly was fraudulently conveyed; (4) injunctive relief is improper; and (5) the home was a gift from the mother to the son. We reverse and render.

I. Factual and Procedural Background

Before appellant Brian Moneyhon's marriage to appellant Cheryl Parrish-Moneyhon, Brian lived with appellee, his seventy-five-year-old mother, Patricia Moneyhon in a Houston home referred to by the parties as "Bash Place." By her own admission, Patricia was dependent on Brian's care, and had been for many years, because she was not in good health.[1] Patricia sold Bash Place, and proceeds from that sale were used to purchase a home in Lake Jackson. The title to the Lake Jackson home was transferred to Brian alone. Brian and Patricia moved to the home in Lake Jackson, which is the home at issue in this case.

Brian and Cheryl were married shortly after he and Patricia moved to Lake Jackson. Cheryl moved into the Lake Jackson home with Brian and Patricia. In the months that followed, Brian and Cheryl's relationship with Patricia deteriorated, which the couple attributed to Patricia's declining health and growing demands. The couple believed it was in Patricia's best interest for her to live in a facility that was better-equipped to meet her needs, and they served Patricia with a notice of eviction in hope that she would move to an assisted-living facility. Upon receiving the eviction notice, Patricia sued Brian and Cheryl, seeking an injunction against the couple to prevent her eviction.

Patricia petitioned the district court to determine ownership of the home and to declare a constructive trust. In her petition for injunction, Patricia made the following factual allegations:

- Patricia agreed to sell her Bash Place home and purchase the Lake Jackson home.
- The proceeds from the sale of Bash Place were dispersed to Patricia and Brian, with the bulk of the proceeds transferred to a title company in Lake Jackson.
- Patricia received roughly $49,000 by check, which was endorsed by Brian and deposited in a bank. Brian subsequently withdrew or spent the money to Patricia's damage.
- Patricia and Brian discussed the purchase of the Lake Jackson home with the understanding that they would reside there together. Each of them continuously have lived together at the Lake Jackson home since moving to the home in November 2004.
- Brian used the proceeds of the sale of Bash Place to purchase the Lake Jackson home. All of the money used for the purchase of the Lake Jackson home was Patricia's.
- Brian, by deed transfers, purposely transferred an undivided one-half interest in the Lake Jackson home to Cheryl, which was done without Patricia's consent or approval to Patricia's damage.
- In March 2006, the couple gave Patricia a thirty-day eviction notice, requesting her to vacate the premises of the Lake Jackson home.

Patricia also petitioned for the district court to declare a constructive trust, based on the following allegations:

- Patricia sold her Bash Place home. Unbeknownst to Patricia, Brian and Cheryl arranged for the purchase of the Lake Jackson home using entirely the proceeds from the sale of the Bash Place home. Brian took title to the Lake Jackson property.
- The couple, through a series of conveyances, transferred the home to each other. The couple obtained the property in complete disregard to Patricia's rights by promising

or representing to Patricia that Patricia would own the property, but "if anything ever happened" to Patricia, Brian would receive the property. Brian promised to let Patricia live the rest of her life at the Lake Jackson home.

- After Patricia learned of the couple's "plan to dispossess [her] and own the property," Brian promised Patricia that he would convey the property to her. The couple did not convey the Lake Jackson home to Patricia.

- Brian's promises were material representations because Patricia did not agree that Brian would own the property to Patricia's exclusion. The couple's representations were false because they never intended to reconvey the property to Patricia, though the representations were made with the intent that Patricia would act upon them.

- Patricia fully performed on the agreement, and Brian and Cheryl breached the agreement by failing to fulfill the expressed promises and representations made. Brian and Cheryl collaborated with each other to obtain title to the Lake Jackson property using all of Patricia's funds.

- Patricia has been injured and deprived of her funds and property because she relied on the couple's promises and representations. The couple has been unjustly enriched by being permitted to stay on the Lake Jackson property. A constructive trust is the only remedy to prevent their unjust enrichment at Patricia's expense.

- Because the couple's conduct was fraudulent and malicious, Patricia is owed exemplary damages to deter similar conduct by the couple in connection with a home-equity mortgage on the Lake Jackson home.[2]

The couple denied Patricia's allegations and alleged that the Lake Jackson home was Brian's sole and separate property, in which he conveyed an undivided one-half interest to Cheryl just before their marriage. The couple alleged that they permitted Patricia to reside in the Lake Jackson home until she began verbally and physically assaulting the couple, and then they sought to evict Patricia. They also filed a counterclaim, alleging trespass to try title and that Patricia made an unconditional gift of the home to Brian.

After a bench trial, the trial court made the following findings:

- Clear and convincing evidence shows Patricia did not intend to make an absolute gift of the Lake Jackson home to Brian to her exclusion.

- A fiduciary relationship existed between Patricia and Brian, and Brian breached the relationship in failing to disclose factual information about Medicare and estate taxes and potential effects from the transaction.

- The conveyance to Brian from Patricia was a fraudulent conveyance.

The trial court issued a permanent injunction in favor of Patricia and ordered the couple to convey the Lake Jackson home to Patricia. The trial court ordered that Patricia take nothing for exemplary damages or for attorney's fees. The couple now appeals the trial court's judgment.

II. Issues and Analysis

Did the trial court err in rendering judgment based on the existence and breach of a fiduciary duty?

In their first issue, Brian and Cheryl complain that the trial court erred in awarding Patricia relief based on a finding that Brian owed Patricia a fiduciary duty and breached that duty. According to Brian and Cheryl, because Patricia did not assert a claim for breach of a fiduciary duty, and the issue was not tried by consent, the trial court's finding is in error.

A trial court's judgment must conform to the pleadings. Tex. R. Civ. P. 301. Pleadings must give reasonable notice of the claims asserted. *SmithKline Beecham Corp. v. Doe,* 903 S.W.2d 347, 354B55 (Tex. 1995). A reviewing court should liberally construe the petition to contain any claims that reasonably may be inferred from the specific language as used in the petition and uphold the petition as to those claims, even if an element of a claim is not specifically alleged. *See id.* In making this determination, however, a reviewing court cannot use a liberal construction of the petition as a license to read into the petition a claim that it does not contain. *San Saba Energy, L.P. v. Crawford,* 171 S.W.3d 323, 338 (Tex. App. CHouston [14 Dist.] 2005, no pet.). The petition must give fair and adequate notice of the claims being asserted, and, if the reviewing court cannot reasonably infer that the petition contains a claim, then it must conclude the petition does not contain this claim, even under a liberal construction. *See SmithKline Beecham Corp.,* 903 S.W.2d at 354B55. It is against this standard that we must analyze Patricia's pleadings to determine if they may be construed as containing a claim for breach of fiduciary duty.

Although Patricia pleaded for equitable relief in the form of a constructive trust, even under a liberal construction, Patricia's live petition for constructive trust cannot be said to contain any allegation or even a mention of the existence of a fiduciary relationship[3] or the breach of a fiduciary relationship.[4] Because the trial court's judgment awarded title to Patricia based on a breach of a fiduciary duty, the judgment did not conform to the pleadings, and the trial court erred in granting such relief in the absence of pleadings to support such relief or trial by consent.[5] *See* Tex. R. Civ. P. 301; *Binder v. Joe,* 193 S.W.3d 29, 32 (Tex. App.CHouston [1st Dist.] 2005, no pet.). If issues not raised by the pleadings are tried by express or implied consent of the parties, these issues shall be treated as if they had been raised by the pleadings. *See* Tex. R. Civ. P. 67, 301; *Baltzer v. Medina,* 240 S.W.3d 469, 476 (Tex. App.CHouston [14th Dist.] 2007, no pet.). To determine whether the issue was tried by consent, the court must examine the record not for evidence of the issue, but rather for evidence of trial of the issue. *Greene v. Young,* 174 S.W.3d 291, 301 (Tex. App.CHouston [1st Dist.] 2005, pet. denied). Thus, absent record evidence that a breach-of-fiduciary-duty claim was tried by consent, the judgment on that claim cannot stand.

The record utterly fails to support trial by consent of a breach-of-fiduciary-duty claim. At no point did any party present evidence of a fiduciary relationship based on trust or confidence. Though the record indicates that Patricia depended on Brian for care and that he shared a joint checking account with her, nothing in the record indicates that the parties were trying the issue of whether Patricia and Brian's relationship involved such a high degree of trust and confidence as to give rise to a fiduciary duty or that Brian breached such a fiduciary duty.[6] To the contrary, it was only during closing arguments that Patricia's trial counsel mentioned B for the first time B a "confidential relationship" between Brian and Patricia. Prior to the close of evidence, however, no party presented evidence or made any reference to this alleged confidential relationship. Thus, we can only conclude that the issue of the existence or breach of a fiduciary duty was not tried by consent of the parties. Absent either trial by consent or pleadings to support a breach-of-fiduciary-duty claim, the trial court erred in granting Patricia relief on this basis. *See Baltzer,* 240 S.W.3d at 476. Accordingly, we sustain Brian and Cheryl's first issue.

May the trial court's judgment be affirmed based on any other claim?

In Brian and Cheryl's second issue, they assert that the trial court did not find that they committed actual fraud and that the judgment may not be affirmed based on Patricia's actual fraud claims. Patricia asserts that the trial court did find in her favor as to the actual fraud claims based on the trial court's finding "the conveyance to Brian D. Moneyhon from Patricia Moneyhon a [sic] fraudulent conveyance." Based on statutory amendments, what used to be called a "fraudulent conveyance" is now called a "fraudulent transfer" under the Uniform Fraudulent Transfer Act. *See* TEX. BUS. & COMM. CODE ANN. §24.001, et seq. (Vernon Supp. 2008). Claims under this statute are brought by one or more creditors to challenge transfers made by a debtor. *See id.* Claims under the Uniform Fraudulent Transfer Act do not match up with the allegations in Patricia's pleadings. In her petition,

Patricia does not purport to assert any claims under the Uniform Fraudulent Transfer Act, and liberally construing the petition to contain any claims that reasonably may be inferred from its language, we cannot reasonably conclude that Patricia has pleaded any claims under this statute. On appeal, Patricia agrees that the trial court was not referring to the Uniform Fraudulent Transfer Act when it found a "fraudulent conveyance."

The trial court's intent in finding a "fraudulent conveyance" is explained in a letter that the trial court sent to counsel. In this letter the trial court explains its decision, stating that,

> since the Court has found that Patricia had no intent to convey the property unconditionally to her son, and because of Brian's breach of the fiduciary relationship to his mother in failing to completely disclose factual information concerning Medicaid and estate taxes and his failure to disclose the potential affects of transaction, [sic] the Court hereby finds the conveyance to Brian from Patricia a fraudulent conveyance.

We conclude that the trial court's subsequent finding of a "fraudulent conveyance" reflected its findings of no gift and a breach of fiduciary duty. In the context of this record, we cannot reasonably conclude that the trial court found that Brian and Cheryl committed actual fraud. Accordingly, we sustain Brian and Cheryl's second issue.

Because the trial court did not find any element of Brian and Cheryl's other pleaded claims, these claims cannot provide a basis for affirming the trial court's judgment. *See* TEX. R. CIV. P. 299; *Vickery v. Comm'n for Lawyer Discipline*, 5 S.W.3d 241, 252 (Tex. App. CHouston [14th Dist.] 1999, pet. denied). The only claim on which the trial court's judgment is based is a breach-of-fiduciary-duty claim that was not pleaded or tried by consent. Therefore, the equitable relief awarded in the trial court's order, conveying title in the Lake Jackson home to Patricia, necessarily must be reversed. *See W & F Transp., Inc. v. Wilhelm*, 208 S.W.3d 32, 46B7 (Tex. App.CHouston [14th Dist.] 2006, no pet.) (reversing and rendering a take-nothing judgment because jury's findings did not support liability against two appellants). Accordingly, the trial court's judgment is reversed.[7]

III. Conclusion

The trial court awarded relief based on the existence and breach of a fiduciary duty. This theory, however, was neither pleaded nor tried by consent. The trial court did not find any elements of Patricia's other claims that would support the relief it granted; therefore, Patricia's other claims cannot provide a basis for affirming the trial court's judgment. For this reason, we reverse the trial court's judgment and render judgment that Patricia take nothing against Brian and Cheryl.

/s/ Kem Thompson Frost
Justice

Panel consists of Justices Anderson, Frost, and Guzman.

NOTES

1. This court learned at oral argument that Patricia passed away after the parties' appellate briefs were filed. Accordingly, this court will proceed to adjudicate the appeal as if Patricia were still alive, and this court will use Patricia's name on all papers. *See* TEX. R. APP. P. 7.1(a). This court's judgment will have the same force and effect as if rendered when Patricia was living. *See* id.

2. Patricia contends that Brian and Cheryl, through a series of deeds, conveyed title in the Lake Jackson home to each other, and they applied for a home-equity loan using that property as collateral.

3. A formal fiduciary relationship arises as a matter of law in certain situations, for example, between attorney and client. *See Swinehart v. Stubbeman, McRae, Sealy, Laughlin, & Browder, Inc.*, 48 S.W.3d 865, 878 (Tex. App.CHouston [14th Dist.] 2001, pet. denied). An informal relationship may give rise to a fiduciary duty when one person trusts in and relies on another, whether the relationship is a moral, social, domestic, or purely personal one. *See Schlumberger Tech. Corp. v. Swanson*, 959 S.W.2d 171, 176 (Tex. 1997). However, not every relationship involving a high degree of trust

and confidence rises to the stature of a fiduciary relationship. *See id.* at 176B77. Texas courts do not create such a duty lightly. *See id.*

4. During oral argument, Patricia's appellate counsel urged this court to consider an affidavit by Patricia, included in the record in support of Patricia's initial pleadings, as evidence that she alleged the existence of a fiduciary duty. Presuming that we may consider the affidavit as part of the live pleadings, any allegations in the affidavit support pleadings for misrepresentation, but do not support any alleged pleadings for the existence or breach of a fiduciary relationship.

5. Patricia asserts that Brian and Cheryl must have been aware that her petition contained a claim for breach of fiduciary duty because, in her petition, Patricia sought a constructive trust and, Patricia asserts, such relief is only available when a fiduciary duty has been breached. This argument lacks merit. A constructive trust is available in other circumstances, for example, as a remedy for actual fraud. *See Swinehart*, 48 S.W.3d at 878.

6. Patricia argues on appeal that Brian and Cheryl, themselves, presented evidence concerning the issue of a fiduciary relationship, citing evidence of the joint bank account shared by Brian and Patricia, Brian's presence at the closing for both the Bash Place and Lake Jackson homes, and Brian's testimony of long-term care and financial support of multiple elderly family members, including Patricia. However, any evidence that could be construed as supporting the existence or breach of a fiduciary duty was elicited to prove or disprove fraud, an allegation upon which Patricia sought equitable relief as reflected in the pleadings. The doctrine of trial by consent does not apply when the evidence of an unpleaded matter is relevant to the pleaded issues because it would not be calculated to elicit an objection. *In re J.M.*, 156 S.W.3d 696, 705 (Tex. App.CDallas 2005, no pet.); *RE/Max of Tex., Inc. v. Kater Corp.*, 961 S.W.2d 324, 328 (Tex. App.CHouston [1st Dist.] 1997, pet. denied).

7. Because we sustain the first two issues, we need not and do not address Brian and Cheryl's remaining issues.

Chapter **nine**

SPECIALIZED TRUSTS AND GIFTS

As stated in the prior chapter on trusts, a trust is an estate planning vehicle in which a person, called the trustor, transfers property to a trustee. The trustee then holds the property in the trust ("in trust") for the benefit of certain third parties, called beneficiaries. A trust is essentially a contract between the trustor and the trustee in which the trustee agrees to manage the trust property and distributes the assets pursuant to the agreement's terms.

Trusts may be created in a will, and are therefore called ***testamentary trusts.*** They also may be stand-alone documents, of which there are two basic types:

- revocable trusts (also called inter vivos or living trusts), meaning they can be altered or amended
- **irrevocable trusts,** meaning that once put into effect, they may not be altered or amended

Trustors often have specific goals in mind when preparing a trust. Some want to protect their spouses and family from a creditor's reach, while others want to shield their dollars from the long arm of the Internal Revenue Service. Still others want to ensure that a loved one would get extra attention, especially monetary assistance, should the need arise. Sometimes a family member gets government assistance due to handicaps and disabilities, but the family wants to supply a little extra to that person without fear that government benefits will be lost.

In this chapter, we will treat the trusts as stand-alone documents, with a trustor creating a trust that specifically addresses these issues; however, it is possible to add provisions to existing inter vivos and testamentary trusts that would effectuate these goals.

Spendthrift Trust

Assume that Hannah Gross is a 74-year-old woman with three grown children, Daniel, Barbara, and Scott, and five grown grandchildren: Gail, Marsha, Lori, Annie, and Harold. Unfortunately, Daniel and his son, Harold, do not know how to keep money in their wallets. Harold has a penchant for expensive dinners and cigars, while Daniel has a predilection for exorbitantly priced toys, such as cars and home theater equipment. Both have run up a tremendous amount of debt.

Hannah is preparing a trust for the benefit of her children and grandchildren, but wants to protect the trust's assets from the hands of all creditors, including those of Daniel and Harold. How does she accomplish this task?

Hannah executes a **spendthrift trust**. A spendthrift trust includes a provision that protects the trust principal and unpaid income from creditors and from a beneficiary's own foolishness. The provision itself restricts the trust assets as much as is possible by law, in such a way that they do not become the beneficiary's until he or she actually receives the income or portion of the principal. Since the assets are not the beneficiary's until distributed to the beneficiary, the beneficiary's creditors cannot claim a right in them. The following is an illustration of a spendthrift trust provision:

> *Example:*
>
> No beneficiary of this trust shall have the right or power to anticipate, by assignment or otherwise, any income or principal given to such beneficiary by this trust, nor in advance of actually receiving the same, have the right or power to sell, transfer, encumber, or in anywise charge same; nor shall such income or principal, or any portion of the same, be subject to any execution, garnishment, attachment, insolvency, bankruptcy, or legal proceeding of any character, levy, or sale, or in any event or manner be applicable or subject, voluntarily or involuntarily, to the payment of such beneficiary's debts.

Notice that this clause also prevents the beneficiary from selling or otherwise giving away his or her potential interest in the trust's assets. This wording ensures that a beneficiary, strapped for cash, will not sell his or her right to future income or give it to a creditor (hypothecate or assign his or her rights), further hurting his or her precarious financial situation. For another example of a spendthrift trust clause, see Figure 8.1, Section 11.4 as shown in Chapter 8.

CASE 9.1 **SUMMARY**

Although disturbing in its outcome, this case illustrates the effectiveness of spendthrift trust provisions.

Scheffel v. Krueger, 146 N.H. 669, 782 A.2d 410 (NH. 2001)

SUBSEQUENT HISTORY: [*1] Application for Rehearing Denied November 1, 2001. Released for Publication November 5, 2001.

The plaintiff, Scheffel, filed suit against individually and as mother and [*2] next friend of Cory C., appeals a Superior Court (Hollman, J.) order dismissing her trustee process action against Citizens Bank NH, the trustee defendant. See RSA 512:9-b (1997). The Court affirmed.

In 1998, the plaintiff, Scheffel, individually and as mother and "next friend" of Cory, filed suit asserting tort claims against the defendant, Krueger. In her suit, Scheffel alleged that Krueger sexually assaulted Cory, videotaping the assault and broadcasting it over the Internet. (The conduct also formed the basis for criminal charges against the defendant. State v. Krueger, 776 A.2d 720.) The trial court entered a default judgment against Krueger and ordered him to pay $551,286.25 in damages. To satisfy the judgment against Krueger, Scheffel sought attachment of Krueger's beneficial interest in the Kyle Krueger Irrevocable Trust (trust), which had been established for Krueger by his grandmother in 1985.

Under the terms of the trust, the trustee was to pay all of the net income from the trust to Krueger, at least quarterly, or more frequently if Krueger requested in writing. The trustee was authorized to pay any of the principal to Krueger if in the trustee's sole discretion the funds were necessary for Krueger's "maintenance, support and education". Krueger could not invade the principal until he reached the age of fifty, which will not occur until April 6, 2016. In addition, Krueger was prohibited from making any voluntary or involuntary transfers of his interest in the trust. Article VII of the trust instrument specifically provided:

> No principal or income payable or to become payable under any of the trusts created by this instrument shall be subject to anticipation or assignment by any beneficiary thereof, or to the interference or control of any creditors of such beneficiary or to be taken or reached by any legal or equitable process in satisfaction of any debt or liability of such beneficiary prior to its receipt by the beneficiary.

Krueger asserted that the spendthrift provision barred Scheffel's claim against the trust. The trial court found that the provision was enforceable under RSA 564:23 and dismissed the action.

Scheffel's argument on appeal was that the New Hampshire legislature did not intend RSA 564:23 to shield the trust assets from tort creditors, especially when the beneficiary's conduct constituted a criminal act.

"RSA 564:23, I, provides:

In the event the governing instrument so provides, a beneficiary of a trust shall not be able to transfer his or her right to future payments of income and principal, and a creditor of a beneficiary shall not be able to subject the beneficiary's interest to the payment of its claim."

According to the appellate court, RSA 564:23

> provides two exceptions to the enforceability of spendthrift provisions. The provisions "shall not apply to a beneficiary's interest in a trust to the extent that the beneficiary is the settlor and the trust is not a special needs trust established for a person with disabilities," RSA 564:23, II, and "shall not be construed to prevent

> the application of RSA 545-A or a similar law of another state [regarding fraudulent transfers]," RSA 564:23, III.

Based on these exceptions, the appellate court stated that the spendthrift provision was enforceable unless Krueger is also the trustor or the assets were fraudulently transferred to the trust. Neither exception applied. Scheffel then argued that the legislature did not intend for RSA 564:23 to shield the trust assets from tort creditors. The appellate court stated however that the statute

> plainly states that "a creditor of a beneficiary shall not be able to subject the beneficiary's interest to the payment of its claim." RSA 564:23, I. Nothing in this language suggests that the legislature intended that a tort creditor should be exempted from a spendthrift provision. Two exemptions are enumerated in sections II and III. Where the legislature has made specific exemptions, we must presume no others were intended.

Scheffel then argued that public policy required the court to create a tort creditor exception to the statute. The appellate court found that it could not and would not.

Scheffel then argued that the trust did not qualify as a spendthrift trust under RSA 564:23 "because the trust document allows the beneficiary to determine the frequency of payments, to demand principal and interest after his fiftieth birthday, and to dispose of the trust assets by will" and that the rights granted permitted Krueger to exert too much control over the trust assets. The appellate court disagreed.

Finally, Scheffel argued that the trust's purpose to provide for the defendant's support, maintenance and education can no longer be fulfilled because Krueger was likely to remain incarcerated for a period of years. The trial court found that the trust's purpose "may still be fulfilled while the defendant is incarcerated and after he is released," and the appellate court agreed.

The appellate court affirmed the trial court's decision to dismiss the action.

Sprinkling and Spray Trusts

Richard Wiggins is a single father with three children, Fred, Taylor, and Nikki, ages 26, 22, and 16, respectively. He executes a trust that will effectuate his goals, which include assisting his children with their educational needs, and any other reasonable monetary needs they may have. Richard names his friend and business associate, George Dunkin, as the trustee. In the trust agreement, Richard gives George total discretion to distribute the income, and if necessary the principal, to any of Richard's children.

This type of trust is called a **sprinkling trust or spray trust**, so called because the trustee has the discretion to "sprinkle and spray" the income and/or principal from a trust as the trustee sees fit among a group of beneficiaries. Because the trustee has the sole discretion to make the determination regarding how the trust assets are distributed, this type of trust is also called a **discretionary trust**.

Example: Richard Wiggins's trust states in part that the trustee is authorized

in the sole discretion of the Trustee, at any time and from time to time, to distribute all or any part of the net income and/or principal of such trust to any one (1) or more of the beneficiaries of such trust in such proportion and amounts as the Trustee shall from time to time determine, in the sole discretion of the Trustee, to be desirable for the best interests of any said beneficiary, or to accumulate all or any part of such net income and the same to the principal of such trust to be held, administered and distributed as a part thereof; provided, however, no distribution shall be made pursuant to the provisions of this Section which would discharge or satisfy a legal obligation of the Grantor.

Advantages

- Allows the trustee the ability to distribute the trust assets to the beneficiaries the trustee believes are most deserving and needy; releases the trustor from the obligation of making the allocation decision himself or herself. Perhaps, at the time of the trust's execution, the trustor sees that there will be a need in the future, but is uncertain about the actual dollar amounts that may be required later.

    Example: Richard knows that his youngest child will need college tuition in two years, but does not know how much will be necessary. Giving his trustee total discretion frees him from giving his daughter an amount or percentage of the trust that may turn out to be too much or too little when the tuition is finally needed.

- Allows for unforeseen or unwelcome events at the time of the trust's execution.

    Example: Richard's second child is in a car accident three years after the trust's execution. His medical and rehabilitation expenses are enormous. If Richard had left his son 25% of the trust income to be paid quarterly, the amount may not be sufficient to cover those expenses. By giving the trustee total discretion, George can pay all of the trust's income for the benefit of that son.

- Allows the trustee to distribute income to those beneficiaries in lower tax brackets, saving trust assets from income tax.

    Example: When Richard's trust takes effect, his children are 17, 23, and 27, respectively. The oldest child has a thriving business as a stockbroker and is financially secure. If trust income passed to him, it would be taxed at a higher rate because of his higher income. George may choose to give a larger portion of the trust income to the other children because they earn substantially less, securing a lower tax bracket for the trust income.

- Sprinkling and spray trusts have a built-in spendthrift provision, shielding trust principal from creditors.
- Sprinkling trusts may also save estate taxes.

Disadvantages

- The sprinkling or spray trust's foremost advantage may also be seen as its principal disadvantage. The trustee is given a tremendous amount of power when the trustor gives the trustee sole discretion to allocate trust assets to the beneficiaries. That sole control, in some instances, may be a disadvantage. A trustee who dislikes a beneficiary, or does not think a beneficiary's needs are worthy or necessary, may withhold trust income from that beneficiary.

    Example: Richard's son, Taylor, wants to spend his senior year of college abroad. Although studying abroad is a widely accepted practice, the university he will attend is highly regarded, it would greatly enhance his educational needs, and he has received a partial scholarship, George does not want him to go. He refuses Taylor's request for a portion of the trust income to pay for the year. Since Taylor cannot pay for the portion of the tuition not covered by the scholarship, he must decline the invitation to go abroad to study.

- Trusts such as these occasionally give rise to lawsuits in which some of the beneficiaries claim the trustee shows favoritism to one or two of the beneficiaries, to the detriment of the others.

Marital Deduction Trust

Anyone may arrange his affairs so that his taxes shall be as low as possible; he is not bound to choose that pattern which best pays the treasury. There is not even a patriotic duty to increase one's taxes. Over and over again the Courts have said that there is nothing sinister in so arranging affairs as to keep taxes as low as possible. Everyone does it, rich and poor alike and all do right, for nobody owes any public duty to pay more than the law demands.

~~*Judge Learned Hand (1872–1961), Judge, U.S. Court of Appeals, Gregory v. Helvering, 69 F.2d 809, 810 (2d Cir. 1934), aff'd, 293 U.S. 465, 55 S.Ct. 266, 79 L.Ed. 596 (1935).*

The Marital Deduction

The ***marital deduction*** is a deduction permitted by the Internal Revenue Service. The deduction is available only to legally married couples and provides that property left to a surviving spouse either outright or in trust may pass to the surviving spouse tax free. The marital deduction is unlimited meaning that upon the death of the first spouse, that spouse may pass ALL of his or her property to the surviving spouse with no federal estate tax consequences whatsoever.

To obtain the marital deduction:

- The people must be married at the time of the death of the first spouse and local state law determines what the definition of marriage is, and if the people are legally married under that law. (This has an effect with the battles over same-sex marriage which is discussed in Chapter 7.)

- The property must be included in the decedent's gross estate for the marital deduction to apply. Property that is subject to a special power of appointment or irrevocable life insurance trust may not be used to satisfy the marital deduction.

- The surviving spouse must be or become a U.S. citizen by the time the federal estate tax return is filed, and the noncitizen surviving spouse must be a U.S. resident at all times after the first spouse's death and before citizenship is granted.

It is important to note, however, that the marital deduction only applies to the first spouse to die and not the surviving spouse, so that the marital deduction is a deferral of the federal estate tax, not an elimination of the estate tax. The assets remaining in the surviving spouse's estate upon his or her death ARE subject to federal estate taxes.

Example of what happens without estate planning if Congress does not make changes to the estate tax laws: Donald Rivers and Margie Rivers have approximately $12.4 million worth of assets. Assume $11.4 million of the assets belong to Donald.

Donald dies in January 2012, leaving everything to Margie upon his death. Since the marital deduction for property left to a surviving spouse is unlimited, no estate tax accrues at the time of Donald's death because he left everything to Margie.

Then, in January 2013, Margie dies and Congress has still not adjusted the estate tax provisions, meaning that the exemption rate will be $1 million. Donald has left Margie $11.4 million. Upon her death, due to good financial planning, Margie still has the $12.4 million because she has lived off the interest only. She has no debt. Since we are assuming that Congress has not changed the estate tax exemption, Margie will get an exemption of $1 million, leaving a taxable estate of $11.4 million. The maximum tax rate set for 2013 is 55% and Fred, Taylor, and Nikki may have to insure that the estate pays approximately $5 million in estate taxes. No, that is not a misprint. Because Donald and Margie did no serious estate planning, upon Margie's death almost one-half of their combined wealth will be paid in taxes.

Estate planning techniques may be used then, to arrange the couples' assets to insure that the estates of both spouses pay the least amount of federal estate tax.

Marital and Family Trusts

A common way to gain the benefit of the marital deduction, and lessen the blow of taxation upon the second spouse to die, is to set up a trust. Initially, the trust is often a "one pot" trust in which all assets are held in a single revocable trust. Because it is revocable, the spouses retain total control over the assets and may amend or revoke the trust, in part or in full, at any time during their joint lifetimes.

Upon the death of the first spouse to die, however, the trust document itself sets up a scenario in which the trust assets are split into two portions. The surviving spouse is the beneficiary of both portions of the trust, with the children as beneficiaries of the remaining interest.

- One portion of the trust becomes irrevocable and is called the ***bypass trust*** or ***credit shelter trust***. This portion of the trust is funded with the deceased spouse's exemption amount.

Example: Let's revisit Donald and Margie Rivers. In January of 2012, Donald Rivers dies. This portion of the trust will be funded with $6,280,000. This amount of money is the irrevocable portion of the trust and not subject to estate taxes upon Donald's death, taking full advantage of his estate tax credit. This amount is arrived at by taking the amount Donald had at his death, $11.4 million and subtracting the $5,120,000 of the estate tax exemption.

Language in this portion of the trust gives the surviving spouse limited control and access to the funds in this portion of the trust, insuring that the assets in this portion of the trust will not be included in the surviving spouse's taxable estate upon his or her death. This is why it is called a bypass or credit shelter trust, because it bypasses or shelters the assets from estate taxation. This portion of the trust is often called the family trust because it benefits the remainder of the family as well as the spouse.

Example: Donald and Margie's trust states in part:

ARTICLE III—IRREVOCABLE PROVISIONS
Upon the death of the first Co-Trustor to die, hereinafter called the "Deceased Spouse", the then surviving Co-Trustor, hereinafter called the "Surviving Spouse", shall have the power to amend, revoke and/or terminate TRUST A (the marital deduction trust) only, and TRUST B (the exemption equivalent trust), hereinafter established, may not be amended, revoked or terminated. On revocation of TRUST A, all of its assets shall be delivered to the Surviving Spouse. Revocation and amendment shall be made by written instrument filed with the Trustee.

- The remainder of the trust assets are often given to the surviving spouse outright. Most times the funds are left in trust but with total control to the surviving spouse. This insures that if the surviving spouse desires to leave the funds in trust and becomes incapacitated, the successor trustee can handle the assets on the surviving spouse's behalf.

Example: Donald's trust states in part:

D. I give the residue of my real and personal estate to my Trustee to be divided (along with any assets coming to my Trustee from other sources at my death) into two separate shares, called the Marital Share and the Family Trust, according to the directions in Article III. However, if my wife does not survive me, the Marital Share shall be eliminated and all the assets shall constitute the Family Trust.

1. Marital Share. My Trustee shall distribute the Marital Share outright to my wife.

2. Family Trust. My Trustee shall administer the Family Trust upon these directions:

   a. Pay the net income to my wife during her lifetime in quarterly or more frequent installments and pay to her as much of the principal as my Trustee may deem necessary for her support in reasonable comfort, and for her medical, dental, hospital and nursing expenses and expenses of invalidism.

   b. Upon my wife's death (or my death if my wife predeceases me), distribute the principal and any undistributed income of the Family Trust to my then living descendants.

c. If at the death of the survivor of my wife and me, or the termination of a child's separate trust, there is no living beneficiary designated to take the assets held in the trust, distribute the principal and any undistributed income to the persons who would then be my distributees under the laws of Anystate then in effect as if I had then died without a will, unmarried and owning the assets.

Determination of the marital deduction amounts must be determined based upon what a family's preferences are.

Examples of clauses for marital deduction amount and family or bypass amount:

Article III. Division into Marital Share and Family Trust. If my wife survives me, then as of my death my Trustee shall divide the trust assets (but excluding assets used to make the payments described in Article IV) into the Marital Share and the Family Trust as follows:

A. The Marital Share shall consist of the following fractional share of the trust assets: The numerator of the fraction shall be a figure equal to (1) such portion, if any, of the unlimited marital deduction allowable to my estate as may be necessary to reduce to zero (or if that is not possible, to a minimum) the federal estate tax on my estate after taking into account all other deductions, exclusions, the unified credit, and the state death tax credit or deduction (but only to the extent that the use of the state death tax credit or deduction does not incur or increase any state death taxes otherwise payable by my estate) finally allowed for federal estate tax purposes less (2) the aggregate value as finally determined for such purposes of all property and interests in property included in my gross estate that qualify for the marital deduction and that pass or have passed to, or for the benefit of my wife on or before my death, other than as a part of the Marital Share. The denominator of the fraction shall be a figure equal to the value of the trust assets calculated on the basis of values as finally determined for federal estate tax purposes.

[Providing for a larger amount in the family trust]

OR

The Marital Share shall consist of the smallest amount of the unlimited marital deduction allowable to my estate as may be necessary to reduce to zero (or if that is not possible, to a minimum) the federal estate tax on my estate after taking into account all other deductions, exclusions, the unified credit, and the state death tax credit or deduction (but only to the extent that the use of the state death tax credit or deduction does not incur or increase any state death taxes otherwise payable by my estate) finally allowed for federal estate tax purposes.

[Providing for the larger amount of the estate to go into the family trust]

OR

The Marital Share shall consist of the greater of (1) and (2), as follows: (1) one-half of the trust assets; and (2) the following fractional share of the trust assets: The numerator of the fraction shall be a figure equal to (i) such portion, if any, of the unlimited marital deduction allowable to my estate as may be necessary to reduce to zero (or if that is not possible, to a minimum) the federal estate tax on my estate after taking into account all other deductions, exclusions, the unified credit, and the state death tax credit or deduction (but only to the extent that the use of the state death tax credit or deduction does not incur or increase any state death taxes otherwise payable by my estate) finally allowed for federal estate tax purposes less (ii) the aggregate value as finally determined for such purposes of all property and interests in property included in my gross estate that qualify for the marital deduction and that pass or have passed to, or for the benefit of my wife on or before my death, other than as a part of the Marital Share. The denominator of the fraction shall be a figure equal to the value of the trust assets calculated on the basis of values as finally determined for federal estate tax purposes. [Providing the wife with more money in the marital share.]

B.   The Family Trust shall consist of the remaining trust assets.

C.   In making the division, my Trustee shall not distribute to the Marital Share any property or the proceeds of any property that are not capable of qualifying for the marital deduction. Except to the extent that the Marital Share cannot be satisfied by other property qualifying for the marital deduction, my Trustee shall not distribute to the Marital Share any property in respect of which any tax is payable to a foreign country by reason of my death. Subject to the restrictions of this paragraph, my Trustee may select trust assets to be allocated to the Marital Share and the Family Trust as my Trustee may determine, valuing the assets selected as of the date or dates of distribution.

Example: Let's see what happens when Donald and Margie do some estate planning using a marital deduction trust. When Donald dies, the remaining $5,120,000 is given to Margie outright to do with as she pleases. What this means, however, is that when Margie dies in 2013, even if she does no further estate planning and Congress does not extend the law so that the estate tax exemption in 2013 is only $1 million, Donald and Margie's children only pay $1.5 million in estate taxes. A still substantial sum to be sure but much less than with no estate planning whatsoever. See Figure 9.4 to see what happened to the estates of more famous people than Donald and Margie whose estates paid a fair sum to the IRS in estate taxes.

Qualified Terminable Interest Property (QTIP) Trust

A **qualified terminable interest property trust** or ***QTIP*** trust is a tax provision that allows a trustor to create a trust giving a life interest of all the income of the trust to a surviving spouse, with the remainder of the trust property passing to someone other than the surviving spouse upon that spouse's death. A QTIP trust is particularly desirable for spouses in second marriages where each spouse desires to leave as much of his or her estate to his or her children and heirs. The Internal Revenue Code provides that a surviving spouse has a qualifying income for life if:

• the surviving spouse is entitled to all the income from the property, payable annually or at more frequent intervals, or has a usufruct interest for life in the property (in Louisiana),

- no person has a power to appoint any part of the property to any person other than the surviving spouse (although the surviving spouse can give it to other people once he or she has been given the income outright), and
- the trustee makes an election to treat the property as QTIP property.

[I.R.C. §2056(b)(7)]

Example: Steven and Jane Newberry have been married for 25 years and have no children together. Jane has three children from a prior marriage, and Steven has no children. Jane wants to provide for Steven upon her death, but wants her children to ultimately receive her property. If Jane were to leave her property to Steven outright, Steven would be under no obligation to leave any of it to Jane's children upon his death. Jane can create a QTIP trust instead. The QTIP would pass all income from the trust to Steven during his life. During his lifetime the trust property could not be given to anyone other than Steven. Upon Steven's death, the entire trust would pass to Jane's children.

The Trust Jane sets up in part states:

The Trustee shall pay the net income of the Marital Trust to my husband during his lifetime in quarterly or more frequent installments and may pay to my husband as much of the principal as the Trustee may deem necessary for his support, health, and maintenance.

THE PROFESSIONAL PARALEGAL

In 1991, the American Bar Association adopted Model Guidelines for the Utilization of Legal Assistant Services, which is available for download at http://www.abanet .org/legalservices/paralegals/. This is a model code pertaining directly to paralegals but your jurisdiction may not have a specific set of ethical rules for paralegals that are codified in your state statutes or codes. The National Federation of Paralegal Associations ("NFPA") and National Association of Legal Assistants ("NALA") are the two primary national professional paralegal associations, and membership in either is voluntary. Both organizations have developed their own codes of ethical conduct for their memberships that are similar to the ABA Model Guidelines.

Despite lacking a mandatory ethics code of their own, paralegals are still required to comply with the Rules of Professional Conduct, albeit somewhat indirectly as their supervising attorney must insure that the Rules of Professional Conduct for lawyers is always complied with in the law office setting.

To learn more about paralegal ethics see *ETHICS: Top Ten Rules for Paralegals* and *Ethics for the Legal Professional, 6th Edition* both by Deborah K. Orlik and published by Pearson Prentice Hall Legal, as well as Chapter 14 of this textbook.

Life Insurance Trust

In a **life insurance trust**, the trustor creates an irrevocable trust in which the trust is the named insurance beneficiary on a life insurance policy, with the trustor as the insured. This type of trust is also called an ILIT (pronounced eye-lit). Upon the trustor's death, the insurance company pays the proceeds directly to the trust.

An ILIT can be set up in two ways:

- The trustor can transfer an existing policy to the trust. In this situation, the trustor is giving a gift of the insurance policy to the trust beneficiaries. This is a form of pourover trust because the gift pours over into an existing trust. It is important to note that unless the trustor transfers the actual ownership of the insurance policy to the trust or otherwise relinquishes his or her rights to ownership in the policy by writing a letter to the insurance company and filling out a change of beneficiary form, the insurance proceeds will be included in the trustor's estate for tax purposes. Once the trustor transfers ownership of the policy to the trust, it will not be included in the trustor's estate. Unless the policy is paid up, the trustor must contribute a small amount to the trust each year so that it remains funded and so the trustee can make premium payments on the policy.

- Create a trust and have the trustee purchase the insurance outright. In this situation, either the policy is paid up on purchase or the trustor makes periodic payments which are a gift during that year.

ILITs are exceptional estate planning tools because under most circumstances, the insurance proceeds are not considered part of the trustor's estate upon his or her death.

Example: Amanda Taylor wants to provide for her grandchildren, Harold and Maude. She creates an irrevocable life insurance trust (an ILIT) and then has the trust purchase life insurance on her own life with Harold and Maude as the sole beneficiaries of the trust in the face amount of $3 million. The premiums are $25,000 a year. Upon Amanda's death, the $3 million insurance proceeds will belong to Harold and Maude subject to the terms of the trust but will not be included in Amanda's estate.

Crummey Notice and Powers

Because the trustor of an ILIT usually makes annual premium payments to keep the insurance policy current, the payments are considered gifts to the beneficiaries by the Internal Revenue Service. The IRS determined that the gift would only be a present gift and the life insurance proceeds not part of the decedent's estate if the beneficiaries had a right to demand the premium gifts. Present gift quite literally means at the time the gift is made—"now." The value of this type of arrangement is that each year the trustor is removing the value of the premium amounts from his or her estate, AND the life insurance proceeds aren't included in the estate upon death either.

The method by which the beneficiaries may make demand is called **Crummey powers** and the notice they must receive from the trustee is called a **Crummey notice.** Trustors hope that the beneficiaries will not withdraw their share of the premiums since the benefit of the life insurance proceeds will likely be greater, and also because the premiums will go unpaid. However, the notice must be given each time a premium payment (gift) is made to the trust, and each beneficiary must be given a reasonable time to make demand.

Crummey powers and notice derive their name from a United States Court of Appeal, 9th Circuit case called *Crummey v. Commissioner,* 397 F.2d 82 (9th Cir.

1968). Based on the decision in *Crummey,* after the trustor pays the insurance premiums, the trustee must give notice to each trust beneficiary, the Crummey notice, informing the beneficiaries that the payment (gift) was made and that they have a right to withdraw their share of the payment for a specified period of time so that the gift is deemed a present interest. If the gift is a present interest, the trustor may take the premium payments under an annual gift tax exclusion and will file a gift tax return for each beneficiary (see Chapter 12 for information on estate and gift tax).

Figure 9.1   Crummey Notice to Child

June 17, 2012

Nikki Wiggins
456 Elm Street
Anytown, Anystate

RE: Richard Wiggins Irrevocable Life Insurance Trust Agreement Dated February 13, 2005 with George Dunkin as Trustee

Dear Ms. Wiggins:

You are hereby notified that on June 17, 2009 by transfer of the following policies of insurance in the face amounts specified, Richard Wiggins has made a donation to the trust created by him dated February 13, 2005. Under the terms of this trust, you have the annual power to withdraw the greater of $5,000 or five percent (5%) of the trust property subject to the power. This annual power of withdrawal is limited by the equal withdrawal powers of you and your brothers Fred Wiggins and Taylor Wiggins. Your power of withdrawal is exercisable only by written notice to the Trustee within thirty (30) days of either receipt of this notice or knowledge of the donation; or the actual date of the donation.

Please acknowledge receipt of this letter by signing it and returning it to my attention. A self-addressed stamped envelope has been enclosed for your convenience. A copy of this letter is also enclosed for your records.

Sincerely,

George Dunkin, Trustee

Acknowledged:

I hereby acknowledge my right to withdraw the contribution to the Richard Wiggins Irrevocable Life Insurance Trust Agreement Dated February 13, 2005 with George Dunkin as Trustee that was made on June 17, 2012.

_____

Nikki Wiggins, Donee

_____

Date

Charitable Trusts

Charitable trusts, so called because they benefit charitable organizations, are created to benefit the public at large instead of individuals. For this reason, they are also called *public trusts*. To be eligible as a charitable gift, the trust must comply with three specific requirements:

- The trust must be made for religious, scientific, charitable, literary, or educational purposes. The beneficiary must not be an individual. It usually helps when the charity is a charity with charitable status through the Internal Revenue Code as a 501(c)(3) company although this is not required. Section 501(c)(3) describes the most common charitable entities as a

  > corporation, community chest, fund or foundation organized and operated for religious, charitable, scientific, testing for public safety, literary or educational purposes or to foster national or international sports competition or for the prevention of cruelty to animals or children, no part of the net earnings of which inure to the benefit of any private shareholder or individual, no substantial part of which is carrying on propaganda or attempting to influence legislation and which does not intervene in or participate in any political campaign.

- The trustor must intend to create a public trust. A charitable purpose must be specified in the trust agreement.
- The beneficiaries must be an indefinite class. This means that the individuals who ultimately benefit from the gift must be unascertainable. According to the Internal Revenue Service's Revenue Ruling 59-310, 1959-2 CB 146, "charity in the legal sense of the term includes benefits which are for an indefinite number of persons and are for the relief of the poor, the advancement of religion, the advancement of education, or erecting or maintaining public buildings or works or otherwise lessening the burdens of government." Upon the death of the trustor, the funds in the trust are not part of the trustor's estate for taxation purposes.

Example: Mitchell Rodgers creates a charitable trust whose purpose is to purchase art supplies for poor children with artistic potential. Any individual who meets the criteria of the trust would be eligible for the art supplies.

Example: Mitchell Rodgers creates a charitable trust for the benefit of Habitat for Humanity in which all of the trust assets will be used to further Habitat's mission to eliminate poverty housing from the earth by building and renovating decent, affordable housing.

Charitable Remainder Trusts

When a trustor creates a **charitable remainder trust,** he or she intends to retain the income for his or her lifetime for him or herself or a beneficiary of the trustor's choice (children, nieces, and nephews, for example) and upon his or her, or the beneficiary's death, the principal remaining in the trust is distributed to an already named charity.

Charitable Remainder Annuity Trust

In a **charitable remainder annuity trust**, also called a CRAT, a fixed amount of income totaling not less than 5% nor more than 50% of the initial net fair market value of the trust is paid at least annually to one or more beneficiaries. This amount is fixed at the time the trust is created and can never change regardless of the needs of the beneficiary in later years. Should the income become insufficient to pay the beneficiary, the difference will be paid from the principal. Should the income be in excess of the fixed amount, however, the excess becomes part of the trust principal and will not be paid to the beneficiary. The remainder of the property is given to the charity upon the death of the beneficiary.

Charitable Remainder Unitrust

Like an annuity trust, in a **charitable remainder unitrust**, also called a CRUT, a fixed amount of income totaling not less than 5% nor more than 50% of the net fair market value of the trust property as valued annually is paid to one or more beneficiaries. Unlike an annuity trust, this amount is not fixed for the life of the beneficiary. When the trust property's value increases, causing an increase in the income, the beneficiary receives the greater amount. The remainder of the property is given to the charity upon the death of the beneficiary.

Charitable Lead Trusts

Charitable lead trusts are another form of irrevocable trust. Considered a mirror image of the charitable remainder trust, in a lead trust the grantor donates cash or some other income-producing asset to an irrevocable trust. The trustee then pays income to a named charity for a period of time, after which the trust principal is paid to a specified remainder beneficiary. This person may not be the grantor but is often the grantor's spouse, children, or grandchildren. Charitable lead trusts may be guaranteed annuity trusts, in which the organization receives a guaranteed (fixed) payment at least annually for a term of years or for the life of a person or persons. These are also called charitable lead annuity trusts (CLAT). A charitable lead trust may also be a unitrust interest in which the charitable organization receives a fixed percentage of the net fair market value of the property determined annually for a set term or for the life of a person or persons. These are also called charitable lead unitrusts (CLUT).

Cy Pres Doctrine

Often a person leaves property in trust for a charity, but years later the charity no longer exists or otherwise merges with another charity. The **cy pres doctrine**, which means "as near as possible," allows a court to find a charity with either the same or a similar purpose to give the charitable trust income and principal. The use of the doctrine is dependent upon whether the trustor's intent was general or specific.

> *Example:* Mitchelle Rodgers created a charitable trust in which she gave $1 million to a no-kill pet shelter. Unfortunately, Michelle's gift of financial support was not enough to keep the charity's good work afloat, and the shelter terminated its existence. A court would likely determine that a general

intent exists and the court will find another charity that does the same type of work. If the court finds, however, that Michelle intended to create the trust solely for that particular animal shelter, the court will not substitute another charity and the trust will terminate at which point the remainder beneficiaries will receive the remainder of the trust assets.

Special Needs Trusts

Special needs trusts, also called supplemental needs trusts, are designed to benefit a person with disabilities. When a person is disabled, to receive government benefits or assistance, the person must be considered impoverished. Government benefits may include Supplemental Security Income (SSI), Social Security Disability Insurance (SSDI), Medicaid, subsidized housing, occupational rehabilitation, and allowances so that the disabled person can meet his or her costs of housing, utilities, clothing, laundry, household supplies, personal essentials, food, and transportation. Benefits may be lost if the person receives assets through gift or inheritance that would render the disabled person no longer impoverished and in need of assistance. An increase in a disabled person's assets over the allowed amount of even $1 can jeopardize the person's benefit status.

> *Example:* Joshua's adult son, Joe, is disabled and receives SSI and other benefits. Joe's grandfather, John, leaves all his grandchildren $25,000 each in his will upon his death. The inheritance of $25,000 may cause Joe to lose all of his benefits.

A special needs trust may be established to insure that the disabled person, often a child, may receive the funds in trust, however, and not lose government benefits and assistance. The funds create a "safe harbor" for those assets because the trust purpose specifically states that it is meant to provide supplemental and extra care only, and not intended to provide basic care for the disabled person and is not meant to provide any care or assistance for those items that are covered by government benefits.

Totten Trusts

As discussed in Chapter 2, Totten Trusts, also known as Pay-on-death (POD) accounts, are actually savings accounts that a depositor, called the trustee, opens for the benefit of another, called the beneficiary (*notice that the creator of the account is not called a trustor!*). During the depositor's lifetime, the depositor may withdraw any or all of the money deposited in the account and is considered the rightful owner of the assets on account. Upon the depositor's death, the money automatically passes to the possession of the beneficiary and does not become part of the depositor's estate.

> *Example:* Sara opens a savings account at First Fidelity Savings and Loan for minor child, Tina. The account shows the depositor as "Sara Small for the benefit of Tina Small." This is all that is necessary to designate a POD account or Totten trust.

> As a matter of note, if such an account is set up with a brokerage firm, the account is called a Transfer on Death account, or TOD, instead but it operates in the same manner.

Figure 9.2   Alan Shapiro Irrevocable Special Needs Trust

THIS TRUST is dated as of this _____ day of _____, 2009, made and entered into by and between the following:

Settlor: ILENE SHAPIRO (hereinafter called "Settlor").

Trustee: ILENE SHAPIRO (hereinafter called "Trustee").

Alternate Trustee: COURTNEY SHAPIRO (also hereinafter called "Trustee" or "Successor Trustee").

WITNESSETH:

WHEREAS, the Settlor, as Conservator for Alan Shapiro by Letters of Qualification certified on May 1, 2007, petitioned the Circuit Court of Anycounty, Anystate on April 20, 2009 and obtained an Order in said Court enabling the Settlor to create a special needs trust for Alan Shapiro; and

WHEREAS, the Settlor desires to create a special needs trust to hold such property itemized and described in "Exhibit A" attached hereto and made a part hereof, together with such monies, life insurance, securities and other assets as the Trustee may hereafter at any time hold or acquire hereunder (all of said property being hereinafter referred to as the "Trust Estate") for the purposes hereinafter set forth.

NOW, THEREFORE, in consideration of the premises and the mutual covenants herein contained, the Settlor agrees to execute such further instruments as shall be necessary to transfer said property to the Trust and the Trustee agrees to hold the Trust estate, IN TRUST, NEVERTHELESS, for the following uses and purposes and subject to the terms and conditions hereinafter set forth:

Article I—Definitions

A. Additions to Corpus

The Settlor, or any other person with the consent of the Trustee, may add to the principal of the Trust created herein by donation, deed, will or otherwise. Such additions shall be covered by the provisions hereof, the same as if originally included herein.

B. Laws Governing

This Agreement shall be construed, enforced and regulated in all respects by the laws of the State of Anystate and in the Courts of the State of Anystate.

C. Beneficiary

ALAN (hereinafter called "ALAN") is a handicapped or disabled person receiving Supplemental Security Income from the Social Security administration Medicaid benefits. During his lifetime, he shall be considered the prime and first beneficiary of this Trust for all purposes and the Trustee shall consider him as the Trustee's primary interest and responsibility. However, all income and principal of the trust estate during the lifetime of ALAN shall be administered, rearranged, held, applied and/or distributed only in strict conformity with the provisions of Article II-C hereof as this trust is made expressly to supplement and not replace any governmental assistance

(continued)

Figure 9.2 (continued)

available or which may in the future be available to ALAN. ALAN is the brother and ward of Settlor.

D. Name of Trust

This Trust shall, for convenience, be known by the name following and it shall be sufficient that it be referred to as such in any deed, assignment, bequest or devise by that name, to wit:

Alan Shapiro Irrevocable Special Needs Trust

E. Education

The term "education" shall include all forms of education including but not limited to, public or private schools, primary or secondary, college, advanced college or post-college, commercial, vocational, technical, business or art education; or otherwise.

Article II—Administration During Lifetime of Settlor

A. Life Insurance

The Settlor may, but need not necessarily, name the Trust Estate as beneficiary of life insurance policies. Furthermore, the Settlor may directly maintain life insurance policies, change beneficiaries thereon, borrow against same, receive dividends thereon, pledge and hypothecate such policies as security for undertakings, exercise any option granted under such policies and may withdraw such policies from this Trust as the owner of the policies wishes.

B. Irrevocability

This trust agreement is irrevocable and may not be changed, amended, altered or revoked except as expressly provided herein. Notwithstanding any provision hereof to the contrary, the Settlor may amend this Agreement to change Trustee, provide replacement or successor Trustee or to comply with provisions of law as may be constituted from time to time. Furthermore, any trustee may amend this agreement to name a replacement or successor trustee to himself or herself in the event of the death, incompetence, or resignation of the amending trustee and/or may amend this agreement to comply with provisions of law or may be constituted from time to time. All amendments shall be made in writing and delivered to the Settlor and ALAN, if living.

C. Lifetime Benefit to or for Ted

During the lifetime of ALAN the Trustee shall manage, invest and reinvest the portion of the Residuary Trust meant for him, collect the income thereof and shall, in the absolute discretion of the Trustee, pay over or apply all of such part of the income and/or principal thereof as the Trustee deems necessary, wise or prudent for: (i) ALAN's use, care, support, maintenance or general welfare or apply same for any such purposes; and (ii) any taxes of any nature, source or amount levied or assessed against ALAN, the Trust Estate, this Trust or the income of ALAN. All undistributed income shall be added to principal. ALAN, from time to time, may refuse receipt of any such

(continued)

Figure 9.2 (continued)

payment or application and may direct that no payment or application be made in his behalf.

Notwithstanding any provision of this Trust Agreement to the contrary, the whole of ALAN's share, income and principal, is only to be used for ALAN's special needs. A Trustee shall have no discretion, to pay or apply income and/or principal to or for the benefit of ALAN for any purpose other than for the special needs of ALAN. The term "special needs" refers to the requisites for maintaining ALAN's good health, safety, and welfare when, in the discretion of the Trustee, such requisites are not being provided by any public or quasi-public agency, office, or department of any state or of the United States. "Special needs" shall include, but not be limited to, medical and dental expenses, insurance therefor, travel, entertainment, programs of training and education, hobby supplies, luxuries, housing, nursing services, psychological and/or psychiatric services, care monitoring and/or management, roommate provision, nurses aides, podiatry and/or chiropractic services, and/or clothing and other daily necessities. This trust is created expressly for ALAN's extra and supplemental care, maintenance, support, and education in addition to and over and above the benefits ALAN receives or may receive from any local, state, or federal government, or from any private agencies, any of which provide services or benefits to disabled or incapacitated persons. It is the express purpose of this Trust that funds be used solely to supplement other benefits received by ALAN and not supplant same. The Trustee shall have no discretion to pay or provide health, food, and home expenses to or for ALAN paid or provided by government or quasi-governmental sources.

It is further the intent of this Trust that no part of the corpus of the trust created herein shall be used to supplant or replace public assistance benefits of any county, state, federal or governmental agency. For purposes of determining ALAN's eligibility for such benefits, no part of the principal or income of the trust estate shall be considered available to ALAN. In the event the Trustee is requested by any department or agency to release principal or income of the trust to or on behalf of ALAN to pay for equipment, medication, or services that other organizations or agencies are authorized to provide, or in the event Trustee is requested by any department or agency administering such benefits to petition the court or any other administrative agency for the release of trust principal or income for this purpose, the Trustee shall deny such request and is directed to defend, at the expense of the trust estate, any contest of this Agreement or other attack of any nature. The Trustee shall have complete discretion with regard to the defense of any such claim, including the management of all litigation which may result. Trustee also shall be authorized, in the Trustee's complete discretion, to settle, in whole or in part, or otherwise compromise any such claim or litigation.

The Trustee, when applying funds for the benefit of ALAN, may apply or give funds to care managers and/or monitors, social service organizations and other professionals who provide care management, personal services or care monitoring services for ALAN. Moreover, the Trustee may pay housing expenses and expenses of live-in care management or a live-in monitor for ALAN.

Note that these paragraphs specifically relate to the fact that the trust assets may only be used for those items of supplemental and extra care for Ted and not for his basic care and those items that are covered by his government benefits.

(continued)

Figure 9.2 (continued)

Should ALAN abandon a home which may be owned by the Trust for benefit of ALAN, or should the Trustee believe that it is not economically sound or otherwise feasible for ALAN to continue to reside in said home, the Trustee may sell the home, after making proper provision for ALAN's living arrangements, and apply the net proceeds to the share of ALAN in the Residuary Trust, to be held pursuant to the provisions of this Agreement.

Article III—Administration Upon Death of Settlor and/or Disabled Person

A. Collection of Insurance Proceeds

The Trustee shall collect the proceeds of any life insurance policies subject hereto when they, by the terms thereof, become payable to the Trust or to the Trustee in their fiduciary capacity, adding any proceeds thereof to the principal of the Trust Estate. Full authority is given to the Trustee to take legal action to collect all such insurance proceeds and to be reimbursed for the costs thereof and any personal liability they may incur due to such litigation from the Trust Estate. No insurance company shall be required to inquire into or take notice of any of the provisions of this Trust Agreement or to see to the application or distribution of the policy proceeds and the receipt of the Trustee or any of them to such insurance company shall be effectual to release and discharge the insurance company for any payment so made and shall be binding upon the beneficiaries of this Trust.

B. Expenses and Cost of Estate Settlement

Upon the death of ALAN, the Trustee shall comply with all laws regarding Trustee's duties and laws as to creditor claims of his Estate and may pay or settle from the Trust Estate all or part of the just debts, funeral, administrative, and inheritance and/or estate tax expenses of his estate and Trust administration as the Trustee deems necessary, wise and/or prudent.

Article IV—Trust Termination

Upon the death of ALAN the balance of the Trust Estate, after the payments aforesaid, if any, this Trust will terminate. At that point, Trustee will distribute free of trust the remaining balance of the Trust Estate to COURTNEY SHAPIRO and MINA SHAPIRO.

Article V—General Provisions

A. Payments to or for Beneficiaries

The Trustee has the sole and absolute discretion to make payments of principal and/or income to a beneficiary of this Trust in one (1) or more of the following four (4) ways as the Trustee deems best in their opinion: (i) directly to such beneficiary; (ii) to the legally appointed guardian or conservator of such beneficiary; (iii) to some relative or friend of the beneficiary for the care, support and/or education of such beneficiary; and/or (iv) by the Trustee, using such amounts directly for such beneficiary's care, support and/or education.

(continued)

Figure 9.2   (continued)

B. Spendthrift Provisions

No disposition, charge, or encumbrance of either the income or principal of any of the separate shares in trust or any part thereof, by any beneficiary hereunder (including the Settlor as beneficiary hereunder) by way of anticipation shall be of any validity or legal effect or be in anywise regarded by the Trustee, and no such income or principal, or any part, shall in anywise be liable to any claim of any creditor for any such beneficiary except in those cases where all of the credit extended, liability, claim, and/or the assignment of the beneficiary's interest hereunder as collateral therefore has first been approved unanimously by all Trustees in the absolute discretion of Trustees. In exercising such discretion, the Trustee shall ascertain whether or not it would appear to be in the best interest of the beneficiary or same would appear to be in the contemplation of the Settlor that credit be accepted, the claim or liability be allowed and collateral given and may, without stated reason, decline to approve such credit, liability, claim and/or assignment.

C. Protection Against Perpetuities

All distributions required by this Trust Agreement and the final accounting of the Trust must be accomplished and finished as provided in this Agreement and, in any event, no later than twenty-one (21) years after the last to die of the expressly named individual beneficiaries noted in Article IV hereof or, if such beneficiaries are all charities, then twenty-one (21) years after the death of the Settlor.

Article VI—Powers and Duties of Trustee

A. Investments and Duties

The Trustee and each Successor Trustee shall have all powers and authority conferred upon Trustee by the laws of the State of Anystate besides such additional powers and authority conferred by the provisions of this Agreement. In exercising such powers the Trustee shall be bound to do only what a reasonably prudent person would do in like circumstances and to make prudent investments.

The Trustee of each Trust established hereunder (including any Successor Trustee) shall have the continuing, absolute, discretionary power to deal with any property, real or personal, held in such Trusts. Such power may be exercised independently and without the prior or subsequent approval of any Court or judicial authority, and no person dealing with such Trustee shall be required to inquire into the propriety of any of the actions of such Trustee. The Trustee shall not be limited to the type, amount, and character of investments in which the Trustee may invest the funds of this Trust, so long as the Trustee uses reasonable prudence and judgment in the selection of investments. In the event there are Co-Trustees hereof, such Co-Trustees are authorized to arrange that any account with any third party titled in the name of the Trustee or this Trust can be dealt with by less than all of the said Co-Trustees; for example, an account or asset that is titled in the name of all Co-Trustees or this Trust can be established or issued in such manner as

(continued)

Figure 9.2   (continued)

to allow for the signature of less than all of the Co-Trustees, including, but not limited to, only one of the Co-Trustees, to act upon such asset or account. The Trustee shall have the following general powers, in addition to, and not by way of limitation of, the powers provided by law:

1. **Retention:** To retain any property for any period whether or not the same be of the character permissible for investments by fiduciaries under any applicable law, and without regard to any effect the retention may have upon the diversification of the investments.

2. **Sell:** To sell, transfer, exchange, convert or otherwise dispose of, or grant options with respect to any security or property, real or personal, including homestead property, held as part of the Trust Estate, at public or private sale, with or without security, in such manner, at such time or times, for such purposes, for such prices and upon such terms, credits, and conditions as the Trustee may deem advisable.

3. **Invest:** To invest and reinvest all or any part of the Trust Estate in any property and undivided interests in property, wherever located, including bonds, debentures, notes, secured or unsecured, stocks of corporations regardless of class, interests in limited partnerships, real estate or any interest in real estate whether or not productive at the time of investment, interests in trusts, investment trusts, whether of the open and/or closed fund types, and insurance contracts on the life of any beneficiary or annuity contracts for any beneficiary, without being limited by any statute or rule of law concerning investments by fiduciaries.

4. **Liquidity:** To render liquid the Trust Estate or any trust created hereunder, in whole or in part at any time or from time to time, and hold cash or readily marketable securities of little or no yield for such period as the Trustee may deem advisable.

5. **Lease:** To lease any such property beyond the period fixed by statutes for leases made by a Trustee and beyond the duration of the Trust Estate or any Trust created hereunder.

6. **Securities:** To join in or become a party to, or to oppose, any reorganization, readjustment, recapitalization, foreclosure, merger, voting trust, dissolution, consolidation or exchange, and to deposit any securities with any committee, depository or trustee, and to pay any and all fees, expenses, and assessments incurred in connection therewith, and to charge the same to principal, to exercise conversion, subscripting or other rights, and to make any necessary payments in connection therewith, or to sell any such privileges.

7. **Vote:** To vote in person at meeting of stock or security holders, or any adjournment of such meetings, or to vote by general or limited proxy with respect to any such shares of stock or other securities held by the Trustee.

8. **Nominee:** To hold securities in the name of a nominee without indicating the trust character of such holding, or unregistered, or in such form as will pass by delivery.

(continued)

Figure 9.2   (continued)

9. **Claims:** To pay, compromise, compound, adjust, submit to arbitration, sell or release any claim or demands of the Trust Estate, or any Trust created hereunder, against others, or of others against the same as the Trustee may deem advisable, including the acceptance of deeds of real property in satisfaction of bonds and mortgages, and to make any payments in connection therewith which the Trustee may deem advisable.

10. **Real Property:** To possess, manage, sell, insure against loss by fire or other casualties, develop, subdivide, control, partition, mortgage, lease or otherwise deal with any and all real property, including homestead property; to satisfy and discharge or extend the term of any mortgage thereon; to execute the necessary instruments and covenants to effectuate the foregoing powers, including the giving or granting of options in connection therewith; to make improvements, structural or otherwise, or abandon the same if deemed to be worthless or not of sufficient value to warrant keeping or protecting; to abstain from the payment of taxes, water rents, assessments, repairs, maintenance or upkeep of the same; to permit to be lost by tax sale or other proceeding or to convey the same for a nominal consideration or without consideration; to set up appropriate reserves out of income for repairs, modernization and upkeep of buildings, including reserves for depreciation and obsolescence, and to add such reserves to principal, and, if the income from the property itself should not suffice for such purposes, to allow in determining the federal estate tax payable by Settlor's estate, to advance any income of the Trust for the amortization of any mortgage on property held in the Trust.

11. **Distributions:** To make distributions in cash or in kind, or partly in cash and partly in kind and to divide, partition, allocate or distribute particular assets or undivided interests therein, without any obligation to make proportionate distributions or to distribute to all beneficiaries property having an equivalent income tax basis, and without regard to any provision of law expressing a preference for distribution in kind, and to value such property to the extent permitted by law, and to cause any share to be composed of cash, property or undivided fractional shares in property different in kind from any other share.

12. **Instruments:** To execute and deliver any and all instruments in writing which are deemed advisable to carry out any of the foregoing powers. No party to any such instrument in writing signed by the Trustee shall be obliged to inquire into its validity.

13. **Trust Funds:** To invest any part or all of the principal of the Trust Estate in any common trust fund, legal or discretionary, which may be established and operated by and under the control of the Trustee.

14. **Allocations:** To determine, irrespective of statute or rule of law, what shall be fairly and equitably charged or credited to income and what to principal notwithstanding any determination by the courts or by any custom or statute, and whether or not to establish depreciation reserves.

(continued)

Figure 9.2 (continued)

15. **Possession:** To allow temporary possession by and make available personal property for the personal use of any beneficiary hereof; if any item(s) of personal property are held in trust by the Trustee for the benefit of such beneficiary.

16. **Employ Experts:** To employ legal counsel, accountants and agents deemed advisable by the Trustee and to pay them reasonable compensation.

17. **Distributions:** Notwithstanding any provision of the Virginia Code to the contrary, a Trustee: (i) may make discretionary distribution of income, or principal, to or for the benefit of such Trustee if otherwise provided in this Agreement; and (ii) may make discretionary allocations of receipts or expenses as between principal and income.

B. Shares

Notwithstanding anything herein to the contrary, the Trustee shall administer any and all Trusts created herein as separate and distinct, but commonly administered shares.

C. Compensation and Accounting

1. **Compensation:** The Trustee shall be entitled to receive fair and reasonable compensation from the Trust Estate (payable at convenient intervals selected by the Trustee) considering: (i) the duties, responsibilities, risks, and potential liabilities undertaken; (ii) the nature of its estate; (iii) the time and effort involved; and (iv) the customary and prevailing charges for services of a similar character at the time and at the place the services are performed. The Trustee shall also receive reimbursement for all reasonable expenses incurred in management and protection of the Trust Estate.

2. **Accounting:** Each Trustee shall render to Settlor, ALAN, and each other Trustee full accounting of such act, payment, distribution, or investment within thirty (30) days of such action. If there are no other Trustees and Settlor is deceased or incompetent, the said acting Trustee shall render such full accounting to the beneficiaries named or alluded to in this Trust Agreement's Article IV.

D. Disability or Incompetency

1. **Definition:** Any Trustee (including Settlor who acts as a Trustee) shall be automatically and forthwith discharged and removed from authority and duties of a fiduciary or trustee hereunder should he or she be deemed disabled or incompetent as defined herein. A Trustee or Settlor ("the questionable trustee") shall be deemed so disabled or incompetent to act as a trustee if any other Trustee hereunder shall receive in his possession any one of the following: **(a)** a writing from the questionable trustee's physician and a writing from a member of the questionable trustee's immediate family or another Trustee stating that the questionable trustee is too disabled or incompetent to make rational or prudent judgments or handle his personal affairs; **(b)** a court order which he deems

(*continued*)

Figure 9.2 (continued)

jurisdictionally proper and currently applicable holding that the questionable trustee is legally incompetent to act in his own behalf or appointing a guardian or conservator of his person and/or property to act for him; **(c)** duly executed, witnessed, and acknowledged written certificates of two (2) licensed physicians (each of whom represents that he or she is certified by a recognized medical board), each certifying that he has examined the questionable trustee and has concluded that, by reason of accident, physical or mental illness, progressive or intermittent physical or mental deterioration or other similar cause, the questionable trustee is incompetent or disabled to act rationally and prudently in the questionable trustee's best interests, the interests of the Settlor or the interest of other beneficiaries hereunder; **(d)** evidence deemed credible and currently applicable that the questionable trustee has disappeared, is unaccountably absent or is being detained under duress and, thus, unable to effectively and prudently look after his financial interests or that of the Settlor or other beneficiaries hereunder; **(e)** proof that the questionable trustee is an inmate of or has entered into confinement, residence, or daily care of a skilled or custodial nursing home, mental institution, jail, or prison; or **(f)** proof that the questionable trustee (or someone in his behalf) has applied for, is being considered for, intends to apply for or is entitled to receive (but for availability of payments or distributions to be made or which may be made under this Agreement) governmental assistance funds based on financial need of such questionable trustee, by reason of the questionable trustee's health, physical, or mental condition.

2. **Restoration of Trusteeship Authority:** If any of the writings, proofs, certificates, or order as noted above in this Subparagraph D be negated, changed, canceled or abrogated to the benefit of the questionable trustee, the questionable trustee (even if it is Settlor) who was removed from fiduciary authority shall automatically be restored to full fiduciary power and authority and rights of decision or election reserved to him by this Agreement.

Article VII—Appointment of Trustee

A. Appointment

Settlor hereby nominates and appoints ILENE SHAPIRO as Trustee of this Trust.

B. Appointment of Successor

1. **Succession:** Upon the death, incompetency, resignation, or discharge of the above named Trustee, the Successor Trustee shall succeed to the position of Trustee. The Settlor may, however, appoint one or more other or replacement Successor Trustees by amendment to this Agreement. A Trustee, Settlor or Beneficiary may amend this Agreement to provide for replacement trustee as noted above in the Agreement.

(continued)

Figure 9.2 (continued)

2. **Resignation:** Any Trustee or Successor Trustee may resign by instrument in writing.
3. **Rights:** Any Successor Trustee shall have all the rights, powers, duties, and discretion conferred or imposed on the original Trustee. No Trustee shall be liable for any act or omission unless the same be due to such Trustee's own default. In no event shall a corporate trustee be a corporation owned or controlled by any beneficiary hereof.
4. **Responsibility:** Any Successor Trustee shall become responsible for the applicable Trust Estate only when, as and if the same shall be received by said Trustee and, in determining such estate, such Trustee shall only be responsible to make a reasonable inquiry from the records of the prior Trustee which are available.
5. **New Appointment:** If none of the above named Trustees or Successor Trustees shall be serving as such, whether by reason of death, resignation, incompetency or discharge, the then current income beneficiary or beneficiaries who are of legal age and the guardians of any incompetent or minor then current income beneficiary or beneficiaries shall appoint a Successor Trustee. Such Successor Trustee must be one (1) or more of such competent beneficiaries of legal age, a trust company, bank or attorney qualified to act as such, and if a bank or trust company, must possess trust powers, and such Successor Trustee must be approved by all such beneficiaries unanimously. In the event the current income beneficiary or beneficiaries shall fail to so designate promptly a Successor Trustee, the then acting Trustee or any beneficiary shall apply to a court of proper jurisdiction for such appointment and for settlement of account. In no event shall such Successor Trustee be a beneficiary who is to be paid his or her share of income and/or principal over a period of time rather than in one sum or who is defined as a minor in this Agreement. In no event shall ALAN SHAPIRO be a Trustee.
6. **Signatures and Decisions:** Except as noted in Article V-B as to creditor claims, all acts, deeds and transactions, including but not limited to, banking, securities, and real estate transactions of any kind, nature or amount, with regard to this Trust Agreement or pursuant thereto, shall require the signature of only one (1) Trustee even though there may be Co-Trustee available to act.

C. Bond

It is Settlor's request and direction that no bond or other security shall be required of any Trustee named hereunder.

D. Discretion

Each decision, act, transaction, and deed of a named Trustee herein shall be deemed discretionary and not subject to judicial review in any jurisdiction unless a fraudulent, wanton, criminal or gross negligent act of a Trustee is first proven against him. No Trustee shall be liable or responsible for an erroneous act or omission made in good faith.

(continued)

Figure 9.2   (continued)

Article VIII—Miscellaneous

The paragraph and article headings used herein are for convenience only and shall not be resorted to for interpretation of this Trust. Wherever the context so requires, the masculine gender shall include the feminine and neuter gender (and vice versa) and the singular shall include the plural (and vice versa). Wherever the terms "Settlors" or "Trustees" (plural) are noted they shall also mean "Settlor" or "Trustee" (singular), as the case may be, and vice versa, unless the context would preclude such interpretation. If any portion of this Trust is judicially held to be void or unenforceable, the balance of this Trust shall nevertheless be carried into effect.

IN WITNESS WHEREOF, the parties specified above as Settlor, the Trustee, and the Successor Trustee have signed and sealed this Trust Agreement as of the _____ day of _____, 2009.

_____
ILENE SHAPIRO, Settlor and Trustee

_____
COURTNEY SHAPIRO, Successor Trustee

The foregoing instrument, consisting of ten (10) typewritten pages and "Exhibit A" attached, was signed, sealed, published and declared by the Settlor in our presence and the presence of each other and we, at the Settlor's request and in Settlor's presence and in the presence of each other, have hereunto subscribed our hands as witnesses this _____ day of _____, 2009.

_____
Witness

_____
Witness

STATE OF ANYSTATE
COUNTY OF ANYCOUNTY

Before me personally appeared ILENE SHAPIRO as Settlor above noted, to me well known and known to me to be the person described in and who executed the foregoing Trust Agreement and who acknowledged to and before me that she executed said instrument in the capacities and for the purposes therein expressed.

WITNESS my hand and official seal this _____ day of _____, 2009.

_____
Notary Public

My Commission expires: _____
My registration number: _____

ACCEPTANCE BY TRUSTEE

The undersigned hereby accept the trust imposed by this Trust Agreement and agree to serve as Trustee or Successor Trustee upon the terms and conditions therein set forth.

(*continued*)

Figure 9.2   (continued)

SIGNED, SEALED, AND DELIVERED IN THE PRESENCE OF:

_____   _____

Witness   ILENE SHAPIRO

_____   _____

Witness   COURTNEY SHAPIRO

EXHIBIT "A"
of the
ALAN SHAPIRO IRREVOCABLE
SPECIAL NEEDS TRUST
dated

_____

TEN ($10.00) DOLLARS

Lady Bird Deeds

As discussed in Chapter 2, a Lady Bird deed is an enhanced life estate deed in which the holder of the life estate also retains the right to transfer the property, by sale or gift, without obtaining the consent of the owner of the remainder interest. If the life estate holder transfers the property, the remainder interest is destroyed, which is different from a traditional life estate. In a traditional life estate, the life estate owner cannot transfer more than his or her interest without the consent of remaindermen. However, if the life estate holder dies before taking any action to transfer the property by sale or gift, it acts as a traditional life estate and passes to the remaindermen.

This is considered a better form of life estate in the instances where a parent, attempting to avoid probate, transfers an interest in her property to her children retaining a life estate to herself. However, the parent has to get the children's consent to mortgage, sell, or gift the property away, sometimes being unable to obtain that consent.

> _Example:_ Carol owns 100 N. Main Street in fee simple. She executes a deed conveying the house to herself and her children. The pertinent part of the deed states
>
> > Carol Shorter, Grantor, for and in consideration of the sum of Ten Dollars ($10.00) cash in hand paid by the Grantee, and other good and valuable consideration, the receipt and sufficiency of which are hereby acknowledged, hereby grants and conveys, without warranty, unto Carol Shorter, Grantee, a life estate in the following described real property, then to Marsha Shorter Wilde and Marta Shorter as joint tenants with right of survivorship.

In this example, Carol's intention was most likely an estate planning tool to convey the property to her children upon her death without the house having to be part of a probate process. However, because it is a traditional life estate, she needs the consent of her children to mortgage the property or sell it.

However, see this example: Carol owns 100 N. Main Street in fee simple. She executes a deed conveying the house to herself and her children. The pertinent part of the deed states

> Carole Shorter, Grantor, for and in consideration of the sum of Ten Dollars ($10.00) cash in hand paid by the Grantee, and other good and valuable consideration, the receipt and sufficiency of which are hereby acknowledged, hereby grants and conveys, without warranty, unto Carol Shorter, Grantee, a life estate, without any liability for waste, with full power and authority in said life tenant to sell, convey, mortgage, lease, or otherwise dispose of the property described herein, in fee simple, with or without consideration, without joinder of the remaindermen, and with full power and authority to retain any and all proceeds generated thereby, and upon the death of the life tenant, the remainder, if any, to Marsha Shorter Wilde and Marta Shorter as joint tenants with right of survivorship as grantees.

This is an example of an enhanced life estate in which Carol retains all ownership rights and does not need her children's consent to handle the property however she likes.

Lady Bird deeds are not valid in but a handful of states. They are called Lady Bird deeds because President Johnson allegedly used this type of deed to convey property to his wife.

Revocable Transfer on Death Deeds

Revocable transfer on death deeds (TOD deeds or *beneficiary deeds*) are similar to "Lady Bird" deeds in that an owner of property deeds the property to a beneficiary but the transfer happens only upon the owner's death. It remains revocable by the owner until that time. Five states have a statutory form for this type of deed: Arizona, Arkansas, Nevada, New Mexico, and Ohio. Four others guide the owner with statutory language that is required to make it a valid TOD deed: Colorado, Kansas, Missouri, and Wisconsin.

Proponents of this type of transfer note its simplicity and its affordability. It is fully revocable during the owner's lifetime, unlike a life tenant deed or a joint with right of survivor deed. All the owner has to do is record the deed and it is valid. Revocation is generally by a formally recorded revocation document, a new TOD document, or an outright sale or transfer to someone other than the owner. The beneficiary does not have to be given notice of the transfer to him or to the revocation.

Opponents note the inherent problems with TOD deeds. One problem is how to determine the owner's capacity. A deed requires contractual capacity while a will execution only requires testamentary capacity, which is a lower standard. Most importantly, however, because they are not subject to probate contest, a person claiming that the transfer was not valid has no mechanism to contest before the property passes to the beneficiary as operation of law. By the time someone contests, the beneficiary could have even sold the property. Other opponents believe that unscrupulous family members can get a simple form at the big box store and induce an older relative into making this type of transfer and it wouldn't be put to the same scrutiny as a will properly drafted by an attorney. Opponents also note that since this only applies to real property, the owner still has to deal with his other property through regular channels and therefore incurs even more cost than necessary.

Pet Trusts

Trusts for pets are becoming more commonplace. Upon death, a deceased person may not leave assets directly to a pet. A **pet trust** is a trust in which an amount is left to a living person, essentially in trust, for the benefit of the care of the pet. Thirty-nine states and the District of Columbia recognize pet trusts. Hotel heiress and billionaire Leona Helmsley left her maltese, Trouble, $12 million, but her heirs fought the bequest in court. Ultimately, Trouble, who lives in Florida with Carl Lekic, the general manager of the Helmsley Sandcastle Hotel, got $2 million, and $10 million went to Mrs. Helmsley's multibillion-dollar charitable foundation. Lawyers Weekly USA stated that the average amount left by pet owners to their pets is $25,000.

Figure 9.3   Massachusetts Trusts for the Care of Animals, Chapter 203, Section 3C

Section 3C. (a) A trust for the care of animals alive during a settlor's lifetime shall be valid. Unless the trust instrument provides for an earlier termination, the trust shall terminate upon the death of the animal or, if the trust was created to provide for the care of more than 1 animal alive during the settlor's lifetime, upon the death of the last surviving animal.

(b) Except as otherwise expressly provided in the trust instrument, no portion of the principal or income shall be converted to the use of the trustee, other than reasonable trustee fees and expenses of administration, or to any use other than for the benefit of covered animals.

(c) A court may reduce the amount of property held by the trust if it determines that the amount substantially exceeds the amount required for the intended use and the court finds that there will be no substantial adverse impact in the care, maintenance, health or appearance of the covered animal. The amount of the reduction shall pass as unexpended trust property in accordance with subsection (d).

(d) Upon reduction or termination, the trustee shall transfer the unexpended trust property in the following order:
    (1) as directed in the trust instrument;
    (2) to the settlor, if living;
    (3) if the trust was created in a nonresiduary clause in the transferor's will or in a codicil to the transferor's will, under the residuary clause in the transferor's will; or
    (4) to the settlor's heirs in accordance with chapter 190.

(e) If a trustee is not designated in the trust instrument or no designated trustee is willing or able to serve, the court shall name a trustee. The court may order the transfer of the property to another trustee if the transfer is necessary to ensure that the intended use is carried out. The court may also make other orders and determinations as are advisable to carry out the intent of the settlor and the intended use of the trust.

(continued)

Figure 9.3   (continued)

> (f) The intended use of the principal or income may be enforced by an individual designated for that purpose in the trust instrument, by the person having custody of an animal for which care is provided by the trust instrument, by a remainder beneficiary, or by an individual appointed by a court upon application to it by an individual or charitable organization.
>
> (g) The settlor or other custodian of an animal for whose benefit the trust was created may transfer custody of the animal to the trustee at or subsequent to the creation of the trust.
>
> (h) A trust created under this section shall be exempt from chapter 184A and the common law rule against perpetuities.

Gifts

What is a Gift and Why Is Gifting Important in Estate Planning?

What is a gift? A **gift** is a transfer of property to another person without any consideration or benefit given in return for the property. A gift may be as simple as a birthday present to your child or friend, or as complicated as a large sum of money to a charity. When you give a gift, you are not expecting anything in return for it and the gift is irrevocable, meaning you cannot take it back. A gift with strings attached may not really be a gift at all.

For estate planning purposes, gifts are made to friends, family, and charities so that the monetary value of certain property is removed from the donor's (the person making the gift) estate at the time of death. Planning for death may seem odd or "creepy" to some, but without adequate planning, some families may pay a great deal of money to the government in taxes. Gifting during life insures that money is removed from a person's estate and they get the added benefit of seeing their donee reap the benefit of the gift.

The Internal Revenue Code provides that, in addition to the lifetime gift tax exemption, for 2012, at $5,120,000 unified with the estate tax exemption (meaning $5,120,000 total for both) and in 2013 of $1 million, a person may make an unlimited number of gifts to an unlimited number of persons (donees) each year. In order not to pay gift tax on those gifts that do not qualify or are in excess of the lifetime exemption, they must be for no more than $13,000 per person. Gifts that are eligible for the annual exemption must be gifts of a present interest. A present interest includes:

- Outright gifts.
- Life estates or life income interests.
- Certain trusts for minors.
- Gifts made to a minor's custodian under the Uniform Gift to Minors Act in which the minor is the owner of gifted property, but the property is held, managed, and distributed by a custodian until the minor reaches the age of majority (state law controls). When the child reaches the age of

majority, the property is given to the now adult child outright and free of the custodial management and control.

- Gifts to trusts with Crummey powers.
- Gifts of life insurance policies, despite the fact that the face amount of the insurance is not going to be received by the beneficiary until either the policy matures or the insured dies.

Certain gifts are exempt from taxation by the Internal Revenue Service:

- Tuition or medical expenses you pay for someone else. For example, no matter how large an amount was paid for the benefit of someone else's education, the amount remains nontaxable.
- Gifts made between spouses.
- Gifts to political organizations.

For 2012 and beyond, the annual gift tax exemption amount is $13,000. Congress may change this amount, however, and it is best to consult the IRS website (www.irs.gov) to determine what the annual exclusion rate will be in the future. As already stated, this is a good way for people to transfer wealth to family and others without having the property subject to estate taxes upon death.

Example: Thomas Tuttle has ten children and grandchildren. He can give each child and grandchild $13,000 in 2012 and transfer $130,000 out of his estate. Married couples can effectively transfer twice that amount each year.

Example: Thomas and Theresa Tuttle have ten children and grandchildren. Thomas can give each child and grandchild $13,000 in 2012, and so can Theresa. Between them they can transfer $260,000 out of their joint estate in 2012 without paying any gift tax.

Note that Thomas cannot give $19,500 to each of his five children and $6500 to each of his five grandchildren. Although the total amount of the gifts adds up to $130,000, any gift in excess of $13,000 would be subject to tax unless it could be offset by the lifetime exemption.

Figure 9.4   Estate Shrinkage of Famous People Who Failed to Plan

Name	Gross Estate	Total Settlement	Net Estate	Percent Shrinkage
Franklin D. Roosevelt	1,940,099	574,867	1,365,232	30%
Humphrey Bogart	910,146	274,234	635,912	30%
Clark Gable	2,806,526	1,101,038	1,705,488	30%
Dean Witter	7,451,055	1,830,717	5,620,338	25%
Walt Disney	23,004,851	6,811,943	16,192,908	30%
Marilyn Monroe	819,176	448,750	370,426	55%
Elvis Presley	10,165,434	7,374,635	2,790,799	73%
J. P. Morgan	17,121,482	11,893,691	5,227,791	69%
John D. Rockefeller Sr.	26,905,182	17,124,988	9,780,194	64%
Frederick Vanderbilt	76,838,530	42,846,112	33,992,418	56%

SUMMARY

Specialized trusts are created to effectuate the trustor's many goals. Often they are created to protect the trust property from creditors and from taxes while providing income for spouses, children, and other family members. Other trusts are created to benefit the public, through the use of charitable trusts.

Spendthrift trusts protect trust property from a beneficiary's creditors. Trustors create spendthrift trusts when their loved ones spend money unwisely, often leaving many creditors in their wake. The spendthrift provisions prevent the creditors from obtaining the trust principal and prevent the beneficiary from alienating his or her interests in the trust.

Sprinkling trusts, also called spray trusts or discretionary trusts, give total discretion to the trustee. The trustee is permitted to pay all of the trust income, and sometimes trust principal, to one or a few beneficiaries who need the money the most, withholding income from those the trustee believes do not need the income.

Marital deduction trusts enable a trustor to pass his or her estate to his or her surviving spouse with the smallest tax bite possible, making use of the deceased spouse's estate exemption credit and the unlimited marital deduction. This insures that not only will the deceased spouse's estate has a reduced taxable estate, it allows the surviving spouse to potentially lower his or her taxable estate upon death as well. One type of marital deduction trust permits the trustor to pass the estate to a surviving spouse for life and then to children and other beneficiaries. Another type of marital deduction trust is a **qualified terminable interest trust** or QTIP trust, which allows the trustor to create a trust which gives a life interest of the trust income to the surviving spouse, while passing the principal to someone else after the spouse's death. These are often used by spouses in second marriages, so that the children from the first marriage are assured an inheritance from their parent.

A life insurance trust (ILIT) is a vehicle in which this irrevocable trust is funded by life insurance on the trustor's life with the trust as the beneficiary. The trust itself owns the policy and upon the trustor's death, the life insurance proceeds become part of the trust. They are then distributed to the beneficiaries pursuant to the trust's provisions. The major benefit of ILITs is that the proceeds are not included in the insured's estate for tax purposes upon the insured's death, and the annual premium payments are gifts of a present interest which remove the premiums from the insured's estate for gift and estate tax purposes.

Charitable gifts are those given to charities for the good of the public at large and not for individuals. A charitable remainder trust is a method of providing income for the trustor during his or her lifetime with the remainder of the trust assets being distributed to a charity upon the trustor's death. Charitable remainder trusts include charitable remainder annuity trusts (CRAT), charitable remainder unitrusts (CRUT), charitable lead annuity trusts (CLAT), and charitable lead unitrusts (CLUT). Pet owners often look for means to take care of their pets after the owner dies. This may be achieved through a pet trust. Although not legal in all states, in those where a pet trust is available, the owner may leave a sum of money to a person for the benefit of the pet's care.

Gifts—transfers of property to another person without any consideration or benefit given in return for the property—are often made during a person's life so that sums of money and wealth will not be taxable upon the person's death. Gifting during life ensures that money is removed from a person's estate and they get the added benefit of seeing their donees reap the benefit of the gifts.

KEY TERMS

charitable remainder trusts	discretionary trusts	Crummey powers
gifts	spendthrift trusts	Crummey notice
pet trusts	qualified terminable interest trust	sprinkling or spray trusts
charitable remainder annuity trusts	charitable remainder unitrusts	irrevocable trusts
life insurance trust	cy pres doctrine	special needs trusts

REVIEW **QUESTIONS**

1. What are the advantages and disadvantages of a sprinkling or spray trust?
2. List the different types of marital deduction trusts.
3. What is a charitable remainder trust?
4. What are Crummey powers?
5. What is the cy pres doctrine?
6. What is the purpose of a spendthrift trust?
7. What is the purpose of a pet trust?
8. What is a special needs trust?
9. What is an ILIT?
10. What is a charitable remainder unitrust?
11. What is the purpose of a gift?

PROJECT

1. Bobbie and Donald Black have been married for 25 years and have three children, Tina, age 23, Todd, age 20, and Ted, age 18. Bobbie and Donald have a very lucrative printing business. The Bobbie's live a comfortable life, and through proper investment planning, will also have a comfortable retirement. They have come to your supervising attorney's office to update their estate plan, which they realize is long overdue. Their current estate plan consists only of reciprocal wills leaving everything to each other and to their children in equal shares if the spouse predeceases. The Black's estate is currently valued at $4 million. Tina is pregnant with her first child, and Todd is a junior in college with plans to continue on to medical school. Ted is just about to graduate from high school. Tina and her husband have just bought their first home. Bobbie and Donald have confided that Todd is a "good kid," but they've had to bail him out of credit card debt more than once. Bobbie and Donald want to provide for their retirement years and for their children's and grandchildren's education, as well as other day-to-day needs. They also want to save as much in taxes as possible.

   Your attorney has asked you to prepare a memo regarding all the possible issues that may arise with Bobbie and Donald. Assume that neither of them will die before 2013. Address the needs for their retirement and for their concerns for their children and grandchildren. Discuss the need for wills, advance directives, and trusts or trust provisions that may be advantageous to them.

2. Review the Boys and Girls Club case below. Summarize the case. Do you think the decision is fair? Why or why not?

MyLegalStudiesLab™   http://www.mylegalstudieslab.com
MYLEGALSTUDIESLAB VIRTUAL LAW OFFICE EXPERIENCE ASSIGNMENTS
Complete the pre-test, study plan, and post-test for this chapter and answer the Legal Applications questions as assigned.

These will help you confirm your mastery of the concepts and their application to legal scenarios. Then complete the Virtual Law Office assignments as assigned by your instructor. These assignments are designed to develop your workplace skills and result in producing documents for inclusion in your portfolio.

Boys and Girls Club of Petaluma v. Walsh, 169 Cal.App.4th 1049 (2008):

BOYS AND GIRLS CLUB OF PETALUMA et al., Plaintiffs and Respondents, v. JAMES J. WALSH, as Cotrustee, etc., et al., Defendants and Appellants.

(Superior Court of Sonoma County, No. SPR74933, Elaine M. Rushing, Judge.)
(Opinion by Jones, P.J., with Needham, J., and Dondero, J., concurring.)

Opinion Jones, P.J.-

Subject to one exception, Probate Code section 15403, subdivision (a)[1] gives the probate court the authority to modify or terminate an irrevocable trust "if all beneficiaries . . . consent[.]" The exception to this general rule is found in subdivision (b), which provides that even if all beneficiaries consent, a court cannot modify or terminate a trust where "the continuance of the trust is necessary to carry out a material purpose of the trust" unless "the court, in its discretion, determines that the reason for doing so under the circumstances outweighs the interest in accomplishing a material purpose of the trust." (§15403, subd. (b).)

In this appeal we must interpret and apply section 15403 to a charitable trust (the Trust) created by Laurence Moore (Moore) in 1993. In the Trust, Moore designated five beneficiaries: The Salvation Army, Guide Dogs for the Blind, Hospice of Petaluma, Boys and Girls Club of Petaluma, and Face to Face of Sonoma County. Among other powers, the Trust gave the trustees broad discretion in two areas: (1) the "discretion to determine the relative amounts or percentages" given to these beneficiaries of the Trust, "including the power to . . . make [a] distribution to one or more of them to the exclusion of others;" and (2) the discretion to name additional beneficiaries and distribute the Trust to them.

Before his death in 2003, Moore named James J. Walsh and Michael E. Wood as successor trustees. After Moore's death, a contentious dispute arose regarding the successor trustees' discretion to identify beneficiaries of the Trust. Over the trustees' objection, the probate court modified the Trust in 2007 pursuant to section 15403. In ordering the modification without first deciding the trustees' petition to ascertain beneficiaries, the probate court gave effect to a settlement agreement reached by the beneficiaries listed in the Trust and a group of other charitable organizations referenced in a hand-written document Moore prepared after the execution of his Trust, and dated four days after his last amendment.

The successor trustees appealed.

There are two questions before us. The first question is whether "all beneficiaries" of the Trust consented to the modification in accordance with section 15403, subdivision (a). The answer to this question is yes. The second question before us is whether the broad discretion conferred upon the trustees constitutes a "material purpose" which would prevent a probate court from modifying the Trust pursuant to section 15403, subdivision (b). The answer to this question is no.

Accordingly, we affirm the probate court's order modifying the Trust.

Factual and Procedural Background

Moore Creates the Trust

Moore created the Trust on March 8, 1993. The Trust was to "be organized and operated exclusively for charitable purposes" and its property was "irrevocably dedicated to charitable purposes[.]" Article V of the Trust provided as follows:

A. Charitable Beneficiaries. The [T]rust shall terminate upon the later of the Grantor's death or ten (10) years from the date this [T]rust is executed. Upon termination [of the Trust], the Trustees shall distribute the entire remaining balance of the [T]rust in such proportions as the Trustees determine in their discretion to the following charitable organizations:

1. THE SALVATION ARMY (Northern California Division).

2. GUIDE DOGS FOR THE BLIND.

3. HOSPICE OF PETALUMA.

4. BOYS AND GIRLS CLUB OF PETALUMA.

5. FACE TO FACE OF SONOMA COUNTY.

6. Such other charitable organization or organizations similar to one or more of the above-named charities, as the Trustees determine in their discretion, provided that such other charities are organized and operated exclusively for charitable purposes within the meaning of Section 501(c)(3) of the Internal Revenue Code and are qualified to receive contributions deductible under Section 170(c)(2) and Section 2055 of the Internal Revenue Code or successor provisions.

B. Distributions. The Trustees are authorized to make the distributions under this Article over a reasonable period of time as determined in the Trustees' discretion, provided that during such distribution period the remaining trust estate shall continue to be managed as provided herein. The Trustees shall have the discretion to determine the relative amounts or percentages to be given to the respective charitable organizations, including the power to distribute more to some of the charities than others, or to make distribution to one or more of them to the exclusion of others.

Moore retained the power to amend the Trust "in whole or in part, by a writing delivered to the Trustee." Moore amended the Trust twice, both times to change the trustees. In a document dated September 8, 1995, and entitled, "Amendment," Moore amended the Trust to name Walsh and Wood (appellants) as successor trustees.[2]

The Discovery of the Disbursement Schedule

Moore died in April 2003. Shortly thereafter, Moore's niece, Marsha J. Moore (Marsha), claimed an interest in Trust assets. During the litigation with Marsha, appellants found several documents in Moore's files, including a handwritten letter from Moore to his then attorney, Robert J. Kwasneski. The letter, dated September 10, 1995, stated, "Enclosed is [a] copy of the disbursement schedule we discussed. There will be changes, of course, as time passes, but I will rest easier with this in place." The letter attached a document entitled, "Schedule For Cash Disbursements to be made Annually as Provided For in the . . . Trust Following the Death of Its Grantor" (Disbursement Schedule). The Disbursement Schedule listed 18 organizations[3] and designated the distributions that each organization would receive annually.

In January 2004, appellants filed a petition for construction of trust documents (petition for construction) seeking construction of the Trust "in light of" the Disbursement Schedule. Appellants acknowledged that they were "unable to locate any evidence that [Moore] did not intend the provisions of [the Disbursement Schedule] to guide [their] discretion." They also noted that the Disbursement Schedule "provide[d] for annual ongoing distributions of the Trust income. [A]nd name[d] charitable beneficiaries in addition to those identified in the [T]rust. . . ." Appellants argued that the Disbursement Schedule "appear[ed] to create an ambiguity" in the Trust because it contemplated "an indefinite term. [A]nd . . . contemplates charitable beneficiaries different from those" listed in the Trust.

Appellants File a Petition to Ascertain Beneficiaries and the Battle Begins

Appellants eventually settled the litigation with Marsha in February 2006 and the Trust received approximately $4.6 million. Shortly thereafter, appellants began to focus on ascertaining beneficiaries and distributing the Trust. In April 2006, they dismissed their petition for construction[4] and filed a petition to ascertain beneficiaries. Appellants stated that they "wish[ed] to be clear" whether the Disbursement Schedule amended the Trust; they explained that they sought "guidance to determine the beneficiaries of the Trust."

But the five beneficiaries listed in the Trust – the Salvation Army, Guide Dogs for the Blind, Hospice of Petaluma, Boys and Girls Club of Petaluma, and Face to Face of Sonoma County – had a different idea. They contended that the Disbursement Schedule did *not* amend the Trust and, as a result, the court should compel appellants to distribute the Trust in "equal shares" to each of them. In November 2006, they filed a petition to compel appellants to distribute the Trust to them and only them (distribution petition). Appellants opposed the distribution petition. They characterized it as "premature" and argued that the legal effect of the Disbursement Schedule must be determined before distributing the Trust. Appellants explained that by ruling on the petition to ascertain beneficiaries, "the Court will answer a basic question crucial to the administration of the [T]rust: 'Who are the beneficiaries of the Trust?' Until that question is answered, the Trustees cannot move forward with distribution, although they are eager to do so." Appellants also argued that granting the distribution petition would preclude them from exercising their discretion to determine Trust beneficiaries and the amounts those beneficiaries would receive. In addition, several respondents opposed the distribution petition, claiming that the Disbursement Schedule amended the Trust to name additional beneficiaries.

In the spring of 2007, appellants and respondents participated in two mediations; both were unsuccessful. The court set a trial date to resolve the petition to ascertain beneficiaries and the distribution petition and ordered the parties to attend a mandatory settlement conference. At the settlement conference, respondents negotiated a settlement among themselves. The settlement agreement defined all respondents as "Beneficiaries" of the Trust and set forth a "percentage beneficial interests" that each beneficiary would receive annually. The settlement agreement also provided that "[t]he Trust shall be modified to reflect the terms of this Settlement Agreement." Appellants did not approve of, nor agree to, the settlement.

The Court Modifies the Trust

In September 2007, respondents filed a petition to modify the Trust (petition to modify). They contended that the court had the authority to modify the Trust pursuant to section 15403, subdivision (a), because "all twenty beneficiaries of the Trust agree to the proposed modifications." The California Attorney General (Attorney General) filed a statement of "No Position."

Appellants opposed the petition to modify. They urged the probate court to deny the petition to modify because "'all the beneficiaries' of the Trust have not consented – indeed, they have not yet even been identified. . . . " In addition, appellants argued that the proposed modification: (1) precluded any charitable organization other than respondents from being considered a beneficiary of the Trust; and (2) prevented appellants "from carrying out the clearly stated purpose and intent of the Trust."

Following a hearing, the probate court granted the petition to modify. The court's November 15, 2007 order stated,

> This matter has been before the Court since May 5, 2003. Section 15403(a) of the Probate Code provides that, unless the continuance of the trust is necessary to carry out a material purpose of the trust, 'if all beneficiaries of an irrevocable trust consent, they may compel modification or termination of the trust upon petition to the court.' Having carefully considered the petition and the trustee's opposition, the Court finds that all beneficiaries have agreed to the proposed modifications and that there is no material purpose of the [T]rust which would necessitate its continuance beyond the distributions to those beneficiaries. [¶] Therefore, the Court hereby approves the modifications [to] the [T]rust embodied in the beneficiaries' settlement agreement. The parties are ordered to confer and agree upon a comprehensive form of order which approves the modifications and which addresses any other . . . matters in this case.

On December 3, 2007, the court entered an order modifying the Trust and dismissing the petition to ascertain beneficiaries and the distribution petition. Appellants timely appealed. In April 2008 – and after appellants appealed – the Attorney General filed a "Consent to Modification of Trust" with the probate court. In it, the Attorney General stated that it "represents the People of the State of California, the ultimate beneficiaries of charity" and that on behalf of the "ultimate beneficiaries of charity, [it] does hereby CONSENT" to the modification of the trust "consistent with the Court's December 3, 2007 Order." We have taken judicial notice of the Attorney General's "Consent to Modification of Trust." The Attorney General has also filed a letter brief in this Court "in support of upholding the trial court's modification of the . . . Trust."

Discussion

Appellants contend the probate court erred in modifying the Trust for two reasons. First, they argue section 15403, subdivision (a), precluded the court from modifying the Trust because all beneficiaries have not been identified and, as a result, could not have consented to the modification. Second, appellants contend that the order modifying the Trust contravenes section 15403, subdivision (b), because the reason for the modification does not outweigh the material purpose of the Trust, specifically their discretion to identify beneficiaries and to distribute the Trust to those beneficiaries.

I. Standard of Review

"An appeal lies from any order made appealable by the Probate Code." (*Esslinger v. Cummins* (2006) 144 Cal.App.4th 517, 522 (*Cummins*); Code Civ. Proc., §904.1, subd. (a)(10).) With two exceptions not relevant here, "the Probate Code permits an appeal to be taken from any final order under Probate Code section 17200 et seq. . . . " (*Cummins, supra,* at p. 522.) An order "[a]pproving or directing the modification or termination of the [T]rust" constitutes a final order under section 17200. (§17200, subd. (b)(13).) The order modifying the Trust is therefore appealable.

The parties disagree on the appropriate standard to review the probate court's application of section 15403, subdivision (a).[5] Appellants contend this case presents "a mixed issue of law and fact" and urge us to apply an " 'independent review' standard." Respondents, however, contend that probate court's ruling with respect to section 15403, subdivision (a), should be reviewed for abuse of discretion pursuant to sections 17200, subdivision (b)(13), and 17206.

[1] The issue of whether all beneficiaries consented to the modification within the meaning of section 15403, subdivision (a), is a question of statutory interpretation and is a pure question of law. (*People ex rel. Lockyer v. Shamrock Foods Co.* (2000) 24 Cal.4th 415, 432; see also *Patton v. Sherwood* (2007) 152 Cal.App.4th 339, 345 (*Sherwood*) [interpretation of section 24 "presents a question of law"].) The first step in statutory construction "is to scrutinize the actual words of the statute, giving them a plain and commonsense meaning." (*Murillo v. Fleetwood Enterprises, Inc.* (1998) 17 Cal.4th 985, 990, internal citations omitted; see also *Olson v. Automobile Club of Southern California* (2008) 42 Cal.4th 1142, 1147.) "If the statutory language is unambiguous, 'we presume the Legislature meant what it said, and the plain meaning of the statute governs.' " (*People v. Toney* (2004) 32 Cal.4th 228, 232, quoting *People v. Robles* (2000) 23 Cal.4th 1106, 1111.)

II. The Order Modifying the Trust Complied with Section 15403, Subdivision (a)

We must first ascertain the meaning of the phrase "all beneficiaries . . . of the trust" set forth in section 15403, subdivision (a). Section 24 defines a beneficiary as "a person to whom a donative transfer of property is made or that person's successor in interest. . . ," including "a person who has any present or future interest, vested or contingent." (§24, subd. (c).) In the context of a charitable trust, section 24 defines a beneficiary as "any person entitled to enforce the trust." (§24, subd. (d).) Applying section 24, we conclude the five beneficiaries named in the trust instrument – The Salvation Army, Guide Dogs for the Blind, Hospice of Petaluma, Boys and Girls Club of Petaluma, and Face to Face of Sonoma County – are beneficiaries who have a "present or future interest, vested or contingent" in the Trust. (§24, subd. (c).) Even if they hold mere "future interests" or "contingent interests," the five named beneficiaries are entitled to enforce the trust pursuant to the plain language of section 24, subdivision (d). These five entities do not lack the status of beneficiaries merely because appellants have not exercised their powers as successor trustees to select the five, or other charitable organizations.

Appellants contend that respondents could not consent to the modification because they "had no vested claim to assets of the Trust, and, in fact, no claim to be beneficiaries at all." To support this argument, appellants rely on *Estate of Quinn* (1958) 156 Cal.App.2d 684, 687-688. In that case, a will directed the residue of the decedent's estate to "'go to charity'" but did not identify a specific charitable purpose or appoint a trustee to select the charity or charities. (*Id.* at p. 685.) The trial court designated three charities. The charities and the decedent's heirs later agreed to receive equal shares of the residue, despite the fact that the will directed the residue to "'go to charity.'" (*Ibid.*) The Attorney General appealed, contending that "the entire residue" of the estate "should have been awarded to charity" and that no portion of the estate should have gone to the heirs. (*Ibid.*)

The appellate court agreed. It held that "[n]either the failure to appoint a trustee . . . nor the failure to designate a specific charitable purpose . . . prevents a court from effectuating the will of the testator." (*Estate of Quinn, supra,* 56 Cal.App.2d at p. 687.) The court also rejected the heirs' claim that the charities consented to the settlement and relinquished their share of the estate residue. (*Id.* at p. 688.) The court explained that the "'consent' of the designated charities" did not sanction diverting "any portion of the residue to a noncharitable purpose" because the interest of the charities had not "vested. . . . The court could have eliminated the charities mentioned and substituted other charities at any time prior to the filing of the decree of distribution." (*Id.* at pp. 689–690.)

Estate of Quinn has no application here for several reasons. First, *Estate of Quinn* stands for the proposition that a charitable bequest is valid even where it does not specify the charity, or the charitable purpose. (See, e.g., *Estate of Clementi* (2008) 166 Cal.App.4th 375, 385; *Estate of Gatlin* (1971) 16 Cal.App.3d 644, 648.) The issue in *Estate of Quinn* was whether the failure to appoint a trustee and designate a charitable purpose prevented the court from giving effect to the testator's will, not whether charities may consent to a proposed distribution. In fact, appellants concede that "*Estate of Quinn* can be distinguished on the grounds that the central issue [in that case] was whether all the assets should have gone to charities rather than being shared with an heir, an issue not raised in the present case." Second, *Estate of Quinn* was decided almost 30 years before section 15403 was enacted.[6] As a result, it has no bearing on whether the probate court properly applied section 15403 here.[7]

Appellants urge an additional ground to reverse the ruling granting the petition to modify. They contend that section 21102, subdivision (a), "compelled" the probate court "to hear and decide" their petition to ascertain beneficiaries before considering the petition to modify. According to appellants, the rationale for this rule in section 21102 is that not all beneficiaries could consent to the modification because appellants had not yet identified all beneficiaries. Appellants urge that it was "'a miscarriage of justice'" to modify the trust pursuant to section 15403 without first making a determination of whether Moore had intended to amend the Trust with his Disbursement Schedule.[8]

[2] We disagree. Section 21102, subdivision (a), is found within Part 1 of Division 11 of the Probate Code, which deals with "Rules for Interpretation of Instruments." (§§21101-21135.) It provides that "[t]he intention of the transferor as expressed in the instrument controls the legal effect of the dispositions made in the instrument." Section 21102 does not require a probate court to hear and decide a petition to ascertain beneficiaries before a petition to modify. The cases appellants cite do not establish otherwise. Moreover, subdivision (b) of section 21202 provides that the "rules of construction in this part apply where the intention of the transferor is *not* indicated by the instrument." (Italics

added.) Here, the Trust expresses Moore's intent. The Trust states that it is to "be organized and operated exclusively for charitable purposes" and that its property is "irrevocably dedicated to charitable purposes[.]" As a result, we must reject appellants' argument that section 21102 required the probate court to determine their petition to ascertain beneficiaries before considering respondents' petition to modify.

Moreover, section 17202 enables a probate court to "dismiss a petition if it appears that the proceeding is not reasonably necessary for the protection of the interests of the trustee or beneficiary." As stated above, "all beneficiaries" consented to the modification within the meaning of section 15403, subdivision (a). As a result, appellants' petition to ascertain beneficiaries was "not reasonably necessary for the protection" of the beneficiaries' interests. Under the facts of this case, the probate court was not required to elevate the interest of appellants, the successor trustees, in exercising their power to choose beneficiaries and allocate trust assets over the interest of the named charitable beneficiaries in accomplishing a distribution and closure of the proceedings.

III. The Order Modifying the Trust Did Not Contravene Section 15403, Subdivision (b)

[3] As stated above, section 15403, subdivision (b) creates an exception to the general rule set forth in subdivision (a). Pursuant to subdivision (b), a court may not modify or terminate a trust where "the continuance of the trust is necessary to carry out a material purpose of the trust . . . unless the court, in its discretion, determines that the reason for doing so under the circumstances outweighs the interest in accomplishing a material purpose of the [T]rust." (§15403, subd. (b).)

Here, the probate court determined that there was "no material purpose of the [T]rust which would necessitate its continuance beyond the distributions to those beneficiaries." Appellants contend the court was incorrect and that the modification contravenes section 15403, subdivision (b). According to appellants, the modification "impaired" a material purpose of the Trust, specifically, their "broad discretion" to identify beneficiaries and to distribute the Trust to those beneficiaries. Respondents disagree and argue that appellants' discretion was not a material purpose of the trust.

Assuming for the sake of argument that appellants' discretion is a material purpose, the reasons for modifying the Trust clearly outweigh the interest in permitting appellants to exercise their discretion.[9] Moore created the Trust with the intent that his estate would be "dedicated to charitable purposes[.]" The Trust directed the trustees to "distribute the trust estate as provided in Article V of this trust," specifically, to make distributions to the beneficiaries "over a reasonable period of time as determined in the Trustees' discretion." Moore died in April 2003. Over five years have passed since his death, and not a penny of his estate has been "dedicated to charitable purposes" or distributed to charitable organizations. While we are mindful that appellants spent much of the intervening time litigating with Marsha, we also recognize that remanding this case to the probate court to permit appellants to identify beneficiaries and determine whether the Disbursement Schedule amended the Trust, would be costly and time-consuming; it would further delay the distribution of an estate likely to be further diminished by litigation expenses. The modification unquestionably accomplishes Moore's overriding goal of dedicating [sic] the Trust to charity.

Appellants' reliance on *Estate of Gilliland* (1974) 44 Cal.App.3d 32, 40 (*Gilliland*), does not alter our conclusion. In that case, the decedent's nieces and nephews reached an agreement with various charities to distribute the decedent's estate. (*Id.* at p. 36.) The probate court approved the agreement, concluding that it was in the "best interests" of the trust to approve the agreement. (*Ibid.*) The trustees appealed, contending that "the probate court committed error in approving the [ ] agreement made without their consent, which would result, if executed, in a substantial modification of the trust as created in the will without recognizable justification for such modification." (*Ibid.*)

The appellate court agreed and reversed the order approving the settlement. (*Gilliland, supra,* 44 Cal.App.3d at p. 36.) The *Gilliland* court explained that "'the [probate] court should not permit a deviation simply because the beneficiaries request it where the main purpose of the trust is not threatened and no emergency exists or is threatened,' [citation], for the power to modify a trust must be exercised 'sparingly and only in the clearest of cases' [citation]. Deviation is not justified merely because it would be more advantageous to the beneficiaries or would offer an expedient solution to problems of trust management." (*Id.* at p. 39, quoting *Crocker-Citizens National Bank v. Younger* (1971) 4 Cal.3d 202, 211.) *Gilliland* is inapposite for two reasons. First, it was decided before section 15403 was enacted and, as a result, it is of limited value here. Second, and unlike *Gilliland,* there were "recognizable justification[s]" for the modification at issue here, specifically avoiding the cost, delay, and potential for further litigation associated with permitting appellants to exercise their discretion to select different or additional beneficiaries.

[4] By impliedly concluding that the reasons for the modification outweighed the interest in accomplishing a material purpose of the Trust, the probate court did not – as appellants argue – "inappropriately put expediency ahead of the principles of trust law embodied in . . . section 15403." The probate court simply concluded that the time had finally come to honor Moore's intent and distribute his estate to charity. Section 15403, subdivision (b) "gives the court some discretion in applying the material purposes doctrine . . . " and was "intended to provide some degree of flexibility in applying the material purposes doctrine in situations where transfer of the beneficiary's interest is not restrained." (Cal. Law Revision Comm., 54 West's Ann. Prob. Code, foll. §15403, p. 576.) The probate court properly exercised its discretion here.

Disposition

The order modifying the Trust is affirmed. Respondents are awarded costs on appeal.

Needham, J., and Dondero, J., concurred.

"Note that these paragraphs specifically relate to the fact that the trust assets may only be used for those items of supplemental and extra care for Ted and not for his basic care and those items that are covered by his government benefits."

NOTES

1. Unless otherwise noted, all further statutory references are to the Probate Code.
2. The relevant amendment states that Moore "revokes . . . and amends Paragraph A of Article VI" to appoint appellants as co-trustees. Paragraph A of Article VII is titled "Appointment of Trustee," while Article VI speaks to a different subject, "Trustee Powers."
3. The organizations listed in the Disbursement Schedule are: (1) Sonoma State University; (2) Hillsdale College; (3) Walla Walla College; (4) Auburn Adventist Academy; (5) Pine Hills Junior Academy; (6) KQED/Ch. 9-Signal Society; (7) Petaluma Boys and Girls Club; (8) Habitat for Humanity; (9) U.S. Naval Academy Alumni Association; (10) U.C. Berkeley Alumni Association; (11) University of Texas M.D. Anderson Cancer Center; (12) Canine Companions for Independence; (13) Guide Dogs for the Blind; (14) Council on Aging; (15) Hospice of Petaluma; (16) Petaluma Kitchen; (17) St. Anthony Foundation; and (18) Humane Society of Sonoma County. Guide Dogs for the Blind, Hospice of Petaluma, and Boys and Girls Club of Petaluma are named in the Trust and in the Disbursement Schedule. The Salvation Army and Face to Face of Sonoma County are named in the Trust but are not listed in the Disbursement Schedule. Together, the Trust and the Distribution Schedule list 20 charitable organizations. These organizations are respondents in this appeal.
4. Appellants apparently believed that the issues raised in the petition for construction, "the identities of the beneficiaries and the duration of the [T]rust[,]" could "be resolved outside the courtroom."

5. The parties agree that the court's application of section 15403, subdivision (b), is reviewed for abuse of discretion.

6. Former section 15403 was added by the Legislature in 1986. (Stats. 1986, ch. 820, §40, p. 2756; repealed by Stats. 1990, ch. 79, §14, p. 934 (Assem. Bill No. 759).) The current version of section 15403 continued former section 15403 without change. (Stats. 1990, ch. 79, §14, p. 934 (Assem. Bill No. 759); 54 West's Ann. Prob. Code (1991) foll. §15403, p. 576.)

7. While the petition to modify was pending in the probate court, the Attorney General filed a statement of "No Position." After appellants filed their notice of appeal, however, the California Attorney General filed a "Consent to Modification of Trust" in the probate court. Citing *Holt v. College of Osteopathic Physicians & Surgeons* (1964) 61 Cal.2d 750, 754, the Attorney General stated that it represents the People of the State of California, the ultimate beneficiaries of charity, and that it thereby gave all beneficiaries, named and unnamed, representation in the modification proceeding. By consenting to the modification on behalf of all unnamed beneficiaries, the Attorney General argued that the strictures of section 15403, subdivision (a), were satisfied. (See generally, *Sherwood, supra,* 152 Cal.App.4th at p. 346.) Thus, the Attorney General has endorsed the trial court's order. We took judicial notice of the Attorney General's consent. We do not rely on it, because it was not before the probate court.

8. Appellants assert a variation of this argument when they argue that until "'all the beneficiaries'" were identified by the Trustees — which might include beneficiaries from a class of "other [unnamed] charitable organization or organizations" — it was error for the probate court to authorize a section 15403 modification. We reject this point for the same reasons we reject its close cousin, which emphasized the five entities' lack of a "vested interest," as we have already explained.

9. Because we reach this conclusion, we need not determine whether appellants' discretion is a "material purpose" of the Trust. We note, however, that section 15403 does not define "material purpose." The parties have not cited, and we have not found, any cases defining "material purpose" in the context of section 15403.

Chapter **ten**

THE PERSONAL REPRESENTATIVE

The function of a **personal representative**, also called the *executor*, is to collect the testator's property, manage it, and pay debts and expenses of the estate during the probate process, and ultimately distribute the property pursuant to the testator's will, or if the decedent died intestate, to distribute the property pursuant to state statute (wherein the personal representative is usually called the *administrator*). Usually, the task of being a personal representative is straightforward. It can, however, be a difficult task if the beneficiaries and heirs are squabbling or demanding, or when the testator had many debts or assets.

For these reasons, the personal representative must be capable of handling the demands of administering the testator's estate. The testator usually chooses a spouse or a child, to act as personal representative, but sometimes will choose a corporate entity, such as a bank trust department instead.

The surviving spouse, child, or friend, recently learning that he or she has been chosen for this task, is unfamiliar with the probate and estate administration processes and often needs help. The paperwork and forms are daunting. The paralegal is often called upon to assist the personal representative in the administration of the testator's estate, which includes assisting in filling out paperwork, contacting life insurance companies, and talking to human resource personnel as well as general hand-holding of the personal representative during the process.

Types of Personal Representatives
Named in the Will

When the person named to administer the decedent's estate is so named in the will, he or she may be called:

- personal representative
- executor (**executrix** is the female form but is not commonly used anymore because the masculine is used in a gender neutral manner for all individuals)

- independent executor
- successor personal representative or alternate personal representative (or executor), if not the first choice

The choice of title is dependent upon statutory language so it is imperative of a paralegal to know which term is used in his or her state statute.

A testator may appoint a corporate entity, such as a bank trust department, as personal representative instead of a person.

Example: Bobbie Black's will states in part:

I hereby nominate and appoint First Bank of Anytown, or its successors or assigns, as my personal representative under this my Last Will and Testament.

Use of the terminology "successors or assigns" permits the bank to be personal representative under circumstances in which the entity has changed names or ownership. Otherwise, if the bank had changed names or ownership, a new person or entity would have to be appointed.

Intestate Decedent

When a decedent dies without a will, he or she is intestate. Not having executed a will means that no personal representative has been named. In this situation, a person or entity must be appointed to administer the decedent's estate. This person is given a different title than the one named in a will; usually that title is that of administrator.

State statute determines the priority list used to select the administrator, but customarily, the surviving spouse will be appointed first, adult children will be appointed second, followed by remaining next of kin or heirs. If all possible appointments fail because no next of kin are living, or if none accept the responsibility or qualify, the court may appoint any other person who has expressed an interest in administering the estate. This includes friends and even creditors of the decedent. If none of the people in this category step forward or qualify, the court will appoint a public administrator. The public administrator is determined by state statute and may be a local attorney or someone in public office designated to take over when no one else does; for example, in West Virginia, that person, strangely enough, can even be the County Sheriff.

Successor Personal Representative

Choosing an alternate, or successor personal representative, while not legally necessary, is a prudent decision for any testator to make. If for any reason, the testator's first choice cannot or is unwilling to serve, the alternate named may take over after being sworn and given testamentary letters, eliminating the process of having an administrator appointed.

Example: Roberta Carter's will states in part:

I nominate and appoint my husband, DONALD CARTER, to be my Executor. If he should, for any reason, fail to qualify, or having qualified, cease to act in such capacity, I nominate and appoint DONALD CARTER, JR., to be my alternate Executor, as my husband's successor, upon like terms. If administration of my estate should be necessary in any jurisdiction where my Executor is unable to qualify, or if my Executor deems it necessary for any other reason, I give to my Executor the power to designate any individual or corporation with trust powers to serve with my Executor or in my Executor's stead. I request that no security or bond be required of any Executor, except for any corporate executor named or appointed in the preceding sentence, which shall be required to post security or a bond. References in my will to my "Executor" are to the one or ones acting at the time, except where otherwise specifically provided.

Notice that the testator provides that the personal representative may designate another individual or corporation to fulfill the duties if for some reason either the personal representative or the alternate cannot. The provision also states that an individual personal representative should not have to post a bond or security, but a corporate entity will post one.

Administrator with Will Annexed

When a testator dies, and his or her choice or choices for personal representative either predeceased him or her or fail to qualify and no other person has been named in the will or appointed by the personal representative(s), the person finally chosen to administer the estate is called the administrator with the will annexed or **administrator cum testamento annexo** (although most often, the person is just called "administrator"). This is usually abbreviated "administrator c.t.a."

Example: When Roberta Carter died, she named her husband, Donald, as her personal representative of her will. Unfortunately, Donald predeceased Roberta. Her successor personal representative was their son, Donald Jr. Donald Jr. could not act for some reason and declined the nomination. Roberta's will did not provide for another alternate personal representative. Tina petitioned to administer the estate and was appointed. Because Tina was not named in Roberta's will as personal representative, she was given the title administrator with will annexed (administrator c.t.a.).

Special Administrator

A special administrator is appointed in emergency situations. The regular appointment process may be very slow in some jurisdictions, and there are occasions when the need for someone to administer the estate is immediate. The special administrator is appointed only for the time it takes to complete the regular appointment process and only for a special purpose. The special administrator's powers will end as soon as the regular personal representative or administrator is appointed.

Administrator Pendente Lite or Administrator Ad Litem

An **administrator pendente lite** is appointed when there is a will contest, and when the court hearing the contest believes that the personal representative should not handle the administration of the estate during the pendency of the suit. While the suit is pending, the administrator pendente lite will serve as a temporary administrator. His or her sole function is to preserve the estate's assets during the pendency of the lawsuit.

An ***administrator ad litem*** is appointed for lawsuits other than a will contest. When the decedent dies, he or she may have had an interest in, or have been a party to, a lawsuit. The administrator ad litem is appointed to represent the decedent in the lawsuit until the personal representative named in the will or administrator of an intestate testator can be properly appointed, at which time, the personal representative will step in and represent the estate in the lawsuit.

Appointment

When the personal representative is appointed, he or she is given a document called **Letters Testamentary**, also called Letters of Appointment. This document is a formal authority establishing the personal representative's right to represent the decedent's estate in all matters. If an administrator is appointed, the document is called **Letters of Administration** instead.

The personal representative or administrator will take an oath stating that he or she will faithfully fulfill his or her fiduciary duties. In some jurisdictions, the personal representative will take the oath before a notary public by written affidavit, while in other jurisdictions he or she is required to take the oath in person. Once the oath is taken and the letters of appointment are granted, the personal representative has the duty and obligation to administer the deceased's estate.

Personal Representative's Duties

The paramount duties of the personal representative (or administrator) are to collect the decedent's assets and preserve them; pay any debts, taxes, and estate expenses; and then distribute the assets according to the will provisions or intestate succession.

The bundle of obligations the personal representative has is called "***fiduciary duties.***" These duties require the personal representative to act in good faith solely on behalf of the estate and its beneficiaries. This is a position of trust and loyalty and must be undertaken with proper regard for the position, as well as the obligations that come with the position.

Of course, the personal representative's actual duties must necessarily be broad. Otherwise, the personal representative would be unable to collect assets, preserve them, and distribute them properly. Wills generally state that the personal representative is granted all powers allowed by law and incorporate all such laws into the will by reference, meaning that, even if they are not enumerated, they are nonetheless part of the will.

Example: Richard Wall's will states in part:
In addition to the powers granted by law, I grant my Executor the powers set forth in Section 15.1-2 of the Code of Anystate, as in force from time to time, and I incorporate that Code Section in my will by this reference.

A will may also enumerate a laundry list of powers the personal representative may invoke, if necessary, to carry out his or her role and fulfill his or her obligations to the estate. Most wills also contain a blanket clause that this list is not exclusive and that any other power enumerated by state statute, and not specifically forbidden in the will, is also permitted. A list of potential duties of the personal representative includes the following:

- Locate the will and if the original cannot be found, have a safe deposit opened to find it. Hire an attorney to assist with the probate.
- Notify post office of death and have mail forwarded to the personal representative.
- Obtain taxpayer ID number for estate.
- Open an estate bank account.
- Give notice to heirs and beneficiaries (and to anyone who has demanded notice) with proof of notice to court, as well as a list of those who received the notice.
- Give notice to known creditors. Notice by publication may also be required for any unknown creditors of the probate of the estate. Publication is generally in a newspaper of general circulation in the county where the probate is filed. It is usually published once a week, two weeks in a row. An affidavit of publication is then sent from the newspaper and the personal representative files that affidavit with the court as proof of publication.
- Notify all other possible interested parties, including the decedent's business associates, banks, investment advisors, accountants, and lawyers of the appointment.
- Search for assets of decedent, which entails going through all of the decedent's records and belongings, and opening and inventorying the decedent's safe deposit box, if any.
- The personal representative also often has the responsibility of selling the decedent's real estate if there is no surviving spouse living on the premises. Real estate must be secured and locks are usually changed to insure that anxious heirs do not help themselves to assets that don't belong to them. Sometimes the personal representative will have to manage leasehold property that belonged to the decedent as well. It should be noted that in some states the will must state that the personal representative has the power of sale over the real estate or a court will have to give the representative an order granting that authority. An administrator must always get an order granting the power of sale over real estate if a sale is required.
- Obtain copies of all of decedent's records including bank statements, brokerage statements, canceled checks, and income tax returns.
- Establish values for all stocks and bonds, and all other assets as of decedent's date of death. The personal representative will usually enlist financial advisors and appraisers for this task. The personal representative will also have to determine how to collect the assets from each source, and deposit all the assets in the estate bank account.
- Coordinate with decedent's business partners, if any, regarding winding up of decedent's business, if there was a business. If the decedent had a business, the personal representative will have to determine which of the business's assets belong to the decedent upon his or her death. These assets will have to be valued and collected as well. If the decedent was a sole proprietor, the personal representative will have the task of either winding up

the business or selling it off to another, and depositing all the proceeds therefrom into the estate bank account.

- Collect all assets that were still due and owing to the decedent or the estate, and are held by others (such as retirement and life insurance accounts, which while they are not probate assets, often fall to the personal representative to obtain for the heirs or beneficiaries).

- Fill out paperwork for life insurance, annuity, and retirement and pension account disbursals, unless the beneficiary does it himself or herself.

- Notify Social Security Administration (SSA) and Veterans Administration of death, and obtain any death benefits as well as refund payments made after the date of death (if the decedent's check was deposited electronically, SSA will automatically electronically draft any funds paid after the decedent's death).

- Determine whether claims against the estate are valid. Valid claims should be paid if possible (if the estate is insolvent, this may not be possible). If necessary negotiate with the creditor to pay the claim.

- Prepare an inventory and appraisal of assets of the estate. Hire an appraiser when necessary. The inventory includes reasonable detail and estimated value of each asset. If an appraiser has been hired, a copy of the appraisal documents must be included with the inventory when it is filed with the court (not all states require that it be filed instead only requiring notification and copies to those beneficiaries and heirs that request the inventory).

- Determine priority of payment of assets for taxes and any allowances, such as family and homestead allowances. Determine distribution of remaining assets.

- Keep records of all receipts and disbursements of the estate.

- Prepare an estate accounting, which lists the value and distribution of the estate assets, including all amounts paid from the estate to pay bills as well as taxes and distributions to heirs and beneficiaries.

- Arrange for burial or cremation of decedent.

- Close out decedent's personal bank accounts.

- Cancel decedent's cable, satellite, utilities, cell phone, memberships in organizations, and other of decedent's obligations that will no longer be necessary.

- Arrange for care of decedent's spouse, if decedent was spouse's caretaker.

- Cancel decedent's credit cards.

- Notify Medicare of the death, as well as Medicaid, if decedent was receiving Medicaid benefits.

- Clean out closets, storage units, and all other places where decedent stored assets and hold an estate sale, if necessary.

- Pay all lawful debts of the decedent and the estate, and sell assets as may be necessary to pay all such debts and expenses of the estate.

- Manage all of the estate's assets and comply with the prudent investor rules in doing so. The personal representative must always act in a fiduciary capacity. The personal representative must always keep a detailed account of all funds taken in and paid out of the estate. These details will be needed for the estate accountings.

- Prepare and file all applicable tax returns, including the decedent's last income tax returns (state and federal), income tax returns of the estate and estate tax returns, if required, and pay any taxes due. The personal representative may hire an accountant to prepare the documents on his or her behalf.
- Make distributions of estate assets to the beneficiaries as required, and make a final distribution of the estate assets when authorized to do so.
- All other tasks necessary to disburse decedent's assets and pay and close decedent's financial obligations.

As can be seen, these powers are very broad and are given in such a manner so that personal representative can discharge his or her duties fully. A personal representative may never have need of all of these duties, but the comprehensive nature of them insures that the personal representative will always have whatever powers may be necessary without having to petition a clerk or court to do so.

Some states require a personal representative to sign an affidavit swearing that he or she will uphold the responsibilities of office. Others ask the personal representative to actually swear in person before the judge or a clerk of court.

THE PROFESSIONAL PARALEGAL

The paralegal often takes an active role in assisting the personal representative in his or her job as fiduciary. The paralegal may draft necessary documents and letters, speak with banks and other institutions, prepare and file estate tax returns, and otherwise assist the supervising attorney guide the personal representative during the estate administration process.

Bond

In most states, the personal representative must post a bond or security unless excused from giving the bond. Excuse from a bond is generally only granted if the testator's will explicitly states that a bond is not required, as shown in the example in the section on appointment of the personal representative. Some states will require a bond of a non-resident of the state regardless of what the decedent's will states. A *bond*, also called a **surety bond**, is the written promise by the personal representative that he or she will faithfully perform his or her duties. This promise is secured by an amount of money set by the clerk or court appointing the personal representative. The bond is usually an insurance policy insuring that if the personal representative breaches his or her duties in any way (but most times is for theft or squandering the assets), the policy will pay for the damages. If the personal representative obtains a traditional bond, the insurance company will keep a portion of the amount paid as its fee and refund the remainder; however, if it has to pay on the policy, the personal representative will have to pay whatever amount is required pursuant to the policy requirements. This requires an application and a showing by the personal representative that he or she has decent credit. A personal representative can be denied a bond due to poor credit history. In some circumstances, the clerk or court may instead require a percentage of the amount set as "bond" to be paid into a registry instead. The percentage is returned when the estate administration is over, and the personal representative is discharged by the court. If the personal representative fails to perform his or her duties, the remaining sum will be paid to the court as a penalty.

Figure 10.1 California Affidavit of the Personal Representative

DE-147

ATTORNEY OR PARTY WITHOUT ATTORNEY *(Name, state bar number, and address):*

John Jones, 121
Main Street,
Noplace, CA
11111, Bar ID
#1234567

TELEPHONE NO.: 555-555-1234   FAX NO. *(Optional):*

E–MAIL ADDRESS *(Optional):* jjones@jonespc.com

ATTORNEY FOR *(Name):* Mandy Livermore, Personal Representative

SUPERIOR COURT OF CALIFORNIA, COUNTY OF

STREET ADDRESS:

MAILING ADDRESS:

CITY AND ZIP CODE:

BRANCH NAME:

ESTATE OF *(Name):*

DECEDENT

DUTIES AND LIABILITIES OF PERSONAL REPRESENTATIVE
and Acknowledgment of Receipt

CASE NUMBER:

To keep other people from seeing what you entered on your form, please press the Clear This Form button at the end of the form when finished.

DUTIES AND LIABILITIES OF PERSONAL REPRESENTATIVE

When the court appoints you as personal representative of an estate, you become an officer of the court and assume certain duties and obligations. An attorney is best qualified to advise you about these matters. You should understand the following:

1. MANAGING THE ESTATE'S ASSETS

a. Prudent investments
You must manage the estate assets with the care of a prudent person dealing with someone else's property. This means that you must be cautious and may not make any speculative investments.

b. Keep estate assets separate
You must keep the money and property in this estate separate from anyone else's, including your own. When you open a bank account for the estate, the account name must indicate that it is an estate account and not your personal account. Never deposit estate funds in your personal account or otherwise mix them with your or anyone else's property. Securities in the estate must also be held in a name that shows they are estate property and not your personal property.

c. Interest-bearing accounts and other investments
Except for checking accounts intended for ordinary administration expenses, estate accounts must earn interest. You may deposit estate funds in insured accounts in financial institutions, but you should consult with an attorney before making other kinds of investments.

d. Other restrictions
There are many other restrictions on your authority to deal with estate property. You should not spend any of the estate's money unless you have received permission from the court or have been advised to do so by an attorney. You may reimburse yourself for official court costs paid by you to the county clerk and for the premium on your bond. Without prior order of the court, you may not pay fees to yourself or to your attorney, if you have one. If you do not obtain the court's permission when it is required, you may be removed as personal representative or you may be required to reimburse the estate from your own personal funds, or both. You should consult with an attorney concerning the legal requirements affecting sales, leases, mortgages, and investments of estate property.

2. INVENTORY OF ESTATE PROPERTY

a. Locate the estate's property
You must attempt to locate and take possession of all the decedent's property to be administered in the estate.

b. Determine the value of the property
You must arrange to have a court-appointed referee determine the value of the property unless the appointment is waived by the court. You, rather than the referee, must determine the value of certain "cash items." An attorney can advise you about how to do this.

c. File an inventory and appraisal
Within four months after Letters are first issued to you as personal representative, you must file with the court an inventory and appraisal of all the assets in the estate.

Page 1 of 2

Form Adopted for Mandatory Use
Judicial Council of California
DE-147 [Rev. January 1, 2002]

DUTIES AND LIABILITIES OF PERSONAL REPRESENTATIVE
(Probate)

Probate Code, § 8404

(continued)

Figure 10.1 (continued)

ESTATE OF (Name):	CASE NUMBER:
ROLAND LIVERMORE DECEDENT	

d. File a change of ownership
At the time you file the inventory and appraisal, you must also file a change of ownership statement with the county recorder or assessor in each county where the decedent owned real property at the time of death, as provided in section 480 of the California Revenue and Taxation Code.

3. NOTICE TO CREDITORS

You must mail a notice of administration to each known creditor of the decedent within four months after your appointment as personal representative. If the decedent received Medi-Cal assistance, you must notify the State Director of Health Services within 90 days after appointment.

4. INSURANCE

You should determine that there is appropriate and adequate insurance covering the assets and risks of the estate. Maintain the insurance in force during the entire period of the administration.

5. RECORD KEEPING

a. Keep accounts
You must keep complete and accurate records of each financial transaction affecting the estate. You will have to prepare an account of all money and property you have received, what you have spent, and the date of each transaction. You must describe in detail what you have left after the payment of expenses.

b. Court review
Your account will be reviewed by the court. Save your receipts because the court may ask to review them. If you do not file your accounts as required, the court will order you to do so. You may be removed as personal representative if you fail to comply.

6. CONSULTING AN ATTORNEY

If you have an attorney, you should cooperate with the attorney at all times. You and your attorney are responsible for completing the estate administration as promptly as possible. **When in doubt, contact your attorney.**

NOTICE:	1. This statement of duties and liabilities is a summary and is not a complete statement of the law. Your conduct as a personal representative is governed by the law itself and not by this summary.
	2. If you fail to perform your duties or to meet the deadlines, the court may reduce your compensation, remove you from office, and impose other sanctions.

ACKNOWLEDGMENT OF RECEIPT

1. I have petitioned the court to be appointed as a personal representative.

2. My address and telephone number are (specify):

   435 Palm Street, Noplace, CA 11111. 555-555-2345

3. I acknowledge that I have received a copy of this statement of the duties and liabilities of the office of personal representative.

Date: July 1, 2012

Mandy Livermore	▶	
(TYPE OR PRINT NAME)		(SIGNATURE OF PETITIONER)

Date: July 1, 2012

	▶	
(TYPE OR PRINT NAME)		(SIGNATURE OF PETITIONER)

CONFIDENTIAL INFORMATION: If required to do so by local court rule, you must provide your date of birth and driver's license number on supplemental Form DE-147S. (Prob. Code, § 8404(b).)

DE-147 [Rev. January 1, 2002]	**DUTIES AND LIABILITIES OF PERSONAL REPRESENTATIVE** (Probate)	Page 2 of 2

For your protection and privacy, please press the Clear This Form button after you

Save This Form	Print This Form	Clear This Form

Figure 10.2 Montana Affidavit of the Personal Representative

Acknowledgement of Fiduciary Relationship and Obligations
Personal Representative, Guardian, or Conservator
MCA §72-3-109

By signing, accepting, or acting under this appointment, I acknowledge that I will assume the duties and responsibilities of a fiduciary and that I must work exclusively for the benefit of the decedent's estate and its beneficiaries, the ward under any guardianship, or the protected person under any conservatorship. I also acknowledge that the primary duty of a personal representative, guardian, or conservator is the duty of loyalty to and protection of the best interests of the estate, ward, or protected person. Therefore, I acknowledge that:

- I may not use any of the property or other assets of the decedent's estate, ward, or protected person for my own personal benefit;

- I must direct any benefit derived from this appointment to the decedent's estate, ward, or protected person; and

- I must avoid conflicts of interest and must use ordinary skill and prudence in carrying out the duties of this appointment."

I declare under penalty of perjury under the laws of the state of Montana that the foregoing is true and correct.

Signed this _____ day of _____, 20____

Signature of applicant _____

State of Montana County of _____

This instrument was signed before me on _____

by_____
   Print name of signer(s)

_____
Notary Signature

[Montana notaries must complete the following, if not part of stamp.]

_____
Printed Name

Notary Public for the State of Montana

Residing at_____

My Commission expires:_____, 20_____

As stated earlier, the requirement of posting a bond may be waived if the testator excuses the personal representative in the will. When the named personal representative is a family member or trusted friend, a bond is an unnecessary expense and in fact, does not guarantee that the estate will not be mismanaged.

Except in extreme cases, or when a corporate executor is named, most testators take advantage of the clause and excuse the personal representative's bond. If it appears that the estate is being mismanaged or the personal representative is about to betray his or her trust, the beneficiaries may petition the clerk or court to require a bond to be posted, or remove the personal representative before harm can occur.

Resignation, Discharge, or Removal of Personal Representative

A personal representative must fulfill his or her obligations until either removed or discharged. A personal representative will act unless and until he or she resigns or is discharged or removed, or if he or she becomes incapacitated or dies while the estate is still pending. If the personal representative becomes incapacitated or dies, his or her own representative or agent must do whatever is necessary to preserve the estate's assets and give them to the successor personal representative or administrator as soon as possible.

Resignation

A personal representative may ask to be discharged before he or she has fulfilled his or her obligations by filing a written resignation. To resign, the personal representative must first offer a complete accounting of the estate. He or she will not be allowed to resign until the accounting is examined and approved, and shows that the estate has been administered in a proper manner. If no successor is available, the personal representative must continue his or her duties until an administrator is appointed, or until the estate is discharged, whichever occurs first.

Removal

The court may remove the personal representative when it is in the best interest of the estate. Mismanagement of the estate, breach of fiduciary duties, and violation of a court order are all grounds for **removal**. In addition, if the personal representative is unsuitable or incapable of performing his or her duties, or becomes incapacitated and of unsound mind, he or she may be removed. Beneficiaries of the estate or any other person with an interest in the estate may petition for the removal. A hearing is held to determine if removal for cause is required.

Discharge

After the estate has been administered and the personal representative has performed all necessary duties, the personal representative petitions for **discharge**. Discharge releases the personal representative from all liability pertaining to the administration of the estate as long as those matters have been fully and fairly disclosed to all involved parties and to the clerk or court. Discharge will be discussed again in the chapter on the probate process.

Liability of the Personal Representative
Surcharge

A question about whether or not the personal representative may be held personally accountable for the actions he or she takes in his or her capacity as personal representative often arises. If the personal representative fails to properly administer the decedent's estate, he or she may be liable to the beneficiaries or heirs for his or her mistakes. A remedy that may be assessed is called a **surcharge**. A surcharge is imposed against the personal representative to restore the estate's losses as a result of the personal representative's failure to act appropriately.

However, if the personal representative collects, manages, and distributes the estate in a proper manner, he or she will not be held personally responsible for any problems that may arise. In order for the personal representative to be held personally liable for the losses, a breach of duty must be found.

CASE 10.1 **SUMMARY**

In the Matter of the Estate of LOUIS F. LANIER, Deceased.
Court of Appeals of Michigan (2000) (unpublished opinion)

Sakowski served as the temporary personal representative of Lanier's estate during which time he was involved in the estate's medical malpractice claim against William Beaumont Hospital. The case mediated for $25,000 which Sakowski accepted but the hospital rejected the award. The hospital responded with an offer of $3000. The attorney handling the malpractice claim never told Sakowski about the offer. The estate didn't respond to the offer which according to Michigan law acted as a rejection of the offer. At trial, the jury found for the hospital and the hospital's motion for costs and fees settled for $10,636.70.

Szymanksi, the estate's successor personal representative asked the probate court to surcharge Sakowski for his failure to notify the heirs about the $3000 offer. The court ordered Sakowski to reimburse for the $10,636.70 expended in costs and fees.

On appeal, Sakowski contended that the probate court erred in assessing the surcharge against him. The appellate court concluded that the probate court abused its discretion in imposing the surcharge stating that "[a]n independent personal representative shall not be surcharged for any good faith act of administration or distribution if the act in question was authorized at the time."

The court stated that at no time was Sakowski "derelict in attending to his responsibilities" with regard to the malpractice action and could not find that Sakowski violated any of his duties to the estate.

As for Sakowski's failure to notify the heirs about the $3,000 offer, the appellate court stated

> [R]espondent can hardly be blamed for failing to inform others of facts of which he was not aware. In any case, the probate court erred in concluding that respondent had a duty to consult Lanier's heirs with regard to the offer of judgment. As an independent personal representative, respondent had the authority to make decisions regarding settlement of decedent's claims and was not obligated to obtain the consent of the heirs or any other interested persons.

As long as the personal representative acts reasonably and in good faith, there is no personal liability for decreases in an estate's value or loss of an asset. It is only when there is a breach of fiduciary duty, such as negligence, delay, or self-dealing, that a personal representative will be held personally liable and accountable to the beneficiaries of the estate.

SUMMARY

Different titles attach to the position of a person, or corporate entity, that handles the collection, management, and distribution of the decedent's estate from jurisdiction to jurisdiction, but the responsibilities are the same regardless. The personal representative's immense obligations to the decedent's estate, beneficiaries, and heirs are called fiduciary duties. The powers the personal representative has are very broad, and include paying all the just debts of the estate, collecting all monies owed to the estate, collecting and valuing all assets of the estate, preparing tax returns, managing the estate assets so that they are productive, preparing inventories and accountings, and eventually distributing the estate's assets to the beneficiaries named in the testator's will or to the heirs if the decedent died intestate. As a fiduciary, the personal representative is accountable to the beneficiaries, to the heirs, and to the clerk or court that authorized the personal representative to administer the estate during its administration. The paralegal may be called upon to assist the supervising attorney and the personal representative in fulfilling these very important duties.

KEY TERMS

personal representative	surety bond	executrix
discharge	removal	surcharge
letters of administration	administrator cum testamento	letters testamentary
administrator pendente lite	annexo	

REVIEW QUESTIONS

1. What basic requirements must a person fulfill before she or he can be appointed as a personal representative?
2. Explain why a personal representative may be required to post a bond.
3. What are five duties of the personal representative?
4. When may a personal representative be removed?
5. Explain the different types of personal representatives.
6. What is the concept of surcharge?

PROJECTS

1. Look up your state statutes. What is your state's label (title) for the person authorized to administer an estate?
2. Look up your state statutes. Which statute enables the person authorized to administer an estate as personal representative (or executor) to act? Which statute enables an administrator to act?
3. Read Case 10.2 below. Briefly explain the case and the court's determination.

CASE 10.2 SUMMARY

Fall v. Miller
Court of Appeals of Indiana, First District.
April 24, 1984. Rehearing Denied May 31, 1984.

Statement of the Case

Petitioner-appellant William L. Fall (Fall) appeals a decision of the Putnam Circuit Court overruling specific legatee Fall's petition objecting to the Final Account and proposed distribution of the estate of Leah Curnutt (Decedent) prepared by respondent-appellee Constance Miller (Executrix).

We reverse.

Statement of the Facts

On November 6, 1980, the decedent died testate, and by the terms of her will, bequeathed certain corporate stock to Fall. During the course of the administration, though the gross estate was in excess of $80,000.00 and the debts and expenses were less than $25,000.00, and though there was no necessity to sell the stock, the Executrix filed her petition with the court, without Fall's knowledge and consent, to sell the stock, falsely alleging therein that it was necessary to do so to pay debts of the estate. The court granted its petition and in March, 1981, the Executrix sold the stock for $33,476.29.

However, in November, 1981, the attorney for the Executrix candidly acknowledged in a letter to Fall that a mistake had been made and promised Fall compensation for or substitution for the erroneously sold stock. Thereafter, without Fall's knowledge and consent, the Executrix reacquired on the market equal shares of the same stock for $24,671.63. In her final accounts she proposed to distribute those shares to Fall and retain the $8,804.60 profit to be divided between herself and other residuary legatees. From an adverse ruling on his objections to the final accounts challenging that proposal, Fall appeals.

Issues

Fall presents two issues on appeal. He claims the trial court erred in:
   I. Permitting the Executrix and other residuary legatees to keep and share the profits derived from dealing in his stock.
   II. Not awarding interest on a specific legacy. [omitted]

Discussion and Decision

Issue I: Specific Legacy

Both parties agree that the stock is a specific legacy and enjoys priority over general and residuary bequests, and that general and residuary bequests abate before specific bequests under IND.CODE 29-1-17-3. However, the Executrix argues that Fall is only entitled to receive his distribution in kind, which he did, and so her fiduciary duty is satisfied, and Fall is not entitled to any of the profit.

We first observe that the term "fiduciary" includes a personal representative. IND. CODE 29-1-1-3. Further, it is conceded that the Executrix had no right to sell the stock and it was a breach of her duty to do so. A personal representative is regarded as a trustee appointed by law for the benefit of and the protection of creditors and distributes. 13 I.L.E. Executors and Administrators Secs. 3 and 71 (1959). Under IND.CODE 29-1-16-1, a personal representative "shall not be entitled to any profit by the increase . . ." in the assets of the estate, and is liable for "negligent or willful" acts.

There is a thread which runs through the law governing fiduciary relationships which forbids a person standing in a fiduciary capacity to another from profiting by dealing in the property of his beneficiary. In Brown v. Brown, (1956) 235 Ind. 563, 135 N.E.2d 614, the Court discussed constructive trusts:

It has also long been the law that an executor cannot mingle estate funds with his own money, and he cannot make a profit for himself from the use of estate funds. Forsyth v. Woods, (1871) 11 Wall. 484, 20 L.Ed. 207. Furthermore, a personal representative is personally liable for all profits derived from property of the decedent's estate. Evans v. Hardy, (1881) 76 Ind. 527; Hendrix v. Hendrix, (1879) 65 Ind. 329; and 31 Am.Jur.2d, Executors and Administrators,

Sec. 267. Where an executor converts assets of an estate, he is chargeable with the value of the converted property and all the profits made during the period of conversion. Cates v. Cates, (1958) 268 Ala. 6, 104 So.2d 756. A legatee may either charge the personal representative with the value of the converted property or elect to claim and pursue the property for which it has been exchanged. Jose v. Lyman, (1944) 316 Mass. 271. 55 N.E.2d 433. The executor shall be held accountable for any profits realized from the use of the estate's money. Walls v. Walker, (1869) 37 Cal. 424.

In Indiana, an executor is personally liable for loss where he deposits trust funds in a bank in his individual name. Corya v. Corya, (1889) 119 Ind. 593, 22 N.E. 3. The fiduciary character of an executor extends to all legatees, and he cannot purchase the legacy of any of them for his benefit or the benefit of the other legatees. Goodwin v. Goodwin, (1874) 48 Ind. 584. The Indiana Probate Code specifically charges the personal representative with the responsibility of collecting and preserving all assets of the decedent's estate. IND.CODE 29-1-1-1. Furthermore, a personal representative who sells personal property of the estate does so at his peril. IND.CODE 29-1-5-8 and 29-1-16-1.

Title to decedent's personal property vests in the executor where it remains until the property is sold and the proceeds applied to the payment of the decedent's debts and the expense of administration, or until it is distributed to the heirs. However, the executor does not have absolute power over the personal property, but must dispose of it in the manner and mode prescribed by statute or by order of the Court. Root v. Blackwood, (1950) 120 Ind.App. 545, 94 N.E.2d 489.

The executrix cites no relevant authority whatsoever to support her acts. We conclude that the above authorities are clearly applicable to the case at bar. The executrix held Fall's stock in a fiduciary capacity, and wrongly sold it, even if by mistake. Neither she nor anyone claiming through her should be permitted to retain the profits or fruits of the transaction. Fall, as equitable owner of the stock, subject only to abatement for payment of debts, is entitled to his stock and all profits made by the executrix in wrongfully dealing in it.

One rationale for the rule is that the property which generated the profit belonged to Fall and in equity and good conscience the profit should belong to him. A more persuasive rationale is that if a fiduciary is not allowed to retain any gain or profit from wrongful, speculative, or self-dealing transactions in his beneficiary's property and at the same time can be held liable for any loss incurred, an effective deterrent to such activity exists.

Any other rule would only encourage residuary legatees in control of the estate to speculate in estate assets. Policy forbids such conduct.

For the above reasons, this cause is reversed and the court is ordered to enter a judgment for Fall.

Judgment reversed.

MyLegalStudiesLab™ http://www.mylegalstudieslab

MYLEGALSTUDIESLAB VIRTUAL LAW OFFICE EXPERIENCE ASSIGNMENTS

Complete the pre-test, study plan, and post-test for this chapter and answer the Legal Applications questions as assigned.

These will help you confirm your mastery of the concepts and their application to legal scenarios. Then complete the Virtual Law Office assignments as assigned by your instructor. These assignments are designed to develop your workplace skills and result in producing documents for inclusion in your portfolio.

Chapter **eleven**

ESTATE ADMINISTRATION

Overview of the Probate Process

When a person dies, his or her estate must be administered. This means that the decedent's debts must be paid, any money due to the decedent must be collected, his or her real and personal property must be collected and valued, and then the property must be distributed as set forth in the decedent's will or by descent and distribution. This process is called **probate**. Probate literally means "to prove." The estate will be proved through a legal process that will collect and distribute the decedent's property to the appropriate beneficiaries and heirs after debts are paid.

The probate process generally consists of three phases:

1. pre-probate
2. the actual probate of the will (or if no will, descent and distribution of the estate)
3. estate administration

In the pre-probate phase, the decedent's will must be located. Many times the decedent's family brings a copy of the will to the attorney's office when they arrive for their appointment. If the will was executed many years prior to the decedent's death, it is important to determine if it has been superseded by a new will or supplemented by a codicil. Once this phase is completed, the attorney will begin probate proceedings. If the will cannot be located, the attorney will have to begin proceedings through intestate succession.

THE PROFESSIONAL PARALEGAL

Sometimes family members think that the decedent had a will, but one cannot be found. The attorney may request that notices be printed in local and out-of-town newspapers. These notices are requests that anyone with knowledge of the decedent's will should contact the attorney's office. Sometimes, it's the family members who cannot be found. The notice printed will then ask that anyone who is related to, or knows the family history of the decedent, may contact the attorney's office.

The paralegal must keep addresses, phone numbers, and advertising rates for all local papers readily available and be prepared to place notices in the appropriate newspapers.

The second phase is the actual probate of the estate. During this phase, the attorney or personal representative will file the will with the clerk and insure that the will is declared to be the legal and valid will of the decedent. Once that task is accomplished, the court will issue testamentary letters to the personal representative. Testamentary letters authorize the personal representative to conduct all business necessary to the administration of the estate. During this phase, all beneficiaries or heirs of the estate will be notified about the probate proceeding and be afforded the opportunity to be heard. Will contests occur during this phase.

The third phase is the **estate administration**. During this phase, the personal representative collects the decedent's property and money owed and pays all of the decedent's lawful debts. Taxes due to or owed by the estate will be paid. Finally, the remaining property will be distributed to the appropriate beneficiaries or heirs, according to the terms of the will or if the decedent was intestate, according to descent and distribution. The term "probate" is often used to mean both the probate and estate administration of the decedent's estate. In this book, we refer to the clerk and probate court for probate filings; however, it should be noted that the proper venue for filing of estate administration is determined by jurisdiction. Other venues for filing and administration of estates may be the Commissioner of Fiduciary Accounts or the Surrogate Court.

Preliminary Duties of the Law Office

The legal team, especially the paralegal, must perform certain duties before probate and estate administration. The paralegal must remember that each state has its own probate documentation and forms. If the supervising attorney does not have the proper forms, they can be obtained in numerous probate form books and, in many cases, directly from the state online. It is important that the paralegal become familiar with the most common probate forms to be an effective part of the legal team.

Obtaining the Death Certificate

Before the clerk or court will entertain any probate proceeding, the personal representative has to prove that the person whose estate for which probate is being sought is really deceased. This is usually done through the presentment of a *death*

THE PROFESSIONAL PARALEGAL

The probate process affords the paralegal a vast amount of responsibility as an integral part of the legal team. The paralegal will assist the personal representative in locating the will, if necessary; arrange for conferences between family members and other beneficiaries; assist the personal representative in the administration of the estate; and otherwise assist the supervising attorney in the preparation and filing of all probate and taxation documentation. The personal representative and probate court personnel will most likely have the greatest contact with the paralegal during the administration of the decedent's estate.

certificate. Most families obtain copies of the death certificate from the funeral home, which can take as little as one week, but in some instances more than a month. If, for some reason, no copies are available, the paralegal may obtain one from the appropriate county or state agency, such as a department of health or department of vital statistics. A copy of a record or report stating that the person is presumed dead is evidence of that person's death and may substitute for a death certificate. As a practical matter, whenever possible, the personal representative will want to get a minimum of 10 certificates as they are needed to present to banks, motor vehicle departments, Social Security Administration, life insurance companies, pension plans, and any other person or entity that will need proof of death.

If not done by the funeral home, the law office will either instruct the family or personal representative to contact Social Security Administration (SSA) and Veterans Administration (VA) regarding the decedent's death, or will contact the SSA and the VA on their behalf. The family must be informed that in some instances, benefit payments that have already been made to the decedent by check, or by direct deposit, may have to be returned.

Example: William Bright dies at 11:58 P.M. on October 31, 2011. His November 2011 Social Security check will be deposited to his checking account at midnight November 1, 2011. The personal representative or surviving spouse or family must return the money. Since William's check was direct deposited, SSA will automatically withdraw the money within a few days' notice of William's death. The family should be alerted to this and not spend the money.

Finding the Will

Some families know exactly where to find the decedent's will. In other cases, finding the will is an exercise in frustration. Some places that a decedent may have a will include:

- The Decedent's Home or Office

The first place that a family looks for the will is at the decedent's home or office. This is, for the most part, the easiest method of finding the will to carry out as a surviving spouse or child usually has easy access to the property. When the family cannot find the will in the "usual places" one looks, the more unusual places should be searched, such as under the mattress, the freezer or refrigerator, a hidden wall or floor safe, inside books and coffee cans, or even in the trunk or glove compartment in the decedent's car.

● The Safe Deposit Box

Should the decedent's family be unable to locate the last will or believes that it is in the decedent's safe deposit box, the attorney must obtain an order granting permission to have the safe deposit box opened. The reason an order is necessary is that when a person dies, the bank automatically seals the box to prevent pilferage of the contents by anyone before the new rightful owners of those contents can be determined. Unless a personal representative can show the bank official testamentary letters, which statutorily authorize the personal representative the right to access the safe deposit box, they will not open the box unless an order granting permission to do so is tendered. When the box is opened, a bank official may accompany the person granted access. Only the document presumed to be the will may be removed from the safe deposit box at this time. All other documents and assets must stay in the box until a personal representative or administrator is granted access.

● The Court House

In some states, a will may be deposited with the clerk for safekeeping. This is not done as routinely as in the past, but it may pay to call the clerk's office and see if the will is filed there.

Allowances

At this time, the supervising attorney may also petition to obtain family allowance allotments as permitted by state law. The attorney will determine if the family's hardship is sufficient to be afforded the allowance at this time, or if they can wait until the petition is filed. In general, the surviving spouse and minor children of the decedent are entitled to a reasonable allowance in money out of the estate for their maintenance during the period of the estate's administration.

Guardianship of Minors

If the decedent left minor children and the children's other natural parent is absent, it will be essential to have a guardian appointed for the children. If the will has provided for the children's **guardianship**, that person can petition for permission to fulfill his or her duty before the will is probated. Otherwise, any competent adult may petition to be the children's guardian, although most courts favor the natural parent and relatives, such as adult siblings and grandparents, over non-family members.

Figure 11.1   South Dakota Uniform Laws §29A-3-302

§29A-3-302. Informal probate—Duty of clerk—Effect of informal probate. Upon receipt of an application requesting informal probate of a will, the clerk, upon making the findings required by §29A-3-303 shall issue a written statement of informal probate if at least one hundred twenty hours have elapsed since the decedent's death. Informal probate is conclusive as to all persons until superseded by an order in a formal testacy proceeding. No defect in the application or procedure relating there to which leads to informal probate of a will renders the probate void.

Figure 11.2 Order to Open Safe Deposit Box

Estate of	NO._____
BOBBIE BLACK,	**ORDER DIRECTING BANK**
	TO OPEN SAFETY BOX &
Deceased.	**RELEASE WILL**

SUPERIOR COURT OF WASHINGTON FOR _____ COUNTY

      THE COURT, having heard and considered the *Petition for Order to Open Safety Box and Release Will* presented by Petitioner DONALD BLACK; showing that Decedent died on January 1, 2011, was then a resident of _____ County, Washington and left property in Washington subject to probate; and alleging (i) that Decedent signed a Will, in which he/she nominated Petitioner as his/her Personal Representative, and had access to and deposited the Will in the Safety Box described below; (ii) that as a result of Decedent's death, such Safety Box has become inaccessible; and (iii) that the Bank named below has control over such Safety Box; and because if Decedent left a Will, it needs to be promptly filed with the Court as required by law; good cause thereby having been shown for the Petition;

ORDERS:

Bank Branch
Bank Name
Street Addr.
City, WA ZIP

     1. To permit Petitioner, at his/her expense, to open at that Branch Safety Box No. 123-456-789.

     2. To deliver any purported Will, Codicil, or other estate document(s) of Decedent contained in that Box to Petitioner upon his/her delivery of a receipt therefor to the Bank.

     3. The Bank, at its expense, may concurrently make and retain a photocopy of the documents.

DONE IN OPEN COURT on

_____
Judge/Commissioner of the Superior Court

Presented by:

_____
      Petitioner

(continued)

Figure 11.2   (continued)

Order Directing Bank to Open Safety Box & Release Will County LR 98.04(d) Page 2 of 2	[Your Name, Address, & Phone]

Lost Wills

In the prior section, we discussed how to go about finding a decedent's will. But what happens if a will everyone assumed existed, cannot be found?

Examine this scenario:

Ann Little dies in February 2009. Her daughter, Ruth, knows that her mom had a will prepared in 2001, but when she and her brother, Michael, look in every place they can think of, including the safe deposit box and the filing cabinets at Ann's office, all they find is a copy of the will. They never find the original. Can they probate the copy asserting that the original is lost?

Probating a lost will is often a difficult task. The initial presumption in most jurisdictions is that the testator destroyed it deliberately. Is it possible that the testator:

- revoked the will? Ann may have revoked it by destroying it. She may have run it through her shredder and never thought about the copy.

- innocently destroyed the will? Was there evidence of a fire in Ann's house or office which destroyed the will?
- misplaced the will?

State law will determine if a lost will copy can be probated instead of the original; however, certain tasks can be clearly stated. The person who wants to have the copy of the will probated, contending that the original was lost, must present:

- a copy of the will;
- a proof of the will's execution and validity, by either
  - witnesses who will authenticate that the copy is a true and correct copy of the lost or destroyed will, often the lawyer who drafted the will and a member of her staff. The evidence of the witnesses has to show that, it is more likely than not, that the will was lost or destroyed (preponderance of the evidence). The witnesses also have to testify as to the contents of the will; or
  - a "self-proving" affidavit at the end of the will.

Often the witness signs an affidavit under the penalty of perjury in a form similar to the following example:

Example: I, Ruth Little Bingham, have attached to this *Affidavit* what I believe to be a true and correct copy of Decedent's Will. The original of the Will has not been found, and I believe it to have been lost under circumstances such that its loss does not have the effect of revoking the Will.

The circumstances surrounding the loss of Decedent's Will are as follows:

[Narrative regarding the circumstances, i.e., fire at home in 2005, shredded old files shredded the will]

I believe the original of Decedent's Will was lost under circumstances such that its loss does not have the effect of revoking the Will because of the following reasons:

[Narrative regarding how the above circumstances did not mean that the Decedent wanted to revoke, and did revoke, the will, i.e., the fire at the home in 2005 had the effect of severely damaging all the boxes in the basement where the will was likely kept with all of Ann Little's paperwork and files]

It should be noted that sometimes, it is just as easy, or easier, to consider the decedent to be intestate. Questions that may be asked to determine if it would be easier to have the decedent declared intestate, include:

- Who would be the beneficiaries under the will? Who would be the heirs by state descent and distribution laws? Are they the same, or would the outcome be so different that the decedent would have objected?
- Who would be the personal representative under the will? Is there a difference of who would file to be the administrator of an intestate estate? Would it be so vastly different that the decedent would have objected to the administrator handling the estate?
- How old is the copy of the will? Consider this example:

Example: Beverly Nash is an elderly woman who has been incapacitated for years. Her husband Daniel has been taking care of her, but the truth is that Beverly has been in a nursing facility for the prior 5 years and doesn't know who Daniel is. Beverly and Daniel moved fairly frequently due to Daniel's military career and job changes. Beverly had a will executed in 1969, but after looking high and low, Daniel determines that both his and Beverly's wills cannot be found, probably due to the many moves over the years; but he does find an old and faded copy of the will. Daniel makes an appointment with a lawyer and tells the lawyer that he knows that the lawyer that drafted the will and the witnesses are all deceased.

Under the terms of the copy of the will, all of Beverly's property was to be given to Daniel if he survived, and then to their children, Marie and Edward. The will provided for guardianship for the children, who are now grown with children and grandchildren of their own.

In this instance, it is far easier to have Beverly declared intestate than to prove the copy of the lost will. It is likely that Daniel will receive all of the assets of Beverly's estate under state intestacy laws and to insure that it happens, the children can sign waivers and disclaimers of any interest they may have in their mother's estate (belt with suspenders perhaps).

CASE 11.1 **SUMMARY**

Gifford v. Bank of the Southwest, 712 S.W.2d 182 (Tex. App. Houston [14th Dist.] 1986)

Gifford's husband executed his Last Will and Testament in November of 1943, and deposited it with the San Jacinto National Bank. San Jacinto was also appointed executor of the will. San Jacinto merged with another bank which then merged into the Bank of the Southwest. Gifford's husband died in February of 1974. On many occasions prior to his death, Mr. Gifford told his wife that the bank was to be the corporate executor of his estate. Gifford stated that she knew the terms of the will and that it should have been on deposit with the Bank of the Southwest since, "I had a copy of the original [w]ill that was dated in 1943 and placed in the Trust Department of San Jacinto Bank, and my husband told me that the Bank of the Southwest was [e]xecutor of the [w]ill." The will provided that Mr. Gifford's entire estate was to pass to his wife.

A few days after her husband's death, Gifford called the bank concerning the will and was told that the will could not be located. Gifford and her son called the bank several times and were told that the bank had still not found the will.

Gifford contended that since the bank failed to tender the will, she was required to probate Mr. Gifford's

estate as if he was intestate. In May of 1974, the probate court divided Mr. Gifford's estate with one-half passing to Gifford and one-half to her son.

In November of 1982, Gifford received a letter from the bank's trust department addressed to Mr. Gifford. The letter stated that the bank "valued Mr. Gifford's involvement in its trust group and requested information to help the Bank update its trust department records." Gifford called the bank about the letter and learned that the bank had found the will.

In July of 1984, Gifford sued the bank for breach of its contract of bailment. The bank asserted that her cause of action was barred due to the statute of limitations.

Gifford argued that the cause of action accrued in November of 1982, when she learned that the bank located the will. The bank asserted that the cause of action accrued in 1974, when Gifford learned that the bank couldn't locate the will.

The Court found that Gifford

was fully aware of the facts giving rise to her cause of action in May 1974, when her husband's estate was probated without the will that should have been in the Bank's possession. A statute of limitations begins to run at the time the wrong was or should have been discovered, not from the date of the wrongful act or omission. Here appellant knew in 1974 that the Bank should have had the will. She made demand on the Bank at that time for delivery. As a result of the Bank's failure to deliver, appellant suffered injury. These facts were sufficient to allow appellant to sue the Bank for a breach of its contract of bailment. They were known to her in 1974, and her cause of action against the Bank accrued at that time. She did not need to allege that the Bank actually possessed the will in 1974. She was required to allege merely that a bailment existed and that the Bank, as bailee, failed to return the bailed property. Since appellant was aware of the facts giving rise to her cause of action in 1974, the suit she filed in 1984 is barred by limitations. . . .

Was the decision correct?

Should the attorney that assisted with the administration of the intestate estate be sued for malpractice? Do you think that action would also be barred by the statute of limitations?

Small Estate Settlement

Small estate settlement, also called *informal probate* or **summary administration**, occurs when the estate's value does not exceed a small sum as set by state statute. Small estate administration occurs when the total probate estate does not exceed a certain amount of money. For example, in New York, the amount is $30,000 and only applies to personal property, while in South Carolina, an informal probate is one that does not require a court hearing but is otherwise similar to a formal probate in other jurisdictions. The procedure for small estate administration is relatively simple. After a petition is filed, an order for informal administration is granted. Once the debts are paid and the property is distributed, the estate is closed. The process takes from a few weeks to a few months, unlike formal probate, which can continue for a year or more. It is important to determine if state law requires notice to be given to interested parties. While most states do not require notice to other beneficiaries or heirs, notice to creditors is required (discussed below). If a creditor is not properly notified, it does not lose its right to claim the debt owed after the estate is closed. It is important to note, however, that not all states have a summary administration process. In many jurisdictions, administration of an estate is the same whether the estate is worth $10,000 or 10 million dollars and in those instances, a formal probate is usually required.

Figure 11.3 Oregon Statute Regarding Small Estates

ORS 114.515 Value of estate; where affidavit filed; fee; amended affidavit; supplemental affidavit.

1. If the estate of a decedent meets the requirements of subsection (2) of this section, any of the following persons may file an affidavit with the clerk of the probate court in any county where there is venue for a proceeding seeking the appointment of a personal representative for the estate:

    (a) One or more of the claiming successors of the decedent.

    (b) If the decedent died testate, any person named as personal representative in the decedent's will.

    (c) The Director of Human Services, the Director of the Oregon Health Authority or an attorney approved under ORS 114.517, if the decedent received public assistance pursuant to ORS chapter 411 or 414 or received care at an institution as defined in ORS 179.010, and it appears that the assistance or the cost of care may be recovered from the estate of the decedent.

(continued)

Figure 11.3   (continued)

2. An affidavit under this section may be filed only if:

   (a) The fair market value of the estate is $275,000 or less;

   (b) Not more than $75,000 of the fair market value of the estate is attributable to personal property; and

   (c) Not more than $200,000 of the fair market value of the estate is attributable to real property.

3. An affidavit under this section may not be filed until 30 days after the death of the decedent.

4. An affidavit filed under the provisions of this section must contain the information required in ORS 114.525 and shall be made a part of the probate records. If the affiant is an attorney approved by the Director of Human Services or the Director of the Oregon Health Authority, a copy of the document approving the attorney must be attached to the affidavit.

5. In determining fair market value under this section, the fair market value of the entire interest in the property included in the estate shall be used without reduction for liens or other debts.

6. The clerk of the probate court shall charge and collect the fee established under ORS 21.145 for the filing of any affidavit under this section.

7. Any error or omission in an affidavit filed under this section may be corrected by filing an amended affidavit within four months after the filing of the affidavit.

8. One or more supplemental affidavits may be filed at any time after the filing of an affidavit under this section for the purpose of including property not described in the original affidavit. Copies of all previously filed affidavits must be attached to the supplemental affidavit and all information required in ORS 114.525 must be reflected in the supplemental affidavit. A supplemental affidavit may not be filed if by reason of the additional property described in the supplemental affidavit any limitation imposed by subsection (2) of this section is exceeded.

Formal Probate Administration

When the value of the decedent's estate exceeds the statutory maximum for an informal probate administration, the estate must go through formal probate. In many states, there is no distinction between informal or summary administration and **formal administration**. In those jurisdictions, all estates must follow the statutory requirements for formal administration of the estate.

We have relied heavily on California forms in this textbook, but you should always rely on your state's forms. In some jurisdictions, your supervising attorney must purchase the forms from the state for use. In some jurisdictions, such as California, Florida, and South Carolina, probate is heavily form driven. In other states, the process only requires a few forms. This may be due to how the proceedings take place. For example, in states like California, Florida, New York, and South Carolina, you have a probate court (Surrogate Court in New York). Therefore, you file petitions and orders and other documents that are actual pleadings requesting that certain steps may be taken or have been taken. In states like Virginia and West Virginia, the only court proceedings necessary are in will contest situations, and otherwise everything is handled through a fiduciary commissioner or supervisor. The only forms filed are inventories and accountings, and even those are sent to the commissioner or supervisor before being forwarded by that party to the clerk for filing in the court records. Therefore, it is very important to understand what the basic procedures are for your state.

Petition

Intestate Decedent   When a decedent dies intestate, someone must file a petition for administration. This person is usually the surviving spouse or a child of the decedent, but it may be any relative, anyone that reasonably believes that he or she will be considered an heir of the estate, or a person or company that is a creditor of the decedent. The petition asks to be appointed as the administrator for the decedent's estate.

Testate Decedent   When the decedent is testate, the person who was nominated in the will to be the personal representative usually files the probate petition; although if the nominated personal representative is deceased or otherwise refuses, the named successor, or if none is named, any other relative, named beneficiary, person that reasonably believes that he or she will be considered an heir of the estate, or a person or company that is a creditor of the decedent may also petition to be named to administer the will. If not named in the will, this person is an administrator with will annexed (administrator c.t.a.).

Almost every petition for probate, whether for a testate or intestate decedent, will require the petitioner to state the following:

- the name and address of the petitioner
- the name and domicile of the decedent
- the decedent's date of death and age
- the potential beneficiaries' names, addresses, and relationship to the decedent
- the court's jurisdiction

Other requirements for the petition may include:

- the decedent's Social Security number (often redacted to the last four numbers)
- the approximate value of the estate assets
- the date of the decedent's last will and testament (if testate)
- a declaration that a diligent search had been made for the will (if intestate)

If the decedent's will is available, but its custodian refuses to produce it, potential beneficiaries have the right to ask the court to compel its production. In some states, willfully withholding the will from the probate court may be met with criminal charges.

Figure 11.4   Application for Informal Probate (Michigan)

Approved, SCAO		JIS CODE: IPA
STATE OF MICHIGAN **PROBATE COURT** **COUNTY OF**	**APPLICATION FOR INFORMAL PROBATE** **AND/OR APPOINTMENT OF PERSONAL** **REPRESENTATIVE (TESTATE/INTESTATE)**	**FILE NO.**

Estate of _____

1. I, _____ , am interested in the estate and make this application as
   Name of applicant

   _____ .
   Relationship to decedent, i.e., heir, devisee, child, spouse, creditor, beneficiary, etc.

2. Decedent information: _____ _____ _____ **XXX-XX-** _____
   Date of death   Time (if known)   Date of birth   Last four digits of SSN

   Domicile (at date of death): _____ _____ _____
   City/Township/Village   County   State

3. ☐ A death certificate has been issued, and a copy is attached.
   ☐ No death certificate is available. Attached is alternative documentation of the decedent's death.

4. So far as I know or could ascertain with reasonable diligence, the names and addresses of the heirs and devisees of the decedent and other interested persons, the relationship to the decedent, and the ages of any who are minors are as follows:
   (required testimony forms are attached)

NAME	ADDRESS	RELATIONSHIP	AGE (if minor)

Of the interested persons listed above, the following are under legal disability or otherwise represented and presently have or will require representation:

NAME	LEGAL DISABILITY	REPRESENTED BY Name, address, and capacity

5. ☐ a. Venue is proper in this county because the decedent was domiciled in this county on the date of death.
   ☐ b. The decedent was not domiciled in Michigan, but venue is proper in this county because property of the decedent was located in this county at the date of death.

(PLEASE SEE OTHER SIDE)

Do not write below this line - For court use only

PC 558 (9/07)   **APPLICATION FOR INFORMAL PROBATE AND/OR APPOINTMENT OF PERSONAL REPRESENTATIVE**
         (TESTATE/INTESTATE)   MCL 700.1309, MCL 700.3301, MCL 700.3311, MCL 700.3614, MCR 5.302, MCR 5.309

(continued)

Figure 11.4   (continued)

6. ☐ a. The decedent died intestate and after exercising reasonable diligence, I am unaware of any unrevoked testamentary instrument relating to property located in this state as defined under MCL 700.1301.

☐ b. I am aware of an unrevoked testamentary instrument relating to property located in this state as defined under MCL 700.1301, but the instrument is not being probated because (if this statement is true, the probate register must deny this application

according to MCL 700.3311):_____
The instrument   ☐ is attached to this application.   ☐ is already in the court's possession.

☐ c. The decedent's will, dated _____ , with codicil(s) dated _____ ,
is/are offered for probate and ☐ is/are attached to this application.   ☐ is/are already in the court's possession.

☐ d. An authenticated copy of the will and codicil(s), if any, probated in _____ County,
_____ is/are offered for probate, and documents establishing its probate are attached to this application.
State

7. To the best of my knowledge, I believe that the instrument(s) subject to this application, if any, was/were validly executed and is the decedent's last will. After exercising reasonable diligence, I am unaware of an instrument revoking the will or codicil(s).

☐ 8. A personal representative has been previously appointed in _____ County, _____
and the appointment has not been terminated. The personal representative's name and address are: State

_____   _____
Name   Address

_____
City, state, zip

☐ 9. I nominate_____ , as personal representative, who is qualified and has the
Name

following priority for appointment:_____ . His/her address is:_____
Address

_____ .
City, state, zip

☐ 10. Other persons have prior or equal right to appointment as personal representative. They are:

_____   _____
Name   Name

_____   _____
Name   Name

Suitable renunciations, nominations, and/or a Notice of Intent to Seek Informal Appointment and proof of its service have been or will be filed.

☐ 11. The will expressly requests that the personal representative serve with bond.

☐ 12. A special personal representative is necessary because_____ .

I REQUEST:

☐ 13. Informal probate of the will.

☐ 14. Informal appointment of the nominated personal representative   ☐ with   ☐ without   bond.

☐ 15. The appointment of a special personal representative pending the appointment of the nominated personal representative.

I declare under the penalties of perjury that this application has been examined by me and that its contents are true to the best of my information, knowledge, and belief.

_____
Date

_____   _____
Attorney signature   Applicant signature

_____   _____
Attorney name (type or print)   Bar no.   Applicant name (type or print)

_____   _____
Address   Address

_____   _____
City, state, zip   Telephone no.   City, state, zip   Telephone no.

Figure 11.5   Probate Statutes by State

Alabama	Title 43 Chapter 2 Administration of Estates
	Title 43 Chapter 8 Probate Code
Alaska	Title 13 Decedents' Estates, Guardianships, Transfers and Trusts
	Title 13 Chapter 16 Probate of Wills and Administration
Arizona	Title 14 Trusts, Estates, and Protective Proceedings
Arkansas	Title 28 Wills, Estates and Fiduciary Relationships
California	California Probate Code
Colorado	Title 15 Probate, Trusts and Fiduciaries
Connecticut	Title 45 Probate Courts and Procedure
District of Columbia	Division III Title 18 Wills
	Division III Title 19 Descent Distribution and Trusts
	Division III Title 20 Probate and Administration of Decedents' Estates
Florida	Title XLII Estates and Trusts
Georgia	Title 53 Wills, Trusts, and Administration of Estates
Hawaii	Title 30A Uniform Probate Code
Idaho	Title 15 Uniform Probate Code
Illinois	Chapter 755 Estates
	Chapter 760 Trusts and Fiduciaries
Indiana	Title 29 Probate
	Title 30 Trusts and Fiduciaries
Iowa	Title XV Chapter 633 Probate Code
	Title XV Chapter 634 Private Foundations and Charitable Trusts
	Title XV Chapter 635 Administration of Small Estates
	Title XV Chapter 636 Sureties-Fiduciaries-Trusts-Investments
Kansas	Chapter 59 Probate Code
Kentucky	Chapter 140 Inheritance and Estate Taxes
	Chapter 386 Administration of Trusts—Investments
	Chapter 391 Descent and Distribution
	Chapter 394 Wills
	Chapter 395 Personal Representatives
	Chapter 396 Claims Against Decedents' Estates

(*continued*)

Figure 11.5   (continued)

Louisiana	<u>Book III, Title I</u> of Successions <u>Uniform Probate Law</u>
Maine	<u>Title 18</u> Decedents' Estates and Fiduciary Relations <u>Title 18A</u> Probate Code
Maryland	<u>Titles 1–16</u> Estates and Trusts
Massachusetts	<u>MGL Part II, Title II</u> Descent and Distribution, Wills, Estates
Michigan	<u>Chapters 701–713</u> Probate Code
Minnesota	<u>Chapters 524–532</u> Estates of Decedents; Guardianships
Missouri	<u>Title XXXI, Chapters 456–475</u> Trusts and Estates of Decedents
Montana	<u>Title 72</u> Estates, Trusts and Fiduciary Relationships
Nebraska	<u>Chapter 30</u> Decedents' Estates; Protection of Persons and Property
Nevada	<u>Title 12</u> Wills and Estates of Deceased Persons <u>Title 13</u> Guardianships; Conservatorships; Trusts
New Hampshire	<u>Title 56</u> Probate Courts and Decedents' Estates
New Jersey	<u>Titles 3A and 3B</u> Administration of Estates—Decedents and Others
New Mexico	<u>Chapter 45</u> Uniform Probate Code <u>Chapter 46</u> Fiduciaries and Trusts
New York	<u>Chapter 17-B</u> Estates, Powers and Trusts
North Carolina	<u>Chapter 41</u> Estates <u>Chapter 47</u> Probate and Registration
North Dakota	<u>Title 30.1</u> Uniform Probate Code
Ohio	<u>Title XXI</u> Courts—Probate—Juvenile
Oklahoma	<u>Title 58</u> Probate Procedure <u>Title 84</u> Wills and Succession
Oregon	<u>Chapter 111</u> Probate Law <u>Chapter 112</u> Intestate Succession and Wills <u>Chapter 113</u> Initiation of Estate Proceedings

(continued)

Figure 11.5 (continued)

	Chapter 114 Administration of Estates
	Chapter 115 Claims, Actions, and Suits Against Estates
Pennsylvania	Title 20 Decedents, Estates and Fiduciaries
Rhode Island	Title 33 Probate Practice and Procedure
South Dakota	Title 29A Uniform Probate Code
	Title 55 Fiduciaries and Trusts
South Carolina	Title 21 Estates, Trusts, Guardians and Fiduciaries
	Title 62 Probate Code
Tennessee	Title 30 Administration of Estates
	Title 31 Descent and Distribution
	Title 32 Wills
	Title 35 Fiduciaries and Trust Estates
Texas	Texas Probate Code
	Texas Probate Code Chapter V Estates of Decedents
	Texas Probate Code Chapter IV Execution and Revocation of Wills
	Texas Probate Code Chapter XIII Guardianship
Utah	Title 22 Fiduciaries and Trusts
	Title 75 Uniform Probate Code
Vermont	Title 14 Decedents' Estates and Fiduciary Relations
Virginia	Title 64.1 Wills and Decedents' Estates
Washington	Title 11 Probate and Trust Law
West Virginia	Chapter 41 Wills
	Chapter 42 Descent and Distribution
	Chapter 44 Administration of Estates and Trusts
Wisconsin	Chapter 701 Trusts
	Chapter 853 Wills
	Chapters 851–882 Probate
Wyoming	Title 2 Wills, Decedents' Estates and Probate Code
	Title 2 Chapter 2 Probate Court
	Title 2 Chapter 6 Wills
	Title 2 Chapter 7 Administration of Estates

Figure 11.6   Petition for Probate (California)

DE-111

ATTORNEY OR PARTY WITHOUT ATTORNEY *(Name, State Bar number, and address):*

FOR COURT USE ONLY

TELEPHONE NO.:   FAX NO. *(Optional):*

E-MAIL ADDRESS *(Optional):*

ATTORNEY FOR *(Name):*

SUPERIOR COURT OF CALIFORNIA, COUNTY OF

STREET ADDRESS:

MAILING ADDRESS:

CITY AND ZIP CODE:

BRANCH NAME:

ESTATE OF *(Name):*

DECEDENT

PETITION FOR ☐ **Probate of Will and for Letters Testamentary**
☐ **Probate of Will and for Letters of Administration with Will Annexed**
☐ **Letters of Administration**
☐ **Letters of Special Administration** ☐ **with general powers**
☐ **Authorization to Administer Under the Independent Administration of Estates Act** ☐ **with limited authority**

CASE NUMBER:

HEARING DATE:

DEPT.:   TIME:

1. Publication will be in *(specify name of newspaper):*
   a. ☐ Publication requested.
   b. ☐ Publication to be arranged.
2. **Petitioner** *(name each):*   **requests that**
   a. ☐ decedent's will and codicils, if any, be admitted to probate.
   b. ☐ *(name):*
      be appointed
      (1) ☐ executor
      (2) ☐ administrator with will annexed
      (3) ☐ administrator
      (4) ☐ special administrator ☐ with general powers
      and Letters issue upon qualification.
   c. ☐ full ☐ limited authority be granted to administer under the Independent Administration of Estates Act.
   d. (1) ☐ bond not be required for the reasons stated in item 3d.
      (2) ☐ $ bond be fixed. The bond will be furnished by an admitted surety insurer or as otherwise provided by law. *(Specify reasons in Attachment 2 if the amount is different from the maximum required by Prob. Code, § 8482.)*
      (3) ☐ $ in deposits in a blocked account be allowed. Receipts will be filed. *(Specify institution and location):*

3. a. Decedent died on *(date):*   at *(place):*
      (1) ☐ a resident of the county named above.
      (2) ☐ a nonresident of California and left an estate in the county named above located at *(specify location permitting publication in the newspaper named in item 1):*

   b. Street address, city, and county of decedent's residence at time of death *(specify):*

Page 1 of 4

Form Adopted for Mandatory Use
Judicial Council of California
DE-111 [Rev. March 1, 2008]

PETITION FOR PROBATE
(Probate—Decedents Estates)

Probate Code, §§ 8002, 10450;
www.courtinfo.ca.gov

American LegalNet, Inc.
www.Forms*Workflow*.com

(continued)

Figure 11.6 (continued)

ESTATE OF *(Name):*	CASE NUMBER:
DECEDENT	

3. c. **Character and estimated value of the property of the estate** *(complete in all cases):*

 (1) Personal property: $

 (2) Annual gross income from

   (a) real property: $

   (b) personal property: $

 (3) **Subtotal** *(add (1) and (2)):* $

 (4) Gross fair market value of real property: $

 (5) (Less) Encumbrances: $( )

 (6) Net value of real property: $

 (7) **Total** *(add (3) and (6)):* $

 d. (1) ☐ Will waives bond. ☐ Special administrator is the named executor, and the will waives bond.

  (2) ☐ All beneficiaries are adults and have waived bond, and the will does not require a bond.
   (Affix waiver as Attachment 3d(2).)

  (3) ☐ All heirs at law are adults and have waived bond. *(Affix waiver as Attachment 3d(3).)*

  (4) ☐ Sole personal representative is a corporate fiduciary or an exempt government agency.

 e. (1) ☐ Decedent died intestate.

  (2) ☐ Copy of decedent's will dated: ☐ codicil dated *(specify for each):*

   are affixed as Attachment 3e(2).

   (Include typed copies of handwritten documents and English translations of foreign-language documents.)

   ☐ The will and all codicils are self-proving (Prob. Code, § 8220).

 f. **Appointment of personal representative** *(check all applicable boxes):*

  (1) Appointment of executor or administrator with will annexed:

   (a) ☐ Proposed executor is named as executor in the will and consents to act.

   (b) ☐ No executor is named in the will.

   (c) ☐ Proposed personal representative is a nominee of a person entitled to Letters.
    (Affix nomination as Attachment 3f(1)(c).)

   (d) ☐ Other named executors will not act because of ☐ death ☐ declination
    ☐ other reasons *(specify):*

    ☐ Continued in Attachment 3f(1)(d).

  (2) Appointment of administrator:

   (a) ☐ Petitioner is a person entitled to Letters. *(If necessary, explain priority in Attachment 3f(2)(a).)*

   (b) ☐ Petitioner is a nominee of a person entitled to Letters. *(Affix nomination as Attachment 3f(2)(b).)*

   (c) ☐ Petitioner is related to the decedent as *(specify):*

  (3) ☐ Appointment of special administrator requested. *(Specify grounds and requested powers in Attachment 3f(3).)*

 g. Proposed personal representative is a

  (1) ☐ resident of California.

  (2) ☐ nonresident of California *(specify permanent address):*

  (3) ☐ resident of the United States.

  (4) ☐ nonresident of the United States.

DE-111 [Rev. March 1, 2008]	**PETITION FOR PROBATE** (Probate—Decedents Estates)	Page 2 of 4

(continued)

Figure 11.6 (continued)

	DE-111
ESTATE OF *(Name)*:	CASE NUMBER:
DECEDENT	

4. ☐ Decedent's will does not preclude administration of this estate under the Independent Administration of Estates Act.

5. a. Decedent was survived by *(check items (1) or (2), and (3) or (4), and (5) or (6), and (7) or (8))*

    (1) ☐ spouse.

    (2) ☐ no spouse as follows:

        (a) ☐ divorced or never married.

        (b) ☐ spouse deceased.

    (3) ☐ registered domestic partner.

    (4) ☐ no registered domestic partner.

        (See Fam. Code, § 297.5(c); Prob. Code, §§ 37(b), 6401(c), and 6402.)

    (5) ☐ child as follows:

        (a) ☐ natural or adopted.

        (b) ☐ natural adopted by a third party.

    (6) ☐ no child.

    (7) ☐ issue of a predeceased child.

    (8) ☐ no issue of a predeceased child.

  b. Decedent ☐ was ☐ was not survived by a stepchild or foster child or children who would have been adopted by decedent but for a legal barrier. *(See Prob. Code, § 6454.)*

6. *(Complete if decedent was survived by (1) a spouse or registered domestic partner but no issue (only **a** or **b** apply), or (2) no spouse, registered domestic partner, or issue. (Check the **first** box that applies):*

  a. ☐ Decedent was survived by a parent or parents who are listed in item 8.

  b. ☐ Decedent was survived by issue of deceased parents, all of whom are listed in item 8.

  c. ☐ Decedent was survived by a grandparent or grandparents who are listed in item 8.

  d. ☐ Decedent was survived by issue of grandparents, all of whom are listed in item 8.

  e. ☐ Decedent was survived by issue of a predeceased spouse, all of whom are listed in item 8.

  f. ☐ Decedent was survived by next of kin, all of whom are listed in item 8.

  g. ☐ Decedent was survived by parents of a predeceased spouse or issue of those parents, if both are predeceased, all of whom are listed in item 8.

  h. ☐ Decedent was survived by no known next of kin.

7. *(Complete only if no spouse or issue survived decedent.)*

  a. ☐ Decedent had no predeceased spouse.

  b. ☐ Decedent had a predeceased spouse who

    (1) ☐ died not more than 15 years before decedent and who owned an interest in **real property** that passed to decedent,

    (2) ☐ died not more than five years before decedent and who owned **personal property** valued at $10,000 or more that passed to decedent,

    *(If you checked (1) or (2), check only the **first** box that applies):*

      (a) ☐ Decedent was survived by issue of a predeceased spouse, all of whom are listed in item 8.

      (b) ☐ Decedent was survived by a parent or parents of the predeceased spouse who are listed in item 8.

      (c) ☐ Decedent was survived by issue of a parent of the predeceased spouse, all of whom are listed in item 8.

      (d) ☐ Decedent was survived by next of kin of the decedent, all of whom are listed in item 8.

      (e) ☐ Decedent was survived by next of kin of the predeceased spouse, all of whom are listed in item 8.

    (3) ☐ neither (1) nor (2) apply.

8. Listed on the next page are the names, relationships to decedent, ages, and addresses, so far as known to or reasonably ascertainable by petitioner, of (1) all persons mentioned in decedent's will or any codicil, whether living or deceased; (2) all persons named or checked in items 2, 5, 6, and 7; and (3) all beneficiaries of a trust named in decedent's will or any codicil in which the trustee and personal representative are the same person.

DE-111 [Rev. March 1, 2008]

PETITION FOR PROBATE
(Probate—Decedents Estates)

Page 3 of 4

(continued)

Figure 11.6   (continued)

ESTATE OF *(Name)*:		CASE NUMBER:	DE-111
	DECEDENT		

8.   Name and relationship to decedent   Age   Address

☐ Continued on Attachment 8.

9.   Number of pages attached: _____

Date:

_____   ►   _____
(TYPE OR PRINT NAME OF ATTORNEY)   (SIGNATURE OF ATTORNEY)*

* (Signatures of all petitioners are also required. All petitioners must sign, but the petition may be verified by any one of them (Prob. Code, §§ 1020, 1021; Cal. Rules of Court, rule 7.103).)

I declare under penalty of perjury under the laws of the State of California that the foregoing is true and correct.

Date:

_____   ►   _____
(TYPE OR PRINT NAME OF PETITIONER)   (SIGNATURE OF PETITIONER)

                                                                     ►   _____
(TYPE OR PRINT NAME OF PETITIONER)   (SIGNATURE OF PETITIONER)

☐ Signatures of additional petitioners follow last attachment.

DE-111 [Rev. March 1, 2008]

PETITION FOR PROBATE
(Probate—Decedents Estates)

Page 4 of 4

Notice to Other Interested Parties

Once the petition has been filed, the personal representative must file a notice to all interested parties. An interested party is anyone who would reasonably expect to be affected by the outcome of the probate of the decedent's estate. Interested persons can request that notices and copies of all pleadings be forwarded to them; however, some will waive their right to notice and not expect to receive any notification in the future.

Notice served upon interested parties is determined by state statute and may include:

- mail requiring a signed receipt, such as certified mail or return receipt requested
- overnight delivery that requires a signature before the carrier will turn over the package
- in some instances, by publishing the notice in a newspaper of general circulation or by hand delivery

Notice of the estate administration to the decedent's creditors is given by mail to those who are known creditors, and by publication in a newspaper of general circulation to those that are unknown to the personal representative.

Proof of Will

While the method of proving a will varies from state to state, some consistencies exist. As was discussed in Chapter 4, a self-proving will does not require the personal representative to produce a witness at the time the petition for probate is filed. The self-proof affidavit's function is to negate the necessity for any witness to either testify in open court or sign an affidavit or oath when the will is produced for the probate court. The affidavit saves a great deal of time and in many cases a great deal of heartache and frustration, because it is often impossible to find witnesses when it is time to probate the will. Sometimes witnesses have predeceased the decedent. Sometimes the witness has become incompetent and cannot testify or otherwise take an oath. Witnesses' memories may have become faulty after a period of years. Many times the witness was a law office receptionist, secretary, or paralegal, who, after witnessing so many wills, does not remember the testator or the will's execution, years later. In today's mobile society, the witness may have moved to not only another city, but to another state or country. Witnesses may change their surnames due to marriage or divorce, making them difficult to track down.

Still other times, producing a witness in open court can be a costly endeavor for the decedent's estate if the witness must be brought to the city where the will is being probated. Expenses that many estates cannot afford often include food, lodging, and transportation. A self-proof affidavit substitutes for the testimony of the witnesses, negating the need to produce a witness to testify that the testator was of sound mind and knew that he or she was signing a will and that he or she did so in the witnesses' presence.

If a self-proving affidavit was executed, a witness will only be required to testify if a will contest ensues.

When a self-proof affidavit has not been executed, the probate court will require the testimony of at least one witness in open court or the execution of an affidavit, which is dependent upon state statute. The witness will be required to testify as to the testator's competence at the time the will was signed. If the witness is only required to sign an affidavit, but lives outside the state in which the probate is being administered, a special commissioner may have to be appointed. The commissioner is someone in the other jurisdiction, usually a notary public in that jurisdiction, who is granted the authority to administer an oath on behalf of clerk or court. This can be a time-consuming as well as costly process. It is another valid reason to have the witnesses execute a self-proof affidavit at the time of the will's execution.

At this time, the clerk or court will admit the will to probate if it finds the will to be valid.

Bond and Testamentary Letters

While some states require all personal representatives to post a bond, many do not under two circumstances:

- The decedent's will has a provision that specifically states a bond is not required. When a clause in the will specifically states that the personal representative should not have to post a security or bond, one is not required, although in some states, such as Virginia, a bond is required for a non-resident personal representative regardless of the will's provision.
- The bond is waived because all beneficiaries agree that the personal representative should not have to post bond.

After it is determined whether or not the personal representative must post bond, and it is posted if required, the clerk or court will issue **testamentary letters**. Testamentary letters, also called letters of administration, are the proof that the personal representative needs to administer the estate. Once the letters are issued, the personal representative has the power to perform his or her duties, which, as discussed in Chapter 9, include collecting the decedent's assets; collecting debts owed to the decedent, and paying those due; managing the estate during the time of administration; and distributing the estate to the beneficiaries.

Obtaining Tax Identification Number for the Estate

Each estate must obtain a tax identification number from Internal Revenue Service (IRS) called an Employee Identification Number or EIN. The paralegal will use Internal Revenue Form SS-4 to obtain the EIN, and file the form according to the instructions on the IRS website (the place of filing changes periodically and it's best to review the instructions to insure you are sending the form to the correct mailing address, or faxing it to the correct telephone number). IRS Form SS-4 may currently be found online at http://www.irs.gov/pub/irs-pdf/fss4.pdf.

Inventory

Once the personal representative has been given testamentary letters, he or she will file an inventory of the decedent's estate with the clerk or court. The **inventory** is a detailed list of the decedent's property that includes not only the description of each item of real and personal property of the estate, but also the estimated value of each item. The description of each item must include information like bank account numbers, serial numbers for stocks and bonds, Vehicle Identification Numbers (VINs) and state registration numbers for all cars, and legal descriptions

Figure 11.7 Letters Granting Authority to Probate (California)

DE-150

ATTORNEY OR PARTY WITHOUT ATTORNEY *(Name, state bar number, and address)* :	TELEPHONE AND FAX NOS.:	*FOR COURT USE ONLY*

ATTORNEY FOR *(Name)*:

SUPERIOR COURT OF CALIFORNIA, COUNTY OF

STREET ADDRESS:

MAILING ADDRESS:

CITY AND ZIP CODE:

BRANCH NAME:

ESTATE OF *(Name)*:

DECEDENT

CASE NUMBER:

LETTERS

☐ **TESTAMENTARY**	☐ **OF ADMINISTRATION**
☐ **OF ADMINISTRATION WITH WILL ANNEXED**	☐ **SPECIAL ADMINISTRATION**

LETTERS

1. ☐ The last will of the decedent named above having been proved, the court appoints *(name)*:

    a. ☐ executor.

    b. ☐ administrator with will annexed.

2. ☐ The court appoints *(name)*:

    a. ☐ administrator of the decedent's estate.

    b. ☐ special administrator of decedent's estate

        (1) ☐ with the special powers specified in the *Order for Probate.*

        (2) ☐ with the powers of a general administrator.

        (3) ☐ letters will expire on *(date)*:

3. ☐ The personal representative is authorized to administer the estate under the Independent Administration of Estates Act ☐ **with full authority** ☐ **with limited authority** (no authority, without court supervision, to (1) sell or exchange real property or (2) grant an option to purchase real property or (3) borrow money with the loan secured by an encumbrance upon real property).

4. ☐ The personal representative is not authorized to take possession of money or any other property without a specific court order.

WITNESS, clerk of the court, with seal of the court affixed.

(SEAL)

Date:

Clerk, by

_____
(DEPUTY)

AFFIRMATION

1. ☐ PUBLIC ADMINISTRATOR: No affirmation required (Prob. Code, § 7621(c)).

2. ☐ INDIVIDUAL: **I solemnly affirm** that I will perform the duties of personal representative according to law.

3. ☐ INSTITUTIONAL FIDUCIARY *(name)*:

    I solemnly affirm that the institution will perform the duties of personal representative according to law. I make this affirmation for myself as an individual and on behalf of the institution as an officer. *(Name and title)*:

4. Executed on *(date)*:

    at *(place)*: , California.

▶ _____
(SIGNATURE)

CERTIFICATION

I certify that this document is a correct copy of the original on file in my office and the letters issued the personal representative appointed above have not been revoked, annulled, or set aside, and are still in full force and effect.

(SEAL)

Date:

Clerk, by

_____
(DEPUTY)

Form Approved by the
Judicial Council of California
DE-150 [Rev. January 1, 1998]
Mandatory Form [1/1/2000]

LETTERS
(Probate)

Probate Code, §§ 1001, 8403,
8405, 8544, 8545;
Code of Civil Procedure, § 2015.6

Figure 11.8 Inventory (Ohio)

BARRETT BROTHERS, SPRINGFIELD, OHIO 1-800-322-7711

PROBATE COURT OF ______________ COUNTY, OHIO

ESTATE OF ____, DECEASED

CASE NO. __________________

INVENTORY AND APPRAISAL

[R.C. 2115.02]

To the knowledge of the fiduciary the attached schedule of assets in decedent's estate is complete. The fiduciary determined the value of those assets whose values were readily ascertainable and which were not appraised by the appraiser, and that such values are correct.

The estate is recapitulated as follows:

Tangible personal property .... $______________

Intangible personal property .... $______________

Real Estate .... $______________

Total .... $______________

Automobile transferred to surviving spouse under R.C. 2106.18 .... $______________

[Check if applicable] ☐ The surviving spouse is the sole legatee and devisee under decedent's will, and has not manifested an intention to take against it. It is therefore unnecessary to cite the surviving spouse to make an election.

______________________________ ______________________________

Attorney Fiduciary

Attorney Registration No. ______________

APPRAISER'S CERTIFICATE

The undersigned appraiser, appointed by the Court, appraised those assets whose values were not readily ascertainable, indicated on the attached schedule by a check in the column "Appraiser" opposite each such item, and states that such values are correct.

____

Appraiser

FORM 6.0 - INVENTORY AND APPRAISAL 3/1/96

(*continued*)

Figure 11.8 (continued)

WAIVER OF NOTICE OF TAKING OF INVENTORY
[R.C. 2115.04]

The undersigned surviving spouse hereby waives notice of the time and place of taking the inventory of decedent's estate.

_____
Surviving Spouse

WAIVER OF NOTICE OF HEARING ON INVENTORY
[Use when notice is required by the Court or deemed necessary by the fiduciary]

The undersigned, who are interested in the estate, waive notice of the hearing on the inventory.

_____   _____

_____   _____

_____   _____

_____   _____

_____   _____

_____   _____

ENTRY SETTING HEARING

The Court sets _____ at _____ o'clock _____.M., as the date and time for hearing the inventory of decedent's estate.

_____   _____
Date   Probate Judge

for all real estate. The supervising attorney and personal representative will often look to the paralegal for guidance during this phase of administration, which can be quite a rigorous and daunting responsibility for the personal representative. This is usually required to be filed within 90 days of obtaining testamentary letters.

THE PROFESSIONAL PARALEGAL

It is in the best interest of the paralegal to have a list of possible real estate appraisers, stock brokers, numismatists, philatelists, certified public accountants, and other professionals who are well versed in the appraisal of tangible and intangible personal property.

Estate Expenses, Debts, Taxes, Notice to Creditors, and Claims Against the Estate

The personal representative must also assist in determining the extent of any expenses, debts, and taxes that are due by the estate. All claims against the estate that were legal and owed by the decedent at the time of death, as well as estate taxes, are paid from the estate assets. The assets are liquidated based upon express provision in the state statutes for payment of all debts in a process called *abatement*. **Abatement** is discussed in Chapter 3, and refers to a reduction in the sums or gifts to a beneficiary to pay the taxes and debts of the estate. If the decedent's will specifically refers to the order of liquidation, however, the will controls.

Creditors must be given notification that an estate has been opened and be given the opportunity to file a claim against the estate. Each state has a different timetable for when the notice must be given but generally it is done immediately after receiving testamentary letters. For known creditors, the notice is sent to them directly by mail, usually certified. A notification is also published in a local newspaper of general circulation informing unknown creditors of the probate and telling them who they may contact for further information or where to send the claim for payment. Publication usually entails a notice in the newspaper once a week for two or three consecutive weeks. Creditors usually have between 6 and 12 months to file their claim or be barred.

Payment of claims usually occurs in the following order:

- Costs and expenses of administration. All costs and expenses incurred by the personal representative for the administration of the decedent's estate are paid first.
- Reasonable funeral expenses. If the cost of the decedent's funeral was not pre-paid through pre-paid funeral services or through life insurance, the personal representative will be required to pay those expenses with the collected estate assets.
- Debts and taxes with federal preference.
- Medical and hospitalization expenses of the decedent's last illness that are valid and reasonable.
- Debts and taxes with state preference.
- Other creditors' claims.

The personal representative also has to keep track of when to file the various tax returns as discussed in Chapter 12. Returns to be filed include the last income tax return of the decedent, income tax return of the estate, and the estate tax return.

Accountings

Personal representatives, in addition to the initial inventory, must file regular accountings, usually annually. In most cases, the first accounting is also the final accounting but sometimes, estates stay open for longer than a one-year period.

The **accounting** is a report of all transactions made by the personal representative during the administration of the estate. All receipts and disbursements, including payment and settlement of debts, expenses, and taxes, as well as those transactions in which distribution is made to various beneficiaries, are documented in the final accounting.

When the personal representative is ready to distribute all of the estate's assets to the appropriate beneficiaries or heirs, a final accounting will be filed. In many states, the final accounting is all that is necessary to close the estate. In others, a petition for discharge must be filed with the probate court after the final accounting has been made and accepted by the court. If the beneficiaries waive the final accounting, the personal representative will immediately petition for discharge, usually prompting a swift grant of the order for discharge by the court.

Distribution to Beneficiaries and Discharge of the Estate

What most beneficiaries and heirs wait for, and sometimes annoy the personal representative over, is when they will receive "their money"; however, beneficiaries and heirs only take distribution of the estate once all of the debts, taxes, and claims, as shown above, have been paid. In some instances, an estate is insolvent or nearly so, and the estate will make little or no distribution. In most instances, an estate is not distributed until the waiting period for creditors to make claims has expired. If any distribution is made before that time, the personal representative asks the beneficiaries or heirs to provide a refunding bond, which provides that if a claim arises, the beneficiary will refund the money to the estate so the claim can be paid. Most times, the personal representative does not make any distributions until the estate is beyond the creditors' waiting period, however, as the personal representative could be held personally liable for the shortage in the estate, but for that refunding bond and getting the money back from a beneficiary that already spent it is too difficult a task.

Once all the assets have been distributed, the personal representative will be discharged. *Discharge* means that the personal representative (or administrator) will be released from his or her obligations to the estate and all future claims against the estate are barred.

Ancillary Administration

Ancillary administration is required when a decedent was domiciled in one jurisdiction but has real property located in another, at the time of death. When this occurs, a probate proceeding of the decedent's real property located in the other jurisdiction is required, in addition to the probate in the state of domicile. This probate proceeding does not attempt to distribute all of the decedent's property, however. The sole purpose of this probate proceeding is to determine the proper distribution of the real property located outside the jurisdiction of the probate court of the decedent's domicile. This type of proceeding is required because the court located in the decedent's place of domicile is prohibited from making distribution decisions about real property not within its jurisdictional limits or boundaries. The concept of ancillary jurisdiction is also covered in Chapter 13.

Figure 11.9   Sample Final Accounting

In the City of Anytown, State of Anystate First and Final Proposed Settlement Report of Donald Black as Executor of the Estate of Bobbie Black, Deceased

ASSETS PER APPRAISEMENT: $1,045,372.97

RECEIPTS:

1. 9/17/10, Anytown Nursing Facility, Refund $2,100.00
2. 2/27/11, Social Security Payment   787.00

DISBURSEMENTS:

1. 7/7/10, Anytown Funeral Home, Funeral Expense $4,486.75
2. 7/7/10, Anytown Religious Center, Funeral Expense   100.00
3. 7/7/10, Organist, Funeral Expense   100.00
4. 7/7/10, Anytown Flowers, Funeral Expense   57.75
5. 9/22/10, John Smith, Esq., Legal Fee, Probate Expense   1,800.00
6. 9/22/10, Clerk's Office, Probate Expense   175.00
7. 9/22/10, Clerk's Office, Filing Fee, Probate Expense   20.00
8. 9/26/10, Anytown Bank, Estate Acct Check Printing Fee,
   Probate Exp.   18.00
9. 9/26/10, United States Postal Service, Postage, Probate Expense   11.54
10. 10/7/10, Anytown Pharmacy, Medical Expense   224.21
11. 10/17/10, United States Postal Service, Postage, Probate Expense   5.21
12. 11/5/10, John Smith, Esq., Legal Fee, Probate Expense   780.00
13. 12/11/10, Dr. Everett Jones, Medical Expense   200.00
14. 12/12/10, John Smith, Esq. Legal Fee, Probate Expense   781.00
15. 12/12/10, United States Postal Service, Postage, Probate Expense   72.94
16. 1/31/11, Anytown Monuments, Cemetery Plot Monument,
    Funeral Expense   381.75
17. 2/11/11, John Smith, Esq., Legal Fees, Probate Expense   820.00
18. 3/27/11, United States Treasury, Income Taxes, Probate Expense   835.00
19. 3/31/11, United States Postal Service, Postage, Probate Expense   11.37
20. 4/11/11, John Smith, Esq., Legal Fee, Probate Expense   340.00
21. 5/21/11, John Smith, Esq., Legal Fee, Probate Expense   340.00
22. 6/1/11, Rupert Jones, CPA, Est. Inc. Tax Return, Prob. Exp.   550.00
23. 6/4/11, John Smith, Esq., Legal Fee, Probate Expense   769.50

DISTRIBUTION OF ASSETS:

NONE

(continued)

Figure 11.9 (continued)

ASSETS ON HAND:

1. Anystate Securities, as of 6/4/11	$63,605.17
2. Anytown Bank	$30,774.78

TOTAL RECEIPTS (included in Assets on Hand):	**$2,937.00**
TOTAL DISBURSEMENTS:	**$12,880.02**
TOTAL DISTRIBUTIONS:	**$00.00**
TOTAL ASSETS ON HAND:	**$94,379.95**

PROPOSED DISTRIBUTIONS:

1. Donald Black, Estate Distribution	$ 92,863.95
2. John Smith, Esq. Final Legal Fees	800.00
3. United States Treasury, Income Taxes, Probate Expense	300.00
4. Rupert Jones, CPA, Est. Inc. Tax Return, Probate Expense	375.00
5. Clerk's Office, Approval of Settlement of Accounts	30.00
6. Clerk's Office, Recording Settlement of Accounts	11.00

TOTAL PROPOSED DISTRIBUTIONS: $94,379.95

VERIFICATION

I, Donald Black, Fiduciary of the Estate of Bobbie Black, deceased, do hereby affirm that the foregoing is a true, correct, complete report of all receipts and disbursements made from the estate. I further affirm that I have exercised due diligence in the investigation of any and all claims against this estate and to the best of my knowledge and belief I state there are no other claim/debts due or owing against this estate.

_____

DONALD BLACK, Fiduciary

STATE OF ANYSTATE

CITY OF ANYTOWN

Taken, subscribed and sworn to before me the undersigned Notary Public, by DONALD BLACK, Fiduciary of the Estate of Bobbie Black, this _____ day of _____, 2011.

_____

Notary Public

My Commission Expires: _____

My Cert No.: _____

Example: Greg Goode was domiciled in Anytown, Anystate, at the time of his death. His daughter Tina, hired a lawyer in Anytown to begin probate. During the initial conference with Tina, the lawyer determined that Greg owned a condo in Sun City, Arizona, where Greg went for vacations and to where he intended to retire. The attorney must file an ancillary, or secondary, probate proceeding in the appropriate Arizona court so that Greg's property in Arizona can be properly distributed, since the court in Anystate does not have jurisdiction over the Arizona real property.

Figure 11.10 Order of Discharge (Michigan)

Approved, SCAO

OSM CODE: DIS

STATE OF MICHIGAN PROBATE COURT COUNTY CIRCUIT COURT - FAMILY DIVISION	ORDER OF DISCHARGE	FILE NO.

In the matter of _____

1. Date of hearing: _____ Judge: _____

Bar no.

2. It appears the fiduciary in this matter has fully performed the duties required by law.

IT IS ORDERED:

3. _____ , _____

Name   Title

is discharged and bond, if any, cancelled.

4. The matter/estate ☐ is closed.
☐ is not closed.

_____
Date

_____
Judge

_____
Attorney name (type or print)   Bar no.

_____
Address

_____
City, state, zip   Telephone no.

Do not write below this line - For court use only

PC 597 (9/03) **ORDER OF DISCHARGE**   MCL 330.1626, MCL 700.3612, MCL 700.5431, MCL 700.5426(4), MCL 700.5310, MCR 5.311(B)(3)

In most instances, the court with ancillary jurisdiction will require exemplified or authenticated copies of the original probate procedures documents, including the will and testamentary letters. Exemplified copies are also referred to as triple-sealed copies. These are filed with the petition for the ancillary jurisdiction. The purpose for an ancillary jurisdiction is to transfer the title to the real property held in the other state in a manner that leaves no cloud on the title, meaning that there are no irregularities in the title preventing sale or conveyance to another.

SUMMARY

When a person dies, the decedent's debts must be paid; any money due to the decedent must be collected; and the decedent's real and personal property must be collected and valued. When those tasks are completed, the remaining property must be distributed to the beneficiaries or heirs as set forth in either the decedent's will or by descent and distribution. This is accomplished through a process called probate, which means "to prove."

During the pre-probate phase, the personal representative, with assistance from the lawyer and especially from the paralegal, will perform a number of tasks including obtaining the decedent's death certificate and finding the decedent's will and codicils. If necessary, the personal representative will petition the probate court for permission to open the decedent's safe deposit box or to search the decedent's home or office. At this time, the attorney will determine if the decedent's estate may be probated by informal or formal proceedings, as provided by state statute.

If the attorney concludes that the estate can be probated through informal proceedings, a petition for small estate or summary administration will be filed with the clerk or court. A notice to creditors will be given to all known creditors and published in a newspaper of general circulation. Once the petition is filed, the court will grant an order of small estate or summary administration, and the personal representative will distribute the estate's assets to the beneficiaries or heirs. Then the estate will be discharged. This is a simple and cost-effective process.

When the attorney concludes that the estate must be probated through formal administration, a petition is filed. The as-yet-to-be-appointed personal representative must then prove the validity of the decedent's will. This is done through a witness's affidavit or testimony in open court. After the will is admitted to probate, the court appoints the personal representative as the legal fiduciary to administer the estate. The personal representative must post a bond unless the decedent's will made express provision to the contrary, or all of the will's beneficiaries and other interested parties agree that the bond may be waived. If a will, is lost, the personal representative will have to go through various steps to prove the will. A copy of the will, as well as testimony by witnesses to the execution of the will and to the terms of the will, must be presented before a copy of a will may be admitted to probate as the actual will of a decedent.

Once the personal representative is appointed, he or she is granted testamentary letters. The letters evidence the personal representative's legal right to administer the decedent's estate. Administering the estate includes collecting all of the estate assets, paying all the debts and taxes of the estate, managing the assets during the estate administration proceedings, and distributing the remaining assets to the appropriate beneficiaries or heirs. After the assets are distributed, the court will discharge the personal representative and close the estate.

Ancillary jurisdiction is a proceeding that allows for the probate of real property that was not located in the jurisdiction in which the decedent was domiciled at the time of death. A separate proceeding is held in the jurisdiction in which the real property is actually located because the court in the jurisdiction of the decedent's domicile is prohibited from distributing property outside its jurisdiction.

KEY TERMS

probate
estate administration
guardianship
ancillary administration

testamentary letters
accounting
formal administration
inventory

summary administration
abatement

REVIEW **QUESTIONS**

1. What is probate?
2. What consequences might be there if a will's custodian fails to turn the will over to the probate court after the decedent's death?
3. What is the purpose of a self-proof affidavit?
4. What is an inventory?
5. When would a personal representative have to institute an ancillary jurisdiction proceeding?
6. What are testamentary letters?
7. What is a summary administration?
8. What is an EIN?
9. What steps might have to be undertaken to find the will of a decedent?
10. What expenses and debts of an estate may be paid by the personal representative?
11. What steps are required to prove a lost will?

PROJECTS

1. Draft a memo for clients which explains the probate process. If discussed in your class, include specific tasks that are performed in your jurisdiction.
2. Obtain copies of the relevant probate court forms for your state and review them.
3. Review the following case regarding ancillary administration. What were the findings of the Supreme Court of Wisconsin regarding the decedent's domicile?

MyLegalStudiesLab™   http://www.mylegalstudieslab
MYLEGALSTUDIESLAB VIRTUAL LAW OFFICE EXPERIENCE ASSIGNMENTS

Complete the pre-test, study plan, and post-test for this chapter and answer the Legal Applications questions as assigned.

These will help you confirm your mastery of the concepts and their application to legal scenarios. Then, complete the Virtual Law Office assignments as assigned by your instructor. These assignments are designed to develop your workplace skills and result in producing documents for inclusion in your portfolio.

CASE 7.2

In the Matter of the ESTATE of Eric TRESSING, a/k/a Eric J. Tressing, Deceased.

OAK PARK TRUST & SAVINGS BANK, Ancillary Personal Representative, Joseph M. Tressing, Lawrence T. Crown and Sally Crown, Respondents,

v.

Esther P. TRESSING, Appellant.
   273 N.W.2d 271
   Supreme Court of Wisconsin.
   Decided Jan. 9, 1979.
   DAY, Justice.

This is an appeal from a judgment of the county court of Walworth County, the Honorable John D. Voss, presiding, entered July 30, 1976, which determined that the deceased was domiciled in Riviera Beach, Florida, at the time of his death which we affirm. The appeal is also taken from the order granting ancillary probate of the estate and issuing ancillary letters to Oak Park Trust and Savings Bank of Oak Park, Illinois. We affirm that part of the order allowing ancillary probate of the will of the deceased but reverse that part of the order naming Oak Park Trust and Savings Bank as ancillary personal representative and remand for further proceedings.

The principal question raised on this appeal is whether the finding of the trial court that the deceased, Eric Tressing, was domiciled in the state of Florida at the time of his death is against the great weight and clear preponderance of the evidence. We hold such finding is not against the great weight and clear preponderance of the evidence and accordingly we affirm the judgment declaring him to be such a resident. The second question is whether or not the order granting ancillary rather than primary probate was proper? [sic] We hold that it was.

part of opinion omitted

The issues presented here arose when Esther P. Tressing, widow of the deceased filed a petition on February 10, 1976 for intestate administration (with attached copy of will and codicil) and for will and codicil to be admitted to probate if produced at time of hearing and requesting that letters be issued to her as personal representative. Oak Park Trust and Savings Bank filed an objection to the issuance of such letters and in turn petitioned that letters of ancillary administration be issued to it. The petition by Esther Tressing alleged that the deceased was domiciled in Wisconsin at the time of death whereas the petition of the Oak Park Trust and Savings Bank alleged the deceased was domiciled in Florida at the time of death. The court after taking testimony denied both of her requests and issued an order for ancillary probate naming the Oak Park Trust and Savings Bank as ancillary personal representative. The court made fourteen findings of fact in support of its ruling that the deceased at the time of death was a Florida domiciliary. The court said " . . . the court does conclude that the deceased attempted to and succeeded in changing his domicile and legal residence from Wisconsin to Florida in 1972 for the following reasons:. . . ."

There then followed the fourteen specific findings that the deceased prior to death (1) made two declarations of domicile in Florida dated March 1, 1972 and November 6, 1972; (2) voted in Florida in 1972; (3) leased an apartment in Florida on an annual basis from March 1, 1972 until the time of his death which lease was still in effect the date of trial, March 27, 1976; (4) made two wills and one codicil commencing "I, Eric J. Tressing of the county of Palm Beach in state of Florida do hereby make public and declare" etc.; (5) registered his personal automobile in Florida; (6) had a Florida's driver's license; (7) established a bank account in Florida; (8) procured a safety deposit box in Florida; (9) the death certificate gave his Florida address; (10) notified his accountant and his attorney of change of permanent residence; (11) his Federal Income Tax returns bore the Florida address and were filed in Georgia, the proper place for filing such Florida returns; (12) never had a bank account in Wisconsin and named no Wisconsin charities in his wills; (13) transferred his Blue Cross and Blue Shield insurance to Jacksonville, Florida; (14) ". . . almost all of the foregoing were admitted by his widow on cross-examination."

The court in its decision of July 19, 1976 noted the arguments of Mrs. Tressing that the decedent was a Wisconsin resident and that the deceased (1) did not file tax return on tangible property in Florida; (2) maintained a telephone credit card with the Lake Geneva, Wisconsin address and at all times from 1966 to date of death was listed in the Lake Geneva telephone directory; (3) maintained a Lake Geneva Sentry "courtesy check-cashing card;" (4) continued his membership in the American Association of Retired Persons with his Lake Geneva address; (5) maintained his various Lake Geneva area fraternal memberships through 1975; (6) in 1972, rented an automobile in Florida and on the rental contract showed his home address to be Lake Geneva and also his Wisconsin driver's license number; (7) renewed his American Economy insurance policy dated December 4, 1972 giving Lake Geneva as his address; (8) the tax forms of the deceased were mailed to him at his Lake Geneva address (although the tax forms, themselves, showed his Florida address); (9) deceased's Illinois attorney corresponded with deceased at Lake Geneva on important trust matters; (10) the Oak Park Trust & Savings Bank checking accounts dealt with him as a Lake Geneva resident since 1972; (11) various medical bills and statements were directed to the Lake Geneva address; (12) a Pfizer stock certificate dated January 26, 1973 showed his address to be Lake Geneva; (13) various drug receipts and miscellaneous statements were introduced showing the Lake Geneva address.

The standard for review that this court must apply in reviewing trial court findings is strict. The fact that this court might have reached a different conclusion in a given case by its own balancing of the inferences and possible conclusions to be drawn from evidence presented is not the standard to be applied. Two trial courts faced with identical conflicting evidence may reach opposite conclusions. Yet it could be said that neither court's findings was in fact against the great weight and clear preponderance of the evidence.

Seventy years ago this court in Ott v. Boring, 139 Wis. 403, 407, 121 N.W. 126, 128 (1909) said:

> Hence the rule that there must not only be a preponderance of evidence against such determination, but there must be a clear preponderance. The significance of the word 'clear' is not always fully appreciated. Manifestly, that requires the preponderance to be so apparent as to manifestly outweigh any probable legitimate influence upon the triers of those advantages for discovering the truth which the reviewing tribunal cannot have . . .

This court has repeatedly said that findings of fact by the trial court will not be upset on appeal unless they are clearly erroneous and against the great weight and clear preponderance of the evidence. In re Estate of Taylor, 81 Wis. 2d 687, 696, 260 N.W.2d 803 (1978). To command reversal, such evidence and support of a contrary finding must itself constitute the great weight and clear preponderance of the evidence. In re Estate of Jones, 74 Wis.2d 607, 611, 615, 247 N.W.2d 168 (1976).

Eric Tressing, the deceased, and his wife Esther Tressing, the appellant in this case, were married in 1957. In 1966, the Tressings moved from Illinois to Lake Geneva, Wisconsin where the deceased owned a 220 acre farm. They lived in a modern ranch style house on the farm. There was another dwelling on the farm which was sometimes occupied by tenants. Mr. Tressing participated in some of the farm work, although there was a dispute in the testimony as to the extent of such involvement and the skill exercised when it was done. The Tressings socialized with family and friends in that area and Mr. Tressing was active in a fraternal organization.

In 1967, the Tressings established a pattern of traveling to Florida for the winter months and this pattern continued until close to Mr. Tressing's death. They usually left Wisconsin in late December, although in 1972, they did not make the trip until February. They would return to Wisconsin in late April. For several years they would stay in a motel until they found a furnished apartment for their stay in Florida. Dissatisfaction with these arrangements resulted in leasing a two bedroom unfurnished apartment on an annual basis in 1972. At about this time Mr. Tressing advised his wife he wanted to establish Florida residency. She testified she had no interest in becoming a Florida resident and asked him how he could do that since he had a home in Wisconsin and a farm here. His reply was to the effect that he knew what he was doing and to let him handle it. Other facts with regard to Mr. Tressing's activities between Florida and Wisconsin are set forth above from the findings of the trial court. In April 1973, Mr. Tressing became ill. Upon returning from Florida, he went to Chicago for medical help and received a diagnosis that he was suffering from a brain tumor. He underwent surgery in Chicago, and after two and one-half months of convalescence he returned to Lake Geneva with Mrs. Tressing in August, 1973. In late December, 1973, the Tressings went as usual to Florida and returned in April, 1974. They made their final trip to Florida in December, 1974, and returned in April, 1975. In September, 1975, Mr. Tressing's health began to fail. He was again hospitalized in Chicago for a month beginning October 10th, he then went to Lake Geneva for approximately a month and then returned to Illinois and entered a nursing home in December. He died at the nursing home on January 21, 1976. The death certificate, signed by

Mrs. Tressing, showed Mr. Tressing's address as Florida though Mrs. Tressing testified that her daughter was the one who supplied the address for that certificate.

In Estate of Daniels, 53 Wis.2d 611, 193 N.W.2d 847 (1972), this court said "where two homes are owned, domicile is determined by intention and physical acts are considered to express which residence is to be considered the permanent home as the domicile." This was a modification from the earlier rule as expressed in Will of Eaton, 186 Wis. 124, 133, 202 N.W. 309, 312 (1925) where the court held that once a domicile is established it is not lost until a new one is acquired and that where an actual domicile has been established, two things are necessary to create a new domicile, "first, an abandonment of the old domicile; and, second, the intention and establishment of a new domicile . . . "

In this time of great mobility of our population a residence may be owned in more than one state and ownership is not the prime requirement. Whether it is ownership or rental of a condominium or ownership of a mobile home parked on a rented area in a trailer park, the mere fact that a fee simple interest in residential property may exist in another jurisdiction is not determinative of whether a new domicile has been established. Particularly in retirement years people may have more than one place where they reside for a greater or lesser part of the year and whether they follow the sun or follow the snow, the place of physical habitation and the nature of the relationship to it, whether owned or leased, is only one of the indicia of residence along with others that establishes where the domicile of one may be for tax purposes. From an examination of the fourteen points relied on by the trial court in concluding that domicile was in Florida compared to the thirteen points raised by the widow and cited by the judge in his opinion in arguing for a finding of Wisconsin domicile, this court cannot say that the conclusion of the trial judge is against the greater weight and clear preponderance of the evidence.

The second question is did the trial court abuse its discretion in granting ancillary probate instead of primary probate, or as Esther Tressing's brief refers to it, "original" probate.

We conclude that the trial court acted properly within its discretion in granting ancillary probate. Wisconsin has adopted the Uniform Probate of Foreign Wills Act as sec. 868.01, Stats. (1975). In pertinent part, it provides:

. . . (5) Original probate; when allowed. Original probate of the will of a testator who died domiciled outside this state, which upon probate may operate upon any property in this state and is valid under the laws of this state, may be granted if the will does not stand rejected from probate or establishment in the jurisdiction where the testator died domiciled, or stands rejected from probate or establishment in the jurisdiction where the testator died domiciled solely for a cause which is not ground for rejection of a will of a testator who died domiciled in this state. The court may delay passing on the application for probate under this subsection pending the result of probate or establishment or contest at the domicile or on the application for probate under sub. (1).

> (6) Proof of will by probate in nondomiciliary jurisdiction. If a testator dies domiciled outside this state, an authenticated copy of his will and of the probate or establishment there of in a jurisdiction other than the one in which he died domiciled shall be sufficient proof of the contents and legal sufficiency of the will to authorize the admission of the will to probate under sub. (5) if no objection is made thereto. This subsection does not authorize the probate of any will which would not be admissible to probate under sub. (5), nor, in case objection is made to the will, to relieve proponent from offering proof of the contents and legal sufficiency of the will except that the original will need not be produced unless the court so orders.

The will of Mr. Tressing was admitted in Illinois which no one in this law-suit claims was his domicile. We conclude that sub. (6) of sec. 868.01, Stats. applies. The Commissioners Note to sub. (6), 8 Uniform Laws Annotated, p. 601 comments:

> This section is designed simply to facilitate proof in case that the only prior probate is in another ancillary jurisdiction and there is no objection to the will. It permits the court to dispense with the production of the original even if objection is made to the

will. However, probate in another ancillary jurisdiction has only prima facie effect and a local contest is permitted. Compare Sections 1, 2 and 3 where the prior probate is at the domicile.

Sub. (6) refers the reader back to sub. (5). This section is explained in MacDonald, Wisconsin Probate Law, Vol. 1, pp. 101-102 (1972):

> There can be no question but that the proper place for original probate is at the domicile of the testator, wherever that may be, and it was accordingly considered that the will should only be admitted to probate in Wisconsin after probate at the place of domicile, as a 'foreign' will, upon the record of probate at the place of domicile, in accordance with the statutes relating to probate of foreign wills. Under the statutes, however, (sec. 868.01(5)), the Wisconsin court may admit the will to probate if it is valid under the laws of this state and does not stand rejected in the state where the testator died domiciled. If it is rejected in that state solely for a cause which is not ground for rejection in Wisconsin it may be granted original probate in Wisconsin. Having admitted the will to probate the Wisconsin court may proceed as with an original administration as to both real and personal property within the county until such time as the will is probated and representatives are appointed at the domicile; after which remaining personalty may be transferred to the domiciliary representatives and the subsequent Wisconsin administration handled as an ancillary administration.

"Original probate" as used in sec. 868.01(5), Stats. is not the equivalent of domiciliary or primary probate; rather, it is an ancillary proceeding since it applies by its own terms to testators who die domiciled in states other than Wisconsin. As used in secs. 868.01(5) and (6), "original probate" means first in time. Thus, Wisconsin courts may act upon property located in the state, even though the will has not yet been admitted to probate in the state of domicile, provided other conditions of the statutes are met. This conclusion is underscored by the fact that the title of Chapter 868 is "Ancillary Procedures."

Mr. Tressing's will was admitted to probate in Illinois and that admission is not being contested. Sec. 868.03(3), Stats. provides that the court may deny the application for ancillary letters if it appears that the estate may be settled conveniently without ancillary administration. However, there is Wisconsin property involved in this case, and the trial court properly found that ancillary probate was necessary.

part of opinion omitted

Judgment affirmed. Order affirmed in part and reversed in part and remanded for further proceedings.

Chapter **twelve**

TAX CONSIDERATIONS IN ESTATE ADMINISTRATION

OBJECTIVES

At the end of this chapter, the student will understand:

- the fiduciary's duties concerning the decedent's taxes
- the decedent's final income tax return
- the estate's federal income tax return
- how the decedent's estate is valued
- a few post-mortem estate planning techniques

When someone dies, it becomes the responsibility of the personal representative (or administrator) to file all necessary tax forms and pay any taxes required by the Internal Revenue Service (IRS) and state taxing authorities. The determination concerning what items are taxable and actual tax computations are usually performed by the attorney or accountant for the estate. This does not preclude the paralegal from the process, however. Paralegals keep track of all the estate assets and expenditures. Paralegals also assist the personal representative in filling out the tax forms required by the Internal Revenue Service and state taxing authority, and insure that all filings are done properly and promptly. In this text, we will focus primarily on federal tax returns, as state tax returns vary by jurisdiction. Paralegals also assist with post-mortem (after death) estate planning, which usually focuses on tax planning and savings.

The Fiduciary's Obligations

The personal representative is responsible for filing all tax forms with the Internal Revenue Service. Should the personal representative fail to file the proper forms in a timely manner, the personal representative will be held personally liable for all interest and penalties the Internal Revenue Service assesses. If the personal representative distributes the decedent's estate to the beneficiaries before any taxes due are paid, he or she will be held personally responsible for payment of the taxes.

Two forms are generally filed with Internal Revenue Service before any others and are filed not only by large estates, but by small estates that have no tax liability as well:

- Form 56, "Notice Concerning Fiduciary Relationship"
- Form SS-4, "Application for Employer Identification Number"

THE PROFESSIONAL PARALEGAL

Paralegals may want to become acquainted with IRS Publication 559, "Survivors, Executors, and Administrators," a free publication that informs those people involved in winding up a decedent's tax liabilities. Publication 559 includes a list of all tax forms that may be required including samples of each, and instructions on how to fill them out. Publication 559 also includes a checklist of all the forms and their due dates.

All Internal Revenue Service forms may be found online at: *www.irs.gov*. A sample of IRS forms, current until date of publication, may be found in Appendix D. Many of the forms are now filled in PDF forms, which are a great tool. Unfortunately, you cannot save your work for a number of them and that means that either you leave the screen up until your supervisor reviews it or you have to retype the forms over again. This is fine for SS-4 and W-9 forms which are short; however, it would be impossible for an SS-760. Firms that handle a number of estate tax issues usually have dedicated software just for that purpose and those programs, properly updated, will have the newest IRS forms as well, and the means for the program to handle your calculations.

Notification of Decedent's Death to IRS

When the decedent dies, the personal representative may want to notify Internal Revenue Service of that fact. The form used is Form 56, "Notice Concerning Fiduciary Relationship." Form 56 is a simple one-page document that identifies the decedent, the personal representative (or administrator), and which notices should be sent to the personal representative. This form is not required by Internal Revenue Service regulations, but will ensure that any notices and communications from the Internal Revenue Service will be sent directly to the personal representative and not to the decedent's former address. It is a tremendous time-saver and will prevent the possibility that taxes will not be timely paid and interest and penalties incurred.

Tax Identification Number Application

A form that the personal representative must file with Internal Revenue Service as soon as possible is Form SS-4, "Application for Employer Identification Number," which is nothing more than an application for a tax identification number for the estate. It is common knowledge that all taxpayers in the United States are identified by the Internal Revenue Service not by our names but by identification numbers instead. Individuals have Social Security numbers. Other entities, such as corporations and partnerships as well as anyone who has employees, have employer identification numbers (EINs).

Estates, being a taxable entity, must also have identification numbers. Since Social Security numbers are reserved for individuals only, employer identification numbers are used for estates. The identification number must be used on all forms and correspondence sent to Internal Revenue Service. The **EIN** should be applied for immediately after obtaining testamentary letters, as it will be necessary to open an estate bank account as well as file tax returns. Obtaining an EIN is a simple process which can be done online, by fax, and by mail (although online and fax are used by attorneys and accountants due to the almost instantaneous result). EINs are also required for certain types of trusts so this is a very important form for a paralegal to become familiar with.

It should be noted that all IRS forms have instructions either at the end of the form or in a separate booklet and should be read for clarification and to insure that forms are being sent to the correct IRS facility. It should also be noted that *many attorneys do not assist in the preparation of income, or even estate tax returns, favoring the use of a trusted accountant to handle all tax matters.* Nonetheless, it is important to understand the procedures that have to be followed and the ramifications of various tax elections, as clients must still be counseled about what tasks must be completed. A client that doesn't know that as personal representative, he has to file tax returns will not know to contact an accountant either. It is the law office's responsibility to instruct the client in all matters.

Income Tax Returns

When a decedent dies, the personal representative is responsible for paying the decedent's final income taxes, if any. All decedents must have a final federal tax return filed on his or her behalf as well as a final state income tax return for those states with state income taxes.

Decedent's Final Federal Income Tax Return

Example: When Bobbie Black died in February 2011, she had not filed her 2010 income tax return yet. In fact, she was in no hurry and hadn't even made an appointment with her accountant. Bobbie was divorced and the mother of three adult children, Tina, Todd, and Ted. Since Bobbie died before the April 15, 2011 deadline for 2010 taxes, must a 2010 tax return be filed for her?

Yes. Bobbie's death in February 2011 does not excuse her from paying her taxes due to the United States Treasury for 2010. The personal representative of Bobbie's estate is responsible for filing the return by April 15, 2011 just as any other federal tax return must be filed by that time.

If no personal representative has yet been appointed, a relative or friend may file instead. In this case, it would be appropriate for one of Bobbie's children to file the 2010 income tax return on behalf of Bobbie's estate.

If the decedent was married at the time of death, a joint income tax return may be filed with the surviving spouse as long as the surviving spouse did not remarry before the end of the taxable year. If a joint return is filed, the decedent's income until date of death and the surviving spouse's income through December 31st must be claimed. The surviving spouse can also file a separate return on the behalf of the decedent.

> *Example:* Gary Morgan was married to Pamela White Morgan at the time of his death May 21, 2012. Pamela has not remarried. Pamela intends to file their joint tax return by April 15, 2013.

The income tax form used to file the decedent's final income tax is IRS **Form 1040**, which is the same form used by all taxpayers filing income tax returns. Only two things distinguish the filing from a regular income tax return: The return is marked "Final Return," and the time period for which income is being reported is generally shorter than one full year, since the income tax period ends on the date of the decedent's death. If a tax refund is due, a Form 1310, "Statement of Person Claiming Refund Due a Deceased Taxpayer," must also be filed in order to receive the refund.

Decedent's Final State Income Tax Return

The personal representative must also file a **final income tax return** when the state in which the decedent was domiciled has a state income tax. State requirements are too numerous to illustrate in detail. If the jurisdiction in which the paralegal works exacts an income tax, he or she must consult the state's statutes and codes, as well as any state-specific manuals, to determine when the returns must be made on behalf of the decedent and his or her estate, and what forms must be filed. Alaska, Florida, Nevada, South Dakota, Texas, Washington, and Wyoming do not have a state income tax and New Hampshire and Tennessee tax only dividend and interest income.

Federal Income Tax Return of the Estate

> *Example:* Winona Strayer died in February 2011. By the time of her death, she had earned commissions from her job in IT, dividends on her stocks and bonds, as well as other income. In addition, during the pendency of the probate administration, the stocks and bonds continued to accrue dividends, the estate bank account earned interest, and the sale of Winona's residence incurred a gain, meaning that it was sold for more than its value. Assume Winona's estate will be closed and the personal representative released in April of 2013. Winona's estate, therefore, must file an income tax return in April of 2011, 2012, and one for 2013, which is due on the 15th day of the 4th month after the estate is closed, in this case on August 15, 2013.

As already discussed, the personal representative's job is to distribute the decedent's assets either to the beneficiaries under a valid will or to the decedent's heirs by descent and distribution should the decedent die intestate, as soon as is practical. While the estate is being administered, however, the personal representative has the responsibility of making certain that the estate's assets produce income and do not lose value. A personal representative, therefore, must account for all of the income that accrued to the decedent from the beginning of the tax year until the date of death. Income includes unpaid wages and salary; income from any businesses in which the decedent may have been involved; trust income; rents, royalties, and dividends; and any gains from the sale of real or personal property. In the example above, Winona's estate has taxable income from January 1, 2011 until the date that the personal representative is released from his or her duties by the clerk or the court. For each tax year, or portion of a tax year that an estate is being administered, the personal representative must file a U.S. Fiduciary Income Tax Return [IRS Form 1041] on behalf of the decedent's estate. The filing date is April 15th if the tax year is a calendar year; on the 15th day of the 4th month after the end of the tax year when a fiscal year is used; and upon the closing of an estate, on the 15th day of the 4th month after the estate is closed.

Post-Mortem Estate Planning

Of course, all estate planning should be done during life. However, as we have already discussed, people often don't plan at all and die intestate, or they plan but plan poorly. Post-mortem or after death estate planning are the terms used to describe various techniques, which are used to lessen the consequences that occur when there is no planning or poor planning. Poor planning is usually the result of minimal estate planning, that is, simple wills or everything held jointly with right of survivorship, when in fact, more rigorous planning should have been done because either the estate or the beneficiaries need to save taxes. **Post-mortem estate planning** is therefore often referred to as post-mortem tax planning.

> *Example:* Tim and Joann Moore are a wealthy couple with three adult children, Charity, Hope, and Faith. If Tim and Joann executed simple wills in which they left everything to each other and then alternatively to their children, they may have a problem if Tim died in 2009 and their jointly held estate was worth more than $7 million.
>
> If Tim dies in 2013 without a change in the tax laws (discussed in this chapter under the section on the exclusion amount), and their jointly held estate is worth more than $2 million, Joann will have possible estate tax issues to contend with.
>
> To complicate matters, if Tim dies in January 2013 without a change in the tax laws, and Joann dies soon thereafter in March 2013, their children will inherit the entire $7 million. Perhaps, Charity is wealthy herself and doesn't really need the money. In fact, inheriting the money would only add to her tax problems. Perhaps, Faith lives in a state with an inheritance tax that will eat up any share he receives from his parents' estates.

> *Example:* Change the above fact-pattern just a bit, Tim and Joann Moore are not exceptionally wealthy but are very comfortable. They both die in 2013 and their wealthy children, Charity, Hope, and Faith (each having done very well in their careers) inherit the property from both parents, largely stocks and mutual funds. None of them really need the property or the increased income tax base they will have due to the dividends the property pays each year.

Can some of these issues be alleviated? Perhaps they can, with the use of various post-mortem estate planning techniques.

The most common post-mortem estate planning techniques are:

- Disclaimer clauses in a will or trust, in which the beneficiary has the right to disclaim, or refuse a gift of property. The beneficiary is then considered to have predeceased the executor (trustor) of the will (or the trust), allowing the property to pass to the alternate beneficiary or to deliberately lapse and be given to a residuary beneficiary.

Example: Any beneficiary or the legal representative of any deceased beneficiary shall have the right, within the time prescribed by law, to disclaim any benefit or power under my will. When property is to be distributed to the descendants of a person and, one such descendant disclaims his interest in all or a portion of such property, the disclaimed interest, determined as if the disclaimant were living at the time of distribution, shall be distributed to the then living descendants of the disclaimant; provided, however, that if the disclaimant has no descendants then living, the interest shall be distributed as if the disclaimant had predeceased the event that results in the distribution of the property.

- If a charity is the successor beneficiary, the primary beneficiary can disclaim so that the estate gets a charitable deduction pursuant to Internal Revenue Code §2055.

- Apportionment of taxes to insure that the residuary isn't adversely affected by having to pay the largest share of the tax burden, or that a beneficiary subject to inheritance taxes doesn't have a large tax burden.

- Marital deduction clauses and trusts, whereby specific assets are funneled to the family trust so that they are not taxed in the decedent's estate.

- Expenses of the estate taken on the income tax return of the decedent instead because to do so will assist in lowering the estate's income taxes to be paid that tax year. This is often done when there is an income tax due but no estate tax.

- Deduction of medical and dental expenses. Pursuant to The Internal Revenue Code [26 U.S.C. §213c] the decedent's medical and dental expenses may be deducted on the decedent's final income tax return. The expenses must be paid within a one-year period beginning with the day after the date of death. The surviving spouse or personal representative making this choice (election) must attach a statement to the income tax return saying that the expenses have not been and will not be claimed on the estate tax return since the decision to deduct them on the income tax return precludes their inclusion on the estate tax return.

- Valuation of the decedent's assets. Assets can be valued at the date of death or six months after the date of death, known as the alternate valuation date. If the value of the property has gone down in the six months after the decedent's death, the estate may save considerable money in taxes by valuing the property six months after death. The downside to this is that all assets must be valued at either date of death or six months after death. There is no selection of specific assets for this treatment.

- Qualified Terminable Interest Property (QTIP) election. If property is passing to a surviving spouse as the outright owner as qualified terminable interest property, it automatically qualifies for the estate tax marital deduction and no election has to be made to claim it.

- Claim of dower or courtesy where allowed by law, or claim of an elective share if such an election will increase the marital deduction, an amount that is exempt from estate taxes.

- If taxes are owed, asking for additional time to pay them. An extension to pay the estate tax may be granted by the IRS for a 12-month period for "reasonable cause."
- Power of appointment. As stated in Chapter 5, a power of appointment is created when a donor conferred the authority upon the donee to select and nominate who will receive property or its income either by will or in a trust, called the appointee. In some circumstances, the donee is given the authority to select himself or herself as the beneficiary. The holder of a general power of appointment (the donee) is treated for estate tax purposes as if he or she is the owner of the property subject to the power, whether or not the power is exercised, meaning whether or not the donee actually gives the property to the appointee. (If the power is not exercised, the person that obtains the property is called the taker in default.) This has the consequence of subjecting a decedent's estate to taxation of property that he or she didn't own at the time of his or her death and that he or she never owned during life! Merely having the appointment power as the donee determines that the property is includable in the decedent's estate. It does allow for planning, however, in which the power may be exercised in favor of those that will most benefit from the appointment. A special or limited power of appointment that is not exercised does not have the effect of causing the property to be included in the decedent's estate.

What are Estate Taxes?

According to the Internal Revenue Service "[T]he estate tax is a tax on your right to transfer property at your death. It consists of an accounting of everything you own or have certain interests in at the date of death." Estate taxes are, therefore, paid upon the transfer of the decedent's property to the beneficiaries or the heirs at law. These taxes are paid by the personal representative on behalf of the estate.

The Federal Estate Tax Return

The personal representative must file federal **estate tax returns** and state estate tax returns if required by the jurisdiction. This section will only describe the federal estate tax. The paralegal must, however, learn more about the estate tax requirements in his or her state.

The estate tax return is filed on Internal Revenue Service *Form 706*, "United States Estate (and Generation-Skipping Transfer) Tax Return," which must be filed within nine months of the decedent's death. If the nine-month time limit imposed will be difficult or impossible to meet, Form 4768, "Application for Extension of Time to File U.S. Estate Tax Return," is filed. It is important to file this form as soon as possible since the Service must rule on the extension before the estate tax return (Form 706) is due.

Form 706 is the primary return for federal estate taxation and may be the most important tax form for a paralegal to master if he or she intends to work in the estate planning field. The Internal Revenue Service has a number of free pamphlets and booklets available on how to prepare this form. It is highly recommended that these booklets should be obtained and studied before preparing the first Form 706 and that they be kept on hand for future reference. Law offices that prepare estate tax returns usually have tax return software which often comes with its own collection of information on how to prepare the return.

Form 706 is divided into five categories:

- Part I, "Decedent and Executor," asks for all information about the decedent, such as name, domicile at the time of death, and name and address of the personal representative.
- Part II, "Tax Computation," requires the computation of the total tax that is due by the estate. The personal representative must complete 19 schedules before Part II can be prepared. Discussion of the schedules is presented later in this chapter.
- Part III, "Elections by the Executor," refers to certain tax elections the personal representative may take. The form only requires an affirmative or negative response to questions such as, "Do you elect alternative valuation?"
- Part IV, "General Information," means general information about the estate. Items such as the decedent's death certificate must be attached. Part IV asks for information concerning the decedent's occupation at time of death, marital status, whether gift tax returns had ever been filed, and the names of any estate beneficiaries other than a surviving spouse.
- Part V, "Recapitulation," is the summarization of all the totals as computed for each of the 19 schedules.

A copy of Form 706 as current at time of publication may be found in the Appendix. The Internal Revenue Service website, www.irs.gov, has copies of all IRS forms, many of which are in fill-in format or online filing format. These forms are updated annually so it is important to always use the newest IRS form available.

Decedent's Gross Estate

In order to determine what, if any, estate taxes are due and owing on an estate, the gross estate of the decedent must be calculated. The gross estate is all of the property owned by the decedent at the time of death, as well as the value of any interest the decedent may have in property. Examples of property included in the gross estate are individually owned property, jointly held property, pensions and annuities, and life insurance. A property's value may be either:

- the fair market value on the date of death or
- the value on an alternate valuation date.

In general, the value of the property for estate tax purposes is the **fair market value** (FMV). FMV is the price that a buyer would be willingly to pay if the seller was not under pressure to sell, and both parties were aware of all relevant information concerning the sale. In other words, the price must be determined based upon an arm's length transaction without any coercion, or the need to sell at a "fire sale" in which prices are deeply discounted due to a need to sell quickly.

If the personal representative chooses, he or she may elect to use the **alternate valuation** method to determine the value of the decedent's property instead.

The alternate valuation method allows the personal representative to value the property six months after death if the value of the property has gone down in the six months after the decedent's death. When this method is used, the tax liability is reduced if the estate property's total value has decreased in the six months since death. The downside to this is that all assets must be valued at either date of death or six months after death. There is no selection of specific assets for this treatment.

Example: Jennifer Craig owned a house at the time of her death worth $300,000. Shortly after her death, housing values in Jennifer's neighborhood decreased substantially due to the downturn in the housing market. Six months after her death, Jennifer's house was only worth $150,000. It would be unfair to use the value of her house at the time of her death because it would create an unfair tax liability. Jennifer's personal representative may want to use the alternate valuation method, assuming that the value of the remainder of Jennifer's estate did not increase in the six months after her death.

If the majority of a decedent's property increased in the six months after death, and the aggregate increase in that property's value is more than the aggregate decrease in the other property, the personal representative would not elect the alternate valuation method.

Example: When Jennifer died, she owned the following property:

Item	Value at Time of Death
house	$300,000
stocks and bonds	$250,000
personal effects	$50,000
car	$27,000
Total Value	$627,000

Six months after her death, the value of each item of property was as follows:

Item	Value at Time of Death
house	$150,000
stocks and bonds	$450,000
personal effects	$45,000
car	$20,000
Total Value	$665,000

As explained in the prior example, Jennifer's house decreased in value because of a downturn in the housing market. The value of most of Jennifer's other property also decreased in value. Due to a bull stock market, however, the value of Jennifer's stock portfolio increased substantially. Since the aggregate value of Jennifer's property six months after her death is greater than the aggregate value of the property at the time of her death, Jennifer's personal representative will not elect the alternate valuation method.

After the decedent's gross estate is determined, all of the exemptions, deductions, and claims must also be determined, allowing for the calculation of the decedent's taxable estate. The taxable estate is the one upon which the federal estate tax is imposed. Credits are subtracted directly from the tax imposed. The estate will pay the balance or net tax due.

Schedules Relating to Assets

Schedule A: Real Estate. Schedule A identifies all the real estate owned solely by the decedent at the time of his or her death. It also includes the value of any property the decedent owned a share in as a tenant in common. As discussed in Chapter 2, real estate includes the land, buildings, crops that have not been harvested, mineral rights, and any fixtures attached to the property. Schedule A requires that the real estate be identified well enough so that the Internal Revenue Service can inspect the property to determine its value if need be. The fair market value (FMV) model is used to determine the value of real estate. Since the value used is the real estate's FMV, the *total* value of the property is indicated on Schedule A. Real estate that is mortgaged should be included on the schedule. The mortgage will then be deducted on Schedule E.

Schedule A-I: Real Estate Used in Farming or Closely Held Business. The Service allows a special use valuation for property used in farming or closely held businesses. The personal representative is permitted to value the real property according to its actual use, rather than its highest or best use. This is an election that is made and should only be used with care, as the value of the property at the time the beneficiaries or heirs take title to the property may affect their gains or losses upon sale. If this schedule is required, the services of an accountant or other tax expert will almost certainly be required.

Schedule B: Stocks and Bonds. All stocks and bonds that the decedent owned must be listed in complete detail. The information on the stocks includes the exact name of the corporation, the number of shares, whether they were common or preferred stocks, the par value, price per share, the exchange upon which the stocks are sold, that is, NYSE, AMEX, OTC, and the CUSIP (Committee on Uniform Security Identification Procedure) number, if it is available. The CUSIP number is a 9-digit number that is assigned to all stocks and bonds traded on major exchanges. It is most often located on the face of the stock certificate. If the stock is not publicly traded, the company's state and date of incorporation as well as the corporation's principal place of business must be given. Of course, most securities, including bonds and mutual funds, are now held in book entry form, meaning that instead of actual stock certificates, investors have their securities registered in their names without the issuance of physical certificates. The ownership is either electronically registered directly on the brokerage firm's books or those of their transfer agent. This allows buys and sells to be handled efficiently and eliminates the risk of losing or misplacing certificates. Book entry form also streamlines the process of determining the information for the estate tax return because the broker will not have to research each individual stock certificate. The information required for bonds includes the name of the obligor, quantity, and denomination of each type, interest rate, initial due date, date of maturity, principal exchange upon which the bond is sold, and the CUSIP number. If the bond is not listed, the business office of the obligor must be given. As with stocks, if they are in book entry form, the process of determining the information will be streamlined.

Stocks and bonds are listed according to their fair market value on the date of death. For securities, the fair market value is the mean between the highest and lowest selling prices quoted on the valuation date.

Example: On the day Bobbie Black died, she owned shares of stock in IBM. The highest selling price on that date was 125. The lowest selling price that day was 113. The fair market value is 119 ((125 + 113)/2 = 119).

Schedule C: Mortgages, Notes, and Cash. All interests owned by the decedent in mortgages (in some jurisdictions called deeds of trust), promissory notes, contracts to sell land, cash, and bank accounts must be accounted for on Schedule C. These are not debts of the decedent but interests in which someone owes the decedent money for loans the decedent made.

Information required on mortgages includes the original face value, unpaid principal balance, date when mortgage was executed, maturity date, name of the maker (who owes the money), a description of the property that is mortgaged, rate of interest, and interest dates.

Information on promissory notes includes the maker's name (the person stating that he or she owes money to the decedent, "I, John Smith, owe Two Thousand Dollars [$2000.00] to Jane Doe"), date given, principal amount, maturity date, rate of interest, and amount of unpaid interest and principal remaining.

Mortgages and notes are valued at their discounted rates. The discount rate is the amount a person would pay to purchase the note immediately, even if it would not be due for several years. The discount rate is not the face value. The bank must issue an order indicating what the value is. The order is attached to Form 706.

Example: When Kate died, she held a note from Carter, evidencing a loan Kate gave to Carter. The face value of the note was $15,000 but the bank has indicated that the discount rate is only $11,000 because the note will not come due for another 2 years. Kate's personal representative will indicate the value on Schedule C as $11,000 and attach a copy of the bank's order to the tax return.

Contracts to sell land are included on Schedule C and include the interest owned by the decedent, name of the buyer, date of the contract, property description, sale price, initial payment, installment amounts, and termination date.

Cash includes the location of all cash whether decedent had possession, or had deposited the money in a bank, in a safe deposit box, or with another person.

All bank accounts, except those held in joint tenancy, must be scheduled on Schedule C. The name and address of the depositor, amount on deposit, whether it is a savings or checking account, rate of interest, amount of interest accrued, and that payable as of the date of death, as well as the account number, must be included.

Schedule D: Insurance on Decedent's Life. As already discussed, insurance policies are non-probate assets and the insurance proceeds pass immediately to the beneficiary. If the decedent retains incidents of ownership in the policy, the estate will be responsible for taxes on the value of the proceeds. Incidents of ownership are indications that the decedent retained actual ownership rights in the property. Incidents of ownership include the following:

1. naming "the estate" as the beneficiary
2. having the right to cancel or surrender the policy
3. retaining the right to change the beneficiary
4. having the right to assign the policy
5. having the right to pledge the policy
6. having the right to borrow against the policy

When the decedent is deemed to have retained ownership and control of the life insurance policy and its proceeds, the policy is considered a taxable asset of the decedent's estate. Even if the decedent transferred the life insurance policy to someone else within three years of death, the value of the policy will be included in the taxable estate. Form 712, "Life Insurance Statement," must be obtained from the insurance company for each life insurance policy listed. The forms are attached to the schedule.

Schedule E: Jointly Held Property. All property held jointly, either as joint tenant with right of survivorship or as tenants by the entirety, must be included in Schedule E. If the property was jointly held with a surviving spouse, only one-half of the property's value must be declared, regardless of who paid for the property. If the property was held with anyone other than a surviving spouse, the entire value of the property must be declared unless the other joint owner can prove that he or she furnished all or part of the purchase price or that the property was acquired by gift, devise, bequest, or inheritance. In addition, any property found in a safe deposit box must be declared at full value unless the surviving joint tenant can prove ownership of the property.

Example: Phyllis owned a summer cottage jointly with her sister, Alice. At the time of the purchase, Phyllis paid two-thirds of the purchase price and alice paid one-third of the purchase price. When Phylllis died, Alice had to prove that she paid one-third of the cottage's purchase price. Once she proved that she did, only two-thirds of the cottage's value, the amount that Phyllis contributed to the purchase price, was declared on Schedule E. However, see the next example.

Example: Phyllis purchased a summer cottage and put it in both her and her sister, Alice's name as joint tenants with right of survivorship. When Phyllis died, the entire value of the cottage must be declared on Schedule E since Alice did not pay any of the cottage's purchase price. Now however see the difference in the outcome with this example:

Example: Assume that Phyllis was married to Philip at the time of her death. They owned a home valued at $300,000. Phyllis's husband was a stay at home dad for their entire marriage. Despite the fact that Philip never paid any money toward the house, only $150,000, or one-half, of the home's value will be declared on Schedule E because the surviving joint tenant is a surviving spouse.

Schedule F: Other Miscellaneous Property. Any property not declared on any other schedule is included on Schedule F. Usually this includes but is not limited to the following:

1. tangible personal property, such as automobiles, jewelry, art, clothing, and furniture
2. insurance on the life of another
3. income tax refunds
4. uncashed checks payable to the decedent
5. interests in other trusts and estates
6. reversionary and remainder interests
7. farm machinery, livestock, farm products, and growing crops that have been severed from the land, meaning they have been harvested

8. patents, copyrights, and royalties
9. Social Security payments
10. debts due the decedent
11. interest in businesses, such as sole proprietorships and partnerships

Schedule G: Transfers during Decedent's Life. Any transfer the decedent made during his or her lifetime in which he or she retained the benefits of the property, such as transfers in which the decedent retained a life estate to property or its income, must be declared on Schedule G. In addition, property the decedent transferred within three years of his or her death must be declared as well. This includes any property transferred to a living trust.

Property for which the decedent engaged in a bona fide sale for adequate and full consideration is not included in Schedule G, however.

> *Example:* Monica established an educational trust for her grandchildren two years before her death. Despite the fact that she retained no interest in the property, having made her son, Robert, the trustee, the property will be included in Schedule G because the transfer occurred within three years of Monica's death.

Schedule H: Powers of Appointment. The value of property over which the decedent possessed, exercised, or released a general power of appointment is declared on Schedule H. A general power of appointment is a power that can be exercised in favor of the decedent, his or her estate, his or her creditors, or his or her estate's creditors. Special powers of appointment in which the power could only be exercised in favor of other specifically named persons are not part of the decedent's estate and need not be declared.

> *Example:* Shawn's grandmother left a sizable estate at the time of her death. By the terms of the will, Shawn was given a power of appointment to distribute the property to whomever he chose, including himself. Since he was given a general power of appointment, this property is declared on Schedule H of Shawn's Form 706 when he dies.

> *Example:* Shawn's grandmother left a sizable estate at the time of her death. By the terms of the will, Shawn was given a power of appointment to distribute the property to any or all of certain named great-grandchildren. Since Shawn was given a special power of appointment and did not have the unfettered discretion to distribute the property to himself but only to the specifically named grandchildren, the property is not declared on Schedule H of Shawn's Form 706 when he dies.

Schedule I: Annuities. The value of annuities that will be received by a beneficiary of the decedent must be declared on Schedule I. **Annuities** are contracts between a person and an insurance company. The person makes a lump-sum payment or series of payments, and in return the insurance company agrees to make periodic payments to the person either immediately or at some date in the future. If the annuity terminates at the decedent's death and does not pay a death benefit to another beneficiary, the annuity is not included in the decedent's taxable estate and is not declared. The value of the annuity is determined by the insurance company that issued the annuity policy. The company will issue a letter which is then attached to the schedule.

Example: Michael's grandfather worked for 35 years until retirement. Upon retirement, Grandfather was paid an annuity on a monthly basis. When Grandfather died 10 years later, the annuity ceased. The value of the annuity is not included in Grandfather's estate and not recorded on his Schedule I. However, see the different outcome in this example.

Example: Michael's grandfather worked for 35 years until retirement. Upon retirement, Grandfather was paid an annuity on a monthly basis. When Grandfather died 10 years later, the annuity continued to pay Grandmother a monthly income until her death seven years after Grandfather. Since this annuity continued beyond Grandfather's date of death, the value of the annuity is declared on Grandfather's Schedule I.

Schedules Relating to Deductions

After the gross estate is calculated, certain items are deducted. The amount that remains is the taxable estate, or **adjusted gross estate**. The deductions are itemized on Schedule J through Schedule O.

Schedule J: Funeral Expenses and Expenses Incurred in Administering Property Subject to Claims. All reasonable expenses associated with a funeral service, including burial, headstone, mausoleum, cost of transporting the body to the place of burial, and payment to clergy officiating at the funeral are included in Schedule J. Whether or not the expenses are reasonable is based upon the size of the decedent's estate. As discussed earlier, these expenses may be deducted on the decedent's final income tax return as well, so the personal representative will have to determine where the deductions will have the most benefit to the decedent's estate.

Administration of probate expenses are also declared on Schedule J. These **administrative expenses** include legal fees, accountant's fees, court filing fees, appraisal fees, and any expenses incurred for collecting, maintaining (such as utility, rent, and insurance payments), and selling the estate's assets.

Schedule K: Debts of the Decedent, and Mortgages and Liens. Any reasonable debt of the decedent at the time of death may be declared on Schedule K. Debts are divided into secured and unsecured. Secured debts are those in which property was pledged as collateral, including car loans and mortgages. Unsecured debts are those in which no collateral was pledged, such as credit card debts, medical expenses, and taxes that accrued prior to the decedent's death. Any debt that is in dispute, however, may not be declared on this schedule.

Schedule L: Net Losses during Administration and Expenses Incurred in Administering Property Not Subject to Claims. If a loss occurred during the administration of the estate, such as a fire or theft, it may be declared on Schedule L.

Schedule M: Bequests and the like to Surviving Spouse. Any property left to the surviving spouse is declared on this schedule. All property left to the surviving spouse qualifies for the marital deduction, which as previously discussed, is unlimited. Decisions regarding whether or not the entire value of the marital deduction will be taken should be discussed with a tax attorney, CPA, or accountant. The qualified terminable interest property deduction election and a qualified domestic trust (regarding foreign spouses so they can get the marital deduction) is made on Schedule L as well.

Schedule N: Qualified ESOP Sales. This deduction was repealed. If for some reason you are using an old Form 706, leave this schedule blank.

Schedule O: Charitable, Public, and Similar Gifts and Bequests. Charitable gifts are those that are given to groups that are organized under §501(c)(3) of the Internal Revenue Code. Such groups are devoted to the advancement of religion, education, literature, charity, and science. Any gift to a §501(c)(3) organization may be declared on Schedule O. Gifts to any other type of organization will not be considered for this deduction.

Schedules Relating to Credits

Credits directly reduce the amount of taxes that are due by the decedent's estate.

Schedule P: Credit for Foreign Death Taxes. If the decedent was a citizen of the United States but was obligated to pay death taxes to a foreign country, usually because he or she was residing in that foreign country at the time of death, a credit may be claimed on Schedule P.

Schedule Q: Credit for Tax on Prior Transfers. This schedule has been repealed. If for some reason you are using an old Form 706, leave this schedule blank.

Schedule R: Generation-Skipping Transfer Tax. Generation-skipping transfers (GSTs) are very complicated and were discussed in Chapter 9. In these types of transfers, the beneficiaries (called "skip" persons) are two or more generations removed from the grantor, now the deceased. The most common example of this type of provision is when a grantor leaves a trust for the benefit of his children and his grandchildren. The grandchildren are two generations removed from the grantor. If it appears that a GST transfer tax may apply to the decedent's estate, a tax professional should be consulted.

Schedule U: Qualified Conservation Easement Exclusion. **Conservation easements** are contracts which permanently restrict the future use and development of land. They are created, among other reasons, to:

- retain or protect the land for the public and economically benefit the natural, scenic, or open space value of the land
- protect wildlife
- ensure that land remains available for agricultural, forest, recreational, or open-space use
- preserve the land's historical, architectural, archeological, or cultural use

An owner of real property that creates such an easement gives up some of his or her ownership rights in the property, whereby the owner is restricted ever after from developing the land or changing its use, pursuant to the terms of the agreement.

Certain tax benefits are created, however. The owner often gets a tax credit on state income taxes. In addition, because the land's use is now restricted, the value of the land is reduced. The Internal Revenue Code also provides that the lesser of the applicable percentage of the value of land (after certain reductions) or $500,000 per estate, not per tract of land, may be excluded from the owner's estate upon his or her death if it meets certain criteria; for example, the exclusion does not apply if the sole purpose is historic preservation. The personal representative may elect to donate an easement to capture the benefit of the exclusion, thereby using another post-mortem estate planning technique.

The conservation easement exclusion must be elected on Schedule U of Form 706.

Exclusion Amount

The Economic Growth and Tax Relief Reconciliation Act of 2001 (EGTRRA) has provided for more than one trillion dollars in tax cuts over a 10-year period. Among other provisions, EGTRRA changed the concept of a unified rate schedule for estate and gift tax transfers, so that the rate schedules for estates and gifts are now separate. The rate corresponds to a tax credit that will be received on an estate tax return, except for 2012, when Congress unified them again for one year only. This amount is what a person may give away during his or her lifetime (by gift) or in his or her estate (at death). Interestingly, EGTRRA was set to sunset, or be automatically repealed with respect to estate tax transfers, on December 31, 2010; however, Congress enacted the Tax Relief, Unemployment Insurance Reauthorization and Job Creation Act of 2010. This extended most of the EGTRRA "tax cuts" for two more years. At date of publication, it continues to be a question mark for estate planning attorneys, financial advisors, and accountants alike if Congress will permit the new cuts to sunset or will amend it before the law sunsets. This has caused a conundrum for estate planners trying to plan for the eventual death of a client and not really knowing how the law will affect the client's estate. The new law passed in 2010 provided for a maximum tax rate of 35% with a $5 million exclusion. The **exclusion amount** is adjusted for inflation for decedents that die in 2012. The new law also allowed those estates of decedents dying after December 31, 2009 but before January 1, 2011 the option to elect to apply either the 35% maximum rate and $5 million exclusion or no estate tax under EGTRRA. Because of the confusion, estates were also given an extension to file the returns.

Congress did not repeal the gift tax in 2010 but the law also provided that for gifts made after December 31, 2010, gift and estate taxes were combined into what is called a unifed credit, applying a maximum rate of 35% with a $5 million exclusion. This means that in 2011 and 2012, a person could gift up to $5 million dollars to family and others but then would have no estate tax exclusion remaining (adjusted for inflation in 2012, it is $5,120,000).

A person may always gift a separate amount each year; in 2012, the rate is $13,000 per donor, per person. The Internal Revenue Service may continue to adjust this rate for inflation. The exclusion rate in any given year is posted on the Internal Revenue Service website. Figure 12.1 shows the rate schedule for the estate tax exemption.

Figure 12.1   Applicable Exclusion Amount
Schedule for Estate Transfers

2001	$ 675,000
2002–2003	$1,000,000
2004–2005	$1,500,000
2006–2008	$2,000,000
2009	$3,500,000
2010	Repealed
2011	$5,000,000
2012	$5,120,000
2013	$1,000,000

The top tax rates are shown in Figure 12.2. As you can see, the rate that an estate may be taxed is quite high. However, less than 3% of estates actually pay an estate tax according to the Urban Institute-Brookings Tax Policy Center and the Center on Budget Policies and Priorities.

The broader topic of estate and gift tax will not be further discussed in this book as it could fill a book of its own due to its complexity.

Figure 12.2   Top Gift and Estate Tax Rates for
Years 2003 Through 2011

Year	Top Gift and Estate Tax Bracket
2003	49%
2004	48%
2005	47%
2006	46%
2007	45%
2008	45%
2009	45%
2010	35% (Gift Tax Only)
2011	35%
2012	35%
2013	55%

SUMMARY

As can be seen from the lengthy discussion in this chapter, the personal representative's responsibility to the decedent's estate is great. The personal representative first informs the Internal Revenue Service of the decedent's death. Then the personal representative has a fiduciary duty to prepare the decedent's final federal income tax return and state income tax return, if required. Since the decedent's Social Security number is not used by the decedent's estate for estate tax purposes, the personal representative must obtain an Employer Identification Number (EIN) for the estate. The EIN is used by Internal Revenue as a method of identifying any artificial entity, such as corporations, partnerships, and estates. If the estate is open for any length of time, it is likely that it will be income producing, necessitating the need for the personal representative to file a federal and, if required, state income tax return for the estate for each year the estate is in administration. The personal representative must value the estate, and if required, file a federal estate tax return (Form 706) for the estate as well as a state estate tax return if necessary. Form 706 is the primary tax return in the estate planning field. The paralegal can have an invaluable role in helping the attorney and the client maneuver through the maze that is Form 706. Learning how to prepare Form 706, as well as all the other taxation forms, will be advantageous to any paralegal who works in the estate planning and probate field. All Internal Revenue Service forms can be found at the IRS website www.irs.gov.

KEY TERMS

post-mortem estate planning
EIN
final income tax return

estate tax return
conservation easement
alternate valuation

fair market value
annuity
exclusion amount

REVIEW **QUESTIONS**

1. What kinds of gifts are subject to federal gift tax?
2. What is the purpose of a generation-skipping tax?
3. What is qualified terminable interest property?
4. What is the difference between an estate and an inheritance tax?
5. Define decedent's *gross estate*.
6. What is U.S. Treasury Form 706?
7. Define *fair market value*.
8. What is the alternate valuation method?
9. Why do people create conservation easements?
10. Which schedules relate to
    a. funeral and administrative expenses?
    b. powers of appointment?
    c. insurance on the decedent's life?
    d. mortgages on the decedent's residence?
11. What is the purpose of the employer identification number and how does the personal representative apply for one?

PROJECTS

1. Prepare a Form SS-4 for the following:

   Bobbie Black, died Anytown, Anystate, February 11, 2009. Husband Donald Black, who has qualified as the personal representative under her will on March 12, 2009. They lived at 100 S. Main Street, Anytown, Anystate. The third-party designee is your instructor (acting as supervising attorney).

2. Does your state require state income and estate tax returns? Note the statute number(s) for future reference and become familiar with the forms required.

MyLegalStudiesLab™   http://www.mylegalstudieslab

MYLEGALSTUDIESLAB VIRTUAL LAW OFFICE EXPERIENCE ASSIGNMENTS

Complete the pre-test, study plan, and post-test for this chapter and answer the Legal Applications questions as assigned.

These will help you confirm your mastery of the concepts and their application to legal scenarios. Then, complete the Virtual Law Office assignments as assigned by your instructor. These assignments are designed to develop your workplace skills and result in producing documents for inclusion in your portfolio.

Chapter **thirteen**

THE PROBATE COURT AND UNIFORM LAWS

OBJECTIVES

At the end of this chapter, the student will understand:

- what the probate court is
- the probate court's function
- the probate court's jurisdiction
- the Uniform Probate Code and other Uniform Laws
- the concept of domicile
- the concept of venue
- ancillary jurisdiction and its function in probate matters

All estate matters fall within the jurisdiction of a probate system. Probate courts may be given different names from state to state, that is, in New York it is the Surrogate Court, but their function remains constant, that of estate administration. With the exception of those states wherein estate administration is handled by a clerk's office and fiduciary commissioners, all probates function within a state court system because *the federal courts lack jurisdiction concerning the probate of wills*. In this book, we will refer to the process where to file a probate and where the probate process takes place as a probate "court," even if in your jurisdiction the probate function is handled through a different administrative office or agency.

Jurisdiction

All courts must obtain jurisdiction over the matters before them. When a court has jurisdiction, it has the authority to make all decisions affecting the parties in that matter and, for estate administration matters, the estate that is being probated. Should a court fail to obtain jurisdiction, any decisions it makes concerning the matter will be invalid.

As stated in the introduction, only states have jurisdiction over probate matters. This is based upon the United States Constitution. As indicated on the U.S. Courts website, maintained by the Administrative Office of the U.S. Courts on behalf of the Federal Judiciary (www.uscourts.gov), federal courts hear the following types of cases:

- the constitutionality of a law;
- cases involving the laws and treaties of the U.S.;
- ambassadors and public ministers;
- disputes between two or more states;
- admiralty law; and
- bankruptcy cases.

In general then, unless the case involves those types of cases, a state court will have the jurisdiction over the case, including probate matters. As ruled in Marshall v. Marshall, 392 F.3d 7118 {9th Cir. 22004), "[T]hus, the probate exception reserves to state probate courts the probate or annulment of a will and the administration of a decedent's estate; it also precludes federal courts from endeavoring to dispose of property that is in the custody of a state probate court."

For more information on the federal judiciary, please see http://www .uscourts.gov/federalcourts/understandingthefederalcourts/Jurisdiction.aspx.

Domicile

In order to decide which state court to file the probate, the attorney needs to determine the decedent's domicile. **Domicile** is the legal residence of the decedent at the time of death. While a decedent may have lived in more than one place, that is, two homes in different states, only one residence will be classified as his or her domicile, and is defined as *the home a person returns to following temporary absences and at which he or she intends to stay indefinitely.* A person may have only one domicile. Even if a person lives overseas, or in the Sun Belt (Arizona or Florida, for example) for six months of the year, that person's domicile is where the person lives for legal purposes. Domicile may be proved by evidence, such as:

- the address used to file federal and state income tax returns
- driver's license address
- voter registration
- motor vehicle registration
- passport registration address
- ownership or lease of real property
- bank accounts

While no one item is determinative of domicile, the intent to call a jurisdiction home coupled with the evidence of that intent is usually enough.

Example: Roger Rarebit owns a home in Boston, Massachusetts. He also is a snowbird, staying in Miami, Florida from October through March. He puts his Boston address as his permanent residence for tax purposes and has his passport address listed as Boston, Mass. His domicile is Massachusetts despite the extended period of time he spends in Florida.

Example: If Roger had a home in Boston but lived in Florida all but one month of the year, one might consider Florida his domicile despite the fact that he filed his income tax returns using the Massachusetts address (although frankly, it would be unlikely a certified public accountant (CPA) would advise this). In this sort of instance, the attorney would want to carefully decide which state would provide a better tax treatment for Roger's estate upon his death.

Example: If Roger only had an apartment in Boston and owned a home in Florida but still used the Boston address for his Internal Revenue Service (IRS) filings and voted in Massachusetts, the attorney will likely use the Boston address as the domiciliary address for purposes of probate.

In most all instances, attorneys will look to where the decedent registered to vote and what address he or she used for filings with the IRS as strong indicators of intent to live in a place permanently.

Once you have determined that your matter is properly within a state court's jurisdiction because of the decedent's domicile, you have to determine what type of jurisdiction the state court has.

There are two types of jurisdiction:

- in rem
- in personam

In Rem Jurisdiction

In rem, which is Latin for "against the thing," gives a court authority to hear a case over *items*. Specifically, **in rem jurisdiction** gives the probate court jurisdiction over the decedent's personal property and real property. It does not, however, give jurisdiction over people—just property. For example, a New Mexico probate court will not have jurisdiction over real property in Texas because obviously, the real property is affixed to the geographic location that is Texas. However, in probate matters, personal property usually follows the domicile of the decedent, meaning that even if a decedent had a bank account in Texas, the New Mexico probate court could render a decision about the property. The following case summary discusses the determination of which state court has jurisdiction over a bank account. It is not likely the decision rendered would have been the same if the argument had been over Vermont real estate. In that instance, it is more likely that an ancillary probate would have been necessary (more on ancillary probate in Chapter 11 and later in this chapter).

CASE 13.1 **SUMMARY**

In re Estate of Charles A. Piche, 697 A.2d 674 (Vt. 1997)

The Vermont State Employees Credit Union (VSECU) appealed a decision of the Washington Probate Court, arguing that the probate court did not have subject matter jurisdiction to determine title to Piche's VSECU account. Both Piche's personal representative and his nephew, the stated beneficiary on a designation-of-beneficiary card filed at VSECU, claimed title to the account. The appellate court held that the probate court had jurisdiction to determine title to personal property where the issue is necessary and incidental to the determination of other matters within the probate court's jurisdiction.

Piche died testate in January 1996 in Washington State. His will named his nephew beneficiary of two life insurance policies, one issued by VSECU and the other by the State of Vermont. Piche left the remainder of his estate in equal portions to his nephew and two others. He also left a signature card and a designation-of-beneficiary card, naming his nephew beneficiary of all sums paid under the VSECU life insurance policy "and all monies on deposit" at VSECU.

The executor filed a petition for declaratory judgment asking the probate court to declare the rightful owner of a VSECU account containing $51,810. The court concluded "that the determination of the ownership of the account in question among the heirs and legatees is within the declaratory judgment jurisdiction of the probate court" and that the account was an asset of the estate. VSECU appealed.

VSECU argued that while the probate court had primary exclusive jurisdiction over the probate of wills and the settlement of estates, the jurisdiction was "special and limited."

The appellate court held that the probate court had jurisdiction to determine title to personal property where the issue is necessary and incidental to the determination of other matters within the probate court's jurisdiction. The appellate court stated that VSECU's argument "urges a result that runs counter to the sound, practical, and efficient administration of estates."

The appellate court conceded that while VSECU was literally correct that Vermont case law had not "squarely decided" whether a probate court has subject matter jurisdiction to determine title to property, "it failed to recognize opinions of this Court that have necessarily been predicated on such jurisdiction."

The appellate court stated that "determining title to personal property, or "what is 'in' and what is 'out' of the probate estate is a common aspect of estate administration." The stated beneficiary on the designation-of-beneficiary card filed with VSECU

was a beneficiary under the will, and therefore, the probate court could determine if the nephew or the estate was entitled to the account.

The appellate court concluded that "by forcing parties to litigate their title disputes in a separate court, we prolong the probate process and increase its cost." The appellate court found that the probate court had jurisdiction to determine title to personal property and that "to find otherwise would deprive the probate court of the ability to function efficiently and effectively and result in many contested cases having hearings in the superior court before the settlement of the estate could proceed. We decline to complicate the probate process by precluding the probate court from deciding matters that are necessary and incidental to the effective administration of estates."

A Note About Ancillary Jurisdiction   As discussed in Chapter 11, sometimes a lawyer will be required to have a separate probate proceeding filed in another state as well as in the decedent's domiciliary location. This is required because the decedent owned real property in a second location. As indicated in Chapter 11, ancillary jurisdiction does not attempt to distribute all of the decedent's property. The sole purpose of this probate proceeding is to determine the proper distribution of the real property located in the second jurisdiction because the court located in the decedent's place of domicile is prohibited from making distribution decisions about real property not within its jurisdictional limits or boundaries. **Ancillary jurisdiction** then is about obtaining the proper *in rem* jurisdiction over the decedent's estate.

Example: Our friend, Robert Rarebit owned a house in Boston, Massachusetts but had otherwise moved to Miami, Florida. His domicile for purposes of his estate is Florida and that is where the primary probate proceeding will take place. However, the Florida probate court cannot make a determination about Robert's Boston home. In that instance, an ancillary probate administration will be handled in Massachusetts because the Massachusetts court has proper in rem jurisdiction over the house in Boston.

In Personam Jurisdiction

In personam jurisdiction refers to the authority a court has over the parties themselves. In most instances, a court must obtain jurisdiction over the persons involved in a matter as well as in rem jurisdiction concerning the property involved. Since probate is almost always a situation in which all that is necessary is for the probate court to have jurisdiction over the decedent's property, in personam jurisdiction is rarely an issue in non-contested probate proceedings.

When estate litigation is involved, in personam jurisdiction may be required, however. Courts automatically gain in personam jurisdiction over plaintiffs to lawsuits since they choose the court in which to file and therefore are agreeing to submit themselves to the court's jurisdiction. Jurisdiction over a defendant or respondent to the lawsuit is obtained by service of process.

Figure 13.1 Probate Statutes by States Following the Uniform Probate Code

Alaska	Title 13 Decedents' Estates, Guardianships, Transfers and Trusts Title 13 Chapter 16 Probate of Wills and Administration
Arizona	Title 14 Trusts, Estates and Protective Proceedings
Colorado	Title 15 Probate, Trusts and Fiduciaries
Florida	Title XLII Estates and Trusts
Hawaii	Title 30A Uniform Probate Code
Idaho	Title 15 Uniform Probate Code
Maine	Title 18 Decedents' Estates and Fiduciary Relations Title 18A Probate Code
Massachusetts	MGL c.190B, s.2-101 et seq.
Minnesota	Chapters 524–532 Estates of Decedents; Guardianships
Montana	Title 72 Estates, Trusts and Fiduciary Relationships
Nebraska	Chapter 30 Decedents' Estates; Protection of Persons and Property
New Mexico	Chapter 45 Uniform Probate Code Chapter 46 Fiduciaries and Trusts
North Dakota	Title 30.1 Uniform Probate Code
South Carolina	Title 21 Estates, Trusts, Guardians and Fiduciaries Title 62 Probate Code
South Dakota	Title 29A Uniform Probate Code Title 55 Fiduciaries and Trusts
Utah	Title 22 Fiduciaries and Trusts Title 75 Uniform Probate Code

Service of Process

Service of process is the procedure used to give notice of the lawsuit to the defendant. The most common form of service is through a process server, who is either a law enforcement officer or a privately hired individual who is certified, licensed, or registered to perform this role on behalf of the court system. Service of process requires that the process server give the defendant a summons, which is the notification of a pending lawsuit, and a copy of the complaint or petition. Other methods of service may be necessary, should personal service be impossible.

Methods of **substitute service** include:

- publication in a newspaper of general circulation,
- publication by first-class certified mail, return receipt requested,

Figure 13.2   Venue for Probate (Florida Statutes)

---

§733.101 Venue of probate proceedings.

(1) The venue for probate of wills and granting letters shall be:
 (a) In the county in this state where the decedent was domiciled.
 (b) If the decedent had no domicile in this state, then in any county where the decedent's property is located.
 (c) If the decedent had no domicile in this state and possessed no property in this state, then in the county where any debtor of the decedent resides.

(2) For the purpose of this section, a married woman whose husband is an alien or a nonresident of Florida may establish or designate a separate domicile in this state.

(3) Whenever a proceeding is filed laying venue in an improper county, the court may transfer the action in the same manner as provided in the Florida Rules of Civil Procedure. Any action taken by the court or the parties before the transfer is not affected by the improper venue.

- affixing a copy of the summons and petition to the defendant's front door, and
- serving the state's Secretary of State (when the defendant is a business with ties to the state).

The paralegal who is asked to assist with the process of obtaining substituted service must be familiar with his or her state's substituted service requirements since not all methods are available in all states or in all circumstances. Permission is usually needed by the court and is granted upon a showing that reasonable effort had been made to make service on the defendant and that all efforts had failed.

Note that in some jurisdictions the parties are called petitioner and respondent instead of plaintiff and defendant.

Venue

An issue related to jurisdiction is venue. **Venue** is the proper forum in which a case should be filed. Venue usually refers to the city or county that will hear the case. That means that the city or county where the decedent resided will likely be the proper venue for the probate filing.

Example: Robert Reed was domiciled in the State of California at the time of his death. California's probate courts have in rem jurisdiction over Robert's property. The question that remains, however, is in which probate court should the administration of his estate take place? The court with the proper venue is the court in which the case should be filed. If Robert lived in Los Angeles at the time of his death, the probate court in Los Angeles County will be the proper forum or venue.

Example: If our friend Roger Rarebit's proper domicile was Boston, Massachusetts, his estate's venue would be Suffolk County. If his proper domicile was Miami, Florida, his estate's venue would be Miami-Dade County.

Registry with the Court Clerk

Once it is determined which court has jurisdiction over an estate and which court venue is proper, the personal representative will file the petition for probate with the clerk of the court. In some states, the clerk's office is called the registry of probate or the clerk of the fiduciary supervisor, or some other name; but nonetheless, the petition is always filed with a clerk's office.

The court clerk, or registrar, is responsible for filing and maintaining all documents relating to each case being probated in that jurisdiction. The clerk maintains the documents, compiles indices so all the documents are accessible, and ensures that they are available to the public for viewing during regular business hours. In effect, the clerk does all routine clerical work that facilitates the function of the probate process.

It is important to determine if your state has a separate probate clerk's office. In larger jurisdictions it is not unusual for there to be a separate clerk for probate, as well as family or criminal, so that the clerk's office may focus on those tasks common to those areas of law. This is important because these offices may not be housed in the same location and you want to save yourself time and trouble when filings need to be done. If your state uses a separate clerk's office for probate, you don't want to be in the wrong place at 4:58 P.M. when you have a 5:00 P.M. deadline and the probate clerk is five floors down or in a different building a block away, or even across town.

Uniform Probate Laws

As you are undoubtedly aware, the United States is comprised of 50 separate state governments with 50 separate legislatures, plus the District of Columbia and various territories. The state legislatures and council of the District of Columbia have the task of making laws that will benefit their constituents. Often, these laws differ from the laws of other states, even those that border them. This may cause difficulties when a person cannot be certain if the laws of his or her home state pertaining to a particular field of law are different from those of another state in which he or she must do business.

Uniform Laws are laws that were proposed by the National Conference of Commissioners on Uniform State Laws. The National Conference is comprised of representatives from each state, with the goal of compiling uniform laws on various subjects that would have the effect of standardizing and modernizing the law in those subject areas.

After the laws are drafted, they are proposed to the individual state legislatures in the hope that the states will adopt them and enact them into law. In this fashion, the laws of the 50 states would be uniform, hence the name Uniform Laws. It is important to note that while many states adopt Uniform Laws wholly, others only enact them in part. State legislatures often amend the Uniform Laws to such a degree as to defeat the purpose of uniformity between state laws. Nonetheless, to the extent that these Uniform Laws are adopted, they do promote the standardization of laws in the United States.

Figure 13.3 Minnesota Statutes §524.1-307 Registrar Powers

The acts and orders which this chapter specifies as performable by the registrar shall be performed by a judge of the court or by a person, including the court administrator, designated by the court by a written order filed and recorded in the office of the court.

In addition to acts specified in this chapter to be performed by the registrar, the registrar may take acknowledgments, administer oaths, fix and approve bonds, provide information on the various methods of transferring property of decedents under the laws of this state, issue letters in informal proceedings and perform such other acts as the court may by written order authorize as necessary or incidental to the conduct of informal proceedings. Letters, orders and documents issued by the registrar may be certified, authenticated or exemplified by the registrar or in the same manner as those issued by the court. All files shall be maintained by the court administrator. The probate registrar shall not render advice calling for the exercise of such professional judgment as constitutes the practice of law.

There are many Uniform Laws relating to wills, trusts, and estate administration, such as the Uniform Simultaneous Death Act; the Uniform Gift to Minors Act; and the Uniform Durable Power of Attorney Act, which was discussed in Chapter 6.

The Uniform Probate Code (UPC) is another such Uniform Law. Unlike the Uniform Powers of Attorney Act (UPOAA) which has been adopted in all jurisdictions, currently only 18 states follow the Uniform Probate Code in its entirety, those being Alaska, Arizona, Colorado, Florida, Hawaii, Idaho, Maine, Massachusetts, Michigan, Minnesota, Montana, Nebraska, New Jersey, New Mexico, North Dakota, South Carolina, South Dakota, and Utah. Other states have partially adopted it or used it as a basis for its laws. Massachusetts was the most recent adoptee of the UPC. Therefore, unlike the UPOAA, there is no uniformity among the states regarding probate. While the UPC is a standard by which court and lawyers look to when looking for solutions to difficult questions and certainly when researching for arguments and strategies in will contests, as a paralegal you must learn your state's laws to be certain of how a court will view a matter before it.

Example: Bobbie Black executes a will in New Jersey. The following year, she moves to Arizona to get away from the cold in winter. She does not execute another will in Arizona. Bobbie dies two years after her move. If we assume that the laws in New Jersey, where the will was executed, are different from the laws of Arizona, where shall the will be probated? The personal representative and the attorney handling the probate may have concerns about Bobbie's dispositions and the consequences of them. It is possible that the dispositions made in the New Jersey document will not be beneficial to her estate in Arizona. Perhaps a document drafted in Arizona by an Arizona attorney would have protected her assets better. This is not to disparage the work of the New Jersey lawyer. If Bobbie had instead moved from Arizona to New Jersey, a New Jersey document drafted by a New Jersey attorney might have protected Bobbie's assets better. It should be noted that all wills that are validly executed in the state of execution are valid in each other jurisdiction. If Bobbie had moved from Alaska to Arizona, her will would likely be handled the same way because both Alaska and Arizona have adopted the UPC *in toto*.

SUMMARY

The probate court is responsible for the administration of all estate matters. The court must obtain jurisdiction over the estate property, which is called in rem jurisdiction. When litigation is involved, the court must also obtain jurisdiction over the litigants, called in personam jurisdiction. An issue related to jurisdiction is venue, which is the proper forum for the estate administration. The proper venue is usually the probate court in the city or county in the state in which the decedent was domiciled at the time of death. Domicile relates to the place a person returns to after short absences with the intent to remain indefinitely. It is the supervising attorney's responsibility to determine the decedent's proper domicile. Once the proper forum is determined, the personal representative

will file a petition asking for the estate to be opened for probate administration. The filings are made with the clerk of the court, who in different jurisdictions may have a different title, such as registrar or clerk of the fiduciary supervisor.

Uniform Probate Laws are drafted and proposed by the National Conference of Commissioners on Uniform State Laws. These Uniform Laws are then referred to each state, which may or may not adopt them. If they are adopted, they promote the standardization and modernization of laws in the United States. There are Uniform Laws on various subjects including those relating to wills, trusts, and estate administration, one of which is the Uniform Probate Code (UPC).

KEY **TERMS**

in personam jurisdiction
in rem jurisdiction
venue

domicile
ancillary jurisdiction
service of process

substitute service
Uniform Laws

REVIEW **QUESTIONS**

1. For what purpose was the Uniform Probate Code, as well as other Uniform Laws, drafted?

2. What is in rem jurisdiction?

3. Define *domicile*.

4. Why is ancillary jurisdiction important?

5. Why do federal courts lack jurisdiction over probate matters?

6. What is the job of the probate clerk or registrar?

7. What is in personam jurisdiction?

8. What are examples of evidence of domicile?

9. How do you determine the proper venue for a probate administration?

PROJECTS

1. Determine the name and location of the probate court in your city or county. Is the location different from that of the regular civil courts in your county?

2. Determine where probate documents are filed. Is this location different from where regular civil documents are filed?

3. Review the case located at http://www.denverprobatecourt.org/cases/pdf/05PR1191Murphy.pdf.
   Why did the court dismiss the suit? Explain.

MyLegalStudiesLab™   http://www.mylegalstudieslab

MYLEGALSTUDIESLAB VIRTUAL LAW OFFICE EXPERIENCE ASSIGNMENTS

Complete the pre-test, study plan, and post-test for this chapter and answer the Legal Applications questions as assigned. These will help you confirm your mastery of the concepts and their application to legal scenarios. Then, complete the Virtual Law Office assignments as assigned by your instructor. These assignments are designed to develop your workplace skills and result in producing documents for inclusion in your portfolio.

Chapter **fourteen**
PARALEGALS AND ETHICS

OBJECTIVES

At the end of this chapter, the student will understand:

- what the purpose of ethics is
- what are the rules of professional conduct
- what is the unauthorized practice of law
- what it means to practice law without a license
- what rules the paralegal must follow to avoid unauthorized practice of law
- what steps the paralegal should take to insure that she isn't misrepresenting herself as a lawyer
- what working under supervision entails
- what giving advice means
- what confidentiality is and how to preserve it

So you are studying to be a paralegal. You want to do a great job and be the very best paralegal you can be, maybe be the best in your firm. You may have seen any number of the TV shows depicting the life of the lawyer, law firms, and its employees. Maybe you're a fan of a new show that hires a guy that isn't a lawyer but is being passed off as one—by his own boss? What do you think about that behavior? Do you think it's wrong? Do you know what the consequences for being caught would be? Should he get thrown out of the firm? Get sued by clients? Get a criminal conviction?

Why Do We Have to Have Ethical Rules Anyway?

From the Preamble of the Ohio Rules of Professional Conduct: "Lawyers play a vital role in the preservation of society. A lawyer's conduct should conform to the requirements of the law, both in professional service to clients and in the lawyer's business and personal affairs. A lawyer should use the law's procedures only for legitimate purposes and not to harass or intimidate others. A lawyer should demonstrate respect for the legal system and for those who serve it, including judges, other lawyers, and public officials. Adjudicatory officials, not being wholly free to defend themselves, are entitled to receive the support of the bar against unjustified criticism. Although a lawyer, as a citizen, has a right to criticize such officials, the lawyer should do so with restraint and avoid intemperate statements that tend to lessen public confidence in the legal system. While it is a lawyer's duty, when necessary, to challenge the rectitude of official action, it is also a lawyer's duty to uphold legal process."

Figure 14.1   New York Lawyer's Code of Professional Responsibility. Preamble.
(Published by the New York State Bar Association)

The continued existence of a free and democratic society depends upon recognition of the concept that justice is based upon the rule of law grounded in respect for the dignity of the individual and the capacity of the individual through reason for enlightened self-government. Law so grounded makes justice possible, for only through such law does the dignity of the individual attain respect and protection. Without it, individual rights become subject to unrestrained power, respect for law is destroyed, and rational self-government is impossible.

Lawyers, as guardians of the law, play a vital role in the preservation of society. The fulfillment of this role requires an understanding by lawyers of their relationship with and function in our legal system. A consequent obligation of lawyers is to maintain the highest standards of ethical conduct.

In fulfilling professional responsibilities, a lawyer necessarily assumes various roles that require the performance of many difficult tasks. Not every situation which the lawyer may encounter can be foreseen, but fundamental ethical principles are always present for guidance. Within the framework of these principles, a lawyer must with courage and foresight be able and ready to shape the body of the law to the ever-changing relationships of society.

The Code of Professional Responsibility points the way to the aspiring and provides standards by which to judge the transgressor. Each lawyer's own conscience must provide the touchstone against which to test the extent to which the lawyer's actions should rise above minimum standards. But in the last analysis it is the desire for the respect and confidence of the members of the profession and of the society which the lawyer serves that should provide to a lawyer the incentive for the highest possible degree of ethical conduct. The possible loss of that respect and confidence is the ultimate sanction. So long as its practitioners are guided by these principles, the law will continue to be a noble profession. This is its greatness and its strength, which permit of no compromise.

A Note on the American Bar Association Model Rules of Professional Conduct and the State Rules

The rules that are shown in this chapter are from individual states. These rules are similar to the Model Rules of Professional Conduct promulgated by the American Bar Association (ABA). According to the ABA website, California is the only state that does not follow the format of the ABA Model Rules. The **Rules of Professional Conduct** provide a foundation of ethical rules, either inspirational or mandated, that lawyers and lawyers' staff should or must follow. Lawyers are held to a standard of conduct becoming to the profession and their office staff are held to this standard indirectly. The Rules therefore are the means by which lawyers may be disciplined if they fail to uphold that standard but the Rules also illuminate what is best and good about the legal profession as shown in the preambles of the Ohio Rules and the New York State Bar Association. As stated by Missouri Chief Justice Michael A. Wolff in his Law Matters column dated February 26, 2007, "Viewers of popular television shows about lawyers are likely to be left with some strange impressions of lawyers' ethics. From some shows, they even may get the impression that there aren't any. For example, although Denny Crane and Alan Shore are witty and acerbic and entertaining, they likely would be disbarred if they were lawyers anywhere other than on television's "Boston Legal" show. That is because real clients have the right to expect competent, ethical representation from the lawyers they hire."

Perhaps one of the best explanations of attorney ethics, and why we have them, is from Peter MacFarlane, writing in the *Journal of the South Pacific*, commenting on Australian lawyers; however, the words are just as true for American lawyers. First, he asked as we do, why is **ethics** important to the practice of law? He answered, "[F]irst because lawyers are integral to the working-out of the law and the Rule of Law itself is founded on principles of justice, fairness and equity. If lawyers do not adhere and promote these ethical principles then the law will fall into disrepute and people will resort to alternative means of resolving conflict. The Rule of Law will fail with a rise of public discontent.

Second, lawyers are professionals. This concept conveys the notion that issues of ethical responsibility and duty are an inherent part of the legal profession. It has been said that a profession's most valuable asset is its collective reputation and the confidence which that inspires. The legal profession especially must have the confidence of the community."

The Oregon Rules of Professional Conduct, newly updated in January 2012, can be found at http://www.osbar.org/rulesregs/ and are instructive as they explain the comparison of the Oregon Rules and ABA Model Rules.

Unauthorized Practice of Law (UPL)

When you read the introduction to this chapter and read the scenario about the show currently on TV, did you say "no" to that last question asking if you could be convicted of a crime for practicing law without a license? You would be wrong. Practicing law without a license may be a crime and for the lawyer that supervises you could be grounds for a reprimand or suspension from practice as well. The most egregious of cases might even get your supervising attorney disbarred. (In the TV show plot above, our fictitious lawyer/supervisor would most likely be disbarred when he and his sidekick are discovered.)

The California Business and Professional Code Section 6125 states that "No person shall practice law in California unless the person is an active member of the State Bar." Every state has a similar statute clearly stating that only someone licensed in the jurisdiction may practice law there. A manual for prosecutors in the Office of the District Attorney for Los Angeles County issued for the public in February 2004 quoted *State Bar of California v. Superior Court*, 207 Cal.323,331 (1929): "*The profession and practice of the law … is … a matter of public interest and concern,* not only from the viewpoint of its relation to the administration of civil and criminal law, but also from that of the contacts of its membership with the constituent membership of society at large, whose interest is to be safeguarded … *the membership, character and conduct of those entering in and engaging in the legal profession have long been regarded as the proper subject of legislative regulation and control.*" (Emphasis added and edits made by the District Attorney's Office)

So this begs the question, what is the practice of law because how can you know if you are engaging in the **unauthorized practice of law**, commonly called UPL, if you don't know what the practice of law is.

What Is the Practice of Law?

On its website, the Oregon State Bar states that "[T]he 'practice of law' is defined in decisions of the Oregon Supreme Court and generally includes, among other things:

- appearing on behalf of others in Oregon courts and administrative proceedings;
- drafting or selecting legal documents for another when informed or trained discretion must be exercised to meet the person's individual needs;
- advising someone of his or her legal rights in a particular situation;
- having a law office in Oregon regardless of where clients are located;
- acting as an immigration consultant unless authorized by federal law to do so; and
- holding oneself out as a lawyer."

State bar associations and/or state supreme courts throughout the United States generally agree that these points indicate what the **practice of law** entails. State bar associations take UPL very seriously and as shown in the following case, writing a will for a "client" without a license is very serious business indeed.

CASE 14.1 **SUMMARY**

State of Indiana Ex Rel., Indiana State Bar Association v. United Financial Systems Corporation, et. al., 926 N.E.2d 8 (Ind. 2010).

The Indiana State Bar Association (ISBA) brought suit against United Financial Systems Corporation and many individuals (UFSC) for the unauthorized practice of law. ISBA wanted an order enjoining UFSFC from UPL and requiring them to disgorge fees collected from their UPL.

The Court explained UFSC's business model in full. Essentially, UFSC was an insurance marketing agency and in 1995, they started marketing and selling estate planning services including wills and trusts to prospective clients. From October 2006 through May 2009, they sold 1306 estate plans grossing over $2.7 million in Indiana alone.

They did this by mailing prospective clients (client(s)) about avoiding probate. When the client responded, a UFSC sales representative, called an Estate Planning Assistant or a Health Planning Assistant (Assistant) met with the client, gaining access to financial information which they used later

to sell the client insurance products. The Assistant made a commission on the sales and so of course, they pushed the most expensive plans. The Assistants were not licensed attorneys and they were not directly supervised by attorneys.

Upon receiving all the information it was sent to UFSC's in-house counsel, McInerney and then he sent the information to one of their "panel attorneys" who drafted the documents. The court noted that the panel attorneys were paid a flat fee of $225 and that generally there was no contact between the client and the panel attorney beyond the drafting of the documents and one initial phone call.

The panel attorneys sent the documents back to UFSC whereupon a Financial Planning Assistant was paid $75 to deliver the documents and assist the client in executing them. These Assistants made most of their money from sales of UFSC insurance products and had a sales quota.

The Court flatly stated "that preparing and drafting a will, and giving advice regarding the contents and effect of a will, constitute the practice of law" as do "drafting and preparing testamentary and trust documents."

The Court found that despite UFSC's protestations, the use of attorneys in its business model so marginalized the professional judgment of the attorneys "as to cross the line of permissible practices". It therefore held that they indeed engaged in the unauthorized practice of law and was to be enjoined from further UPL.

The Court stated that "the respondents should be prohibited from retaining fees for unauthorized practices to as "to deter similar conduct in the future, and, ultimately to protect the public." It stated that the "prohibition against unauthorized practice of law would be much less effective if an offending party were permitted to retain fees collected for unauthorized services."

The court specifically determined that disgorgement was appropriate "irrespective of the actual harm" and that some of the clients may have received an adequate product did not "alter the illegality of UFSC's conduct." The case was remanded to the Commissioner to determine what the amounts being refunded should be.

How Do Paralegals Avoid Practicing Law?

Paralegals Must Identify Themselves as Paralegals

Lawyers need never identify themselves as lawyers, as long as they are licensed in that jurisdiction. Paralegals are always obligated to identify themselves as non-lawyers. How do they do this? Of course, paralegals must verbally identify themselves.

Example: On a phone call: "Hello Mrs. Smith, this is Adam Sanchez and I'm a paralegal assisting Mr. Jones on your case."

Example: In person: "Hi! I'm Adam Sanchez, paralegal with Jones and Jones downtown."

Other ways of identification:

- business cards
- letterhead and on signature lines of letters
- telephone directories for firms, whether in a book or online
- firm's website
- LinkedIn or other social media sites
- e-mail
- office door signs
- name tags at business functions; it is not proper to write only "Adam Sanchez, Jones & Jones." Always add "Paralegal" or "Legal Assistant." Remember, your lawyer supervisor may put "attorney at law" after his name but he's not required to do so.

Paralegals Should Always Work Under Supervision

Except when state statute provides otherwise (in very limited circumstances), a paralegal must work under direct supervision of a licensed attorney. This means that your supervising lawyer is responsible for your behavior at the firm and even outside the firm if you are giving anyone the impression that you are anything but a paralegal.

Lawyers are required to adhere to rules of professional conduct as provided by either a state bar association or the state supreme court, which usually monitors lawyers' conduct and licensing and may be disciplined for violating those rules.

Figure 14.2   Indiana Rules of Professional Conduct. Rule 5.3. Responsibilities
Regarding Nonlawyer Assistants

With respect to a nonlawyer employed or retained by or associated with a lawyer:

(a) a partner, and a lawyer who individually or together with other lawyers possess comparable managerial authority in a law firm shall make reasonable efforts to ensure that the firm has in effect measures giving reasonable assurance that the person's conduct is compatible with the professional obligations of the lawyer;

(b) a lawyer having direct supervisory authority over the nonlawyer shall make reasonable efforts to ensure that the person's conduct is compatible with the professional obligations of the lawyer; and

(c) a lawyer shall be responsible for conduct of such a person that would be a violation of the Rules of Professional Conduct if engaged in by a lawyer if:

    (1) the lawyer orders or, with the knowledge of the specific conduct, ratifies the conduct involved; or

    (2) the lawyer is a partner or has comparable managerial authority in the law firm in which the person is employed, or has direct supervisory authority over the person, and knows of the conduct at a time when its consequences can be avoided or mitigated but fails to take reasonable remedial action.

Discipline may include a private or public reprimand, a suspension, or disbarment in the most egregious of circumstances.

Lawyers are then required to take all reasonable measures to insure that your conduct, as well as all employees' conduct, is consistent with those rules of conduct. So while you are not held directly responsible under a lawyer's rules of conduct, you are indirectly responsible to uphold them.

Don't Give Advice!

Paralegals usually find themselves in trouble when they advise clients without the direct supervision of a lawyer. What is legal advice? If you listen to the client's story, apply your knowledge and judgment to that story and then give the client your opinion about what you think the client should do to protect his or her rights and obligations; and/or suggest a course of action, you have given advice. When paralegals meet with clients, the paralegal should only obtain information and if the client asks a question, the proper response is "I will have Mr. Jones speak with you about that."

As a paralegal you should never recommend a course of action about how to proceed with a matter, explain what a client's legal rights are, or interpret legal documents or laws. This is not just true for giving advice to clients. It is true for the stranger in the grocery store, your friends, your family, and anyone else that asks you for advice because you work in a law office. You may be tempted. You will be armed with a college degree and the knowledge of the area of law, but don't be disillusioned that you can give advice under any circumstance. You can't. **Don't get sucked in. You may not give that advice no matter how much you want to.**

Only Draft Documents on Behalf of Your Supervising Attorney

This is another area that paralegals get sucked into easily. A friend or family member will beg you to assist in drafting a document. If you work as a paralegal in the estate planning field, you will be asked to assist with drafting wills and especially powers of attorney. Perhaps your aunt went to the big box store, got a form, and wanted you to help fill it out. It would be so simple. It couldn't cause any harm, could it?

Don't do it!! Under no circumstances should you assist a person by filling out a form for them or help them with filling it out. You certainly may not draft a document for another person without direct attorney supervision and review. You may fill out a form or draft one for yourself, just as your friend can fill out his or her own form. Pro se (doing for oneself) is permissible. For someone else, you are practicing law without a license.

It is also important that when your supervising attorney has you draft documents for clients that the attorney then review your work. To do otherwise would be the unauthorized practice of law by you and a lack of supervision on his part. At best, your drafting of the document will not cause harm but at the worst, the document may not provide the client with the proper outcome. Your supervising attorney may be sanctioned by the bar but also may be sued by the client for malpractice. Although you cannot be sanctioned by the bar and will not likely be sued for negligence, although you can be, it is not in your best interest to put your career in jeopardy by doing tasks that only lawyers can do.

Do Not Make Court Appearances

This may seem ridiculous but it actually happens. A paralegal should never represent a case before the bench at any time. Your supervising lawyer should never ask you to and you should not do it. If there is a situation in which your lawyer cannot attend a hearing, either call the judge's assistant or go to the assistant's office to address the issue and ask for a postponement due to unforeseen circumstances. Lawyers get detained in other matters sometimes and you will have to make phone calls of this sort on their behalf. Hopefully, you can reach the opposing counsel who will then ask for the postponement on your lawyer's behalf instead. However, if your lawyer forgot a court hearing, your lawyer may have to take his lumps. Do not try to rescue him by attending in his stead.

Do Not Retain the Client

A paralegal may not retain clients. Only a lawyer may retain the clients. A paralegal that retains clients, even on behalf of a lawyer, may be committing UPL.

Don't Set Fees

Related to retaining a client is setting the fee the client will pay for the services to be rendered. Paralegals must not set fees and must always defer to the lawyer for the proper fee. It is up to your supervising lawyer to determine what the fee is for each situation and what your billing rate will be. Billing rates are often based upon expertise and at some firms, the rate for a paralegal is set firm-wide. When a client has a question about his or her bill, always defer the question to the lawyer for response.

Don't Take Money or Gifts from a Client

Of course, if the client hands you a check for payment of an invoice, that's perfectly permissible but never take money from the client unless the client was properly billed for that money and then give the money directly to the lawyer or to the office manager or billing person at the firm. Never keep money or a "tip" from a client. Accepting any money from the client could be seen as fee splitting and lawyers are prohibited from splitting client fees with anyone other than another lawyer. You are entitled only to salary and wages. It is also wise to find out what the firm's policy on gifts from clients is. If a client offers you a gift, make sure that your supervising lawyer approves it.

What Are the Penalties for Unauthorized Practice of Law?

Penalties for UPL vary from state to state. As you saw in the Indiana case summarized in Case Summary 14.1, the offending parties were enjoined from further business and had to pay back, or disgorge, all funds earned in the commission of UPL. In some states, you may be convicted of a crime, however. See Figure 14.3 for a statute from Florida regarding penalties for unauthorized practice of law. The American Bar Association conducted a survey of UPL for 2011–2012. You may download the PDF form at http://www.americanbar.org/groups/professional_responsibility.html.

Figure 14.3 Florida Statutes Section 454.23. Penalties

Any person not licensed or otherwise authorized to practice law in this state who practices law in this state or holds himself or herself out to the public as qualified to practice law in this state, or who willfully pretends to be, or willfully takes or uses any name, title, addition, or description implying that he or she is qualified, or recognized by law as qualified, to practice law in this state, commits a felony of the third degree, punishable as provided in s. 775.082, s. 775.083, or s. 775.084.

[Note: s. 775.082, s. 775.083, or s. 775.084. refer to the actual penalties for various crimes. In this instance, UPL carries punishment terms up to 5 years in jail and up to a $5000 fine per offense. If the person is a habitual offender, he or she may be subject to enhanced penalties.]

What Is a Paralegal Permitted to Do?

Guideline 9.10 from the Indiana Rules of Professional Conduct states a paralegal's duties very well. Note that these are directed at the lawyer, not the paralegal; although according to this Guideline, the paralegal is bound by these rules as well.

Figure 14.4 Guideline 9.10 of the Indiana Rules of Professional Conduct

All lawyers who employ non-lawyer assistants in the state of Indiana shall assure that such non-lawyer assistants conform their conduct to be consistent with the following ethical standards:

(a) A non-lawyer assistant may perform any task delegated and supervised by a lawyer so long as the lawyer is responsible to the client, maintains a direct relationship with the client, and assumes full professional responsibility for the work product.

(b) A non-lawyer assistant shall not engage in the unauthorized practice of law.

(c) A non-lawyer assistant shall serve the public interest by contributing to the delivery of quality legal services and the improvement of the legal system.

(d) A non-lawyer assistant shall achieve and maintain a high level of competence, as well as a high level of personal and professional integrity and conduct.

(e) A non-lawyer assistant's title shall be fully disclosed in all business and professional communications.

(f) A non-lawyer assistant shall preserve all confidential information provided by the client or acquired from other sources before, during, and after the course of the professional relationship.

(g) A non-lawyer assistant shall avoid conflicts of interest and shall disclose any possible conflict to the employer or client, as well as to the prospective employers or clients.

(h) A non-lawyer assistant shall act within the bounds of the law, uncompromisingly for the benefit of the client.

(i) A non-lawyer assistant shall do all things incidental, necessary, or expedient for the attainment of the ethics and responsibilities imposed by statute or rule of court.

(j) A non-lawyer assistant shall be governed by the Indiana Rules of Professional Conduct.

(k) For purposes of this Guideline, a non-lawyer assistant includes, but shall not be limited to: paralegals, legal assistants, investigators, law students.

Duty of Confidentiality

A lawyer and her staff owe each and every client the duty of confidentiality. **Confidentiality** refers to the information that the client tells the lawyer and her staff. This may be regarding information from correspondence, documents, and consultations. The duty to maintain the confidence occurs even if the law firm eventually declines the representation. As pointed out in Rule 1.6 of the Georgia Rules of Professional Conduct (Figure 14.5), the purpose behind keeping a client's confidences is that "[T]he client is thereby encouraged to communicate fully and frankly with the lawyer even as to embarrassing or legally damaging subject matter." While a client may waive his or her right to confidentiality, it is always best to not divulge client information. In some instances, it may be divulging confidences by just telling someone that the client is the client.

A paralegal must always be on his or her guard when discussing client matters. A spouse, significant other, roommate, or friend may want you to "dish the dirt" but refrain from doing so. It is important never to give enough information to people outside the firm so that the outsider can figure out who the client is.

The duty to maintain client confidences lasts forever.

How Does a Paralegal Refrain from Breaching Client Confidentiality?

- Not talking about clients and their cases in public
- Not forwarding client e-mails to friends or family
- Protecting computers from viruses that may "forward" confidential information
- Not allowing non-firm members to sit at your desk
- Making sure the computer is passcoded and that you have a screensaver that will prevent prying eyes from seeing your work product
- Files should be out of reach of non-firm members so that they don't inadvertently see information that may be important
- Get the client's permission to speak to others that may help the case (although your supervising attorney should be the one to do this, not you)
- Refraining from talking shop with other paralegals, friends, spouses, and family about your work, except in very broad terms, and always be careful when you do so

There are limited exceptions to confidentiality. These include divulging information if there is reasonable belief that the client will cause bodily injury to someone else or is about to commit a crime. It is best, however, that if you believe this situation is occurring to discuss it with your supervising attorney and let the attorney handle the matter.

Figure 14.5 is from the Georgia Rules of Professional Conduct. The Comments are well worth reading as they further explain why lawyers are held to this very important rule and why the paralegal, by extension, also is held to this rule.

Figure 14.5   Georgia Rule 1.6 Confidentiality of Information

a. A lawyer shall maintain in confidence all information gained in the professional relationship with a client, including information which the client has requested to be held inviolate or the disclosure of which would be embarrassing or would likely be detrimental to the client, unless the client gives informed consent, except for disclosures that are impliedly authorized in order to carry out the representation, or are required by these Rules or other law, or by order of the Court.

b.
   1. A lawyer may reveal information covered by paragraph (a) which the lawyer reasonably believes necessary:
      i to avoid or prevent harm or substantial financial loss to another as a result of client criminal conduct or third party criminal conduct clearly in violation of the law;
      ii to prevent serious injury or death not otherwise covered by subparagraph (i) above;
      iii to establish a claim or defense on behalf of the lawyer in a controversy between the lawyer and the client, to establish a defense to a criminal charge or civil claim against the lawyer

(continued)

Figure 14.5   (continued)

based upon conduct in which the client was involved, or to respond to allegations in any proceeding concerning the lawyer's representation of the client;

    iv   to secure legal advice about the lawyer's compliance with these Rules.

   2. In a situation described in paragraph (b)(1), if the client has acted at the time the lawyer learns of the threat of harm or loss to a victim, use or disclosure is permissible only if the harm or loss has not yet occurred.

   3. Before using or disclosing information pursuant to paragraph (b)(1), if feasible, the lawyer must make a good faith effort to persuade the client either not to act or, if the client has already acted, to warn the victim.

  c. The lawyer may, where the law does not otherwise require, reveal information to which the duty of confidentiality does not apply under paragraph (b) without being subjected to disciplinary proceedings.

  d. The lawyer shall reveal information under paragraph (b) as the applicable law requires.

  e. The duty of confidentiality shall continue after the client-lawyer relationship has terminated.

The maximum penalty for a violation of this Rule is disbarment.

Comment

[1]   The lawyer is part of a judicial system charged with upholding the law. One of the lawyer's functions is to advise clients so that they avoid any violation of the law in the proper exercise of their rights.

[2]   The observance of the ethical obligation of a lawyer to hold inviolate confidential information of the client not only facilitates the full development of facts essential to proper representation of the client but also encourages people to seek early legal assistance.

[3]   Almost without exception, clients come to lawyers in order to determine what their rights are and what is, in the maze of laws and regulations, deemed to be legal and correct. The common law recognizes that the client's confidences must be protected from disclosure. Based upon experience, lawyers know that almost all clients follow the advice given, and the law is upheld.

[4]   A fundamental principle in the client-lawyer relationship is that the lawyer maintain confidentiality of information relating to the representation. The client is thereby encouraged to communicate fully and frankly with the lawyer even as to embarrassing or legally damaging subject matter.

[4A] Information gained in the professional relationship includes information gained from a person (prospective client) who discusses the possibility of forming a client-lawyer relationship with respect to a matter. Even when no client-lawyer relationship ensues, the restrictions and exceptions of these Rules as to use or revelation of the information apply, e.g. Rules 1.9 and 1.10.

[5]   The principle of confidentiality is given effect in two related bodies of law, the attorney-client privilege (which includes the work product doctrine) in the law of evidence and the rule of confidentiality established in professional ethics. The attorney-client privilege applies in judicial and other proceedings in which a lawyer may be called as a witness or otherwise required to produce evidence concerning a client. The rule of client-lawyer confidentiality applies in situations other than those where evidence is sought from the lawyer through compulsion of law. Rule 1.6 applies not merely to matters communicated in confidence by the client but also to all information gained in the professional relationship, whatever its source. A lawyer may not disclose such information except as authorized or required by the Rules of Professional Conduct or other law. See also Scope. The requirement of maintaining confidentiality of information gained in the professional relationship applies to government lawyers who may disagree with the client's policy goals.

(continued)

Figure 14.5 (continued)

Authorized Disclosure

[6] A lawyer is impliedly authorized to make disclosures about a client when appropriate in carrying out the representation, except to the extent that the client's instructions or special circumstances limit that authority. In litigation, for example, a lawyer may disclose information by admitting a fact that cannot properly be disputed, or in negotiation by making a disclosure that facilitates a satisfactory conclusion.

[7] Lawyers in a firm may, in the course of the firm's practice, disclose to each other information relating to a client of the firm, unless the client has instructed that particular information be confined to specified lawyers.

[7A] A lawyer's confidentiality obligations do not preclude a lawyer from securing confidential legal advice about the lawyer's personal responsibility to comply with these Rules. In most situations, disclosing information to secure such advice will be impliedly authorized for the lawyer to carry out the representation. Even when the disclosure is not impliedly authorized paragraph (b)(1)(iv) permits such disclosure because of the importance of a lawyer's compliance with the Rules of Professional Conduct.

Disclosure Adverse to Client

[8] The confidentiality rule is subject to limited exceptions. In becoming privy to information about a client, a lawyer may foresee that the client intends serious harm to another person. The public is better protected if full and open communication by the client is encouraged than if it is inhibited.

[9] Several situations must be distinguished. First, the lawyer may not knowingly assist a client in conduct that is criminal or fraudulent. See Rule 1.2(d). Similarly, a lawyer has a duty under Rule 3.3(a)(4) not to use false evidence.

[10] Second, the lawyer may have been innocently involved in past conduct by the client that was criminal or fraudulent. In such a situation the lawyer has not violated Rule 1.2(d), because to "knowingly assist" criminal or fraudulent conduct requires knowing that the conduct is of that character.

[11] Third, the lawyer may learn that a client intends prospective conduct that is criminal and likely to result in death or substantial bodily harm. As stated in paragraph (b)(1), the lawyer has professional discretion to reveal information in order to prevent such consequences. The lawyer may make a disclosure in order to prevent death or serious bodily injury which the lawyer reasonably believes will occur. It is very difficult for a lawyer to "know" when such a heinous purpose will actually be carried out, for the client may have a change of mind.

[12] The lawyer's exercise of discretion requires consideration of such factors as the nature of the lawyer's relationship with the client and with those who might be injured by the client, the lawyer's own involvement in the transaction and factors that may extenuate the conduct in question. Where practical, the lawyer should seek to persuade the client to take suitable action. In any case, a disclosure adverse to the client's interest should be no greater than the lawyer reasonably believes necessary to the purpose. A lawyer's decision not to take preventive action permitted by paragraph (b)(1) does not violate this Rule.

Withdrawal

[13] If the lawyer's services will be used by the client in materially furthering a course of criminal or fraudulent conduct, the lawyer must withdraw, as stated in Rule 1.16(a)(1).

[14] After withdrawal the lawyer is required to refrain from making disclosure of the client's confidences, except as otherwise provided in Rule 1.6. Neither this rule nor Rule 1.8(b) nor

(continued)

Figure 14.5 (continued)

Rule 1.16(d) prevents the lawyer from giving notice of the fact of withdrawal, and the lawyer may also withdraw or disaffirm any opinion, document, affirmation, or the like.

[15] Where the client is an organization, the lawyer may be in doubt whether contemplated conduct will actually be carried out by the organization. Where necessary to guide conduct in connection with this Rule, the lawyer may make inquiry within the organization as indicated in Rule 1.13(b).

Dispute Concerning a Lawyer's Conduct

[16] Where a legal claim or disciplinary charge alleges complicity of the lawyer in a client's conduct or other misconduct of the lawyer involving representation of the client, the lawyer may respond to the extent the lawyer reasonably believes necessary to establish a defense. The same is true with respect to a claim involving the conduct or representation of a former client. The lawyer's right to respond arises when an assertion of such complicity has been made. Paragraph (b)(1)(iii) does not require the lawyer to await the commencement of an action or proceeding that charges such complicity, so that the defense may be established by responding directly to a third party who has made such an assertion. The right to defend, of course, applies where a proceeding has been commenced. Where practicable and not prejudicial to the lawyer's ability to establish the defense, the lawyer should advise the client of the third party's assertion and request that the client respond appropriately. In any event, disclosure should be no greater than the lawyer reasonably believes is necessary to vindicate innocence, the disclosure should be made in a manner which limits access to the information to the tribunal or other persons having a need to know it, and appropriate protective orders or other arrangements should be sought by the lawyer to the fullest extent practicable.

[17] If the lawyer is charged with wrongdoing in which the client's conduct is implicated, the rule of confidentiality should not prevent the lawyer from defending against the charge. Such a charge can arise in a civil, criminal or professional disciplinary proceeding, and can be based on a wrong allegedly committed by the lawyer against the client, or on a wrong alleged by a third person; for example, a person claiming to have been defrauded by the lawyer and client acting together. A lawyer entitled to a fee is permitted by paragraph (b)(1)(iii) to prove the services rendered in an action to collect it. This aspect of the rule expresses the principle that the beneficiary of a fiduciary relationship may not exploit it to the detriment of the fiduciary. As stated above, the lawyer must make every effort practicable to avoid unnecessary disclosure of information relating to a representation, to limit disclosure to those having the need to know it, and to obtain protective orders or make other arrangements minimizing the risk of disclosure.

Disclosures Otherwise Required or Authorized

[18] The attorney-client privilege is differently defined in various jurisdictions. If a lawyer is called as a witness to give testimony concerning a client, absent waiver by the client, paragraph (a) requires the lawyer to invoke the privilege when it is applicable. The lawyer must comply with the final orders of a court or other tribunal of competent jurisdiction requiring the lawyer to give information about the client.

[19] The Rules of Professional Conduct in various circumstances permit or require a lawyer to disclose information relating to the representation. See Rules 2.2, 2.3, 3.3 and 4.1. In addition to these provisions, a lawyer may be obligated or permitted by other provisions of law to give information about a client. Whether another provision of law supersedes Rule 1.6 is a matter of interpretation beyond the scope of these Rules, but a presumption should exist against such a supersession.

Paralegals May Engage in Certain Activities and Regulation

Some states have enacted legislation that would allow paralegals to engage in certain activities that would otherwise fall within the definition of the "practice of law." If you live in one of those states, you will be able to engage in such activities without committing UPL. It will be most important to insure that you stay within the framework of the law. For example, on June 15, 2012, the Washington Supreme Court established a framework for the licensing and regulation of non-lawyers to engage in certain activities that otherwise would be the practice of law.

In addition, states are beginning to enact licensing requirements for paralegals. For example, the State of Florida now has a registered paralegal program which does permit the paralegal to perform services for an attorney in the representation of a client, provided that the services do not require the exercise of independent legal judgment; the attorney is responsible for the client and maintains a direct relationship with the client, and the attorney supervises the paralegal. In addition, the work product of the paralegal becomes the attorney's work product and the attorney remains fully responsible for all work done on behalf of the client.

SUMMARY

Paralegal ethics are closely tied to lawyer ethics rules. The lawyer has the direct responsibility to insure that his or her entire staff is performing tasks in an ethical manner and that their behavior conforms to the Rules of Professional Conduct. Rules of Professional Conduct ("Rules") have been promulgated in each state and only California has not adopted the American Bar Association Model Rules of Professional Conduct. The Rules map those standards that an attorney should aspire to as well as those that the attorney must follow or be subject to discipline, which could be a reprimand, a suspension, or disbarment.

Paralegals must not engage in the unauthorized practice of law. To do so could mean a loss of a job certainly but in some situations, could lead to a criminal conviction which may include jail and a fine. Those things that constitute the practice of law are those things that only a lawyer may do. Only a lawyer may give legal advice; prepare documents, such as wills and trusts, or court pleadings; appear in court on behalf of a client; or give legal advice to a client, or anyone else for that matter.

Paralegals must keep client confidences. This means that anything told to a client that the client told the attorney or paralegal, with the express or implied understanding that the information would not be disclosed outside the firm, must be held in confidence. The duty of confidentiality lasts forever. Paralegals should take care to avoid gossiping about client matters to friends, spouses, or family.

KEY TERMS

ethics
Rules of Professional Conduct

unauthorized practice of law
practice of law

confidentiality

REVIEW QUESTIONS

1. Why do we have legal ethics?
2. What is client confidentiality? Why is it so important to the relationship with the client?
3. What are the Rules of Professional Conduct? Are paralegals held responsible under them? Should they be?

4. How may a paralegal prevent misrepresenting herself as a lawyer? Can you think of other ways that are not represented in this book? What are they?
5. May you prepare a will for your spouse or your adult child? Why or why not?

6. May you assist your best friend with filling out a big box store pre-prepared power of attorney? Why or why not?

7. If you commit an ethical violation, is your supervising lawyer going to be sanctioned by the bar or state Supreme Court? Why or why not? Is this, in your opinion, a good outcome?

8. What is a registered paralegal?

9. What constitutes giving legal advice?

10. What does working under direct supervision of a lawyer mean?

PROJECTS

1. Review Rule 1.6 of the Oregon Rules of Professional Conduct, found at http://www. osbar.org/rulesregs/. How does it differ from Rule 1.6 of the Georgia Rules of Professional Conduct? How does it differ from the ABA Model Rules?

2. There are numerous blogs written by paralegals. Do you think that as a paralegal you can write a blog? What do you think your limitations should be based upon the Rules? Will your blog writing cause trouble for your supervising attorney? See http://hunterlipton.com/index.php/news/details/Disciplinary-Panel-Sides-With-the-Virginia-State-Bar-Over-Blogging/ and make the case for and against this Virginia ruling.

MyLegalStudiesLab™ http://www.mylegalstudieslab
MYLEGALSTUDIESLAB VIRTUAL LAW OFFICE EXPERIENCE ASSIGNMENTS
Complete the pre-test, study plan, and post-test for this chapter and answer the Legal Applications questions as assigned.

These will help you confirm your mastery of the concepts and their application to legal scenarios. Then, complete the Virtual Law Office assignments as assigned by your instructor. These assignments are designed to develop your workplace skills and result in producing documents for inclusion in your portfolio.

Appendix A

IMPORTANT CASES CONCERNING THE RIGHT TO DIE

Cruzan v. Director, MDH

497 U.S. 261

CRUZAN, BY HER PARENTS AND CO-GUARDIANS CRUZAN ET UX. v. DIRECTOR, MISSOURI DEPARTMENT OF HEALTH, ET AL. CERTIORARI TO THE SUPREME COURT OF MISSOURI

Argued December 6, 1989
Decided June 25, 1990

REHNQUIST, C.J., delivered the opinion of the Court, in which WHITE, O'CONNOR, SCALIA, and KENNEDY, JJ., joined. O'CONNOR, J., and SCALIA, J., filed concurring opinions. BRENNAN, J., filed a dissenting opinion, in which MARSHALL and BLACKMUN, JJ., joined, STEVENS, J., filed a dissenting opinion.

CHIEF JUSTICE REHNQUIST delivered the opinion of the Court.

Petitioner Nancy Beth Cruzan was rendered incompetent as a result of severe injuries sustained during an automobile accident. Copetitioners Lester and Joyce Cruzan, Nancy's parents and coguardians, sought a court order directing the withdrawal of their daughter's artificial feeding and hydration equipment after it became apparent that she had virtually no chance of recovering her cognitive faculties. The Supreme Court of Missouri held that, because there was no clear and convincing evidence of Nancy's desire to have life-sustaining treatment withdrawn under such circumstances, her parents lacked authority to effectuate such a request. We granted certiorari, 492 U.S. 917 (1989), and now affirm.

On the night of January 11, 1983; Nancy Cruzan lost control of her car as she traveled down Elm Road in Jasper County, Missouri. The vehicle overturned, and Cruzan was discovered lying face down in a ditch without detectable respiratory or cardiac function. Paramedics were able to restore her breathing and heartbeat at the accident site, and she was transported to a hospital in an unconscious state. An attending neurosurgeon diagnosed her as having sustained probable cerebral contusions compounded by significant anoxia (lack of oxygen). The Missouri trial court in this case found that permanent brain damage generally results after 6 minutes in an anoxic state; it was estimated that Cruzan was deprived of oxygen from 12 to 14 minutes. She remained in a coma for approximately three weeks, and then progressed to an unconscious state in which she was able to orally ingest some nutrition. In order to ease feeding and further the recovery, surgeons implanted a gastrostomy feeding and hydration tube in Cruzan with the consent of her then husband. Subsequent rehabilitative efforts proved unavailing. She now lies in a Missouri state hospital in what is commonly referred to as a persistent vegetative state: generally, a condition in which a person exhibits motor reflexes but evinces no indications of significant cognitive function. The State of Missouri is bearing the cost of her care.

After it had become apparent that Nancy Cruzan had virtually no chance of regaining her mental faculties, her parents asked hospital employees to terminate the artificial nutrition and hydration procedures. All agree that such a removal would cause her death. The employees refused to honor the request without court approval. The parents then sought and received authorization from the state trial court for termination. The court found that a person in Nancy's condition had a fundamental right under the State and Federal Constitutions to refuse or direct the withdrawal of "death prolonging procedures." App. to Pet. for Cert. A99. The court also found that Nancy's "expressed thoughts at age twenty-five in somewhat serious conversation with a housemate friend that, if sick or injured, she would not wish to continue her life unless she could live at least halfway normally suggests that, given her present condition, she would not wish to continue on with her nutrition and hydration." Id., at A97–A98.

The Supreme Court of Missouri reversed by a divided vote. The court recognized a right to refuse treatment embodied in the common law doctrine of informed consent, but expressed skepticism about the application of that doctrine in the circumstances of this case. Cruzan v. Harmon, 760 S.W.2d 408, 416–417 (1988) (en banc). The court also declined to read a broad right of privacy into the State Constitution which would "support the right of a person to refuse medical treatment in every circumstance," and expressed doubt as to whether such a right existed under the United States Constitution. Id., at 417–418. It then decided that the Missouri Living Will statute, Mo.Rev.Stat. 459.010 et seq. (1986), embodied a state policy strongly favoring the preservation of life. 760 S.W.2d, at 419–420. The court found that Cruzan's statements to her roommate regarding her desire to live or die under certain conditions were "unreliable for the purpose of determining her intent," id., at 424, "and thus insufficient to support the coguardians['] claim to exercise substituted judgment on Nancy's behalf." Id., at 426. It rejected the argument that Cruzan's parents were entitled to order the termination of her medical treatment, concluding that "no person can assume that choice for an incompetent in the absence of the formalities required under Missouri's Living Will statutes or the clear and convincing, inherently reliable evidence absent here." Id., at 425. The court also expressed its view that "[b]road policy questions bearing on life and death are more properly addressed by representative assemblies" than judicial bodies. Id., at 426.

We granted certiorari to consider the question of whether Cruzan has a right under the United States Constitution which would require the hospital to withdraw life-sustaining treatment from her under these circumstances.

At common law, even the touching of one person by another without consent and without legal justification was a battery. See W. Keeton, D. Dobbs, R. Keeton, & D. Owen, Prosser and Keeton on Law of Torts 9, pp. 39–42 (5th ed. 1984). Before the turn of the century, this Court observed that "[n]o right is held more sacred, or is more carefully guarded by the common law, than the right of every individual to the possession and control of his own person, free from all restraint or interference of others, unless by clear and unquestionable authority of law." Union Pacific R. Co. v. Botsford, 141 U.S. 250, 251 (1891). This notion of bodily integrity has been embodied in the requirement that informed consent is generally required for medical treatment. Justice Cardozo, while on the Court of Appeals of New York, aptly described this doctrine: "Every human being of adult years and sound mind has a right to determine what shall be done with his own body, and a surgeon who performs an operation without his patient's consent commits an assault, for which he is liable in damages." Schloendorff v. Society of New York Hospital, 211 N.Y. 125, 129-30, 105 N.E. 92, 93 (1914). The informed consent doctrine has become firmly entrenched in American tort law. See Dobbs, Keeton, & Owen, supra, 32, pp. 189-192; F. Rozovsky, Consent to Treatment, A Practical Guide 1–98 (2d ed. 1990).

The logical corollary of the doctrine of informed consent is that the patient generally possesses the right not to consent, that is, to refuse treatment. Until about 15 years ago and the seminal decision in In re Quinlan, 70 N.J. 10, 355 A.2d 647, cert. denied sub nom. Garger v. New Jersey, 429 U.S. 922 (1976), the number of right-to-refuse-treatment decisions were relatively few. Most of the earlier cases involved patients who refused medical treatment forbidden by their religious beliefs, thus implicating First Amendment rights as well as common law rights of self-determination. More recently, however, with the advance of medical technology capable of sustaining life well past the point where natural forces would have brought certain death in earlier times, cases involving the right to refuse life-sustaining treatment have burgeoned. See 760 S.W.2d at 412, n. 4 (collecting 54 reported decisions from 1976 through 1988).

In the Quinlan case, young Karen Quinlan suffered severe brain damage as the result of anoxia, and entered a persistent vegetative state. Karen's father sought judicial approval to disconnect his daughter's respirator. The New Jersey Supreme Court granted the relief, holding that Karen had a right of privacy grounded in the Federal Constitution to terminate treatment. In re Quinlan, 70 N.J. at 38–42, 355 A.2d at 662–664. Recognizing that this right was not absolute, however, the court balanced it against asserted state interests. Noting that the State's interest "weakens and the individual's right to privacy grows as the degree of bodily invasion increases and the prognosis dims," the court concluded that the state interests had to give way in that case. Id., at 41, 355 A.2d at 664. The court also concluded that the "only practical way" to prevent the loss of Karen's privacy right due to her incompetence was to allow her guardian and family to decide "whether she would exercise it in these circumstances." Ibid.

After Quinlan, however, most courts have based a right to refuse treatment either solely on the common law right to informed consent or on both the common law right and a constitutional privacy right. See L. Tribe, American Constitutional Law 15-11, p. 1365 (2d ed. 1988). In Superintendent of Belchertown State School v. Saikewicz, 373 Mass. 728, 370 N.E.2d 417 (1977), the Supreme Judicial Court of Massachusetts relied on both the right of privacy and the right of informed consent to permit the withholding of chemotherapy from a profoundly-retarded 67-year-old man suffering from leukemia. Id., at 737-738, 370 N.E.2d at 424. Reasoning that an incompetent person retains the same rights as a competent individual "because the value of human dignity extends to both," the court adopted a "substituted judgment" standard whereby courts were to determine what an incompetent individual's decision would have been under the circumstances. Id., at 745, 752–753, 757–758, 370 N.E.2d at 427, 431, 434. Distilling certain state interests from prior case law—the preservation of life, the protection of the interests of innocent third parties, the prevention of suicide, and the maintenance of the ethical integrity of the medical profession—the court recognized the first interest as paramount and noted it was greatest when an affliction was curable, "as opposed to the State interest where, as here, the issue is not whether, but when, for how long, and at what cost to the individual [a] life may be briefly extended." Id., at 742, 370 N.E.2d at 426.

In In re Storar, 52 N.Y.2d 363, 438 N.Y.S.2d 266, 420 N.E.2d 64, cert. denied, 454 U.S. 858 (1981), the New York Court of Appeals declined to base a right to refuse treatment on a constitutional privacy right. Instead, it found such a right "adequately supported" by the informed consent doctrine. Id., at 376–377, 420 N.E.2d at 70. In In re Eichner (decided with In re Storar, supra), an 83-year-old man who had suffered brain damage from anoxia entered a vegetative state and was thus incompetent to consent to the removal of his respirator. The court, however, found it unnecessary to reach the question of whether his rights could be exercised by others, since it found the evidence clear and convincing from statements made by the patient when competent that he "did not want to be maintained in a vegetative coma by use of a respirator." Id., at 380, 420 N.E.2d at 72. In the companion Storar case, a 52-year-old man suffering from bladder cancer had been profoundly retarded during most of his life. Implicitly rejecting the approach taken in Saikewicz, supra, the court reasoned that, due to such life-long incompetency, "it is unrealistic to attempt to determine whether he would want to continue potentially life-prolonging treatment if he were competent." 52 N.Y.2d at 380, 420 N.E.2d at 72. As the evidence showed that the patient's required blood transfusions did not involve excessive pain and, without them, his mental and physical abilities would deteriorate, the court concluded that it should not "allow an incompetent patient to bleed to death because someone, even someone as close as a parent or sibling, feels that this is best for one with an incurable disease." Id., at 382, 420 N.E.2d, at 73.

Many of the later cases build on the principles established in Quinlan, Saikewicz and Storar/Eichner. For instance, in In re Conroy, 98 N.J. 321, 486 A.2d 1209 (1985), the same court that decided Quinlan considered whether a nasogastric feeding tube could be removed from an 84-year-old incompetent nursing-home resident suffering irreversible mental and physical ailments. While recognizing that a federal right of privacy might apply in the case, the court, contrary to its approach in Quinlan, decided to base its decision on the common law right to self-determination and informed consent. 98 N.J. at 348, 486 A.2d at 1223. "On balance, the right to self-determination ordinarily outweighs any countervailing state interests, and competent persons generally are permitted to refuse medical treatment, even at the risk of death. Most of the cases that have held otherwise, unless they involved the interest in protecting innocent third parties, have concerned the patient's competency to make a rational and considered choice." Id., at 353-354, 486 A.2d at 1225.

Reasoning that the right of self-determination should not be lost merely because an individual is unable to sense a violation of it, the court held that incompetent individuals retain a right to refuse treatment. It also held that such a right could be exercised by a surrogate decisionmaker using a "subjective" standard when there was clear evidence that the incompetent person would have exercised it. Where such evidence was lacking, the court held that an individual's right could still be invoked in certain circumstances under objective "best interest" standards. Id., at 361-368, 486 A.2d at 1229-1233. Thus, if some trustworthy evidence existed that the individual would have wanted to terminate treatment, but not enough to clearly establish a person's wishes for purposes of the subjective standard, and the burden of a prolonged life from the experience of pain and suffering markedly outweighed its satisfactions, treatment could be terminated under a "limited-objective" standard. Where no trustworthy evidence existed, and a person's suffering would make the administration of life-sustaining treatment inhumane, a "pure-objective" standard could be used to terminate treatment. If none of these conditions obtained, the court held it was best to err in favor of preserving life. Id., at 364-368, 486 A.2d at 1231–1233.

The court also rejected certain categorical distinctions that had been drawn in prior refusal-of-treatment cases as lacking substance for decision purposes: the distinction between actively hastening death by terminating treatment and passively allowing a person to die of a disease; between treating individuals as an initial matter versus withdrawing treatment afterwards; between ordinary versus extraordinary treatment; and between treatment by artificial feeding versus other forms of life-sustaining medical procedures. Id., at 369–374, 486 A.2d at 1233–1237. As to the last item, the court acknowledged the "emotional significance" of food, but noted that feeding by implanted tubes is a "medical procedur[e] with inherent risks and possible side effects, instituted by skilled healthcare providers to compensate for impaired physical functioning" which analytically was equivalent to artificial breathing using a respirator. Id., at 373, 486 A.2d at 1236.

In contrast to Conroy, the Court of Appeals of New York recently refused to accept less than the clearly expressed wishes of a patient before permitting the exercise of her right to refuse treatment by a surrogate decisionmaker. In re Westchester County Medical Center on behalf of O'Connor, 72 N.Y.2d 517, 534 N.Y.S.2d 886, 531 N.E.2d 607 (1988) (O'Connor). There, the court, over the objection of the patient's family members, granted an order to insert a feeding tube into a 77-year-old woman rendered incompetent as a result of several strokes. While continuing to recognize a common law right to refuse treatment, the court rejected the substituted judgment approach for asserting it "because it is inconsistent with our fundamental commitment to the notion that no person or court should substitute its judgment as to what would be an acceptable quality of life for another. Consequently, we adhere to the view that, despite its pitfalls and inevitable uncertainties, the inquiry must always be narrowed to the patient's expressed intent, with every effort made to minimize the opportunity for error." Id., at 530, 531 N.E.2d, at 613 (citation omitted). The court held that the record lacked the requisite clear and convincing evidence of the patient's expressed intent to withhold life-sustaining treatment. Id., at 531–534, 531 N.E.2d, at 613–615.

Other courts have found state statutory law relevant to the resolution of these issues. In Conservatorship of Drabick, 200 Cal.App. 3d 185, 245 Cal.Rptr. 840, cert. denied, 488 U.S. 958 (1988), the California Court of Appeal authorized the removal of a nasogastric feeding tube from a 44-year-old man who was in a persistent vegetative state as a result of an auto accident. Noting that the right to refuse treatment was grounded in both the common law and a constitutional right of privacy, the court held that a state probate statute authorized the patient's conservator to order the withdrawal of life-sustaining treatment when such a decision was made in good faith based on medical advice and the conservatee's best interests. While acknowledging that "to claim that [a patient's] right to choose' survives incompetence is a legal fiction at best," the court reasoned that the respect society accords to persons as individuals is not lost upon incompetence, and is best preserved by allowing others "to make a decision that reflects [a patient's] interests more closely than would a purely technological decision to do whatever is possible." Id., at 208, 245 Cal.Rptr., at 854–855. See also In re Conservatorship of Torres, 357 N.W.2d 332 (Minn. 1984). (Minnesota court had constitutional and statutory authority to authorize a conservator to order the removal of an incompetent individual's respirator since in patient's best interests.)

In In re Estate of Longeway, 133 Ill.2d 33, 549 N.E.2d 292 (1989), the Supreme Court of Illinois considered whether a 76-year-old woman rendered incompetent from a series of strokes had a right to the discontinuance of artificial nutrition and hydration. Noting that the boundaries of a federal right of privacy were uncertain, the court found a right to refuse treatment in the doctrine of informed consent. Id., at 43–45, 549 N.E.2d at 296–297. The court further held that the State Probate Act impliedly authorized a guardian to exercise a ward's right to refuse artificial sustenance in the event that the ward was terminally ill and irreversibly comatose. Id., at 45–47, 549 N.E.2d at 298. Declining to adopt a best interests standard for deciding when it would be appropriate to exercise a ward's right because it "lets another make a determination of a patient's quality of life," the court opted instead for a substituted judgment standard. Id., at 49, 549 N.E.2d at 299. Finding the "expressed intent" standard utilized in O'Connor, supra, too rigid, the court noted that other clear and convincing evidence of the patient's intent could be considered. 133 Ill.2d, at 50–51, 549 N.E.2d, at 300. The court also adopted the "consensus opinion [that] treats artificial nutrition and hydration as medical treatment." Id., at 42, 549 N.E.2d at 296. Cf. McConnell v. Beverly Enterprises-Connecticut, Inc., 209 Conn. 692, 705, 553 A.2d 596, 603 (1989) (right to withdraw artificial nutrition and hydration found in the Connecticut Removal of Life Support Systems Act, which "provid[es] functional guidelines for the exercise of the common law and constitutional rights of self-determination"; attending physician authorized to remove treatment after finding that patient is in a terminal condition, obtaining consent of family, and considering expressed wishes of patient).

As these cases demonstrate, the common law doctrine of informed consent is viewed as generally encompassing the right of a competent individual to refuse medical treatment. Beyond that, these decisions demonstrate both similarity and diversity in their approach to decision of what all agree is a perplexing question with unusually strong moral and ethical overtones. State courts have available to them for decision a number of sources—state constitutions, statutes, and common law—which are not available to us. In this Court, the question is simply and starkly whether the United States Constitution prohibits Missouri from choosing the rule of decision which it did. This is the first case in which we have been squarely presented with the issue of whether the United States Constitution grants what is in common parlance referred to as a "right to die." We follow the judicious counsel of our decision in Twin City Bank v. Nebeker, 167 U.S. 196, 202 (1897), where we said that, in deciding "a question of such magnitude and importance . . . it is the [better] part of wisdom not to attempt, by any general statement, to cover every possible phase of the subject."

The Fourteenth Amendment provides that no State shall "deprive any person of life, liberty, or property, without due process of law." The principle that a competent person has a constitutionally protected liberty interest in refusing unwanted medical treatment may be inferred from our prior decisions. In Jacobson v. Massachusetts, 197 U.S. 11, 24–30 (1905), for instance, the Court balanced an individual's liberty interest in declining an unwanted smallpox vaccine against the State's interest in preventing disease. Decisions prior to the incorporation of the Fourth Amendment into the Fourteenth Amendment analyzed searches and seizures involving the body under the Due Process Clause and were thought to implicate substantial liberty interests. See, e.g., Breithaupt v. Abram, 352 U.S. 432, 439 (1957) ("As against the right of an individual that his person be held inviolable . . . must be set the interests of society . . . ").

Just this Term, in the course of holding that a State's procedures for administering antipsychotic medication to prisoners were sufficient to satisfy due process concerns, we recognized that prisoners possess "a significant liberty interest in avoiding the unwanted administration of antipsychotic drugs under the Due Process Clause of the Fourteenth Amendment." Washington v. Harper, 494 U.S. 210, 221–222 (1990); see also id., at 229 ("The forcible injection of medication into a nonconsenting person's body represents a substantial interference with that person's liberty"). Still other cases support the recognition of a general liberty interest in refusing medical treatment. Vitek v. Jones, 445 U.S. 480, 494 (1980) (transfer to mental hospital coupled with mandatory behavior modification treatment implicated liberty interests); Parham v. J.R., 442 U.S. 584, 600 (1979) ("a child, in common with adults, has a substantial liberty interest in not being confined unnecessarily for medical treatment").

But determining that a person has a "liberty interest" under the Due Process Clause does not end the inquiry; "whether respondent's constitutional rights have been violated must be determined by balancing his liberty interests against the relevant state interests." Youngberg v. Romeo, 457 U.S. 307, 321 (1982). See also Mills v. Rogers, 457 U.S. 291, 299 (1982). Petitioners insist that, under the general holdings of our cases, the forced administration of life-sustaining medical treatment, and even of artificially delivered food and water essential to life, would implicate a competent person's liberty interest. Although we think the logic of the cases discussed above would embrace such a liberty interest, the dramatic consequences involved in refusal of such treatment would inform the inquiry as to whether the deprivation of that interest is constitutionally permissible. But for purposes of this case, we assume that the United States Constitution would grant a competent person a constitutionally protected right to refuse lifesaving hydration and nutrition.

Petitioners go on to assert that an incompetent person should possess the same right in this respect as is possessed by a competent person. They rely primarily on our decisions in Parham v. J.R., supra, and Youngberg v. Romeo, supra. In Parham, we held that a mentally disturbed minor child had a liberty interest in "not being confined unnecessarily for medical treatment," 442 U.S., at 600, but we certainly did not intimate that such a minor child, after commitment, would have a liberty interest in refusing treatment. In Youngberg, we held that a seriously retarded adult had a liberty interest in safety and freedom from bodily restraint, 457 U.S., at 320. Youngberg, however, did not deal with decisions to administer or withhold medical treatment.

The difficulty with petitioners' claim is that, in a sense, it begs the question: an incompetent person is not able to make an informed and voluntary choice to exercise a hypothetical right to refuse treatment or any other right. Such a "right" must be exercised for her, if at all, by some sort of surrogate. Here, Missouri has in effect recognized that, under certain circumstances, a surrogate may act for the patient in electing to have hydration and nutrition withdrawn in such a way as to cause death, but it has established a procedural safeguard to assure that the action of the surrogate conforms as best it may to the wishes expressed by the patient while competent. Missouri requires that evidence of the incompetent's wishes as to the withdrawal of treatment be proved by clear and convincing evidence. The question, then, is whether the United States Constitution forbids the establishment of this procedural requirement by the State. We hold that it does not.

Whether or not Missouri's clear and convincing evidence requirement comports with the United States Constitution depends in part on what interests the State may properly seek to protect in this situation. Missouri relies on its interest in the protection and preservation of human life, and there can be no gainsaying this interest. As a general matter, the States—indeed, all civilized nations—demonstrate their commitment to life by treating homicide as serious crime. Moreover, the majority of States in this country have laws imposing criminal penalties on one who assists another to commit suicide. We do not think a State is required to remain neutral in the face of an informed and voluntary decision by a physically able adult to starve to death.

But in the context presented here, a State has more particular interests at stake. The choice between life and death is a deeply personal decision of obvious and overwhelming finality. We believe Missouri may legitimately seek to safeguard the personal element of this choice through the imposition of heightened evidentiary requirements. It cannot be disputed that the Due Process Clause protects an interest in life as well as an interest in refusing life-sustaining medical treatment. Not all incompetent patients will have loved ones available to serve as surrogate decisionmakers. And even where family members are present, "[t]here will, of course, be some unfortunate situations in which family members will not act to protect a patient." In re Jobes, 108 N.J. 394, 419, 529 A.2d 434, 477 (1987). A State is entitled to guard against potential abuses in such situations. Similarly, a State is entitled to consider that a judicial proceeding to make a determination regarding an incompetent's wishes may very well not be an adversarial one, with the added guarantee of accurate factfinding that the adversary process brings with it. See Ohio v. Akron Center for Reproductive Health, post, at 515–516 (1990). Finally, we think a State may properly decline to make judgments about the "quality" of life that a particular individual may enjoy, and simply assert an unqualified interest in the preservation of human life to be weighed against the constitutionally protected interests of the individual.

In our view, Missouri has permissibly sought to advance these interests through the adoption of a "clear and convincing" standard of proof to govern such proceedings. "The function of a standard of proof, as that concept is embodied in the Due Process Clause and in the realm of factfinding, is to instruct the factfinder concerning the degree of confidence our society thinks he should have in the correctness of factual conclusions for a particular type of adjudication." Addington v. Texas, 441 U.S. 418, 423 (1979) (quoting In re Winship, 397 U.S. 358, 370 (1970) (Harlan, J., concurring)). "This Court has mandated an intermediate standard of proof—'clear and convincing evidence'—when the individual interests at stake in a state proceeding are both 'particularly important' and 'more substantial than mere loss of money.'" Santosky v. Kramer, 455 U.S. 745, 756 (1982) (quoting Addington, supra, at 424). Thus, such a standard has been required in deportation proceedings, Woodby v. INS, 385 U.S. 276 (1966), in denaturalization proceedings, Schneiderman v. United States, 320 U.S. 118 (1943), in civil commitment proceedings, Addington, supra, and in proceedings for the termination of parental rights. Santosky, supra. Further, this level of proof, "or an even higher one, has traditionally been imposed in cases involving allegations of civil fraud, and in a variety of other kinds of civil cases involving such issues as. . . lost wills, oral contracts to make bequests, and the like." Woodby, supra, at 285, n. 18.

We think it self-evident that the interests at stake in the instant proceedings are more substantial, both on an individual and societal level, than those involved in a run-of-the-mine civil dispute. But not only does the standard of proof reflect the importance of a particular adjudication, it also serves as "a societal judgment about how the risk of error should be distributed between the litigants." Santosky, supra, at 755; Addington, supra, at 423. The more stringent the burden of proof a party must bear, the more that party bears the risk of an erroneous decision. We believe that Missouri may permissibly place an increased risk of an erroneous decision on those seeking to terminate an incompetent individual's life-sustaining treatment. An erroneous decision not to terminate results in a maintenance of the status quo; the possibility of subsequent developments such as advancements in medical science, the discovery of new evidence regarding the patient's intent, changes in the law, or simply the unexpected death of the patient despite the administration of life-sustaining treatment, at least create the potential that a wrong decision will eventually be corrected or its impact mitigated. An erroneous decision to withdraw life-sustaining treatment, however, is not susceptible of correction. In Santosky, one of the factors which led the Court to require proof by clear and convincing evidence in a proceeding to terminate parental rights was that a decision in such a case was final and irrevocable. Santosky, supra, at 759. The same must surely be said of the decision to discontinue hydration and nutrition of a patient such as Nancy Cruzan, which all agree will result in her death.

It is also worth noting that most, if not all, States simply forbid oral testimony entirely in determining the wishes of parties in transactions which, while important, simply do not have the consequences that a decision to terminate a person's life does. At common law and by statute in most States, the parol evidence rule prevents the variations of the terms of a written contract by oral testimony. The statute of frauds makes unenforceable oral contracts to leave property by will, and statutes regulating the making of wills universally require that those instruments be in writing. See 2 A. Corbin, Contracts 398, pp. 360–361 (1950); 2 W. Page, Law of Wills 19.3–19.5, pp. 61–71 (1960). There is no doubt that statutes requiring wills to be in writing, and statutes of frauds which require that a contract to make a will be in writing, on occasion frustrate the effectuation of the intent of a particular decedent, just as Missouri's requirement of proof in this case may have frustrated the effectuation of the not-fully-expressed desires of Nancy Cruzan. But the Constitution does not require general rules to work faultlessly; no general rule can.

In sum, we conclude that a State may apply a clear and convincing evidence standard in proceedings where a guardian seeks to discontinue nutrition and hydration of a person diagnosed to be in a persistent vegetative state. We note that many courts which have adopted some sort of substituted judgment procedure in situations like this, whether they limit consideration of evidence to the prior expressed wishes of the incompetent individual, or whether they allow more general proof of what the individual's decision would have been, require a clear and convincing standard of proof for such evidence. See, e.g., Longeway, 133 Ill.2d at 50–51, 549 N.E.2d at 300; McConnell, 209 Conn., at 707–710, 553 A.2d at 604–605; O'Connor, 72 N.Y.2d at 529–530, 531 N.E.2d at 613; In re Gardner, 534 A.2d 947, 952–953 (Me. 1987); In re Jobes, 108 N.J. at 412–413, 529 A.2d at 443; Leach v. Akron General Medical Center, 68 Ohio Misc. 1, 11, 426 N.E.2d 809, 815 (1980).

The Supreme Court of Missouri held that, in this case, the testimony adduced at trial did not amount to clear and convincing proof of the patient's desire to have hydration and nutrition withdrawn. In so doing, it reversed a decision of the Missouri trial court, which had found that the evidence "suggest[ed]" Nancy Cruzan would not have desired to continue such measures, App. to Pet. for Cert. A98, but which had not adopted the standard of "clear and convincing evidence" enunciated by the Supreme Court. The testimony adduced at trial consisted primarily of Nancy Cruzan's statements, made to a housemate about a year before her accident, that she would not want to live should she face life as a "vegetable," and other observations to the same effect. The observations did not deal in terms with withdrawal of medical treatment or of hydration and nutrition. We cannot say that the Supreme Court of Missouri committed constitutional error in reaching the conclusion that it did.

Petitioners alternatively contend that Missouri must accept the "substituted judgment" of close family members even in the absence of substantial proof that their views reflect the views of the patient. They rely primarily upon our decisions in Michael H. v. Gerald D., 491 U.S. 110 (1989), and Parham v. J.R., 442 U.S. 584 (1979). But we do not think these cases support their claim. In Michael H., we upheld the constitutionality of California's favored treatment of traditional family relationships; such a holding may not be turned around into a constitutional requirement that a State must recognize the primacy of those relationships in a situation like this. And in Parham, where the patient was a minor, we also upheld the constitutionality of a state scheme in which parents made certain decisions for mentally ill minors. Here again, petitioners would seek to turn a decision which allowed a State to rely on family decisionmaking into a constitutional requirement that the State recognize such decisionmaking. But constitutional law does not work that way.

No doubt is engendered by anything in this record but that Nancy Cruzan's mother and father are loving and caring parents. If the State were required by the United States Constitution to repose a right of "substituted judgment" with anyone, the Cruzans would surely qualify. But we do not think the Due Process Clause requires the State to repose judgment on these matters with anyone but the patient herself. Close family members may have a strong feeling—a feeling not at all ignoble or unworthy, but not entirely disinterested, either—that they do not wish to witness the continuation of the life of a loved one which they regard as hopeless, meaningless, and even degrading. But there is no automatic assurance that the view of close family members will necessarily be the same as the patient's would have been had she been confronted with the prospect of her situation while competent. All of the reasons previously discussed for allowing Missouri to require clear and convincing evidence of the patient's wishes lead us to conclude that the State may choose to defer only to those wishes, rather than confide the decision to close family members.

The judgment of the Supreme Court of Missouri is Affirmed.

JUSTICE O'CONNOR, concurring.

I agree that a protected liberty interest in refusing unwanted medical treatment may be inferred from our prior decisions, see ante at 278–279, and that the refusal of artificially delivered food and water is encompassed within that liberty interest. See ante at 279. I write separately to clarify why I believe this to be so.

As the Court notes, the liberty interest in refusing medical treatment flows from decisions involving the State's invasions into the body. See ante at 278–279. Because our notions of liberty are inextricably entwined with our idea of physical freedom and self-determination, the Court has often deemed state incursions into the body repugnant to the interests protected by the Due Process Clause. See, e.g., Rochin v. California, 342 U.S. 165, 172 (1952) ("Illegally breaking into the privacy of the petitioner, the struggle to open his mouth and remove what was there, the forcible extraction of his stomach's contents . . . is bound to offend even hardened sensibilities"); Union Pacific R. Co. v. Botsford, 141 U.S. 250, 251 (1891). Our Fourth Amendment jurisprudence has echoed this same concern. See Schmerber v. California, 384 U.S. 757, 772 (1966) ("The integrity of an individual's person is a cherished value of our society"); Winston v. Lee, 470 U.S. 753, 759 (1985) ("A compelled surgical intrusion into an individual's body for evidence . . . implicates expectations of privacy and security of such magnitude that the intrusion may be " 'unreasonable' even if likely to produce evidence of a crime"). The State's imposition of medical treatment on an unwilling competent adult necessarily involves some form of restraint and intrusion. A seriously ill or dying patient whose wishes are not honored may feel a captive of the machinery required for life-sustaining measures or other medical interventions. Such forced treatment may burden that individual's liberty interests as much as any state coercion. See, e.g., Washington v. Harper, 494 U.S. 210, 221

(1990); Parham v. J.R., 442 U.S. 584, 600 (1979) ("It is not disputed that a child, in common with adults, has a substantial liberty interest in not being confined unnecessarily for medical treatment").

The State's artificial provision of nutrition and hydration implicates identical concerns. Artificial feeding cannot readily be distinguished from other forms of medical treatment. See, e.g., Council on Ethical and Judicial Affairs, American Medical Association, AMA Ethical Opinion 2.20, Withholding or Withdrawing Life-Prolonging Medical Treatment, Current Opinions 13 (1989); The Hastings Center, Guidelines on the Termination of Life-Sustaining Treatment and the Care of the Dying 59 (1987). Whether or not the techniques used to pass food and water into the patient's alimentary tract are termed "medical treatment," it is clear they all involve some degree of intrusion and restraint. Feeding a patient by means of a nasogastric tube requires a physician to pass a long flexible tube through the patient's nose, throat and esophagus and into the stomach. Because of the discomfort such a tube causes, "[m]any patients need to be restrained forcibly, and their hands put into large mittens to prevent them from removing the tube." Major, The Medical Procedures for Providing Food and Water: Indications and Effects, in By No Extraordinary Means: The Choice to Forgo Life-Sustaining Food and Water 25 (J. Lynn ed. 1986). A gastrostomy tube (as was used to provide food and water to Nancy Cruzan, see ante at 266) or jejunostomy tube must be surgically implanted into the stomach or small intestine. Office of Technology Assessment Task Force, Life-Sustaining Technologies and the Elderly 282 (1988). Requiring a competent adult to endure such procedures against her will burdens the patient's liberty, dignity, and freedom to determine the course of her own treatment. Accordingly, the liberty guaranteed by the Due Process Clause must protect, if it protects anything, an individual's deeply personal decision to reject medical treatment, including the artificial delivery of food and water.

I also write separately to emphasize that the Court does not today decide the issue whether a State must also give effect to the decisions of a surrogate decisionmaker. See ante at 287, n. 12. In my view, such a duty may well be constitutionally required to protect the patient's liberty interest in refusing medical treatment. Few individuals provide explicit oral or written instructions regarding their intent to refuse medical treatment should they become incompetent. States which decline to consider any evidence other than such instructions may frequently fail to honor a patient's intent. Such failures might be avoided if the State considered an equally probative source of evidence: the patient's appointment of a proxy to make health care decisions on her behalf. Delegating the authority to make medical decisions to a family member or friend is becoming a common method of planning for the future. See, e.g., Green, The Legal Status of Consent Obtained from Families of Adult Patients to Withhold or Withdraw Treatment, 258 JAMA 229, 230 (1987). Several States have recognized the practical wisdom of such a procedure by enacting durable power of attorney statutes that specifically authorize an individual to appoint a surrogate to make medical treatment decisions. Some state courts have suggested that an agent appointed pursuant to a general durable power of attorney statute would also be empowered to make health care decisions on behalf of the patient. See, e.g., In re Peter, 108 N.J. 365, 378–379, 529 A.2d 419, 426 (1987); see also 73 Op.Md. Atty. Gen. No. 88–046 (1988) (interpreting Md. Est. & Trusts Code Ann. 13-601 to 13-602 (1974), as authorizing a delegatee to make health care decisions). Other States allow an individual to designate a proxy to carry out the intent of a living will. These procedures for surrogate decisionmaking, which appear to be rapidly gaining in acceptance, may be a valuable additional safeguard of the patient's interest in directing his medical care. Moreover, as patients are likely to select a family member as a surrogate, see 2 President's Commission for the Study of Ethical Problems in Medicine and Biomedical and Behavioral Research, Making Health Care Decisions 240 (1982), giving effect to a proxy's decisions may also protect the "freedom of personal choice in matters of . . . family life." Cleveland Board of Education v. LaFleur, 414 U.S. 632, 639 (1974).

Today's decision, holding only that the Constitution permits a State to require clear and convincing evidence of Nancy Cruzan's desire to have artificial hydration and nutrition withdrawn, does not preclude a future determination that the Constitution requires the States to implement the decisions of a patient's duly appointed surrogate. Nor does it prevent States from developing other approaches for protecting an incompetent individual's liberty interest in refusing medical treatment. As is evident from the Court's survey of state court decisions, see ante at 271–277, no national consensus has yet emerged on the best solution for this difficult and sensitive problem. Today we decide only that one State's practice does not violate the Constitution; the more challenging task of crafting appropriate procedures for safeguarding incompetents' liberty interests is entrusted to the "laboratory" of the States, New State Ice Co. v. Liebmann, 285 U.S. 262, 311 (1932) (Brandeis, J., dissenting), in the first instance.

JUSTICE SCALIA, concurring.

The various opinions in this case portray quite clearly the difficult, indeed agonizing, questions that are presented by the constantly increasing power of science to keep the human body alive for longer than any reasonable person would want to inhabit it. The States have begun to grapple with these problems through legislation. I am concerned, from the tenor of today's opinions, that we are poised to confuse that enterprise as successfully as we have confused the enterprise of legislating concerning abortion—requiring it to be conducted against a background of federal constitutional imperatives that are unknown because they are being newly crafted from Term to Term. That would be a great misfortune.

While I agree with the Court's analysis today, and therefore join in its opinion, I would have preferred that we announce, clearly and promptly, that the federal courts have no business in this field; that American law has always accorded the State the power to prevent, by force if necessary, suicide—including suicide by refusing to take appropriate measures necessary to preserve one's life; that the point at which life becomes "worthless," and the point at which the means necessary to preserve it become "extraordinary" or "inappropriate," are neither set forth in the Constitution nor known to the nine Justices of this Court any better than they are known to nine people picked at random from the Kansas City telephone directory; and hence, that even when it is demonstrated by clear and convincing evidence that a patient no longer wishes certain measures to be taken to preserve her life, it is up to the citizens of Missouri to decide, through their elected representatives, whether that wish will be honored. It is quite impossible (because the Constitution says nothing about the matter) that those citizens will decide upon a line less lawful than the one we would choose; and it is unlikely (because we know no more about "life-and-death" than they do) that they will decide upon a line less reasonable.

The text of the Due Process Clause does not protect individuals against deprivations of liberty simpliciter. It protects them against deprivations of liberty "without due process of law." To determine that such a deprivation would not occur if Nancy Cruzan were forced to take nourishment against her will, it is unnecessary to reopen the historically recurrent debate over whether "due process" includes substantive restrictions. Compare Murray's Lessee v. Hoboken Land and Improvement Co., 18 How. 272 (1856), with Scott v. Sandford, 19 How. 393, 450 (1857); compare Tyson & Bro. v. Banton, 273 U.S. 418 (1927), with Olsen v. Nebraska ex rel. Western Reference & Bond Assn., Inc., 313 U.S. 236, 246–247 (1941); compare Ferguson v. Skrupa, 372 U.S. 726, 730 (1963), with Moore v. East Cleveland, 431 U.S. 494 (1977) (plurality opinion); see Easterbrook, Substance and Due Process, 1982 S.Ct.Rev 85; Monaghan, Our Perfect Constitution, 56 N.Y.U.L.Rev. 353 (1981). It is at least true that no "substantive due process" claim can be maintained unless the claimant demonstrates that the State has deprived him of a right historically and traditionally protected against State interference. Michael H. v. Gerald D., 491 U.S. 110, 122 (1989) (plurality opinion); Bowers v. Hardwick, 478 U.S. 186, 192 (1986); Moore, supra, at 502–503 (plurality opinion). That cannot possibly be established here.

At common law in England, a suicide—defined as one who "deliberately puts an end to his own existence, or commits any unlawful malicious act, the consequence of which is his own death," 4 W. Blackstone, Commentaries *189—was criminally liable. Ibid. Although the States abolished the penalties imposed by the common law (i.e., forfeiture and ignominious burial), they did so to spare the innocent family, and not to legitimize the act. Case law at the time of the Fourteenth Amendment generally held that assisting suicide was a criminal offense. See Marzen, O'Dowd, Crone, & Balch, Suicide: A Constitutional Right?, 24 Duquesne L.Rev. 1, 76 (1985) ("In short, twenty-one of the thirty-seven states, and eighteen of the thirty ratifying states, prohibited assisting suicide. Only eight of the states, and seven of the ratifying states, definitely did not"); see also 1 F. Wharton, Criminal Law 122 (6th rev. ed. 1868). The System of Penal Law presented to the House of Representatives by Representative Livingston in 1828 would have criminalized assisted suicide. E. Livingston, A System of Penal Law, Penal Code 122 (1828). The Field Penal Code, adopted by the Dakota Territory in 1877, proscribed attempted suicide and assisted suicide. Marzen, O'Dowd, Crone, & Balch, supra, at 76–77. And most States that did not explicitly prohibit assisted suicide in 1868 recognized, when the issue arose in the 50 years following the Fourteenth Amendment's ratification, that assisted and (in some cases) attempted suicide were unlawful. Id., at 77–100; id., at 148–242 (surveying development of States' laws). Thus, "there is no significant support for the claim that a right to suicide is so rooted in our tradition that it may be deemed 'fundamental' or 'implicit in the concept of ordered liberty.'" Id., at 100 (quoting Palko v. Connecticut, 302 U.S. 319, 325 (1937)).

Petitioners rely on three distinctions to separate Nancy Cruzan's case from ordinary suicide: (1) that she is permanently incapacitated and in pain; (2) that she would bring on her death not by any affirmative act but by merely declining treatment that provides nourishment; and (3) that preventing her from effectuating her presumed wish to die requires violation of her bodily integrity. None of these suffices. Suicide was not excused even when committed "to avoid those ills which [persons] had not the fortitude to endure." Blackstone, supra, at *189. "The life of those to whom life has become a burden—of those who are hopelessly diseased or fatally wounded—nay, even the lives of criminals condemned to death, are under the protection of the law, equally as the lives of those who are in the full tide of life's enjoyment, and anxious to continue to live." Blackburn v. State, 23 Ohio St. 146, 163 (1873). Thus, a man who prepared a poison, and placed it within reach of his wife, "to put an end to her suffering" from a terminal illness was convicted of murder, People v. Roberts, 211 Mich. 187, 178 N.W. 690, 693 (1920); the "incurable suffering of the suicide, as a legal question, could hardly affect the degree of criminality . . . " Note, 30 Yale L.J. 408, 412 (1921) (discussing Roberts). Nor would the imminence of the patient's death have affected liability. "The lives of all are equally under the protection of the law, and under that protection to their last moment . . . . [Assisted suicide] is declared by the law to be murder, irrespective of the wishes or the condition of the party to whom the poison is administered . . . ." Blackburn, supra, at 163; see also Commonwealth v. Bowen, 213 Mass. 356, 360 (1816).

The second asserted distinction—suggested by the recent cases canvassed by the Court concerning the right to refuse treatment, ante at 270–277—relies on the dichotomy between action and inaction. Suicide, it is said, consists of an affirmative act to end one's life; refusing treatment is not an affirmative act "causing" death, but merely a passive acceptance of the natural process of dying. I readily acknowledge that the distinction between action and inaction has some bearing upon the legislative judgment of what ought to be prevented as suicide—though even there it would seem to me unreasonable to draw the line precisely between action and inaction, rather than between various forms of inaction. It would not make much sense to say that one may not kill oneself by walking into the sea, but may sit on the beach until submerged by the incoming tide; or that one may not intentionally lock oneself into a cold storage locker, but may refrain from coming indoors when the temperature drops below freezing. Even as a legislative matter, in other words, the intelligent line does not fall between action and inaction, but between those forms of inaction that consist of abstaining from "ordinary" care and those that consist of abstaining from "excessive" or "heroic" measures. Unlike action vs. inaction, that is not a line to be discerned by logic or legal analysis, and we should not pretend that it is.

But to return to the principal point for present purposes: the irrelevance of the action–inaction distinction. Starving oneself to death is no different from putting a gun to one's temple as far as the common law definition of suicide is concerned; the cause of death in both cases is the suicide's conscious decision to "pu[t] an end to his own existence." Blackstone, supra, at *189. See In re Caulk, 125 N.H. 226, 232, 480 A.2d 93, 97 (1984); State ex rel. White v. Narick, 170 W.Va. 195, 292 S.E.2d 54 (1982); Von Holden v. Chapman, 87 App. Div.2d 66, 450 N.Y.S.2d 623 (1982). Of course, the common law rejected the action–inaction distinction in other contexts involving the taking of human life as well. In the prosecution of a parent for the starvation death of her infant, it was no defense that the infant's death was "caused" by no action of the parent, but by the natural process of starvation, or by the infant's natural inability to provide for itself. See Lewis v. State, 72 Ga. 164 (1883); People v. McDonald, 49 Hun. 67, 1 N.Y.S. 703 (1888); (5th Dept., App. Div. 1888); Commonwealth v. Hall, 322 Mass. 523, 528, 78 N.E.2d 644, 647 (1948) (collecting cases); F. Wharton, Law of Homicide 134–135, 304 (2d ed. 1875); 2 J. Bishop, Commentaries on the Criminal Law 686 (5th ed. 1872); J. Hawley & M. McGregor, Criminal Law 152 (3d ed. 1899). A physician, moreover, could be criminally liable for failure to provide care that could have extended the patient's life, even if death was immediately caused by the underlying disease that the physician failed to treat. Barrow v. State, 17 Okl.Cr. 340, 188 P. 351 (1920); People v. Phillips, 64 Cal.2d 574, 414 P.2d 353 (1966).

It is not surprising, therefore, that the early cases considering the claimed right to refuse medical treatment dismissed as specious the nice distinction between "passively submitting to death and actively seeking it. The distinction may be merely verbal, as it would be if an adult sought death by starvation instead of a drug. If the State may interrupt one mode of self-destruction, it may with equal authority interfere with the other." John F. Kennedy Memorial Hosp. v. Heston, 58 N.J. 576, 581–582, 279 A.2d 670, 672–673 (1971); see also Application of President & Directors of Georgetown College, Inc., 118 U.S. App. D.C. 80, 88–89, 331 F.2d 1000, 1008–1009 (Wright, J., in chambers), cert. denied, 377 U.S. 978 (1964).

The third asserted basis of distinction—that frustrating Nancy Cruzan's wish to die in the present case requires interference with her bodily integrity—is likewise inadequate, because such interference is impermissible only if one begs the question whether her refusal to undergo the treatment on her own is suicide. It has always been lawful not only for the State, but even for private citizens, to interfere with bodily integrity to prevent a felony. See Phillips v. Trull, 11 Johns. 486 (N.Y. 1814); City Council v. Payne, 2 Nott & McCord 475 (S.C. 1821); Vandeveer v. Mattocks, 3 Ind. 479 (1852); T. Cooley, Law of Torts 174–175 (1879); Wilgus, Arrest Without a Warrant, 22 Mich.L.Rev. 673 (1924); Restatement of Torts 119 (1934). That general rule has of course been applied to suicide. At common law, even a private person's use of force to prevent suicide was privileged. Colby v. Jackson, 12 N.H. 526, 530–531 (1842); Look v. Choate, 108 Mass. 116, 120 (1871); Commonwealth v. Mink, 123 Mass. 422, 429 (1877); In re Doyle, 16 R.I. 537, 539, 18A. 159, 159–160 (1889); Porter v. Ritch, 70 Conn. 235, 255, 39 A. 169, 175 (1898); Emmerich v. Thorley, 54 N.Y.S. 791, 793–794 (1898); State v. Hembd, 305 Minn. 120, 130, 232 N.W.2d 872, 878 (1975); 2 C. Addison, Law of Torts 819 (1876); Cooley, supra, at 179–180. It is not even reasonable, much less required by the Constitution, to maintain that, although the State has the right to prevent a person from slashing his wrists, it does not have the power to apply physical force to prevent him from doing so, nor the power, should he succeed, to apply, coercively if necessary, medical measures to stop the flow of blood. The state-run hospital, I am certain, is not liable under 42 U.S.C. 1983 for violation of constitutional rights, nor the private hospital liable under general tort law, if, in a State where suicide is unlawful, it pumps out the stomach of a person who has intentionally taken an overdose of barbiturates, despite that person's wishes to the contrary.

The dissents of JUSTICES BRENNAN and STEVENS make a plausible case for our intervention here only by embracing—the latter explicitly and the former by implication—a political principle that the States are free to adopt, but that is demonstrably not imposed by the Constitution. "The State," says JUSTICE BRENNAN, "has no legitimate general interest in someone's life, completely abstracted from the interest of the person living that life, that could outweigh the person's choice to avoid medical treatment." Post at 313 (emphasis added). The italicized phrase sounds moderate enough, and is all that is needed to cover the present case—but the proposition cannot logically be so limited. One who accepts it must also accept, I think, that the State has no such legitimate interest that could outweigh "the person's choice to put an end to her life." Similarly, if one agrees with JUSTICE BRENNAN that "the State's general interest in life must accede to Nancy Cruzan's particularized and intense interest in self-determination in her choice of medical treatment," post, at 314 (emphasis added), he must also believe that the State must accede to her "particularized and intense interest in self-determination in her choice whether to continue living or to die." For insofar as balancing the relative interests of the State and the individual is concerned, there is nothing distinctive about accepting death through the refusal of "medical treatment," as opposed to accepting it through the refusal of food, or through the failure to shut off the engine and get out of the car after parking in one's garage after work. Suppose that Nancy Cruzan were in precisely the condition she is in today, except that she could be fed and digest food and water without artificial assistance. How is the State's "interest" in keeping her alive thereby increased, or her interest in deciding whether she wants to continue living reduced? It seems to me, in other words, that JUSTICE BRENNAN's position ultimately rests upon the proposition that it is none of the State's business if a person wants to commit suicide. JUSTICE STEVENS is explicit on the point: "Choices about death touch the core of liberty . . . . [N]ot much may be said with confidence about death unless it is said from faith, and that alone is reason enough to protect the freedom to conform choices about death to individual conscience." Post at 343. This is a view that some societies have held, and that our States are free to adopt if they wish. But it is not a view imposed by our constitutional traditions, in which the power of the State to prohibit suicide is unquestionable.

What I have said above is not meant to suggest that I would think it desirable, if we were sure that Nancy Cruzan wanted to die, to keep her alive by the means at issue here. I assert only that the Constitution has nothing to say about the subject. To raise up a constitutional right here, we would have to create out of nothing (for it exists neither in text nor tradition) some constitutional principle whereby, although the State may insist that an individual come in out of the cold and eat food, it may not insist that he take medicine; and although it may pump his stomach empty of poison he has ingested, it may not fill his stomach with food he has failed to ingest. Are there, then, no reasonable and humane limits that ought not to be exceeded in requiring an individual to preserve his own life? There obviously are, but they are not set forth in the Due Process Clause. What assures us that those limits will not be exceeded is the same constitutional guarantee that is the source of most of our protection—what protects us, for example, from being assessed a tax of 100% of our income above the subsistence level, from being forbidden to drive cars, or from being required to send our children to school for 10 hours a day, none of which horribles is categorically prohibited by the Constitution. Our salvation is the Equal Protection Clause, which requires the democratic majority to accept for themselves and their loved ones what they impose on you and me. This Court need not, and has no authority to, inject itself into every field of human activity where irrationality and oppression may theoretically occur, and if it tries to do so, it will destroy itself.

JUSTICE BRENNAN, with whom JUSTICE MARSHALL and JUSTICE BLACKMUN join, dissenting.

"Medical technology has effectively created a twilight zone of suspended animation where death commences while life, in some form, continues. Some patients, however, want no part of a life sustained only by medical technology. Instead, they prefer a plan of medical treatment that allows nature to take its course and permits them to die with dignity."

Nancy Cruzan has dwelt in that twilight zone for 6 years. She is oblivious to her surroundings and will remain so. Cruzan v. Harmon, 760 S.W.2d 408, 411 (Mo. 1988). Her body twitches only reflexively, without consciousness. Ibid. The areas of her brain that once thought, felt, and experienced sensations have degenerated badly, and are continuing to do so. The cavities remaining are filling with cerebrospinal fluid. The "'cerebral cortical atrophy is irreversible, permanent, progressive and ongoing.'" Ibid. "Nancy will never interact meaningfully with her environment again. She will remain in a persistent vegetative state until her death." Id., at 422. Because she cannot swallow, her nutrition and hydration are delivered through a tube surgically implanted in her stomach.

A grown woman at the time of the accident, Nancy had previously expressed her wish to forgo continuing medical care under circumstances such as these. Her family and her friends are convinced that this is what she would want. See n. 20, infra. A guardian ad litem appointed by the trial court is also convinced that this is what Nancy would want. See 760 S.W.2d at 444 (Higgins, J., dissenting from denial of rehearing). Yet the Missouri Supreme Court, alone among state courts deciding such a question, has determined that an irreversibly vegetative patient will remain a passive prisoner of medical technology—for Nancy, perhaps for the next 30 years. See id., at 424, 427.

Today the Court, while tentatively accepting that there is some degree of constitutionally protected liberty interest in avoiding unwanted medical treatment, including life-sustaining medical treatment such as artificial nutrition and hydration, affirms the decision of the Missouri Supreme Court. The majority opinion, as I read it, would affirm that decision on the ground that a State may require "clear and convincing" evidence of Nancy Cruzan's prior decision to forgo life-sustaining treatment under circumstances such as hers in order to ensure that her actual wishes are honored. See ante at 282–283, 286–287. Because I believe that Nancy Cruzan has a fundamental right to be free of unwanted artificial nutrition and hydration, which right is not outweighed by any interests of the State, and because I find that the improperly biased procedural obstacles imposed by the Missouri Supreme Court impermissibly burden that right, I respectfully dissent. Nancy Cruzan is entitled to choose to die with dignity.

I

A

"[T]he timing of death—once a matter of fate—is now a matter of human choice." Office of Technology Assessment Task Force, Life Sustaining Technologies and the Elderly 41 (1988). Of the approximately two million people who die each year, 80% die in hospitals and long-term care institutions, and perhaps 70% of those after a decision to forgo life-sustaining treatment has been made. Nearly every death involves a decision whether to undertake some medical procedure that could prolong the process of dying. Such decisions are difficult and personal. They must be made on the basis of individual values, informed by medical realities, yet within a framework governed by law. The role of the courts is confined to defining that framework, delineating the ways in which government may and may not participate in such decisions.

The question before this Court is a relatively narrow one: whether the Due Process Clause allows Missouri to require a now-incompetent patient in an irreversible persistent vegetative state to remain on life-support absent rigorously clear and convincing evidence that avoiding the treatment represents the patient's prior, express choice. See ante at 277–278. If a fundamental right is at issue, Missouri's rule of decision must be scrutinized under the standards this Court has always applied in such circumstances. As we said in Zablocki v. Redhail, 434 U.S. 374, 388 (1978), if a requirement imposed by a State "significantly interferes with the exercise of a fundamental right, it cannot be upheld unless it is supported by sufficiently important state interests and is closely tailored to effectuate only those interests." The Constitution imposes on this Court the obligation to "examine carefully . . . the extent to which [the legitimate government interests advanced] are served by the challenged regulation." Moore v. East Cleveland, 431 U.S. 494, 499 (1977). See also Carey v. Population Services International, 431 U.S. 678, 690 (1977) (invalidating a requirement that bore "no relation to the State's interest"). An evidentiary rule, just as a substantive prohibition, must meet these standards if it significantly burdens a fundamental liberty interest. Fundamental rights "are protected not only against heavy-handed frontal attack, but also from being stifled by more subtle governmental interference." Bates v. Little Rock, 361 U.S. 516, 523 (1960).

B

The starting point for our legal analysis must be whether a competent person has a constitutional right to avoid unwanted medical care. Earlier this Term, this Court held that the Due Process Clause of the Fourteenth Amendment confers a significant liberty interest in avoiding unwanted medical treatment. Washington v. Harper, 494 U.S. 210, 221–222 (1990). Today, the Court concedes that our prior decisions "support the recognition of a general liberty interest in refusing medical treatment." See ante at 278. The Court, however, avoids discussing either the measure of that liberty interest or its application by assuming, for purposes of this case only, that a competent person has a constitutionally protected liberty interest in being free of unwanted artificial nutrition and hydration. See ante at 279. JUSTICE O'CONNOR's opinion is less parsimonious. She openly affirms that "the Court has often deemed state incursions into the body repugnant to the interests protected by the Due Process Clause," that there is a liberty interest in avoiding unwanted medical treatment, and that it encompasses the right to be free of "artificially delivered food and water." See ante at 287.

But if a competent person has a liberty interest to be free of unwanted medical treatment, as both the majority and JUSTICE O'CONNOR concede, it must be fundamental. "We are dealing here with [a decision] which involves one of the basic civil rights of man." Skinner v. Oklahoma ex rel. Williamson, 316 U.S. 535, 541 (1942) (invalidating a statute authorizing sterilization of certain felons). Whatever other liberties protected by the Due Process Clause are fundamental, "those liberties that are 'deeply rooted in this Nation's history and tradition'" are among them. Bowers v. Hardwick, 478 U.S. 186, 192 (1986) (quoting Moore v. East Cleveland, supra, at 503 (plurality opinion)). "Such a tradition commands respect in part because the Constitution carries the gloss of history." Richmond Newspapers, Inc. v. Virginia, 448 U.S. 555, 589 (1980) (BRENNAN, J., concurring in judgment).

The right to be free from medical attention without consent, to determine what shall be done with one's own body, is deeply rooted in this Nation's traditions, as the majority acknowledges. See ante at 270. This right has long been "firmly entrenched in American tort law" and is securely grounded in the earliest common law. Ante, at 269. See also Mills v. Rogers, 457 U.S. 291, 294, n. 4 (1982) ("[T]he right to refuse any medical treatment emerged from the doctrines of trespass and battery, which were applied to unauthorized touchings by a physician"). "Anglo-American law starts with the premise of thorough-going self-determination. It follows that each man is considered to be master of his own body, and he may, if he be of sound mind, expressly prohibit the performance of lifesaving surgery or other medical treatment." Natanson v. Kline, 186 Kan. 393, 406–407, 350 P.2d 1093, 1104 (1960). "The inviolability of the person" has been held as "sacred" and "carefully guarded" as any common law right. Union Pacific R. Co. v. Botsford, 141 U.S. 250, 251–252 (1891). Thus, freedom from unwanted medical attention is unquestionably among those principles "so rooted in the traditions and conscience of our people as to be ranked as fundamental." Snyder v. Massachusetts, 291 U.S. 97, 105 (1934).

That there may be serious consequences involved in refusal of the medical treatment at issue here does not vitiate the right under our common law tradition of medical self-determination. It is "a well-established rule of general law . . . that it is the patient, not the physician, who ultimately decides if treatment—any treatment—is to be given at all . . . . The rule has never been qualified in its application by either the nature or purpose of the treatment, or the gravity of the consequences of acceding to or foregoing it." Tune v. Walter Reed Army Medical Hospital, 602 F.Supp. 1452, 1455 (DC 1985). See also Downer v. Veilleux, 322 A.2d 82, 91 (Me. 1974). ("The rationale of this rule lies in the fact that every competent adult has the right to forego treatment, or even cure, if it entails what for him are intolerable consequences or risks, however unwise his sense of values may be to others.")

No material distinction can be drawn between the treatment to which Nancy Cruzan continues to be subject—artificial nutrition and hydration—and any other medical treatment. See ante at 288–289 (O'CONNOR, J., concurring). The artificial delivery of nutrition and hydration is undoubtedly medical treatment. The technique to which Nancy Cruzan is subject—artificial feeding through a gastrostomy tube—involves a tube implanted surgically into her stomach through incisions in her abdominal wall. It may obstruct the intestinal tract, erode and pierce the stomach wall, or cause leakage of the stomach's contents into the abdominal cavity. See Page, Andrassy, & Sandler, Techniques in Delivery of Liquid Diets, in Nutrition in Clinical Surgery 66–67 (M. Deitel 2d ed. 1985). The tube can cause pneumonia from reflux of the stomach's contents into the lung. See Bernard & Forlaw, Complications and Their Prevention, in Enteral and Tube Feeding 553 (J. Rombeau & M. Caldwell eds. 1984). Typically, and in this case (see Tr. 377), commercially prepared formulas are used, rather than fresh food. See Matarese, Enteral Alimentation, in Surgical Nutrition 726 (J. Fischer ed. 1983). The type of formula and method of administration must be experimented with to avoid gastrointestinal problems. Id., at 748. The patient must be monitored daily by medical personnel as to weight, fluid intake and fluid output; blood tests must be done weekly. Id., at 749, 751.

Artificial delivery of food and water is regarded as medical treatment by the medical profession and the Federal Government. According to the American Academy of Neurology:

"The artificial provision of nutrition and hydration is a form of medical treatment . . . analogous to other forms of life-sustaining treatment, such as the use of the respirator. When a patient is unconscious, both a respirator and an artificial feeding device serve to support or replace normal bodily functions that are compromised as a result of the patient's illness." Position of the American Academy of Neurology on Certain Aspects of the Care and Management of the Persistent Vegetative State Patient, 39 Neurology 125 (Jan. 1989). See also Council on Ethical and Judicial Affairs of the American Medical Association, Current Opinions, Opinion 2.20 (1989) ("Life-prolonging medical treatment includes medication and artificially or technologically supplied respiration, nutrition or hydration"); President's Commission 88 (life-sustaining treatment includes respirators, kidney dialysis machines, special feeding procedures). The Federal Government permits the cost of the medical devices and formulas used in enteral feeding to be reimbursed under Medicare. See Pub.L. 99–509, 9340, note following 42 U.S.C. 1395u, p. 592 (1982 ed., Supp. V). The formulas are regulated by the Federal Drug Administration as "medical foods," see 21 U.S.C. 360ee, and the feeding tubes are regulated as medical devices, 21 CFR 876.5980 (1989).

Nor does the fact that Nancy Cruzan is now incompetent deprive her of her fundamental rights. See Youngberg v. Romeo, 457 U.S. 307, 315, 316, 319 (1982) (holding that severely retarded man's liberty interests in safety, freedom from bodily restraint and reasonable training survive involuntary commitment); Parham v. J.R., 442 U.S. 584, 600 (1979) (recognizing a child's substantial liberty interest in not being confined unnecessarily for medical treatment); Jackson v. Indiana, 406 U.S. 715, 730, 738 (1972) (holding that Indiana could not violate the due process and equal protection rights of a mentally retarded deaf mute by committing him for an indefinite amount of time simply because he was incompetent to stand trial on the criminal charges filed against him). As the majority recognizes, ante at 280, the question is not whether an incompetent has constitutional rights, but how such rights may be exercised. As we explained in Thompson v. Oklahoma, 487 U.S. 815 (1988), "[t]he law must often adjust the manner in which it affords rights to those whose status renders them unable to exercise choice freely and rationally. Children, the insane, and those who are irreversibly ill with loss of brain function, for instance, all retain 'rights,' to be sure, but often such rights are only meaningful as they are exercised by agents acting with the best interests of their principals in mind." Id., at 825, n. 23 (emphasis added). "To deny [its] exercise because the patient is unconscious or incompetent would be to deny the right." Foody v. Manchester Memorial Hospital, 40 Conn.Supp. 127, 133, 482 A.2d 713, 718 (1984).

II

A

The right to be free from unwanted medical attention is a right to evaluate the potential benefit of treatment and its possible consequences according to one's own values and to make a personal decision whether to subject oneself to the intrusion. For a patient like Nancy Cruzan, the sole benefit of medical treatment is being kept metabolically alive. Neither artificial nutrition nor any other form of medical treatment available today can cure or in any way ameliorate her condition. Irreversibly vegetative patients are devoid of thought, emotion and sensation; they are permanently and completely unconscious. See n. 2, supra. As the President's Commission concluded in approving the withdrawal of life support equipment from irreversibly vegetative patients:

"[T]reatment ordinarily aims to benefit a patient through preserving life, relieving pain and suffering, protecting against disability, and returning maximally effective functioning. If a prognosis of permanent unconsciousness is correct, however, continued treatment cannot confer such benefits. Pain and suffering are absent, as are joy, satisfaction, and pleasure. Disability is total, and no return to an even minimal level of social or human functioning is possible." President's Commission 181–182.

There are also affirmative reasons why someone like Nancy might choose to forgo artificial nutrition and hydration under these circumstances. Dying is personal. And it is profound. For many, the thought of an ignoble end, steeped in decay, is abhorrent. A quiet, proud death, bodily integrity intact, is a matter of extreme consequence. "In certain, thankfully rare, circumstances the burden of maintaining the corporeal existence degrades the very humanity it was meant to serve." Brophy v. New England Sinai Hospital, Inc., 398 Mass. 417, 434, 497 N.E.2d 626, 635–636 (1986) (finding the subject of the proceeding "in a condition which [he] has indicated he would consider to be degrading and without human dignity" and holding that "[t]he duty of the State to preserve life must encompass a recognition of an individual's right to avoid circumstances in which the individual himself would feel that efforts to sustain life demean or degrade his humanity"). Another court, hearing a similar case, noted:

"It is apparent from the testimony that what was on [the patient's] mind was not only the invasiveness of life-sustaining systems, such as the [nasogastric] tube, upon the integrity of his body. It was also the utter helplessness of the permanently comatose person, the wasting of a once strong body, and the submission of the most private bodily functions to the attention of others." In re Gardner, 534 A.2d 947, 953 (Me. 1987).

Such conditions are, for many, humiliating to contemplate, as is visiting a prolonged and anguished vigil on one's parents, spouse, and children. A longdrawnout death can have a debilitating effect on family members. See Carnwath & Johnson, Psychiatric Morbidity Among Spouses of Patients With Stroke, 294 Brit.Med.J. 409 (1987); Livingston, Families Who Care, 291 Brit.Med.J. 919 (1985). For some, the idea of being remembered in their persistent vegetative states, rather than as they were before their illness or accident, may be very disturbing.

B

Although the right to be free of unwanted medical intervention, like other constitutionally protected interests, may not be absolute, no State interest could outweigh the rights of an individual in Nancy Cruzan's position. Whatever a State's possible interests in mandating life-support treatment under other circumstances, there is no good to be obtained here by Missouri's insistence that Nancy Cruzan remain on life-support systems if it is indeed her wish not to do so. Missouri does not claim, nor could it, that society as a whole will be benefited by

Nancy's receiving medical treatment. No third party's situation will be improved, and no harm to others will be averted. Cf. nn. 6 and 8, supra.

The only state interest asserted here is a general interest in the preservation of life. But the State has no legitimate general interest in someone's life, completely abstracted from the interest of the person living that life, that could outweigh the person's choice to avoid medical treatment. "[T]he regulation of constitutionally protected decisions . . . must be predicated on legitimate state concerns other than disagreement with the choice the individual has made . . . . Otherwise, the interest in liberty protected by the Due Process Clause would be a nullity." Hodgson v. Minnesota, post, at 435 (1990) (Opinion of STEVENS, J.) (emphasis added). Thus, the State's general interest in life must accede to Nancy Cruzan's particularized and intense interest in self-determination in her choice of medical treatment. There is simply nothing legitimately within the State's purview to be gained by superseding her decision.

Moreover, there may be considerable danger that Missouri's rule of decision would impair rather than serve any interest the State does have in sustaining life. Current medical practice recommends use of heroic measures if there is a scintilla of a chance that the patient will recover, on the assumption that the measures will be discontinued should the patient improve. When the President's Commission in 1982 approved the withdrawal of life support equipment from irreversibly vegetative patients, it explained that "[a]n even more troubling wrong occurs when a treatment that might save life or improve health is not started because the health care personnel are afraid that they will find it very difficult to stop the treatment if, as is fairly likely, it proves to be of little benefit and greatly burdens the patient." President's Commission 75. A New Jersey court recognized that families as well as doctors might be discouraged by an inability to stop life-support measures from "even attempting certain types of care [which] could thereby force them into hasty and premature decisions to allow a patient to die." In re Conroy, 98 N.J. 321, 370, 486 A.2d 1209, 1234 (1985). See also Brief for American Academy of Neurology as Amicus Curiae 9 (expressing same concern).

III

This is not to say that the State has no legitimate interests to assert here. As the majority recognizes, ante at 281–282, Missouri has a parens patriae interest in providing Nancy Cruzan, now incompetent, with as accurate as possible a determination of how she would exercise her rights under these circumstances. Second, if and when it is determined that Nancy Cruzan would want to continue treatment, the State may legitimately assert an interest in providing that treatment. But until Nancy's wishes have been determined, the only state interest that may be asserted is an interest in safe-guarding the accuracy of that determination.

Accuracy, therefore, must be our touchstone. Missouri may constitutionally impose only those procedural requirements that serve to enhance the accuracy of a determination of Nancy Cruzan's wishes or are at least consistent with an accurate determination. The Missouri "safeguard" that the Court upholds today does not meet that standard. The determination needed in this context is whether the incompetent person would choose to live in a persistent vegetative state on life-support or to avoid this medical treatment. Missouri's rule of decision imposes a markedly asymmetrical evidentiary burden. Only evidence of specific statements of treatment choice made by the patient when competent is admissible to support a finding that the patient, now in a persistent vegetative state, would wish to avoid further medical treatment. Moreover, this evidence must be clear and convincing. No proof is required to support a finding that the incompetent person would wish to continue treatment.

A

The majority offers several justifications for Missouri's heightened evidentiary standard. First, the majority explains that the State may constitutionally adopt this rule to govern determinations of an incompetent's wishes in order to advance the State's substantive interests, including its unqualified interest in the preservation of human life. See ante at 282–283 and n. 10. Missouri's evidentiary standard, however, cannot rest on the State's own interest in a particular substantive result. To be sure, courts have long erected clear and convincing evidence standards to place the greater risk of erroneous decisions on those bringing disfavored claims. In such cases, however, the choice to discourage certain claims was a legitimate, constitutional policy choice. In contrast,

Missouri has no such power to disfavor a choice by Nancy Cruzan to avoid medical treatment, because Missouri has no legitimate interest in providing Nancy with treatment until it is established that this represents her choice. See supra at 312–314. Just as a State may not override Nancy's choice directly, it may not do so indirectly through the imposition of a procedural rule.

Second, the majority offers two explanations for why Missouri's clear and convincing evidence standard is a means of enhancing accuracy, but neither is persuasive. The majority initially argues that a clear and convincing evidence standard is necessary to compensate for the possibility that such proceedings will lack the "guarantee of accurate factfinding that the adversary process brings with it," citing Ohio v. Akron Center for Reproductive Health, post at 515–516 (upholding a clear and convincing evidence standard for an ex parte proceeding). Ante, at 281–282. Without supporting the Court's decision in that case, I note that the proceeding to determine an incompetent's wishes is quite different from a proceeding to determine whether a minor may bypass notifying her parents before undergoing an abortion on the ground that she is mature enough to make the decision or that the abortion is in her best interest.

An adversarial proceeding is of particular importance when one side has a strong personal interest which needs to be counterbalanced to assure the court that the questions will be fully explored. A minor who has a strong interest in obtaining permission for an abortion without notifying her parents may come forward whether or not society would be satisfied that she has made the decision with the seasoned judgment of an adult. The proceeding here is of a different nature. Barring venal motives, which a trial court has the means of ferreting out, the decision to come forward to request a judicial order to stop treatment represents a slowly and carefully considered resolution by at least one adult and more frequently several adults that discontinuation of treatment is the patient's wish.

In addition, the bypass procedure at issue in Akron, supra, is ex parte and secret. The court may not notify the minor's parents, siblings or friends. No one may be present to submit evidence unless brought forward by the minor herself. In contrast, the proceeding to determine Nancy Cruzan's wishes was neither ex parte nor secret. In a hearing to determine the treatment preferences of an incompetent person, a court is not limited to adjusting burdens of proof as its only means of protecting against a possible imbalance. Indeed, any concern that those who come forward will present a one-sided view would be better addressed by appointing a guardian ad litem, who could use the State's powers of discovery to gather and present evidence regarding the patient's wishes. A guardian ad litem's task is to uncover any conflicts of interest and ensure that each party likely to have relevant evidence is consulted and brought forward—for example, other members of the family, friends, clergy, and doctors. See, e.g., In re Colyer, 99 Wash.2d 114, 133, 660 P.2d 738, 748–749 (1983). Missouri's heightened evidentiary standard attempts to achieve balance by discounting evidence; the guardian ad litem technique achieves balance by probing for additional evidence. Where, as here, the family members, friends, doctors and guardian ad litem agree, it is not because the process has failed, as the majority suggests. See ante at 281, n. 9. It is because there is no genuine dispute as to Nancy's preference.

The majority next argues that where, as here, important individual rights are at stake, a clear and convincing evidence standard has long been held to be an appropriate means of enhancing accuracy, citing decisions concerning what process an individual is due before he can be deprived of a liberty interest. See ante, at 283. In those cases, however, this Court imposed a clear and convincing standard as a constitutional minimum on the basis of its evaluation that one side's interests clearly outweighed the second side's interests, and therefore the second side should bear the risk of error. See Santosky v. Kramer, 455 U.S. 745, 753, 766–767 (1982) (requiring a clear and convincing evidence standard for termination of parental rights because the parent's interest is fundamental, but the State has no legitimate interest in termination unless the parent is unfit, and finding that the State's interest in finding the best home for the child does not arise until the parent has been found unfit); Addington v. Texas, 441 U.S. 418, 426–427 (1979) (requiring clear and convincing evidence in an involuntary commitment hearing because the interest of the individual far outweighs that of a State, which has no legitimate interest in confining individuals who are not mentally ill and do not pose a danger to themselves or others). Moreover, we have always recognized that shifting the risk of error reduces the likelihood of errors in one direction at the cost of increasing the likelihood of errors in the other. See Addington, supra, at 423 (contrasting heightened standards of proof to a preponderance standard in which the two sides "share the risk of error in roughly equal fashion" because society does not favor one outcome over the other). In the cases cited by the majority, the imbalance imposed by a heightened evidentiary standard was not only acceptable, but required because the standard was deployed to protect an individual's exercise of a fundamental right, as the majority admits, ante at 282–283, n. 10. In contrast, the Missouri court imposed a clear and convincing standard as an obstacle to the exercise of a fundamental right.

The majority claims that the allocation of the risk of error is justified because it is more important not to terminate life-support for someone who would wish it continued than to honor the wishes of someone who would not. An erroneous decision to terminate life-support is irrevocable, says the majority, while an erroneous decision not to terminate "results in a maintenance of the status quo." See ante at 283. But, from the point of view of the patient, an erroneous decision in either direction is irrevocable. An erroneous decision to terminate artificial nutrition and hydration, to be sure, will lead to failure of that last remnant of physiological life, the brain stem, and result in complete brain death. An erroneous decision not to terminate life-support, however, robs a patient of the very qualities protected by the right to avoid unwanted medical treatment. His own degraded existence is perpetuated; his family's suffering is protracted; the memory he leaves behind becomes more and more distorted.

Even a later decision to grant him his wish cannot undo the intervening harm. But a later decision is unlikely in any event. "[T]he discovery of new evidence," to which the majority refers, ibid., is more hypothetical than plausible. The majority also misconceives the relevance of the possibility of "advancements in medical science," ibid., by treating it as a reason to force someone to continue medical treatment against his will. The possibility of a medical miracle is indeed part of the calculus, but it is a part of the patient's calculus. If current research suggests that some hope for cure or even moderate improvement is possible within the life-span projected, this is a factor that should be and would be accorded significant weight in assessing what the patient himself would choose.

B

Even more than its heightened evidentiary standard, the Missouri court's categorical exclusion of relevant evidence dispenses with any semblance of accurate factfinding. The court adverted to no evidence supporting its decision, but held that no clear and convincing, inherently reliable evidence had been presented to show that Nancy would want to avoid further treatment. In doing so, the court failed to consider statements Nancy had made to family members and a close friend. The court also failed to consider testimony from Nancy's mother and sister that they were certain that Nancy would want to discontinue to [sic] artificial nutrition and hydration, even after the court found that Nancy's family was loving and without malignant motive. See 760 S.W.2d at 412. The court also failed to consider the conclusions of the guardian ad litem, appointed by the trial court, that there was clear and convincing evidence that Nancy would want to discontinue medical treatment and that this was in her best interests. Id., at 444 (Higgins, J., dissenting from denial of rehearing); Brief for Respondent Guardian Ad Litem 2-3. The court did not specifically define what kind of evidence it would consider clear and convincing, but its general discussion suggests that only a living will or equivalently formal directive from the patient when competent would meet this standard. See 760 S.W.2d at 424–425.

Too few people execute living wills or equivalently formal directives for such an evidentiary rule to ensure adequately that the wishes of incompetent persons will be honored. While it might be a wise social policy to encourage people to furnish such instructions, no general conclusion about a patient's choice can be drawn from the absence of formalities. The probability of becoming irreversibly vegetative is so low that many people may not feel an urgency to marshal formal evidence of their preferences. Some may not wish to dwell on their own physical deterioration and mortality. Even someone with a resolute determination to avoid life-support under circumstances such as Nancy's would still need to know that such things as living wills exist and how to execute one. Often legal help would be necessary, especially given the majority's apparent willingness to permit States to insist that a person's wishes are not truly known unless the particular medical treatment is specified. See ante at 285.

As a California appellate court observed: "The lack of generalized public awareness of the statutory scheme and the typically human characteristics of procrastination and reluctance to contemplate the need for such arrangements however makes this a tool which will all too often go unused by those who might desire it." Barber v. Superior Court, 147 Cal.App. 3d 1006, 1015, 195 Cal.Rptr. 484, 489 (1983). When a person tells family or close friends that she does not want her life sustained artificially, she is "express[ing] her wishes in the only terms familiar to her, and . . . as clearly as a lay person should be asked to express them. To require more is unrealistic, and for all practical purposes, it precludes the rights of patients to forego life-sustaining treatment." In re O'Connor, 72 N.Y.2d 517, 551, 534 N.Y.S.2d 886, 905, 531 N.E.2d 607, 626 (1988) (Simons, J., dissenting). When Missouri enacted a living will statute, it specifically provided that the absence of a living will does not warrant a presumption that a patient wishes continued medical treatment. See n. 15, supra. Thus, apparently not even Missouri's own legislature believes that a person who does not execute a living will fails to do so because he wishes continuous medical treatment under all circumstances.

The testimony of close friends and family members, on the other hand, may often be the best evidence available of what the patient's choice would be. It is they with whom the patient most likely will have discussed such questions and they who know the patient best. "Family members have a unique knowledge of the patient which is vital to any decision on his or her behalf." Newman, Treatment Refusals for the Critically and Terminally Ill: Proposed Rules for the Family, the Physician, and the State, 3 N.Y.L.S. Human Rights Annual 35, 46 (1985). The Missouri court's decision to ignore this whole category of testimony is also at odds with the practices of other States. See, e.g., In re Peter, 108 N.J. 365, 529 A.2d 419 (1987); Brophy v. New England Sinai Hospital, Inc., 398 Mass. 417, 497 N.E.2d 626 (1986); In re Severns, 425 A.2d 156 (Del.Ch. 1980).

The Missouri court's disdain for Nancy's statements in serious conversations not long before her accident, for the opinions of Nancy's family and friends as to her values, beliefs and certain choice, and even for the opinion of an outside objective factfinder appointed by the State, evinces a disdain for Nancy Cruzan's own right to choose. The rules by which an incompetent person's wishes are determined must represent every effort to determine those wishes. The rule that the Missouri court adopted and that this Court upholds, however, skews the result away from a determination that as accurately as possible reflects the individual's own preferences and beliefs. It is a rule that transforms human beings into passive subjects of medical technology.

"[M]edical care decisions must be guided by the individual patient's interests and values. Allowing persons to determine their own medical treatment is an important way in which society respects persons as individuals. Moreover, the respect due to persons as individuals does not diminish simply because they have become incapable of participating in treatment decisions . . . . [I]t is still possible for others to make a decision that reflects [the patient's] interests more closely than would a purely technological decision to do whatever is possible. Lacking the ability to decide, [a patient] has a right to a decision that takes his interests into account." Conservatorship of Drabick, 200 Cal.App. 3d 185, 208, 245 Cal.Rptr. 840, 854–855, cert. denied, 488 U.S. 958 (1988).

C

I do not suggest that States must sit by helplessly if the choices of incompetent patients are in danger of being ignored. See ante at 281. Even if the Court had ruled that Missouri's rule of decision is unconstitutional, as I believe it should have, States would nevertheless remain free to fashion procedural protections to safeguard the interests of incompetents under these circumstances. The Constitution provides merely a framework here: protections must be genuinely aimed at ensuring decisions commensurate with the will of the patient, and must be reliable as instruments to that end. Of the many States which have instituted such protections, Missouri is virtually the only one to have fashioned a rule that lessens the likelihood of accurate determinations. In contrast, nothing in the Constitution prevents States from reviewing the advisability of a family decision by requiring a court proceeding or by appointing an impartial guardian ad litem.

There are various approaches to determining an incompetent patient's treatment choice in use by the several States today, and there may be advantages and disadvantages to each, and other approaches not yet envisioned. The choice, in largest part, is and should be left to the States, so long as each State is seeking, in a reliable manner, to discover what the patient would want. But with such momentous interests in the balance, States must avoid procedures that will prejudice the decision. "To err either way—to keep a person alive under circumstances under which he would rather have been allowed to die, or to allow that person to die when he would have chosen to cling to life—would be deeply unfortunate." In re Conroy, 98 N.J. at 343, 486 A.2d at 1 220.

D

Finally, I cannot agree with the majority that where it is not possible to determine what choice an incompetent patient would make, a State's role as parens patriae permits the State automatically to make that choice itself. See ante at 286 (explaining that the Due Process Clause does not require a State to confide the decision to "anyone but the patient herself"). Under fair rules of evidence, it is improbable that a court could not determine what the patient's choice would be. Under the rule of decision adopted by Missouri and upheld today by this Court, such occasions might be numerous. But in neither case does it follow that it is constitutionally acceptable for the State invariably to assume the role of deciding for the patient. A State's legitimate interest in safeguarding a patient's choice cannot be furthered by simply appropriating it.

The majority justifies its position by arguing that, while close family members may have a strong feeling about the question, "there is no automatic assurance that the view of close family members will necessarily be the same as the patient's would have been had she been confronted with the prospect of her situation while competent." Ibid. I cannot quarrel with this observation. But it leads only to another question: Is there any reason to suppose that a State is more likely to make the choice that the patient would have made than someone who knew the patient intimately? To ask this is to answer it. As the New Jersey Supreme Court observed: "Family members are best qualified to make substituted judgments for incompetent patients not only because of their peculiar grasp of the patient's approach to life, but because of their special bonds with him or her . . . . It is . . . they who treat the patient as a person, rather than a symbol of a cause." In re Jobes, 108 N.J. 394, 416, 529 A.2d 434, 445 (1987). The State, in contrast, is a stranger to the patient.

A State's inability to discern an incompetent patient's choice still need not mean that a State is rendered powerless to protect that choice. But I would find that the Due Process Clause prohibits a State from doing more than that. A State may ensure that the person who makes the decision on the patient's behalf is the one whom the patient himself would have selected to make that choice for him. And a State may exclude from consideration anyone having improper motives. But a State generally must either repose the choice with the person whom the patient himself would most likely have chosen as proxy or leave the decision to the patient's family.

IV

As many as 10,000 patients are being maintained in persistent vegetative states in the United States, and the number is expected to increase significantly in the near future. See Cranford, supra, n. 2, at 27, 31. Medical technology, developed over the past 20 or so years, is often capable of resuscitating people after they have stopped breathing or their hearts have stopped beating. Some of those people are brought fully back to life. Two decades ago, those who were not and could not swallow and digest food died. Intravenous solutions could not provide sufficient calories to maintain people for more than a short time. Today, various forms of artificial feeding have been developed that are able to keep people metabolically alive for years, even decades. See Spencer & Palmisano, Specialized Nutritional Support of Patients—A Hospital's Legal Duty?, 11 Quality Rev.Bull. 160, 160–161 (1985). In addition, in this century, chronic or degenerative ailments have replaced communicable diseases as the primary causes of death. See R. Weir, Abating Treatment with Critically Ill Patients 12–13 (1989); President's Commission 15–16. The 80% of Americans who die in hospitals are "likely to meet their end . . . 'in a sedated or comatose state; betubed nasally, abdominally and intravenously; and far more like manipulated objects than like moral subjects.'" A fifth of all adults surviving to age 80 will suffer a progressive dementing disorder prior to death. See Cohen & Eisdorfer, Dementing Disorders, in The Practice of Geriatrics 194 (E. Calkins, P. Davis, & A. Ford eds. 1986).

"[L]aw, equity and justice must not themselves quail and be helpless in the face of modern technological marvels presenting questions hitherto unthought of." In re Quinlan, 70 N.J. 10, 44, 355 A.2d 647, 665, cert.

denied, 429 U.S. 922 (1976). The new medical technology can reclaim those who would have been irretrievably lost a few decades ago and restore them to active lives.

For Nancy Cruzan, it failed, and for others with wasting incurable disease it may be doomed to failure. In these unfortunate situations, the bodies and preferences and memories of the victims do not escheat to the State; nor does our Constitution permit the State or any other government to commandeer them. No singularity of feeling exists upon which such a government might confidently rely as parens patriae. The President's Commission, after years of research, concluded:

"In few areas of health care are people's evaluations of their experiences so varied and uniquely personal as in their assessments of the nature and value of the processes associated with dying. For some, every moment of life is of inestimable value; for others, life without some desired level of mental or physical ability is worthless or burdensome. A moderate degree of suffering may be an important means of personal growth and religious experience to one person, but only frightening or despicable to another." President's Commission 276.

Yet Missouri and this Court have displaced Nancy's own assessment of the processes, associated with dying. They have discarded evidence of her will, ignored her values, and deprived her of the right to a decision as closely approximating her own choice as humanly possible. They have done so disingenuously in her name, and openly in Missouri's own. That Missouri and this Court may truly be motivated only by concern for incompetent patients makes no matter. As one of our most prominent jurists warned us decades ago: "Experience should teach us to be most on our guard to protect liberty when the government's purposes are beneficent . . . . The greatest dangers to liberty lurk in insidious encroachment by men of zeal, well meaning but without understanding." Olmstead v. United States, 277 U.S. 438, 479 (1928) (Brandeis, J., dissenting). I respectfully dissent.

JUSTICE STEVENS, dissenting.

Our Constitution is born of the proposition that all legitimate governments must secure the equal right of every person to "Life, Liberty, and the pursuit of Happiness." In the ordinary case, we quite naturally assume that these three ends are compatible, mutually enhancing, and perhaps even coincident.

The Court would make an exception here. It permits the State's abstract, undifferentiated interest in the preservation of life to overwhelm the best interests of Nancy Beth Cruzan, interests which would, according to an undisputed finding, be served by allowing her guardians to exercise her constitutional right to discontinue medical treatment. Ironically, the Court reaches this conclusion despite endorsing three significant propositions which should save it from any such dilemma. First, a competent individual's decision to refuse life-sustaining medical procedures is an aspect of liberty protected by the Due Process Clause of the Fourteenth Amendment. See ante at 278–279. Second, upon a proper evidentiary showing, a qualified guardian may make that decision on behalf of an incompetent ward. See, e.g., ante at 284–285. Third, in answering the important question presented by this tragic case, it is wise "not to attempt by any general statement, to cover every possible phase of the subject." See ante at 278 (citation omitted). Together, these considerations suggest that Nancy Cruzan's liberty to be free from medical treatment must be understood in light of the facts and circumstances particular to her.

I would so hold: in my view, the Constitution requires the State to care for Nancy Cruzan's life in a way that gives appropriate respect to her own best interests.

I

This case is the first in which we consider whether, and how, the Constitution protects the liberty of seriously ill patients to be free from life-sustaining medical treatment. So put, the question is both general and profound. We need not, however, resolve the question in the abstract. Our responsibility as judges both enables and compels us to treat the problem as it is illuminated by the facts of the controversy before us.

The most important of those facts are these: "Clear and convincing evidence" established that Nancy Cruzan is "oblivious to her environment except for reflexive responses to sound and perhaps to painful stimuli"; that "she has no cognitive or reflexive ability to swallow food or water"; that "she will never recover" these abilities; and that her "cerebral cortical atrophy is irreversible, permanent, progressive and ongoing." App. to Pet. for Cert.

A94–A95. Recovery and consciousness are impossible; the highest cognitive brain function that can be hoped for is a grimace in "recognition of ordinarily painful stimuli" or an "apparent response to sound." Id., at A95.

After thus evaluating Nancy Cruzan's medical condition, the trial judge next examined how the interests of third parties would be affected if Nancy's parents were allowed to withdraw the gastrostomy tube that had been implanted in their daughter. His findings make it clear that the parents' request had no economic motivation, and that granting their request would neither adversely affect any innocent third parties nor breach the ethical standards of the medical profession. He then considered, and rejected, a religious objection to his decision, and explained why he concluded that the ward's constitutional "right to liberty" outweighed the general public policy on which the State relied:

"There is a fundamental natural right, expressed in our Constitution as the 'right to liberty,' which permits an individual to refuse or direct the withholding or withdrawal of artificial death prolonging procedures when the person has no more cognitive brain function than our Ward and all the physicians agree there is no hope of further recovery while the deterioration of the brain continues with further overall worsening physical contractures. To the extent that the statute or public policy prohibits withholding or withdrawal of nutrition and hydration or euthanasia or mercy killing, if such be the definition, under all circumstances, arbitrarily and with no exceptions, it is in violation of our Ward's constitutional rights by depriving her of liberty without due process of law. To decide otherwise that medical treatment once undertaken must be continued irrespective of its lack of success or benefit to the patient in effect gives one's body to medical science without their [sic] consent.

"The Co-guardians are required only to exercise their legal authority to act in the best interests of their Ward as they discharge their duty and are free to act or not with this authority as they may determine." Id., at A98–A99 (footnotes omitted).

II

Because he believed he had a duty to do so, the independent guardian ad litem appealed the trial court's order to the Missouri Supreme Court. In that appeal, however, the guardian advised the court that he did not disagree with the trial court's decision. Specifically, he endorsed the critical finding that "it was in Nancy Cruzan's best interests to have the tube feeding discontinued."

That important conclusion thus was not disputed by the litigants. One might reasonably suppose that it would be dispositive: if Nancy Cruzan has no interest in continued treatment, and if she has a liberty interest in being free from unwanted treatment, and if the cessation of treatment would have no adverse impact on third parties, and if no reason exists to doubt the good faith of Nancy's parents, then what possible basis could the State have for insisting upon continued medical treatment? Yet, instead of questioning or endorsing the trial court's conclusions about Nancy Cruzan's interests, the State Supreme Court largely ignored them.

The opinion of that court referred to four different state interests that have been identified in other somewhat similar cases, but acknowledged that only the State's general interest in "the preservation of life" was implicated by this case. It defined that interest as follows:

"The state's interest in life embraces two separate concerns: an interest in the prolongation of the life of the individual patient and an interest in the sanctity of life itself." Cruzan v. Harmon, 760 S.W.2d 408, 419 (1988).

Although the court did not characterize this interest as absolute, it repeatedly indicated that it outweighs any countervailing interest that is based on the "quality of life" of any individual patient. In the view of the state-court majority, that general interest is strong enough to foreclose any decision to refuse treatment for an incompetent person unless that person had previously evidenced, in clear and convincing terms, such a decision for herself. The best interests of the incompetent individual who had never confronted the issue—or perhaps had been incompetent since birth—are entirely irrelevant and unprotected under the reasoning of the State Supreme Court's four-judge majority.

The three dissenting judges found Nancy Cruzan's interests compelling. They agreed with the trial court's evaluation of state policy. In his persuasive dissent, Judge Blackmar explained that decisions about the care of chronically ill patients were traditionally private:

"My disagreement with the principal opinion lies fundamentally in its emphasis on the interest of and the role of the state, represented by the Attorney General. Decisions about prolongation of life are of recent origin. For most of the world's history, and presently in most parts of the world, such decisions would never arise, because the technology would not be available. Decisions about medical treatment have customarily been made by the patient, or by those closest to the patient if the patient, because of youth or infirmity, is unable to make the decisions. This is nothing new in substituted decisionmaking. The state is seldom called upon to be the decisionmaker.

"I would not accept the assumption, inherent in the principal opinion, that, with our advanced technology, the state must necessarily become involved in a decision about using extraordinary measures to prolong life. Decisions of this kind are made daily by the patient or relatives, on the basis of medical advice and their conclusion as to what is best. Very few cases reach court, and I doubt whether this case would be before us but for the fact that Nancy lies in a state hospital. I do not place primary emphasis on the patient's expressions, except possibly in the very unusual case, of which I find no example in the books, in which the patient expresses a view that all available life supports should be made use of. Those closest to the patient are best positioned to make judgments about the patient's best interest." Id., at 428.

Judge Blackmar then argued that Missouri's policy imposed upon dying individuals and their families a controversial and objectionable view of life's meaning:

"It is unrealistic to say that the preservation of life is an absolute, without regard to the quality of life. I make this statement only in the context of a case in which the trial judge has found that there is no chance for amelioration of Nancy's condition. The principal opinion accepts this conclusion. It is appropriate to consider the quality of life in making decisions about the extraordinary medical treatment. Those who have made decisions about such matters without resort to the courts certainly consider the quality of life, and balance this against the unpleasant consequences to the patient. There is evidence that Nancy may react to pain stimuli. If she has any awareness of her surroundings, her life must be a living hell. She is unable to express herself or to do anything at all to alter her situation. Her parents, who are her closest relatives, are best able to feel for her and to decide what is best for her. The state should not substitute its decisions for theirs. Nor am I impressed with the crypto-philosophers cited in the principal opinion, who declaim about the sanctity of any life without regard to its quality. They dwell in ivory towers." Id., at 429.

Finally, Judge Blackmar concluded that the Missouri policy was illegitimate because it treats life as a theoretical abstraction, severed from, and indeed opposed to, the person of Nancy Cruzan.

"The Cruzan family appropriately came before the court seeking relief. The circuit judge properly found the facts and applied the law. His factual findings are supported by the record, and his legal conclusions by overwhelming weight of authority. The principal opinion attempts to establish absolutes, but does so at the expense of human factors. In so doing, it unnecessarily subjects Nancy and those close to her to continuous torture which no family should be forced to endure." Id., at 429–430.

Although Judge Blackmar did not frame his argument as such, it propounds a sound constitutional objection to the Missouri majority's reasoning: Missouri's regulation is an unreasonable intrusion upon traditionally private matters encompassed within the liberty protected by the Due Process Clause.

The portion of this Court's opinion that considers the merits of this case is similarly unsatisfactory. It, too, fails to respect the best interests of the patient. It, too, relies on what is tantamount to a waiver rationale: the dying patient's best interests are put to one side, and the entire inquiry is focused on her prior expressions of intent. An innocent person's constitutional right to be free from unwanted medical treatment is thereby categorically limited to those patients who had the foresight to make an unambiguous statement of their wishes while competent. The Court's decision affords no protection to children, to young people who are victims of unexpected accidents or illnesses, or to the countless thousands of elderly persons who either fail to decide, or fail to explain, how they want to be treated if they should experience a similar fate. Because Nancy Beth Cruzan did not have the foresight to preserve her constitutional right in a living will, or some comparable "clear and convincing" alternative, her right is gone forever, and her fate is in the hands of the state legislature instead of in those of her family, her independent neutral guardian ad litem, and an impartial judge—all of whom agree on the course of action that is in her best interests. The Court's willingness to find a waiver of this constitutional right reveals a distressing misunderstanding of the importance of individual liberty.

III

It is perhaps predictable that courts might undervalue the liberty at stake here. Because death is so profoundly personal, public reflection upon it is unusual. As this sad case shows, however, such reflection must become more common if we are to deal responsibly with the modern circumstances of death. Medical advances have altered the physiological conditions of death in ways that may be alarming: Highly invasive treatment may perpetuate human existence through a merger of body and machine that some might reasonably regard as an insult to life, rather than as its continuation. But those same advances, and the reorganization of medical care accompanying the new science and technology, have also transformed the political and social conditions of death: people are less likely to die at home, and more likely to die in relatively public places such as hospitals or nursing homes.

Ultimate questions that might once have been dealt with in intimacy by a family and its physician have now become the concern of institutions. When the institution is a state hospital, as it is in this case, the government itself becomes involved. Dying nonetheless remains a part of "the life which characteristically has its place in the home," Poe v. Ullman, 367 U.S. 497, 551 (1961) (Harlan, J., dissenting). The "integrity of that life is something so fundamental that it has been found to draw to its protection the principles of more than one explicitly granted Constitutional right," id., at 551–552, and our decisions have demarcated a "private realm of family life which the state cannot enter." Prince v. Massachusetts, 321 U.S. 158, 166–167 (1944). The physical boundaries of the home, of course, remain crucial guarantors of the life within it. See, e.g., Payton v. New York, 445 U.S. 573, 589 (1980); Stanley v. Georgia, 394 U.S. 557, 565 (1969). Nevertheless, this Court has long recognized that the liberty to make the decisions and choices constitutive of private life is so fundamental to our "concept of ordered liberty," Palko v. Connecticut, 302 U.S. 319, 325 (1937), that those choices must occasionally be afforded more direct protection. See, e.g., Meyer v. Nebraska, 262 U.S. 390 (1923); Griswold v. Connecticut, 381 U.S. 479 (1965); Roe v. Wade, 410 U.S. 113 (1973); Thornburgh v. American College of Obstetricians and Gynecologists, 476 U.S. 747, 772–782 (1986) (STEVENS, J., concurring).

Respect for these choices has guided our recognition of rights pertaining to bodily integrity. The constitutional decisions identifying those rights, like the common law tradition upon which they built, are mindful that the "makers of our Constitution . . . recognized the significance of man's spiritual nature." Olmstead v. United States, 277 U.S. 438, 478 (1928) (Brandeis, J., dissenting). It may truly be said that "our notions of liberty are inextricably entwined with our idea of physical freedom and self-determination." Ante at 287 (O'CONNOR, J., concurring). Thus we have construed the Due Process Clause to preclude physically invasive recoveries of evidence not only because such procedures are "brutal" but also because they are "offensive to human dignity." Rochin v. California, 342 U.S. 165, 174 (1952). We have interpreted the Constitution to interpose barriers to a State's efforts to sterilize some criminals not only because the proposed punishment would do "irreparable injury" to bodily integrity, but because "[m]arriage and procreation" concern "the basic civil rights of man." Skinner v. Oklahoma ex rel. Williamson, 316 U.S. 535, 541 (1942). The sanctity, and individual privacy, of the human body is obviously fundamental to liberty. "Every violation of a person's bodily integrity is an invasion of his or her liberty." Washington v. Harper, 494 U.S. 210, 237, (1990) (STEVENS, J., concurring in part and dissenting in part). Yet, just as the constitutional protection for the "physical curtilage of the home . . . is surely . . . a result of solicitude to protect the privacies of the life within," Poe v. Ullman, 367 U.S., at 551 (Harlan, J., dissenting), so too the constitutional protection for the human body is surely inseparable from concern for the mind and spirit that dwell therein.

It is against this background of decisional law, and the constitutional tradition which it illuminates, that the right to be free from unwanted life-sustaining medical treatment must be understood. That right presupposes no abandonment of the desire for life. Nor is it reducible to a protection against batteries undertaken in the name of treatment, or to a guarantee against the infliction of bodily discomfort. Choices about death touch the core of liberty. Our duty, and the concomitant freedom, to come to terms with the conditions of our own mortality are undoubtedly "so rooted in the traditions and conscience of our people as to be ranked as fundamental," Snyder v. Massachusetts, 291 U.S. 97, 105 (1934), and indeed are essential incidents of the unalienable rights to life and liberty endowed us by our Creator. See Meachum v. Fano, 427 U.S. 215, 230 (1976) (STEVENS, J., dissenting).

The more precise constitutional significance of death is difficult to describe; not much may be said with confidence about death unless it is said from faith, and that alone is reason enough to protect the freedom to conform choices about death to individual conscience. We may also, however, justly assume that death is not life's simple opposite, or its necessary terminus, but rather its completion. Our ethical tradition has long regarded an appreciation of mortality as essential to understanding life's significance. It may, in fact, be impossible to live for anything without being prepared to die for something. Certainly there was no disdain for life in Nathan Hale's most famous declaration or in Patrick Henry's; their words instead bespeak a passion for life that forever preserves their own lives in the memories of their countrymen. From such "honored dead we take increased devotion to that cause for which they gave the last full measure of devotion."

These considerations cast into stark relief the injustice, and unconstitutionally, of Missouri's treatment of Nancy Beth Cruzan. Nancy Cruzan's death, when it comes, cannot be an historic act of heroism; it will inevitably be the consequence of her tragic accident. But Nancy Cruzan's interest in life, no less than that of any other person, includes an interest in how she will be thought of after her death by those whose opinions mattered to her. There can be no doubt that her life made her dear to her family, and to others. How she dies will affect how that life is remembered. The trial court's order authorizing Nancy's parents to cease their daughter's treatment would have permitted the family that cares for Nancy to bring to a close her tragedy and her death. Missouri's objection to that order subordinates Nancy's body, her family, and the lasting significance of her life to the State's own interests. The decision we review thereby interferes with constitutional interests of the highest order.

To be constitutionally permissible, Missouri's intrusion upon these fundamental liberties must, at a minimum, bear a reasonable relationship to a legitimate state end. See, e.g., Meyer v. Nebraska, 262 U.S., at 400; Doe v. Bolton, 410 U.S. 179, 194–195, 199 (1973). Missouri asserts that its policy is related to a state interest in the protection of life. In my view, however, it is an effort to define life, rather than to protect it, that is the heart of Missouri's policy. Missouri insists, without regard to Nancy Cruzan's own interests, upon equating her life with the biological persistence of her bodily functions. Nancy Cruzan, it must be remembered, is not now simply incompetent. She is in a persistent vegetative state, and has been so for seven years. The trial court found, and no party contested, that Nancy has no possibility of recovery, and no consciousness.

It seems to me that the Court errs insofar as it characterizes this case as involving "judgments about the 'quality' of life that a particular individual may enjoy," ante, at 282. Nancy Cruzan is obviously "alive" in a physiological sense. But for patients like Nancy Cruzan, who have no consciousness and no chance of recovery, there is a serious question as to whether the mere persistence of their bodies is "life" as that word is commonly understood, or as it is used in both the Constitution and the Declaration of Independence. The State's unflagging determination to perpetuate Nancy Cruzan's physical existence is comprehensible only as an effort to define life's meaning, not as an attempt to preserve its sanctity.

This much should be clear from the oddity of Missouri's definition alone. Life, particularly human life, is not commonly thought of as a merely physiological condition or function. Its sanctity is often thought to derive from the impossibility of any such reduction. When people speak of life, they often mean to describe the experiences that comprise a person's history, as when it is said that somebody "led a good life." They may also mean to refer to the practical manifestation of the human spirit, a meaning captured by the familiar observation that somebody "added life" to an assembly. If there is a shared thread among the various opinions on this subject, it may be that life is an activity which is at once the matrix for and an integration of a person's interests. In any event, absent some theological abstraction, the idea of life is not conceived separately from the idea of a living person. Yet, it is by precisely such a separation that Missouri asserts an interest in Nancy Cruzan's life in opposition to Nancy Cruzan's own interests. The resulting definition is uncommon indeed.

The laws punishing homicide, upon which the Court relies, ante, at 280, do not support a contrary inference. Obviously, such laws protect both the life and interests of those who would otherwise be victims. Even laws against suicide presuppose that those inclined to take their own lives have some interest in living, and, indeed, that the depressed people whose lives are preserved may later be thankful for the State's, intervention. Likewise, decisions that address the "quality of life" of incompetent, but conscious, patients rest upon the recognition that these patients have some interest in continuing their lives, even if that interest pales in some eyes when measured against interests in dignity or comfort. Not so here. Contrary to the Court's suggestion, Missouri's protection of life in a form abstracted from the living is not commonplace; it is aberrant.

Nor does Missouri's treatment of Nancy Cruzan find precedent in the various state law cases surveyed by the majority. Despite the Court's assertion that state courts have demonstrated "both similarity and diversity in their approach" to the issue before us, none of the decisions surveyed by the Court interposed an absolute bar to the termination of treatment for a patient in a persistent vegetative state. For example, In re Westchester County Medical Center on behalf of O'Connor, 72 N.Y.2d 517, 534 N.Y.S.2d 886, 531 N.E.2d 607 (1988), pertained to an incompetent patient who "was not in a coma or vegetative state. She was conscious, and capable of responding to simple questions or requests sometimes by squeezing the questioner's hand and sometimes verbally." Id., at 524–525, 531 N.E.2d at 609–610. Likewise, In re Storar, 52 N.Y.2d 363, 420 N.E.2d 64 (1981), involved a conscious patient who was incompetent because "profoundly retarded with a mental age of about 18 months." Id., at 373, 420 N.E.2d, at 68. When it decided In re Conroy, 98 N.J. 321, 486 A.2d 1209 (1985), the New Jersey Supreme Court noted that "Ms. Conroy was not brain dead, comatose, or in a chronic vegetative state," 98 N.J. at 337, 486 A.2d at 1217, and then distinguished In re Quinlan, 70 N.J. 10, 355 A.2d 647 (1976), on the ground that Karen Quinlan had been in a "persistent vegetative or comatose state." 98 N.J. at 358–359, 486 A.2d at 1228. By contrast, an unbroken stream of cases has authorized procedures for the cessation of treatment of patients in persistent vegetative states. Considered against the background of other cases involving patients in persistent vegetative states, instead of against the broader—and inapt—category of cases involving chronically ill incompetent patients, Missouri's decision is anomalous. In short, there is no reasonable ground for believing that Nancy Beth Cruzan has any personal interest in the perpetuation of what the State has decided is her life. As I have already suggested, it would be possible to hypothesize such an interest on the basis of theological or philosophical conjecture. But even to posit such a basis for the State's action is to condemn it. It is not within the province of secular government to circumscribe the liberties of the people by regulations designed wholly for he purpose of establishing a sectarian definition of life. See Webster v. Reproductive Health Services, 492 U.S. 490, 566–572 (1989) (STEVENS, J., dissenting).

My disagreement with the Court is thus unrelated to its endorsement of the clear and convincing standard of proof for cases of this kind. Indeed, I agree that the controlling facts must be established with unmistakable clarity. The critical question, however, is not how to prove the controlling facts but rather what proven facts should be controlling. In my view, the constitutional answer is clear: the best interests of the individual, especially when buttressed by the interests of all related third parties, must prevail over any general state policy that simply ignores those interests. Indeed, the only apparent secular basis for the State's interest in life is the policy's persuasive impact upon people other than Nancy and her family. Yet, "[a]lthough the State may properly perform a teaching function," and although that teaching may foster respect for the sanctity of life, the State may not pursue its project by infringing constitutionally protected interests for "symbolic effect." Carey v. Population Services International, 431 U.S. 678, 715 (1977) (STEVENS, J., concurring in part and concurring in judgment). The failure of Missouri's policy to heed the interests of a dying individual with respect to matters so private is ample evidence of the policy's illegitimacy.

Only because Missouri has arrogated to itself the power to define life, and only because the Court permits this usurpation, are Nancy Cruzan's life and liberty put into disquieting conflict. If Nancy Cruzan's life were defined by reference to her own interests, so that her life expired when her biological existence ceased serving any of her own interests, then her constitutionally protected interest in freedom from unwanted treatment would not come into conflict with her constitutionally protected interest in life. Conversely, if there were any evidence that Nancy Cruzan herself defined life to encompass every form of biological persistence by a human being, so that the continuation of treatment would serve Nancy's own liberty, then once again there would be no conflict between life and liberty. The opposition of life and liberty in this case are thus not the result of Nancy Cruzan's tragic accident, but are instead the artificial consequence of Missouri's effort and this Court's willingness, to abstract Nancy Cruzan's life from Nancy Cruzan's person.

IV

Both this Court's majority and the state court's majority express great deference to the policy choice made by the state legislature. That deference is, in my view, based upon a severe error in the Court's constitutional logic. The Court believes that the liberty interest claimed here on behalf of Nancy Cruzan is peculiarly problematic because "[a]n incompetent person is not able to make an informed and voluntary choice to exercise a hypothetical right to refuse treatment or any other right." Ante at 280. The impossibility of such an exercise affords the State, according to the Court, some discretion to interpose "a procedural requirement" that effectively compels the continuation of Nancy Cruzan's treatment.

There is, however, nothing "hypothetical" about Nancy Cruzan's constitutionally protected interest in freedom from unwanted treatment, and the difficulties involved in ascertaining what her interests are do not in any way justify the State's decision to oppose her interests with its own. As this case comes to us, the crucial question—and the question addressed by the Court—is not what Nancy Cruzan's interests are, but whether the State must give effect to them. There is certainly nothing novel about the practice of permitting a next friend to assert constitutional rights on behalf of an incompetent patient who is unable to do so. See, e.g., Youngberg v. Romeo, 457 U.S. 307, 310 (1982); Whitmore v. Arkansas, 495 U.S. 149, 161–164 (1990). Thus, if Nancy Cruzan's incapacity to "exercise" her rights is to alter the balance between her interests and the State's, there must be some further explanation of how it does so. The Court offers two possibilities, neither of them satisfactory.

The first possibility is that the State's policy favoring life is by its nature less intrusive upon the patient's interest than any alternative. The Court suggests that Missouri's policy "results in a maintenance of the status quo," and is subject to reversal, while a decision to terminate treatment "is not susceptible of correction" because death is irreversible. Ante, at 283. Yet this explanation begs the question, for it assumes either that the State's policy is consistent with Nancy Cruzan's own interests or that no damage is done by ignoring her interests. The first assumption is without basis in the record of this case, and would obviate any need for the State to rely, as it does, upon its own interests rather than upon the patient's. The second assumption is unconscionable. Insofar as Nancy Cruzan has an interest in being remembered for how she lived rather than how she died, the damage done to those memories by the prolongation of her death is irreversible. Insofar as Nancy Cruzan has an interest in the cessation of any pain, the continuation of her pain is irreversible. Insofar as Nancy Cruzan has an interest in a closure to her life consistent with her own beliefs rather than those of the Missouri legislature, the State's imposition of its contrary view is irreversible. To deny the importance of these consequences is in effect to deny that Nancy Cruzan has interests at all, and thereby to deny her personhood in the name of preserving the sanctity of her life.

The second possibility is that the State must be allowed to define the interests of incompetent patients with respect to life-sustaining treatment because there is no procedure capable of determining what those interests are in any particular case. The Court points out various possible "abuses" and inaccuracies that may affect procedures authorizing the termination of treatment. See ante at 281–282. The Court correctly notes that, in some cases, there may be a conflict between the interests of an incompetent patient and the interests of members of her family. A State's procedures must guard against the risk that the survivors' interests are not mistaken for the patient's. Yet the appointment of the neutral guardian ad litem, coupled with the searching inquiry conducted by the trial judge and the imposition of the clear and convincing standard of proof, all effectively avoided that risk in this case. Why such procedural safeguards should not be adequate to avoid a similar risk in other cases is a question the Court simply ignores.

Indeed, to argue that the mere possibility of error in any case suffices to allow the State's interests to override the particular interests of incompetent individuals in every case, or to argue that the interests of such individuals are unknowable and therefore may be subordinated to the State's concerns, is once again to deny Nancy Cruzan's personhood. The meaning of respect for her personhood, and for that of others who are gravely ill and incapacitated, is, admittedly, not easily defined: choices about life and death are profound ones, not susceptible of resolution by recourse to medical or legal rules. It may be that the best we can do is to ensure that these choices are made by those who will care enough about the patient to investigate her interests with particularity and caution. The Court seems to recognize as much when it cautions against formulating any general or inflexible rule to govern all the cases that might arise in this area of the law. Ante at 277–278. The Court's deference to the legislature is, however, itself an inflexible rule, one that the Court is willing to apply in this case even though the Court's principal grounds for deferring to Missouri's legislature are hypothetical circumstances not relevant to Nancy Cruzan's interests.

On either explanation, then, the Court's deference seems ultimately to derive from the premise that chronically incompetent persons have no constitutionally cognizable interests at all, and so are not persons within the meaning of the Constitution. Deference of this sort is patently unconstitutional. It is also dangerous in ways that may not be immediately apparent. Today the State of Missouri has announced its intent to spend several hundred thousand dollars in preserving the life of Nancy Beth Cruzan in order to vindicate its general policy favoring the preservation of human life. Tomorrow, another State equally eager to champion an interest in the "quality of life" might favor a policy designed to ensure quick and comfortable deaths by denying treatment to categories of marginally hopeless cases. If the State in fact has an interest in defining life, and if the State's policy with respect to the termination of life-sustaining treatment commands deference from the judiciary, it is unclear how any resulting conflict between the best interests of the individual and the general policy of the State would be resolved. I believe the Constitution requires that the individual's vital interest in liberty should prevail over the general policy in that case, just as in this.

That a contrary result is readily imaginable under the majority's theory makes manifest that this Court cannot defer to any State policy that drives a theoretical wedge between a person's life, on the one hand, and that person's liberty or happiness, on the other. The consequence of such a theory is to deny the personhood of those whose lives are defined by the State's interests rather than their own. This consequence may be acceptable in theology or in speculative philosophy, see Meyer, 262 U.S., at 401–402, but it is radically inconsistent with the foundation of all legitimate government. Our Constitution presupposes a respect for the personhood of every individual, and nowhere is strict adherence to that principle more essential than in the Judicial Branch. See, e.g., Thornburgh v. American College of Obstetricians and Gynecologists, 476 U.S., at 781–782 (STEVENS, J., concurring).

V

In this case, as is no doubt true in many others, the predicament confronted by the healthy members of the Cruzan family merely adds emphasis to the best interests finding made by the trial judge. Each of us has an interest in the kind of memories that will survive after death. To that end, individual decisions are often motivated by their impact on others. A member of the kind of family identified in the trial court's findings in this case would likely have not only a normal interest in minimizing the burden that her own illness imposes on others but also an interest in having their memories of her filled predominantly with thoughts about her past vitality rather than her current condition. The meaning and completion of her life should be controlled by persons who have her best interests at heart—not by a state legislature concerned only with the "preservation of human life."

The Cruzan family's continuing concern provides a concrete reminder that Nancy Cruzan's interests did not disappear with her vitality or her consciousness. However commendable may be the State's interest in human life, it cannot pursue that interest by appropriating Nancy Cruzan's life as a symbol for its own purposes. Lives do not exist in abstraction from persons, and to pretend otherwise is not to honor but to desecrate the State's responsibility for protecting life. A State that seeks to demonstrate its commitment to life may do so by aiding those who are actively struggling for life and health. In this endeavor, unfortunately, no State can lack for opportunities: there can be no need to make an example of tragic cases like that of Nancy Cruzan.

I respectfully dissent.

[All footnotes omitted.]

Internet Note: To see the footnotes for *Cruzan,* and other interesting United States Supreme Court cases, go to *http://www.findlaw.com.* FindLaw has all U.S. Supreme Court cases from 1837 to the present online for free.

Anderson v. St. Francis-St. George Hospital, Incorporated

Supreme Court of Ohio

Decided October 10, 1996

77 Ohio St.3d 82, 671 N.E.2d 225

MOYER, Chief Justice.

We are presented with the following question: Where a medical provider administers a life-prolonging treatment or procedure to a patient against the patient's instructions, is the medical provider liable for all foreseeable consequential damages resulting from the treatment or procedure? This is a case of first impression, and presents this court with the issues raised by a claim of "wrongful living." In its simplest form, the question becomes: Is "continued living" a compensable injury?

American jurisprudence has developed at least three civil actions relating to the beginning and the extension of life: "wrongful life," "wrongful birth" and wrongful living." Generally, a claim for "wrongful life" is brought by a child seeking damages against a physician or hospital for negligently failing to properly sterilize the parent. See Bowman v. Davis (1976), 48 Ohio St.2d 41, 45, 2 O.O.3d 133, 135, 356 N.E.2d 496, 499, fn. 3.

A "wrongful birth" action is a claim brought by the parents of an impaired child seeking to recover damages for the birth of the child. The parents claim that due to the negligence of the physician, they were prevented from exercising their right to terminate the pregnancy or avoid conception altogether. See Johnson v. Univ. Hospitals of Cleveland (1989), 44 Ohio St.3d 49 51, 540 N.E.2d 1370, 1372.

In a claim for "wrongful living," which is the basis for recovery in this case, the plaintiff does not assert a claim based on a life coming into being. Rather, the plaintiff asserts a right to enforce an informed, competent decision to reject live-saving treatment. This claim is inextricably linked to, and arises directly out of, the right to die recognized in Cruzan v. Director, Missouri Dept. of Health (1990), 497 U.S. 261, 110 S.Ct. 2841, 111 L.Ed.2d 224. Thus, in a "wrongful living" action, the plaintiff is asserting a liberty interest in refusing unwanted medical treatment. It is the denial of this liberty interest, when the medical professional either negligently or intentionally disregards the express wishes of a patient, that gives rise to the wrongful living cause of action.

Some form of valuation of life pervades the legal issue in all three of the causes of action. In reality, a claim of wrongful living is a damages concept, just as a claim for "wrongful whiplash" or "wrongful broken arm," and must necessarily involve an underlying claim of negligence or battery. A negligence claim requires proof of the following elements: duty, breach of duty, causation, and damages. Menifee v. Ohio Welding Products, Inc. (1984), 15 Ohio St.3d 75, 15 OBR 179, 472 N.E.2d 707. A battery claim, while sharing the elements of causation and damages, does not require the proving of a duty and a breach of that duty, but rather an intentional, unconsented-to touching. Love v. Port Clinton (1988), 37 Ohio St.3d 98, 524 N.E.2d 166. Under both claims, a defendant is liable only for harms that are proximately caused by the tortious act. It is the defining of the harm giving rise to damages that is uniquely difficult in a claim of "wrongful living."

Because a person has a right, to die, a medical professional who has been trained to preserve life, and who has taken an oath to do so, is relieved of that duty and is required by a legal duty to accede to a patient's express refusal of medical treatment. Whether intentional or negligent, interference with a person's legal right to die would constitute a breach of that duty to honor the wishes of the patient.

Where a breach of duty has occurred, liability will not attach unless there is a causal connection between the conduct of the medical professional and the loss suffered by the patient.

The standard test for establishing causation is the sine qua non or "but for" test. Thus, a defendant's conduct is a cause of the event (or harm) if the event (or harm) would not have occurred but for that conduct; conversely, the defendant's conduct is not the cause of the event (or harm) if the event (or harm) would have occurred regardless of the conduct. Prosser & Keeton, Law of Torts (5 Ed. 1984) 266.

For purposes of a "wrongful living" cause of action, the event or loss for which the plaintiff seeks damages is neither death nor life, but the prolongation of life. Thus, once it is established that but for the conduct of the medical professional, death would have resulted, the causation element of a "wrongful living" claim is satisfied.

Assuming that the plaintiff can show a duty, breach of the duty, and proximate cause between the breach and the prolongation of life, the difficult issue is what damages flow from the "harm" caused the plaintiff. There is perhaps no issue that better demonstrates the outer bounds of liability in the American civil justice system than this issue.

This court has recognized "the impossibility of a jury placing a price tag" on the benefit of life. Johnson, supra, 44 Ohio St.3d at 58, 540 N.E.2d at 1378. We have also disapproved of awarding damages on the relative merits of "being versus nonbeing. Bowman, supra, 48 Ohio St.2d at 45, 2 0.0.3d at 135, 356 N.E.2d at 499, fn. 3. These views are consistent with the views expressed by the courts of other states. Cockrum v. Baumgartner (1983), 95 Ill.2d 193, 201, 69 Ill.Dec. 168, 172, 447 N.E.2d 385, 389 (finding that human life cannot be a compensable harm, and stating that "the benefit of life should not be outweighed by the expense of supporting it"); Becker v. Schwartz (1978), 46 N.Y.2d 401, 412, 413 N.Y.S.2d 895, 900, 386 N.E.2d 807, 812 (finding courts not equipped to handle the task of comparing the value of life in an impaired state and nonexistence); Lininger v. Eisenbaum (Colo. 1988), 764 P.2d 1202, 1212 (concluding that "life, however impaired and regardless of any attendant expenses, cannot rationally be said to be a detriment" when compared to the alternative of nonexistence).

In Winter's first appeal, the court of appeals properly concluded that there is no cause of action for "wrongful living" and remanded for a determination of several issues related to traditional negligence and battery. 83 Ohio App.3d 221, 614 N.E.2d 841. In the second appeal, the court held that a patient may recover damages based upon the torts of negligence or battery for all the foreseeable consequences of the therapy, including the pain, suffering, and emotional distress beyond that which he normally would have suffered had the therapy not been initiated. The record clearly indicates that Winter would have died on May 30, 1988, without the defibrillation and, consequently, would not have suffered any subsequent medical conditions. Thus, the court of appeals' theory of recovery seems to be identical to the theory of recovery underlying a claim of "wrongful living." Both the law of the case and our holding here make this theory untenable, and damages, if any, must be based strictly on the theories of negligence or battery.

There are some mistakes, indeed even breaches of duty or technical assaults, that people make in this life that affect the lives of others for which there simply should be no monetary compensation. See Heiner v. Moretuzzo (1995), 73 Ohio St.3d 80, 88, 652 N.E.2d 664, 670 (affirming that "not every wrong is deserving of a legal remedy").

Winter's estate now argues that it is not asserting a "wrongful living" claim. Rather, it argues that it is entitled to damages for the stroke suffered by Winter on May 30, 1988, and any injuries, other than continued living, that were the foreseeable results of the "wrongful" resuscitation of Winter. We find this argument to be without merit.

As we have observed, supra, the standard test for establishing causation is the "but for" test. "As a rule regarding legal responsibility, at most this must be a rule of exclusion: if the event would not have occurred 'but for' the defendant's negligence, it still does not follow that there is liability, since other considerations remain to be discussed and may prevent liability. It should be quite obvious that, once events are set in motion, there is, in terms of causation alone, no place to stop." (Footnote omitted.) Prosser, supra, at 266. Accordingly, an act is, not regarded as a cause of an event if the particular event would have occurred without the doing of the act. Id. at 265.

This is the essential point that Anderson avoids. Edward Winter was 82 years old with a history of cardiac problems. The record indicates that a stroke was reasonably foreseeable if Winter survived the ventricular tachycardia he suffered on May 28, 1988. However, the record is devoid of any evidence that the administering of the resuscitative measures caused the stroke. Winter suffered the stroke because the nurse enabled him to survive the ventricular tachycardia. Because the nurse prolonged Winter's life, numerous injuries occurring after resuscitation might be foreseeable, but would not be caused by the defibrillation.

The record supports our conclusion. Anderson never presented any evidence that the defibrillation itself caused or contributed to Winter's suffering a stroke in any way other than by simply prolonging his life. When Anderson's expert witness, Dr. Finley, was asked for his opinion regarding the cause of Winter's stroke, he testified that:

"I think that, in this clinical circumstance, it is more likely than not related to his acute cardiac event, and that in all, probability, given that he was elderly, he had known peripheral vascular and presumably some cerebral vascular disease, that it was very likely connected with his continued rhythm disturbance, and being off the monitor, there really would be no evidence to that effect, but it is, either a spontaneous, completely unrelated cerebral accident, or it is related to his presentation in his hospital course. Given the fairly complicated presentation, I think it is infinitely more likely to be related to the events that were occurring [i e., heart arrhythmias] rather than a second, unrelated event."

In addition, in his 1993 memorandum opposing jurisdiction, Anderson stated to this court that:

"It has never been Plaintiff's position that the resuscitation caused the stroke. Plaintiff's expert will only testify that a stroke is one of the recognized sequelae of sustained ventricular tachycardia and, that if a patient with this medical problem survives the episode, either through spontaneous recovery or resuscitation, the risk can become a reality."

The only damages that appellee may recover are those damages suffered by Winter due directly to the battery. Where the battery was physically harmless, however, the plaintiff is entitled to nominal damages only. Lacey v. Laird (1956), 166 Ohio St. 12, 139 N.E.2d 25, paragraphs one and two of the syllabus.

We also observe that unwanted lifesaving [sic] treatment does not go undeterred. Where a patient clearly delimits the medical measures he or she is willing to undergo, and a health care provider disregards such instructions, the consequences for that breach would include the damages arising from any battery inflicted on the patient, as well as appropriate licensing sanctions against the medical professionals.

In the present case, Winter suffered no damages as a result of the defibrillation of his heart, i.e., no tissue burns or broken bones. Anderson concedes that he is not seeking nominal damages. There is no issue to be decided by the trial court upon remand. Therefore, we reverse the judgment of the court of appeals and enter judgment for appellant.

Judgment reversed.

FRANCIS E. SWEENEY, Sr. and COOK, JJ., concur.
DOUGLAS, J., concurs in judgment.
RESNICK, PFEIFER and BOWMAN, JJ., dissent.
DONNA BOWMAN, J., of the Tenth Appellate District, sitting for STRATTON, J.

DOUGLAS, Justice, concurring.
I concur with the judgment of the majority. Doctors, hospitals and their staffs are in the business of saving lives. Short of ignoring a living will (R.C. 2133.01 et seq.) or a durable power of attorney for health care (R.C. 1337.11 et seq.), medical professionals should not be subjected to liability for carrying out the very mission for which they have been trained and for which they have taken an oath. Maybe such cases as the one before us should be denominated "furthering life" rather than "wrongful living." Applying the positive connotation to an act which continues life where death would have occurred without intervention, what damage could possibly ensue?

The only measure we have in the civil law to compensate a person injured by the wrongful act of another is "damages." Assuming, for purposes of argument only, that the action of the hospital through its staff was negligence and, assuming further, that "damages" should be assessed as a result of the negligence, how would they be computed? Can the preservation of life (furthering life) even be amenable to the "damages" concept? I think not!

Writing for the majority of the court in Johnson v. Univ. Hospitals of Cleveland (1989), 44 Ohio St.3d 49, 58, 540 N.E.2d 1370, 1378, I said:

[W]e are not persuaded to adopt the full recovery rule because the strict rules of tort should not be applied to an action to which they are not suited, such as a wrongful pregnancy case [and wrongful life or furthering life], in which a doctor's tortious conduct permits to occur the birth of a child [or continued life] rather than the causing of an injury.

Even assuming the hospital, acting through its employees, engaged in tortious conduct, a premise I do not accept, there could be no resulting damage for seeing to it that a life was preserved. I believe Johnson is entirely dispositive of this case. In addition, as I said, again writing for a majority of the court, in Heiner v. Moretuzzo (1995), 73 Ohio St.3d 80, 88, 652 N.E.2d 664, 670, if the hospital through its staff was negligent, "the facts of this case remind us that not every wrong is deserving of a legal remedy."

Accordingly, I concur in judgment.

PFEIFER, Justice, dissenting.

Winter told his doctor that he did not wish to be subjected to certain medical treatment, as was his constitutional right. See Cruzan v. Director, Missouri Dept. of Health (1990), 497 U.S. 261, 110 S.Ct. 2841, 111 L.Ed.2d 224. Nevertheless, Winter's instructions were not followed, he was defibrillated, and subsequently suffered a stroke.

Anderson (the administrator of Winter's estate) should have been afforded an opportunity to prove that the hospital was negligent, that Winter's constitutional rights were violated, and that Winter suffered harm as a consequence. It is not certain that Anderson would have proven causation, but it was error to summarily foreclose the opportunity of proof. Medical experts were prepared to testify on behalf of the plaintiff that "it was medically foreseeable that he [Winter] would suffer a stroke during the days immediately following defibrillation." This statement strongly suggests that there was a factual dispute as to causation that ought to have survived summary judgment.

Contrary to the assertion of the majority opinion, the plaintiff was not seeking to recover because Winter's life was prolonged. He was seeking to recover because the hospital staff failed to follow the instructions Winter had given them. He claimed that this negligence increased the likelihood that Winter would suffer a stroke. Not only did Winter suffer a stroke, he was incapacitated from that day until the day of his death. I respectfully dissent.

RESNICK and BOWMAN, JJ., concur in the foregoing dissenting opinion.

No. SC04-925

JEB BUSH, Governor of Florida, et al., Appellants,

vs.

MICHAEL SCHIAVO, Guardian of Theresa Schiavo, Appellee.

September 23, 2004

PARIENTE, C.J.

The narrow issue in this case requires this Court to decide the constitutionality of a law passed by the Legislature that directly affected Theresa Schiavo, who has been in a persistent vegetative state since 1990.[1] This Court, after careful consideration of the arguments of the parties and amici, the constitutional issues raised, the precise wording of the challenged law, and the underlying procedural history of this case, concludes that the law violates the fundamental constitutional tenet of separation of powers and is therefore unconstitutional both on its face and as applied to Theresa Schiavo. Accordingly, we affirm the trial court's order declaring the law unconstitutional.

Facts and Procedural History

The resolution of the discrete separation of powers issue presented in this case does not turn on the facts of the underlying guardianship proceedings that resulted in the removal of Theresa's nutrition and hydration tube. The underlying litigation, which has pitted Theresa's husband, Michael Schiavo, against Theresa's parents, turned on whether the procedures sustaining Theresa's life should be discontinued. However, the procedural history is important because it provides the backdrop to the Legislature's enactment of the challenged law. We also detail the facts and procedural history in light of the Governor's assertion that chapter 2003-418, Laws of Florida (hereinafter sometimes referred to as "the Act"), was passed in order to protect the due process rights of Theresa and other individuals in her position.

---

[1] The trial court, in an extensive written order, declared that the law was unconstitutional as a violation of separation of powers, as a violation of the right of privacy and as unconstitutional retroactive legislation. The Second District Court of Appeal certified this case as one of great public importance and requiring immediate resolution by this Court. We have jurisdiction. See art. V, §3(b)(5), Fla. Const.

As set forth in the Second District's first opinion in this case, which upheld the guardianship court's final order,

> Theresa Marie Schindler was born on December 3, 1963, and lived with or near her parents in Pennsylvania until she married Michael Schiavo on November 10, 1984. Michael and Theresa moved to Florida in 1986. They were happily married and both were employed. They had no children.
>
> On February 25, 1990, their lives changed. Theresa, age 27, suffered a cardiac arrest as a result of a potassium imbalance. Michael called 911, and Theresa was rushed to the hospital. She never regained consciousness.
>
> Since 1990, Theresa has lived in nursing homes with constant care. She is fed and hydrated by tubes. The staff changes her diapers regularly. She has had numerous health problems, but none have been life threatening.

In re Guardianship of Schiavo, 780 So. 2d 176, 177 (Fla. 2d DCA 2001) (*Schiavo I*).

For the first three years after this tragedy, Michael and Theresa's parents, Robert and Mary Schindler, enjoyed an amicable relationship. However, that relationship ended in 1993 and the parties literally stopped speaking to each other. In May of 1998, eight years after Theresa lost consciousness, Michael petitioned the guardianship court to authorize the termination of life-prolonging procedures. *See id.* By filing this petition, which the Schindlers opposed, Michael placed the difficult decision in the hands of the court.

After a trial, at which both Michael and the Schindlers presented evidence, the guardianship court issued an extensive written order authorizing the discontinuance of artificial life support. The trial court found by clear and convincing evidence that Theresa Schiavo was in a persistent vegetative state and that Theresa would elect to cease life-prolonging procedures if she were competent to make her own decision. This order was affirmed on direct appeal, *see Schiavo I,* 780 So. 2d at 177, and we denied review. *See In re Guardianship of Schiavo,* 789 So. 2d 348 (Fla. 2001).

The severity of Theresa's medical condition was explained by the Second District as follows:

> The evidence is overwhelming that Theresa is in a permanent or persistent vegetative state. It is important to understand that a persistent vegetative state is not simply a coma. She is not asleep. She has cycles of apparent wakefulness and apparent sleep without any cognition or awareness. As she breathes, she often makes moaning sounds. Theresa has severe contractures of her hands, elbows, knees, and feet.
>
> Over the span of this last decade, Theresa's brain has deteriorated because of the lack of oxygen it suffered at the time of the heart attack. By mid 1996, the CAT scans of her brain showed a severely abnormal structure. At this point, much of her cerebral cortex is simply gone and has been replaced by cerebral spinal fluid. Medicine cannot cure this condition. Unless an act of God, a true miracle, were to recreate her brain, Theresa will always remain in an unconscious, reflexive state, totally dependent upon others to feed her and care for her most private needs. She could remain in this state for many years.

Schiavo I, 780 So. 2d at 177. In affirming the trial court's order, the Second District concluded by stating:

> In the final analysis, the difficult question that faced the trial court was whether Theresa Marie Schindler Schiavo, not after a few weeks in a coma, but after ten years in a persistent vegetative state that has robbed her of most of her cerebrum and all but the most instinctive of neurological functions, with no hope of a medical cure but with sufficient money and strength of body to live indefinitely, would choose to continue the constant nursing care and the supporting tubes in hopes that a miracle would somehow recreate her missing brain tissue, or whether she would wish to permit a natural death process to take its course and for her family members and loved ones to be free to continue their lives. After due consideration, we conclude that the trial judge had clear and convincing evidence to answer this question as he did.

Schiavo I, 780 So. 2d at 180.

Although the guardianship court's final order authorizing the termination of life-prolonging procedures was affirmed on direct appeal, the litigation continued because the Schindlers began an attack on the final order. The Schindlers filed a motion for relief from judgment under Florida Rule of Civil Procedure 1.540(b)(2) and (3) in the guardianship court, alleging newly discovered evidence and intrinsic fraud. The Schindlers also filed a separate complaint in the civil division of the circuit court, challenging the final judgment of the guardianship court. *See In re Guardianship of Schiavo,* 792 So. 2d 551, 555–56 (Fla. 2d DCA 2001) (*Schiavo II*).

The trial court determined that the post-judgment motion was untimely and the Schindlers appealed. The Second District agreed that the guardianship court had appropriately denied the rule 1.540(b)(2) and (3) motion as untimely. *See Schiavo II,* 792 So. 2d at 558. The Second District also reversed an injunction entered in the case pending before the civil division of the circuit court. *See id.* at 562. However, the Second District determined that the Schindlers, as "interested parties," had standing to file either a motion for relief from judgment under Florida Rule of Civil Procedure 1.540(b)(5) or an independent action in the guardianship court to challenge the judgment on the ground that it is "no longer equitable for the trial court to enforce its earlier order." *Schiavo II,* 792 So. 2d at 560 (quotation marks omitted). Nonetheless, the Second District pointedly cautioned

> that any proceeding to challenge a final order on this basis is extraordinary and should not be filed merely to delay an order with which an interested party disagrees or to retry an adversary proceeding. The interested party must establish that new circumstances make it no longer equitable to enforce the earlier order. In this case, if the Schindlers believe a valid basis for relief from the order exists, they must plead and prove newly discovered evidence of such a substantial nature that it proves either (1) that Mrs. Schiavo would not have made the decision to withdraw life-prolonging procedures fourteen months earlier when the final order was entered, or (2) that Mrs. Schiavo would make a different decision at this time based on developments subsequent to the earlier court order.

Id. at 554.

On remand, the Schindlers filed a timely motion for relief from judgment pursuant to rule 1.540(b)(5). *See In re Guardianship of Schiavo,* 800 So. 2d 640, 642 (Fla. 2d DCA 2001) (*Schiavo III*). The trial court summarily denied the motion but the Second District reversed and remanded to the guardianship court for the purpose of conducting a limited evidentiary hearing:

> Of the four issues resolved in the original trial . . . , we conclude that the motion establishes a colorable entitlement only as to the fourth issue. As to that issue—whether there was clear and convincing evidence to support the determination that Mrs. Schiavo would choose to withdraw the life-prolonging procedures— the motion for relief from judgment alleges evidence of a new treatment that could dramatically improve Mrs. Schiavo's condition and allow her to have cognitive function to the level of speech. In our last opinion we stated that the Schindlers had "presented no medical evidence suggesting that any new treatment could restore to Mrs. Schiavo a level of function within the cerebral cortex that would allow her to understand her perceptions of sight and sound or to communicate or respond cognitively to those perceptions." *Schiavo II,* 792 So. 2d at 560. Although we have expressed some lay skepticism about the new affidavits, the Schindlers now have presented some evidence, in the form of the affidavit of Dr. [Fred] Webber, of such a potential new treatment.

Id. at 645.

The Second District permitted the Schindlers to present evidence to establish by a preponderance of the evidence that the judgment was no longer equitable and specifically held:

> To meet this burden, they must establish that new treatment offers sufficient promise of increased cognitive function in Mrs. Schiavo's cerebral cortex—significantly improving the quality of Mrs. Schiavo's life—so that she herself would elect to undergo this treatment and would reverse the prior decision to withdraw life-prolonging procedures.

Id.

The Second District required an additional set of medical examinations of Theresa and instructed that one of the physicians must be a new, independent physician selected either by the agreement of the parties or, if they could not agree, by the appointment of the guardianship court. *See id.* at 646.

After conducting a hearing for the purpose set forth in the Second District's decision, the guardianship court denied the Schindlers' motion for relief from judgment. *See In re Guardianship of Schiavo*, 851 So. 2d 182, 183 (Fla. 2d DCA 2003) (*Schiavo IV*). In reviewing the trial court's order, the Second District explained that it was "not reviewing a final judgment in this appellate proceeding. The final judgment was entered several years ago and has already been affirmed by this court." *Id*. at 185–86. However, the Second District carefully examined the record:

> Despite our decision that the appropriate standard of review is abuse of discretion, this court has closely examined all of the evidence in this record. We have repeatedly examined the videotapes, not merely watching short segments but carefully observing the tapes in their entirety. We have examined the brain scans with the eyes of educated laypersons and considered the explanations provided by the doctors in the transcripts. We have concluded that, if we were called upon to review the guardianship court's decision de novo, we would still affirm it.

Id. at 186. Finally, the Second District concluded its fourth opinion in the Schiavo case with the following observation:

> The judges on this panel are called upon to make a collective, objective decision concerning a question of law. Each of us, however, has our own family, our own loved ones, our own children. From our review of the videotapes of Mrs. Schiavo, despite the irrefutable evidence that her cerebral cortex has sustained the most severe of irreparable injuries, we understand why a parent who had raised and nurtured a child from conception would hold out hope that some level of cognitive function remained. If Mrs. Schiavo were our own daughter, we could not but hold to such a faith.
>
> But in the end, this case is not about the aspirations that loving parents have for their children. It is about Theresa Schiavo's right to make her own decision, independent of her parents and independent of her husband . . . . It may be unfortunate that when families cannot agree, the best forum we can offer for this private, personal decision is a public courtroom and the best decision-maker we can provide is a judge with no prior knowledge of the ward, but the law currently provides no better solution that adequately protects the interests of promoting the value of life. We have previously affirmed the guardianship court's decision in this regard, and we now affirm the denial of a motion for relief from that judgment.

Id. at 186-87.

We denied review, *see In re Guardianship of Schiavo*, 855 So. 2d 621 (Fla. 2003), and Theresa's nutrition and hydration tube was removed on October 15, 2003.

On October 21, 2003, the Legislature enacted chapter 2003-418, the Governor signed the Act into law, and the Governor issued executive order No. 03-201 to stay the continued withholding of nutrition and hydration from Theresa. The nutrition and hydration tube was reinserted pursuant to the Governor's executive order.

On the same day, Michael Schiavo brought the action for declaratory judgment in the circuit court. Relying on undisputed facts and legal argument, the circuit court entered a final summary judgment on May 6, 2004, in favor of Michael Schiavo, finding the Act unconstitutional both on its face and as applied to Theresa. Specifically, the circuit court found that chapter 2003-418 was unconstitutional on its face as an unlawful delegation of legislative authority and as a violation of the right to privacy, and unconstitutional as applied because it allowed the Governor to encroach upon the judicial power and to retroactively abolish Theresa's vested right to privacy.[2]

---

[2] Because we find the separation of powers issue to be dispositive in this case, we do not reach the other constitutional issues addressed by the circuit court.

ANALYSIS

We begin our discussion by emphasizing that our task in this case is to review the constitutionality of chapter 2003-418, not to reexamine the guardianship court's orders directing the removal of Theresa's nutrition and hydration tube, or to review the Second District's numerous decisions in the guardianship case. Although we recognize that the parties continue to dispute the findings made in the prior proceedings, these proceedings are relevant to our decision only to the extent that they occurred and resulted in a final judgment directing the withdrawal of life-prolonging procedures.[3]

The language of chapter 2003-418 is clear. It states in full:

Section 1. (1) The Governor shall have the authority to issue a one-time stay to prevent the withholding of nutrition and hydration from a patient if, as of October 15, 2003:
  (a) That patient has no written advance directive;
  (b) The court has found that patient to be in a persistent vegetative state;
  (c) That patient has had nutrition and hydration withheld; and
  (d) A member of that patient's family has challenged the withholding of nutrition and hydration.

(2) The Governor's authority to issue the stay expires 15 days after the effective date of this act, and the expiration of the authority does not impact the validity or the effect of any stay issued pursuant to this act. The Governor may lift the stay authorized under this act at any time. A person may not be held civilly liable and is not subject to regulatory or disciplinary sanctions for taking any action to comply with a stay issued by the Governor pursuant to this act.

(3) Upon issuance of a stay, the chief judge of the circuit court shall appoint a guardian ad litem for the patient to make recommendations to the Governor and the court.

Section 2. This act shall take effect upon becoming a law.

Ch. 2003-418, Laws of Fla. Thus, chapter 2003-418 allowed the Governor to issue a stay to prevent the withholding of nutrition and hydration from a patient under the circumstances provided for in subsections (1) (a)–(d). Under the fifteen-day sunset provision, the Governor's authority to issue the stay expired on November 5, 2003. *See id.* The Governor's authority to lift the stay continues indefinitely.

SEPARATION OF POWERS

The cornerstone of American democracy known as separation of powers recognizes three separate branches of government—the executive, the legislative, and the judicial—each with its own powers and responsibilities. In Florida, the constitutional doctrine has been expressly codified in article II, section 3 of the Florida Constitution, which not only divides state government into three branches but also expressly prohibits one branch from exercising the powers of the other two branches:

Branches of Government.—The powers of the state government shall be divided into legislative, executive and judicial branches. No person belonging to one branch shall exercise any powers appertaining to either of the other branches unless expressly provided herein.

"This Court . . . has traditionally applied a strict separation of powers doctrine," *State v. Cotton,* 769 So. 2d 345, 353 (Fla. 2000), and has explained that this doctrine "encompasses two fundamental prohibitions. The first is that no branch may encroach upon the powers of another. The second is that no branch may delegate to another branch its constitutionally assigned power." *Chiles v. Children A, B, C, D, E, & F,* 589 So. 2d 260, 264 (Fla. 1991) (citation omitted).

---

[3] The parties stipulated that the circuit court was authorized to take judicial notice of three orders of the guardianship court. The circuit court relied only on the existence of these orders in finding chapter 2003-418 unconstitutional as applied.

The circuit court found that chapter 2003-418 violates both of these prohibition, and we address each separately below. Our standard of review is de novo. *See Major League Baseball v. Morsani,* 790 So. 2d 1071, 1074 (Fla. 2001) (stating that a trial court's ruling on a motion for summary judgment posing a pure question of law is subject to de novo review).

Encroachment on the Judicial Branch

We begin by addressing the argument that, as applied to Theresa Schiavo, the Act encroaches on the power and authority of the judicial branch. More than 140 years ago this Court explained the foundation of Florida's express separation of powers provision:

> The framers of the Constitution of Florida, doubtless, had in mind the omnipotent power often exercised by the British Parliament, the exercise of judicial power by the Legislature in those States where there are no written Constitutions restraining them, when they wisely prohibited the exercise of such powers in our State.
>
> That Convention was composed of men of the best legal minds in the country—men of experience and skilled in the law—who had witnessed the breaking down by unrestrained legislation all the security of property derived from contract, the divesting of vested rights by doing away the force of the law as decided, the overturning of solemn decisions of the Courts of the last resort, by, under the pretence of remedial acts, enacting for one or the other party litigants such provisions as would dictate to the judiciary their decision, and leaving everything which should be expounded by the judiciary to the variable and ever-changing mind of the popular branch of the Government.

Trustees Internal Improvement Fund v. Bailey, 10 Fla. 238, 250 (1863). Similarly, the framers of the United States Constitution recognized the need to establish a judiciary independent of the legislative branch. Indeed, the desire to prevent Congress from using its power to interfere with the judgments of the courts was one of the primary motivations for the separation of powers established at this nation's founding:

> This sense of a sharp necessity to separate the legislative from the judicial power, prompted by the crescendo of legislative interference with private judgments of the courts, triumphed among the Framers of the new Federal Constitution. The Convention made the critical decision to establish a judicial department independent of the Legislative Branch . . . . Before and during the debates on ratification, Madison, Jefferson, and Hamilton each wrote of the factional disorders and disarray that the system of legislative equity had produced in the years before the framing; and each thought that the separation of the legislative from the judicial power in the new Constitution would cure them. Madison's Federalist No. 48, the famous description of the process by which "[t]he legislative department is every where extending the sphere of its activity, and drawing all power into its impetuous vortex," referred to the report of the Pennsylvania Council of Censors to show that in that State "cases belonging to the judiciary department [had been] frequently drawn within legislative cognizance and determination." Madison relied as well on Jefferson's Notes on the State of Virginia, which mentioned, as one example of the dangerous concentration of governmental powers into the hands of the legislature, that "the Legislature . . . in many instances decided rights which should have been left to judiciary controversy."

Plaut v. Spendthrift Farm, Inc., 514 U.S. 211, 221–22 (1995) (citations omitted).

Under the express separation of powers provision in our state constitution, "the judiciary is a coequal branch of the Florida government vested with the sole authority to exercise the judicial power," and "the legislature cannot, short of constitutional amendment, reallocate the balance of power expressly delineated in the constitution among the three coequal branches." *Children A, B, C, D, E, & F,* 589 So. 2d at 268–69; *see also Office of State Attorney v. Parrotino,* 628 So. 2d 1097, 1099 (Fla. 1993). ("[T]he legislature cannot take actions that would undermine the independence of Florida's judicial . . . offices.")

As the United States Supreme Court has explained, the power of the judiciary is "not merely to rule on cases, but to *decide* them, subject to review only by superior courts" and "[h]aving achieved finality . . . a judicial decision becomes the last word of the judicial department with regard to a particular case or controversy." *Plaut,* 514 U.S. at 218–19, 227. Moreover, "purely judicial acts . . . are not subject to review as to their accuracy by the

Governor." *In re Advisory Opinion to the Governor,* 213 So. 2d 716, 720 (Fla. 1968); *see also Children A, B, C, D, E, & F,* 589 So. 2d at 269 ("The judicial branch cannot be subject in any manner to oversight by the executive branch.").

In *Advisory Opinion,* the Governor asked the Court whether he had the "constitutional authority to review the judicial accuracy and propriety of [a judge] and to suspend him from office if it does not appear . . . that the Judge has exercised proper judicial discretion and wisdom." 213 So. 2d at 718. The Court agreed that the Governor had the authority to suspend a judge on the grounds of incompetency "if the physical or mental incompetency is established and determined within the Judicial Branch by a court of competent jurisdiction." *Id.* at 720. However, the Court held that the Governor did not have the power to "review the judicial discretion and wisdom of a . . . Judge while he is engaged in the judicial process." *Id.* The Court explained that article V of the Florida Constitution provides for appellate review for the benefit of litigants aggrieved by the decisions of the lower court, and that "[a]ppeal is the exclusive remedy." *Id.*

In this case, the undisputed facts show that the guardianship court authorized Michael to proceed with the discontinuance of Theresa's life support after the issue was fully litigated in a proceeding in which the Schindlers were afforded the opportunity to present evidence on all issues. This order as well as the order denying the Schindlers' motion for relief from judgment were affirmed on direct appeal. *See Schiavo I,* 780 So. 2d at 177; *Schiavo IV,* 851 So. 2d at 183. The Schindlers sought review in this Court, which was denied. Thereafter, the tube was removed. Subsequently, pursuant to the Governor's executive order, the nutrition and hydration tube was reinserted. Thus, the Act, as applied in this case, resulted in an executive order that effectively reversed a properly rendered final judgment and thereby constituted an unconstitutional encroachment on the power that has been reserved for the independent judiciary. *Cf. Bailey,* 10 Fla. at 249–50 (noting that had the statute under review "directed a rehearing, the hearing of the case would necessarily carry with it the right to set aside the judgment of the Court, and there would be unquestionably an exercise of judicial power").

The Governor and amici assert that the Act does not reverse a final court order because an order to discontinue life-prolonging procedures may be challenged at any time prior to the death of the ward. In advancing this argument, the Governor and amici rely on the Second District's conclusion that as long as the ward is alive, an order discontinuing life-prolonging procedures "is subject to recall and is executory in nature." *Schiavo II,* 792 So. 2d at 559. However, the Second District did not hold that the guardianship court's order was not a final judgment but, rather, that the Schindlers, as interested parties, could file a motion for relief from judgment under Florida Rule of Civil Procedure 1.540(b)(5) if they sufficiently alleged that it is no longer equitable that the judgment have prospective application. *See id.* at 561. Rule 1.540(b) expressly states that a motion filed pursuant to its terms "does not affect the finality of a judgment." Further, the fact that a final judgment may be subject to recall under a rule of procedure, if certain circumstances can be proved, does not negate its finality. Unless and until the judgment is vacated by judicial order, it is "the last word of the judicial department with regard to a particular case or controversy." *Plaut,* 514 U.S. at 227.

Under procedures enacted by the Legislature, effective both before the passage of the Act and after its fifteen-day effective period expired, circuit courts are charged with adjudicating issues regarding incompetent individuals. The trial courts of this State are called upon to make many of the most difficult decisions facing society. In proceedings under chapter 765, Florida Statutes (2003), these decisions literally affect the lives or deaths of patients. The trial courts also handle other weighty decisions affecting the welfare of children such as termination of parental rights and child custody. *See* §61.13(2)(1), Fla. Stat. (2003). ("The court shall determine all matters relating to custody of each minor child of the parties in accordance with the best interests of the child and in accordance with the Uniform Child Custody Jurisdiction and Enforcement Act."); §39.801(2), Fla. Stat. (2003) ("The circuit court shall have exclusive original jurisdiction of a proceeding involving termination of parental rights."). When the prescribed procedures are followed according to our rules of court and the governing statutes, a final judgment is issued, and all post-judgment procedures are followed, it is without question an invasion of the authority of the judicial branch for the Legislature to pass a law that allows the executive branch to interfere with the final judicial determination in a case. That is precisely what occurred here and for that reason the Act is unconstitutional as applied to Theresa Schiavo.

Delegation of Legislative Authority

In addition to concluding that the Act is unconstitutional as applied in this case because it encroaches on the power of the judicial branch, we further conclude that the Act is unconstitutional on its face because it delegates legislative power to the Governor. The Legislature is permitted to transfer subordinate functions "to permit administration of legislative policy by an agency with the expertise and flexibility to deal with complex and fluid conditions." *Microtel, Inc. v. Fla. Public Serv. Comm'n,* 464 So. 2d 1189, 1191 (Fla. 1985). However, under article II, section 3 of the constitution the Legislature "may not delegate the power to enact a law or the right to exercise unrestricted discretion in applying the law." *Sims v. State,* 754 So. 2d 657, 668 (Fla. 2000). This prohibition, known as the nondelegation doctrine, requires that "fundamental and primary policy decisions . . . be made by members of the legislature who are elected to perform those tasks, and [that the] administration of legislative programs must be pursuant to some minimal standards and guidelines ascertainable by reference to the enactment establishing the program." *Askew v. Cross Key Waterways,* 372 So. 2d 913, 925 (Fla. 1978); *see also Avatar Dev. Corp. v. State,* 723 So. 2d 199, 202 (Fla. 1998) (citing *Askew* with approval). In other words, statutes granting power to the executive branch "must clearly announce adequate standards to guide . . . in the execution of the powers delegated. The statute must so clearly define the power delegated that the [executive] is precluded from acting through whim, showing favoritism, or exercising unbridled discretion." *Lewis v. Bank of Pasco County,* 346 So. 2d 53, 55–56 (Fla. 1976). The requirement that the Legislature provide sufficient guidelines also ensures the availability of meaningful judicial review:

> In the final analysis it is the courts, upon a challenge to the exercise or nonexercise of administrative action, which must determine whether the administrative agency has performed consistently with the mandate of the legislature. When legislation is so lacking in guidelines that neither the agency nor the courts can determine whether the agency is carrying out the intent of the legislature in its conduct, then, in fact, the agency becomes the lawgiver rather than the administrator of the law.

Askew, 372 So. 2d at 918–19.

We have recognized that the "specificity of the guidelines [set forth in the legislation] will depend on the complexity of the subject and the 'degree of difficulty involved in articulating finite standards.'" *Brown v. Apalachee Regional Planning Council,* 560 So. 2d 782, 784 (Fla. 1990) (quoting *Askew,* 372 So. 2d at 918). However, we have also made clear that "[e]ven where a general approach would be more practical than a detailed scheme of legislation, enactments may not be drafted in terms so general and unrestrictive that administrators are left without standards for the guidance of their official acts." *State Dep't of Citrus v. Griffin,* 239 So. 2d 577, 581 (Fla. 1970).

In both *Askew* and *Lewis,* this Court held that the respective statutes under review violated the nondelegation doctrine because they failed to provide the executive branch with adequate guidelines and criteria. In *Askew,* the Court invalidated a statute that directed the executive branch to designate certain areas of the state as areas of critical state concern but did not contain sufficient standards to allow "a reviewing court to ascertain whether the priorities recognized by the Administration Commission comport with the intent of the legislature." 372 So. 2d at 919. The statute in question enunciated the following criteria for the Division of State Planning to use in identifying a particular area as one of critical state concern:

(a) An area containing, or having a significant impact upon, environmental, historical, natural, or archaeological resources of regional or statewide importance.

(b) An area significantly affected by, or having a significant effect upon, an existing or proposed major public facility or other area of major public investment.

(c) A proposed area of major development potential, which may include a proposed site of a new community, designated in a state land development plan.

Id. at 914–15 (quoting section 380.05(2), Florida Statutes (1975)). The Court concluded that the criteria for designation of an area of critical concern set forth in subsections (a) and (b) were defective because they gave the executive agency "the fundamental legislative task of determining which geographic areas and resources [were] in greatest need of protection." *Id.* at 919. With regard to subsection (a), this Court agreed with the district court that the deficiency resulted from the Legislature's failure to "establish or provide for establishing priorities or other means for identifying and choosing among the resources the Act is intended to preserve." *Id.* (quoting *Cross Key Waterways v. Askew,* 351 So. 2d 1062, 1069 (Fla. 1st DCA 1977)). Subsection (b) suffered a similar defect by expanding "the choice to include areas which in unstated ways affect or are affected by any 'major public facility' which is defined in Section 380.031(10), or any 'major public investment,' which is not." *Id.*

Lewis involved a statute that gave the state comptroller the unrestricted power to release banking records to the public that were otherwise considered confidential under the Public Records Act. *See* 346 So. 2d at 55. The statute at issue provided in pertinent part:

> Division records.
>
> All bank or trust company applications, investigation reports, examination reports, and related information, including any duly authorized copies in possession of any banking organization, foreign banking corporation, or any other person or agency, shall be confidential communications, other than such documents as are required by law to be published, and shall not be made public, unless *with the consent of the department,* pursuant to a court order, or in response to legislative subpoena as provided by law.

Lewis, 346 So. 2d at 54 (quoting section 658.10, Florida Statutes (1975)) (alteration in original). This Court held that the law was "couched in vague and uncertain terms or is so broad in scope that . . . it must be held unconstitutional as attempting to grant to the . . . [comptroller] the power to say *what the law shall be.*" 346 So. 2d at 56 (quoting *Sarasota County v. Barg,* 302 So. 2d 737, 742 (Fla. 1974)) (alterations in original).

In this case, the circuit court found that chapter 2003-418 contains no guidelines or standards that "would serve to limit the Governor from exercising completely unrestricted discretion in applying the law to" those who fall within its terms. The circuit court explained:

> The terms of the Act affirmatively confirm the discretionary power conferred upon the Governor. He is given the "authority to issue a one-time stay to prevent the withholding of nutrition and hydration from a patient" under certain circumstances but, he is not required to do so. Likewise, the act provides that the Governor "*may* lift the stay authorized under this act at any time. The Governor *may* revoke the stay upon a finding that a change in the condition of the patient warrants revocation." (Emphasis added). In both instances there is nothing to provide the Governor with any direction or guidelines for the exercise of this delegated authority. The Act does not suggest what constitutes "a change in condition of the patient" that could "warrant revocation." Even when such an undefined "change" occurs, the Governor is not compelled to act. The Act confers upon the Governor the unfettered discretion to determine what the terms of the Act mean and when, or if, he may act under it.

We agree with this analysis. In enacting chapter 2003-418, the Legislature failed to provide any standards by which the Governor should determine whether, in any given case, a stay should be issued and how long a stay should remain in effect. Further, the Legislature has failed to provide any criteria for lifting the stay. This absolute, unfettered discretion to decide whether to issue and then when to lift a stay makes the Governor's decision virtually unreviewable.

The Governor asserts that by enacting chapter 2003-418 the Legislature determined that he should be permitted to act as proxy for an incompetent patient in very narrow circumstances and, therefore, that his discretion is limited by the provisions of chapter 765. However, the Act does not refer to the provisions of chapter 765. Specifically, the Act does not amend section 765.401(1), Florida Statutes (2003), which sets forth an order of priority for determining who should act as proxy for an incapacitated patient who has no advance directive. Nor does the Act require that the Governor's decision be made in conformity with the requirement of section 765.401 that the proxy's decision be based on "the decision the proxy reasonably believes that patient would have made under the circumstances" or, if there is no indication of what the patient would have chosen, in the patient's best interests. §765.401(2)-(3), Fla. Stat. (2003). Finally, the Act does not provide for review of the Governor's decision as proxy as required by section 765.105, Florida Statutes (2003). In short, there is no indication in the language of chapter 2003-418 that the Legislature intended the Governor's discretion to be limited in any way. Even if we were to read chapter 2003-418 in pari materia with chapter 765, as the Governor suggests, there is nothing in chapter 765 to guide the Governor's discretion in issuing a stay because chapter 765 does not contemplate that a proxy will have the type of open-ended power delegated to the Governor under the Act.

We also reject the Governor's argument that this legislation provides an additional layer of due process protection to those who are unable to communicate their wishes regarding end-of-life decisions. Parts I, II, III, and IV of chapter 765, enacted by the Legislature in 1992 and amended several times,[4] provide detailed protections for those who are adjudicated incompetent, including that the proxy's decision be based on what the patient would have chosen under the circumstances or is in the patient's best interest, and be supported by competent, substantial evidence. *See* §765.401(2)-(3). chapter 765 also provides for judicial review if "[t]he patient's family, the health care facility, or the attending physician, or any other interested person who may reasonably be expected to be directly affected by the surrogate or proxy's decision . . . believes [that] [t]he surrogate or proxy's decision is not in accord with the patient's known desires or the provisions of this chapter." §765.105(1), Fla. Stat. (2003).

In contrast to the protections set forth in chapter 765, chapter 2003-418's standardless, open-ended delegation of authority by the Legislature to the Governor provides no guarantee that the incompetent patient's right

---

[4] Prior to this Court's decision in *In re Guardianship of Browning*, 568 So. 2d 4 (Fla. 1990), statutory law provided a procedure by which a competent adult could provide a declaration instructing his or her physician to withhold or withdraw life-prolonging procedures, or designating another to make the treatment decision. *See* §§765.01-765.17, Fla. Stat. (1991). This law had been in effect since 1984.

In 1992, the Legislature repealed sections 765.01-765.17, *see* ch. 92–199, §10 at 1852, Laws of Fla., and enacted Parts I, II, III, and IV of chapter 765. *See id.* §§2–5. The Legislature provided that in the absence of an advance directive, a proxy may make health care decisions for an incapacitated patient. *See* ch. 92–199, §5 at 1850 Laws of Fla.; §765.401 Fla. Stat. (2003). "Health care decisions" include "[i]nformed consent, refusal of consent, or withdrawal of consent to any and all health care, including life-prolonging procedures." Ch. 92–199, §2 at 1840, Laws of Fla.; §765.101(5)(a) Fla. Stat. (2003). When the statute was enacted in 1992, the Legislature defined life-prolonging procedures as:

> any medical procedure, treatment, or intervention which:
> (a) Utilizes mechanical or other artificial means to sustain, restore, or supplant a spontaneous vital function; and
> (b) When applied to a patient in a terminal condition, serves only to prolong the process of dying.

Ch. 92–199, §2 at 1840–41. However, in 1999, the Legislature rewrote the definitions section and defined life-prolonging procedures as:

> any medical procedure, treatment, or intervention, including artificially provided sustenance and hydration, which sustains, restores, or supplants a spontaneous vital function. The term does not include the administration of medication or performance of medical procedure, when such medication or procedure is deemed necessary to provide comfort care or to alleviate pain.

Ch. 99–331, §16 at 3464, Laws of Fla.; §765.101(10), Fla. Stat. (2003).

In order to determine who is to act as a patient's proxy, the Legislature set forth a detailed order of priority. *See* ch. 92–199, §5 at 1851. This order of priority has been amended only once since 1992 to allow a clinical social worker to act as the patient's proxy if none of the other potential proxies are available. *See* ch. 2003-57, §5, Laws of Fla. The Legislature also provided that a "proxy's decision to withhold or withdraw life-prolonging procedures must by supported by clear and convincing evidence that the decision would have been the one the patient would have/chosen had [the patient] been competent." Ch. 92–199, §5 at 1851, Laws of Fla., *see also* §765.401(3), Fla. Stat. (2003).

Finally, the Legislature provided for judicial review of a proxy's decision if "[t]he patient's family, the health care facility, or the attending physician, or any other interested person who may reasonably be expected to be directly affected by the surrogate or proxy's decision . . . believes (1) The surrogate or proxy's decision is not in accord with the patient's known desires or the provisions of this chapter." Ch. 92–199, §2 at 1842, Laws of Fla; §765.105, Fla. Stat. (2003).

to withdraw life-prolonging procedures will in fact be honored. *See In re Guardianship of Browning,* 568 So. 2d 4, 12 (Fla. 1990) (reaffirming that an incompetent person has the same right to refuse medical treatment as a competent person). As noted above, the Act does not even require that the Governor consider the patient's wishes in deciding whether to issue a stay, and instead allows a unilateral decision by the Governor to stay the withholding of life-prolonging procedures without affording any procedural process to the patient.

Finally, we reject the Governor's argument that the Legislature's grant of authority to issue the stay under chapter 2003-418 is a valid exercise of the state's parens patriae power. Although unquestionably the Legislature may enact laws to protect those citizens who are incapable of protecting their own interests, *see, e.g., In re Byrne,* 402 So. 2d 383 (Fla. 1981), such laws must comply with the constitution. chapter 2003-418 fails to do so.

Moreover, the argument that the Act broadly protects those who cannot protect themselves is belied by the case-specific criteria under which the Governor can exercise his discretion. The Act applies only if a court has found the individual to be in a persistent vegetative state and food and hydration have been ordered withdrawn. It does not authorize the Governor to intervene if a person in a persistent vegetative state is dependent upon another form of life support. Nor does the Act apply to a person who is not in a persistent vegetative state but a court finds, contrary to the wishes of another family member, that life support should be withdrawn. In theory, the Act could have applied during its fifteen-day window to more than one person, but it is undeniable that in fact the criteria fit only Theresa Schiavo.

In sum, although chapter 2003-418 applies to a limited class of people, it provides no criteria to guide the Governor's decision about whether to act. In addition, once the Governor has issued a stay as provided for in the Act, there are no criteria for the Governor to evaluate in deciding whether to lift the stay. Thus, chapter 2003-418 allows the Governor to act "through whim, show[] (SIC) favoritism, or exercis[e] (SIC) unbridled discretion," *Lewis,* 346 So. 2d at 56, and is therefore an unconstitutional delegation of legislative authority.

CONCLUSION

We recognize that the tragic circumstances underlying this case make it difficult to put emotions aside and focus solely on the legal issue presented. We are not insensitive to the struggle that all members of Theresa's family have endured since she fell unconscious in 1990. However, we are a nation of laws and we must govern our decisions by the rule of law and not by our own emotions. Our hearts can fully comprehend the grief so fully demonstrated by Theresa's family members on this record. But our hearts are not the law. What is in the Constitution always must prevail over emotion. Our oaths as judges require that this principle is our polestar, and it alone.

As the Second District noted in one of the multiple appeals in this case, we "are called upon to make a collective, objective decision concerning a question of law. Each of us, however, has our own family, our own loved ones, our own children . . . . But in the end, this case is not about the aspirations that loving parents have for their children." *Schiavo IV,* 851 So. 2d at 186. Rather, as our decision today makes clear, this case is about maintaining the integrity of a constitutional system of government with three independent and coequal branches, none of which can either encroach upon the powers of another branch or improperly delegate its own responsibilities.

The continuing vitality of our system of separation of powers precludes the other two branches from nullifying the judicial branch's final orders. If the Legislature with the assent of the Governor can do what was attempted here, the judicial branch would be subordinated to the final directive of the other branches. Also subordinated would be the rights of individuals, including the well established privacy right to self determination. *See Browning,* 568 So. 2d at 11–13. No court judgment could ever be considered truly final and no constitutional right truly secure, because the precedent of this case would hold to the contrary. Vested rights could be stripped away based on popular clamor. The essential core of what the Founding Fathers sought to change from their experience with English rule would be lost, especially their belief that our courts exist precisely to preserve the rights of individuals, even when doing so is contrary to popular will.

The trial court's decision regarding Theresa Schiavo was made in accordance with the procedures and protections set forth by the judicial branch and in accordance with the statutes passed by the Legislature in effect at that time. That decision is final and the Legislature's attempt to alter that final adjudication is unconstitutional as applied to Theresa Schiavo. Further, even if there had been no final judgment in this case, the Legislature provided the Governor constitutionally inadequate standards for the application of the legislative authority delegated in chapter 2003-418. Because chapter 2003-418 runs afoul of article II, section 3 of the Florida Constitution in both respects, we affirm the circuit court's final summary judgment.

It is so ordered.

WELLS, ANSTEAD, LEWIS, QUINCE, CANTERO and BELL, JJ., concur.

IN THIS CASE DUE TO I TS EXPEDITED NATURE ANY REHEARING MOTION SHALL BE FILED NO LATER THAN 10 DAYS FROM THE DATE OF THIS OPINION AND ANY RESPONSE FILED 5 DAYS THEREAFTER. NO REPLY SHALL BE ALLOWED AND NO MOTIONS FOR EXTENSION OF TIME ENTERTAINED.

Certified Judgments of Trial Courts in and for Pinellas County—W. Douglas Baird, Judge, Case No. 03-8212-CI-20—An Appeal from the District Court of Appeal, Second District, Case No. 2D04-2045

Kenneth L. Connor and Camille Godwin of Wilkes and McHugh, P.A., Tampa, Florida, and Robert A. Destro, Washington, D.C. on behalf of Jeb Bush, Governor of the State of Florida; and Charles J. Crist, Jr., Attorney General, George Lemieux, Deputy Attorney General, Chief of Staff, and Jay Vail, Senior Assistant Attorney General, Tallahassee, Florida,

for Appellant

George J. Felos of Felos and Felos, P.A., Dunedin, Florida, Randall C. Marshall, Legal Director of American Civil Liberties Union of Florida, Miami, Florida, and Thomas J. Perrelli and Robert M. Portman of Jenner and Block, LLC, Washington, D.C. on behalf of Michael Schiavo, as Guardian of the person of Theresa Marie Schiavo,

for Appellee

Jan G. Halisky, Clearwater, Florida and William L. Saunders, Jr., Director and Counsel, Washington, D.C. for Center for Human Life and Bioethics at the Family Research Council, Amici Curiae; George K. Rahdert of Rahdert, Steele, Bryan and Bole, P.A., St. Petersburg, Florida and Max Lapertosa, Chicago Illinois for Not Dead Yet, Adapt, The ARC of the United States, Center on Human Policy, Syracuse University, Center on Self Determination, Disability Rights Center, Freedom Clearinghouse, Hospice Patients' Alliance, Mouth Magazine, National Council on Independent Living, National Disabled Students Union, National Spinal Cord Injury Association, Self-Advocates Becoming Empowered, Society for Disability Studies, TASH, World Association of Persons With Disabilities and World Institute on Disability, Amici Curiae; Patricia Fields Anderson, St. Petersburg, Florida, Barbara J. Weller and David Charles Gibbs, III of Gibbs Law Firm, P.A., Seminole, Florida, Jay Alan Sekulow, James H. Henderson, Sr., Walter M. Weber and David A. Cortman, Washington, D.C. for Robert and Mary Schindler, Amici Curiae; Mary L. Wakeman, Russell E. Carlisle, Lauchlin T. Waldoch and Edwin M. Boyer, Tallahassee, Florida for the Academy of Florida Elder Law Attorneys, Inc., and the National Academy of Elder Law Attorneys, Amici Curiae; and Jon B. Eisenberg and David S. Ettinger of Horvitz and Levy, LLP, Encino, California and Bruce G. Howie, St. Petersburg, Florida for 55 Bioethicists Amici Curiae

state of oregon, Plaintiff-Appellee,

v.

JOHN ASHCROFT, Attorney General, in his official capacity as United States Attorney General; **ASA HUTCHINSON,** in his official capacity as Administrator of the Drug Enforcement Administration; **KENNETH W. MAGEE,** in his official capacity as Director of the Drug Enforcement Administration, Portland Office; UNITED STATES OF AMERICA; UNITED STATES DEPARTMENT OF JUSTICE; UNITED STATES DRUG ENFORCEMENT ADMINISTRATION, **Defendants-Appellants,**

v.

PETER A. RASMUSSEN; DAVID MALCOLM HOCHHALTER; RICHARD HOLMES; JAMES ROMNEY; MELISSA BUSH; JOHN DOE **#1,Plaintiffs-Intervenors-Appellees.**

No. 02-35587
D.C. No.
CV-01-01647-JO
OPINION

APPEAL FROM THE UNITED STATES DISTRICT COURT FOR THE DISTRICT OF OREGON ROBERT E. JONES, DISTRICT JUDGE, PRESIDING

Eli D. Stutsman, Portland, Oregon; Nicholas W. van Aelstyn, Heller Ehrman White & McAuliffe, San Francisco, California; and Kathryn L. Tucker, Compassion in Dying Federation, Seattle, Washington, for the patient plaintiffs-intervenors/appellees.

Daniel Avila, Everett, Massachusetts; Gregory S. Baylor, Annandale, Virginia; Thane W. Tienson, Landye Bennet & Brumstein, Portland, Oregon; Mark E. Chopko, Washington, D.C.; Richard E. Coleson, Bobb, Coleson & Bostrom, Terre Haute, Indiana; Rebecca P. Dick, Swidler Berlin Shereff & Friedman, Washington, D.C.; Donald A. Daugherty, Jr., Michael Best & Friedrich, Milwaukee, Wisconsin; Robert A. Free, MacDonald, Hoague & Bayless, Seattle, Washington; Katherine Heekin, Markowitz Herbold Glade & Mehlhaf, Portland, Oregon; Arthur B. LaFrance, Portland, Oregon; Max Lapertosa, Chicago, Illinois; Rita L. Marker, Steubenville, Ohio; Mitchell Olejko, Morrison & Foerster, San Francisco, California; John H. Pickering, Wilmer, Cutler & Pickering, Washington, D.C.; Wesley J. Smith, Oakland, California; William R. Stein, Hughes Hubbard & Reed, Washington, D.C.; Joel H. Thornton, Washington, D.C.; Thomas Triplett, Schwabe Williamson & Wyatt, Portland, Oregon; Harris J. Yale, New York, New York; and Miles J. Zaremski, Schaumburg, Illinois, for the amici.

OPINION

TALLMAN, Circuit Judge:

A doctor, a pharmacist, several terminally ill patients, and the State of Oregon challenge an interpretive rule issued by Attorney General John Ashcroft which declares that physician assisted suicide violates the Controlled Substances Act of 1970 ("CSA"), 21 U.S.C. §§801–904. This so-called "Ashcroft Directive," published at 66 Fed. Reg. 56,607, criminalizes conduct specifically authorized by Oregon's Death With Dignity Act, Or. Rev. Stat. §127.800-897. We hold that the Ashcroft Directive is unlawful and unenforceable because it violates the plain language of the CSA, contravenes Congress' express legislative intent, and oversteps the bounds of the Attorney General's statutory authority. *See* 5 U.S.C. §706(2)(C), (D). The petitions for review are granted.

I

We have original jurisdiction over "final determinations, findings, and conclusions of the Attorney General" made under the CSA. 21 U.S.C. §877. Because the Attorney General maintains that his interpretive rule is a "final determination" and because the Directive orders sanctions for violations of its provisions, we have original jurisdiction pursuant to §877. *See Hemp Indus. Ass'n v. DEA,* 333 F.3d 1082, 1085 (9th Cir. 2003) (holding that an interpretive rule issued by the Attorney General pursuant to the CSA is a "final determination" for jurisdictional purposes because the rule "impos[es] obligations and sanctions in the event of violation [of its provisions]"); *see also City of Auburn v. Qwest,* 260 F.3d 1160, 1171–73 (9th Cir. 2001). We consider the matter transferred to us from the district court pursuant to 28 U.S.C. §1631.[5]

Note: For complete document see http://www.oregon.gov./DHS/ph/pas/fags.html

---

[5] On April 17, 2002, United States District Judge Robert E. Jones entered a permanent injunction against enforcement of the Ashcroft Directive. 192 F. Supp. 2d 1077 (D. Or. 2002). Recognizing that he might lack jurisdiction over the matter, Judge Jones alternatively ordered the petitions for review transferred to us under 28 U.S.C. §1631 ("Whenever a civil action is filed in a court . . . including a petition for review of administrative action . . . and that court finds that there is a want of jurisdiction, the court shall, if it is in the interest of justice, transfer such action or appeal to any other such court in which the action or appeal could have been brought at the time it was filed or noticed[.]"). 192 F. Supp. 2d at 1086–87. Although we conclude that the district court did not have jurisdiction, Judge Jones' opinion on the merits is well reasoned, and we ultimately adopt many of his conclusions.

BAXTER v. STATE, 354 Mont. 234, 224 P.3d 1211 (2009)

Montana Supreme Court

(Decided December 31, 2009. Rehearing denied March 3, 2010)

In this case, the Supreme Court of Montana asked the following question "Whether the District Court erred in its decision that competent, terminally ill patients have a constitutional right to die with dignity, which protects physicians who provide aid in dying from prosecution under the homicide statutes."

Robert Baxter was a retired truck driver who was terminally ill with lymphocytic leukemia with diffuse lymph-adenopathy. He was being treated with multiple rounds of chemotherapy. "As a result of the disease and treatment, Mr. Baxter suffered from a variety of debilitating symptoms, including infections, chronic fatigue and weakness, anemia, night sweats, nausea, massively swollen glands, significant ongoing digestive problems and generalized pain and discomfort. The symptoms were expected to increase in frequency and intensity as the chemotherapy lost its effectiveness. There was no cure for Mr. Baxter's disease and no prospect of recovery. Mr. Baxter wanted the option of ingesting a lethal dose of medication prescribed by his physician and self-administered at the time of Mr. Baxter's own choosing."

The trial court found that "Montana constitutional rights of individual privacy and human dignity, together, encompass the right of a competent, terminally ill patient to die with dignity." In addition, the trial court held that "a patient may use the assistance of his physician to obtain a prescription for a lethal dose of medication. The patient would then decide whether to self-administer the dose and cause his own death." The trial court also held that this included protection from prosecution for the physician that assisted the patient.

The Supreme Court had to determine the physician's culpability. It started by stating that in Montana, suicide is not a crime so that the only person(s) that might be prosecuted for the patient's death would be the physician(s) if they prescribed a lethal dose of medication. The Court then said that the physician would be shielded from homicide liability if the patient gave consent so that the Court needed to determine if the physician could use a statutory consent defense and then if it would be ineffective because such conduct or resulting harm would be against public policy.

The Court said that the physician may be shielded from liability if none of the four statutory exceptions applied. According to the Court consent would be ineffective if "(a) it is given by a person who is legally incompetent to authorize the conduct charged to constitute the offense; (b) it is given by a person who by reason of youth, mental disease or defect, or intoxication is unable to make a reasonable judgment as to the nature or harmfulness of the conduct charged to constitute the offense; (c) it is induced by force, duress, or deception; or (d) it is against public policy to permit the conduct or the resulting harm, even though consented to."

The Court found that the first three exceptions are factual so they focused on the fourth and found that under Montana law, assisting in such a manner was not against public policy. Because the Court found only one case that discussed this matter and it dealt with a drunken brawl, it looked to the State of Washington which has a number of such cases. The Court stated "Washington courts have consistently held that the "public policy" exception applies only to brutish, irrational violence that endangers others."

The Court found that "a physician who aids a terminally ill patient in dying is not directly involved in the final decision or the final act. He or she only provides a means by which a terminally ill patient himself can give effect to his life-ending decision, or not, as the case may be. Each stage of the physician-patient interaction is private, civil, and compassionate. The physician and terminally ill patient work together to create a means by which the patient can be in control of his own mortality. The patient's subsequent private decision whether to take the medicine does not breach public peace or endanger others."

The Court in fact found that the "Terminally Ill Act, by its very subject matter, is an apt statutory starting point for understanding the legislature's intent to give terminally ill patients—like Mr. Baxter—end-of-life autonomy, respect and assurance that their life-ending wishes will be followed. The Terminally Ill Act expressly immunizes physicians from criminal and civil liability for following a patient's directions to withhold or withdraw life-sustaining treatment. Section 50-9-204, MCA. Indeed, the legislature has criminalized the failure to act according to the patient's wishes. Section 50-9-206, MCA. Other parts of the Terminally Ill Act also resonate with this respect for the patient's end-of-life preferences. Section 50-9-205, MCA, explicitly prohibits, "for any purpose," calling the patient's death a "suicide or homicide," and § 50-9-501, MCA, charges the Montana Attorney General with creating a "declaration registry" and waging a statewide campaign to educate Montanans about end-of-life decisionmaking. The statute even establishes a specialized state fund account specifically for the registry and education program."

The Court distinguished between assisting the patient to make end-of-life decisions from assisted suicide or "mercy killings." It stated that the statute did not "condone, authorize, or approve mercy killing or euthanasia." Physician aid in dying is, by definition, neither of these. It was very clear that what is different is that the patient must remain autonomous in his or her decisionmaking.

The link for the case is found on http://www.aclumontana.org/legal/526-baxter-v-state-of-montana which also has amicus briefs, the complaint and other documents regarding the case.

Appendix B

SELECTED WILLS OF FAMOUS PEOPLE

THE WILL OF DIANA, PRINCESS OF WALES

I DIANA PRINCESS OF WALES of Kensington Palace London W8 HEREBY REVOKE all former Wills and testamentary dispositions made by me AND DECLARE this to be my last Will which I make this First day Of June One thousand nine hundred and ninety three.

1 I APPOINT my mother THE HONOURABLE MRS FRANCES RUTH SHAND KYDD of Callinesh Isle of Seil Oban Scotland and COMMANDER PATRICK DESMOND CHRISTIAN JERMY JEPHSON of St James's Palace London SW1 to be the Executors and Trustees of this my Will.

2 I WISH to be buried.

3 SHOULD any child of mine be under age at the date of the death of the survivor of myself and my husband I APPOINT my mother and my brother EARL SPENCER to be the guardians of that child and I express the wish that should I predecease my husband he will consult with my mother with regard to the upbringing education and welfare of our children.

4 (a) I GIVE free of inheritance tax all my chattels to my Executors jointly (or if only one of them shall prove my Will to her or him)
   (b) I DESIRE them (or if only one shall prove her or him)
      (i) To give effect as soon as possible but not later than two years following my death to any written memorandum or notes of wishes of mine with regard to any of my chattels
      (ii) Subject to any such wishes to hold my chattels (or the balance thereof) in accordance with Clause 5 of this my Will
   (c) FOR the purposes of this Clause "chattels" shall have the same meaning as is assigned to the expression "personal chattels" in the Administration of Estates Act 1925 (including any car or cars that I may own at the time of my death)
   (d) I DECLARE that all expenses for the safe custody of and insurance incurred prior to giving effect to my wishes and for packing transporting and insurance for the purposes of the delivery to the respective recipients of their particular chattels shall be borne by my residuary estate

5 SUBJECT to the payment or discharge of my funeral testamentary and administration expenses and debts and other liabilities I GIVE all my property and assets of every kind and wherever situate to my Executors and Trustees Upon trust either to retain (if they think fit without being liable for loss) all or any part in the same state as they are at

the time of my death or to sell whatever and wherever they decide with power when they consider it proper to invest trust monies and to vary investments in accordance with the powers contained in the Schedule to this my Will and to hold the same UPON TRUST for such of them my children PRINCE WILLIAM and PRINCE HENRY as are living three months after my death and attain the age of twenty five years if more than one in equal shares PROVIDED THAT if either child of mine dies before me or within three months after my death and issue of that child are living three months after my death and attain the age of twenty one years such issue shall take by substitution if more than one in equal shares per stirpes the share that the deceased child of mine would have taken had he been living three months after my death but so that no issue shall take whose parent is then living and so capable of taking

6 MY EXECUTORS AND TRUSTEES shall have the following powers in addition to all other powers over any share of the Trust Fund

(a) POWER under the Trustee Act 1925 Section 31 to apply income for maintenance and to accumulate surplus income during a minority but as if the words "my Trustees think fit" were substituted in sub-section (1)(i) thereof for the words "may in all the circumstances be reasonable" and as if the proviso at the end of sub-section (1) thereof was omitted

(b) POWER under the Trustee Act 1925 Section 32 to pay or apply capital for advancement or benefit but as if proviso (a) to sub-section (1) thereof stated that "no payment or application shall be made to or for any person which exceeds altogether in amount the whole of the presumptive or vested share or interest of that person in the trust property or other than for the personal benefit of that person or in such manner as to prevent limit or postpone his or her interest in possession in that share or interest"

7 THE statutory and equitable rules of apportionment shall not apply to my Will and all dividends and other payments in the nature of income received by the Trustees shall be treated as income at the date of receipt irrespective of the period for which the dividend or other income is payable

8 IT is my wish (but without placing them under any binding obligation) that my executors employ the firm of Mishcon de Reya of 21 Southampton Row London WC1B 5HS in obtaining a Grant of Probate to and administering my estate

9 ANY person who does not survive me by at least three months shall be deemed to have predeceased me for the purpose of ascertaining the devolution of my estate and the income thereof

10 IF at any time an Executor or Trustee is a professional or business person charges can be made in the ordinary way for all work done by that person or his firm or company or any partner or employee

The Schedule

MY Executors and Trustees (hereinafter referred to as "my Trustees") in addition to all other powers conferred on them by law or as the result of the terms of this my Will shall have the following powers

1 (a) FOR the purposes of any distribution under Clause 5 to appropriate all or any part of my said property and assets in or toward satisfaction of any share in my residuary estate without needing the consent of anyone

(b) FOR the purposes of placing a value on any of my personal chattels (as defined by the Administration of Estates Act 1925) so appropriated to use if they so decide such value as may have been placed on the same by any Valuers they instruct for inheritance tax purposes on my death or such other value as they may in their absolute discretion consider fair and my Trustees in respect of any of my personal chattels which being articles of national scientific historic or artistic interest are treated on such death as the subject of a conditionally exempt transfer for the purposes of the Inheritance Tax Act 1984 Section 30 (or any statutory modification or re-enactment thereof) shall in respect of any such appropriation place such lesser value as they in their absolute discretion consider fair after taking into account such facts and surrounding circumstances as they consider appropriate including the fact that inheritance tax for which conditional exemption was obtained might be payable by the beneficiary on there being a subsequent chargeable event

(c) TO insure under comprehensive or any other cover against any risks and for any amounts (including allowing as they deem appropriate for any possible future effects of inflation and increasing building costs and expenses) any asset held at any time by my Executors and Trustees And the premiums in respect of any such insurance may be discharged by my Executors and Trustees either out of income or out of capital (or partly out of one and partly out of the other) as my Executors and Trustees shall in their absolute discretion determine and any monies received by my Executors and Trustees as the result of any insurance insofar as not used in rebuilding reinstating replacing or repairing the asset lost or damaged shall be treated as if they were the proceeds of sale of the asset insured PROVIDED ALWAYS that my Executors and Trustees shall not be under any responsibility to insure or be liable for any loss that may result from any failure so to do

2 (a) POWER to invest trust monies in both income producing and non-income producing assets of every kind and wherever situated and to vary investments in the same full and unrestricted manner in all respects as if they were absolutely entitled thereto beneficially

(b) POWER to retain or purchase as an authorized investment any freehold or leasehold property or any interest or share therein of whatever nature proportion or amount (which shall be held upon trust to retain or sell the same) as a residence for one or more beneficiaries under this my Will and in the event of any such retention or purchase my Trustees shall have power to apply trust monies in the erection alteration improvement or repair of any building on such freehold or leasehold property including one where there is any such interest or share And my Trustees shall have power to decide (according to the circumstances generally) the terms and conditions in every respect upon which any such person or persons may occupy and reside at any such property (or have the benefit of the said interest or share therein)

(c) POWER to delegate the exercise of their power to invest trust monies (including for the purpose of holding or placing them on deposit pending investment) and to vary investments to any company or other persons or person whether or not being or including one or more of my Trustees and to allow any investment or other asset to be held in the names or name of such person or persons as nominees or nominee of my Trustees and to decide the terms and conditions in every respect including the period thereof and the commission fees or other remuneration payable therefor which commission fees or other remuneration shall be paid out of the capital and income of that part of the Trust Fund in respect of which they are incurred or of any property held on the same trusts AND I DECLARE that my Trustees shall not be liable for any loss arising from any act or omission by any person in whose favour they shall have exercised either or both their powers under this Clause

(d) POWER to retain and purchase chattels of every description under whatever terms they hold the same by virtue of the provisions of this my Will And in respect thereof they shall have the following powers

(i) To retain the chattels in question under their joint control and custody or the control and custody of any of them or to store the same (whether in a depository or warehouse or elsewhere)

(ii) To lend all or any of the chattels to any person or persons or body or bodies (including a museum or gallery) upon such terms and conditions as my Trustees shall determine

(iii) To cause inventories to be made

(iv) Generally to make such arrangements for their safe custody repair and use as having regard to the circumstances my Trustees may from time to time think expedient

(v) To sell the chattels or any of them and

(vi) To treat any money received as the result of any insurance in so far as not used in reinstating replacing or repairing any chattel lost or damaged as if it were the proceeds of sale of the chattel insured

(e) POWER in the case of any of the chattels of which a person of full age and capacity is entitled to the use but when such person's interest is less than an absolute one

(i) To cause an inventory of such chattels to be made in duplicate with a view to one part being signed by the beneficiary for retention by my Trustees and the other part to be kept by the beneficiary and to cause any such inventory to be revised as occasion shall require and the parts thereof altered accordingly

(ii) To require the beneficiary to arrange at his or her expense for the safe custody repair and insurance of such chattels in such manner as my Trustees think expedient and (where it is not practicable so to require the beneficiary) to make such arrangements as are referred to under paragraph (iv) of sub-clause (d) of this Clause

PROVIDED THAT my Trustees shall also have power to meet any expenses which they may incur in the exercise of any of their powers in respect of chattels out of the capital and income of my estate or such one or more of any different parts and the income thereof as they shall in their absolute discretion determine AND I FURTHER DECLARE that my Trustees shall not be obliged to make or cause to be made any inventories of any such chattels that may be held and shall not be liable for any loss injury or damage that may happen to any such chattels from any cause whatsoever or any failure on the part of anyone to effect or maintain any insurance

IN WITNESS whereof I have hereunto set my hand the day and year first above written

SIGNED by HER ROYAL HIGHNESS)
in our joint presence and)
then by us in her presence)

Codicil to Will

I DIANA PRINCESS OF WALES of Kensington Palace London W8 DECLARE this to be a First Codicil to my Will which is dated the first day of June One thousand nine hundred and ninety three

1 My Will shall be construed and take effect as if in clause 1 the name and address of Commander Patrick Desmond Christian Jermy Jephson were omitted and replaced by the following:

My sister Elizabeth Sarah Lavinia McCorquodale (known as The Lady Sarah McCorquodale) of Stoke Rochford Grantham Lincolnshire NG33 5EB

2 In all other respects I confirm my said Will.

IN WITNESS whereof I have hereunto set my hand this First day of February One thousand nine hundred and ninety six

SIGNED by HER ROYAL HIGHNESS)
in our joint presence and then)
by us in her presence)

WILL OF STEVE JOBS

Sorry folks! By all accounts Steve Jobs, estimated to be worth $7 billion dollars at the time of his death, properly used trusts to effectuate his estate and financial planning. That means that the majority of his wealth distribution is and will likely remain private.

However, if you find anything, feel free to contact the author and she'll be glad to check out the details.

THE WILL OF JERRY GARCIA (OF THE GRATEFUL DEAD)

I, JEROME J. GARCIA, also known as JERRY GARCIA, a resident of Marin County, California, hereby make, publish and declare this to be my Last Will and Testament.

First

REVOCATION OF PRIOR WILLS
I revoke all Wills and Codicils heretofore made by me.

Second

DECLARATIONS
I declare that I am married; my wife's name is DEBORAH KOONS. We have no children by our marriage. I have four children now living from prior relationships, namely HEATHER GARCIA KATZ, born December 8, 1963, ANNABELLE WALKER GARCIA, born February 2, 1970, THERESA ADAMS GARCIA, born September 21, 1974, and KEELIN GARCIA, born December 20, 1987. I have no deceased children leaving issue, and I have not adopted any children. The terms "child" or "children" as used in this Will shall refer only to my children and if any person shall claim and establish any right to participate in my estate other than as provided in this Will, whether as heir or in any other capacity whatsoever, I give and bequeath to each such person the sum of One Dollar ($1.00).

Third

COMMUNITY PROPERTY
I declare my intention to dispose of all property, real and personal, of which I have the right to dispose by Will, including any and all property as to which I may have at the time of my death a power of appointment by Will. I confirm to my wife her interest in our community property. It is my intention by this Will to dispose of all my separate Property and of my one-half (1/2) interest in our community property.

Fourth

PERSONAL PROPERTY
Except as specifically provided herein below, I give my jewelry, clothing, household furniture and furnishings, personal automobiles, books, pictures, objects of art and other tangible articles of a personal nature, or my interest in such property, which I may have at the time of my death, not otherwise specifically disposed of by this Will or in any other manner, together with any insurance on such property, to my wife, if she survives me for sixty (60) days, and if she does not, then to such of my children, by representation, who survive me for sixty (60) days in equal shares as they shall agree, or as my Executor shall, in my Executor's discretion, determine if my children do not agree within one hundered (sic) fifty (150) days of my death.

In the absence of a conflict of interest, my Executor shall represent any child under age eighteen (18) in matter relating to any distribution under this Article FOURTH, including selection of the assets that shall constitute that child's share, and my Executor may, in my Executor's discretion, sell for the child's account any part of that child's share. Any property or its proceeds distributable to a child under age eighteen (18) pursuant to this Paragraph may be delivered without bond to the guardian of such child or to any suitable person with whom he or she resides or who has the care or control of him or her.

If neither my wife nor any of my children shall survive me, then this gift shall lapse and such property, and any insurance thereon, shall become part of the residue of my estate.

Fifth

GUITARS
I give all my guitars made by DOUGLAS ERWIN, to DOUGLAS ERWIN, or to his estate if he predeceases me.

Sixth

DISTRIBUTION OF RESIDUE OF ESTATE

After payment of all my debts, my last illness and funeral expenses, and provision for my child support obligations for KEELIN GARCIA, my marital settlement agreement with CAROLYN ADAMS GARCIA which is being drafted at the time of signing this will, and my agreement with MANASHA MATHESON regarding the house to be owned one-half by her and one-half by the trust established for KEELIN GARCIA which is being drafted at the time of signing this will, my Executor shall divide and distribute the remainder of my estate for my wife/husband and children as follows:

A. If my wife survives me for sixty (60) days, I give her one-third (1/3) of my estate outright and free of trust. If my wife fails to survive me for sixty days this bequest shall lapse and the amount shall be included with the remainder of my estate under paragraph B.

B. I give the remaining two-thirds (2/3) of my estate, or if my wife fails to survive me, my entire remaining estate, to my daughters, my friends, and my brother as follows:

1 The following shares shall be distributed outright and free of trust, by right of representation, to the persons indicated:

> HEATHER GARCIA KATZ ONE-FIFTH (1/5)
> ANNABELLE WALKER GARCIA ONE-FIFTH (1/5)
> SUNSHINE MAY WALKER KESEY ONE-TENTH (1/10)
> CLIFFORD GARCIA ONE-TENTH (1/10)

2 I give to the Trustee hereinafter named, IN TRUST, for the benefit of my younger daughters, THERESA ADAMS GARCIA and KEELIN GARCIA, one-fifth (1/5) of my estate for each, to be held, administered and distributed as a separate trust for each child as follows:

(a) So long as my child is living and is under age twenty-one (21), the Trustee shall pay to or apply for her benefit, as much of the net income and principal of the Trust as the Trustee, in the Trustee's absolute discretion, shall deem necessary for her proper support, health, maintenance and education, after taking into consideration, to the extent the Trustee shall deem advisable, any other income or resources of my child, known to the Trustee. Any net income not distributed shall be accumulated and added to principal.

(b) When the child attains the age of twenty-one (21), the trust share allocated on account of such child shall thereupon be distributed free of trust to that child.

(c) If my child dies prior to receipt of her entire share of principal and income provided herein, and that child is survived by issue, then the remaining principal and income shall be held in trust for those issue under the terms of this subparagraph 2. If my child is not survived by issue, then the remaining principal and income shall be distributed free of trust to the other residual beneficiaries receiving fractional interests in my estate under this paragraph B in proportion to those fractional interests, by right of representation; provided, however, if a part of that balance would otherwise be distributed to a person for whose benefit a trust is then being administered under this Will, that part shall instead be added to that trust and shall thereafter be administered according to its terms.

(d) Whenever provision is made in this Article SIXTH for payment for the "education" of a beneficiary, the term "education" shall be construed to include college and postgraduate study, so long as pursued to advantage by the beneficiary at an institution of the beneficiary's choice; and in determining payments to be made for such college of post-graduate education, the Trustee shall take into consideration the beneficary's related living expenses to the extent that they are reasonable.

(e) Notwithstanding the directions given as to the distribution of income and principal in this Article SIXTH, any trusts established by this Article shall terminate, if they have not previously terminated, twenty-one (21) years after the death of the survivor of the class composed of my wife/husband and all my issue living at my death, and the then remaining principal and undistributed income of such trusts shall be paid to my issue or other beneficiaries then living to whom income payments could be made under such trusts immediately prior to its termination under this clause, such issue to take by right of representation.

Seventh

ULTIMATE DISTRIBUTION

If at the time of my death, or at any later time before full distribution of any Trust established under Article SIXTH, all my issue are deceased, and no other disposition of the property is directed by this Will, the estate or the portion of it then remaining shall there upon be distributed to those persons who would then be my heirs, their identities and respective shares to be determined as though my death had then occurred and according to the laws of the State of California then in effect relating to the succession of separate property not acquired from a predeceased spouse.

Eighth

TRUSTEE'S POWERS

I give to the Trustee of all of the Trusts established under this Will the following powers, in addition to and not in limitation of the common-law and statutory powers, and without application or permission of any court.

A. To retain any property, real or personal, which the Trustee may receive, even though such property (by reason of its character, amount, proportion to the total Trust Estate or otherwise) would not be considered appropriate for a Trustee apart from this provision.

B. To sell, exchange, give options upon, partition, or otherwise dispose of any property which the Trustee may hold from time to time at public or private sale or otherwise, for cash or other consideration or on credit, and upon such terms and for such consideration as the Trustee shall think fit, and to transfer and convey the same free of all trust.

C. To invest and reinvest the Trust Estate from time to time in any property, real or personal, including (without limiting the generality of the foregoing language) securities of domestic and foreign corporations and investment trusts, common trust funds, including those established by any successor corporate fiduciary which acts as Executor and Trustee hereunder, bonds, preferred stocks, common stocks, mortgages, mortgage participation, even though such investment (by reason of its character, amount, proportion to the total Trust Estate or otherwise) would not be considered appropriate for a Trustee apart from this provision, and even though such investment causes a greater proportion of the principal to be invested in investment of one type or of one company than would be considered appropriate for a Trustee apart from this provision; to lend money to any and all persons, including any or all of the beneficiaries hereof, upon such terms and conditions as the Trustee in the Trustee's sole discretion deems proper; in connection with such loans the Trustee may or may not demand security therefor or interest thereon as the Trustee in the Trustee's sole discretion deems proper.

D. To improve any real estate held in the Trust Estate, including the power to demolish any buildings in whole or in part and to erect buildings; to lease real estate on such terms as the Trustee thinks fit, including leases for periods that may extend beyond the duration of the Trusts, and to grant renewals thereof; and to foreclose, extend, assign, partially release and discharge mortgages.

E. To borrow money from any lender even though a successor fiduciary hereunder, execute promissory notes therefor, and to secure said obligations by mortgage or pledge of any of the Trust property.

F. To compromise or arbitrate any claim in favor of or against the Trust Estate; to commence or defend any litigation concerning the Trust Estate which the Trustee in the Trustee's absolute discretion considers prudent, and costs and expenses of such, including reasonable attorney's fees, to be borne by the Trust Estate; to give or receive consideration in any settlement to reduce the rate of return on any investment, with or without consideration; to prepay or accept prepayment of any debt; to enforce, abstain from enforcing, release or modify, with or without consideration, any right, obligation, or claim; to extend and renew any obligation or hold the same after maturity without extension or renewal; to accept deeds in lieu of foreclosure and pay consideration for the same; to determine that any property is worthless or of insufficient value to warrant keeping or protecting, and to abandon any such property or convey the same with or without consideration; and to use any portion of the Trust Estate to protect any other portion of the Trust Estate.

G. To vote all securities held as a part of the Trust Estate, or to join in a voting trust or other lawful form of stockholders' agreements respecting the voting of shares for such period as the Trustee deems proper; to pay all assessments on such securities, to exercise options, subscriptions and conversion rights on such securities, with respect thereto; to employ such brokers, banks, counsel, custodians, attorneys or other agents, and to delegate to them such powers (including, among others, the right to vote shares of stock held in trust) or join in a voting trust or other lawful form of stockholders' agreements respecting the voting of shares for such periods as the Trustee deems proper; and to cause securities held from time to time to be registered in the name of the Trustee, or in the name of the Trustee's nominee with or without mention of the Trust in any instrument of ownership, and to keep the same unregistered or to retain them in condition that they will pass by delivery.

H. To incur and pay all taxes, assessments, costs, charges, fees and other expenses of every kind which the Trustee deems necessary or advisable in connection with the administration of the Trust created hereby, including reasonable Trustee's fees.

I. To join in or oppose any reorganization, recapitalization, consolidation or merger, liquidation or foreclosure, or any plan therefor; to deposit property with, and delegate discretionary power to any committee or depository; to pay assessments, expenses and compensation; and to retain any property issued therein; to exercise or sell conversion or subscription rights, and to retain the property received.

J. To hold, manage, invest and account for the several shares which may be held in trust, either as separate funds or as a single fund, as the Trustee deems proper; if as a single fund, making the division thereof only upon the Trustee's books of account and allocating to each share its proportionate part of the principal and income of the common fund and charging against each share its proportionate part of the common expenses.

K. To keep any or all of the Trust property at any place or places in California or elsewhere in the United States or abroad, or with a depository or custodian at such place or places.

L. In dividing the Trust Estate into shares or in distributing the same, to divide or distribute in cash or in kind as the Trustee thinks fit. For purposes of division or distribution, to value the Trust Estate reasonably and in good faith, and such valuation shall be conclusive on all parties. Where distribution or division is made in kind, the Trustee shall, so far as the Trustee finds practicable, allocate to the beneficiaries proportionate amounts of each kind or security; or other property of the Trust Estate.

M. The Trustee is authorized in the Trustee's discretion to retain from income distributable to any beneficiary an amount equal to the income tax (Federal and State) the Trustee estimates will be imposed upon such income; any sums so withheld shall be applied to the tax liability of such beneficiary. Nothing herein shall be construed as imposing an obligation upon the Trustee to retain any sums for the purpose mentioned, nor that said tax shall be assumed or borne by the assets held for such beneficiary. No liability shall attach to the Trustee if the Trustee acts or fails to act as authorized in Subparagraph M.

N. To partition, without sale, any real or personal property held jointly or in common with others or distributable to one or more persons hereunder; to pay or receive consideration to effect equality of partition; to unite with any other owner in the management, leasing, use of improvement of any property.

O. To determine, as to all property received, whether and to what extent the same shall be deemed to be principal or income and as to all charges or expenses paid, whether and to what extent the same shall be charged against principal or against income, including, without limiting the generality of the foregoing language, power to apportion any receipt or expense between principal and income and to determine what part, if any, of the actual income received upon any wasting investment or upon any security purchased or acquired at a premium shall be retained and added to principal to prevent diminution of principal upon exhaustion or maturity thereof. In this regard, the Trustee in the Trustee's absolute discretion, may, but shall not be required to, if the Trustees deems it proper, allocate receipts or charges and expenses to income or principal according to the Principal and Income Law of the State of California as it may from time to time exist. All allocation of receipts or charges and expenses shall be conclusive on all persons interested in any trusts created hereby.

P. In all matters to administer and invest the Trust Estate as fully and freely as an individual owner might do, without any restrictions to which fiduciaries are ordinarily subject, except the duty to act in good faith and with reasonable care.

Q. The Trustee shall also have the power to do all things necessary to continue any business enterprise, in whatever form, owned or controlled by me upon my death for such period as the Trustee shall deem to be in the best interests of the Trust Estate.

R. The Trustee is authorized to employ attorneys, accountants, investment advisors, specialists and such other agents as he shall deem necessary or desirable. The Trustee shall have the authority to appoint an investment manager or managers to manage all or any part of the assets of the Trust Estate, appointments shall include the power to acquire and dispose of such assets. The Trustee may charge the compensation of such attorneys, accountants, investment advisors, specialists and other agents and any other expenses against the Trust Estate.

Ninth

PAYMENT OF TAXES AND EXPENSES
I direct that all estate, succession or other death taxes, duties, charges or assessments that may by reason of my death be attributable to my probate estate or any portion of it, or to any property or transfers of property outside my probate estate, including but not limited to burial expenses, expenses of last illness, attorney's fees, executor's fees, appraiser's fees, accountant's fees and other expenses of administering my estate shall be paid by the Executor from the estate in the same manner as if said taxes were a debt of my estate, without apportionment, deduction, or reimbursement thereof and without adjustment thereof among my beneficiaries. Provided, however, if there is inadequate cash in my estate to pay such taxes and expenses, then my executor may borrow such funds as I have given authority in Article TWELFTH below.

Tenth

NO CONTEST CLAUSE
If any beneficiary of my Will or any Codicil hereto or of the Trusts created hereunder before or after the admission of this Will to probate, directly or indirectly, contests or aids in the contest of the same or any provision thereof, or contests the distribution of my estate in accordance with my Will or any Codicil, the provisions herein made to or for the benefit of such contestant or contestants are hereby revoked and for the purpose of my Will and any Codicil, said contestant or contestants shall be deemed to have predeceased me.

Eleventh

SPENDTHRIFT PROVISION
Each and every beneficiary under the Trust or Trusts created by this Will is hereby restrained from and is and shall be without right, power, or authority to sell, transfer, pledge, hypothecate, mortgage, alienate, anticipate, or in any other manner affect or impair his, her or their beneficial and legal rights, titles, interests, claims and estates in and to the income and/or principal of said trusts, and the rights, titles, interests and estate of any beneficiary thereunder shall not be subject nor liable to any process of law or court, and all of the income and/or principal under said trusts shall be paid over to the beneficiary in person, or, in the event of the minority or

incompetency of any beneficiary, to the guardian of that beneficiary in such manner as in the Trustee's discretion seems most advisable at the time and in the manner provided by the terms of the Trust.

Twelfth

EXECUTOR'S APPOINTMENT AND POWERS

I hereby nominate and appoint my wife DEBORAH KOONS, and my attorney DAVID M. HELLMAN, as Executor of this Will. If either of them shall be, or become unable or unwilling to act, then the survivor shall act with JEFFREY E. EHLENBACH. No bond or other security shall be required of any person who acts as Executor hereunder.

A. I hereby expressly authorize and empower my Executor to sell and dispose of the whole or any portion of my estate, real or personal, and wherever situate, as and when and upon such terms as my Executor deems proper, at public or private sale, with or without notice, and without first securing any order or court therefor. I further grant to my Executor all the powers granted to the Trustee under Article EIGHTH hereof, insofar as such powers are appropriate for the administration of my estate and the probate of my Will.

B. If my Executor in good faith decides that there is uncertainty as to the inclusion of particular property in my gross estate for federal estate tax purposes, my Executor shall exclude such property from my gross estate in the estate tax return. My Executor shall not be liable for any loss to my estate or to any beneficiary, which loss results from the decision made in good faith that there is uncertainty as to the inclusion of particular property in my gross estate.

C. The decision of my Executor as to the date which should be selected for the valuation of property in my gross estate for federal estate tax purposes shall be conclusive on all concerned.

D. When a choice is available as to whether certain deductions shall be taken as income tax deductions or estate tax deductions, the decision of my Executor in this regard shall be conclusive on all concerned and no adjustment of income and principal account shall be made as a result of such decision.

E. Beginning as of the date of my death and until the establishment of the trusts provided for herein, my Executor shall make such payments of estate income, which is allocable to trust assets, as would be required if the trusts had actually been established at the date of my death.

F. My Executor is authorized to execute and deliver disclaimers under Internal Revenue Code Section 2518 and California Probate Code Sections 260 through 295 or any successor statute.

Thirteenth

TRUSTEE'S APPOINTMENT AND COMPENSATION

I hereby nominate and appoint my wife DEBORAH KOONS, and my attorney DAVID M. HELLMAN, as Trustee of this Will. If either of them shall be, or become unable or unwilling to act, then the survivor shall act with JEFFREY E. EHLENBACH. No bond or other security shall be required of any person who acts as Trustee hereunder.

The individual Trustees shall be entitled to receive reasonable commissions similar to those charged by corporate Trustees in the San Francisco Bay Area. Any successor Trustee shall be entitled to reasonable compensation for its services.

Fourteenth

GUARDIAN

If MANASHA MATHESON does not survive me, I hereby nominate and appoint SUNSHINE MAY WALKER KESEY, as the guardian of KEELIN GARCIA, if she is then a minor. No bond shall be required of any person who acts as guardian hereunder.

Fifteenth

DELAYED DISTRIBUTION

I direct that no interest shall be payable on account of any delay in distributing any devise, bequest, or legacy under my Will or any Codicil thereto.

Sixteenth

DEFINITIONS

The words "Executor," "Trustee," "child," "children," and "beneficiary," as used herein, shall comprehend both the singular and the plural, and the masculine or feminine shall be deemed to include the other wherever the context of this Will requires. This Will and any Codicil shall be interpreted under the California law as in effect at the date of signature of such document.

IN WITNESS WHEREOF, I have hereunto set my hand this May 12, 1994.

Jerome J. Garcia

On the date indicated below, JEROME J. GARCIA, declared to us, the undersigned, that this instrument, consisting of sixteen (16) pages, including the page signed by us as witnesses, was the testators Will and requested us to act as witnesses to it. The testator thereupon signed this Will in our presence, all of us being present at the same time. We now, at the testators request, in the testators presence and in the presence of each other, subscribe our names as witnesses.

It is our belief that the testator is of sound mind and memory and is under no constraint or undue influence whatsoever.

We declare under penalty of perjury that the foregoing is true and correct and that this declaration was executed on May 12, 1994, at San Rafael, California.

David M. Hellman residing at - - - - - -, San Rafael, CA 94901

Tanna Burcher residing at - - - - - -, San Rafael, CA 94901

LAST WILL AND TESTAMENT OF WARREN E. BURGER (FORMER U.S. SUPREME COURT CHIEF JUSTICE)

I hereby make and declare the following to be my last will and testament.

1 My executors will first pay all claims against my estate;

2 The remainder of my estate will be distributed as follows: one-third to my daughter, Margaret Elizabeth Burger Rose and two-thirds to my son, Wade A. Burger;

3 I designate and appoint as executors of this will, Wade A. Burger and J. Michael Luttig.

IN WITNESS WHEREOF, I have hereunto set my hand to this my Last Will and Testament this 9th day of June, 1994.

Warren E. Burger

We hereby certify that in our presence on the date written above WARREN E. BURGER signed the foregoing instrument and declared it to be his Last Will and Testament and that at this request in his presence and in the presence of each other we have signed our names below as witnesses.

Nathaniel E. Brady residing at 120 F St., NW, Washington, DC

Alice M. Khu residing at 3041 Meeting St., Falls Church, VA

THE WILL OF BABE RUTH

I, GEORGE HERMAN RUTH, being of sound and disposing mind, memory and understanding, but mindful of the uncertainty of life, do hereby make, declare and publish this to be my Last Will and Testament, hereby revoking all other wills and codicils thereto by me at any time heretofore made.

FIRST: I direct my Executors hereinafter named to pay all my just debts and funeral expenses as soon after my death as may be practicable.

SECOND: I give and bequeath to my wife, CLARA MAE RUTH, if she shall survive me, all my household furniture, automobiles with the appurtenances thereto, paintings, works of art, books, china, glassware, silverware, linens, household furnishings and equipment of any kind, clothing, jewelry, articles of personal wear and adornment and personal effects, excepting however, souvenirs, mementoes, pictures, scrap-books, manuscripts, letters, athletic equipment and other personal property pertaining to baseball. In the event that my wife, Clara Mae Ruth, shall not survive me, I direct my Executors hereinafter named to divide the said property between my daughters, DOROTHY RUTH SULLIVAN and JULIA RUTH FLANDERS, as my said daughters may agree, or in the event they are unable to agree, to divide the said property between my said daughters as my Executors hereinafter named may, in their absolute discretion determine. The determination of my Executors as to the relative values of such property for the purpose of dividing the same and in the making of such distribution shall be final, conclusive and binding upon all persons interested herein.

THIRD: I give and bequeath to my Executors hereinafter named or either of them who may qualify, all my souvenirs, mementoes, pictures, scrap-books, manuscripts, letters, athletic equipment and other personal property pertaining to baseball, and I request but do not direct my said Executors to divide the same among such persons, corporations and organizations as I may from time to time request or in such manner as they in their sole and uncontrolled discretion may deem proper and fitting.

FOURTH: I give and bequeath to my wife, CLARA MAE RUTH, if she shall survive me, to my daughter, DOROTHY RUTH SULLIVAN, if she shall survive me, and to my daughter, JULIA RUTH FLANDERS, if she shall survive me, each the sum of Five Thousand ($5,000.) Dollars.

FIFTH: I give and bequeath to my sister, MARY H. MOBERLY, now residing in Baltimore, Maryland, if she shall survive me, the sum of Ten Thousand ($10,000.) Dollars.

SIXTH: I give and bequeath to FRANK DELANEY, providing he is in my employ at the time of my death, and to MARY REITH, providing she is in my employ at the time of my death, each the sum of Five Hundred ($500.) Dollars.

SEVENTH: Under the provisions of a certain Indenture or Trust Agreement made and executed by and between me and the President and Directors of The Manhattan Company of 40 Wall Street, Borough of Manhattan, City of New York, dated the 26th day of April, 1927, I reserved the right to designate in and by my last will and testament a new beneficiary to whom the income or principal of the trust fund which is the subject of the said Trust Agreement, shall be paid after my death in the place and stead of my daughter, Dorothy Ruth Sullivan, and my next of kin. Pursuant to such reserved right and in the exercise thereof, I hereby declare and direct that the income and principal of the said trust shall be paid after my death as follows:

A. The income of the said trust fund shall be paid to my wife, CLARA MAE RUTH, during the term of said trust or the life of my said wife, CLARA MAE RUTH, whichever may be the shorter period. After the death of my wife, CLARA MAE RUTH, the income of the said trust during the remainder of the term thereof shall be divided equally between my daughters, DOROTHY RUTH SULLIVAN and JULIA RUTH FLANDERS. If JULIA RUTH FLANDERS shall be deceased, the income which she would have received had she been alive, shall be paid to her issue per stirpes and not per capita, or if there be no issue of said JULIA RUTH FLANDERS then living, all of the income of the said trust shall be paid to my daughter, DOROTHY RUTH SULLIVAN.

B. Upon the termination of the said trust during the lifetime of my wife, CLARA MAE RUTH, I direct the Trustee thereof to purchase from an insurance company authorized to do business in the State of New York, a refund annuity which will pay to my wife, CLARA MAE RUTH, during her lifetime, in equal monthly installments the annual amount of Six Thousand ($6,000.) Dollars, and I further direct the Trustee of the said trust to divide the remainder of the principal of the said trust fund, including any refund payable upon the annuity hereinbefore required to be purchased for the benefit of my wife, CLARA MAE RUTH, into two (2) equal parts; and

(1) To pay one of such equal parts to the issue then living of my daughter, DOROTHY RUTH SULLIVAN, or if she shall leave no issue then surviving, among such persons and in such manner as she may by her last will and testament direct; and

(2) To pay the other of such equal parts to my daughter, JULIA RUTH FLANDERS, if she be then living, or if she be not living, to her issue then surviving, or if she shall leave no issue then surviving, among such persons and in such manner as she may by her last will and testament direct.

EIGHTH: All the rest, residue and remainder of my property and estate, real, personal and mixed, of whatsoever kind, nature or description and wheresoever situate, of which I may die seized and/or possessed or over which I may have any power of disposition or to which I or my estate may be entitled, I give devise and bequeath to my Trustees hereinafter named IN TRUST NEVERTHELESS for the following uses and purposes:

A. To collect and receive the rents, income and profits thereof and to pay the same to my wife CLARA MAE RUTH, as long as she shall live.

B. Upon the death of my wife, CLARA MAE RUTH, or upon my death, if she shall predecease me, I direct my Trustees to pay over, transfer, convey and deliver the principal then remaining in the said trust as follows:

(1) Ten percent (10%) thereof to THE BABE RUTH FOUNDATION, INC., a corporation organized under the Membership Corporations Law of the State of New York and dedicated to the interests of the kids of America.

(2) Forty-five percent (45%) thereof to my daughter, DOROTHY RUTH SULLIVAN, if she be then alive, or if she be not then alive, to her then surviving issue per stirpes and not per capita, or if she leave no issue then surviving, to such persons and in such manner as she may by her last will and testament direct. (3) Forty-five percent (45%) thereof to my daughter, JULIA RUTH FLANDERS, if she be then alive, or if she be not then alive, to her then surviving issue per stirpes and not per capita, or if she leave no issue then surviving, to such persons and in such manner as she by her last will and testament direct.

NINTH: I nominate, constitute and appoint J. PAUL CAREY, II and MELVYN GORDON LOWENSTEIN, and the survivor of them, as Executors of and Trustees under this my Last Will and Testament. Within ninety (90) days from the date upon which one of the above named Executors or Trustees shall first act as sole Executor or sole Trustee of this my Last Will and testament, I direct him, by an instrument in writing duly signed and acknowledged and suitable for recording in the State of New York, to appoint a bank or a trust company which has conducted active business operations in the State of New York for at least 25 years, or which is the successor to a bank or trust company organized under the laws of the State of New York or the United States of America more than 25 years prior to the date of such appointment, to be and become a co-Executor and/or a co-Trustee. In the event that such sole acting Executor or sole acting Trustee shall not have appointed a bank or a trust company as co-Executor or co-Trustee hereunder, as hereinabove directed and within the period hereinabove specified, then I nominate, constitute and appoint THE CHASE NATIONAL BANK OF THE CITY OF NEW YORK, as co-Executor and co-Trustee of this my Last Will and Testament.

TENTH: I direct that if and when any part of the principal or income of any share or portion of my estate shall become payable to any beneficiary who is an infant, such principal or income shall absolutely vest in and belong to such infant, but payment thereof may be deferred, and I authorize my Executors and Trustees, as the case may be, in their sole and uncontrolled discretion, to hold the share of such infant and to retain the custody and control thereof and to administer the same and invest and reinvest such share or portion and the accumulated income therefrom, if any, with all the powers granted in this my Last Will and Testament to the Executors and Trustees, and my Executors and Trustees are further directed to apply such part of the income and principal thereof as in their discretion they may deem necessary and proper for the maintenance, support and education of such infant during minority, and upon such infant attaining majority, to pay over to such infant whatever part of such principal and income and any accumulated income thereon which may then remain in the hands of my said Executors or Trustees, as the case may be. Such application of principal or income, in the discretion of my said Executors or Trustees may be made wholly or in part by said Executors or Trustees paying directly the expenses for the maintenance, support and education of such infant, or by paying such principal or income to such infant or to an adult person of my Executors' or Trustees' selection deemed by them to be the most likely person to make proper application of such principal or income for the infant's benefit; the receipt of the person to whom such payment is made to be a sufficient voucher and discharge to my said Executors or Trustees, as the case may be, for all payments so made by them.

ELEVENTH: In addition to the powers conferred upon my Executors and Trustees by law, or herein elsewhere conferred upon them. I hereby authorize and empower them and successors (a) to retain any investments which I may have at the time of my death, and to invest and reinvest any trusts funds coming into their hands in any stocks, bonds, securities or other property, real or personal, which they in their discretion deem advisable, whether such investments be authorized by the laws of any state or jurisdiction or not, and to hold the same as long as they may deem advisable, with full power to sell and reinvest, and to change securities and investments as they deem best; (b) for the purpose of partitioning or distributing the funds of my estate, and for any other purpose whatsoever, to grant, bargain, sell, convey, mortgage, lease, exchange, or otherwise dispose of as and when they or their successors may deem expedient, any and all property, real, personal or mixed, of which I may be seized or possessed or in or to which I may be in any manner interested or entitled at the time of my death, or of which they may be seized or possessed, entitled to or interested in, as my Executors or Trustees, and upon such disposition thereof, to execute, acknowledge and deliver all necessary and proper deeds or instruments of conveyance for the vesting in the purchases, mortgagee, lessee, or other transferee thereof, the title thereto, in fee or otherwise, and I hereby direct that upon any such disposition thereof, my Executors or Trustees, or the successors of any of them, may take the consideration agreed upon, wholly or partly, in cash, stocks, bonds, notes or any securities which they or their successors shall determine upon, and I expressly direct that no purchases, mortgagee, lessee, or other transferee thereof shall be bound to see to the application of money or other thing of value paid or given therefor; (c) whenever my Executors or Trustees, or the successors of any of them, are required, or shall determine to divide the principal of my estate held by them into shares, so to divide the same without converting it into money, but in their discretion by apportioning the property held, whether the same shall be producing income or not, to such different parts or shares, in such manner as they shall deem fairly and equitably to bring about the division directed or determined upon, the judgment of my said Executors or Trustees concerning the priority of any allotment or distribution of property hereunder shall be final and binding upon all persons interested in my estate, and the determination of my Executors or Trustees as to the value of any such property shall be presumptively correct and shall be final and binding upon all persons in interest, unless clear and convincing proof is adduced showing gross error on the part of my said Executors or Trustees; (d) to consent to and participate in the reorganization, consolidation, merger or other capital readjustment of any corporation, the stocks, bonds or other securities of which they may hold, and to do all things whatsoever necessary, advisable or expedient to enable them to secure the benefits of such reorganization, consolidation, merger or other capital readjustment, including particularly the sale or purchase of any rights incident thereto, and the payment of any amounts necessary. Investments made through the exercise of any such rights, or the proceeds received at the sale thereof, shall be considered principal.

I also further authorize my Executors or Trustees, as the case may be, to vote upon and give proxies to vote upon, any stocks or bonds of corporations that may be owned by me at the time of my death or subsequently acquired by them, upon any question that may lawfully be submitted to the vote of the stockholders or bondholders of such corporation, and in their discretion to subject any such stocks to voting trust agreements, and to accept voting trust certificates in exchange therefor. It is my will and intention that in dealing with the affairs and securities of any corporation in which I shall be interested at the time of my death, either as creditor or stockholder, or with the affairs and securities of any corporation in which my Executors or Trustees, as the case may be, may at any time be interested on behalf of my estate, as creditors or stockholders, my said Executors or Trustees, as the case may be, shall have and may exercise all of the powers that might lawfully be exercised by an individual owning said stock or obligation and acting in his own right and interest.

The Trustees shall be authorized to hold such sum or sums uninvested as they shall see fit.

The Trustees may hold the trust estate or any part thereof as an undivided whole, without separation as between the trusts hereby created, but no such holding shall defer the vesting of any estate in possession, or otherwise, according to the terms hereof.

The Trustees are hereby authorized and empowered to employ such person or persons to assist them in the management and administration of the estate, in an advisory capacity or otherwise, as they shall deem in their sole discretion to be for the best interests of the trust estate and to fix and pay the compensation therefor.

I direct that my Executors and Trustees shall not be required to lay apart any portion of the income or any of the said trust funds for the purpose of keeping the principal thereof intact, or for the purpose of making good any amount paid in premiums on the purchase of securities.

All cash dividends or other cash distributions received from any mining stocks or other wasting investments whether or not of the same kind (notwithstanding such cash dividends or distributions may have been designated or described by the disburser thereof to be in whole or in part a return of capital or a distribution from depletion reserves and whether or not they may be extraordinary dividends or distributions), shall be treated as income without setting apart any portions of such dividends or distributions to maintain intact the principal of any trust fund provided for hereunder. All extraordinary stock dividends and all realized appreciation in the value of stocks, bonds, securities or other property, resulting from the sale or other disposition thereof, shall be considered principal and not income, but ordinary stock dividends paid regularly by a corporation in lieu of, or in addition to regular cash dividends shall be considered income and not principal, PROVIDED, HOWEVER, that the Trustees' determination as to whether any dividend should be apportioned or allocated in whole or in part to principal or income, shall be conclusive and binding upon all persons now or hereafter interested in the trust estate.

I hereby expressly declare that my Executors or Trustees, as the case may be, whichever shall assume to act in the premises, shall have full power to settle and determine all questions which may arise as to my estate, including the power to settle, adjust, compromise or refer to arbitration, any and all claims in favor of or against my estate and to receive and make payment thereof according to such arbitration, settlement, adjustment and compromise, and all the acts of said Executors and/or Trustees in that regard shall be final and conclusive.

I further direct that no bond, undertaking or other security whatsoever, shall be required of my Executors and Trustees, or their successors in any jurisdiction whatsoever, for the discharge of any of their duties hereunder, or for or upon the doing any act which they are empowered to do under or by virtue of the provisions of this my Last Will, or under or by virtue of any law or authority whatsoever.

Except as otherwise herein provided, all of the powers and authority herein conferred, including discretionary power, may be exercised by such of my Executors and Trustees as may qualify, and by the survivor, survivors and successors of them.

The words "income" and "profits" as used in this my Last Will are not intended to include profits realized upon the sale of any of the assets constituting the principal of my estate. Such profits are to be treated as accretions to principal.

In the event that any person named as a legatee under this my Last Will and Testament shall die simultaneously with me, or in or as a result of a common disaster, or in the event that there may be a question as to the survivorship of such person or myself, then for all purposes and intents under this my Last Will and Testament such person shall be deemed to have predeceased me.

TWELFTH: I direct that any Federal or state income tax which may become due from my estate by reason of the profits or accretions which shall accrue to the principal of any trust fund hereunder shall be paid by my Trustees out of the principal of such trust fund and shall not be charged against or paid from the income of any beneficiary of any trust fund under this my Last Will.

THIRTEENTH: I direct that all estate, transfer, succession, inheritance, legacy and similar taxes upon or with respect to so much of my estate as passes by, through or under paragraphs SECOND, THIRD, FOURTH, FIFTH, SIXTH and EIGHTH of this my Last Will, shall be paid out of my residuary estate and there shall be no proration of any such taxes, and I further direct that so much of such estate, transfer, succession, inheritance, legacy and similar taxes as may be assessed against my estate by reason of the inclusion for estate tax purposes of the trust referred to under Paragraph SEVENTH of this my Last Will, or any other assets not passing by, through or under this my Last Will, shall be apportioned to such trust and assets and shall be charged to and paid therefrom.

IN WITNESS WHEREOF, I have hereunto to this, my Last Will and Testament, set my hand and seal this 9th day of August, in the year One Thousand, Nine Hundred and Forty-eight.

George Herman Ruth (L.S.)
In the presence of:
Dorothy Henderson, Herbert P. Polk, F. Van S. Parr, Jr.

SEALED, SUBSCRIBED, PUBLISHED AND DECLARED by the above named Testator, George Herman Ruth, as and for his Last Will and Testament, in the presence of us, and of each of us, who at his request and in his presence and in the presence of each other have hereunto subscribed our names as witnesses the day and year last above written; this clause having first been read to us and we having noted and hereby certifying that the matters herein stated took place in fact and in the order herein stated.

Dorothy Henderson residing at 520A -9th Street Brooklyn, N.Y.
Herbert P. Polk residing at 205 W. 89 Street New York, N.Y.
F. Van S. Parr, Jr. residing at 23 Woodland Way Manhasset, N.Y.

THE LAST WILL AND TESTAMENT OF WILLIAM SHAKESPEARE

"During the winter of 1616, Shakespeare summoned his lawyer Francis Collins, who a decade earlier had drawn up the indentures for the Stratford tithes transaction, to execute his last will and testament. Apparently this event took place in January, for when Collins was called upon to revise the document some weeks later, he (or his clerk) inadvertently wrote January instead of March, copying the word from the earlier draft. Revisions were necessitated by the marriage of [his daughter] Judith . . . The lawyer came on 25 March. A new first page was required, and numerous substitutions and additions in the second and third pages, although it is impossible to say how many changes were made in March and how many *currente calamo,* in January. Collins never got round to having a fair copy of the will made, probably because of haste occasioned by the seriousness of the testators condition, though this attorney had a way of allowing much-corrected draft wills to stand" (@ Schoenbaum 242-6).

Words which were lined-out in the original but which are still legible are indicated by [brackets]. Words which were added interlinearly are indicated by *italic text*. The word "Item" is given in bold text to aid reading and is not so written in the document.

In the name of God Amen I William Shackspeare, of Stratford upon Avon in the countrie of Warr., gent., in perfect health and memorie, God be praysed, doe make and ordayne this my last will and testament in manner and forme followeing, that ys to saye, ffirst, I comend my soule into the hands of God my Creator, hoping and assuredlie beleeving, through thonelie merites, of Jesus Christe my Saviour, to be made partaker of lyfe everlastinge, and my bodye to the earth whereof yt ys made. **Item,** I gyve and bequeath unto my [sonne and] daughter Judyth one hundred and fyftie poundes of lawfull English money, to be paid unto her in the manner and forme foloweng, that ys to saye, one hundred poundes *in discharge of her marriage porcion* within one yeare after my deceas, with consideracion after the rate of twoe shillings in the pound for soe long tyme as the same shalbe unpaied unto her after my deceas, and the fyftie poundes residwe thereof upon her surrendring *of,* or gyving of such sufficient securitie as the overseers of this my will shall like of, to surrender or graunte all her estate and right that shall discend or come unto her after my deceas, or *that shee* nowe hath, of, in, or to, one copiehold tenemente, with thappurtenaunces, lyeing and being in Stratford upon Avon aforesaied in the saied countrye of Warr., being par-cell or holden of the mannour of Rowington, unto my daughter Susanna Hall and her heires for ever. **Item,** I gyve and bequeath unto my saied daughter Judith one hundred and fyftie poundes more, if shee or anie issue of her bodie by lyvinge att thend of three yeares next ensueing the daie of the date of this my will, during which tyme my executours are to paie her consideracion from my deceas according to the rate aforesaied; and if she dye within the saied tearme without issue of her bodye, then my will us, and I doe gyve and bequeath one hundred poundes thereof to my neece Elizabeth Hall, and the fiftie poundes to be sett fourth by my executours during the lief of my sister Johane Harte, and the use and proffitt thereof cominge shalbe payed to my saied sister Jone, and after her deceas the saied l.li. 12 shall remaine amongst the children of my saied sister, equallie to be divided amongst them; but if my saied daughter Judith be lyving att thend of the saied three yeares, or anie yssue of her bodye, then my will ys, and soe I devise and bequeath the saied hundred and fyftie poundes to be sett our *by my executours and overseers* for the best benefitt of her and her issue, and the *stock* not *to be* paied unto her soe long as she shalbe marryed and covert baron [by my executours and overseers]; but my will ys, that she shall have the consideracion yearelie paied unto her during her lief, and, after her ceceas, the saied stocke and consideracion to be paied to her children, if she have anie, and if not, to her executours or assignes, she lyving the saied terme after my deceas. Provided that yf suche husbond as she shall att thend of the saied three years be marryed unto, or att anie after, doe sufficientlie assure unto her and thissue of her bodie landes awnswereable to the porcion by this my will gyven unto her, and to be adjudged soe by my executours and overseers, then my will ys, that the said cl.li. 13 shalbe paied to such husbond as shall make such assurance, to his owne use. **Item,** I gyve and bequeath unto my saied sister Jone xx.li. and all my wearing apparrell, to be paied and delivered within one yeare after my deceas; and I doe will and devise unto her *the house* with thappurtenaunces in Stratford, wherein she dwelleth, for her naturall lief, under the yearlie rent of xij.d. **Item,** I gyve and bequeath unto her three sonnes, William Harte,—Hart, and Michaell Harte, fyve pounds a peece, to be paied within one yeare after my deceas [to be sett out for her within one yeare after my deceas by my executours, with thadvise and direccions of my over-seers, for her best frofitt, untill her mariage, and then the same with the increase thereof to be paied unto her]. **Item,** I gyve and bequeath unto [her] *the saied Elizabeth Hall,* all my plate, *except my brod silver and gilt bole,* that I now have att the date of this my will. **Item,** I gyve and bequeath unto the poore of Stratford aforesaied tenn poundes; to Mr. Thomas Combe my sword; to Thomas Russell esquier fyve poundes; and to Frauncis Collins, of the borough of Warr. in the countie of Warr. gentleman, thirteene poundes, sixe shillinges, and eight pence, to be paied within one yeare after my deceas. **Item,** I gyve and bequeath to [Mr. Richard Tyler thelder] *Hamlett Sadler* xxvj.8. viij.d. to buy him a ringe; to *William Raynoldes gent., xxvj.8. viij.d. to buy him a ringe;* to my dogson William Walker xx8. in gold; to Anthonye Nashe gent. xxvj.8. viij.d. [in gold]; *and to my fellowes John Hemynges, Richard Brubage, and Henry Cundell, xxvj.8. viij.d. a peece to buy them ringes,* **Item,** I gyve, will, bequeath, and devise, unto my daughter Susanna Hall, *for better enabling of her to performe this my will, and towards the perfor-mans thereof,* all that capitall messuage or tenemente with thappurtenaunces, *in Stratford aforesaid,* called the New Place, wherein I nowe dwell, and two messuages or tenementes with thappurtenaunces, scituat, lyeing, and being in Henley streete, within the borough of Stratford aforesaied; and all my barnes, stables, orchardes, gar-dens, landes, tenementes, and hereditamentes, whatsoever, scituat, lyeing, and being, or to be had, receyved, perceyved, or taken, within the townes, hamletes, villages, fieldes, and groundes, of Stratford upon Avon, Oldstratford, Bushopton, and Welcombe, or in anie of them in the saied countie of Warr. And alsoe all that mes-suage or tenemente with thappurtenaunces, wherein one John Robinson dwelleth, scituat, lyeing and being, in the Balckfriers in London, nere the Wardrobe; and all my other landes, tenementes, and hereditamentes whatso-ever, To have and to hold all and singuler the saied premisses, with theire appurtenaunces, unto the saied Susanna Hall, for and during the terme of her naturall lief, and after her deceas, to the first sonne of her bodie lawfullie yssueing, and to the heires males of the bodie of the saied first sonne lawfullie yssueinge; and for defalt of such issue, to the second sonne of her bodie, lawfullie issueing, and to the heires males of the bodie of the saied second sonne lawfullie yssueinge; and for defalt of such heires, to the third sonne of the bodie of the saied Susanna lawfullie yssueinge, and of the heires males of the bodie of the saied third sonne lawfullie yssueing; and for defalt of such issue, the same soe to be and remaine to the ffourth [sonne], ffyfth, sixte, and seaventh sonnes of her bodie lawfullie issueing, one after another, and to the heires males of the bodies of the saied fourth, fifth, sixte, and seaventh sonnes lawfullie yssueing, in such manner as yt ys before lymitted to be and remaine to the first, second, and third sonns of her bodie, and to theire heires males; and for defalt of such issue, the said premisses to be and remaine to my sayed neece Hall, and the heires males of her bodie lawfullie yssueinge; and for defalt of such issue, to my daughter Judith, and the heires males of her bodie lawfullie issueinge; and for defalt of such issue, to the right heires of me the saied William Shackspeare for ever. **Item,** *I gyve unto my wief my second best bed with the furniture.* **Item,** I gyve and bequeath to my saied daughter Judith my broad silver gilt bole. All the rest of my goodes, chattel, leases, plate, jewels, and household stuffe whatsoever, after my dettes and legasies paied, and my funerall expenses dischardged, I give, devise, and bequeath to my sonne in lawe, John Hall gent., and my daughter Susanna, his wief, whom I ordaine and make executours of this my last will and testament. And I doe intreat and appoint *the saied* Thomas Russell esquier and Frauncis Collins gent. to be overseers hereof, and doe revoke all former wills, and publishe this to be my last will and testament. In witness whereof I have hereunto put my [seale] *hand,* the daie and yeare first abovewritten.

Witnes to the publyshing
hereof Fra: Collyns
Julyus Shawe
John Robinson
Hamnet Sadler
Rovert Whattcott

LAST WILL AND TESTAMENT OF FRANCIS ALBERT SINATRA ALSO KNOWN AS FRANK SINATRA

I, FRANCIS ALBERT SINATRA, also known as FRANK SINATRA, declare this to be my Will and revoke all former Wills and Codicils. I am a resident of Riverside County, California.

CLAUSE FIRST: Marital Status and Family

I am married to BARBARA SINATRA, who in this Will is referred to as "my Wife." I was formerly married to NANCY BARBATO SINATRA, to AVA GARDNER SINATRA, and to MIA FARROW SINATRA, and each of said marriages were subsequently dissolved. I have three children, all of whom are the issue of my marriage to NANCY BARBATO SINATRA: NANCY SINATRA LAMBERT, FRANCIS WAYNE SINATRA, and CHRISTINA SINATRA. All of the above-named children are adults. I have never had any other children.

CLAUSE SECOND: Nomination of Executor; Executor's Powers

A. I nominate ELIOT WEISMAN and HARVEY L. SILBERT to act as Co-Executors of this Will. I specifically empower my Co-Executors at any time to designate and appoint any bank or other corporate fiduciary to act as Co-Executor with them, or as Agent on their behalf, and with the further power to change the designation of the said bank or other corporate fiduciary from time to time. If either ELIOT WEISMAN or HARVEY L. SILBERT is unable, unwilling or ceases to act as Co-Executor, I nominate NATHAN S. GOLDEN to act as Co-Executor with the other of them. If two of said three individuals become unable, unwilling or ceases to act as Executor, I nominate CITY NATIONAL BANK, Beverly Hills, California, to act as Co-Executor with the remaining individual, or as sole Executor if all three of said individuals become unable, unwilling, or cease to act hereunder. Whenever the word "Executor" or "Co-Executor" is used in this Will, it shall be deemed to refer to whichever one or more of them is acting from time to time. I direct that no bond shall be required of any Executor or Co-Executor as a condition to qualifying to serve hereunder, whether acting jointly or alone.

B. I authorize my Executor to sell, lease, mortgage or encumber the whole or any part of my estate, with or without notice; to transfer registered securities into street name or to hold them in the name of a nominee, without any liability on the part of my Executor; and at the option and sole discretion of my Executor, to continue to hold, manage and operate any property, business or enterprise that may be an asset of my estate from time to time, whether in corporate, partnership (limited or general) or other form, and whether or not such asset is one in which my Executor is personally interested, the profits or losses therefrom to inure to or be charged against my estate and not my Executor. My Executor shall have absolute discretion as to how much cash, if any, to invest at interest.

C. I authorize my Executor to invest and reinvest funds of my estate, including surplus moneys and the proceeds from the sale of any assets of my estate, in every kind of property, specifically including, but not by way of limitation, corporate or governmental obligations of every kind, securities of any regulated investment trust, and stocks, preferred or common and any common trust fund administered by any corporate fiduciary under this Will.

D. It is my intention that my Executor be permitted to take advantage of all tax savings that the law of any jurisdiction allows, without regard to conflicting interests of those interested in my estate and without making any adjustments among such persons. To that end, I authorize my Executor, in my Executor's absolute discretion, to take any one or more of the following actions as may appear advisable:
1. To join with my Wife in executing joint income tax returns;
2. To value my gross estate for federal estate tax purposes as of the date of my death or as of the alternative valuation date as allowed for such purposes;
3. To claim as estate or inheritance tax deductions, or both, expenses which would otherwise qualify as income tax deductions;
4. To elect to have gifts by my Wife treated as made one-half by me for federal gift tax purposes; and
5. To make any other elections allowed by the Internal Revenue Code or the tax law of applicable jurisdiction.

E. If at my death I hold any stock purchase warrants, stock subscription or conversion rights, or rights under any stock option plan, I authorize my Executor to exercise any or all of those warrants and rights if my Executor, in my Executor's discretion, deems such exercise to be in the best interests of my estate and the beneficiaries thereof, and to borrow money for that purpose if my Executor, in my Executor's discretion, deems it advisable.

F. I authorize my Executor to administer my estate under The California Independent Administration of Estates Act.

G. Upon any preliminary or final distribution of the residue of my estate, my Executor may distribute the residue in undivided interests or in kind, or in money, or partly in any of them at such valuations and according to such method or procedure as my Executor shall determine, including the power to distribute all or part of any particular asset to any beneficiary as my Executor shall determine.

H. All decisions of my Executor made in good faith shall be binding and conclusive on all persons interested in my estate, but shall be subject to such confirmation or Court authority as is required by law.

CLAUSE THIRD: Amount Of Property Disposed Of

I intend that my Will shall govern the disposition of all property wherever situated that I have the power to will at the time of my death, including both my separate property and my one-half interest in such community property as my Wife and I may own at the time of my death.

CLAUSE FOURTH: Payment Of Debts and Taxes

I direct my Executor to pay in full any and all lawful debts which may be owing by me at the time of my death, both secured and unsecured, and regardless of when they might otherwise be due and payable, in the following order of priority and from the following sources:

1 My Executor shall first pay and discharge in full from our community assets, including my Wife's share thereof to the full extent her share is liable for such debts and to the full extent of such community property, any and all debts chargeable to the community estate of myself and my Wife, other than payments in satisfaction of any promissory notes secured by mortgages and/or trust deeds which are a lien on the Rancho Mirage residential real property owned by us.

2 My Executor shall next pay and discharge in full from my share of our community property the full amount of any promissory notes secured by mortgages and/or trust deeds which are a lien on the Rancho Mirage residential real property owned by us, and regardless of whether said real property is owned by us as joint tenants with the right of survivorship, as community property, or as my sole and separate property. If my share of our community property is insufficient to pay said debt in full after payment of our unsecured debts, then any shortfall in payment of this secured debt shall be paid from my separate property. No other debts secured by residential real property in which I have an interest shall be paid in full as a result of my death.

3 I direct that all estate, inheritance or other death taxes occasioned or payable by reason of my death, whether related to the bequests set forth in this will, and whether attributable to property subject to probate administration or not, and all of the expenses of administration of my estate, including but not limited to executor commissions, attorneys fees, court, publication and filing fees, and funeral expenses and expenses of my last illness, if any, shall next be paid from my share of our community property, to the full extent remaining after payment of the debts described in subparagraphs 1 and 2 above. If my share of our community property is insufficient to pay said taxes and expenses, they shall be paid from the residue of my separate property.

CLAUSE FIFTH: Specific Bequests

I make the following specific bequests from my share of our community property to the extent such remains after payment in full of the items described in CLAUSE FOURTH above, and if my share of our community property shall be insufficient to satisfy these bequests, from my separate property:

A. To my former Wife, NANCY BARBATO SINATRA, if she survives me, the sum of Two Hundred Fifty Thousand Dollars ($250,000). If NANCY BARBATO SINATRA does not survive me, this gift shall lapse and shall be considered as part of the residue of my estate.

B. To DOROTHY IJHLEMANN (SIC) of North Hollywood, California, if she survives me, the sum of Fifty Thousand Dollars ($50,000). If DOROTH UHI~EMANN (SIC) does not survive me, this gift shall lapse and shall be considered as part of the residue of my estate.

C. To ELVINA JOUBERT of Rancho Mirage, California, if she survives me, the sum Fifty Thousand Dollars ($50,000). If ELVINA JOUBERT does not survive me, this gift shall lapse and shall be considered as part of the residue of my estate.

D. To JILLY RIZZO, if he survives me, the sum of One Hundred Thousand Dollars ($100,000). If JILLY RIZZO does not survive me, this gift shall lapse and shall be considered as part of the residue of my estate.

E. To my Wife's Son, ROBERT OLIVER MARX, if he survives me, the sum of One Hundred Thousand Dollars ($100,000). If ROBERT OLIVER MARX does not survive me, this gift shall lapse and shall be considered as part of the residue of my estate.

F. To my daughter, CHRISTINA SINATRA, if she survives me, the sum of Two Hundred Thousand Dollars ($200,000). If CHRISTINA SINATRA does not survive me, this gift shall lapse and shall be considered as part of the residue of my estate.

G. To my son, FRANCIS WAYNE SINATRA, if he survives me, the sum of Two Hundred Thousand Dollars ($200,000). If FRANCIS WAYNE SINATRA does not survive me, this gift shall lapse and shall be considered as part of the residue of my estate.

H. To my daughter, NANCY SINATRA LAMBERT, if she survives me, the sum of Two Hundred Thousand Dollars ($200,000). If NANCY SINATRA LAMBERT does not survive me, this gift shall lapse and shall be considered as part of the residue of my estate.

I. To the Trustees of that certain Trust established by me and my former Wife, NANCY BARBATO SINATRA, by Trust Agreement dated December 13, 1983, for the benefit of the children of NANCY SINATRA LAMBERT, the sum of One Million Dollars ($1,000,000), to be added to the assets of said trust and allocated equally between the separate trusts being administered there under for the benefit of my two grandchildren, ANGELA JENIFER LAMBERT and AMANDA KATHERINE LAMBERT.

J. To my Wife, BARBARA SINATRA, provided that we are married and living together at the time of my death, all of my rights as licensor pursuant to that certain License Agreement dated February 29, 1988 with Sheffield Enterprises, Inc., including my twenty-five percent (25%) royalty thereunder, or in the alternative such shares of Capital Stock of Sheffield Enterprises, Inc. as I may have acquired during my lifetime in exchange for said rights. If my Wife does not survive me or we are not married and living together at the time of my death, this gift shall lapse and shall be considered as part of the residue of my estate.

K. To my Wife, BARBARA SINATRA, provided that we are married and living together at the time of my death, my interest in that certain Master Recording entitled "Trilogy," and all rights to royalties and future distribution related there to. If my Wife does not survive me or we are not married and living together at the time of my death, this gift shall lapse and shall be considered as part of the residue of my estate.

L. I give to my children, in undivided interests as tenants in common, upon the principle of representation, my community interest in that certain partnership known as Wilshire—Camden Associates, in which I am a limited partner.

M. I hereby forgive any and all loans or indebtedness which may exist at the time of my death, whether in writing or otherwise, which may be owed to me by any of my children.

CLAUSE SIXTH: Confirmation Of Separate and Joint Tenancy Assets

A. I confirm to my Wife, if she survives me, my interest in the real property situated in Riverside County, California, and commonly known as 70-588 Frank Sinatra Drive, Rancho Mirage, California, including all adjacent guest houses on the grounds thereof, commonly known as 70-200, 70-548, and 70-630 Frank Sinatra Drive, Rancho Mirage, California, which property is held of record by my Wife and I as joint tenants with the right of survivorship.

B. I confirm to my Wife, if she survives me, my interest in the real property situated in Los Angeles County, California, and commonly known as 915 Foothill Road, Beverly Hills, California 90210, which property is held of record by my Wife and I as joint tenants with the right of survivorship.

C. I confirm to my Wife, if she survives me, my interest in the real property situated in Riverside County, California, and commonly known as 1130 Starlight Lane, Rancho Mirage, California, which property is held of record by my Wife and I as joint tenants with the right of survivorship.

D. I confirm to my Wife as her sole and separate property the parcel of real property situated in Riverside County, California, and commonly known as 36928 Pinto Palm Drive, Cathedral City, California.

E. I confirm to my Wife, if she survives me, my interest in the real property situated in Los Angeles County, California, and commonly known as 30966 Broad Beach Road, Malibu, California 90265, subject to all existing encumbrances. If said parcel of real property is not held of record by my Wife and I as joint tenants with the right of survivorship on the date of my death, I give my interest in the said parcel of real property to my Wife, if she survives me and if we are married and living together at the time of my death, and in such event, if my Wife fails to survive me, or we are not married and living together at the time of my death, the above-described real property shall be considered as part of the residue of my estate.

CLAUSE SEVENTH: Gifts Of Tangible Personal Property

A. I give to my Wife, if she survives me, and we are married and living together at the time of my death, all of the silverware, books, displayed paintings, and household furniture and furnishings located in the homes described in CLAUSE SIXTH above, and my interest in any policies of insurance covering the foregoing items of personal property. If my Wife fails to survive me or we are not married and living together at the time of my death, the above-described personal property and any policies of insurance covering such personal property shall be considered as part of the residue of my estate.

B. I give all of my jewelry, art objects, clothing, household furniture and furnishings, personal automobiles (except the 1988 Rolls Royce and the 1990 Mercedes which are the separate property of my Wife), train collections, music and recording collections, memorabilia and other tangible articles of a personal nature, and my interest in any such property not otherwise specifically disposed of by this Will or in any other manner, together with any insurance on such property existing at the time of my death, in the following manner;

1. My Executor shall first return to any child of mine any of such items which said child may have given to me;
2. My Executor shall then honor such written contractual commitments, if any, which I may have entered into during my lifetime for delivery of such items of personal property at my death;
3. I give all of my sheet music to my son, FRANK WAYNE SINATRA;
4. Thereafter each of my Wife, if she survives me and we are married and living together at the time of my death, and each of my children who survive me may designate to my Executor any of the aforementioned items of property which that beneficiary [SIC] desirous of receiving. My Executor shall have all such objects appraised in the manner he deems appropriate, and the appraised value shall be allocated to the requesting beneficiary. My Wife shall be entitled to receive up to a maximum of twenty-five percent (25%) of the total aggregate value of such property, and my children shall be entitled to receive the remaining maximum aggregate value of seventy five percent (75%) of such property, with each of my three children being entitled to receive a maximum of one-third of said remainder, or twenty-five percent (25%) of the total aggregate value of the whole of said property, upon the principle of representation. If my Wife should fail to survive me or we are not married and living together at the time of my death all of said property shall be divided amongst my children. If none of my children or their issue survive me, such property shall be considered as part of the residue of my estate. Notwithstanding the foregoing, my Executor shall have the authority, in my Executor sole and absolute discretion, to distribute any of my personal items and memorabilia to such of my friends and my employees as he may deem appropriate.

C. I give to my Wife, if she survives me and we are married and living together on the date of my death, from my share of our community property remaining after the payment and distribution of all amounts and specific bequests hereinabove in this Will set forth, such additional assets, valued at the date of my death, as equals the total sum of Three Million Five Hundred Thousand Dollars ($3,500,000); provided, however, that if my share of our community property remaining after the payment and distribution of all amounts and specific bequests herein in this Will set forth, is insufficient to provide my Wife with said total sum of Three Million Five Hundred Thousand Dollars ($3,500,000), I give my Wife all of my then remaining community property; provided, further, if my Wife fails to survive me, or we are not married and living together on the date of my death, this gift shall lapse and shall be considered a part of the residue of my estate.

CLAUSE EIGHTH: Power Of Appointment

I hold a limited power of appointment conferred upon me by the Somerset Trust established by that certain declaration of trust dated January 1, 1989 in which I am the Trustor, which power is given me pursuant to numbered paragraph 5 on page 8 of said declaration of trust. I hereby exercise said power of appointment by appointing and giving all assets subject to it in equal shares to CHRISTINA SINATRA, FRANK WAYNE SINATRA, and NANCY SINATRA LAMBERT, or the issue of any of them who do not survive me, according to the principle of representation, and if any of them should predecease me leaving no issue, to the survivors of them.

CLAUSE NINTH: Gift Of Residue

A. I give the residue of my community property estate and all of my separate property remaining after giving effect to the foregoing provisions of this Will, in equal shares to CHRISTINA SINATRA, FRANK WAYNE SINATRA, and NANCY SINATRA LAMBERT, or the issue of any of them who survive me, according to the principle of representation, and if any of them should predecease me leaving no issue, to the survivors of them.

B. If none of my issue survive me, I give the residue of my estate to my heirs, according to the laws of succession of the State of California in force at the date of this Will.

CLAUSE TENTH: No Contest Clause

A. If any devisee, legatee or beneficiary under this Will, or any legal heir of mine or person claiming under any of them directly or indirectly engages in any of the following conduct, then in that event I specifically disinherit each such person, and all such legacies, bequests, devises and interests given under this Will or any trust created by me at any time to that person shall be forfeited as though he or she had predeceased me without issue, and shall augment proportionately the shares of my estate going under this Will to, or in trust for, such of my devisees, legatees and beneficiaries who have not participated in such acts or proceedings:

1. contests this Will or, in any manner, attacks or seeks to impair or invalidate any of its provisions;
2. claims entitlement to any asset of my estate by way of any written or oral contract (whether or not such claim is successful);
3. unsuccessfully challenges the appointment of any person named as an executor or a trustee,
4. objects in any manner to any action taken or proposed to be taken in good faith by my Executor, whether my Executor is acting under court order, notice of proposed action or otherwise, whether such objection is successful or not;
5. objects to any construction or interpretation of my Will, or any provision of it, that is adopted or proposed in good faith by my Executor;
6. unsuccessfully seeks the removal of any person acting as an executor;
7. files any creditor's claim in my estate that is based upon a claim arising prior to the date of this Will (without regard to its validity);
8. claims an interest in any property alleged by executor to belong to my estate (whether or not such claim is successful);
9. challenges the characterization proposed by my Executor of any property as to whether it is separate or community (without regard to the ultimate resolution of the merits of such challenge);
10. challenges the position taken by my Executor as to the validity or construction of any written agreement entered into by me during my lifetime;
11. attacks or seeks to impair or invalidate any of the following:
    a. any designation of beneficiaries for any insurance policy on my life;
    b. any designation of beneficiaries for any pension plan or IRA account;
    c. any trust which I created or may create during my lifetime or any provision thereof;
    d. any gift which I have made or will make during my lifetime;
    e. any transaction by which I have sold any asset to any child or children of mine (whether or not any such attack or attempt is successful);
12. conspires with or voluntarily assists anyone attempting to do any of these things; or
13. refuses a request of my Executor to assist in the defense against any of the foregoing acts or proceedings.

B. Further, if any of my Wife's issue or my grandchildren do any of the things referred to in this CLAUSE TENTH, then any legacy, bequest, device or other interest which would otherwise pass to my Wife or the parents of my grandchildren who so act, as the case may be shall likewise be forfeited, and such forfeiting legatees shall be deemed to have predeceased me without issue.

C. Expenses to resist any contest or other attack of any nature upon any provision of this Will shall be paid from my estate as expenses of administration.

D. In the event that any provision of this CLAUSE TENTH, including any of the provisions of the subparagraphs of paragraph A hereof, is held to be invalid, void or illegal, the same shall be deemed severable from the remainder of the provisions in this CLAUSE TENTH and shall in no way affect, impair or invalidate any other provision in this CLAUSE TENTH. If such provision shall be deemed invalid due to its scope and breadth, such provision shall be deemed valid to the extent of the scope or breadth permitted by law.

CLAUSE ELEVENTH: Conflicts of Interest; Exculpation

The following provisions shall be applicable to any Executor or Co-Executor under this will (hereafter "fiduciary"):

A. Any fiduciary, or any firm with which a fiduciary is affiliated, that performs services in connection with the regular operations of any business, partnership, firm or corporation in which my estate is financially interested may be compensated for services independently of compensation for services as a fiduciary hereunder.

B. The general rule of law whereby actions, decisions, or transactions are held to be void or voidable if a fiduciary is directly or indirectly interested therein in a non-fiduciary capacity shall not be applicable to transactions between my estate and any business entity in which the individual fiduciary is involved. I recognize that the dual role of my fiduciary may result in situations involving conflicts of interest or selfdealing, and it is my express intent that my fiduciary shall not be liable as aforesaid, except in the event of his own bad faith or gross negligence. Notwithstanding the foregoing, all such transactions shall be fair and reasonable. The fiduciary's power hereunder shall be exercised in good faith for the benefit of my estate and in accordance with the usual fiduciary obligations, except that the rule against self-dealing shall not be applicable as provided in this paragraph.

C. A fiduciary who is an attorney, accountant, investment advisor or other professional shall not be disqualified from rendering professional services to my estate and from being compensated on a reasonable basis therefor in addition to any compensation which he or she is otherwise entitled to receive as fiduciary; neither shall a firm with which a fiduciary is associated be disqualified from dealing with, rendering services to or discharging duties for my estate and from being compensated therefor on a reasonable basis.

D. No fiduciary under this Will shall be liable to any person interested in my estate for any act or default of that fiduciary or of any other fiduciary or any other person, unless resulting from that fiduciary's own bad faith or gross negligence.

CLAUSE TWELFTH:

If on the date of the order of distribution of any of my property, the leqatee thereof is a minor, such property may, in my Executor's discretion, be delivered to a custodian chosen by my Executor to be held by such custodian for such minor under the California Uniform Transfers To Minors Act. At the time of such delivery, my Executor may also designate one or more successor custodians to act if such custodian becomes unable, unwilling or ceases to so act, and my Executor may specify whether or not any such custodian or successor custodian shall be required to post bond.

CLAUSE THIRTEENTH: Intepretation of This Will

A. As used in this Will, the terms "child," "children," "grandchild," "grandchildren," and "issue" shall include only children born in wedlock and lawfully adopted children and issue of such children.

B. As used in this Will, and to the extent appropriate, the masculine, feminine and neuter gender shall include the other two genders, the singular shall include the plural, and the plural shall include the singular.

C. If there is no sufficient evidence that my Wife and I died otherwise than simultaneously, it shall be presumed, for the purposes of this Will, that my Wife died before me.

D. For the purposes of this Will, any beneficiary who dies within thirty (30) days after my death shall be deemed to have died before me.

E. No interest shall be paid on any gift, legacy or right to income under this Will or any Codicil to it.

F. The Table of Contents and the headings used herein are solely for the purpose of setting forth the organizational outline of this Will and are not to be considered provisions hereof.

G. If any provision of this Will shall be invalid or unenforceable, the remaining provisions hereof shall subsist and be carried into effect.

H. Except as otherwise specifically provided, the validity and construction of this Will and all rights hereunder shall be governed by the laws of the State of California.

SIGNED at, California, on, 1991.
FRANCIS ALBERT SINATRA
also known as FRANK SINATRA

LAST WILL AND TESTAMENT OF JOHN LENNON

LAST WILL AND TESTAMENT OF JOHN WINSTON ONO LENNON

I, JOHN WINSTON ONO LENNON, a resident of the County of New York, State of New York, which I declare to be my domicile do hereby make, publish and declare this to be my Last Will and Testament, hereby revoking all other Wills, Codicils and Testamentary dispositions by me at any time heretofore made.

FIRST: The expenses of my funeral and the administration of my estate, and all inheritance, estate or succession taxes, including interest and penalties, payable by reason of my death shall be paid out of and charged generally against the principal of my residuary estate without apportionment or proration. My Executor shall not seek contribution or reimbursement for any such payments.

SECOND: Should my wife survive me, I give, devise and bequeath to her absolutely, an amount equal to that portion of my residuary estate, the numerator and denominator of which shall be determined as follows:

1 The numerator shall be an amount equal to one-half (1/2) of my adjusted gross estate less the value of all other property included in my gross estate for Federal Estate Tax purposes and which pass or shall have passed to my wife either under any other provision of this Will or in any manner outside of this Will in such manner as to qualify for and be allowed as a marital deduction. The words "pass", "have passed", "marital deduction" and adjusted gross estate" shall have the same meaning as said words have under those provisions of the Untied States Internal Revenue Code applicable to my estate.

2 The denominator shall be an amount representing the value of my residuary estate.

THIRD: I give, devise and bequeath all the rest, residue and remainder of my estate, wheresoever situate, to the Trustees under a Trust Agreement dated November 12, 1979, which I signed with my wife YOKO ONO, and ELI GARBER as Trustees, to be added to the trust property and held and distributed in accordance with the terms of that agreement and any amendments made pursuant to its terms before my death.

FOURTH: In the event that my wife and I die under such circumstances that there is not sufficient evidence to determine which of us has predeceased the other, I hereby declare it to be my will that it shall be deemed that I shall have predeceased her and that this, my Will, and any and all of its provisions shall be construed based upon that assumption.

FIFTH: I hereby nominate, constitute and appoint my beloved wife, YOKO ONO, to act as the Executor of this my Last Will and Testament. In the event that my beloved wife YOKO ONO shall predecease me or chooses not to act for any reason, I nominate and appoint ELI GARBER, DAVID WARMFLASH and CHARLES PETTIT, in the order named, to act in her place and stead.

SIXTH: I nominate, constitute and appoint my wife YOKO ONO, as the Guardian of the person and property of any children of the marriage who may survive me. In the event that she predeceases me, or for any reason she chooses not to act in that capacity, I nominate, constitute and appoint SAM GREEN to act in her place and stead.

SEVENTH: No person named herein to serve in any fiduciary capacity shall be required to file or post any bond for the faithful performance of his or her duties, in that capacity in this or in any other jurisdiction, any law to the contrary notwithstanding.

EIGHTH: If any legatee or beneficiary under this will or the trust agreement between myself as Grantor and YOKO ONO LENNON and ELI GARBER as Trustees, dated November 12, 1979 shall interpose objections to the probate of this Will, or institute or prosecute or be in any way interested or instrumental in the institution or prosecution of any action or proceeding for the purpose of setting aside or invalidating this Will, then and in each such case, I direct that such legatee or beneficiary shall receive nothing whatsoever under this Will or the aforementioned Trust.

IN WITNESS WHEREOF, I have subscribed and sealed and do publish and declare these presents as and for my Last Will and Testament, this 12th day of November, 1979.

John Winston Ono Lennon

THE FOREGOING INSTRUMENT consisting of four (4) typewritten pages, including this page, was on the 12th day of November, 1979, signed, sealed, published and declared by JOHN WINSTON ONO LENNON, the Testator therein named, as and for his Last Will and Testament, in the present of us, who at his request, and in his presence, and in the presence of each other, have hereunto set our names as witnesses.

(The names of the three witnesses are illegible.)

LAST WILL AND TESTAMENT OF JOHN F. KENNEDY, JR.

I, JOHN F. KENNEDY, JR., of New York, New York, make this my last will, hereby revoking all earlier wills and codicils. I do not by this will exercise any power of appointment.

FIRST: I give all my tangible property (as distinguished from money, securities and the like), wherever located, other than my scrimshaw set previously owned by my father, to my wife, Carolyn Bessette-Kennedy, if she is living on the thirtieth day after my death, or if not, by right of representation to my then living issue, or if none, by right of representation to the then living issue of my sister, Caroline Kennedy Schlossberg, or if none, to my said sister, Caroline, if she is then living. If I am survived by issue, I leave this scrimshaw set to said wife, Carolyn, if she is then living, or if not, by right of representation, to my then living issue. If I am not survived by issue, I give said scrimshaw set to my nephew John B.K. Schlossberg, if he is then living, or if not, by right of representation to the then living issue of my said sister, Caroline, or if none, to my said sister Caroline, if she is then living. Hope that whoever receives my tangible personal property will dispose of certain items of it in accordance with my wishes, however made unknown, but I impose no trust, condition or enforceable obligation of any kind in this regard.

SECOND: I give and devise all my interest in my cooperative apartment located at 20-26 Moore Street, Apartment 9E, in said New York, including all my shares therein and any proprietary leases with respect thereto, to my said wife, Carolyn, if she is living on the thirtieth day after my death.

THIRD: If no issue of mine survive me, I give and devise all my interests in real estate, wherever located, that I own as tenants in common with my said sister, Caroline, or as tenants in common with any of her issue, by right of representation to Caroline's issue who are living on the thirtieth day after my death, or if none, to my said sister Caroline, if she is then living. References in this Article THIRD to "real estate" include shares in cooperative apartments and proprietary leases with respect thereto.

FOURTH: I give and devise the residue of all the property, of whatever kind and wherever located, that I own at my death to the then trustees of the John F. Kennedy Jr. 1983 Trust established October 13, 1983 by me, as Donor, of which John T. Fallon, of Weston, Massachusetts, and I are currently the trustees (the "1983 Trust"), to be added to the principal of the 1983 Trust and administered in accordance with the provisions thereof, as amended by a First Amendment dated April 9, 1987 and by a Second Amendment and Complete Restatement dated earlier this day, and as from time to hereafter further amended whether before or after my death. I have provided in the 1983 Trust for my children and more remote issue and for the method of paying all federal and state taxes in the nature of estate, inheritance, succession and like taxes occasioned by my death.

FIFTH: I appoint my wife, Carolyn Bessette-Kennedy, as guardian of each child of our marriage during minority. No guardian appointed in this will or a codicil need furnish any surety on any official bond.

SIXTH: I name my cousin Anthony Stanislaus Radziwill as my executor; and if for any reason, he fails to qualify or ceases to serve in that capacity, I name my cousin Timothy P. Shriver as my executor in his place. References in this will or a codicil to my "executor" mean the one or more executors (or administrators with this will annexed) for the time being in office. No executor or a codicil need furnish any surety on any official bond. In any proceeding for the allowance of an account of my executor, I request the Court to dispense with the appointment of a guardian ad litem to represent any person or interest. I direct that in any proceeding relating to my estate, service of process upon any person under a disability shall not made when another person not under a disability is a party to the proceeding and has the same interest as the person under the disability.

SEVENTH: In addition to other powers, my executor shall have power from time to time at discretion and without license of court: To retain, and to invest and reinvest in, any kind or amount of property; to vote and exercise other rights of security holders; to make such elections for federal and state estate, gift, income and generation-skipping transfer tax purposes as my executor may deem advisable; to compromise or admit to arbitration any matters in dispute; to borrow money, and to sell, mortgage, pledge, exchange, lease and contract with respect to any real or personal property, all without notice to any beneficiary and in such manner, for such consideration and on such terms as to credit or otherwise as my executor may deem advisable, whether or not the effect thereof extends beyond the period settling my estate; and in distributing my estate, to allot property, whether real or personal, at then current values, in lieu of cash.

LAST WILL AND TESTAMENT OF WHITNEY E. HOUSTON

I, WHITNEY E. HOUSTON, residing in the State of New Jersey, declare this to be my Last Will and Testament and revoke all my prior wills and codicils.

FIRST: I direct that my funeral and cemetery expenses, the expenses of my last illness, all expenses of administration of my estate and all my debts (except mortgage indebtedness and indebtedness secured by any life insurance policy or otherwise secured) that are just and not barred by time be paid by my Executors from my residuary estate.

SECOND:

A. I give my entire interest in all my household furniture and furnishings and other articles of household use or ornament located at any real estate used by me on a full or part-time basis for my residential purposes, together with all my clothing, personal effects, jewelry, and automobiles, and all insurance policies thereon, if any (hereinafter referred to as my "tangible personal property"), to any children of mine who survive me, in such portions as my Executors, in their sole discretion may deem advisable, or sell the same, or any balance thereof, and add the proceeds to my residuary estate.

B. If no child of mine survives me:

(1) I give all jewelry I own at my death to my mother, EMILY CISSY HOUSTON, if she survives me; and

(2) I give the rest of my tangible personal property (or all of my tangible personal property if my mother does not survive me) to those of my mother, EMILY CISSY HOUSTON, my father, JOHN R. HOUSTON, my husband, ROBERT B. BROWN, my brother, MICHAEL HOUSTON, and my brother, GARY HOUSTON, as survive me, to be amicably divided among them as they might agree, in shares as nearly equal as possible.

If my mother, my father, my husband and my said brothers cannot agree on the distribution of any property which would otherwise be distributed to them under this Article SECOND, I direct that such property be sold and the proceeds be added to my residuary estate.

THIRD: The balance of my estate, whether real or personal and wherever situate (referred to as my "residuary estate") shall be disposed of as follows:

A. If any issue of mine survive me, my residuary estate shall be paid to my issue living at my death, per stirpes; provided that any part of my residuary estate passing to a child or more remote descendant of mine who is younger than thirty (30) years of age at my death shall not be paid to him or her outright, but rather I give the same to my Trustees to hold in a separate trust for his or her benefit pursuant to Article FOURTH.

B. If I leave no issue at my death, my residuary estate shall be paid, in equal shares, to those of my mother, EMILY CISSY HOUSTON, my father, JOHN R. HOUSTON, my husband, ROBERT B. BROWN, my brother, MICHAEL HOUSTON, and my brother, GARY HOUSTON, who survive me; provided, however, that as to each of my said brothers (regardless of his age), his share of my residuary estate shall not be paid to him outright, but rather the same shall be paid to my Trustees to hold in a separate trust for the benefit of such brother pursuant to Article FIFTH.

FOURTH: The following are the terms of the separate trusts for the respective benefit of any child or more remote descendant of mine who is younger than thirty (30) years of age, each of whom is hereinafter referred to as the "Beneficiary" of his or her separate trust:

A. My Trustees may, at any time or from time to time, pay to the Beneficiary, or apply for his or her benefit, upon such occasions as my Trustees in their sole discretion shall deem advisable, so much or all (or none) of the entire net income and so much or all (or none) of the principal of the separate trust held for the Beneficiary as my Trustees may deem desirable. At the end of each trust year, my Trustees shall add to the principal of such separate trust any net income not so paid or applied and thereafter the same shall be dealt with as principal for all purposes. Without limiting my Trustees as to occasions upon which payments may be made and without requiring them to make any payment if they deem it inadvisable, I suggest that purposes for which distributions of income and principal might be made include maintenance, educational requirements, engagement, marriage, acquisition of a home, birth of a child, commencement of a new business enterprise or continuance of an existing one, and medical requirements. In granting discretion to my Trustees to make such payments, it is my desire that such discretion be liberally exercised when the occasion, whether one previously specified or not, is such that the interests of the Beneficiary would, in my Trustees' judgment, be best served thereby.

B. My Trustees shall make the following distributions of principal to the Beneficiary from his or her separate trust:

(1) One-tenth (1/10) of the then principal when the Beneficiary reaches the age of twenty-one (21) years;

(2) One-sixth (1/6) of the then principal when the Beneficiary reaches the age of twenty-five (25) years; and

(3) The entire remaining principal, together with all accrued and undistributed income, when the Beneficiary reaches the age of thirty (30) years, whereupon the separate trust held for the Beneficiary shall terminate; provided that if the Beneficiary is at least twenty-one (21) years of age at the time the separate trust is set aside for his or her benefit, one-tenth (1/10) of such separate trust shall then be paid to him or her in lieu of the payment specified in subparagraph "(1)" above; and provided

further that if the Beneficiary is at least twenty-five (25) years old at the time the separate trust is set aside for his or her benefit, one-fourth (1/4) of such separate trust shall then be paid to him or her in lieu of the payments specified in subparagraphs "(1)" and "(2)" above.

C. If the Beneficiary dies before reaching the age of thirty (30) years, the separate trust held for him or her shall terminate and my Trustees shall pay the remaining principal, together with all accrued and undistributed income, to my issue then living, per stirpes; provided, however, that any property payable to a child or more remote descendant of mine who is younger than thirty (30) years of age at the Beneficiary's death shall not be paid to him or her outright, but rather the same shall be paid to my Trustees to hold in a separate trust for his or her benefit pursuant to this Article FOURTH; and provided further that all property payable pursuant to this paragraph to a person who is the Beneficiary of a trust under this Will which is then in existence shall, irrespective of the age of such person, be added in its entirety to the principal thereof to be administered therewith and shall not be paid to him or her outright.

D. If there be no issue of mine living at the Beneficiary's death, such property shall be paid, in equal shares, to those of my mother, EMILY CISSY HOUSTON, my father, JOHN R. HOUSTON, my husband, ROBERT B. BROWN, my brother, MICHAEL HOUSTON, and my brother, GARY HOUSTON, who survive the Beneficiary; provided, however, that as to each of my said brothers (regardless of his age), his share of such property shall not be paid to him outright, but rather the same shall be paid to my Trustees to hold in a separate trust for the benefit of such brother pursuant to Article FIFTH.

E. Notwithstanding any contrary provision in this Will, the separate trust held for the Beneficiary shall terminate, to the extent that it shall not have previously terminated, twenty-one (21) years after the death of the last survivor of my father, JOHN R. HOUSTON, as were living at the date of my death. Upon the termination of such separate trust pursuant to this provision, my Trustees shall pay the entire then principal, together with all accrued and undistributed income, to the Beneficiary thereof.

FIFTH: The following are the terms of the separate trusts for the benefit of each of my brothers, MICHAEL HOUSTON and GARY HOUSTON (each of whom shall be referred to in this Article as the "Beneficiary" of his separate trust).

A. My Trustees may, at any time or from time to time, pay to the Beneficiary, or apply for his benefit, upon such occasions as my Trustees, in their sole discretion shall deem advisable, so much or all (or none) of the net income and so much or all (or none) of the principal of the separate trust held for the Beneficiary as my Trustees may deem desirable. At the end of each trust year, my Trustees shall add to the principal of such separate trust any net income not so paid or applied and thereafter the same shall be dealt with as principal for all purposes. Without limiting my Trustees as to occasions upon which payments may be made and without requiring them to make any payment if they deem it inadvisable, I suggest that purposes for which distributions of income and principal might be made include maintenance, support, care, engagement, marriage, acquisition of a home, birth of a child, commencement of a new business enterprises or continuance of an existing one, medical requirements and vacations. In granting discretion to my Trustees to make such payments of income and principal, it is my desire that such discretion be liberally exercised when the occasion, whether one previously specified or not, is such that the interests of the Beneficiary would, in the judgment of my Trustees, be best served thereby, and that the interests of remaindermen in the principal of the trust shall be disregarded in connection therewith.

B. Upon the Beneficiary's death, the separate trust held for the Beneficiary shall terminate and my Trustees shall pay the remaining principal, together with all accrued and undistributed income, to the same persons, and in the same proportions, as would have inherited such property from me had I then died intestate, the absolute owner thereof, and a resident of the State of New Jersey; provided, however, that notwithstanding the foregoing, under no circumstances shall any part of my estate or the property held in trust under this Will be paid to JOHN R. HOUSTON III.

SIXTH:

A. No assignment, disposition, charge or encumbrance of the income or principal of any trust created herein for the benefit of any beneficiary, or any part thereof, by way of anticipation, alienation or otherwise, shall be valid or in any way binding upon my Trustees and I direct that no beneficiary may assign, transfer, encumber of otherwise dispose of such income or principal, or any part thereof, until the same shall be paid to him or her by my Trustees. No income or principal or any part thereof shall be liable to any claim of any creditor of any beneficiary.

B. If any beneficiary of this Will dies within thirty (30) days after the date of my death or after the date of death of any other person upon whose death such beneficiary would, but for this paragraph, become entitled to receive either income or principal under this Will, then I direct that for the purposes of this Will, such beneficiary shall be deemed to have predeceased me or such other person, as the case may be.

C. Whenever used in this Will, the word "issue" shall include, for all purposes, persons attaining that status by formal adoption, it being my intention to expressly include any extension of the line of descent by means of adoption.

SEVENTH: Distribution of any property under this Will to a person who is a minor or who is under some other legal disability may be made by my Executors and Trustees directly to such person or to any one with whom such person resides or, in the sole discretion of my Executors and Trustees, may be made to such person's parent or spouse or Guardian, Conservator or Committee in whatever jurisdiction appointed, or, in the case of any such person who is younger than twenty-one (21) years of age, whether or not a minor, to a Custodian for such person's benefit under the Uniform Gifts to Minors Act or Uniform Transfers to Minors Act of any of the following States: the State in which I am a resident at my death; the State in which such person resides; the State in which any Executor or Trustee serving hereunder resides; or the State in which any ancestor, sibling, uncle or aunt of such person resides. The receipt by the one to whom distribution is made pursuant to this Article shall be a full discharge in respect of any property so distributed even though such payee may be a fiduciary hereunder. Reference in this Will to a "minor" shall mean a person younger than twenty-one (21) years of age.

EIGHTH: I direct that there shall be no apportionment of any estate, inheritance, transfer, succession, legacy or other death taxes levied or assessed by reason of my death by any governmental authority, domestic or foreign, with respect to any property passing under this Will, or any Codicil hereto, or in respect of any other property passing apart from this Will which may be subject to such taxes. All such taxes, together with interest and penalties thereon, if any, shall be paid as an administration expense from my residuary estate disposed of in Article THIRD, without apportionment among the beneficiaries of my residuary estate. For purposes of this paragraph, such taxes shall not include any generation skipping transfer taxes which may be payable under Chapter 13 of the Code. I expressly recognize that any reduction in tax attributable to property qualifying for the Federal estate tax marital deduction shall inure to the benefit of all recipients of my residuary estate, and not just to the benefit of the recipient of the property qualifying therefor.

NINTH: I confer upon my Executors and Trustees all powers and discretion conferred generally upon fiduciaries by Section 3B:14–23 of the Statutes of the State of New Jersey, and other provisions of this Will, and in addition, without limiting the foregoing, my Executors and my Trustees shall have the following powers and discretion with respect to all property of whatever kind at any time held by them, including income held by them until its distribution, which they may exercise as they deem advisable:

A. To retain, sell (at private or public sale), purchase, exchange, invest and reinvest in bonds, preferred or common stocks, money market funds, certificates of deposit, mortgages, interests in any kind of investment trust, or other evidences or rights, interests or obligations, secured or unsecured, foreign or domestic, or any other property, real or personal and whether or not in the nature of a wasting asset; and to retain and insure the same for any period of time without liability therefor;

B. To retain investments, cash or property of which I may die possessed, or which may be received by them, for such length of time as to them may seem proper, without liability by reason of such retention and without limitation as to the length of such time;

C. To employ and to pay the compensation of such agents, accountants, custodians, experts and counsel, legal or investment (including any firm with which a fiduciary hereunder may be associated), and to delegate discretionary powers to, and rely upon information or advice furnished by, such agents, accountants, custodians, experts or counsel;

D. To improve, lease (for any term, whether or not beyond the term of the administration of my estate or of any trust created hereunder or the term fixed by any law), partition or otherwise deal with or dispose of any real or personal property or any interest therein; to make alterations in, renovations, and extraordinary improvements to any building now or hereafter located on any such property or to demolish the same; to construct new buildings; and to enter into contracts or grant options (for any period) with respect to any of the foregoing;

E. To consent to the modification, renewal or extension of any note, whether or not secured, or any bond or mortgage, or any term or provision thereof, or any guarantee thereof, or to the release of such guarantee; to release obligors on bonds secured by mortgages or to refrain from instituting suits or actions against such obligors for deficiencies; to use property held under this Will for the protection of any investment in real property or in any mortgage on real property;

F. To abandon any property, real or personal, which they shall deem to be worthless or not of sufficient value to warrant keeping or protecting; to abstain from the payment of taxes, water rents, assessments, repairs, maintenance and upkeep of such property; to permit such property to be lost by tax sale or other proceeding, or to convey any such property for nominal or no consideration;

G. To exercise or dispose of any or all options, privileges or rights appurtenant or incident to the ownership of any property; to vote, assent, subscribe, convert property of any other nature; to become a party to, or deposit securities or other property under, or accept securities issued under, any voting trust agreement;

H. To oppose, assent to or participate in any reorganization, readjustment, recapitalization, liquidation, partial liquidation, consolidation, merger, dissolution, sale or purchase of assets, lease, mortgage, contract or other action or proceeding by any corporation and, in connection therewith, to subscribe to new securities issued pursuant thereto or exchange any property for any other property or pay any assessments or other expenses; to delegate discretionary powers to any reorganization, protective or similar committee;

I. To borrow money from any party, including any fiduciary hereunder, whether for the purpose of raising funds to pay taxes, to purchase property, to exercise stock options, or otherwise, and to give or not to give security therefor;

J. To consent to the election by any corporation to be taxed as an "S" corporation under the Internal Revenue Code as it may from time to time exist (or to continue any such election if such election is in effect at the time of my death);

K. To make any loans, either secured or unsecured, in such amounts, and upon such terms, and at such rates of interest, and to such persons, firms or corporations as in the exercise of their discretion they may determine;

L. To invest, reinvest, exchange and carry on any business conducted by me or in which I may be interested as a shareholder, partner or otherwise, for any period of time; to sell or liquidate the same; or to incorporate any such business;

M. To hold property in the name of a nominee or unregistered or in such form as will pass by delivery;

N. To foreclose any mortgage or mortgages, and to take title to the property or any part thereof affected by such mortgage or, in their discretion, to accept a conveyance of any property in lieu of foreclosure, and to collect the rents and income therefrom, either through a receiver or directly, and to protect such property against foreclosure under any mortgage that shall be a prior lien on said property, or to redeem from foreclosure under any such mortgage, as well as to protect any such property against nonpayment of taxes, assessments or other liens;

O. To claim administration and other expenses and losses as deductions either in income tax returns of my estate and/or in any estate tax return, whichever would in their opinion result in the payment of the lowest aggregate of such taxes, without requiring reimbursement of the principal of my residuary estate because of any increase in the estate tax caused by deducting the same in income tax returns, or without making any other adjustments of income or principal, and regardless of the effect that such action on their part may have on the interest of the various beneficiaries under this Will, although my Executors may make such adjustments if they so determine in their absolute discretion;

P. To satisfy any legacy hereunder, whether such legacy be general, pecuniary, residuary or otherwise, with any property, including an undivided interest in property, and to allot any property, including an undivided interest in property, to any separate trust created hereunder whether or not the same kind of property is used in the satisfaction of any other such legacy or as allocated to other trusts created hereunder;

Q. To allocate any federal exemption from the federal generation-skipping transfer tax to any property with respect to which I am the transferor for purposes of said tax, whether or not such property passes under this Will or outside this Will, including, but not limited to, any property which I have transferred during my life to which I did not make an allocation and any property over which I have a general power of appointment, regardless of whether I exercise such power of appointment, and to exclude any such property;

R. My Executors and my Trustees shall be deemed to have acted within the scope of their authority, to have exercised reasonable care, diligence and prudence, and to have acted impartially as to all persons interested including, but not limited to tax elections, unless the contrary be proved by affirmative evidence, and in the absence of such proof shall not be liable for loss arising from depreciation or shrinkage in value of any property herein authorized to be held or acquired.

TENTH: In addition to the powers and discretion conferred upon my fiduciaries by Article NINTH, as to each and any corporation, partnership or other business entity, public or private (including any successor thereto), in which my fiduciaries, as such, hold or acquire any interest (each such corporation, partnership or other business entity being hereafter referred to as the "Entity"), I authorize my fiduciaries to retain the shares thereof or interest therein for as long as they deem it to be in the best interests of my estate or the trusts held under this Will, regardless of the fact that such shares or interest might produce no income, regardless of any duty to diversify investments, and notwithstanding any other fiduciary obligation which might require them to dispose of such shares or interest, other than the obligation to act with reasonable care.

In addition, I authorize my fiduciaries, to the extent permitted by law, to exercise their rights and powers as holders of such shares or interest to effect the continued operation of the Entity or the sale or other disposition of the Entity or of its assets or business, or, in their sole discretion, to sell, exchange, offer for redemption or otherwise dispose of the shares or interest in the Entity owned by my estate or the trusts held under this Will, or to effect the liquidation or dissolution of the Entity, at such time or times and upon such terms and conditions as shall, in the opinion of my fiduciaries, be in the best interests of my estate or of the trusts held under this Will.

So long as my fiduciaries continue to hold any interest in the Entity, I authorize and empower them to participate in the management of the Entity to the extent that their interest therein enables them to do so, without liability or responsibility for any loss resulting from the exercise of the powers hereby granted, or they may delegate their managerial authority to others, whether by means of employment agreements or other arrangements, and they may enter into voting trusts and grant irrevocable proxies, as they deem advisable.

Consequently and to these ends, I expressly authorize my fiduciaries to select, vote for and remove directors of the Entity (if the Entity is a corporation); to take part in the management of the Entity and, to the extent permitted by law, in their managerial capacity to fix, determine or change the policy thereof; to name or change officers, the managing personnel and/or the operating personnel; to employ new management; to reduce, expand, limit or otherwise change the business or type of merchandise dealt in or property invested in and investments held by or product manufactured by or service rendered by the Entity; to require the employees and/or the officers of the Entity to file bonds for the faithful performance of their duties; to determine the amount of bond or bonds to be secured; to select the bonding company; to employ expert outside and disinterested accountants or engineers to make a full and complete survey or appraisal of the Entity's business and its prospects in the trade; to employ investment or legal counsel (including any firm with which a fiduciary hereunder may be associated) whenever my fiduciaries shall deem it advisable; to charge the cost of all such services against the interest in the Entity held by my fiduciaries or to vote or take other action to require the Entity owning said business to pay such expenses; to contribute additional working capital or to subscribe to additional stock as they may see fit; and to take all steps and perform all acts which they shall deem necessary or advisable in connection therewith.

Any one or more of my fiduciaries may act as an officer, director, manager or employee of the Entity, and my fiduciaries are specifically authorized to exercise their rights inhering in their ownership, as such fiduciaries, for the election or appointment of any person or persons, including themselves, as directors, officers, managers and the like. Any such fiduciary who may serve as an officer, director, manager or employee of the Entity shall be entitled to receive compensation for such services notwithstanding that my fiduciaries may themselves (whether individually or as fiduciaries hereunder) be in a position to determine or control the determination of the amount of such compensation, and I direct that no such person shall be required to furnish any bond in connection with any such employment.

In providing as I have, I am aware that conflicts of interest may arise by reason of service hereunder on the part of my fiduciaries and as an officer, director, manager or employee of the Entity. Nevertheless, I have so provided because I have absolute confidence in their business judgment and integrity. It is my intention that any such fiduciary shall, in all respects, be free to exercise the powers and discretion herein conferred as fully and unrestrictedly as if there were no such conflicting interests. With this thought in mind, I expressly exempt my fiduciaries from the adverse operation of any rule of law which might otherwise apply to them in the performance of their fiduciary duties by reason of a conflict of interest. Without limiting the generality of the foregoing, I specifically direct that they shall not have any greater burden of justification in respect of their acts as fiduciaries by reason of a conflict of interest than they would have in the absence of any such conflict.

For purposes of this Will the term "fiduciaries" shall include my Executors, my Trustees, and any one or more of them and any Successor Executor or Successor Trustee.

ELEVENTH: I appoint my attorney, SHELDON PLATT, as Executor of my Will.

I appoint my sister-in-law, DONNA HOUSTON, and my attorney, SHELDON PLATT, as Trustees under this Will.

I appoint my husband, ROBERT B. BROWN, as Guardian of the person and property of my minor children. If my husband shall fail or cease to act for any reason, I appoint my sister-in-law, DONNA HOUSTON, as Guardian in his place.

If ancillary probate of this Will in any jurisdiction is required, I appoint as my Ancillary fiduciaries the same persons who are then serving as my Domiciliary fiduciaries. My Ancillary fiduciaries shall have the same powers and discretion as are conferred upon my Domiciliary fiduciaries.

Except as hereinabove provided in this Article, the last acting individual sole Trustee for whom no designated successor shall be available to act for any reason whatsoever may designate pursuant to a written instrument executed by him or her during his or her lifetime, one or more individuals and/or corporate banking institutions as co-Trustee, to serve with such individual or to succeed such individual as Trustee, in the event he or she shall cease to act for any reason whatsoever.

I direct that no fiduciary (including an Ancillary fiduciary) serving hereunder, whether as Executor, Trustee or Guardian, or as successor thereto, shall be required to file or furnish any bond or other security, any provision of law to the contrary notwithstanding.

All references in this Will to my "Executors", "Trustees" and "Guardians" and the pronouns and verbs corresponding thereto, shall be deemed to include all Successors, and shall be deemed to refer to each Executor, Trustee and Guardian serving hereunder at any time and shall be construed in the masculine or feminine and in the singular or plural, whichever construction is consistent with facts prevailing at any given time.

IN WITNESS WHEREOF, I have hereunto set my hand and seal this 3rd day of February, in the year One Thousand Nine Hundred and Ninety-Three.

_____(L.S.)

SUBSCRIBED, PUBLISHED and DECLARED by the above-named Testatrix, WHITNEY E. HOUSTON, as and for her Last Will and Testament in the presence of us, who, at her request, in her presence and in the presence of each other, have hereunto subscribed our names as witnesses, this 3rd day of February in the year One Thousand Nine Hundred and Ninety-Three.

residing at_____

residing at_____

residing at_____

I, WHITNEY E. HOUSTON, as testatrix, sign my name to this instrument this 3rd day of February, 1993, and being first duly sworn, do hereby declare to the undersigned authority that I sign and execute this instrument as my Last Will and Testament and that I sign it willingly, that I execute it as my free and voluntary act for the purposes therein expressed, and that I am 18 years of age or older, of sound mind, and under no constraint or undue influence.

_____
Whitney E. Houston Testatrix

SILVIA M AYALA VEJA, THOMAS L. WEISENBECK and JEROME H. LIST, the witnesses, being first duly sworn, do each hereby declare to the undersigned authority that the testatrix signs and executes this instrument as her Last Will and Testament and that she signs it willingly, and that each of us states that in the presence and hearing of the testatrix he hereby signs this Will as witness to the testatrix's signing, and that to the best of our knowledge the testatrix is 18 years of age or older, of sound mind, and under no constraint or undue influence.

_____
Witness

_____
Witness

_____
Witness

STATE OF NEW JERSEY

COUNTY OF MORRIS

Subscribed, sworn to and acknowledged before me by WHITNEY E. HOUSTON, the testatrix, and subscribed and sworn to before me by SILVIA M AYALA VEJA, THOMAS L. WEISENBECK and JEROME H. LIST, witnesses this 3rd day of February, 1993.

_____
Jordan S. Weitberg
An Attorney-at-Law of New Jersey

CODICIL DATED APRIL 14, 2000

TO LAST WILL AND TESTAMENT OF WHITNEY E. HOUSTON
EXECUTED ON FEBRUARY 3, 1993

I, WHITNEY E. HOUSTON, a resident of the State of New Jersey declare this to be a codicil to my Last Will and Testament executed on February 3, 1993.

I hereby delete therefrom, the first and second grammatical paragraphs of paragraph Eleventh of my said Last Will and Testament, which provide as follows, and which shall have no further force or effect:

"I appoint my attorney, Sheldon Platt, as executor of my Will.

"I appoint my sister-in-law, Donna Houston, and my attorney, Sheldon Platt, as trustees under this Will".

and substitute the following in their place:

"I appoint Emily Cissy Houston as executor of my Will.

"I appoint my sister-in-law, Donna Houston, and my brother, Michael Houston, as trustees under this Will."

In all other respects, I hereby ratify, confirm and adopt my said Last Will and Testament executed on February 3, 1993.

Dated: _____, 2000

_____
WHITNEY E. HOUSTON

SUBSCRIBED, PUBLISHED and DECLARED by the above-named Testatrix, WHITNEY E. HOUSTON, as and to her Codicil to her Last Will and Testament in the presence of us, who, at her request, in her presence and in the presence of each other, have hereunto subscribed our names as witnesses, this _____ day of _____ in the year Two Thousand.

residing at_____

residing at_____

residing at_____

LAST WILL AND TESTAMENT OF ANNA NICOLE SMITH

I, VICKIE LYNN MARSHALL, also known as Vickie Lynn Smith, and Vickie Lynn Hogan, and Anna Nicole Smith, a resident of Los Angeles County, California, declare that this is my Will. I revoke all prior Wills and Codicils. I hereby dispose of all property that I am entitled to dispose of by Will and exercise all general powers of appointment that I am entitled to exercise. I have not entered into a contract to make or not revoke a Will.

1.

ARTICLE I

FAMILY DECLARATIONS AND STATUTORY DISINHERITANCE
I am unmarried. I have one child DANIEL WAYNE SMITH. I have no predeceased children nor predeceased children leaving issue.

Except as otherwise provided in this Will, I have intentionally omitted to provide for my spouse and other heirs, including future spouses and children and other descendants now living and those hereafter born or adopted, as well as existing and future stepchildren and foster children.

* END OF ARTICLE *

2.

ARTICLE II

DISPOSITION OF ESTATE

All of the property of my estate (the "residue"), after payment of any taxes or other expenses of my estate as provided below, including property subject to a power of appointment exercised hereby, shall be distributed to HOWARD STERN, ESQ., to hold in trust for my child under such terms as he and a court of competent jurisdiction may declare, such that my children are distributed sufficient sums for the health, education, and support according to their accustomed manner of living from either the income or principal of the trust until age twenty-five; and are at that time given one-third of all of the income of the trust and one-third of the principal of the trust as then constituted; and at thirty are given one-half of the income from the trust and one-half of the principal of the trust as then constituted; and at thirty-five are given all of the principal of the trust. If, in the discretion of the Trustee, the amount remaining in the Trust is too small to efficiently administer, he may give all of the corpus of the Trust to my child at once.

* END OF ARTICLE *

3.

ARTICLE III

PROVISIONS REGARDING EXECUTORS

3.1 Nomination of Executor.

I nominate as Executor and as successor Executors of this Will those named below. Each successor Executor shall serve in the order and priority designated if the prior designated Executor fails to qualify or ceases to act.

First: HOWARD STERN, ESQ.
Second: RON RALE, ESQ.
Third: ERIC JAMES LUND, ESQ.
Fourth: Wells Fargo Bank (Sandra K. Von Paul) or its successors by merger, consolidation, or otherwise.

3.2 Power to Nominate Executor.

If all of the foregoing Executors are unable or unwilling to act, the majority of the adult beneficiaries under this Will shall have the power to designate as successor Executor any corporate fiduciary having assets under management of at least Two Hundred Fifty Million Dollars ($250,000,000). Such designation shall be filed with the court in which this Will is probated.

3.3. Waiver of Bond.

I request that no bond be required of any Executor nominated above, including nonresidents, whether such Executor is acting alone or together with another.

3.4. Powers of Executor.

My Executor shall have the following powers in addition to all powers now or hereafter conferred by law, and except as otherwise expressly provided, shall have the broadest and most absolute permissible discretion in exercising all powers. I intend and direct that the probate court uphold any action taken by my Executor, absent clear and convincing evidence of bad faith or gross negligence.

3.4.1. Independent Administration.

My Executor may administer my estate with full authority under the California Independent Administration of Estates Act.

3.4.2. Tax Elections and Decisions.

My Executor may value my gross estate for federal estate tax purposes as of the date of my death or any permissible alternate valuation date, my claim any items of expense as income or estate tax deductions, or both, and may make such other tax elections or tax oriented decisions as my Executor believes will achieve an overall reduction in taxes. No compensating adjustments shall be made among my beneficiaries or between income and principal accounts by reason of the elections and decisions authorized by the preceding sentence, except as my Executor deeds equitable, and no such election or decision shall be subject to challenge absent clear and convincing evidence of gross negligence or bad faith.

3.4.3. Disclaimers.

My Executor may disclaim all or any portion of any bequest, devise or trust interest provided for me under any Will or Trust. In particular, I authorize and encourage my Executor to try to obtain overall tax savings, even though this may change the ultimate recipients of the property that is disclaimed.

3.4.4. Limitations on Tax Elections and Decisions.

No person serving as Executor for federal tax purposes, hereunder or pursuant to the terms of the Trust, shall have authority to make or participate in any tax election or decision if the power to do so would result in his or her having a general power of appointment (for federal gift and estate tax purposes) over property with respect to which he or she would (or might) not otherwise have such a general power, and in such event such authority shall pass to the next successor fiduciary who is not so disqualified.

3.4.5. Management and Administrative Powers of Executor.

Subject to any express limitation stated elsewhere in this will, I hereby grant to my Executor all administrative powers that may legally be granted to an Executor under California law as of the date of my death, including, without limitation and to the extent that I am permitted to do so by California law. Without limiting any of the foregoing, I specifically provide that my Executor shall have the broadest and most unrestricted powers to sell, lease or retain any property, make investments, make tax elections and tax oriented decisions, defer distributions, retain professional advisors and compensate them from my estate, or continue or restructure any business. I also direct that my Executor obtain court approval only as my Executor deems appropriate or if such approval is required by law despite any provision in a Will purporting to eliminate the need for such approval, it being my desire that, whenever possible, my Executor rely on Notices of Proposed Action or Waivers of Notice and Consents, unless my Executor desires court approval.

3.5. Resignation of Executor.

My Executor may resign at any time (a) by filing a written instrument with the court having jurisdiction over my estate, or (b) by giving written notice to all successor Executors.

3.6. Successor Executors.

All authority, titles and powers of the original Executor shall automatically pass to a successor Executor. A successor Executor may accept as correct or contest any accounting made by any predecessor Executor; provided that a successor Executor shall be obligated to inquire into the propriety of any act or omission of a predecessor if so requested in writing by a Trustee of the Trust, any Protector of the Trust, or any adult beneficiary or the guardian of a minor beneficiary of the Trust within ninety (90) days of the date that the successor is appointed.

3.7. Liability of Executor.

No Executor, other than a corporate Executor, shall be liable to any person interested in my estate for any act or default of my Executor or any other person, or for any obligation of my estate, unless it results from my Executor's own bad faith, willful misconduct, or gross negligence. My estate shall indemnify my Executor from any liability with respect to which my Executor is held harmless pursuant to the preceding sentence. I specifically indemnify my Executor, including any corporate Executor, from any personal liability for any clean-up costs relating to property held in my estate that contains toxic substances, and direct that any such clean-up costs be paid from my estate in proportion to its interest in the toxic property. Furthermore, if my Executor suspects that property held in my estate may present toxic clean-up problems, my Executor may obtain an environmental assessment, and my estate shall pay for such assessment. Prior to appointment, a nominated Executor may obtain court authority for such assessment, and be reimbursed from the residue of my estate therefor. Such assessment shall also be obtained before any purchase of any property by my estate if my Executor suspects toxic contamination, the cost of such assessment to be paid from my estate.

3.8. Executor's Authority to Transfer to Trust.

I hereby authorize my Executor (or the person nominated to serve as Executor even if no Letters Testamentary are issued) to transfer to the Trustee of the Trust any asset and to execute any document in connection with any such transfer to the extent necessary or appropriate to carry out any assignment of assets to the Trust.

3.9. Co-Executors.

If more than one person is serving as Executor, one Executor acting alone may transfer securities and execute all documents in connection therewith; open accounts with one or more bank and savings and loan associations; authorize deposit or withdrawal of funds to or from accounts; and sign checks. Transfer agents, corporations and financial institutions dealing with a single Executor as provided in the preceding sentence shall have no liability as a consequence of dealing with only one Executor. My Executor may delegate any ministerial duties to any Co-Executor.

* END OF ARTICLE *

4.

ARTICLE IV

GENERAL PROVISIONS

4.1. No Interest.

No interest shall be paid on any gift hereunder, except to the extent necessary to qualify for the marital deduction.

4.2. Life Insurance Policies.

4.2.1. Collection of Proceeds.

Upon the death of any person insured under a policy of insurance payable to my Executor, my Executor may exercise any option provided in the policy, and receive all sums due under the terms of the policy. To facilitate receipt of such sums, my Executor may execute receipts and other instruments, and compromise disputed claims; provided, however, that if payment of a claim is contested, my Executor shall not be obligated to take any action for collection until my Executor has been personally indemnified to my Executor's satisfaction against any liability or expense, including attorney's fees; provided, further, that my Executor may use any funds in my Executor's hands to pay the expenses, including attorney's fees, to collect the proceeds of a policy, and may reimburse himself, herself or itself for advances made for this purpose. No insurance company shall have any obligation to inquire into the application of the proceeds of any policy. Upon payment to my Executor of the amounts due under a policy, an insurance company shall be relieved of all further liability thereunder.

4.3. Construction.

4.3.1. Number and Gender.

In all matters of interpretation, the masculine, feminine and neuter shall each include the other, as the context indicates, and the singular shall include the plural and vice versa.

4.3.2. Headings.

The headings in this Will are inserted for convenient reference and shall be ignored in interpreting this Will.

4.3.3. Severability of Provisions.

If any provision hereof is unenforceable, the remaining provisions shall remain in full effect.

4.4. Governing Law.

The validity, interpretation, and administration of this Will shall be governed by the laws of the State of California in force from time to time.

* END OF ARTICLE *

5.

ARTICLE V

TAXES AND OTHER EXPENSES OF MY ESTATE

5.1. Payment from Trust.

All federal estate and other death taxes imposed and all expenses and charges incidental thereto, shall be payable by the Executor out of the residue of the estate, without charge against or reimbursement from any beneficiary; but excluding the taxes referred to in the following subsections 5.1.1 through 5.1.13 below, which shall be paid as provided below.

5..1..2. (sic) Any additional taxes under Section 2032A(c) of the Code, which shall be paid or bonded by the recipients of the property subject to special use valuation as provided in Section 2032A(c)(5);

5..1..2. Any tax under Section 2036 of the Code caused by my retaining any interest subject to Section 2036 of the Code, which shall be paid as provided in Section 2207B of the Code;

5..1..3. Any taxes under Section 2039 of the Code;

5..1..4. Any tax under Section 2041 of the Code caused by my possession of a general power of appointment not validly exercised by me during my lifetime or in this Will, imposed upon or in relation to any property or interest therein included in my gross estate for federal estate tax purposes, which shall be paid as provided in Section 2207 of the Code;

5..1..5. Any tax under Section 2042 of the Code with respect to any policy of insurance if the Deceased Trustor did not possess the right to change the beneficiary of such policy on the date of my death, which shall be paid as provided in Section 2206 of the Code;

5..1..6. Any taxes under Section 2056A(b) of the Code, which shall be computed and paid as provided in Section 2056A(b) of the Code;

5..1..7. Any taxes caused by failure to make a full election under Section 2056(b)(7) of the Code with respect to any portion of the Marital Gift. Such taxes shall be paid from the portion of the Marital Gift as to which such election is not made or from any separate Trust created to hold such portion;

5..1..8. Any generation-skipping transfer taxes under Section 2601 et seq. of the Code, which shall be computed as provided in Section 2601 et seq. of the Code and be paid as provided in Section 2603 of the Code;

5..1..9. Any taxes under Section 2701 et seq. of the Code;

5..1..10. Any tax under Section 4980A(d) of the Code.

5..1..11. Any tax caused by my possession of a vested reversion or remainder interest that has been deferred under Section 6163 of the Code; and,

5..1..12. Any state death tax imposed on property subject to the taxes described in Subsections 5.1.1. through 5.1.13 above.

The foregoing taxes excluded from payment from the Residuary Amount shall be charged against and paid from the property and interests with respect to which such taxes are imposed, or by the recipients or owners of such property and interests within thirty (30) days after a written demand from the Trustee, as the Trustee deems appropriate. Except as otherwise provided above with respect to certain of the taxes imposed by the Code, the amounts to be paid pursuant to the preceding sentence shall be computed on a pro-rata basis based on the ratio of (a) the value for federal estate tax purposes of the property and interests with respect to which such taxes are imposed, to (b) the value of the my taxable Estate for federal estate tax purposes, multiplied by (c) the sum of the total estate and other death taxes payable, i.e (a/b) x c. Notwithstanding the foregoing, none of the taxes listed in Subsections 5.1.1 through 5.1.13 above shall be payable (directly or indirectly) by or from a gift to or in trust for the Survivor if the effect of such payment would be to cause an increase in the overall death taxes payable by reason of my death nor shall any such taxes be payable (directly or indirectly) by or from a gift to any charitable entity if the effect of such payment would be to reduce the charitable deduction allowable to my Estate.

5.2. Tax Deductions and Elections.

After reasonable consultation with the Trustee of the trust, my Executor may take any action and make any election to minimize the tax liabilities of my estate or the beneficiaries of the Trust. Except as otherwise expressly provided herein, my Executor shall have the power (but not the obligation) to make adjustments to compensate for the consequences of any tax election or any investment or administrative decision that my Executor believes has had the effect of directly or indirectly preferring one beneficiary or group of beneficiaries over another. No decision of my Executor regarding tax matters shall be subject to challenge by any person or entity, unless the party affected can clearly prove that the decision was grossly negligent or made in bad faith.

* END OF ARTICLE *

6.

ARTICLE VI

NO CONTEST; DISINHERITANCE

6.1. Contestants Disinherited.

If any legal heir of mine, any person claiming under any such heir, or any other person, in any manner, directly or indirectly, contests or attacks this Will or the Trust or any of the provisions of said instruments, or conspires with or assists anyone in any such contest, or pursues any creditor's claim that my Executor reasonably deems to constitute a contest, any share or interest in my estate or the Trust is revoked and shall be disposed of as if the contesting beneficiary had predeceased me without descendants, and shall augment proportionately the shares of my estate passing to or in trust for my beneficiaries who have not participated in such acts. This Article shall not apply to a disclaimer. Expenses to resist a contest or other attack of any nature shall be paid from my estate as expenses of administration.

6.2. General Disinheritance.

Except as otherwise provided herein and in the Trust, I have intentionally omitted to provide for any of my heirs, or persons claiming to be my heirs, whether or not known to me.

* END OF ARTICLE *

7.

ARTICLE VII

OFFICE OF GUARDIAN

7.1. Nomination of Guardian of the Person.

I nominate HOWARD STERN as guardian and successor guardian of the person of my minor child DANIEL WAYNE SMITH:

Any such nominee who is a resident of a state other than California may, at the nominee's election, file a petition for appointment in such other state and/or in California. I request that any court having jurisdiction permit the guardian to change the residence and domicile of my minor children to the jurisdiction where the guardian resides.

I give the guardian of the person of my minor children the same authority as a parent having legal custody and authorize the guardian to exercise such authority without need for notice, hearing, court authorization, instructions, approval or confirmation in the same manner as a parent having legal custody. I request that no bond be required because of the grant of these independent powers.

7.2. Waiver of Bond.

I request that no bond be required of any guardian nominated above.

* END OF ARTICLE *

Signature Clause. I subscribe my name to this Will at Los Angeles, California, on this_____30th_____ day of _____July_____, 2001.

_____/S/ Vicki Lynn Marshall_____VICKI LYNN MARSHALL

LAST WILL AND TESTAMENT OF ELVIS PRESLEY

I, Elvis A. Presley, a resident and citizen of Shelby County, Tennessee, being of sound mind and disposing memory, do hereby make, publish and declare this instrument to be my last will and testament, hereby revoking any and all wills and codicils by me at any time heretofore made.

Item I

Debts, Expenses and Taxes

I direct my Executor, hereinafter named, to pay all of my matured debts and my funeral expenses, as well as the costs and expenses of the administration of my estate, as soon after my death as practicable. I further direct that all estate, inheritance, transfer and succession taxes which are payable by reason under this will, be paid out of my residuary estate; and I hereby waive on behalf of my estate any right to recover from any person any part of such taxes so paid. My Executor, in his sole discretion, may pay from my domiciliary estate all or any portion of the costs of ancillary administration and similar proceedings in other jurisdictions.

Item II

Instruction Concerning Personal Property: Enjoyment in Specie

I anticipate that included as a part of my property and estate at the time of my death will be tangible personal property of various kinds, characters and values, including trophies and other items accumulated by me during my professional career. I hereby specifically instruct all concerned that my Executor, herein appointed, shall have complete freedom and discretion as to disposal of any and all such property so long as he shall act in good faith and in the best interest of my estate and my beneficiaries, and his discretion so exercised shall not be subject to question by anyone whomsoever.

I hereby expressly authorize my Executor and my Trustee, respectively and successively, to permit any beneficiary of any and all trusts created hereunder to enjoy in specie the use or benefit of any household goods, chattels, or other tangible personal property (exclusive of choses in action, cash, stocks, bonds or other securities) which either my Executor or my Trustees may receive in kind, and my Executor and my Trustees shall not be liable for any consumption, damage, injury to or loss of any tangible property so used, nor shall the beneficiaries of any trusts hereunder or their executors of administrators be liable for any consumption, damage, injury to or loss of any tangible personal property so used.

Item III

Real Estate

If I am the owner of any real estate at the time of my death, I instruct and empower my Executor and my Trustee (as the case may be) to hold such real estate for investment, or to sell same, or any portion therof, as my Executor or my Trustee (as the case may be) shall in his sole judgment determine to be for the best interest of my estate and the beneficiaries thereof.

Item IV

Residuary Trust

After payment of all debts, expenses and taxes as directed under Item I hereof, I give, devise, and bequeath all the rest, residue, and remainder of my estate, including all lapsed legacies and devices, and any property over which I have a power of appointment, to my Trustee, hereinafter named, in trust for the following purposes:

(a) The Trustees is directed to take, hold, manage, invest and reinvent the corpus of the trust and to collect the income therefrom in accordance with the rights, powers, duties, authority and discretion hereinafter set forth. The Trustee is directed to pay all the expenses, taxes and costs incurred in the management of the trust estate out of the income thereof.

(b) After payment of all expenses, taxes and costs incurred in the management of the expenses, taxes and costs incurred in the management of the trust estate, the Trustee is authorizes to accumulate the net income or to pay or apply so much of the net income and such portion of the principal at any time and from time to time to time for health, education, support, comfortable maintenance and welfare of: (1) My daughter, Lisa Marie Presley, and any other lawful issue I might have, (2) my grandmother, Minnie Mae Presley, (3) my father, Vernon E. Presley, and (4) such other relatives of mine living at the time of my death who in the absolute discretion of my Trustees are in need of emergency assistance for any of the above mentioned purposes and the Trustee is able to make such distribution without affecting the ability of the trust to meet the present needs of the first three numbered categories of beneficiaries herein mentioned or to meet the reasonably expected future needs of the first three classes of beneficiaries herein mentioned. Any decision of the Trustee as to whether or not distribution, to any of the persons described hereunder shall be final and conclusive and not subject to question by any legatee or beneficiary hereunder.

(c) Upon the death of my Father, Vernon E. Presley, the Trustee is instructed to make no further distributions to the fourth category of beneficiaries and such beneficiaries shall cease to have any interest whatsoever in this trust.

(d) Upon the death of both my said father and my said grandmother, the Trustee is directed to divide the Residuary Trust into separate and equal trusts, creating one such equal trust for each of my lawful children then surviving and one such equal trust for the living issue collectively, if any, of any deceased child of mine. The share, if any, for the issue of any such deceased child, shall immediately vest in such issue in equal shares but shall be subject to the provisions of Item V herein. Separate books and records shall be kept for each trust, but it shall not be necessary that a physical division of the assets be made as to each trust.

The Trustee may from time to time distribute the whole or any part of the net income or principal from each of the aforesaid trusts as the Trustee, in its uncontrolled discretion, considers necessary or desirable to provide for the comfortable support, education, maintenance, benefit and general welfare of each of my children. Such distributions may be made directly to such beneficiary or to the guardian of the person of such beneficiary and without repsonsibilty (sic) on my Trustee to see to the application of nay (sic) such distributions and in making such distributions, the Trustee shall take into account all other sources of funds known by the Trustee to be available for each respective beneficiary for such purpose.

(e) As each of my respective children attains the age of twenty-five (25) years and provided that both my father and my grandmother are deceased, the trust created hereunder for such child care terminate, and all the remainder of the assets then contained in said trust shall be distributed to such child so attaining the age of twenty-five (25) years outright and free of further trust.

(f) If any of my children for whose benefit a trust has been created hereunder should die before attaining the age of twenty- five (25) years, then the trust created for such a child shall terminate on his death, and all remaining assets then contained in said trust shall be distributed outright and free of further trust and in equal shares to the surviving issue of such deceased child but subject to the provisions of Item V herein; but if there be no such surviving issue, then to the brothers and sisters of such deceased child in equal shares, the issue of any other deceased child being entitled collectively to their deceased parent's share. Nevertheless, if any distribution otherwise becomes payable outright and free of trust under the provisions of this paragraph (f) of the Item IV of my will to a beneficiary for whom the Trustee is then administering a trust for the benefit of such beneficiary under provisions of this last will and testament, such distribution shall not be paid outright to such beneficiary but shall be added to and become a part of the trust so being administered for such beneficiary by the Trustee.

Item V

Distribution to Minor Children

If any share of corpus of any trust established under this will become distributable outright and free of trust to any beneficiary before said beneficiary has attained the age of eighteen (18) years, then said share shall immediately vest in said beneficiary, but the Trustee shall retain possession of such share during the period in which such beneficiary is under the age of eighteen (18) years, and, in the meantime, shall use and expend so much of the income and principal for the care, support, and education of such beneficiary, and any income not so expended with respect to each share so retained all the power and discretion had with respect to such trust generally.

Item VI

Alternate Distributees

In the event that all of my descendants should be deceased at any time prior to the time for the termination of the trusts provided for herein, then in such event all of my estate and all the assets of every trust to be created hereunder (as the case may be) shall then distributed outright in equal shares to my heirs at law per stripes.

Item VII

Unenforceable Provisions

If any provisions of this will are unenforceable, the remaining provisions shall, nevertheless, be carried into effect.

Item VIII

Life Insurance

If my estate is the beneficiary of any life insurance on my life at the time of my death, I direct that the proceeds therefrom will be used by my Executor in payment of the debts, expenses and taxes listed in Item I of this will, to the extent deemed advisable by the Executor. All such proceeds not so used are to be used by my Executor for the purpose of satisfying the devises and bequests contained in Item IV herein.

Item IX

Spendthrift Provision

I direct that the interest of any beneficiary in principal or income of any trust created hereunder shall not be subject to claims of creditors or others, nor to legal process, and may not be voluntarily or involuntarily alienated or encumbered except as herein provided. Any bequests contained herein for any female shall be for her sole and separate use, free from the debts, contracts and control of any husband she may ever have.

Item X

Proceeds From Personal Services

All sums paid after my death (either to my estate or to any of the trusts created hereunder) and resulting from personal services rendered by me during my lifetime, including, but not limited to, royalties of all nature, concerts, motion picture contracts, and personal appearances shall be considered to be income, notwithstanding the provisions of estate and trust law to the contrary.

Item XI

Executor and Trustee

I appoint as executor of this, my last will and testament, and as Trustee of every trust required to be created hereunder, my said father.

I hereby direct that my said father shall be entitled by his last will ant testament, duly probated, to appoint a successor Executor of my estate, as well as a successor Trustee or successor Trustees of all the trusts to be created under my last will and testament.

If, for any reason, my said father be unable to serve or to continue to serve as Executor and/or as Trustee, or if he be deceased and shall not have appointed a successor Executor or Trustee, by virtue of his last will and testament as stated -above, then I appoint National Bank of Commerce, Memphis, Tennessee, or its successor or the institution with which it may merge, as successor Executor and/or as successor Trustee of all trusts required to be established hereunder.

None of the appointees named hereunder, including any appointment made by virtue of the last will and testament of my said father, shall be required to furnish any bond or security for performance of the respective fiduciary duties required hereunder, notwithstanding any rule of law to the contrary.

Item XII

Powers, Duties, Privileges and Immunities of the Trustee

Except as otherwise stated expressly to the contrary herein, I give and grant to the said Trustee (and to the duly appointed successor Trustee when acting as such) the power to do everything he deems advisable with respect to the administration of each trust required to be established under this, my last will and Testament, even though such powers would not be authorized or appropriate for the Trustee under statutory or other rules of law. By way of illustration and not in limitation of the generality of the foregoing grant of power and authority of the Trustee, I give and grant to him plenary power as follows:

(a) To exercise all those powers authorized to fiduciaries under the provisions of the Tennessee Code Annotated, Sections 35-616 to 35-618, inclusive, including any amendments thereto in effect at the time of my death, and the same are expressly referred to and incorporated herein by reference.

(b) Plenary power is granted to the Trustee, not only to relieve him from seeking judicial instruction, but to the extent that the Trustee deems it to be prudent, to encourage determinations freely to be made in favor of persons who are the current income beneficiaries. In such instances the rights of all subsequent beneficiaries are subordinate, and the Trustee shall not be answerable to any subsequent beneficiary for anything done or omitted in favor of a current income beneficiary may compel any such favorable or preferential treatment. Without in anywise minimizing or impairing the scope of this declaration of intent, it includes investment policy, exercise of discretionary power to pay or apply principal and income, and determination principal and income questions;

(c) It shall be lawful for the Trustee to apply any sum that is payable to or for the benefit of a minor (or any other person who in the Judgment of the Trustee, is incapable of making proper disposition thereof) by payments in discharge of the costs and expenses of educating, maintaining and supporting said beneficiary, or to make payment to anyone with whom said beneficiary resides or who has the care or custody of the beneficiary, temporarily or permanently, all without intervention of any guardian or like fiduciary. The receipt of anyone to whom payment is so authorized to be made shall be a complete discharge of the Trustees without obligation on his part to see to the further application hereto, and without regard to other resource that the beneficiary may have, or the duty of any other person to support the beneficiary;

(d) In Dealing with the Trustee, no grantee, pledge, vendee, mortgage, lessee or other transference of the trust properties, or any part therof, shall be bound to inquire with respect to the purpose or necessity of any such disposition or to see to the application of any consideration therefore paid to the Trustee.

Item XIII

Concerning the Trustee and the Executor

(a) If at any time the Trustee shall have reasonable doubt as to his power, authority or duty in the administration of any trust herein created, it shall be lawful for the Trustee to obtain the advice and counsel of reputable legal counsel without resorting to the courts for instructions; and the Trustee shall be fully absolved from all liability and damage or detriment to the various trust estates of any beneficiary thereunder by reason of anything done, suffered or omitted pursuant to advice of said counsel given and obtained in good faith, provided that nothing contained herein shall be construed to prohibit or prevent the Trustee in all proper cases from applying to a court of competent jurisdiction for instructions in the administration of the trust assets in lieu of obtaining advice of counsel.

(b) In managing, investing, and controlling the various trust estates, the Trustee shall exercise the judgment and care under the circumstances then prevailing, which men of prudence discretion and judgment exercise in the management of their own affairs, not in regard to speculation, but in regard to the permanent disposition of their funds, considering the probable income as well as the probable safety of their capital, and, in addition, the purchasing power of income distribution to beneficiaries.

(c) My Trustee (as well as my Executor) shall be entitled to reasonable and adequate and adequate compensation for the fiduciary services rendered by him.

(d) My Executor and his successor Executor and his successor Executor shall have the same rights, privileges, powers and immunities herein granted to my Trustee wherever appropriate.

(e) In referring to any fiduciary hereunder, for purposes of construction, masculine pronouns may include a corporate fiduciary and neutral pronouns may include an individual fiduciary.

Item XIV

Law Against Perpetuities

(a) Having in mind the rule against perpetuities, I direct that (notwithstanding anything contained to the contrary in this last will and testament) each trust created under this will (except such trust created under this will (except such trusts as have heretofore vested in compliance with such rule or law) shall end, unless sooner terminated under other provisions of this will, twenty-one (21) years after the death of the last survivor of such of the beneficiaries hereunder as are living at the time of my death; and thereupon that the property held in trust shall be distributed free of all trust to the persons then entitled to receive the income and/or principal therefrom, in the proportion in proportion in which they are then entitled to receive such income.

(b) Notwithstanding anything else contained in this will to the contrary, I direct that if any distribution under this will become payable to a person for whom the Trustee is then administering a trust created hereunder for the benefit of such person, such distribution shall be made to such trust and not to the beneficiary outright, and the funds so passing to such trust shall become a part thereof as corpus and be administered and distributed to the same extent and purpose as if such funds had been a part of such a trust at its inception.

Item XV

Payment of Estate and Inheritance Taxes

Notwithstanding the provisions of Item X herein, I authorize my Executor to use such sums received by my estate after my death and resulting from my personal services as identified in Item X as he deem necessary and advisable in order to pay the taxes referred to in Item I of my said will.

In WITNESS WHEREOF, I, the said ELVIS A. PRESLEY, do hereunto set my hand and seal in the presence of two (2) competent witnesses, and in their presence do publish and declare this instrument to be my Last Will and Testament, this 3rd day of March, 1977.

[Signed by Elvis A. Presley] ELVIS A. PRESLEY

The foregoing instrument, consisting of this and eleven (11) preceding typewritten pages, was signed, sealed, published and declared by ELVIS A.PRESLEY, the Testator, to be his Last Will and Testament, in our presence, and we, at his request and in his presence and in the presence of each other, have hereunto subscribed our names as witnesses, this 3 day of March, 1977, at Memphis, Tennessee.

[Signed by Ginger Alden] Ginger Alden residing at 4152 Royal Crest Place

[Signed by Charles F. Hodge] Charles F. Hodge residing at 3764 Elvis Presley Blvd.

[Signed by Ann Dewey Smith] Ann Dewey Smith residing at 2237 Court Avenue.

State of Tennessee

County of Shelby

Ginger Alden, Charles F. Hodge, and Ann Dewey Smith, after being first duly sworn, make oath or affirm that the foregoing Last Will and Testament, in the sight and presence of us, the undersigned, who at his request and in his sight and presence, and in the sight and presence of each other, have subscribed our names as attesting witnesses on the 3 day of March, 1977, and we further make oath or affirm that the Testator was of sound mind and disposing memory and not acting under fraud, menace or undue influence of any person, and was more than eighteen (18) years of age; and that each of the attesting witnesses is more than eighteen (18) years of age.

[Signed by Ginger Alden] Ginger Alden

[Signed by Charles F. Hodge] Charles F. Hodge

[Signed by Ann Dewey Smith] Ann Dewey Smith

Sworn To And Subscribed before me this 3 day of March, 1977.

Drayton Beecker Smith II Notary Public

My commission expires:

August 8, 1979

Admitted to probate and Ordered Recorded August 22, 1977

Joseph W. Evans, Judge

Recorded August 22, 1977

B.J. Dunavant, Clerk

By: Jan Scott, D.C.

LAST WILL AND TESTAMENT OF GEORGE WASHINGTON

JULY 9, 1799

In the name of God, amen!

I, George Washington of Mount Vernon, a citizen of the United States and lately President of the same, do make, ordain and declare this instrument, which is written with my own hand and every page thereof subscribed with my name, to be my last Will and Testament, revoking all others.

Imprimus. All my debts, of which there are but few, and none of magnitude, are to be punctually and speedily paid, and the legacies hereinafter bequeathed are to be discharged as soon as circumstances will permit, and in the manner directed.

Item. To my dearly beloved wife, Martha Washington, I give and bequeath the use, profit and benefit of my whole estate, real and personal, for the term of her natural life, except such parts thereof as are specially disposed of hereafter—my improved lot in the town of Alexandria, situated on Pitt and Cameron Streets, I give to her and her heirs forever, as I also do my household and kitchen furniture of every sort and kind with the liquors and groceries which may be on hand at the time of my decease, to be used and disposed of as she may think proper.

Item. Upon the decease of my wife, it is my will and desire, that all the slaves which I hold in my own right shall receive their freedom. To emancipate them during her life, would tho earnestly wished by me, be attended with such insuperable difficulties, on account of their intermixture by marriages with the dower negroes as to excite the most painful sensations—if not disagreeable consequences from the latter while both descriptions are in the occupancy of the same proprietor, it not being in my power under the tenure by which the dower Negroes are held to manumit them. And whereas among those who will receive freedom according to this devise there may be some who from old age, or bodily infirmities and others who on account of their infancy, that will be unable to support themselves, it is my will and desire that all who come under the first and second description shall be comfortably clothed and fed by my heirs while they live and that such of the latter description as have no parents living, or if living are unable, or unwilling to provide for them, shall be bound by the Court until they shall arrive at the age of twenty-five years, and in cases where no record can be produced whereby their ages can be ascertained, the judgment of the Court upon its own view of the subject shall be adequate and final. The negroes thus bound are (by their masters and mistresses) to be taught to read and write and to be brought up to some useful occupation, agreeably to the laws of the Commonwealth of Virginia, providing for the support of orphans and other poor children—and I do hereby expressly forbid the sale or transportation out of the said Commonwealth of any slave I may die possessed of, under any pretense, whatsoever—and I do moreover most positively, and most solemnly enjoin it upon my executors hereafter named, or the survivors of them to see that this clause respecting slaves and every part thereof be religiously fulfilled at the epoch at which it is directed to take place without evasion, neglect or delay after the crops which may then be on the ground are harvested, particularly as it respects the aged and infirm, seeing that a regular and permanent fund be established for their support so long as there are subjects requiring it, not trusting to the uncertain provisions to be made by individuals. And to my mulatto man, William (calling himself William Lee) I give immediate freedom or if he should prefer it (on account of the accidents which have befallen him and which have rendered him incapable of walking or of any active employment) to remain in the situation he now is, it shall be optional in him to do so. In either case, however, I allow him an annuity of thirty dollars during his natural life which shall be independent of the victuals and clothes he has been accustomed to receive; if he chooses the last alternative, but in full with his freedom, if he prefers the first, and this I give him as a testimony of my sense of his attachment to me and for his faithful services during the Revolutionary War.

Item. To the Trustees (Governors or by whatsoever other name they may be designated) of the academy in the town of Alexandria, I give and bequeath, in trust, four thousand dollars, or in other words twenty of the shares which I hold in the Bank of Alexandria towards the support of a free school, established at, and annexed to the said academy for the purpose of educating such orphan children, or the children of such other poor and indigent persons as are unable to accomplish it with their own means, and who in the judgment of the trustees of the said seminary, are best entitled to the benefits of this donation. The aforesaid twenty shares I give and bequeath in perpetuity—the dividends only of which are to be drawn for and applied by the said Trustees for the time being, for the uses above mentioned, the stock to remain entire and untouched unless indications of a failure of the said bank should be so apparent or discontinuance thereof should render a removal of this fund necessary, in either of these cases the amount of the stock here devised is to be vested in some other bank or public institution Whereby the interest may with regularity and certainty be drawn and applied as above. And to prevent misconception, my meaning is, and is hereby declared to be that, these twenty shares are in lieu of and not in addition to the thousand pounds given by a missive letter some years ago in consequence whereof an annuity of fifty pounds has since been paid towards the support of this institution.

Item. Whereas by a law of the Commonwealth of Virginia, enacted in the year 1785, the Legislature thereof was pleased (as an evidence of its approbation of the services I had rendered the public, during the Revolution—and partly, I believe in consideration of my having suggested the vast advantages which the community would derive from the extension of its inland navigation, under legislative patronage) to present me with one hundred shares, of one hundred dollars each, in the incorporated company established for the purpose of extending the navigation of James River from tide water to the mountains; and also with fifty shares of one hundred pounds sterling each in the corporation of another company likewise established for the similar purpose of opening the navigation of the River Potomac from tide water to Fort Cumberland; the acceptance of which, although the offer was highly honorable and grateful to my feelings, was refused, as inconsistent with a principle which I had adopted, and had never departed from, namely not to receive pecuniary compensation for any services I could render my country in its arduous struggle with Great Britain for its rights; and because I had evaded similar propositions from other States in the Union—adding to this refusal, however, an intimation, that, if it should be the pleasure of the Legislature to permit me to appropriate the said shares to public uses, I would receive them on those terms with due sensibility—and this it having consented to in flattering terms, as will appear by a subsequent law and sundry resolutions, in the most ample and honorable manner, I proceed after this recital for the more correct understanding of the case to declare—

That as it has always been a source of serious regret with me to see the youth of these United States sent to foreign countries for the purpose of education, often before their minds were formed or they had imbibed any adequate ideas of the happiness of their own, contracting too frequently not only habits of dissipation and extravagance, but principles unfriendly to republican government and to the true and genuine liberties of mankind, which thereafter are rarely overcome. For these reasons it has been my ardent wish to see a plan devised on a liberal scale which would have a tendency to spread systematic ideas through all parts of this rising Empire, thereby to do away local attachments and state prejudices as far as the nature of things would, or indeed ought to admit, from our national councils. Looking anxiously forward to the accomplishment of so desirable an object as this is (in my estimation), my mind has not been able to contemplate any plan more likely to effect the measure than the establishment of a university in a central part of the United States to which the youth of fortune and talents from all parts thereof might be sent for the completion of their education in all the branches of polite literature in arts and sciences—in acquiring knowledge in the principles of politics and good government and (as a matter of infinite importance in my judgment) by associating with each other and forming friendships in juvenile years, be enabled to free themselves in a proper degree from those local prejudices and habitual jealousies which have just been mentioned and which when carried to excess are never failing sources of disquietude to the public mind and pregnant of mischievous consequences to this country—under these impressions so fully dilated—

Item. I give and bequeath in perpetuity the fifty shares which I hold in the Potomac Company (under the aforesaid Acts of the Legislature of Virginia) towards the endowment of a university to be established within the limits of the District of Columbia, under the auspices of the general Government, if that Government should incline to extend a fostering hand towards it, and until such seminary is established, and the funds arising on these shares shall be required for its support, my further will and desire is that the profit accruing therefrom shall whenever the dividends are made be laid out in purchasing stock in the Bank of Columbia or some other bank at the discretion of my executors, or by the Treasurer of the United States for the time being under the direction of Congress, provided that honorable body should patronize the measure. And the dividends proceeding from the purchase of such stock is to be vested in more stock and so on until a sum adequate to the accomplishment of the object is obtained, of which I have not the smallest doubt before many years pass away, even if no aid or encouraged is given by legislative authority or from any other source.

Item. The hundred shares which I held in the James River Company I have given and now confirm in perpetuity to and for the use and benefit of Liberty Hall Academy in the County of Rockbridge, in the Commonwealth of Virginia.

ITEM. I release, exonerate and discharge the estate of my deceased brother, Samuel Washington [1], from the payment of the money which is due to me for the land I sold to Philip Pendleton (lying in the County of Berkley) who assigned the same to him the said Samuel, who by agreement was to pay me therefor. And whereas by some contract (the purport of which was never communicated to me) between the said Samuel and his son, Thornton Washington [2], the latter became possessed of the aforesaid land without any conveyance having passed from me either to the said Pendleton, the said Samuel or the said Thornton, and without any consideration having been made, by which neglect neither the legal or equitable title has been alienated; it rests therefore with me to declare my intentions concerning the premises—and these are to give and bequeath the said land to whomsoever the said Thornton Washington (who is also dead) devised the same or to his heirs forever, if he died intestate. Exonerating the estate of the said Thornton, equally with that of the said Samuel from payment of the purchase money, which with interest agreeably to the original contract with the said Pendleton would amount to more than a thousand pounds—and whereas two other sons of my said deceased brother Samuel—namely, George Steptoe Washington [3] and Lawrence Augustine Washington [4]—were by the decease of those to whose care they were committed, brought under my protection, and in consequence have occasioned advances on my part for their education at college and other schools, for their board, clothing, and other incidental expenses to the amount of near five thousand dollars over and above the sums furnished by their estate, which sum may be inconvenient for them or their father's estate to refund—I do for these reasons acquit them and the said estate from the payment thereof—my intention being that all accounts between them and me and their father's estate and me shall stand balanced.

ITEM. The balance due to me from the estate of Bartholomew Dandridge [5], deceased (my wife's brother), and which amounted on the first day of October, 1795, to four hundred and twenty-five pounds (as will appear by an account rendered by his deceased son, John Dandridge [6], who was the executor of his father's will) I release and acquit from the payment thereof. And the negroes (then thirty-three in number) formerly belonging to the said estate who were taken in execution—sold—and purchased in, on my account . . . and ever since have remained in the possession and to the use of Mary, widow of the said Bartholomew Dandridge with their increase, it is my will and desire shall continue and be in her possession, without paying hire or making compensation for the same for the time past or to come during her natural life, at the expiration of which, I direct that all of them who are forty years old and upwards shall receive their freedom, all under that age and above sixteen shall serve seven years and no longer, and all under sixteen years shall serve until they are twenty-five years of age and then be free. And to avoid disputes respecting the ages of any of these negroes they are to be taken to the Court of the county in which they reside and the judgment thereof in this relation shall be final and a record thereof made, which may be adduced as evidence at any time thereafter if disputes should arise concerning the same. And I further direct that the heirs of the said Bartholomew Dandridge shall equally share the benefits arising from the services of the said negroes according to the tenor of this devise upon the decease of their mother.

ITEM. If Charles Carter who intermarried with my niece, Betty Lewis [7], is not sufficiently secured in the title to the lots he had of me in the town of Fredericksburg, it is my will and desire that my executors shall make such conveyances of them as the law requires to render it perfect.

ITEM. To my nephew, William Augustine Washington [8], and his heirs (if he should conceive them to be objects worth prosecuting) . . . a lot in the town of Manchester (opposite to Richmond) No. 265—drawn on my sole account and also the tenth of one or two hundred acre lots and two or three half-acre lots in the city and vicinity of Richmond, drawn in partnership with nine others, all in the lottery of the deceased William Byrd are given—as is also a lot which I purchased of John Hood conveyed by William Willie and Samuel Gordon, trustees of the said John Hood, numbered 139 in the town of Edenburgh in the county of Prince George, State of Virginia.

ITEM. To my nephew, Bushrod Washington [9], I give and bequeath all the papers in my possession which relate to my civil and military administration of the affairs of this Country—I leave to him also such of my private papers as are worth preserving; and at the decease of my wife and before, if she is not inclined to retain them, I give and bequeath my library of books and pamphlets of every kind.

ITEM. Having sold lands which I possessed in the State of Pennsylvania and part of a tract held in equal right, with George Clinton, late Governor of New York, in the State of New York—my share of land and interest in the Great Dismal Swamp and a tract of land which I owned in the County of Gloucester; withholding the legal titles thereto until the consideration money should be paid—and having moreover leased and conditionally sold (as will appear by the tenor of the said leases), all my lands upon the Great Kanawha and the tract upon Difficult Run in the County of Loudon, it is my will and direction that whensoever the contracts are fully and respectively complied with according to the spirit, true intent, and meaning thereof on the part of the purchaser, their heirs, or assigns, that then and in that case conveyances are to be made agreeably to the terms of the said contracts and the money arising therefrom when paid to be vested in bank stock, the dividends whereof, as of that also which is already vested therein, is to inure to my said wife during her life but the stock itself is to remain and be subject to the general distribution hereafter directed.

ITEM. To the Earl of Buchan I recommit, "The Box made of the oak that sheltered the Great Sir William Wallace after the battle of Falkirk"—presented to me by his Lordship in terms too flattering for me to repeat—with a request "To pass it, on the event of my decease to the man in my country who should appear to merit it best, upon the same conditions that have induced him to send it to me"—whether easy or not to select the man who might comport with his Lordship's opinion in this respect, is not for me to say, but conceiving that no disposition of this valuable curiosity, can be more eligible than the recommitment of it to his own cabinet agreeably to the original design of the Goldsmith's Company of Edinburgh, who presented it to him, and at his request, consented that it should be transferred to me; I do give and bequeath the same to his Lordship, and in case of his decease, to his heir with my grateful thanks for the distinguished honor of presenting it to me, and more especially for the favorable sentiments with which he accompanied it.

ITEM. To my brother, Charles Washington [10], I give and bequeath the gold-headed cane left me by Doctor Franklin in his will—I add nothing to it because of the ample provision I have made for his issue. To the acquaintances and friends of my juvenile years, Lawrence Washington and Robert Washington [11] of Chotanck, I give my other two gold-headed canes, having my arms engraved on them, and to each (as they will be useful where they live), I leave one the spy glasses which constituted part of my equipage during the late war. To my compatriot in arms and old and intimate friend Doctor Craik, I give my bureau (or as the cabinet makers called it tambour secretary) and the circular chair, an appendage of my study. To Doctor David Stuart I give my large shaving and dressing table, and my telescope. To the Reverend, now Bryan Lord Fairfax I give a Bible in three large folio volumes with notes, presented to me by the Right Reverend Thomas Wilson, Bishop of Sodor and Man. To General de la Fayette I give a pair of finely wrought steel pistols taken from the enemy in the Revolutionary War. To my sisters in law, Hannah Washington [12] and Mildred Washington [13]; to my friends Eleanor Stuart; Hannah Washington of Fairfield and Elizabeth Washington of Hayfield, I give each a mourning ring of the value of one hundred dollars. These bequests are not made for the intrinsic value of them, but as mementos of my esteem and regard. To Tobias Lear [14] I give the use of the farm which he now holds in virtue of a lease from me to him and his deceased wife (for and during their natural lives) free from rent during his life, at the expiration of which it is to be disposed as is hereafter directed. To Sally B. Hanyie (a distant relation of mine) I give and bequeath three hundred dollars. To Sarah Green, daughter of the deceased Thomas Bishop, and to Ann Walker, daughter of John Alton, also deceased, I give each one hundred dollars in consideration of the attachment of their fathers to me, each of whom having lived nearly forty years in my family. To each of my nephews, William Augustine Washington [8], George Lewis [15], George Steptoe Washington [3], Bushrod Washington [9], and Samuel Washington [16], I give one of the swords or cutteaux of which I may die possessed, and they are to choose in the order they are named. These swords are accompanied with an injunction not to unsheath them for the purpose of shedding blood except it be for self-defense, or in defense of their Country and its rights, and in the latter case to keep them unsheathed, and prefer falling with them in their hands to the relinquishment thereof.

And now, having gone through these specific devises, with explanations for the more correct understanding of the meaning and design of them, I proceed to the distribution of the more important parts of my estate, in manner following.

First. To my nephew, Bushrod Washington [9], and his heirs (partly in consideration of an intimation to his deceased father, while we were bachelors and he had kindly undertaken to superintend my estate, during my military services in the former war between Great Britain and France, that if I shall fall therein, Mt. Vernon (then less extensive in dominion than at present, should become his property) I give and bequeath all that part thereof which is comprehended within the following limits—viz.—beginning at the ford of Dogue Run near my mill and extending along the road and bounded thereby as it now goes, and ever has gone since my recollection of it, to the ford of little hunting Creek, at the gum spring until it comes to a knowl opposite to an old road which formerly passed through the lower field of Muddy Hole Farm; at which, on the north side of the said road are three red or Spanish oaks marked as a corner, and a stone placed—thence by a line of trees to be marked rectangular to the black line, or outer boundary of the tract between Thomson Mason and myself, thence with that line easterly (now double ditching with a post and rail fence thereon) to the run of little hunting Creek, thence with that run, which is the boundary of the lands of the late Humphrey Peake and me, to the tide water of the said Creek thence by that water to Potomac River, thence with the River to the mouth of Dogue Creek, and thence with the said Dogue Creek to the place of beginning, at the aforesaid ford, containing upwards of four thousand acres, be the same more or less together with the mansion house, and all other buildings and improvements, thereon.

Secondly. In consideration of the consanguinity between them and my wife, being as nearly related to her as to myself, as on account of the affection I had for, and the obligation I was under to their father when living, who from his youth had attached himself to my person and followed my fortunes through the vicissitudes of the late Revolution, afterwards devoting his time to the superintendence of my private concerns for many years whilst my public employments rendered it impracticable for me to do it myself, thereby affording me essential services, and always performing them in a manner the most filial and respectful; for these reasons I say, I give and bequeath to George Fayette Washington and Lawrence Augustine Washington [17] and their heirs my estate east of little hunting creek lying on the River Potomac, including the farm of 360 acres, leased to Tobias Lear as noticed before and containing in the whole, by deeds, two thousand and twenty-seven acres be it more or less which said estate, it is my will and desire should be equitably and advantageously divided between them, according to quantity, quality and other circumstances when the youngest shall have arrived at the age of twenty-one years, by three judicious and disinterested men, one to be chosen by each of the brothers and the third by these two. In the mean time if the termination of my wife's interest therein should have ceased the profits, arising therefrom are to be applied for their joint uses and benefit.

Third. And whereas it has always been my intention, since my expectation of having issue has ceased, to consider the grand children of my wife in the same light as I do my own relations and to act a friendly part by them, more especially by the two whom we have reared from their earliest infancy, namely, Eleanor Parke Custis [18] and George Washington Parke Custis [19]; and whereas the former of these hath lately intermarried with Lawrence Lewis [35], a son of my deceased sister Betty Lewis, by which union the inducement to provide for them both has been increased—wherefore I give and bequeath to the said Lawrence Lewis and Eleanor Parke Lewis, his wife, and their heirs, the residue of my Mount Vernon estate, not already devised to my nephew Bushrod Washington comprehended within the following description—viz.—all the land north of the road leading from the ford of Dogue Run to the Gum Spring as described in the devise of the other part of the tract to Bushrod Washington until it comes to the stone and three red or Spanish oaks on the knowl—thence with the rectangular line to the back line (between Mr. Mason and me)—thence with that line westerly, along the new double ditch to Dogue Run, by the tumbling dam of my mill—thence with the said Run to the ford aforementioned to which I add all the land I possess west of the said Dogue Run and Dogue Creek bounded, easterly and southerly thereby—together with the mill, distillery, and all other houses and improvements on the premises making together about two thousand acres be it more or less.

Fourth. Actuated by the principle already mentioned, I give and bequeath to George Washington Parke Custis [19], the grand son of my wife and my ward, and to his heirs, the tract I hold on four mile Run in the vicinity of Alexandria containing one thousand, two hundred acres, more or less—and my entire square, numbering twenty-one, in the city of Washington.

Fifth. All the rest and residue of my estate, real and personal, not disposed of in manner aforesaid—in whatsoever consisting—wheresoever lying, and wheresoever found—a schedule of which as far as is recollected, with a reasonable estimate of its value is hereunto annexed—I desire may be sold by my executors at such times, in such manner, and in such credits (if an equal valid and satisfactory distribution of the specific property cannot be made without) as, in their judgment shall be most conducive to the interests of the parties concerned, and the monies arising therefrom to be divided into twenty-three equal parts and applied as follows—viz.:

To William Augustine Washington [8], Elizabeth Spotswood [20], Jane Thornton [21], and the heirs of Ann Ashton [22]; son and daughters of my deceased brother Augustine Washington, I give and bequeath four parts—that is—one part to each of them.

To Fielding Lewis [23], George Lewis [15], Robert Lewis [24], Howell Lewis [25], and Betty Carter [7], sons and daughter of my deceased sister, Betty Lewis, I give and bequeath five other parts—one to each of them.

To George Steptoe Washington [3], Lawrence Augustine Washington [4], Harriot Parke [26], and the heirs of Thornton Washington [2], sons and daughter of my deceased brother Samuel Washington [1], I give and bequeath other four parts, one part to each of them.

To Corbin Washington [27], and the heirs of Jane Washington [28], I give and bequeath two parts—one part to each of them.

To Samuel Washington [16], Frances Ball [29], and Mildred Hammond [30], son and daughters of my brother Charles Washington I give and bequeath three parts—one part to each of them. And to George Fayette Washington [17], Charles Augustine Washington [31] and Maria Washington [32], sons and daughter of my deceased nephew, George Augustine Washington, I give one other part—that is—to each a third of that part.

To Elizabeth Parke Law [33], Martha Parke Peter [34], and Eleanor Parke Lewis [18], I give and bequeath three other parts—that is, a part to each of them.

And to my nephew, Bushrod Washington [9], and Lawrence Lewis [35], and to my ward, the grandson of my wife [19], I give and bequeath one other part—that is a third part to each of them. And if it should so happen, that any of the persons whose names are here enumerated (unknown to me) should now be deceased, or should die before me, that in either of these cases, the heirs of such deceased persons shall, notwithstanding derive all the benefit of the bequest, in the same manner as if he, or she was actually living at the time.

And by way of advice, I recommended it to my executors not to be precipitate in disposing of the landed property (herein directed to be sold) if from temporary causes the sale thereof should be dull, experience having fully evinced, that the price of land (especially above the Falls of the Rivers and on the Western Waters) have been progressively rising, and cannot be long checked in its increasing value—and I particularly recommend it to such of the legatees (under this clause of my will) as can make it convenient, to take each a share of my stock in the Potomac Company in preference to the amount of what it might sell for; being thoroughly convinced myself, that no uses to which the money can be applied will be so productive as the tolls arising from this navigation when in full operation (and this from the nature of things it must be 'ere long) and more especially if that of the Shenandoah is added thereto.

The family vault at Mount Vernon requiring repairs, and being improperly situated besides, I desire that a new one of brick, and upon a larger scale, may be built at the foot of what is commonly called the vineyard inclosure—on the ground which is marked out—in which my remains, with those of my deceased relatives (now in the old vault) and such others of my family as may choose to be entombed there, may be deposited. And it is my express desire that my corpse may be interred in a private manner, without parade or funeral oration.

Lastly. I constitute and appoint my dearly beloved wife, Martha Washington, my nephews, William Augustine Washington [8], Bushrod Washington [9], George Steptoe Washington [3], Samuel Washington [16], and Lawrence Lewis [35], and my ward, George Washington Parke Custis [19] (when he shall have arrived at the age of twenty years), executrix and executors of this Will and Testament. In the construction of which it will readily be perceived that no professional character has been consulted or has had any agency in the draught— and that, although it has occupied many of my leisure hours to digest and to through it into its present form, it may notwithstanding, appear crude and incorrect. But having endeavored to be plain and explicit in all the devises—even at the expense of prolixity, perhaps of tautology, I hope, and trust, that no disputes will arise concerning them; but if contrary to expectation the case should be otherwise from the want of legal expression, or the usual technical terms, or because too much or too little, has been said on any of the devises to be consonant with law, my will and direction expressly is, that all disputes (if unhappily any should arise) shall be decided by three impartial and intelligent men, known for their probity and good understanding; two to be chosen by the disputants, each having the choice of one, and the third by those two—which three men thus chosen, shall unfettered by law, or legal constructions declare their sense of the testator's intention; and such decision is, to all intents and purposes to be as binding on the parties as if it had been given in the Supreme Court of the United States.

In witness of all and of each of the things herein contained I have set my hand and seal this ninth day of July, in the year one thousand, seven hundred and ninety-nine, and of the independence of the United States, the twenty-fourth.

LAST WILL AND TESTAMENT
OF
HEATH ANDREW LEDGER

I Karen Frances TYSOE Justice of the Pcaoe of 52 Rocokion Road, Claremont, Western Australia, hereby certify this to be a true and correct copy of the original of the Last Will and Testament of Health Andrew LEDGER dated 12th April 2003.

11th February 2008

_____

K.F. Tysoe, IP

TESTATOR _____   WITNESS _____

                                      WITNESS _____

I HEATH ANDREW LEDGER of 3 Armstrong Road, Applecross, Western Australia Declare this to be my will.

1. I REVOKE all earlier wills and codicils.

2. In this Will unless otherwise required by the context or subject matter.

"Duties" means all death, estate, succession or other duties or taxes payable in respect of my death or the passing of property under this Will, but does not include any tax imposed by the Income Tax Act 1986, as amended, substituted, or re-enacted from time to time or any other Act imposing a tax upon incomes;

"Residuary Estate" has the meaning ascribed to it by Clause 5;

"Trustee" means the executor or executors of this Will and the trustee or trustees for the time being of any trusts arising under it.

3. I APPOINT ROBERT JOHN COLLINS Company Director of 215 Roberts Road, Subiaco in the State of Western Australia and WILLIAM MARK DYSON Chartered Accountant of 359 Marine Terrace, Geraldton in the said State to be the Joint Executors and Trustees of this my Will.

4. I DIRECT that any joint loan by myself and any other person to the Ledger Investment Trust be allocated at the sole discretion of my Trustees.

5. My Trustee shall hold all my property not otherwise disposed of by this Will ON TRUST:
    (a) to pay my debts and testamentary and executorship expenses;
    (b) to pay all Duties; and
    (c) as to fifty percent (50%) of my estate to divide it between my sisters KATHERINE ANNE LEDGER, ASHLEIGH KIRSTEN BELL and OLIVIA JANE LEDGER in equal shares PROVIDED THAT if any of them are under the age of eighteen (18) years I direct my Trustee to hold their respective entitlement under this Will in trust until they reach the age of eighteen (18). I further instruct my Trustee at his sole discretion to apply from the Corpus or Income of my said sisters' respective entitlements to their education and well being during their minority, including but not limited to education fees, books and a motor vehicle if my Trustee considers it necessary for the purpose of attending a place of education or employment. If one of my said sisters should predecease me then the remaining sisters shall be entitled to the share that the deceased sister would otherwise have taken hereunder.
    (d) to hold the remainder of my estate ("Residuary Estate") and to divide it between my parents KIM FRANCIS LEDGER and SALLY ANNE BELL in equal shares, and if one parent should predecease the other or die before me then the remaining parent shall be entitled to the equal share that the other parent would otherwise have taken hereunder.

6. Except to the extent inconsistent with the terms and provisions in this Will, the powers conferred on my Trustee by the Trustee's Act 1962–1978 as amended from time to time are in augmentation of the powers conferred by this Will.

7. My Trustee will have the following powers in connection with my estate:

    (a) to retain the identity of any asset, to sell any asset at any, time, and to distribute the assets in specie;

TESTATOR _____   WITNESS _____

                                                 WITNESS _____

(b) until the absolute vesting of any share or interest in a beneficiary under this Will to apply from time to time the whole or any part of the income from that share or interest with recourse if necessary to the capital of that share or interest for or towards the proper maintenance, education, advancement, benefit or support of that beneficiary and to make payments for that purpose to the beneficiary or to the parent, guardian or carer of that beneficiary without being responsible to see to the application of those payments; and

(c) without limitation and as if my Trustee were beneficially entitled to my Residuary Estate to invest, change or retain investments including unsecured interest free loans or any non-income producing asset.

8. If:

(a) one or more persons hae (sic) died and one or more deaths are presumed; or

(b) two or more deaths are presumed; and

(c) the order of deaths, whether the deaths are proved or presumed, is uncertain; the provisions of Section 120 of the Property Law Act 1969 will apply.

IN WITNESS WHERE OF I have hereunto set my land to this my Will (contained on this and the preceding page of paper)

this 12th day April of 2003.

SIGNED by the Testator in our presence}
and signed by us no witnesses in the}
presence of the Testator and of each other}

_____
Testator

_____
Witness Signature

_____
Witness Signature

_____
Witness Signature

_____
Witness Signature

LAST WILL AND TESTAMENT OF MARILYN MONROE

I, MARILYN MONROE, do make, publish and declare this to be my Last Will and Testament.

FIRST: I hereby revoke all former Wills and Codicils by me made.

TESTATOR _____

WITNESS _____

WITNESS _____

SECOND: I direct my Executor, hereinafter named, to pay all of my just debts, funeral expenses and testamentary charges as soon after my death as can conveniently be done.

THIRD: I direct that all succession, estate or inheritance taxes which may be levied against my estate and/or against any legacies and/or devises hereinafter set forth shall be paid out of my residuary estate.

FOURTH:

  (a) I give and bequeath to BERNICE MIRACLE, should she survive me, the sum of $10,000.00.
  (b) I give and bequeath to MAY REIS, should she survive me, the sum of $10,000.00.
  (c) I give and bequeath to NORMAN and HEDDA ROSTEN, or to the survivor of them, or if they should both predecease me, then to their daughter, PATRICIA ROSTEN, the sum of $5, 000.00. it being my wish that such sum be used for the education of PATRICIA ROSTEN.
  (d) I give and bequeath all of my personal effects and clothing to LEE STRASBERG, or if he should predecease me, then to my Executor hereinafter named, it being my desire that he distribute these, in his sole discretion, among my friends, colleagues and those to whom I am devoted.

FIFTH: I give and bequeath to my Trustee, hereinafter named, the sum of $100,000.00, in Trust, for the following uses and purposes:

  (a) To hold, manage, invest and reinvest the said property and to receive and collect the income therefrom.
  (b) To pay the net income therefrom, together with such amounts of principal as shall be necessary to provide $5,000.00 per annum, in equal quarterly installments, for the maintenance and support of my mother, GLADYS BAKER, during her lifetime.
  (c) To pay the net income therefrom, together with such amounts of principal as shall be necessary to provide $2,500.00 per annum, in equal quarterly installments, for the maintenance and support of MRS. MICHAEL CHEKHOV during her lifetime.
  (d) Upon the death of the survivor between my mother, GLADYS BAKER, and MRS. MICHAEL CHEKHOV to pay over the principal remaining in the Trust, together with any accumulated income, to DR. MARIANNE KRIS to be used by her for the furtherance of the work of such psychiatric institutions or groups as she shall elect.

SIXTH: All the rest, residue and remainder of my estate, both real and personal, of whatsoever nature and wheresoever situate, of which I shall die seized or possessed or to which I shall be in any way entitled, or over which I shall possess any power of appointment by Will at the time of my death, including any lapsed legacies, I give, devise and bequeath as follows:

  (a) to MAY REIS the sum of $40,000.00 or 25% of the total remainder of my estate, whichever shall be the lesser,
  (b) To DR. MARIANNE KRIS 25% of the balance thereof, to be used by her as set forth in ARTICLE FIFTH (d) of this my Last Will and Testament.
  (c) To LEE STRASBERG the entire remaining balance.

SEVENTH: I nominate, constitute and appoint AARON R. FROSCH Executor of this my Last Will and Testament. In the event that he should die or fail to qualify, or resign or for any other reason be unable to act, I nominate, constitute and appoint L. ARNOLD WEISSBERGER in his place and stead.

EIGHTH: I nominate, constitute and appoint AARON R. FROSCH Trustee under this my Last Will and Testament. In the event he should die or fail to qualify, or resign or for any other reason be unable to act, I nominate, constitute and appoint L. Arnold Weissberger in his place and stead.

Marilyn Monroe (L.S.)

SIGNED, SEALED, PUBLISHED and DECLARED by MARILYN MONROE, the Testatrix above named, as and for her Last Will and Testament, in our presence and we, at her request and in her presence and in the presence of each other, have hereunto subscribed our names as witnesses this 14th day of January, 1961

Aaron R. Frosch residing at 10 West 86th St. NYC

Louise H. White residing at 709 E. 56 St., New York, NY

LAST WILL OF MICHAEL JOSEPH JACKSON

NOTE: According to Reuters, February 19, 2011, Michael Jackson's estate generated $310 million in revenue from album sales, a film, merchandising, and other products since the "Thriller" singer died in 2009. He had paid $159 million to pay down his debt, estimated at more than $400 million. Debts included a $900,000 payment to Forest Lawn Memorial cemetery, $27.2 million in taxes, and $4 million in mortgage payments on his properties.

I, MICHAEL JOSEPH JACKSON, a resident of the State of California, declare this to be my last Will, and do hereby revoke all former wills and codicils made by me.

I

I declare that I am not married. My marriage to DEBORAH JEAN ROWE JACKSON has been dissolved. I have three children now living. PRINCE MICHAEL JACKSON, JR, PARIS MICHAEL KATHERINE JACKSON and PRINCE MICHAEL JOSEPH JACKSON, IL I have no other children, living or deceased.

II

It is my intention by this Will to dispose of all property which I am entitled to dispose of by will. I specifically refrain from exercising all powers of appointment that I may possess at the time of my death.

III

I give my entire estate to the Trustee or Trustees then acting under that certain Amended and Restated Declaration of Trust executed on March 22, 2002 by me as Trustee and Trustor which is called the MICHAEL JACKSON FAMILY TRUST, giving effect to any amendments thereto made prior to my death. All such assets shall be held, managed and distributed as a part of said Trust according to its terms and not as a separate testamentary trust.

If for any reason this gift is not operative or is invalid, or if the aforesaid Trust fails or has been revoked, I give my residuary estate to the Trustee or Trustees named to act in the MICHAEL JACKSON FAMILY TRUST, as Amended and Restated on March 22, 2002, and I direct said Trustee or Trustees to divide, administer, hold and distribute the trust estate pursuant to the provisions of said Trust, as hereinabove referred to as such provisions now exist to the same extent and in the same manner as though that certain Amended and Restated Declaration of Trust, were herein set forth in full, but without giving effect to any subsequent amendments after the date of this Will. The Trustee, Trustees, or any successor Trustee named in such Trust Agreement shall serve without bond.

IV

I direct that all federal estate taxes and state inheritance or succession taxes payable upon or resulting from or by reason of my death (herein "Death Taxes") attributable to property which is part of the trust estate of the MICHAEL JACKSON FAMILY TRUST, including property which passes to said trust from my probate estate shall be paid by the Trustee of said trust in accordance with its terms. Death Taxes attributable to property passing outside this Will, other than property constituting the trust estate of the trust mentioned in the preceding sentence, shall be charged against the taker of said property.

V

I appoint JOHN BRANCA, JOHN McCLAIN and BARRY SIEGEL as co-Executors of this Will. In the event of any of their deaths, resignations, inability, failure or refusal to serve or continue to serve as a co-Executor, the other shall serve and no replacement need be named. The co-Executors serving at any time after my death may name one or more replacements to serve in the event that none of the three named individuals is willing or able to serve at any time.

The term "my executors" as used in this Will shall include any duly acting personal representative or representatives of my estate. No individual acting as such need post a bond.

I hereby give to my Executors, full power and authority at any time or times to sell, lease, mortgage, pledge, exchange or otherwise dispose of the property, whether real or personal comprising my estate, upon such terms as my Executors shall deem best, to continue any business enterprises, to purchase assets from my estate, to continue in force and pay insurance premiums on any insurance policy, including life insurance, owned by my estate, and for any of the foregoing purposes to make, execute and deliver any and all deeds, contracts, mortgages, bills of sale or other instruments necessary or desirable therefor. In addition, I give to my Executors full power to invest and reinvest the estate funds and assets in any kind of property, real, personal or mixed, and every kind of investment, specifically including, but not by way of limitation, corporate obligations of every kind and stocks, preferred or common, and interests in investment trusts and shares in investment companies, and any common trust find administered by any corporate executor hereunder, which men of prudent discretion and intelligence acquire for their own account.

VI

Except as otherwise provided in this Will or in the Trust referred to in Article III hereof, I have intentionally omitted to provide for my heirs. I have intentionally omitted to provide for my former wife, DEBORAH JEAN ROWE JACKSON.

VII

If at the time of my death I own or have an interest in property located outside of the State of California requiring ancillary administration, I appoint my domiciliary Executors as ancillary Executors for such property. I give to said domiciliary Executors the following additional powers, rights and privileges to be exercised in their sole and absolute discretion, with reference to such property: to cause such ancillary administration to be commenced, carried on and completed; to determine what assets, if any, are to be sold by the ancillary Executors; to pay directly or to advance funds from the California estate to the ancillary Executors for the payment of all claims, taxes, costs and administration expenses, including compensation of the ancillary Executors and attorneys' fees incurred by reason of the ownership of such property and by such ancillary administration; and upon completion of such ancillary administration, I authorize and direct the ancillary Executors to distribute, transfer and deliver the residue of such property to the domiciliary Executors herein, to be distributed by them under the terms of this Will, it being my intention that my entire estate shall be administered as a unit and that my domiciliary Executors shall supervise and control, so far as permissible by local law, any ancillary administration proceedings deemed necessary in the settlement of my estate.

VIII

If any of my children are minors at the time of my death, I nominate my mother, KATHERINE JACKSON as guardian of the persons and estates of such minor children. If KATHERINE JACKSON fails to survive me, or is unable or unwilling to act as guardian, I nominate DIANA ROSS as guardian of the persons and estates of such minor children.

I subscribe my name to this Will this _____7_____ day of ___July___, 2002.

Signed 'Michael Joseph Jackson'

On the date written below, MICHAEL JOSEPH JACKSON, declared to us, the undersigned, that the foregoing instrument consisting of five (5) pages, including the page signed by us as witnesses, was his Will and requested us to act as witnesses to it. He thereupon signed this Will in our presence, all of us being present at the same time. We now, at his request, in his presence and in the presence of each other, subscribe our names as witnesses.

Each of us in now more than eighteen (18) years of age and a competent witness and resides at the address set forth after his name.

Each of us is acquainted with MICHAEL JOSEPH JACKSON. At this time, he is over the age of eighteen (18) years and, to the best of our knowledge, he is of sound mind and is not acting under duress, menace, fraud, misrepresentation or undue influence.

We declare under penalty that the perjury that the foregoing is true and correct.

Executed on July 7th, 2002 at 5:00 p.m., Los Angeles

LAST WILL AND TESTAMENT OF PAUL NEWMAN

I, PAUL NEWMAN, also known as PAUL L. NEWMAN, of Westport, Connecticut, make, publish and declare this to be my last will and testament. I hereby revoke all wills and codicils to wills which I have made previously.

Section 1: Tangible Personal Property:

1.1 *Airplane and Race Cars*:   I direct the executors to sell any airplane and all race cars which I own at the time of my death at public auction or private sale, as the executors shall deem advisable in order to realize their fair market value. I authorize the executors to engage one or more appraisers or auctioneers knowledgeable about such items to assist the executors in determining both an appropriate value and the best method for marketing such items. The net proceeds thereof shall pass under Section 6 as a part of my residuary estate.

1.2 *Oscars and other Theatrical Awards*:   I bequeath all oscars and other theatrical awards which I own at the time of my death to Newman's own Foundation, a Delaware corporation organized exclusively for purposes described under section 501(c)(3) of the Internal Revenue code (or to its successor in interest), hereinafter referred to as "Newman's Own Foundation."

1.3 *Other Tangible Personal Property*:   I bequeath to my wife, Joanne Woodward Newman (also known as Joanne Woodward), if she survives me, all tangible personal property which I own at the time of my death other than any property effectively sold and/or bequeathed as provided under subsections 1.1 and 1.2 above, including without limitation all household furnishings, musical instruments, works of art, personal effects and automobiles, together with any prepaid insurance or proceeds of insurance thereon. If my wife does not survive me, I bequeath such tangible personal property and insurance to my descendants who survive me, in shares *per stirpes,* to be divided among them as the executors shall determine, in proportions which shall reflect the value of each descendant's stirpital share as nearly as may be practicable; *provided, however,* that the share of any grandchild or more remote descendant of mine who has not attained age 35 at the time of my death shall be distributed to the then trustee under the Amended and Restated Newman Living Trust Number One of even date established by me as settlor and trustee and signed by me prior to the execution of this will ("my Trust Agreement"), to be held and administered in a separate trust for the benefit of such person under subsection 3.12 and the succeeding provisions of my Trust Agreement as my Trust Agreement hereafter may be further amended.

1.4 *Memorandum*:   I may leave a memorandum containing suggestions for the disposition of certain items of my tangible personal property, but such memorandum shall not be legally binding on the legatees named in this Section.

Section 2: Promissory Notes: If my wife, Joanne woodward Newman, does not survive me, I bequeath any promissory notes payable to me (i) by any daughter of mine who survives me, and (ii) by Cora Casem, presently of Fresh Meadows, New York, if she survives me, to the debtor of each such promissory note, together with any accrued and unpaid interest thereon.

Section 3: Specific Bequest: If my wife, Joanne woodward Newman, survives me, I bequeath (A) any property interests which I own at the time of my death in (i) coleytown productions, Inc., (ii) Aspetuck Productions, Ltd., (iii) Newman Foreman Productions, Inc., and (iv) any other entity that receives royalties, profit participations or residuals representing payment for my services rendered as an actor and (B) any other right to receive royalties, profit participations or residuals representing payment for my services rendered as an actor to the then trustee under my Trust Agreement, to be held and administered in Marital Trust B for the benefit of my wife under Subsection 3.8 and the succeeding provisions of my Trust Agreement as my Trust Agreement hereafter may be further amended. If my wife does not survive me, I bequeath such property interests to Newman's own Foundation. In addition, I direct that the executors shall have no rights to sell any of such property interests passing under this section.

Section 4: Property Interests: I bequeath (i) all of my publicity and IP Rights (as defined below), (ii) my entire interest in Newman's Own, Inc. (or its successor in interest), (iii) my entire interest in Salad King, Inc. (or its successor in interest), and (iv) my entire interest in No Limit, LLC (or its successor in interest) to Newman's Own Foundation. The term "Publicity and IP Rights" as used throughout my will shall mean those intellectual property and related tangible or intangible property rights that I may own at the time of my death or in which I may have any interest at the time of my death or in which I may have any interest at the time of my death relating to my name, signature, image (still and moving, photographed and drawn), voice, persona, performances, and various related trademarks and copyrights together with the goodwill associated with any such rights, and including any applications or registrations for such rights, any rights of publicity, any rights to receive payments associated with such intellectual property rights and such rights of publicity, including royalties, profit participations or residuals, any rights to enforce and sue for past and future infringement or violation of such rights, and, to the extent transferable, any rights granted to me in connection with any license or other agreements to which I am a party, other than any property interests effectively bequeathed under Section 3 above.

Section 5: Real Estate: I devise and bequeath to my wife, Joanne Woodward Newman, if she survives me, absolutely and in fee simple, all real estate and interests in real estate, wherever situated, which are owned and used by me at the time of my death as my principal residence, as a seasonal residence or as an office (including without limitation any interest in a condominium or cooperative), together with any prepaid insurance or proceeds of insurance thereon, but subject to any mortgage or other debt secured by such property.

Section 6: Residuary Estate: I devise and bequeath all the residue of my estate, both real and personal, wherever situated, including any property not effectively bequeathed or devised under the foregoing provisions of this will but excluding any property over which I have a power of appointment, to the then trustee under my Trust Agreement, to be administered under the terms thereof as it hereafter may be further amended.

Section 7: Appointment of Executors: I appoint Brian Murphy, presently of Manhattan Beach, California, Robert H. Forrester, presently of Avon, Connecticut, and such individual (other than a daughter of mine) selected by majority vote of my daughters, who survive me, to be the co-executors of my estate. If Brian Murphy, Robert H. Forrester or such individual selected by majority vote of my daughters fails to qualify or ceases to serve as an executor, the other or others of them shall serve as co-executors or sole executor, as the case may be, with all the same powers, discretions and immunities.

I empower the executors to act as ancillary executors of my estate or to appoint any qualified person or corporation to act as ancillary executor in any jurisdiction.

I direct that no bond or other security shall be required of any person or corporation serving as executor or ancillary executor.

Section 8: Powers of Executors: In addition to all powers and discretions conferred upon the executors by other provisions of this will or by law, I hereby grant to the executors all the powers of the Connecticut Fiduciary Powers Act set forth in Connecticut General Statutes $45a-234, and the following additional powers of that Act set forth in Connecticut General Statutes $45a-235: (2) Buy Insurance and Annuities; (3) Invest in Partnerships, etc.; (6) Form Corporation or Other Entity; (7) Fiduciary May Become Director or Officer; (9) Residential Realty; (10) Deal with Estate and Trust; (11) Suits on Insurance Policies; (12) Advancement of Income; (14) Reduce Interest Rates; (15) Establish and Maintain Reserves; (16) Investment Philosophy; (17) Investment During Estate Administration; (19) Remortgage and Refinance Real Estate; (21) Distribute Directly to Remaindermen; (22) Disclaimer of Power; (23) Comply with Stock Restrictions; (24) Continue Subchapter S Election; (25) Acquire Interest in Trust Asset; (26) Income to Custodian for Minor; and (27) General Powers.

In addition, without limiting the foregoing, I give the executors the following powers:

(A) To enter into any transactions authorized under this Section or by law with the legal representative or trustee of any estate or trust in which any beneficiary hereunder or executor hereof has any beneficial interest, even though the legal representative or trustee of such estate or trust is also an executor hereof;

(B) To allocate any portion of my generation-skipping transfer tax exemption under Section 2631(a) of the Internal Revenue Code to any property as to which I am the transferor, including any property transferred by me during my life as to which I did not make an allocation prior to my death;

(C) To disclaim, in whole or in part, on behalf of my estate any interest in property, real or personal, including any power;

(D) To elect to treat as qualified terminable interest property for purposes of the federal or any state estate tax marital deduction all or any specific portion of any property includable in my gross estate for federal or state estate tax purposes. The executors may make any such election in order to minimize the death taxes payable by my estate and, in addition, shall consider the effect of any such election on the death taxes payable by my wife's estate, especially if she should die before any such election is made;

(E) To exercise the special election under Section 2652(a)(3) of the Internal Revenue Code;

(F) To take any and all reasonable measures to (i) manage and control the use of my publicity and IP Rights, (ii) license or otherwise give permission for approved uses of my publicity and IP Rights, and (iii) prevent uses of my publicity and IP Rights that I either explicitly did not approve during my lifetime or that are inconsistent with those uses I did explicitly approve regardless of whether they were disapproved during my lifetime;

(G) To protect my publicity and IP Rights including taking reasonable measures to decline and oppose any and all uses of my publicity and IP Rights for commercial purposes anywhere in the world except as authorized under paragraph (H) below and except as they were used in photoplays or other performances which I authorized during my lifetime and for advertising and promotion in connection with such photoplays or other performances; *provided, however,* that those photoplays or other performances are performed or published in the same or substantially identical form as in their original release or other form which I authorized during my lifetime;

(H) To take all reasonable measures to prevent any and all uses of my publicity and IP Rights on any product or in connection with the advertising or promotion of any product or service whatsoever except in connection with food products (a) of at least the quality of the current Newman's Own brand of products and

(b) authorized and/or licensed by: (i) No Limit, LLC, Newman's Own Foundation, and/or Newman's Own, Inc., (or their respective successors in interest), or (ii) in connection with fundraising activities for the Hole in the Wall Gang Camp Fund, Inc., Hole in the Wall Foundation or the Association of Hole in the Wall Gang Camps and its member camps (or their respective successors in interest); *provided, however,* that such uses have been approved by No Limit, LLC (or its successor in interest) and/or Newman's Own Foundation and, *provided, further,* that such uses are consistent with the quality of uses made for my publicity and IP Rights during my lifetime;

(I) To not authorize, and to employ all reasonable measures to oppose and prevent, any uses of my publicity and IP Rights in connection with the creation, enhancement or contribution to any virtual performance or reanimation of any performance by me by the use of any technique, technology or medium now in existence or which may be known or created in the future anywhere in the universe; *provided, however,* this power is not intended to prevent the use of any technique or method by which any performance of mine may be restored or otherwise preserved in its existing form;

(J) To appoint one or more advisors for the purpose of conserving and protecting my publicity and IP Rights including without limitation (a) residuals, (b) shares or percentages in profits or other revenue from television programs, films or plays, (c) royalties, (d) ownership or interest in such publicity and IP Rights, or (e) merchandising rights; and

(K) To borrow funds in such amounts and for such purposes as the executors shall deem to be in the best interests of my estate and the beneficiaries thereof; to purchase property on the credit of my estate; and to guarantee any debt or obligation incurred by me or any entity which is owned substantially or entirely, directly or indirectly, by me or my estate, and in connection therewith, to execute and deliver promissory notes or other evidences of such indebtedness or guarantee; to mortgage, pledge, hypothecate or otherwise encumber all or any part of my estate; and to secure payment of such indebtedness or on such guarantee from the assets of my estate. In exercising such authority, I direct the executors to guarantee bank loan indebtedness incurred by Newman's Own, Inc. (or any parent, successor, subsidiary or affiliated company of Newman's Own, Inc.), to finance or otherwise facilitate such entity's purchase of Newman's Own Organics, Inc. (or its successor in interest), provided that such guarantee shall not exceed the amount of is Million Dollars. I authorize the executors to take all necessary actions, including the sale of assets of my estate, as the executors shall determine to be appropriate in exercising this directive. I further specifically authorize the executors to secure such guarantee using assets of my estate to the extent and in such manner as the executors in the executors' discretion shall determine and to pay any bank loan indebtedness on such guarantee in full at such time or times and in such manner as the executors in the executors' discretion shall determine.

All such powers shall be exercisable by the executors without probate court approval. The executors' determination with respect to the exercise of any power or election hereunder shall be conclusive upon all persons affected thereby. The executors shall not be responsible for losses to any person resulting from the good faith exercise of discretion by the executors.

Section 9:   Expenses, Bequests and Taxes:

9.1 *Expenses:*   I direct the executors to pay all of (i) my funeral and related expenses; (ii) the expenses of administering my estate, including the expenses of any ancillary probate proceedings; and (iii) the reasonable expenses incurred in insuring, safeguarding, storing, delivering or transferring any property included in my probate estate.

9.2 *Death Taxes:*   I direct the executors to pay all death taxes (as hereinafter defined), including any interest and penalties thereon, levied or assessed upon or with respect to any property which is included in my estate for the purpose of any such tax, whether such property passes under this will or otherwise.

The term "death taxes" shall mean all legacy, succession, inheritance, transfer and estate taxes, but shall not include generation-skipping transfer taxes imposed under Chapter 13 of the Internal Revenue Code or under any state tax laws.

9.3 *Sources of Payment; Apportionment*:   I direct that no portion of any such expenses or death taxes paid under this Section shall be prorated or apportioned among or charged against the respective devisees, legatees, beneficiaries, transferees or other recipients, or charged against any property which passes to any of them, and I direct the executors to pay such expenses and death taxes from my probate estate, in the same manner as payment of administration expenses.

The executors may direct the trustee under my Trust Agreement to pay to my estate such amounts of trust property as the executors shall determine are required for payment, in part or in full, of (i) any such expenses, (ii) any such death taxes (including any interest and penalties thereon), and (iii) any bequests or devises contained in this will and any codicils thereto.

Notwithstanding the foregoing, if my gross estate as determined for the purpose of any death taxes includes property with respect to which I have a power of appointment, the executors shall recover from such property and/or from the recipient thereof, as the executors shall determine, the *prorata* share of each death tax attributable to such property, in an amount which bears the same ratio to the total of such death tax as the value of such property bears to my taxable estate as determined for the purpose of each death tax. The executors may recover such amounts on or before the due date of any such death tax and on or before the due date of any additional assessments, as may be determined for any such death tax.

Section 10: Will And/Or Trust Agreement Contest: If any beneficiary under this will and/or any codicil hereto ("my will") and/or under my Trust Agreement, shall in any manner, directly or indirectly, attempt to contest the probate or validity of any part or all of my will and/or my Trust Agreement, then such beneficiary shall forfeit and cease to have any right or interest whatsoever under my will, and in such event, I direct that my estate shall be disposed of in all respects as if such beneficiary had predeceased me.

Section 11: General Provisions:

11.1 The underlined captions in this will are for convenience of reference only and shall not be deemed to define or limit the provisions hereof or to affect their construction or application.

11.2 The gender and the number of any word shall be construed to include another gender or number whenever appropriate.

11.3 When a distribution is to be made hereunder to my descendants "in shares *per stirpes*," the initial stirpital division shall be at the level of my children, whether or not any child of mine is living at the time of such distribution.

11.4 With respect to adopted persons other than my children, the terms "grandchildren" and "descendants" shall include only those persons legally adopted before attaining age 18 and those descended from persons so adopted.

11.5 The terms "executor," "executors" and "co-executors" shall mean the fiduciary or fiduciaries appointed by a court of competent jurisdiction to administer my estate.

11.6 The term "Internal Revenue Code" shall mean-the Internal Revenue Code of 1986 (or its successor), as amended to the date of my death.

11.7 In the event that Newman's Own Foundation does not exist or is not an organization described in Sections 170 (c) and 2055 (a) of the Internal Revenue Code at the time of my death, the executors shall distribute any such property which otherwise would have been distributed to it to one or more organizations then described in Sections 170(c) and 2055 (a) as executors shall select in the executors' sole discretion.

11.8 If my wife, Joanne Woodward Newman, and I die under such circumstances that the order of our deaths cannot be determined, she shall be presumed to have survived me.

IN WITNESS WHEREOF, I have hereunto set my hand this 11th day of April, 2008.

_____

Paul Newman

Signed, published and declared by the above-named testator, Paul Newman, as and for his last will and testament, in the presence of us who at the testator's request, in his presence and in the presence of each other have hereunto subscribed our names as witnesses:

_____   of _____

Carolyn Murphy

_____   of _____

Charles T. Wright

STATE OF CONNECTICUT)

: ss.: Westport

COUNTRY OF FAIRFIELD)

The undersigned, being duly sworn, say that they witnessed the execution of the within will of the testator, Paul Newman, and subscribed the same in his presence, in the presence of each other and at the testator's request; that said testator, at the time of signing said will, was of full age and of sound mind and memory, that the testator voluntarily signed said will and declared the same to be his last will and testament in the presence of the said two subscribing witnesses thereto; and that this affidavit is made at the request of the testator.

_____

Carolyn Murphy

_____

Charles T. Wright

Subscribed and sworn to
before me this 11th day
of April, 2008.

_____

Judith M. Keppelman
Notary Public
My commission expires: 6/30/10

FIRST CODICIL TO LAST WILL AND TESTAMENT OF PAUL NEWMAN

I, PAUL NEWMAN, also known as PAUL L. NEWMAN, of Westport, Connecticut, make, publish and declare this to be the first codicil to my will dated April 11, 2008.

First: I revoke in its entirety Section 5 of my will dated April 11, 2008, and substitute the following in its place:

> "*Section 5: Westport Residential Real Estate*: I devise and bequeath to my wife, Joanne Woodward Newman, if she survives me, absolutely and in fee—simple, all real estate and interests in real estate, located in Westport, Connecticut, which are owned and used by me at the time of my death as my principal residence or as a seasonal residence (including without limitation any interest in a residential condominium or cooperative), together with any prepaid insurance or proceeds of insurance thereon, but subject to any mortgage or other debt secured by such property."

Second: In all other respects, I ratify, confirm and republish my will dated April 11, 2008, and I declare that such will and this first codicil together shall constitute my last will and testament.

IN WITNESS WHEREOF, I have hereunto set my hand this 24th day of July, 2008.

_____
Paul Newman

Signed, published and declared by the above-named testator, Paul Newman, as and for the first codicil to his will dated April 11, 2008, in the presence of us who at the testator's request, in his presence and in the presence of each other have hereunto subscribed our names as witnesses:

_____   of _____
Cora Casem

_____   of _____
Myriam Babel

STATE OF CONNECTICUT)

: ss.: Westport

COUNTRY OF FAIRFIELD)

The undersigned, being duly sworn, say that they witnessed the execution of the within first codicil of the testator, Paul Newman, and subscribed the same in his presence, in the presence of each other and at the testator's request; that said testator, at the time of signing said codicil, was of full age and of sound mind and memory; that the testator voluntarily signed said codicil and declared the same to be the first codicil to his will dated April 11,

2008, in the presence of the said two subscribing witnesses thereto; and that this affidavit is made at the request of the testator.

_____

Cora Casem

_____

Myriam Babel

Subscribed and sworn to this
24th day of July, 2008,
before me

_____

Judith M. Keppelman
Notary Public
My commission expires: 06/30/2010

Appendix C
INTERNET WEBSITES

Since the last edition of this book (and certainly since the first!) the Internet has changed dramatically. Searching for things online has in some ways become much easier and more user friendly, especially with generalized search engines such as Google and Bing, which have vast databases. In others, it is just as difficult due to the need to sift through lists and lists of items that may or may not have anything to do with your search terms.

To make things a little easier for you, we have compiled some Internet web addresses that may be of use or interest to you. Note that web addresses often change over time; however, these web addresses were correct at the time of publication.

Cornell Law School Legal Information Institute

One of the best sites online for legal items for a number of years has been the Cornell Law School Legal Information Institute (LII), http://www.law.cornell.edu. On the Cornell website you can search for a lawyer, the Constitution as well as state constitutions, federal and state statutes and codes, federal and state law case opinions, as well as overviews of certain areas of legal practice. The site is comprehensive, accurate, and easy to navigate. In addition to the Cornell website, you may find legal information at the web addresses listed below.

Federal Law

- Public Bills and Resolutions: Thomas, named after Thomas Jefferson, at the Library of Congress: http://thomas.loc.gov/
- United States Code: House of Representatives, Office of the Law Revision Counsel: http://uscode.house.gov/
- United States Code: GPO Access, a service of the U.S. Government Printing Office: http://www.gpoaccess.gov/uscode/index.html
- United States Code: Cornell Law School Legal Information Institute (LII): http://www.law.cornell.edu/uscode/
- Federal Cases: GPO Access, a service of the U.S. Government Printing Office: http://www.gpoaccess.gov/judicial.html
- Supreme Court Cases: United States Supreme Court website: http://www.supremecourtus.gov/opinions/opinions.html
- Lower Federal Courts: U.S. Courts website, maintained by the Administrative Office of the U.S. Courts: http://www.uscourts.gov/courtlinks/
- Other Judiciary Links, Federal: U.S. Courts website, maintained by the Administrative Office of the U.S. Courts: http://www.uscourts.gov/courtlinks/#other

State Law

Cornell's LII website has links to all state statute and code websites. In addition to the websites listed below, you can search for individual state statutes, codes, cases, and other resources using a general search engine such as Google, Bing, or Yahoo!.

- State Statutes and Codes: Cornell Law School Legal Information Institute (LII) main page with links to individual state information: http://www.law.cornell.edu/statutes.html
- State Statutes and Codes: http://www.whpgs.org/f.htm
- State Statutes and Codes as well as Cases: Findlaw: http://www.findlaw.com/11stategov/index.html
- State Statutes and Codes and other State Resources: Mega Law: http://www.megalaw.com/states.php
- State Cases: Cornell Law School Legal Information Institute (LII) main page with links to individual state information: http://www.law.cornell.edu/opinions.html

Cornell LII Uniform Probate Law Locator

The Cornell LII website has an entire web page dedicated to the Uniform Probate Laws and it is probably the best single source for the UPL: http://www.law.cornell.edu/uniform/probate.html

Search Engines

We all know that if you say "search engine," the immediate thought is "Google." Over the last few years, Google has overtaken all search engines and is used almost exclusively by Internet users. The term "google" is now a verb in the dictionary, having been added to both the Oxford English Dictionary and the Merriam-Webster Dictionary in 2006. Google is a very good engine to use for searching most topics, including legal topics. A few other search engines are listed here for those who want to use other sources.

General Search Engines

- Google: http://www.google.com. The king of search engines, Google has supplanted all others.
- Bing: http://www.bing.com. A relatively new search engine from Microsoft that has a good interface and works very nicely.
- Metacrawler: http://www.metacrawler.com. Metacrawler presumably searches the major search engines so you don't have to do separate searches.
- Mamma: http://www.mamma.com. "The Mother of All Search Engines" is an aggregator like Metacrawler.
- Dogpile Another aggregator: http://www.dogpile.com
- Yahoo! Search: http://search.yahoo.com/
- Ask: http://www.ask.com/?o=0&l=dir

Legal Search Engines

- Lawcrawler: http://lawcrawler.findlaw.com/
- Law Guru: http://www.lawguru.com
- Hieros Gamos: http://www.hg.org/
- Public Legal, a product of the Internet Legal Resource Group: http://www.ilrg.com/
- Findlaw: http://www.findlaw.com. Acquired by Thompson Reuters (West) in 2001. A mixture of free and for pay information.

Miscellaneous Sites of Interest

- The Empowered Paralegal: http://theempoweredparalegal.com/Blog. This blog has a very good list of state paralegal associations, other blogs, paralegal organizations, and links to all of them.
- Estate Planning Links: http://www.EstatePlanningLinks.com. Created in 1995, this site is maintained by attorney Dennis Toman in Greensboro, North Carolina.
- National Academy of Elder Law Attorneys: http://www.naela.com/. NAELA was, according to its website, "founded in 1987 as a professional association of attorneys who are dedicated to improving the quality of legal services provided to seniors and people with special needs." The website has a great deal of information regarding estate planning and elder law. Some of the information is "members only."
- The American College of Trust and Estate Counsel: http://www.actec.org/. The American College of Trust and Estate Counsel (ACTEC) is a nonprofit association of lawyers established in 1949. ACTEC has a page devoted to public access documentation.
- Wills, Trusts, and Estates Prof Blog, edited by Gerry W. Beyer, Governor Preston E. Smith, Regents Professor of Law, Texas Tech University School of Law: http://lawprofessors.typepad.com/trusts_estates_prof/. Professor Beyer's blog is very informative and also has links to other blogs around the country with a focus on estate planning. This is a personal favorite of mine as a Texas Tech University School of Law alumnus.
- American Bar Association Real Property, Trust, and Estate Law Section: http://www.abanet.org/rppt/
- JURIST: http://jurist.law.pitt.edu. According to its website, JURIST "is a Web-based legal news and real-time legal research service powered by a mostly volunteer team of over 30 part-time law student reporters, editors, and Web developers led by law professor Bernard Hibbitts at the University of Pittsburgh School of Law in Pittsburgh, Pennsylvania." A visit to this website is very enlightening.
- LinkedIn Law: Part of the LinkedIn social media site, LinkedIn Law provides an array of legal articles on various topics.
- The Estrin Report: http://estrinlegaled.typepad.com/. A blog written by a paralegal for paralegals. The blogger for this blog also writes *SUE*, For Women in Litigation, http://www.suemagazine.com; and *KNOW*, The Magazine for Paralegals, http://www.knowparalegal.com
- New York Paralegal Blog: http://www.newyorkparalegalblog.com/

IRS Form 706: United States Tax Return

This form may be viewed and downloaded from www.pearsonhighered.com/careers <http://www.pearsonhighered.com/careers> .

The form will be replaced each year as new IRS forms become available.

Glossary

A

Abatement: Process of selling estate property to pay debts.

Adeem: To revoke a gift made in a will; to take away.

Ademption: Loss of testamentary gift because the testator no longer owns the property at death.

Adjusted gross estate: Value of a decedent's estate after deducting administrative and funeral expenses, as well as the claims of creditors and losses incurred by the estate.

Administrative expenses: Expenses incurred in the management of a decedent's estate, such as attorney's fees, probate filing fees, and the personal representative's fee for managing the estate.

Administrator: Person appointed by a court to represent the estate of a decedent that died intestate.

Administrator cum testamento annexo (CTA): Person appointed by the court when a will fails to name an executor or when any of the named executors fail to complete the administration of the estate.

Administratrix: Female personal representative. See Administrator.

Advance directives: Those documents used to inform family, friends, and medical personnel about the kind of medical care and treatment a person desires if he or she becomes terminally ill or otherwise incapacitated.

Advancement: Inter vivos gift to children in anticipation of their share of a parent's estate. This amount may be deducted from the child's share of the estate.

Affiant: Person who makes, subscribes, and files an affidavit.

Affidavit: Sworn written statement as to particular events that is made before a notary public.

Affinity: Relationship by marriage.

Agent: Another name for the attorney in fact under a power of attorney.

Alternate valuation: Tax rule that allows assets to be valued at either the date of death or six months after death.

Ambulatory: Revocable or subject to change.

Anatomical gift: The donation of a person's body or its organs after the death of the person.

Ancillary administration: Estate administration that occurs in the state where property is located if it is not located within the domiciliary state.

Ancillary administrator: The personal representative appointed when an ancillary administration is necessary. (Feminine: Ancillary administratrix)

Anti-lapse statute: Laws that provide for the passage of gifts to deceased heirs to go to their own heirs; countering or minimizing the effect of a lapse.

Apportionment clause: A clause in a will that allocates the tax burden among the residuary estate and the beneficiaries of the will. Otherwise, the taxes would come only from the residuary.

Ascendant: Lineal ancestor.

Attestation: Clause signed by the witnesses of a will.

Attorney in fact: The person given the authority to perform an act or acts as stated in a power of attorney. This person need not be an attorney. May also be known as an agent.

B

Bailment: Delivery of personal property to someone for a specific purpose but without transferring title to that person.

Beneficiary: The person that receives property under a will or the holder of the equitable title under a trust.

Bequest: A gift of personal property under a will.

Bond: Evidence of indebtedness secured by property, the person who receives a bond will pay interest until the loan is repaid. It is also a means of posting security with a court and is used to ensure a fiduciary's performance.

C

Certificate of deposit (CD): A long-term savings account.

Cestui que trust: The beneficiary of a trust.

Charitable trust: A trust created for a public charitable purpose. Also called a public trust.

Chose in action: A form of intangible property, evidence of a person's right to sue based on his or her ownership interest in intangible property.

Class gift: A gift given to a group of persons, uncertain in number, such as "all of my grandchildren."

Codicil: A document that formally amends a will.

Community property: A method of holding property acquired during marriage in which each spouse owns 1/2 of the property outright. Community property is only valid in 10 states: Texas, New Mexico, Idaho, Washington, Louisiana, Nevada, Arizona, Colorado, Wisconsin, and Alaska.

Concurrent ownership: Two or more persons each owning an undivided interest in property.

Condition precedent: A condition or event that must occur before an obligation becomes binding.

Condition subsequent: A condition or event that will cause an existing agreement to either continue or terminate once the condition occurs.

Consanguinity: Relationship determined by blood.

Conservator: A person that is appointed to take care of the property of an incompetent or a minor.

Constructive trust: A form of implied trust that is imposed by a court to right a wrong.

Contingent remainder: A remainder that is dependent upon the happening of an event.

Conveyance: Transfer of real property.

Corpus: Trust property.

Crummy trust: An irrevocable life insurance trust that allows the trustor to pay premiums with tax free dollars.

Curtesy: Widower's right to property of his deceased wife. No longer accepted in most jurisdictions, having been replaced by other legal methods of protecting surviving spouses.

D

Death certificate: A document issued by a government agency evidencing a person's death.

Decedent: The deceased person.

Declaration of trust: Instrument that creates an inter vivos trust.

Deed: The document used to evidence the owner of title to real property.

Deed of trust: A method of transferring real property in which the seller retains the legal title to the property while the buyer obtains equitable title. The buyer obtains the legal title to the property when the purchase price is paid in full.

Demonstrative legacy: Testamentary gift of money from a particular source.

Dependent relative revocation (DRR): Doctrine which states that if a newer will is found invalid, an earlier valid will can be revived and probated instead.

Descendant: A person who is of the issue of an ancestor; issue.

Descent and distribution: Laws that provide how inheritances are regulated.

Devise: Testamentary gift of real property.

Devisee: Recipient of a testamentary gift of real property.

Discretionary income: Disposable income.

Discretionary trust: Trust in which the trustee is given broad powers of discretion with respect to investments and distribution of the trust income.

Domicile: Legal home as opposed to a residence. Usually evidenced by the place from which a person files income taxes.

Donee: Recipient of a gift.

Donor: Person who gives the gift to the donee.

Dower: The widow's interest in the property of her deceased husband. No longer accepted in most jurisdictions, having been replaced by other legal methods of protecting surviving spouses.

Durable Power of Attorney: Power of Attorney that remains in effect even if the principal becomes incapacitated.

E

Elective share: The right a surviving spouse has in the estate of the deceased spouse. See also Right of election.

Equitable title: Title giving the beneficiary the right to enjoy trust property subject to limitations imposed by the trustor.

Escheat: The process by which the state inherits a decedent's property when there are no living relatives.

Estate: Property of a decedent; interest in land.

Estate administration: The process in which a decedent's assets are collected, debts are paid, and the net worth is distributed.

Estate for years: An estate for a fixed and determinate period, such as a lease for two years.

Estate planning: The process in which a person determines how his or her assets will be distributed and how debts and taxes will be paid after death.

Estate tax: Tax imposed upon the estate for the privilege of passing on the property of the estate after death.

Execute: Sign, as in affixing one's signature to a will or a contract.

Executor: Personal representative of a will, masculine.

Executrix: Personal representative of a will, feminine. Not routinely used; masculine form now used as neutral form in most cases.

Exordium clause: A will's introductory paragraph.

Express trust: Trust created by the voluntary and deliberate act of the trustor.

F

Family allowance: Laws that insure that a family (spouse and minor children) may keep personal property of the decedent and gives them a monthly cash allowance for living expenses before any debts are paid or property of the estate is distributed.

Fee: Estate in land. Also fee simple or fee simple absolute.

Fee simple: The greatest and largest estate that anyone can have in land.

Fee simple defeasible: An interest in land that may come to an end.

Fiduciary: Person in a position of trust.

Fixture: Personal property that is so permanently attached to real property that it becomes part of the realty.

Form 706: Federal estate tax return.

Form 1040: Federal income tax return.

Form 1041: Federal income tax return for estates.

Form SS-4: Application for Employer Identification Number; number given by IRS to identify a decedent's estate.

Fraud: Method used to induce a person to sign a will in which certain facts are misrepresented.

Freehold: An estate in land for an indefinite period.

G

General legacy: Testamentary gift of a fixed sum of money from the general assets of the estate.

General power of appointment: Right of the donee to pass the donor's property to whomever the donee chooses.

Generation skipping transfer: Transfers in property that benefit persons two or more generations removed from the grantor, which are subject to special tax rules and regulations.

Gift: Transfer of property without consideration.

Grantee: Recipient of real property.

Grantor: Transferor of real property.

Guardian: Person named in a will or appointed by a court to have custody and take care of incapacitated persons or minors. Guardians of the person care for the person, while guardians of the property care for the incapacitated person's or minor's property.

Guardian ad litem: Adult appointed by a court to represent persons under an incapacity during litigation.

H

Health care proxy: Document in which a person designates a surrogate to have the legal authority to make medical decisions on his or her behalf if the person is incapacitated and cannot make the decisions.

Heir: Inheritor of property of a deceased person.

Holographic will: A will which is drafted solely in the handwriting of the testator.

I

Illegitimate: Born out of wedlock.

Implied trust: Trust created by operation of law.

Incorporation by reference: When a document mentions another document by specific language so that that external document is considered part of the current document.

Informal probate proceedings: Probate for small estates permitted in certain jurisdictions; sometimes called summary administration.

Inheritance tax: A tax imposed by some states in which the beneficiary of a decedent's property is taxed on the transfer of the property.

In personam jurisdiction: A court's authority over the individual involved in a lawsuit.

In rem jurisdiction: A court's authority over property.

Intangible personal property: Personal property that evidences ownership in something of value but has no value by itself, for example stock certificates which have no real value but are evidence of ownership in a corporation, which may have great value.

In terrorem clause: Penalty clause. Clause in which a testator states that if any beneficiary contests the will, the beneficiary's portion will be forfeited. Not valid in some jurisdictions.

Inter vivos trust: A trust created to take effect while the trustor is alive. Also called a living trust.

Intestacy: Death without a valid will.

Intestate, *n.*: A person that dies without a valid will.

Intestate, *vb.*: To die without a valid will.

Intestate succession: The process of determining who will inherit the property of a person who dies without a valid will.

Irrevocable trust: A trust that may not be revoked by the trustor once it has been created.

Issue: Direct lineal descendants.

J

Joint tenancy: Title to property held by more than one person with a right of survivorship.

Joint will: One will used for two persons.

L

Lady Bird Deed: An enhanced life estate deed; named for Lady Bird Johnson because President Johnson was said to have used this type of deed to convey some land to her.

Lapse: Provision in a will indicating that if a recipient of a gift under the will predeceases the testator, the gift becomes part of the residuary of the estate.

Leasehold: Tenancy in real property for a fixed period.

Legacy: Testamentary gift of money.

Legal list: Statutory group of safe and risk-free investments.

Legal title: Title held by a trustee for the benefit of others.

Legatee: Recipient of money under a will.

Letters of administration: The court's authorization of the administrator's right to act on behalf of a deceased's estate.

Letters testamentary: The court's authorization of the personal representative's right to act on behalf of a deceased's estate.

Life estate: A tenancy which allows a person to own real property for his or her life only.

Life estate pur autre vie: A tenancy which allows a person to own real property for the life of someone else.

Living trust: See Inter vivos trust.

Living will: A document which allows a person to determine if and when life sustaining procedures will be instituted in the instance that the person has a terminal illness.

M

Marital deduction: Tax provision permitting property to go to a surviving spouse tax free.

Minor: A person who is under the age of majority.

Mutual will: Identical wills executed by two persons. Distinguishable from a joint will in which two people execute one document.

N

No contest clause: See In terrorem clause.

Non-probate asset: Property that passes to a decedent's heirs without having to go through the probate process; property that passes by operation of law.

Nuncupative will: An oral will.

P

Partition: Method of dividing the interests joint owners have in real property.

Per capita: When an heir takes property in his or her own right; all heirs of the same degree of kinship receive an equal share of a decedent's estate.

Personal property: Property that is movable and touchable. All property that is not classified as real property; includes both tangible and intangible property.

Personal representative: The person with the fiduciary responsibility to administer a decedent's estate. Also called an executor.

Per stirpes: Taking property by right of representation.

Pourover will: Clause in a will which leaves the testator's property to the trustee of a living trust.

Power of appointment: The legal right given to a person to appoint successor beneficiaries, including oneself.

Power of attorney: A written document that authorizes a person to act as the agent for another.

Precatory language: Words such as "would hope," "recommend," "desire," "wish," and "would like you," which are not binding.

Principal: Trust property.

Probate: Process in which a decedent's will is proved valid; entire process of validating the will; appointing the personal representative; and distributing the decedent's estate.

Probate assets: That property of the decedent which must be distributed through the jurisdiction of the probate court.

Q

Qualified terminable interest property (QTIP):   Property given to a surviving spouse that qualifies as a marital deduction although the spouse's interest is not absolute.

R

Real property: Land and any fixtures on the land.

Reciprocal wills: See Mutual will.

Remainder: The balance of an estate after all provisions of a will have been fulfilled.

Remainderman: Person in whom property eventually vests; the person in whom legal and equitable title merge.

Res: Trust property.

Residuary: Clause in a will which disposes of all remaining assets after all debts are satisfied and all gifts are fulfilled.

Resulting trust: Implied trust in which trust property is held for the benefit of the person who paid for the property.

Reversion: When the property vests again in the trustor after belonging to someone else for a period of time.

Reversionary interest: The interest that the trustor holds; a remainder held by the trustor.

Revocable living trust: Trust in which the trustor retains the power to revoke.

Right of election: The right of a surviving spouse to choose a statutory share of the decedent spouse's estate instead of the assets left to him or her in the decedent spouse's will.

Right of representation: The right of a child to receive his or her parent's share of an estate that the parent would have received if he or she were still living.

Right of survivorship: Rule of joint tenancy that upon the death of one tenant, the deceased tenant's share of property passes to the remaining tenants. The last surviving joint tenant owns the property outright.

Rule against perpetuities: Fixes the time within which a future interest must pass. The rule states that the interest must pass within a time limited by a life or lives in being plus 21 years.

S

Self-proving will: A will in which the witnesses attest to the validity of the will's execution via a separate affidavit sworn to by a notary public.

Separate property: Property owned free and clear from the rights and control of another; in community property states, separate property is all property that is not community property and usually includes gifts and inheritances.

Settlor: Trustor of personal property trust.

Severalty: Sole; one; in context of property, if owned in severalty, the property is owned individually.

Simultaneous death clause: Clause which indicates when and how property is to be distributed if the testator and beneficiary die in a common disaster.

Sound mind: Having the mental capacity to execute a document, such as a will.

Special power of appointment: A power of appointment that prevents the donee from giving the property over which the donee has been given the power to himself or herself or to his or her estate.

Specific devise: A testamentary gift of real property.

Specific legacy: A testamentary gift of specific personal property.

Spendthrift trust: Trust which prevents a beneficiary from alienating his or her interests in the trust. Effect is to keep the beneficiary from selling his or her interests and keeping creditors from capturing the trust assets.

Spray trust: Discretionary trust. See Sprinkling trust.

Sprinkling trust: Discretionary trust in which the trustee has the sole discretion to determine how the income or principal will be distributed to the trust beneficiaries.

Subscribe: To sign.

Subscribing witness: The witness to a will that sees the testator execute it.

T

Tangible personal property: Personal property that is movable and touchable.

Tax credit: Deduction from taxes.

Tax deduction: Amount reducing the value of taxes and taxable property.

Tenancy: Right to real property.

Tenancy at sufferance: Holding possession of real property without the consent of the owner or landlord but having originally obtained the property lawfully, for example, a tenancy at will.

Tenancy at will: Holding possession of real property with the consent of the owner or landlord.

Tenancy by the entirety: A form of joint tenancy that is only available to a husband and wife.

Tenancy in common: Ownership in property by two or more persons in which each owner has an undivided interest in the property without a right of survivorship.

Testamentary capacity: The testator's knowledge of the nature and extent of his or her property and the objects of his or her bounty.

Testamentary trust: A trust created by a will.

Testator: Will creator; person who dies with a valid will.

Testimonium clause: Last clause in a will.

Totten trust: Bank account held "in Trust" for another.

Trustee: Fiduciary who holds legal title to trust property for the benefit of the equitable title holders.

Trustor: Trust creator.

Trust property: All property held in trust.

U

Undue influence: Influence by one party on another that is exerted to such a degree that the latter party is not exercising his or her free will.

W

Will: A document in which the creator disposes of all his or her property upon his or her death.

Will contest: Challenge to a will that is being admitted to probate.

Index